Creating Meaning Through Literature and the Arts

An Integration Resource for Classroom Teachers

Second Edition

CLAUDIA E. CORNETT
Professor Emerita, Wittenberg University

Merrill
Prentice Hall

Upper Saddle River, New Jersey
Columbus, Ohio

Library of Congress Cataloging-in-Publication Data

Cornett, Claudia E.

   Creating meaning through literature and the arts: An integration resource for classroom teachers—2nd ed. / Claudia E. Cornett.

      p. cm.

   Includes bibliographical references and index.

   ISBN 0-13-097777-2

   1. Arts—Study and teaching. 2. Literature—Study and teaching. 3. Interdisciplinary approach in education. I. Title.

LB1591 .C67 2003

372.64—dc21   2002023036

Vice President and Publisher: Jeffery W. Johnston
Editor: Linda Ashe Montgomery
Production Editor: Mary M. Irvin
Design Coordinator: Diane C. Lorenzo
Project Coordinator and Text Design: Ann Mohan, WordCrafters Editorial Services, Inc.
Cover Designer: Setting Pace
Cover Photo: Mural by students at Lady's Island Elementary School
Production Manager: Pamela D. Bennett
Director of Marketing: Ann Castel Davis
Marketing Manager: Krista Groshong
Marketing Coordinator: Tyra Cooper

All photos supplied by the author.

This book was set in Galliard by Carlisle Communications, Ltd., and was printed and bound by Hamilton Printing. The cover was printed by Phoenix Color Corp.

Pearson Education Ltd.
Pearson Education Australia Pty. Limited
Pearson Education Singapore Pte. Ltd.
Pearson Education North Asia Ltd.
Pearson Education Canada, Ltd.
Pearson Educación de Mexico, S.A. de C.V.
Pearson Education—Japan.
Pearson Education Malaysia Pte. Ltd.
Pearson Education, *Upper Saddle River, New Jersey*

Merrill
Prentice Hall

10 9 8 7 6 5 4 3 2 1
ISBN 0-13-097777-2

With love to Charles, my Pygmalion,
who made me laugh, brought me supper,
and believes I can do anything.

Foreword

There is a quiet but determined movement throughout K–12 education in the United States led by teachers who have discovered the power of integrating the arts into their teaching. Each year more teachers are incorporating the arts into their classrooms, often in partnership with arts specialists. These educators are using a variety of teaching strategies that lead to active student participation. This, in turn, leads to livelier classrooms.

Because our lives do not naturally fall into 30–50 minute segments during which we focus on one subject at a time, many educators are also taking a second look at integrating multiple disciplines in their instruction, with an eye on making learning more meaningful for students. These ideas—teaching by integrating subjects and using the arts to integrate disciplines—are not new to education; indeed, they have been advocated by arts groups and many educational institutions for years.

In the 1960s, arts education began to enjoy the spotlight through the work of such organizations as the National Endowment for the Arts and the John D. Rockefeller III Fund. Since then, educators and arts organizations have worked together more closely to provide arts education experiences for students. Over the intervening years, hundreds of arts organizations have made it part of their mission to support the classroom teacher in efforts to teach in, through, and about the arts.

However, practitioners in the arts education field have begun to realize that professional development in the arts is valued not only by experienced teachers, but also by university students learning to become teachers. Indeed, professional development in the arts for practicing teachers is such a growing field precise-ly because classwork in the arts is limited or nonexistent for preservice teachers. It is time to provide more resources and information about the arts and integration at the undergraduate level. With this book, Claudia Cornett has provided such a resource.

Creating Meaning through Literature and the Arts: An Integration Resource for Classroom Teachers will be helpful to preservice teachers but will also serve as a valuable resource for veteran teachers who are new to the concept of arts integration. In this text, educators will find basic information about the four arts disciplines—dance, drama, visual art, and music—and how to integrate them with children's literature. Readers will find strategies and lesson plans for interdisciplinary teaching, resource lists, and an extensive bibliography. Readers will enjoy Dr. Cornett's incorporation of "Take Action" text inserts, which suggest points for class discussion, and "News Bulletins," which highlight arts and education research and facts. In addition, readers will witness integration through classroom vignettes placed at the beginning of some chapters. In these vignettes, actual classroom observations are described in which the arts are being integrated into teaching and learning.

As educators hear the cry for education reform, school change, and school improvement with ever-increasing frequency, many have turned to the arts. With this book, Dr. Cornett has provided a tool to guide teachers on the path toward making the arts a meaningful part of the classroom experience.

Barbara Shepherd
Program Manager
The Kennedy Center's Partners in Education

Preface

The arts do matter in their own right . . . but also as instruments of cognitive growth and development and as agents of motivation for school success. In this light, unfair access to the arts for our children brings consequences of major importance to our society. (Catterall, Chapleau, & Iwanaga, 1999)

THE PURPOSE OF THIS BOOK

Since the events of September 11, 2001, we now look at our work in education with a different eye. Of what value will higher student achievement on standardized measures be if our children aren't safe? What can educators do to prepare students to be more adept at solving the unknown problems ahead of them? How can renewed feelings of patriotism be coupled with increased respect for the diverse peoples of the world? How can children be taught democratic values for freedom and justice using pedagogic processes consistent with these values—methods that encourage students to think openly, take risks, consider choices, and make fair decisions? As we face these teaching challenges in the 21st century, we see a greater need to use our innate creative problem-solving abilities than at any other time in history. The future beckons with a plethora of educational promises and problems. Our challenge is to digest the growing mountain of learning research and convert it to thoughtful, artful practice.

One thing we have learned through the ages is that human beings are at their best when laughing, dancing, singing, painting, potting, and pretending. The most important aspects of civilization are preserved not in percentiles, stanines, or grades, but in imaginative literature, art, drama, dance, and music. And these are the ancient learning rhythms that draw contemporary children. The arts were, and remain, the most basic and most essential forms of human communication. The arts are ways to create meaning about our deepest feelings and most significant thoughts. To ignore or minimize their value by compartmentalizing them in our classrooms into "specials" on Tuesdays or an annual class play is to deny

their power in teaching and learning. This is why increasing numbers of schools have chosen to integrate the arts as primary strategies to increase student achievement, especially in reading and writing. A substantial body of research supporting the impact of the arts on learning is now readily available through publications such as *Champions of Change: The Impact of the Arts on Learning* (Fiske, 1999).

The goal of this text, the second edition of *Creating Meaning Through Literature and the Arts,* is to help pre-service education majors and practicing teachers meaningfully integrate literature, art, drama, dance, and music throughout the curriculum by providing a basic knowledge of the arts, clear reasons for integration, and specific how-to arts integration principles. Teaching *with, about, in,* and *through* the arts implies an alternative approach to the traditional role of classroom teachers who teach science, social studies, math, and language arts/reading using the arts only as enjoyable add-on activities. It is no longer thinkable to cram children into rows of desks and allow them to see school as a lifeless, dull place compared to an outside world filled with emotional and stimulating visual images, concert-quality CDs and entertainment, and fashion designs produced by creative geniuses. It is our role as teachers to make school every bit as engaging, with compelling stories, songs, images, and movement in all lessons.

Because this is an introductory text, I have used my background in alternative learning strategies and many years in undergraduate teacher education to scaffold for readers with structuring devices, repetition, use of examples, and mnemonic devices. My hope is to empower readers to use their own creative abilities to discover patterns and use the ordinary in extraordinary ways in their teaching. Included, therefore, are actual teacher stories, lesson plans, tools to plan "original" lessons and units, and compendia of "seed starter" strategies in each chapter that describe a specific art form and in the chapter on integrating these arts with one another. A special emphasis is placed on active reader engagement through "Take Action" text features that invite readers to transform information and personalize its meaning. Finally, differentiated instruction is addressed throughout the text using a model to particularize instruction by employing ten different adjustments to meet students' diverse needs.

HOW THE TEXT IS ORGANIZED

The book is organized into 14 chapters. Chapters 1 and 2 provide necessary historical and theoretical background to understand WHAT is included in arts integration, WHY the arts are important in education, and HOW teachers can use research and the experiences of others to create an integrated arts program. These two chapters introduce basic frameworks that are applied in the remaining arts chapters, including implications from brain research, the *National Standards,* a leveled concept of arts integration (teaching *with, about, in,* and *through* the arts), the creative problem-solving process, four unit structures, a two-pronged integrated lesson plan, 10 principles of integration, and 10 particular strategies for differentiating instruction.

Next are 10 paired chapters on integrating the arts of literature, art, drama, dance, and music. One chapter of each pair deals with *why, how,* and *what* parts of the art form should be integrated. WHY includes an overview of the theories, beliefs, and research that support the art's use, as well as a discussion of the art form's unique contribution to student learning. In the WHAT sections, the necessary knowledge base for a classroom teacher is discussed, with focus on basic content, including literary elements such as plot and theme and art elements such as color, line, and shape. Also included in the WHAT sections are summaries of the *National Standards for the Arts* and the *Standards for the English Language Arts* to guide teachers in planning for goals concerning what students should know and be able to do in each arts area.

The HOW section forms the bulk of the chapter. It consists of general principles of integration applied to each art area. HOW is organized around a model for integration built on daily arts routines; types of integrated units; and other specific structures for creating meaning through the arts in science, social studies, math, reading, and language arts. Assessment is addressed in the chapters under the heading of "Evi-dence to Document and Assess Student Progress." Adaptations for students with special needs are suggested as well.

Following each of these introductory chapters for each art form is a black-banded chapter containing *Seed Strategies* that are adaptable for most elementary and middle school age and stage levels. These are brief idea starters, offered in the belief that teachers must choose and adapt *all* teaching activities to meet unique student needs. The *Seed Strategies* are organized into (1) energizers and warm-ups, (2) strategies to teach arts concepts and elements, and (3) strategies to integrate the arts in science, social studies, math, and reading/language arts.

Chapter 13 is a separate compendium of strategy seeds for integrating the arts with one another in 10 combinations.

Finally, Chapter 14 deals with assessment and other common questions that classroom teachers ask as they begin to integrate the arts. Topics include censorship, worries about materials, and concerns about diluting the arts through integration.

SPECIAL FEATURES

I would not be true to my roots in literacy pedagogy if I did not supply the following features to activate prior knowledge; establish the importance of particular information; engage readers in cognitive, affective, and kinesthetic ways; and structure response and reflection opportunities.

Post It Pages

One- or two-page summaries throughout the book pull together information that teachers can use over and over to integrate the arts. For example, "News Bulletins" give a quick look at research and current school programs that integrate the arts across the curriculum. Examples of integrated lesson plans appear on "Post It Pages." Post It Pages are set up so that they can be photocopied for ready reference. A Table of Post It Pages is provided right after the Table of Contents so the reader can readily locate them.

Quotes

The powerful words of artists and teachers are presented to provoke thought and give rhythm to the reading material. These can be culled for classroom use as "quotes of the day."

Classroom Snapshots

A basic principle of arts integration is to experience the art first and then isolate its components for study, so the story of one teacher's journey opens most chapters and makes the possible more personal. These vignettes are *whole* art forms that show how creative teachers craft lessons that meaningfully mingle art and math, science and drama, literature and dance, and social studies and art. A basic principle of arts integration is to experience the art first and then isolate its components for study so the story of one teacher's journey opens most chapters and makes the possible more personal. These vignettes are *whole* art forms that show how creative teachers craft lessons that meaningfully mingle art and math, science and drama, literature and dance, and social studies and art.

Photographs

I can't pass up the opportunity to say it: "A picture is worth a thousand words." The faces of students and teachers tell the integrated arts story throughout the book.

Children's Literature

Children's literature is both an art form and one of the basic integration principles used in all arts chapters. Recommendations about specific books and strategies for using children's literature to integrate art, music, drama, and dance appear in every chapter. Poetry writing, sharing, and storytelling are emphasized in special chapter sections.

"Take Action" Tickets

These "tickets" are inserted throughout the text, inviting readers to pause and "do." For deep learning to occur, there is no substitute for acting on information. The tickets provide some ways to do so. They are numbered so that they can be assigned to or chosen by students more easily.

Teacher Resources

At the end of each chapter, teachers can preview resources for special materials or information for arts integration. These include videos; Internet addresses; and addresses of organizations and sources for music, computer software, and multicultural information. More comprehensive resources are listed in the appendixes.

Appendixes

Special items in the appendixes include the following:

Bibliography of Arts-Based Children's Literature. An extensive bibliography of children's literature, grouped by arts areas, is included to help teachers locate appropriate books, stories, and poems related to visual arts, drama, dance, and music.

Bibliography of Award-Winning Children's Books. A bibliography of Newbery and Caldecott winners is provided because these books have been judged to be high-quality literature and are usually available in public libraries and schools. For beginning teachers, the bibliography is useful for finding fine picture books to use for art integration and powerful fiction and nonfiction with arts connections. The books are labeled by genre and approximate age level to aid teachers in selecting books for genre units.

Arts Organizations, Addresses, and Internet Sites. These specific addresses are provided to help teachers find everything from lesson plans to chat rooms on arts integration.

Assessment Tools. Examples of a checklist, an interest inventory, and other tools appear in this appendix. Assessment recommendations are also given in the "Evidence to Document and Assess Student Progress" sections of chapters 2, 3, 5, 7, 9, and 11.

Discipline Prevention and Intervention Strategies. Because classroom discipline is always one of the top concerns of beginning teachers, I've included a summary of common strategies that veteran teachers use to create a positive classroom environment. In addition, this appendix presents basic ways to deal with problems that are bound to occur during instruction.

Bibliography of Recommended Reading and Viewing. This is a resource for specific teaching ideas and materials, as well as for locating additional research on arts integration. In this appendix, books, articles, and videos are categorized by relevant topics in integrating the arts.

◆ REFERENCES

Catterall, J. S., Chapleau, R., & Iwanaga, J. (1999). General involvement and intensive involvement in music and theater arts. In E. Fiske (Ed.), *Champions of change: The impact of the arts on learning* (p. 17). Washington, DC:

Arts Education Partnership and President's Committee on the Arts and Humanities.

Fiske, E. (Ed.). (1999). *Champions of change: The impact of the arts on learning.* Washington, DC: Arts Education Partnership and President's Committee on the Arts and Humanities.

ACKNOWLEDGMENTS

No one ever writes a book alone. I wish to thank all those who traveled with me on this journey. Bethany Gray was my research assistant for the first edition, and her help was invaluable. I wish also to thank my faculty aide, Becca Hoffmeister, who was often given the impossible to do and did it. I feel blessed to have taught at Wittenberg University, where so many wonderful secretaries and students were always ready to find obscure references and tackle any typing task. Thanks to all the students in my education courses who were my guinea pigs. In their field experiences and student teaching, they have reinforced my belief in the power of the arts to energize and humanize the curriculum.

I could not possibly list all the principals and classroom teachers who have contributed to this book. Of particular importance to the second edition were Terry Bennett, principal of Lady's Island Elementary School (LIES), and the teachers at LIES who contributed lesson plans and pictures: J. Samuels, N. Beyer, C. Kotarsky, A. Wirz, D. Smith, A. Peterson, C. Crabb, and Ms. Koverman. In addition, I thank Kristy Smith, the Arts Coordinator for Beaufort County Schools, for her many contributions. Principal Marni Gochenour and the teachers at Kenwood Heights Elementary were collaborators with me and my undergraduate students in integrating the arts throughout the curriculum for many years. In particular, Punky Turner, Beverly Phillips, and Myra Hoak must be recognized for their commitment to the arts and their help in establishing our Arts Alive Resource Collection at Wittenberg. Photos from their classrooms also illustrate the book. Sarah Bennett is acknowledged for her photographic artistry in taking wonderful pictures, especially the stunning one using the sculpture by artist Michel Zurbuchen of Yellow Springs, Ohio.

I wish to thank Carol Sykes, Mary Irvin, and Linda Montgomery at Prentice Hall for being good shepherds. I am also very grateful to have been able to work with WordCrafters and their skillful staff, who provided me wisdom and guidance throughout the production process. In particular, I wish to acknowledge Ann Mohan. Her attention to detail and professionalism were much appreciated.

Of course, first and last, time present and time past, there is my husband, Charles, to whom this book is dedicated. He does indeed give me roots and wings and did a considerable amount of the research for this second edition. Finally, there is a gentle, persistent soul in Arizona who made this book possible. I offer my heartfelt thanks to Colette Kelly for her willingness to take a chance on me. I'm glad we found each other.

Claudia E. Cornett

Contents

CHAPTER 5

INTEGRATING VISUAL ART THROUGHOUT THE CURRICULUM 152

CHAPTER 6

ART SEED STRATEGIES 199

CHAPTER 7

INTEGRATING DRAMA THROUGHOUT THE CURRICULUM 225

CHAPTER 8

DRAMA SEED STRATEGIES 258

Special Features

MOST FREQUENTLY USED POST IT PAGES BY CATEGORY

1

An Introduction to Teaching With, About, In, and Through the Arts

◆ SCHOOL SNAPSHOT

Beaufort's Best Kept Secret

The arts are not an educational option; they are basic.
            John Goodlad

The flamboyant mural across the front of Lady's Island Elementary School (LIES) is one sign that this is no ordinary school. In fact LIES is the first of its kind in the district. It is a site-based, deregulated, school of choice in which arts infusion is the guiding philosophy implemented in grades K–5.

Inside the front doors dozens of American flags, painted on ceiling tiles, greet visitors. A primary class sits on a big rug next to a piano and a sign that reads "Sing Your Way to Reading." A huge shrimp sculpture comically gazes down the center hall while children's mobiles dance overhead. The hall walls are covered with every sort of student art from cartoons to portraits to abstracts. Much of it is framed. Over each classroom door is a teacher's name on a large artist's palette. All this before you even reach the office.

This is Terry Bennett's school. It is obvious how he feels about his job as principal of LIES—he smiles all the time. The school hums with productivity. It is a place full of energy: happy teachers and students. But just 3 years ago this little school on an island in South Carolina was in turmoil. Changes in racial makeup, caused by a new elementary school built in a bedroom community, left LIES with just over 200 students— 75 percent on free or reduced lunch. There had been a massive faculty exodus with almost 50 percent leaving. It was a school without a focus and Terry was to be its new principal.

How did Terry lead the transition to arts integration? He outlined the process step by step.

STEP ONE Identify Strengths. "When I came here in 1999 I knew we needed a focus. I started by having many conversations and discussions with teachers, parents, and school leaders. I didn't ask about problems. I already had that information. I wanted to identify strengths. I didn't begin with the idea that we were going to infuse the arts. The arts just emerged as areas of expertise and interest. Also, I noticed there just weren't any discipline problems coming from the art and music classes. That told me something."

Terry Bennett, principal, Lady's Island Elementary School

Step Two Gather Research. Terry went looking for connections between the arts and academics. "I was surprised to find so much. The National Assessment of Educational Progress in Arts Education showed that students who received classroom arts instruction outperformed other students. Another study by the Wolf Trap Institute for Early Learning through the Arts explained how arts prepare young children for their first years of school. Brain research is showing that stimuli provided by pictures, songs, movement, and drama are essential for the young to develop to their full potential. These activities are the languages of the child, the multiple ways in which kids understand and interpret the world. The arts pave the way for the child to use language to read, and to write.

"Because of the nature of our school population I was most interested in the research on the positive impact on at-risk students. Shirley Brice Heath of Stanford University found that at-risk students who are actively engaged in the arts had improved self-esteem and confidence, took leadership roles, and improved their overall performance. I shared all this with the teachers and parents. I even wrote a letter to the local newspaper outlining how James Catterall analyzed the records of 25,000 students as they moved from grade 8 to grade 10 and found significant correlations between the arts and higher grades, higher scores on standardized tests, better attendance rates, and participation in community affairs. Catterall also found that students from poorer families improved more rapidly than other students when they were involved in the arts. Of course, everyone is impressed by College Board reports that show students who studied the arts more than 4 years scored 59 points higher on the verbal and 44 points higher on the math portions of the SAT than nonarts students. That is 103 points higher on the SAT!"

Step Three Mission Statement.* Terry contacted the South Carolina Arts in the Basic Curriculum (ABC) coordinator and she presented benefits of arts integration to the LIES faculty. "Her message was that we could address problems with attendance, achievement, and teacher turnover by using the arts as our mission. The music teacher and I then attended a workshop to develop a mission statement. That was our first year together as a school team. The next summer we sent a group from LIES to the same workshop."

Step Four Plan of Action. "I'm not an artist. What I am is a leader. My staff needed someone to suggest and to push them—to support them. By 2000 we had developed a schoolwide plan to bring in artists in residence and to integrate the arts throughout the traditional academic curriculum."

Step Five Staff Development. "Our arts specialists have taken on leadership roles from the beginning and have a regular place on every faculty meeting agenda. We also worked with our Arts Coordinator, Kristy Smith, to bring in outside consultants at the start of the 2000 school year. Our focus there was to give classroom teachers arts integration strategies. We've also visited other arts-based elementary schools to get ideas."

Step Six Implementation. "During the 00–01 school year we jumped in. We're not 'there' yet, but teachers are going toward more and more integrated units and there is an increasing tie-in between what goes on between arts classrooms and regular classrooms. Eventually we want a scheduled time for arts specialists and classroom teachers.

"We've got kindergarten students studying Warhol and Rodin. The classroom teachers try to do units on local artists, too, like Jonathan Green. Projects and performances are emphasized because they encourage students to apply complex knowledge and skills from several areas simultaneously. We work a lot with the Beaufort Arts Council. We have after school clubs, too, like strings. One child was in my office whining about something the other day and I said, jokingly, 'Let me play my fiddle.' She said, 'You're not holding it right!'

"In addition to art and music, students now have dance once a week in place of PE—the dance teacher uses the PE standards, too. The dance teacher is actually dance certified, too! Next year we'll add a drama specialist."

Step Seven Maturation and Evaluation. "Our enrollment is up to 320 students! Sixty-one of those are 'out-of-zone' students who have come because of our arts focus. Our gifted and talented program now

*LIES mission statement and beliefs can be viewed on its website at *www.ladysislandelementary.com.*

identifies and develops artistic abilities. I notice how the students are happier. Every child likes some art form and they touch on each every day. With happiness comes better attendance. I hear kids say things like, 'I don't want to be absent on Monday because my class has art on Monday.' Our fifth graders recently won the Beaufort County Academic Challenge and four of our students are in the state elementary honors choir—the only ones in Beaufort County!

"Of course we're proud of our test scores. On the Palmetto Achievement Challenge Test (PACT) all of our students were above the 50th percentile. On the fourth grade English Language Arts portion 96.2 percent were at the 'basic' or above level—just 3.8 percent did not pass. That's compared to 19.5 percent not passing for the district. At third grade in math 90% were at basic or above. Ten percent didn't passed compared to 36.1 percent districtwide who didn't pass. I attribute the test scores to arts infusion. Teachers are teaching a new way, but emphasizing state standards. We're teaching the same things, but teaching them differently."

WHAT'S AHEAD?

"We believe what Richard Riley, U.S. Secretary of Education said, 'The creativity of the arts and the joy of music should be central to the education of every American child.' In the summer of 2002 LIES will break ground on a new wing designed around our arts mission. A new music room, drama room, and dance space are planned. Our commitment to the arts is paramount. The arts must become part of every child's education. They are the driving force at Lady's Island Elementary School—Beaufort's Best Kept Secret!"

INTRODUCTION

The Sense and Soul of the Curriculum

It is, in fact, nothing short of a miracle that the modern methods of instruction have not yet entirely strangled the holy curiosity of inquiry; for this delicate little plant, aside from stimulation, stands mainly in need of freedom; without this it goes to rank and ruin without fail. It is a very grave mistake to think that the engagement of seeing and searching can be promoted by means of coercion and a sense of duty.
Albert Einstein

The very idea that we can change our schools and make them more effective centers of learning without educating children in the arts is simply false.. . .
National Endowment for the Arts, 1995

From Charleston, South Carolina, to Los Angeles, California, schools are now using the arts as essential teaching tools—not just in the occasional art class or interdisciplinary unit but as pedagogical mainstays. These elementary and middle schools describe themselves as "arts based," "arts integrated," "arts infusion," "Arts PROPEL," "interdisciplinary," "arts plus," or "A1 schools." While the labels are diverse, these programs share a common belief: Literature, visual art, drama, dance, and music have the power to energize and humanize the curriculum. Integrated arts schools are acting on research that confirms how arts experiences help "level the educational playing field" for disadvantaged students as well. The arts are returning from a "long exile on the curricular fringe of public education" and are now an acknowledged part of national strategies to transform schools (Bruce, 1996, p. 4).

The impetus for integrating the arts into the classroom teacher's strategy repertoire has a lot to do with changing academic and social expectations for students. Expectations have risen, while test scores remain flat or have declined in many districts. In the quest for promising solutions, educational leaders have rediscovered the "transforming power of the arts" in the mounting research that connects the arts to increases in academic achievement (Boston, 1996; Fiske, 1999).

"[T]he arts and humanities are poised to become leading contenders in the school-reform sweepstakes" (Larson, 1997, p. 91). Why? Schools with strong arts programs enjoy the benefits of increased student motivation to learn, better attendance among students and teachers, increased graduation rates, broader multicultural understanding, revitalized faculty, greater student engagement, growth in use of higher-order thinking and problem-solving skills, and increased creative capacities (Larson, 1997, p. 97). As an example, daily attendance increased to 94 percent, and 83 percent of the students achieved at or above national norms in reading and math after the arts were integrated into the curriculum at the Guggenheim Elementary School in inner-city Chicago. Of course, making sure kids are *in* school is of significant educational, social, and economic value; the annual cost of truancy to the nation is $228 billion—85 percent of all daytime crime is committed by truant youth. Then there is the cost to train unskilled youth that drop out—about $30 billion annually (Bruce, 1996, p. 6).

The potential for the arts to invigorate learning is demonstrated in the academic superiority of students in schools that devote 25 percent or more of the curriculum to arts courses (Perrin, 1994).

> The arts contribute to an overall culture of excellence in a school. They are an effective means of connecting children to each other and helping them gain an understanding of the creators who preceded them. They provide schools with a ready way to formulate relationships across and among traditional disciplines and to connect ideas and notice patterns. Works of art provide effective means for linking information in history and social studies, mathematics, science and geography . . . opening lines of inquiry, revealing that art, like life, is lived in a complex world not easily defined in discrete subjects. (J. Paul Getty Trust, 1993)

As change has happened on the school front, calls for revamping teacher preparation have become more demanding. Escalating world and national problems, along with the breakneck speed of technological change, prompted authors of a recent national report to call for us to "reclaim the soul of America" and direct our energies to "what matters most" (National Commission of Teaching and America's Future). Other reform proposals, like that of the Core Knowledge Foundation, are also on the change agenda. Unfortunately, the arts are not systematically included in discussions of "what matters most" and "core knowledge." Maxine Greene (1997), professor emerita at Columbia University's Teachers College, argues that "it is difficult to accept a call for excellent teaching and 'teaching for America's future' that pays no heed to the awakenings the arts make possible . . . to teach for the future requires a break from the routine and the ordinary, from the merely repetitive. And the arts, of all forms, may awaken teachers-to-be from the 'anesthetic' " (p. 14).

While collaborative models, like The Kennedy Center's Partners in Education, assist districts and arts agencies in providing professional development for *in-*service teachers—with emphasis on bringing artists into classrooms—little is being done to prepare practicing teachers and *pre-*service education majors to use the arts as *daily* integral content and modes of teaching and learning. A more forward-thinking concept of arts integration goes beyond using art, singing, or drama, exclusively for self-expression. In this book a new vision is presented in which the arts are seen as indispensable sources of cultural and historical information, givers of diverse perspectives and values, and invaluable communication vehicles.

Literature, art, drama, dance, and music have historically been the chief means through which people constructed meaning. The arts are "fundamental to what it means to be an educated person. To lack an education in the arts is to be profoundly disconnected from our history, from beauty, from other cultures, and from other forms of expression" (Larson, 1997, p. 99). How can we, as one national commission demands, cause students to "forge shared values, to understand and respect others' perspectives, to learn and work at high levels of competence, to take risks and persevere against the odds, to work comfortably with people from diverse background, and to continue to learn throughout life" without giving teachers tools to achieve these goals? Our world art treasury stands ready to reignite the imagination and passion inherent in its creators. The arts are among our most powerful instructional tools and they are indispensable to standards-based educational reform.

The Arts: Remarkable Meaning Makers

For thousands of years the arts have brought people together in celebration, worship, festivals, and weddings. Story, art, drama, dance, and music uniquely engage our senses and sensibilities, making us active participants in ways of knowing impossible through other domains. Outside the school arena the arts have long been tapped for their problem-solving potential. For example, in Springfield, Ohio, community leaders decided the arts were the most likely means of "discovering common ground" and used their drawing power to unite diverse groups. Since 1997 Culturefest has broadened respect for cultural traditions through storytelling, music, art making, and dancing. In Houston, Texas, walls of graffiti created by angry youth were transformed into stunning art murals by the city's youth—making an eyesore into an area of beauty.

From their early beginnings, humans seemed compelled to express ideas and feelings through the arts. Today 30,000-year-old paintings survive on cave walls in southern France (Chauvet, Deschamps, &

Hilliare, 1996) and folktales from every culture proclaim the importance of the arts in human history. These enduring art forms illuminate customs, commonalities, and differences. For example, there are more than 300 versions of the familiar "Cinderella" story, and Mother Goose rhymes like "Eeny meeny miny mo" recall ancient counting out rituals for human sacrifice. What drives us to use the arts to explain ourselves, answer questions, console each other, and create meaning? The answer has much to do with doing the impossible—trying to define art. No one could presume to offer a definition agreeable to all, but we can consider unique aspects of the arts and their special contributions—how literature, music, art, drama, and dance *are* remarkable meaning makers.

Consider the ways we construct meaning using literature and visual art. Poetry uses words, as does prose, but is different in the kind and degree of intended *emotional* impact.

1. "Our feature is blackened swordfish with grilled vegetables." (restaurant menu)

2. Mahi machi   swordfish steak
   Shrimp scampi   crab cakes
   Blackened broiled   potato-breaded
   I love fish, except with heads-on.

Example 1 is prose. It gives customers important information, but the author probably spent little time selecting each word for its emotional impact. The second example also gives information, but the author used the poetic devices of rhyme and assonance (repetition of vowel sounds) that cause a smile or the urge to read it again—just for the sound of it. We suspect the poet intended both *sound* and *sense* to be shared; the language is creative and offers a unique view of the topic. We *feel* something about the words, perhaps surprise at the poet's inventiveness.

Like poetry, visual art can communicate ideas *and* feelings, but without words. Visual images, left open to interpretation, cause fine art, or even decorative art, to engage us intellectually and emotionally. Visualize Leonardo da Vinci's *Mona Lisa* and, for contrast, the red and white label of a Campbell's soup can. Both pieces include the art elements of color, shape, size, and texture in their compositions. Campbell's Soup Company undoubtedly works hard to use art to get attention and create a design associated with "m-m-m good" feelings. Red is a warm color, set off with white, and is even faintly patriotic. The touch of gold adds a classy feel. Now contrast engagement with the label and response to Andy Warhol's *paintings* of soup cans.

Warhol's and da Vinci's painting are classified as *fine* art partly because they provoke a different kind and degree of cognitive and affective involvement than similar art used in advertisements. Fine art may be less understandable to some and may intentionally confuse, disconcert, or give cognitive dissonance. We wonder about the *Mona Lisa*, "How did he do that?" "Why is she smiling?" "Who is she?" "Why did he use those colors?" "How did he get that expression on her face?" Such art mysteries have intrigued people for four centuries, so much so that the *Mona Lisa* is one of the few paintings in the world shielded with protective glass.

Teachers who use the arts as meaning-making tools take advantage of the unique power of literature, music, art, drama, and dance to deeply affect students intellectually and emotionally. In arts-infused classrooms, students are active in productive ways. Students are engaged physically and mentally through additional learning modes because the arts possess special motivational properties and celebrate multiple interpretations. For example, in an arts-based plant unit insights about the photosynthetic process, and knowledge about characteristics of plants versus animals, can be more comprehensively developed through music, dance, and poetry. Textbooks and worksheets do not have the potential to engage students as deeply as the arts do. Nor do traditional tests reveal as much as a project or a performance can about a student's problem-solving skills. The arts are learning and teaching vehicles without match in their abilities to engage the mind and body. Students can consider artistic properties of any topic and *transform* subject matter through paintings, songs, poems, and dances. Imagine a fourth grade showing what they *know* and *feel* about converting sunshine and water

---

TAKE ACTION 1
WHY DO WE CREATE?

The film *Why Man Creates* suggests that we are compelled to create. Think of artists you know and experiences you've had creating through the arts. Add ideas to this list, give examples from your life or argue some of the points. *We create to*

◆ Construct personal meaning and search for "truth."

◆ Make beauty or express an idea esthetically.

◆ Have fun and play!

into energy, using the communication vehicles of pantomime and dance. Imagine a teacher who knows how to assess science standards using criteria to *observe* student presentations. Imagine students eager to come to school and voluntarily doing homework to prepare for learning performances. Imagine this and you've grasped the core of the integrated arts concept.

Teaching *With, About, In,* and *Through* the Arts

Because of the mounting evidence linking the arts to basic learning, some researchers refer to the arts as the "fourth R."
(Murfee, 1995, p. 4)

Arts specialists know how the arts offer a distinctive means to actively make meaning. Now, growing numbers of elementary and middle classroom teachers are using the arts to infuse science, social studies, and math with energy and relevance. A debate does still persist among some who argue *for* "arts for arts sake" and *against* the use of the arts as practical means of communicating, but Harvard University arts educator, Rudolf Arnheim (1989), has called for a "rapproachment" between applied and fine arts. He has declared the distinction between the two to be pernicious, leading to

> the notion that crafts like architecture are not quite art and that painting and sculpture are privileged to exist for no other purpose than their own sake, that is, for the mere pleasure of their appearance. . . . the arts . . . are an indispensable means of making us cope with the challenges of human experience. This is the entirely practical function of the arts, and unless it is lived up to, they cannot claim as much of a right to exist as other human activities. In other words, unless art is applied art, it is not truly art at all. (p. 54)

Fortunately, numerous school–arts partnerships have formed to create balanced and realistic perspectives on the potential role of the arts in education. The worth of the arts as unique disciplines, with specialist teachers in each discipline, is important, but a *balanced* perspective includes preparing classroom teachers to include the arts as content disciplines and *means* of learning—as alternative modes for expressing and understanding self, others, and the world. This entails teaching *with, about, in,* and *through* the arts. It is the role of classroom teachers in arts integration that is the focus of this book. This role is addressed through sections in each chapter on WHAT should be taught,

WHY, and HOW by generalists who plan to work at elementary and middle school levels.

WHY Integrate the Arts?

In each chapter, *Post It Pages* summarize newsworthy research that teachers need to know and share about arts integration. The first of seven *News Bulletin* summaries appears in Post It Page 1–1.

Reasons to Integrate the Arts

1. The arts are fundamental to all cultures and time periods.

Very little that has come down through the ages has not in some way filtered through something that we can all identify as the arts.
Sherri Geldin, Director, Wexner Art Center,
Columbus, Ohio

The arts are our cultural legacy, a kind of museum of collective memories. The arts are a heritage that stands as a monument to our creativity and resiliency. The history of the human species is told most eloquently through story, song, picture, and dance. The subject matter of the arts connects people to people, and so we can better understand the joys and sorrows of our ancestors. Think how the musical play, *Les Miserables,* increases audience members' perspectives on French history and gives poignant vicarious experiences of suffering caused by poverty and loss. Demographic projections for the next 40 years predict that minorities, with diverse cultures, will become the majority in the United States. Currently, some 90 languages are now spoken by Los Angeles schoolchildren. To live in harmony requires appreciation for societal contributions every culture makes. One source for such understanding is the arts. They are natural components of interdisciplinary and integrated learning, providing a neutral ground to learn about varied and multiple communication symbols, content disciplines, values, and beliefs.

2. The arts were the first and remain the *primary* forms of human communication. The arts teach us that all thoughts and feelings cannot be reduced to words. Through music, art, theatre, dance, and literature we are given special opportunities to look outward to understand others and inward to understand ourselves. The arts give voice to ideas and feelings in ways no other communication can, largely because

NEWS BULLETIN

Research You Can Use

◆ Grades of students involved in the arts are generally higher than those who aren't (*Champions of Change*, 2000; National Center for Education Statistics).

◆ The College Board reported that for the 1999 and 2000 school years SAT scores for students who studied visual art show a 47-point advantage in math and 31 points for the verbal portion over nonarts students. Students with music backgrounds averaged 49 points higher on combined verbal and math scores. In 1999 students with drama and dance backgrounds scored 44 points and 27 points higher, respectively.*

◆ Students educated in the 130 arts-based Waldorf schools outperformed national averages on the SAT (Oppenheimer, 1999).

◆ *New York.* An integrated arts curriculum called "Learning to Read through the Arts" yielded an improvement of one to two months in reading skills for each month students participated. Writing skills also improved. Numerous schools and districts across the country have adopted the program (Office of Educational Research, New York City Board of Education, 1993).

◆ *Los Angeles.* All 3,500 students who participated in a program that integrated the arts into literature and social studies wrote higher-quality essays, showed more conceptual understanding of history, and made more interdisciplinary references than nonparticipating students (Aschbacher & Herman, 1991).

◆ *Hamilton, Ohio.* Elementary students involved in the SPECTRA arts program made more gains in reading vocabulary, comprehension, and math comprehension as compared to a control group. Creativity measures were four times higher and gains continued during a second-year evaluation (Luftig, 1994).

◆ *Sampson County, North Carolina.* Standardized test scores went up 2 years in a row when the only thing that changed was the introduction of the arts (Hanna, 1992).

◆ *Arizona.* Stereotypical views toward minority cultures were decreased through arts instruction centered around Native American music and culture (Edwards, 1994).

◆ *Los Angeles, Boston, and Cambridge, Massachusetts.* In the arts-based "Different Ways of Knowing" program, 920 elementary students in 52 classrooms had significant gains in achievement and motivation. Students increased personal effort and were more engaged; there were more student-initiated discussions and more time devoted to literacy and problem solving. High-risk students in the program only one year gained 8 percentile points on standardized language arts tests; those with 2 years gained 16 points. Arts students had significantly higher grades in language arts, math, reading, and social studies. Nonarts students showed no gains (Catterall, 1995).

◆ *Wilmington, North Carolina.* Student disciplinary actions dropped from 130 to 50 and suspensions from 32 to 3 during the first year of involvement in the A1 School Program of arts integration. In addition, state writing test scores for fourth graders improved 30 percentile points (jumped from 35th to 65th).

◆ As many as one-third of today's students will be employed in an arts-related occupation. [Rexford Brown, p. 8, quoted in) Boston (1996)]. Arts education is important for core workplace competencies: Skills such as creative problem solving, responsibility, self-esteem, and sociability are developed through the arts (Boston, 1996; U.S. Labor Department report, "Secretary's Commission on Achieving Necessary Skills").

---

*For more information about SAT scores and college bound seniors for 1999–2000 go to (http://www.collegeboard.org/prof/). Click the "search" button and enter "national report."

they are driven by emotion and passion. The intellect, heart, and body are holistically engaged as the arts offer a unique means of knowing, thinking, and feeling *based in* imagination and cognition.

3. The arts develop the brain and give students the chance to "be smart in different ways" (Gardner, 1993).

The potential for greatness may be encoded in the genes, but whether that potential is realized . . . is etched by experience in those critical early years.

Nash, 1997, p. 56

Childhood experiences build the brain's circuits for music, art, language, math, and emotion. The brain has unrivaled power to make meaning from the messages it receives, but certain "doors to development" can be opened only during childhood. Studies of the emotional system show that it is completely wired by puberty. Frontal brain lobes responsible for cognition develop until about age 16. Unfortunately, missed chances to develop brain capacities result in lifelong handicaps. Children who see no beauty nor hear no music may spend a lifetime mute to the power of the arts to give perspective, solace, and ecstasy.

Gardner's theory of "multiple intelligences" dovetails with the concept of how the arts can act as expanded ways of knowing and expressing. Indeed, four of Gardner's eight intelligences are arts based: musical, visual (art), body-kinesthetic (drama/dance), and verbal (literature), with the other four being arts connected (logical, interpersonal, intrapersonal, and naturalistic). The arts open avenues for understanding and expression by drawing us into shared views with artists, actors, musicians, and poets. The result is more varied and unique perspectives. So we say "a picture is worth a thousand words" in terms of giving us an expanded understanding. Students who learn to play a keyboard or use paint or a slab of marble to communicate and solve problems are using kinds of "intelligence," as well.

All of us have used our arts "intelligences" at points in our lives. For example, most adults learned the alphabet through music—the alphabet song. We now know that engaging arts intelligences can make *most* learning more memorable. It is not just theory. In Connecticut, elementary students keep sketch journals and use drawing to plan writing. The arts served as creative, enjoyable, effective mnemonics for students in Kansas who wrote math raps to learn long division and for high school students to review important biology concepts (see examples in Chapter 12) as they prepared for state tests. Finally, in Montrose, New York, and Salt Lake City, Utah, drama is used to make social studies and science "lived through" experiences by having students become historical figures and simulate life on a space station (see video, *The Truth about Teachers*). Because the arts are hands-on, experiential, and problem focused, students in arts-based classes develop more creative problem-solving and higher-order thinking skills—essential "smarts" for life in the 21st century.

4. There is a strong positive relationship between the arts and academic success. *Champions of Change: The Impact of the Arts on Learning* (Fiske, 1999) is an important research document, which includes the results of an examination of the records of 25,000 students. The report summarizes consistently more favorable outcomes for students involved in the arts: higher achievement (earning mostly As and Bs and scoring in the top two quartiles on standardized tests), staying in school, better attitudes, and less television viewing time. In addition,

substantial and significant differences in achievement and in important attitudes and behaviors between youth highly involved in the arts . . . and those with little or no arts engagement . . . the achievement differences between high- and low-arts youth were also significant for economically disadvantaged students. Twenty of the differences we found favoring arts-involved students were significant at the p < .0001 level. . . . the odds of the differences being caused by pure chance were smaller than one in one thousand. (p. 3)

Active engagement is a key to academic success. The participative nature of the arts counters the passive habits that television and computers have developed in Americans. For additional examples of the effects on grades and test scores for those students actively involved in arts-based learning, see the *News Bulletin* in Post It Page 1–1.

5. The arts are avenues of achievement for students who might otherwise not be successful.

The arts teach young people how to learn by giving them the first step: the desire to learn.

Richard Riley, U.S. Department Secretary of Education

The arts can be a "feel good" alternative for students who turn to drugs and other destructive means to "get high." Tom Stang, a veteran teacher in an art-based program for troubled youth at Phoenix Academy/Drug Rehabilitation Center believes "if there is one thing I have learned as a teacher, it is that the arts are the soul of the education program" (Larson, 1997, p. 94). Problem students often become the high achievers in arts-learning settings. Success in the arts can be a bridge to success in other areas of learning, as is demonstrated in the case studies of disadvantaged urban students in New York City who were involved in ArtsConnection (Oreck, 1999). Students reported and were observed to use more self-regulatory behaviors and had a sense of identity that made them more confident and resilient. One elementary student explained, "It's like I became addicted to dance" (Oreck, p. 70).

Imagine Leonardo da Vinci in an average American school. "This illegitimate son of a poor woman, a left-handed writer who loved to draw and challenge conventional thought, would be labeled an at-risk special education candidate . . ." (Murfee, 1995, p. 8). Just as sports encourage many to stay in school, the arts can provide motivation to learn. A sculpture project in social studies or learning to play the recorder in music class can be reasons to come to school. The great teachers from children's literature come to mind here: Jesse's music teacher, Miss Edmunds, in *Bridge to Terabithia*, (Paterson, 1979), who gave him hope by helping him find beauty in his dismal life; Mr. Isobe, in *Crow Boy,* (Yashima, 1965), who tacked up an outcast child's art and changed Chibi's life with a stage performance.

The arts can uplift and elevate us to soar spiritually and emotionally from the hope that comes from a good laugh, a beautiful song, or a satisfying painting. Enthusiasm is sparked by playing with ideas and creative discovery, and the arts release creative energy—motivational energy to fuel progress toward productive goals. The potential effects of this motivation? Higher attendance rates, decreased dropout rates, fewer discipline problems, and happier students and teachers (Aschbacher & Herman, 1991).

6. The arts develop cooperation, perseverance, self-regulation, discipline and the value for hard work—important skills for personal life and success in the workplace. Imagine a day without the arts—no musical wakeup, no framed art at home, no drama on television or in theaters, no dancing, and no singing in the shower. The arts should be as prominent inside school as they are outside. The arts are an enormous, often unacknowledged, part in daily life, comprising a $300 billion business. There are arts-related career opportunities, ranging from interior decorating to teaching. The *nonprofit* arts industry alone employs over a million and a half people.

The world of work both needs and wants artistic thinkers and creative problem solvers. The business world now puts a premium on those who can employ diverse problem-solving approaches—people who will readily use intuition, as well as analysis, synthesis, and evaluation to solve problems and make judgments (Boston, 1996). Involvement in the arts prepares students to solve future problems—a lot by encouraging risk taking, experimentation, and freedom to fail. As Aristotle observed, "Art loves chance. He who errs willingly is the artist." In the real world of work, questions and problems seldom have but one answer. The arts prepare students to attend to multiple solutions, to take new tacts, and to capitalize on mistakes. Our economy depends on individuals who can imagine and produce products sought around the globe. The unique language, special symbol systems, and variety of technologies that students must master to become successful in the arts prepares them for a world guaranteed to change in unimaginable ways.

Through arts experiences such as mural making, music ensembles, and theatre productions students learn to cooperate and work as a team in ways critical to the success of both corporations and family units. Through the arts, students learn to respect unusual points of view and see that relationships among people and ideas matter. Connections are emphasized as is the importance of the *form* used to express ideas and feelings. This was illustrated in the outpouring of patriotism after September 11, 2001, in the forms of spontaneous singing of "God Bless America" when a flag was raised in Grand Central Station and the proliferation of flag art on cars, windows, and garments. These art forms express different aspects of patriotism in unique ways. As Marshall McLuhan told us in the 1970s, the "medium is the message."

Students encouraged to create and respond through the arts have special opportunities to make conceptual leaps as they learn to focus on the whole, as well as the parts, to achieve understanding. Teachers who frequently decry students' lack of attention to detail and undeveloped concern for others should consider the potential of the arts to develop student sensitivity and responsibility, as well. What's more, a strong life-connected lesson from the arts is that *quality* matters as much if not more than *quantity*. Blessed with so many *things*, students may not have learned that a nuance creates a large difference. The arts help refocus on the tremendous potential of a single word or slight gesture that can speak volumes, as Mr. Spock's raised eyebrow demonstrates. Arts educator, Elliot Eisner, reminds us that "the subtle is significant."

"Not all art is easily grasped, immediately gratifying, or even necessarily pleasant. The satisfaction and sense of fulfillment that result from coming to terms with a work of art and experiencing its resonance in our own lives is a form of pleasure and intellectual challenge simply unavailable elsewhere" (August Heckscher, President's Commission on National Goals, 1960). Self-discipline is required to master an instrument and learn lines for a school play. These skills transfer to academic learning. Students involved in the arts learn to value sustained work and understand its connection to excellence. Unlike extrinsic rewards provided by teachers or parents, the rewards from the arts are intrinsic—a good feeling of having done it yourself and the pride of *independent* problem solving. According to Richard Riley, former U.S. Secretary of Education, "The arts create a climate of high expectations, respect for quality, and a sense of how work leads to experienced achievement" (Fiske, 1999, p. 6).

7. The arts focus on alternative forms of assessment and evaluation. Quality and quantity of progress in the arts have long been measured by exhibitions, portfolios, and performances. As arts integration has evolved, classroom teachers have begun to see how "making learning visible" through the arts yields clearer indicators of the kind and degree of learning that has happened. Arts-based projects and products offer alternatives to tests as effective and more comprehensive means of documenting student growth throughout the curriculum.

8. Goals 2000, the *National Assessment* and the *National Standards for the Arts* (1994) call for arts-based education for all children.

Perhaps what makes their findings so significant is that they all address ways that our nation's educational goals may be realized though enhanced arts learning.
Richard Riley, Secretary of U.S. Department of Education
(quoted in Fiske, 1999, p. 6)

These national initiatives are discussed next and provide additional impetus for integrating the arts. How so? Specialists alone will not be able to help children meet these goals, partly because of the small number of specialists in schools and because of the limited time specialists have to teach the arts. When classroom teachers become arts collaborators, children benefit from increased time spent with the arts and have the opportunity to view the arts as learning tools used throughout the curriculum, and life, on a daily basis. Note: For examples of arts standards developed

at the state level, contact the Ohio Department of Education (Columbus, Ohio). Kentucky also has state standards for the arts that have been widely implemented. Wisconsin's Model Academic Standards for the Arts can be ordered online: (*http://www.dpl.state. wi.us/dpl/dltcl/els/pubsales/arts.html*).

Goals 2000

More than 100 national organizations from the education, arts, corporate and private foundation and government sectors have formed the Goals 2000 Arts Education Partnership to ensure that the arts become a "vital component of every child's education."
Council of Chief State School Officers,
One Massachusetts Avenue, NW, Suite 700,
Washington, DC 2001

The enactment of the bipartisan *Goals 2000: Educate America Act of 1994* included the arts as core disciplines in which all American children are expected to be competent. The full statement of the national goals follows (Post It Page 1–2), but, in a nutshell, the goals state:

- Children will be ready to learn when they come to school, be graduating from high school at a 90 percent rate, be competent in core academic subjects (including arts domains), be first in the world in math and science, and be educated in safe, disciplined, and drug-free schools.
- All adults will be ready to be employed in the country's work force.
- There will be appropriate professional development for educators.
- Parents will be increasingly involved in their children's education.

While the arts connection is obvious for the core subjects competency goal, there are important relationships between arts integration and *all* the goals. Preliminary research findings "demonstrate that arts experiences in early childhood help prepare children for their first years of school" (Welch, 1995, p. 157). Arts experiences make children ready to learn in many ways. Children who hear and sing nursery rhymes (literature and music) have a language foundation on which teachers can build reading and writing skills. This literary heritage invites children to move as parents and teachers sing "Ring around the rosie" or "London Bridge is falling down." Children dance, sing, laugh, and learn to love language and school.

POST IT PAGE 1–2

NATIONAL EDUCATION GOALS

By the Year 2000 . . .

◆ *School readiness.* All children in America will start school ready to learn.

◆ *School completion.* The high school graduation rate will increase to at least 90 percent.

◆ *Student achievement and citizenship.* All students will leave grades 4, 8, and 12 having demonstrated competency over challenging subject matter, including English, mathematics, science, foreign languages, civics and government, economics, arts, history, and geography, and every school in America will ensure that all students learn to use their minds well so that they may be prepared for responsible citizenship, further learning, and productive employment in our nation's modern economy.

◆ *Mathematics and science.* U.S. students will be first in the world in mathematics and science achievement.

◆ *Adult literacy and lifelong learning.* Every adult American will be literate and will possess the knowledge and skills necessary to compete in a global economy and exercise the rights and responsibilities of citizenship.

◆ *Safe, disciplined, and alcohol- and drug-free schools.* Every school in the United States will be free of drugs, violence, and the unauthorized presence of firearms and alcohol and will offer a disciplined environment conducive to learning.

◆ *Teacher education and professional development.* The nation's teaching force will have access to programs for the continued improvement of its professional skills to prepare all American students for the next century.

◆ *Parental participation.* Every school will promote partnerships that will increase parental involvement and participation in promoting the social, emotional, and academic growth of children.

Source: [On-line]. Available: *Gopher://gopher.ed.gov:00/00/initiative/goals/overview/file.*

Children who have the chance to explore chalk, paint, collage materials, and clay learn to take risks, experiment, and problem solve. The delight in manipulating color, line, shape, and texture can last a lifetime, be the start of an avocation in the arts, or lead to one of hundreds of arts-related careers, from designing automobiles, furniture, or clothes to making picture books for children.

Children who start school expecting success and who continue to enjoy learning have a greater chance of staying in school; "arts programs are related to dropout prevention and staying in school" (Welch, 1995, p. 157). Programs such as the Duke Ellington School's in Washington, D.C., are examples of how the arts motivate students to be successful: Ninety percent of the participants in the Boys Choir of Harlem go on to college (Gregorian, 1997). But the signs of being at risk develop early, so we can't wait until high school to make learning relevant and exciting. As Howard Gardner showed in his book *Creating Minds* (1993), it is often those unconventional "creative spir-

its" such as Einstein and Freud who make the breakthroughs in science and math; we cannot afford to lose creative thinkers who may dismiss science and math as dismal piles of dates, facts, and graphs. Instead, students can be shown how to learn math and science using musical intelligence, by kinesthetic means (dance/drama), or through the visual arts, giving them more means to enjoy learning and more reasons to return to the arts in the future. Teachers need to teach *to* interests, as well as develop new interests by presenting subject matter differerently.

An additional connection to *Goals 2000* relates to the goal of safe, disciplined, and drug-free schools. Research studies link arts-based education to a safe and orderly school environment (Welch, 1995). The arts transform the learning environment and schools become places of discovery (see "School Snapshot," p. 7). The school culture is changed, conditions for learning improve, and there is more integration and collaboration among teachers and disciplines. Even the physical appearance of a school building and its classrooms change as teachers take on more facilitative roles; the dynamics between teachers and students is altered.

Self-discipline and the arts go hand in hand, as anyone who ever learned to play an instrument knows. Thousands of hours of practice are necessary to "become good." College students who remember "forced lessons" by well-meaning parents are often thankful that they persisted. One student's journal entry speaks for so many others: "At first I just wanted to make my parents proud and I loved the applause at recitals. Eventually I found out I could get so much out of just playing—for myself. I could relax, escape, and really just change from a negative mood to a positive frame of mind by sitting down and playing for an hour or so. Other kids got high or zoned out with drugs or booze. I guess I just got high on music!" We can't tell students to "just say no." Children have to be shown ways to feel good besides sticking a destructive substance up their noses, down their throats, or in their veins.

The "Standards" Movement: National Standards for the Arts

National and state standards documents drive curriculum development, assessment strategies, and instruction in today's classrooms. Both teachers and artists need to be mindful of publications that articulate performance and content standards in curricular areas, including each of the arts disciplines.

As mentioned previously, an important justification for viewing the arts as teaching tools is the formulation of the *National Standards for the Arts* in 1994. Developed by the Consortium of National Arts Education Associations, the document is the result of an extended process of consensus building and included a review of state-level arts education frameworks, national forums, and examination of standards of other countries. The *Standards* represent agreement on what U.S. students should *know and be able to do* by the time they complete high school. (See Post It Page 1–2.) The *Standards* are voluntary and are currently being used at state and local levels as reform initiatives progress. Some states have already adopted them or developed their own versions.

The *Standards* address four arts disciplines: dance, music, theater, and the visual arts. Grouped by grade levels K–12, they suggest a basic body of knowledge and skills required to make *sense* and make *use* of the arts. The knowledge and skills are organized into these broad areas: (1) communication in each art form, (2) ability to think critically about art forms, (3) acquaintance with exemplary works of art from a variety of

TAKE ACTION 2

LOOK AHEAD

Find the *National Standards* for literature, music, art, drama/theater, or dance in the WHAT section in Chapters 3, 5, 7, 9, and 11 of this book. Do a self-assessment, using one set, to see how well you'd do if you had to meet these goals.

cultures and periods, and (4) ability to relate types of arts knowledge and skills within and across arts disciplines. While the *Standards* specify desired results, they do not dictate *how* the goals are to be reached— that's left up to local school districts.

In this book, examples of general statements in the *National Standards* for each arts area are included. All the strategies in the chapters meet one or more of the standards. The literature chapter has a *Post It Page* on national standards prepared by the National Council of the Teachers of English and the International Reading Association. A full copy of the *National Standards* is available from MENC (Music Educators National Conference). See the appendix for the address or visit their website.

National Assessment

[In a] society that values measurements and uses data-driven analysis to inform decisions about allocation of scarce resources, photographs of smiling faces are not enough to gain or even retain support. Such images alone will not convince skeptics . . .
Champions of Change, Preface

With the setting of goals and standards comes assessment—the process of collecting evidence so a determination can be made about the extent to which standards are being met. On the one hand, teachers may feel threatened by assessment that makes student achievement public. But if teachers are clear about the goals of instruction, it is more likely that instruction will be focused. A clear destination makes the success of the learning journey more likely.

The final reason for planning arts integration has to do with assessment in the arts. For over 20 years the National Assessment of Educational Progress (NAEP), known as the *Nation's Report Card*, has been the nation's barometer of achievement for student performance in reading, writing, math, and science. Groups of students in grades 4, 8, and 12 across the country are tested to determine how students measure up against standards for essential subjects. In the spring of 1997, assessment in the four arts was added and eighth graders were tested. Plans are on the table to add the fourth and twelfth grades to this periodic national measurement. The assumption is that if something is worth assessing, we must or should be teaching it as well.

WHAT DO TEACHERS NEED TO KNOW AND DO TO TEACH *WITH, ABOUT, IN, AND THROUGH* THE ARTS?

In February 1997 arts advocate Jane Remer spoke to The Kennedy Center Partners in Education at its annual conference on using the arts as teaching tools. At that Washington, D.C., meeting, she discussed the concept of teaching *with* and *about* the arts. Remer's idea was expanded to teaching *with, about, in,* and *through* the arts and is used as a paradigm to organize integration in this book. Teachers can begin at a modest level and teach *with* the arts by adding daily arts routines or centers and stations. More integration happens when teachers plan lessons *about* arts content so that students are involved *in* the arts in more mindful ways. The fullest integration is teaching *through* the arts and involves creating an esthetic classroom environment in which substantial content units are planned using the arts as both learning tools and unit centers. But to derive instructional implications for teaching *with, about, in,* and *through* the arts, planning needs to be grounded in respected teaching and learning theories. The next section provides an overview of essential knowledge relevant to arts integration, including trail-blazing *brain research,* Gardner's *multiple intelligence,* Erikson's *life stages,* Piaget's *developmental stages,* Maslow's *hierarchy of needs,* Vygotsky's *social development,* and the *creative problem-solving process.*

Brain Research: Changing Views of Development

Nearly every time I go to the bookstore there's another new book on being smart. Multiple intelligences theory has ignited interest in a nascent field that now includes emotional intelligence [Daniel Goleman's (1995) *Emotional Intelligence: Why It Can Matter*

More Than IQ was a best seller], moral intelligence, creative intelligence, practical intelligence (see Yale University's [Robert Sternberg's (1997) *Successful Intelligence How Practical and Creative Intelligence Determine Success in Life*], and Gardner's new addition to his magnificent seven, "naturalistic intelligences."

How do these expanded, more inclusive views of intelligence connect to arts integration? New views consider cultural, social, and environmental factors that raise or lower intellectual capabilities, including significant arts experiences, such as learning to play keyboards. Pioneering brain research, such as T. Berry Brazelton's, have revealed hidden links between brain activity and how the brain comes to be structured. The growth of children's brains is now visible from microscopic analyses of PET scans, MRIs, and autopsies. The brain actually grows like a budding and branching tree, depending on which areas are stimulated. By adulthood the connections in the brain are estimated to number more than 100 trillion.

Horizontal Kittens and Brain Pruning. Brain neurons start as a spaghetti-like mass. In early childhood they begin to hook up according to sensory input. Music is heard and a link is made, beautiful colors and shapes surround a child and connections happen, or a baby is rocked or cuddled and another circuit is wired. The key is not simple exposure but a pattern of repeated stimuli that sculpts the brain. "Deprived of a stimulating environment, a child's brain suffers . . . children who don't play much or are rarely touched develop brains 20% to 30% smaller than normal" (Nash, 1997, p. 51).

Windows of development for particular abilities begin to close as early as age 10 as a "draconian pruning" of excess brain synapses starts (Nash, 1997, p. 50). Some neurons may actually die; experiments showed how kittens remained blind in one eye when the eye, sewn shut at birth, was reopened. In other tests, kittens surrounded by only horizontal or only vertical visual images actually grew to be cats that could not see lines that were not a part of their kittenhood. The horizontal cats ran right into vertical bars as if they didn't exist (Hubel, 1988). In the same manner, children born with cataracts became permanently blind in affected eyes if the clouded lens was not removed by age 2. The window for human visual acuity development lasts until about age 8. If a child's environment stimuli is meager, fewer neural connections will be made so it's "use them or you lose them."

What we eventually do and become depends on how each of the brain's billions of neurons link to thousands of other neurons. Each child's brain can form quadrillions of connections, but the number and strength depend on the "transformative power of repeated experience." Startlingly, emotionally deprived babies develop "sad brains" when the center for joy and happiness (left frontal lobe) does not receive stimulation to "get on line."

> Each time a baby tries to touch a tantalizing object or gazes intently at a face or listens to a lullaby, tiny bursts of electricity shoot through the brain, knitting neurons into circuits as well defined as those etched onto silicon chips. . . . When the brain does not receive the right information—or shuts it out—the result can be devastating. (Nash, 1997, p. 54)

HOW Can Teachers Use the Brain Research to Accomplish Arts Integration?

Good teachers know that lecturing on the American Revolution is far less effective than acting out a battle.
          Robert Sylwester, University of Oregon

The thrust of this book is on HOW to implement arts integration. There is a HOW section in each chapter and separate chapters for each art form consisting solely of strategy ideas. Here are a few ideas to introduce the HOW of arts integration.

1. Make the arts an integral part of the elementary curriculum. If schools were structured based on brain research, the school and classroom environment would be alive with visual and auditory stimulation. Songs and movement would be integrated throughout the curriculum. Instrumental music would invite children into classrooms and set the tone for learning. Student passivity during lectures would be replaced with hands-on art and drama activities. It would be common for students to work in groups to write their own songs, poems and stories. Project and performance-based learning would drive the curriculum, making assessment of thinking processes (strategies and skills) and products (information and concepts) more like that in the workplace.

2. Use the power of emotions to release memory proteins. Teachers need to be intentional in their efforts to engage students in experiences that called for feelings to be felt and expressed. For example, literature and art discussions should focus on asking for multiple interpretations; artmaking would be with diverse media and about feelings and ideas chosen by students. On a simple level, background music,

dance, and creative movement all trigger emotional as well as intellectual responses. Dramatic play and exploration of art materials have the potential to alter brain chemistry because they create a feeling of optimism and well-being—play taps into brain chemicals involved in pleasure: Dopamine causes elation and excitement, and endorphin and norepinephrine heighten attention (Brownlee, 1997).

3. Use music to stimulate cognitive development.

[The] . . . fundamental components of music are inherently mathematical in nature.
          Catterall, 2000, p. 10

Accumulated studies in neuroscience in the past decade link music and cognitive development (Rauscher & Shaw, 1997), and significant relationships between math achievement and music performance in elementary students have been found (Klinedinst, 1991). Anaylsis of music at a basic level reveals obvious connections between music and mathematics (Bahna-James, 1991). Catterall (1999, pp. 9–12) explains the relationships:

1. Learning to read music involves associating abstract concepts of time, rhythm and pitch with notation symbols. Mathematical reasoning is involved when children work with the concept of fractions in the context of whole, half notes, distances of notes within scales, etc.

2. Keyboard training alone (versus computer games, simple arithmetic and singing) has a "significant effect on children's ability to classify and recognize similarities and relationships between objects." Preschoolers who received instruction for eight months scored 34 percent higher in spatial–temporal ability than other preschoolers (Rauscher, Shaw, Levine, Wright, Dennis, & Newcomb, 1997). Music, like mathematics, requires recognition of patterns and relationships. In other words, "mastering a musical instrument aids in developing mathematical understanding" (p. 10).

3. "Students concentrating in instrumental music do substantially better in mathematics than those with no involvement in music . . . low SES students with high involvement in music do better than the average student" (p. 11). "By grade 12, the differentials increasingly favor students heavily involved in instrumental music . . . thirty three percent of high-music low SES students test at high levels of mathematics proficiency . . . and only 15.5 percent of no music, low SES students" (p. 12).

The window for shaping the brain area for music is from 3 to 10 years of age, and exposing children to music rewires neural circuits (research at University of Konstanz in Germany): "The amount of somatosensory cortex dedicated to the thumb and fifth finger of the left hand was significantly larger than in nonplayers [string instrument players]" (Begley, 1996, p. 57). The younger the child is when lessons begin, the more the cortex develops. And, there is evidence that these circuits endure; consider those who successfully return to an instrument later in life after childhood exposure. What's more, the circuits for math reside in the brain near those for music, possibly accounting for the correlations between music exposure and math performance. One author concluded that "when children exercise cortical neurons by listening to classical music, they are also strengthening circuits used for mathematics." He believes the "Mozart effect" may be a result of exciting "inherent brain patterns [used] in complex reasoning tasks" (Begley, 1996 p. 57).

Additional brain research implications direct educators to

1. *Encourage an early love and command of words.* It is now clear that children at younger ages than previously thought are capable of using language, music, art, movement, and drama to make meaning; the optimum learning "window" is 10 years, beginning at birth. We should tap into these capacities and not teach down to children. Instead of back to the basics, we need to move forward to a future rich in arts-based learning, including daily poetry sharing, reading aloud, singing, storytelling, and dramatic conversations to stimulate growth in the auditory cortex.

2. *Create a nonthreatening, "synapse stimulating" environment.*

Stress causes the brain's amygdala to flood the brain with chemicals potentially harmful to development of the cortex, which causes problems with understanding. The arts have the power to relax and calm through the use of background music or strategic use of color on classroom walls. In addition, arts integration philosophy is grounded in beliefs about encouraging students to take risks, experiment, and feel free to fail.

Studies of animals raised with playmates, toys, and hands-on stimulus showed that privileged animals grew 25 percent more brain synapses than rats deprived of stimuli. The human brain is a malleable mass with infinite potential. It is childhood experiences that stimulate "which neurons are used, that wire the circuits of the brain as surely as a programmer at a keyboard reconfigures the circuits in a computer. Which keys are typed—which experiences a child has—determines whether the child grows up intelligent or dull, fearful or self-assured, articulate or tongue-tied" (Begley, 1996, p. 56).

3. *Give opportunities to move during learning.* Restricted physical activity inhibits brain and development (Begley, 1996, p. 61). For example, a child in a body cast until age 4 never learns to walk smoothly. Drama and dance are possible avenues to allow students to learn kinesthetically—to use movement essential to development.

Multiple Intelligences (MI) Theory

Strong support for arts-based learning comes from the work of researcher Howard Gardner (1983; 1993), who developed the theory that we don't have one fixed intelligence but at least eight separate ones (see Post It Page 1–3). His work with normal and gifted children, as well as brain-injured adults, led him to dispute the prevalent view of intelligence as a single general capacity used to deal with life situations (Armstrong, 2000; Blythe & Gardner, 1990). Instead, Gardner defines intelligence as the capacity to solve problems and create products that would be valued in a cultural setting. Four of the eight intelligences (verbal, visual/spatial, musical, and body/kinesthetic) are parallel to the arts domains of literature (verbal linguistic), visual art, music, and dance and drama (body/kinesthetic). The other four are linked: logical, inter- and intrapersonal are necessary for working with problem solving in all arts areas, working with people, and doing self-examination. Thus, Gardner's theory views the arts as distinct modes of thinking that fall under the umbrella of intelligence.

While Gardner posits that we all have capacities in all eight domains, he believes we usually have strengths in certain ones. Unfortunately, American schools tend to teach mainly to and through verbal and logical intelligences. Gardner believes it is "educational malpractice to continue to serve education in the same way to all consumers" and urges teachers to draw on students' stronger intelligences as vehicles for working in less dominant areas; musically inclined students might be taught fractions by using eighth, quarter, and whole notes and listening to the varying values. Musically smart students could compose melodies or rhythms to express ideas they are learning or as mnemonics. Here are sample songs from students: prepositions ("Yankee Doodle"): *Out, from, under, in between, over, of, into, through*); bodily processes ("Turkey in the Straw"): *Oh, the bile from the liver it emulsifies the fats. Oh, the bile from the liver it emulsifies the fats. Oh, the bile from the liver it emulsifies the fats, and it does it in the small intestine.* Try thinking from a musical point of view. Hum or imagine a melody Charlotte (in *Charlotte's Web*) might have sung as she spun her web.

Gardner further argues that *real* understanding does not happen unless a person transforms ideas and skills from one domain to another. Indeed, "intelligences seldom operate in isolation" (Blythe & Gardner, 1990, p. 33). Such a view of understanding is an important reason to use the arts since they are ways of *transforming* ideas and feelings using verbal and nonverbal modes.

HOW Can Teachers Apply MI Theory?

Here are practical ways to implement multiple intelligences theory.

Assess Intelligences Informally. Use the information in Post It Page 1–3 to construct a self-assessment checklist or ask students to raise their hands as you ask, *How many of you*

1. Can draw? See pictures in your head? Enjoy TV, movies, art? (visual)
2. Like to read? Listen to stories? (verbal/word smart)
3. Like sports? Like to make things with your hands? (body/kinesthetic)
4. Like to do math and science experiments? (logical/math)
5. Like to listen to music, sing, or play an instrument? (musical)
6. Like to have many friends? Enjoy being with groups? (interpersonal/people–person)
7. Like to work alone? Like to sit and think about yourself? (intrapersonal)
8. Like to be outside? Be around animals and nature? (naturalistic)

Plan to Use All Eight Intelligences. Set up eight centers or stations that give students alternative ways to "show they know" in the eight different ways to learn skills and content. Code lesson plans to note which intelligences are the focus. Use the ideas in the following chapters to present lessons in new ways, and structure alternative response options for students. (See HOW strategies sections of all chapters.)

Use the Eight-Minute Energizer (Armstrong, 1994). Give one minute to each intelligence area as a classroom routine:

TAKE ACTION 3
HOW ARE YOU SMART?

Use the information from the previous and following sections to decide your strongest "intelligences."

MI LESSON PLANNING

PLANNING	Monday	Tuesday	Wednesday	Thursday	Friday
Verbal/words					
Visual/art					
Music					
Inter/group					
Intra/individual					
Logic/math					
Kinesthetic/drama/dance					
Naturalistic					

1. *Visual:* Make pictures in your head: places, colors. Take a fantasy journey.

2. *Verbal:* Write down all the words you can think of that start with a letter or rhyme (pick a category). Make up a poem or riddle.

3. *Musical:* Hum or sing together. Play a piece of music and move to it.

4. *Intrapersonal:* Think about a goal. What would you like to do and how could you do it? How could you be a better person or student?

5. *Interpersonal:* Get a partner and give each other honest compliments.

6. *Logical:* Do quick math (e.g., add, subtract, multiply in your head).

7. *Kinesthetic:* Do toe touches, waist stretches, sky reaches, jumping jacks.

8. *Naturalistic:* Use a magnifying glass to study a plant or animal (picture) for 30 seconds and then share all the things you noticed.

Use Clear Assessment and Evaluation Criteria. Students need to have criteria for evaluation *in advance* so (1) they can explore many ways to meet the criteria and (2) any product can be examined against the criteria by the teacher or students. Optimally, evaluation criteria will be jointly developed and applied to projects, performances, portfolios of work, written materials, and other products. The key is deciding what goals

---

POST IT PAGE 1–3

GARDNER'S EIGHT INTELLIGENCES

Verbal: "Word lovers" (T. S. Eliot,* Paul Lawrence Dunbar) GOOD AT and LIKE TO

See and hear words, talk and discuss, tell stories, read and write (poetry, literature), memorize (names, facts), use or appreciate humor, use word play, and do word puzzles.

Visual: "Imagers" (Mary Cassatt, Pablo Picasso*) GOOD AT and LIKE TO

Think in pictures and see spatial relationships, draw, build, design and create, daydream and imagine, look at pictures, watch movies, read maps and charts, and do mazes and puzzles.

Musical: "Music lovers" (Igor Stravinsky,* Louis Armstrong) GOOD AT and LIKE TO

Sing, hum, and listen to music, play instruments, respond to music (tap rhythms), compose music, pick up sounds, remember melodies, and notice pitches and rhythms.

Interpersonal: "People–people" (Muhatma Gandhi,* Mother Teresa) GOOD AT and LIKE TO

Have lots of friends, join groups, talk out or mediate and resolve conflicts, empathize and understand, share, compare, relate, cooperate, interview others, and lead and organize.

Intrapersonal: "Loners" (Sigmund Freud,* James Baldwin) GOOD AT and LIKE TO

Reflect on feelings, intentions, dreams, and goals, work alone, have own space and self-pace work, pursue own interests, and do original thinking.

Logical: "Reasoners" (Albert Einstein,* Marie Curie) GOOD AT and LIKE TO

Experiment, ask questions, problem solve, figure out how things work, explore abstract relationships and discover patterns, categorize and classify, reason and use logic (inductive and deductive), do math, and play logic games.

Kinesthetic: "Body Movers" (Martha Graham,* Alvin Ailey) GOOD AT and LIKE TO

Move and use body to communicate, touch and use hands, face, gestures, do hands-on learning; kinesthetic–tactile activities, sports, dance, drama, and act.

Naturalistic: "Nature lovers" (Jacques Cousteau; Jane Goodall) GOOD AT and LIKE TO

Have and raise pets, visit zoos and parks, study animals and nature, garden, be out of doors.

---

*The exemplars that Gardner uses in *Creating Minds* (1993) each expressed *extreme* "intelligence" in at least one of the areas, but used some of all intelligences, as well. None was particularly successful in traditional school settings.

or competencies are to *be achieved* in a learning event, not just describing what students will *experience*. It is preposterous to grade any project unless students know, *in advance,* the concepts and skills that the project should show. This emphasis on clear criteria liberates creative thinking by giving focus to the problem-solving process and is a preparation for life, in which time, materials, money, and who you work with are limitations that force us to work with what they have.

Inform Parents about Multiple Intelligences.　Use Post It Page 1–3 to have parents evaluate themselves. Plan presentations and newsletters to let them know about this and other research on learning.

Set Goals with Students.　Teach lessons or a unit on the different ways to be smart. Create a form with goal blanks under each category so that students can fill in eight goals. Ellison (1992) found it useful to include a sentence description for each intelligence. Invite students to think of how to achieve goals in different ways and encourage the use of all intelligences by taking time each week to discuss what's been tried in each (Source for display posters: *"Have You Used Your Seven Intelligences Today?"* Illinois Renewal Institute, 200 E. Ward Street, Suite 274, Palatine, IL 60067, 1-800-348-4474, or a seven-poster set from Zephyr Press, 3316 N. Chapel Ave., Box 6606-A, Tucson, AZ 85728-6006).

Locate People Resources.　Find authors, artists, athletes, or fictional characters (Charlotte in *Charlotte's Web* is verbal and kinesthetic) or use Gardner's eight exemplars from *Creating Minds* (1993) (see Post It Page 1–3) to study the different intelligences. Students can also find peer examples using a Bingo game format. Make cards with different intelligence characteristics in each box. Students circulate and find names of peers that fit in each. Finally, a "Career Day" can be organized around invited guests from each of the eight intelligences to round out the search for people with diverse strengths.

Make Apprenticeships Available.　Visual students can be mentored by local artists and musical students by community members involved in the music industry. A combination of shadowing a mentor, discussing, and being coached on projects forms powerful learning opportunities.

Use Project Work.　Students can be given the choice of a topic or interest and whether to work alone or with a group as means of encouraging the use of their strengths. Ask students to think of ways to respond or *show they know* using different intelligences, and offer

---

TAKE ACTION 4

ARTS INTELLIGENCES

You are a third grade teacher and want to use arts intelligences to help students work on multiplying by 5s. Think of an activity for each of the arts intelligences:
　　For example,

Musical: Sing to "Row row row your boat": *Five times one is fi-i-ive, five times two is ten, five times three is fi-if-teen and five times four is twenty.* Music focus: melody.

Dance/movement: Give small groups problems (e.g., 5 × 5 is 25). Ask them to show this with body shapes and moves. Dance focus: shapes and moves.

Art: Use collage to create art with combinations of five. Art focus: use of space.

Literature/creative writing: Pattern poetry = each line has five beats/syllables. The title is the number of lines *times* the beats.

> *"Four Times Five Is Twenty"*
> *I love to do math*
> *It makes my mom laugh*
> *When I multiply*
> *Two times five is ten. HA!*

Drama: "One liners": each student "becomes a product" and orally expresses how he came to be. *"I am fifty and my parents are five times ten."* Drama focus: use of voice and body (e.g., fifty might be interpreted to be older through body and voice).

---

options, besides traditional reports, to present information (writing stories, poems, songs, constructing games from information, making charts, drawings, sculptures, miming, and creative dance).

Team Plan with Teachers Who Have Strengths Different from Your Own.　Plan with the art or music teacher to discover alternative means of achieving lesson goals.

Contact Schools Putting MI Theory into Operation.　Schools using MI theory include the Key School in Indianapolis and Arts PROPEL schools in

Pittsburgh. Field trips can also be taken to places that focus on a particular intelligence (e.g., symphony for music, art museum for art, library for verbal, dance concert for body).

Erikson's Stage Theory

Erik Erikson was a brilliant psychologist who spent his early years studying art. At an invitation from Sigmund Freud to study psychoanalysis, he changed his direction and in 1950 published *Childhood and Society,* a classic book about the influence of culture on child development. He concluded that all cultures place common demands on individuals, and each person develops a sense of self and relationships to others in response to *crises.* Erikson organized these crises into eight stages.

The first crisis is faced when a child must learn to *trust* to become *hopeful.* During the toddler period, the child must resolve the conflict between *autonomy* and *shame and doubt.* If autonomy and independence are developed, the child will have a sense of *will.* During the preschool years, the child struggles with *initiative versus guilt* and develops a strong *sense of purpose* if he is supported in attempts to take initiative. When a child starts school, she is usually struggling with the conflicts between *industry* and *inferiority.* If this crisis is successfully resolved, there is a growing sense of *competence.* During the adolescent years, the crisis is between *self-identify* and *role confusion,* with successful resolution leading to what Erikson termed *fidelity* or a kind of being true to yourself. The final crises are beyond the scope of this book but involve *intimacy versus isolation* (young adults) to gain acceptable love relationships, *generativity versus rejectivity* (adults) to learn caring; and *integrity versus despair* (mature adults) to gain wisdom (Erikson, 1950).

HOW Can Teachers Use Erikson's Stages?

The arts can play important roles in the successful crisis resolution encountered in each stage. In general, teachers need to (1) create a safe classroom climate that encourages risk taking, and not publicly humiliate or embarrass children by using methods such as writing names on the board for bad behavior, (2) give adequate think time so that more students try to answer questions, and (3) dignify incorrect responses to signify respect for efforts that are sincere. [For example, if the student sincerely responded *"Abraham Lincoln freed the slaves"* when asked *"What do you know about the first president?"* a teacher might say, *"Lincoln was an important president, but not the first president."* This gives accurate information and allows the child to save face.] Finally, children, like adults, struggle to feel competent and want to have a sense of purpose. Here are examples of how arts integration can contribute to developing a sense of industry and competence (the two major crises for primary and intermediate children).

◆ During early childhood (ages 2–6) the crisis of *initiative versus guilt* is successfully confronted by building on the independence (autonomy) developed in the previous stage. The arts offer opportunities for children to actively pursue activities that are intrinsically rewarding and involve use of the imagination. Making and acting on individual choices develops as students are invited to engage in dramatic play. Drama and dance help children explore grown-up roles and ways of moving without having to feel uncomfortable about making mistakes. Through arts experiences children learn that not every activity in school has to yield a "correct" product that, when done "wrong," produces feelings of shame and guilt.

◆ The arts enable students to discover the pleasure and pride resulting from being productive, working hard, and not giving up, which support the developmental crisis about *industry versus inferiority* during the elementary years. The arts allow students to create their own unique products through which they can feel that they are conquering the materials and skills of the world. Teachers can promote a sense of industry through the arts by allowing students to choose individual and group projects, to compose stories and perform poems, and to produce art responses such as sculptures and paintings in social studies and science units. In addition, through group work in drama, dance, music, and art, students have opportunities to develop feelings of competence in peer interactions. Difficulty with any of these challenges can lead to damaging feelings of inferiority. *Note:* A 35-year study of 450 males found a correlation between willingness to work hard in childhood and later success in life in personal relationships, adjustment, and income (Valliant & Valliant, 1981).

Piaget's Stages of Cognitive Development

Jean Piaget, a Swiss biologist and epistemologist, is famous for a four-stage theory based on observing children. He reasoned that the key stimulus for development was interaction with the environment. Piaget thought that, along with genetically programmed biological changes, touching, seeing, hearing, tasting, smelling, and moving and interacting with people cause children to make discoveries that alter world perceptions. In other words, children develop intellectually by experimenting—which appears to be play to adults. He believed children mentally organize reality into psychological structures used to understand and called these cognitive structures *schema*. A person either *assimilates* new information into schema or creates new or modifies old cognitive structures through the process of *accommodation*—thinking is adjusted based on new information. For example, a child might not recognize a bean bag chair as a chair and call it a "ball" because he is trying to understand using old schema. Once the child is shown how to sit in the chair, this new information is assimilated. Accommodation occurs if new information is added about the category of "furniture." In most learning there is both assimilation and accommodation.

Piaget thought these stages were natural and sequential, building on one another in a progression toward more complex thinking (see Post It Page 1–4). Since part of our genetic predisposition toward cognitive development involves continually trying to achieve an equilibrium when something is not understandable, we are motivated to make sense. But Piaget cautioned against trying to hurry up development because he believed it took too long to teach something to a child who was not ready to learn, and he offered general flexible age guidelines to gauge readiness (Piaget, 1980). While Piaget believed a child's thinking would be consistent with his or her developmental stage across situations, more recent research has demonstrated that children show characteristics of one stage in certain situations and then think at a higher or lower stage in other situations. For example, Gelman (1979) reported incidences of 4-year-olds speaking in simpler sentences when they talked to 2-year-olds, indicating they considered the needs of the younger child. This behavior was thought by Piaget to not develop until around age 7. Finally, it is worth noting that many individuals never reach the final stage of development called *formal operations*.

HOW Can Teachers Use Piaget's Theory for Arts Integration?

When teachers work with school-aged students in preoperational and concrete operational stages, they should:

Provide Hands-on Experiences. Visual aids, such as overhead transparencies, charts, timelines, diagrams, pictures, objects, and drama and dance strategies make learning more concrete. It is important to show and use examples, but *not* provide models to copy.

Give Short, Focused Explanations, Followed by Application. Teachers can use minilessons lasting 5–7 minutes and then involve students in applying what was taught. For example, a minilesson on pantomime can show how to use the face, body, and in-place movements to "become" a character. Students may then think of real-life or fictional characters and, in pairs, become "frozen statues" of characters. Characters can be tapped to come alive and do in-place moves. Teachers should coach with descriptive feedback during pantomimes to stretch creative thinking and ask students to discuss observations about themselves and others to promote depth of understanding. This is effective guided instruction that leads students to more thoughtful participation.

Start with Shorter Assignments and Engage Students. Gradually increasing length and complexity causes students to feel successful. Arts activities can start with short energizers to activate experiences related to upcoming lessons. For example, open questions like "What do you know about museums?" or "What do think of when I say the word *dance*?" can be used. Before assemblies and arts performance, *preview* or give *cue sheets* (Kennedy Center strategy) to teach about what is to be experienced. By giving *listen fors* (a character's line or a musical segment), students are more likely to be actively engaged and can then make more discoveries during performances.

Take Field Trips and Invite Guests to Give Rich Concrete Experiences. Museums, concerts, and plays are all examples of rich experiences that can extend the curriculum, especially if pretrip and posttrip activities are planned to cause students to be active meaning makers. Guest artists, storytellers, and musicians can give students direct experiences, and students can prepare interview questions, in advance, to develop language arts skills.

POST IT PAGE 1–4

PIAGET'S STAGES OF COGNITIVE DEVELOPMENT

Sensorimotor Intelligence: Birth to 2 Years

◆ Uses all senses to explore the world. Nonverbal communication.

◆ Gains understanding that objects exist even when not seen. (Remove a toy from a very young child and it won't be missed because she can't see it. Once the child gains *object permanence,* she remembers the toy and will cry to get it back.)

◆ Moves from mere reflex actions to ability to direct actions toward a goal. *Example:* Sees something and tries to get it by crying and crawling.

Preoperational: 2 to 7 Years

◆ Begins to carry out mental actions or operations that require forming and using images and symbols. *Example:* Uses symbols for objects and people. Likes fantasy and imaginative play, makes mental images, and likes to pretend.

◆ Rapid language and concept growth occurs (2,000-word vocabulary by age 4 is common).

◆ Trouble reversing actions or understanding how objects can change shape but still be the same object (doesn't think a tall glass of milk poured into a short fat glass is still the same amount; being able to think from more than one perspective comes later).

◆ Understanding other points of view is difficult since the child is egocentric (centered on own experiences). May happily talk to themselves. Thinks everyone thinks, feels, and sees as they do.

Concrete Operation: 7 to 11 Years (Hands-on Thinking)

◆ Basic concepts of objects, numbers, time, space, and causality are developed.

◆ Reversibility (two-way thinking) develops. Can classify by different categories. Understands how a group can be a subset of another (animals and plants are both "living things").

◆ Uses concrete objects to draw conclusions. Basic logic develops but is tied to physical reality; abstract and hypothetical problem solving is not attainable.

Formal Operation: 11 to 15 Years

◆ Can make predictions, think hypothetically, do metacognition (think about own thinking process and self-question).

◆ Understands sarcasm, puns, argumentation, and abstract thinking. Generates diverse solutions for problems and can evaluate alternatives based on many criteria (e.g., moral, legal, economic). Can form and test hypotheses; uses scientific method.

Source: Data for chart from Ginsberg & Opper, 1969; Piaget, 1950, 1952, 1954.

Coach Students Before and During Arts Experiences. When children are given specific language to understand basic arts elements, they can use these concepts to create new personal meaning. For example a teacher can give labels to concepts that children exhibit: "Yes, when you draw one figure on top of another it looks like the one on top is closer. That is called *overlapping.*"

Create a Life-Centered Curriculum.   Life is a series of problems, and arts-based school learning is focused on use of the creative problem-solving process. Post It Page 1–6 summarizes the process.

Provide Opportunities to Explore Ideas and Think in a Variety of Forms.   Literature, art, drama, dance, and music all have distinct ways of thinking, including special language and symbol systems. Each permits different ways of expressing and receiving information and gives students many opportunities to use the important skill of grouping or classifying. By teaching basic arts elements, we expand capabilities to think in different categories. For example, once students know that dance includes locomotor and nonlocomotor movements, they can brainstorm some of each and experiment with a greater range of movement.

Encourage Students to Construct Their Own Meaning.   Fat, or open, questions like "What makes you think that?" "How do you know that?" "What do you see?" "What have you discovered?" and "Why?" cause students to do more thinking than closed ones requiring yes or no answers. Active learning strategies that engage independent thinking, like *Think–pair–share* after questions, get students to first think of their own answers, then partner and share. Another active learning strategy, *every pupil response,* can be used in every lesson: Ask for "thumbs up" or a signal for all to *show* they have a response; wait for everyone to signal on an important question before calling on anyone. Riddles, jokes, mindbogglers, question of the day, and other puzzles challenge students to use logic and leaps of imagination to "get it." In addition, humor is intrinsically motivating, requires no grade, points, or outside reward to engage students, and may trigger further creative problem solving, such as students writing their own arts riddles (Cornett, 2001).

Maslow's Hierarchy of Needs

In the 1970s, Abraham Maslow proposed a theory of motivation that has helped educators understand why children do what they do—or don't do. Maslow observed that his subjects seemed to be motivated by what they *needed.* He proceeded to categorize the needs people sought to fulfill and organized them into a hierarchy, with the basic needs for surviving, like food, clothes, and a place to live, on the bottom (see Post It Page 1–5). Once lower-level survival needs and safety needs were met, he believed people moved up the ladder. He thought the three top levels, including

the need for beauty, represented needs that were *never* filled, so people continued to always seek more in these areas, unlike the low-level needs that are ignored once fulfilled.

HOW Can Teachers Use Maslow's Hierarchy?

Maslow's information on needs-based motivation suggests that children who are hungry, thirsty, too hot (un-air-conditioned schools), afraid, or worried about their home life have difficulty engaging in arts activities requiring focus on higher-order esthetic needs. Teachers can help children get lowest needs met through school breakfast and lunch programs and referrals to social agencies. Comfort and safety needs (second level) can be met through strategies such as telling students that mistakes are okay, giving second chances after genuine effort, and offering choice, such as where to sit to learn. Humor in the form of appropriate riddles, gentle teasing, and the teacher making fun of his or her own mistakes can relax students. While we strive for students to think they are individuals with unique and different ideas, the need for group approval is very powerful (third level). Many seek to conform and copy ideas from peers. This is a particular problem in the arts, where uniqueness is highly valued, but where students often feel fearful about being different. Teachers can share stories about artists who have taken risks by being different (e.g., cubism was thought ridiculous by many of Picasso's contemporaries) and celebrate novel responses with clear descriptive feedback: "Joe painted his sky with orange and red in it." The need for group approval can also be met by forming *learning circles* to allow students to collaborate on projects, such as writing songs or poems.

Children are not easily pigeonholed and may have needs operating simultaneously at many of Maslow's levels. Stories about artists who deny themselves survival and safety needs to pursue intellectual achievement, esthetic needs, and self-fulfillment can help students think about the motivational power of higher-order needs. For example, students might discuss why Monet and other Impressionists made paintings others thought looked unfinished. (See short biographies of artists, writers, and musicians by Kathleen Krull in the arts-based bibliography in the appendix.)

Finally, while we are motivated to *get* some things, many activities are motivating in and of themselves. Teachers can design a classroom around arts experiences that require no extrinsic rewards (food, candy, stickers) because they are *intrinsically* motivating. Just

MASLOW'S HIERARCHY OF NEEDS

Highest level = Self-fulfillment
 Esthetic needs for beauty and order
 Knowledge and intellectual needs
 Approval and recognition from others
 Belonging, love, acceptance by others
 Physical and psychological safety
Lowest level = Survival needs: food, clothes, water, shelter

Source: Maslow (1970).

---

being in a beautiful room can be emotionally and intellectually satisfying. With the help of students, teachers can make the classroom beautiful with plants, artwork, background music, and potpourri. Another powerful intrinsic motivator is interest, which can be developed through regular times to work on interest-based projects and offering choice whenever possible. Intellectual achievement is encouraged by allowing time and other opportunities to pursue independent projects involving the arts; students might study a person or topic in the arts that connects to units. Teachers can make it a habit to encourage being curious and wondering by having a "Wonder Box" to drop questions and topics that students would like to learn about or information they would like to share (facts about artists or artworks can cause otherwise apathetic students to become excited about learning).

Vygotsky's Social Development

Russian psychologist Lev Vygotsky (1978; 1986) is another researcher who has given educators a theory from which important arts integration strategies can be derived. Unlike Piaget, Vygotsky thought teachers and other mentors could and should intervene in children's learning and act as *scaffolds* to bridge the gap between where a child *was* functioning and a stage just out of reach, but attainable. He called this developmental position the *zone of proximal development* (ZPD) and demonstrated how students can often solve problems with some help (cues, suggestions, steps, encouragement) from others when they cannot do so independently.

HOW Can Teachers Use Vygotsky's ZPD?

The critical idea is to observe students to determine when they can proceed independently, when others might offer some assistance to expedite success, and when the problem or activity is not appropriate at all for a child. Determining this match involves teachers in *instructional* creative problem solving, estimated to occur thousands of times each day in each teacher's classroom. Vygotsky believed social interactions with others boosted intellectual growth, so the implication is to plan arts experiences in which students can work in pairs, triads, quads, and as a whole group. By listening to each other tell what they see in a piece of art or hear in a piece of music, everyone has the chance to get another perspective and make new connections (*peer scaffolding*). For example, "Junior Great Books" literature discussions start with an open question that the questioner *really* wants to discuss because the answer is unknown. For example, "Why did Jack go up the beanstalk the third time when he already had all the money he would ever want?" While there are clues in the story, there is not *an* answer, so students must interpret based on text clues. This co-construction of meaning leaves everyone, including the teacher, with ideas beyond individual realms of meaning.

Creativity and Creative Problem Solving

We are overwhelmed with contemporary problems. Solutions can't be remembered because they never existed: How *do* you stop terrorism? We must *create* new solutions. Who is to do this creative problem solving in the future? Our children, of course, and to focus teaching on fact worksheets and nasty looks is not a strategy for success. In this section, information about creativity and creative problem solving is provided to offer ideas for success. Moreover, integration of the arts rests on the ability to use the creative problem-solving process; the arts, in turn, advance creativity.

One of our most pressing societal needs is to determine what aspects of creativity can be influenced and what might even be directly taught. We're not sure where creativity comes from, exactly what it is, or how it develops. We could just sit back and wait for Plato's muses to visit us or, taking a cue from behaviorist B. F. Skinner, wait for it to happen and then reinforce it with stamps and stickers. Neither waiting nor rewarding seems wise. We can start work mindful that the known "truths of the universe" were born of personal struggle and honed by ancient practices like noticing *patterns*. Creativity emerges from time spent looking closely at details and listening intensely to gather data that yield *realizations*. These gifts of the mind can be intentionally used and taught. By teaching creative thinking we do more than "disturb the universe"; we create it and, in some sense, control it. Of course, using the creative process without considering the consequences can be frightful, as the Jewish folktale of the golem reminds us: Man's creativity, mindless of morality, is a destroyer. (One version, *The Golem* by Wisniewski, won the Caldecott Medal for picture books in 1997.)

Enhancing creativity through the arts rests on developing habits that include celebrating differences of mind, spirit, and body; inviting students to choose within moral limits; and using the motivational power of personal interest that can change the world—I think here of Philo Farnsworth reading old science magazines he found in the attic of his family's Iowa farmhouse. Time to pursue a teenage fascination with electrons led him to envision the rows of his plowed field as a metaphor for the creation of the cathode ray tube, which gave us television. We can begin with a cultivation of creative thinking strategies and a commitment to depth of knowledge in domains where creative work is to be done. We can acknowledge that no one creates in a vacuum or without building on foundations others laid. And we can begin by valuing creativity and using it as a high-placed criterion for sorting out what goes in and should come out of curricula— curricula currently too jam packed to allow substantive

creative meaning making. Author and teacher Alane Starko (1995) believes that

> the most reasonable course of action is to support and encourage characteristics associated with creativity whenever possible. At the very least, our classrooms should be more flexible, responsive, attuned to the wonder around us. At best, we may make a difference in the creativity of a young person who may one day bring greater knowledge or beauty into the world. (p. 93)

Creative Problem Solving and Life.   It is common to associate creative thinking with artists. The arts invite all of us to explore the unusual and create something different, even if it's just another interpretation of a movie. But creative thinking is also an everyday survival skill, a kind of thinking crucial for success in the 21st century. Whether we are deciding how to stretch a budget or attempting to deal with ways to make air travel safer, we use innate abilities to creatively solve problems. Indeed, the most troublesome problems will only be solved by creative thinking— divergent, original thinking that examines issues from new perspectives. There is no textbook chapter nor Internet site that has the solution to global terrorism. Remembering facts and rote skill application, too often the focus in elementary math, science, and social studies, are not sufficient for children who face a future fraught with unthinkable problems. Therefore, a major part of the school day needs to be spent engaging students in creative problem solving; the arts provide the most fertile ground for growing this indispensable higher-order thinking.

What Is Creativity?   The most important things in life are hard to define: love, happiness, art. Creativity is no exception. But many have tried. I especially like Perkins' (1988) definition because it implies that everyday people have what it takes to be creative. He believes creativity is simply "using ordinary resources of the mind in extraordinary ways" (p. 38). To use one's experiences, thinking skills, and knowledge of a field in novel and appropriate ways to produce something new, at least new to the individual, seems doable. But, context is very important in arts experiences, and this is especially apparent with regard to what is considered creative. Societies value original products needed by specific groups and cultures. What is thought creative in one culture or time is not valued in another; for example, re-stickable mini notes probably wouldn't have been hot among 12th-century European peasants; common 20th-century conveniences such as the paper clip are not now thought creative, but they must have amazed first users.

Four Creativity Theories or Models. Researchers have tried to make sense out of the elusive concept of creativity through four angles: (1) examining characteristics of creative people, (2) studying the stages or process of creativity, (3) identifying influences on creativity, and (4) developing an interactive theory. Characteristics of creative people, especially adults, have been studied by researchers such as MacKinnon, Torrance, Tardif, and Sternberg. The stages in the development of creativity and the process of creative problem solving interested Plato, who thought creativity to be a mystical process that resulted from divine intervention and was manifested in bursts of insight. Aristotle believed creativity was explainable by natural laws, just like any other thinking process. His theory was later used by Perkins, Guilford, and Weisberg. Other notable theorists using the stages and process approach are Wallas, Csikszentmihalyi, Maslow, and Vygotsky. B. F. Skinner observed creativity to be a function of behavioral influences: Creativity naturally occurred and, if reinforced, was repeated. Finally, an interactive theory presents creativity as an interaction among (1) individuals using cognitive processes such as divergent thinking, (2) functioning in particular domains or fields (e.g., math or science), and (3) their environment (culture and time period). Sternberg, Gardner, Csikszentmihalyi, and Amabile are all proponents of variations on this last theory.

HOW Can Teachers Use the Research on Creativity?

This section provides an overview of theories and possible arts integration strategies.

Characteristics: The Creative Spirit Profile

Creative children look twice, listen for smells, dig deeper, build dream castles, get from behind locked doors, have a ball, plug in the sun, get into and out of deep water, sing in their own key.

Paul Torrance, 1973

Teachers don't go around saying, "I am not able to do math" or "I can't read." If they did, we would question their competence and find it absurd for them to be employed as professionals. But some teachers do say, "I am not creative" and in doing so limit themselves and their students in their use of innate creative capabilities. Belief in the ability to be creative and valu-

ing creativity are key attitudes needed to increase the likelihood that creativity will happen. It is unacceptable for a teacher to claim that she or he does not have important real-life creative thinking skills that students need to be taught. And creative problem solving *is* an essential survival skill.

While it is hard to find agreement about a definition of creativity, there is consensus about which processes are commonly used to arrive at creative products (Post It Page 1–6), and there is a collection of attributes associated with creativity. Studies of highly creative children and adults (the bulk of the studies) yield a profile to use to observe students and plan a classroom environment to encourage creative thinking (Post It Page 1–8). No two people have the same profile and there is no generic creative person. We all possess degrees of most of the characteristics.

Find out what researchers have discovered in studies of people who have produced highly creative work by doing Take Action 5. Teachers may choose to encourage some of the characteristics in themselves and their students, while others may be undesirable features. To become familiar with the characteristics, take time to rate the level you have of each characteristic. There is no "right" or "better" profile, but the characteristics should help crystalize the many dimensions of creativity and show how all people have creative attributes.

Creative characteristics (Csikszentmihalyi, 1990; Dacey, 1989; Gardner, 1993; Getzels & Jackson, 1962; Tardif & Sternberg, 1988) often emerge in childhood and there are high-frequency patterns of:

- First born
- Childhood trauma, such as loss of a parent
- Estranged relationships with family
- Family that values learning and a pattern of clear expectations and few rules
- Early successes
- Likes school, books, collections
- Creative products emerge in 10-year groupings (Gardner)
- Benefits from role models, mentors
- Has a supportive person who understands person's work
- May have strong social peer group or be marginal, i.e., somewhat of an outsider
- Parents had own interests
- Problem finders, not just problem solvers

CREATIVE SPIRIT PROFILE

Directions: Use a scale of 1 = not evident to 5 = very evident to self-evaluate. Follow with goal setting.

Personality Characteristics

_____ 1. Curious and questioning.

_____ 2. Likes to explore. Seeks adventure.

_____ 3. Spontaneous, impulsive, and uninhibited.

_____ 4. Stable, emotionally secure.

_____ 5. Risk taker and courageous. Doesn't care what others think. Uses mistakes to solve problems.

_____ 6. Takes chances, but not reckless.

_____ 7. Loses track of time. Dislikes deadlines.

_____ 8. Self-confident in own worth and work.

_____ 9. Independent and nonconforming. Likes original ideas. Unlikely to follow the crowd.

_____10. Skeptical of authority. Resistant to "right answers." Easily bored with routine.

_____11. Sense of humor. Playful with words and ideas.

_____12. Critical of self. Not often satisfied, but not easily discouraged either. Sets own standards to judge.

_____13. Likes to work alone. May appear aloof. May not fit in or seek out groups.

_____14. Motivated, hardworking, and persistent. Not easily frustrated. Willing to struggle, sustain effort.

_____15. Sense of wonder and delight—almost childlike in this respect.

_____16. Tolerant of ambiguity. Tolerates anxiety. Doesn't need one right answer.

_____17. Broad interests and hobbies.

_____18. Empathetic. Feels others' pain.

_____19. Strong sense of destiny.

Cognitive Characteristics

_____ 20. Fluent: can generate lots of ideas.

_____ 21. Flexible: can shift perspectives easily and change categories quickly.

_____ 22. Original: comes up with unique ideas. Likes to transform ideas.

_____ 23. Elaborates: can flesh out ideas with details.

_____ 24. Observant: Notices details about people, places, things. Senses are acute.

_____ 25. Intelligent: Creativity and intelligence are correlated. Intellect does not guarantee high creativity, but a threshold level is necessary.

_____ 26. Logical: uses details and evidence to support ideas.

_____ 27. Imaginative and resourceful. Can combine ideas in new ways with vivid detail.

_____ 28. Uses hunches and guesses. Intuitive.

_____ 29. Seeks possibilities and variety. Likes divergent thinking and novelty.

_____ 30. First inclination is to explore possibilities versus do critical thinking or say, "It won't work."

_____ 31. Approaches problems playfully. Can become overly excited.

_____ 32. Likes open-endedness. Is a problem finder.

_____ 33. Visualizes. Uses metaphoric thinking to problem solve.

_____ 34. Organizer. Likes to create order from chaos. Prefers complexity and asymmetry.

_____ 35. Goal and task oriented. Focused.

Sources: Barron, 1969; Dacey, 1989; Isaksen and Treffinger, 1985; MacKinnon, 1978; Torrance, 1962; Tardif & Sternberg, 1988.

CREATIVE PROBLEM-SOLVING PROCESS (CPSP)

I. Preparation (Conscious)

1. *Problem is first presented or found.*
2. *Motivated attitude:* "Can do, will do, want to do!" Emotion causes motion.
3. *Problem described:* What is the problem, specifically? "A problem well defined is half solved" (Charles Kettering).
4. *Data gathering:* Input facts by reading, researching, interviewing. Put in hard work. "We can have facts without thinking, but we cannot have thinking without facts" (John Dewey).

II. Creative Thinking

5. *Divergent thinking* (Alex Osborne's "brainstorming"): Quantity first! "The best way to have a good idea is to have lots of ideas" (Linus Pauling, scientist). Generate many ideas. Use webbing and clustering to record ideas.

    a. *Withhold judgment:* Do *not* evaluate or analyze ideas yet or risk shutting down right-brain thinking.
    b. *Be fluent:* Generate lots of ideas.
    c. *Be flexible:* Try different perspectives or categories; examples/nonexamples.
    d. *Be original:* Never take the first idea. Think of what no one else will think of. Stretch. Often the idea right after you seem to run out is the best idea.
    e. *Elaborate:* Add details and examples to ideas.
    f. *Play with ideas:* Experiment! Ask "What if. . .?"
    g. *Use SCAMPER* (Eberle, 1971; Osborne, 1963):
        (1) *Substitute*—change characters, setting, time, place, . . .
        (2) *Combine*—force relationships; e.g., "How are a computer and a tree related?" Connect.
        (3) *Adapt*—compare and think metaphorically. "What is this like?"
        (4) *Modify*—change color, size, shape, . . .
        (5) *Magnify*—add to or make larger.
        (6) *Minify*—make smaller.
        (7) *Put to other uses*—apply differently.
        (8) *Eliminate*—subtract something.
        (9) *Reverse or rearrange*—backward, upside down, inside out.

III. Incubation (Unconscious) and Illumination (Semiconscious)

6. *Rest:* Let the subconscious work. Plan idle time. Get away.
7. *Insight:* A light goes on; "ah-ha" stage.

IV. Evaluation and Action (Conscious)

8. *Judge:* Use preset criteria (time, money, morals) to decide which solutions are best. "The second goal of education is to form minds which can be critical, can verify, and not accept everything they are offered" (Jean Piaget).
9. *Put the idea into action:* Try it. Elaborate. Revise.
10. *Share, publish (make public):* Celebrate.

Sources: Wallace 1926; Czikszentmihalyi, 1990; Dewey, 1920.

The Process of Creative Thinking. An understanding of the process of creative problem solving has emerged from the work of researchers such as Csikszentmihalyi (1990) and Wallace (1926). Here is a glimpse into the process at work.

> *"It takes an enlightened stubbornness to produce anything,"* declared a man with a British accent.
>
> *Trevor Baylis was being interviewed about an invention he created. It all started when he had been watching a TV program on the AIDS problem in Africa. Baylis became "aware" of the ballooning disease statistics and the efforts to educate the African population by radio. The part of the problem that intrigued Baylis was the inability of people to afford or obtain batteries—it cost about a month's salary to buy batteries and some people were actually giving up their rice to buy them. Baylis began to visually imagine being in Africa in a pith helmet with a monocle and glass of gin. This input triggered the image of a wind-up radio.*
>
> *"It just popped into my head,"* he laughed.
>
> *He said it seemed so simple he was sure someone else must have already thought of it. But he investigated and his inquiries showed no one had!*
>
> *"Everyone has a good original idea, but most don't come to fruition because we worry about humiliation, e.g., people laughing, or that our idea is not new,"* he explained.
>
> *So Baylis experimented with different springs and was able to make a radio that would play for 40 minutes with 20 seconds of winding. Now the Third World has a cheap way to use mass communication and the rest of the world is interested, too.*
>
> August 27, 1995 5:30 P.M. on *National Public Radio*

Baylis's story illustrates the *stages* people go through when they do creative problem solving. What's interesting is how we can *manage* our own processes by knowing the conditions necessary to "prime the pump" of imagination. The process begins consciously with an awareness that a problem exists or a desire to do *problem finding*—a personal decision to look for new uses, products, and the like. Next, an unconscious or idle period happens, called *incubation* by some theorists. An "ah-ha" problem solution brings a person back to conscious focus on the problem, followed by testing and evaluation of ideas or solutions. Another way of describing the process is by thinking about the brain hemispheres taking turns working on the problem: left (conscious), right (unconscious), left–right (insight on problem), and finally left again (evaluation).

Think about Baylis and your own experiences as you examine the *creative problem-solving process* in Post It Page 1–6. Use the process to spur yourself as you engage in arts experiences and plan lessons and experiences for students. Display the process (in simplified form) for stu-

dents to refer to as they work. Take time to talk to students about the processes, do minilessons on strategies, and when kids get stuck refer to ways to propel thinking forward (e.g., data gathering, brainstorming, SCAMPER, etc.).

Creativity Killers

To engender creativity, first we must value it.
Sternberg and Lubar, 1991

Unfortunately, parents and teachers often do not look favorably on behaviors peculiar to creativity. Just like Leo Lionni's main character in *Frederick*, children who are loners and want to "do their own thing," rather than conform to adult expectations, may be looked on as troublemakers. It is frightening to read reports detailing how creative thinking declines in children as they move through school. Some studies have even concluded that fourth grade is the peak of creativity for many students. Post It Page 1–7 lists common *creativity squelchers*.

Creativity Boosters

I have no special gift. I am only passionately curious.
Albert Einstein

If we are to facilitate creative thinking, we must teach content in ways that support, rather than threaten, habits and mind-sets that allow creative ideas to blossom. Any subject can be the basis for creative thinking, if we provide students with opportunities to learn information, methods, and strategies and then teach how to use them in new ways. Traditional content teaching that emphasizes facts and single correct answers is not going to help students learn flexibility or originality. However, it is not enough for children to just play with creative puzzles and games. They must know enough about something to question it, change it, elaborate on it, or do something new with it, and they must have been taught strategies to accomplish these tasks. Post It Page 1–8 lists strategies to boost creative thinking.

HOW CAN A TEACHER COORDINATE RESEARCH AND THEORY FOR ARTS INTEGRATION?

A dramatic revolution in cognitive understanding began in the 1970's. Research now substantiates what some teachers and parents already knew intuitively—that the arts are critical to learning.
Murfee, 1995

POST IT PAGE 1–7

CREATIVITY SQUELCHERS

Directions: Think of yourself or a teacher as you examine the attitudes and behaviors that threaten students' psychological safety. Mark the ones that are of particular concern.

◆ Assessment and evaluation: too much, too soon, too often. The cake falls if you open the oven too soon or too often. Even positive evaluations can inhibit next efforts at creative work.

◆ Hovering over students as they work so that they feel watched.

◆ Extrinsic rewards such as stamps, stickers, and praise that block risk taking and focus on "getting things" rather than the worth of the activity itself.

◆ Worry. Fear. Not feeling safe enough to take risks and make mistakes.

◆ Competition, especially when knowledge and skills are great enough to hope for success.

◆ Too much emphasis on the product rather than the process.

◆ Too little choice, especially of *how* to do an assignment or reach a goal.

◆ Too much emphasis on order, neatness, and following directions.

◆ Preponderance of teacher questions that ask for literal answers.

◆ Lack of incubation/wait time.

◆ Insufficient information to incubate.

◆ Rush to judgment about value of ideas. Saying "That won't work" right off the bat.

◆ Adults doing *for* children what they could do, or do partially, themselves (leads to learned helplessness).

◆ Lack of independent study time to pursue ideas of personal interest.

◆ Taking everything too seriously. Teachers that rarely laugh, play, or express a sense of humor.

◆ Stereotyped or dictated art activities such as coloring books. Emphasis on "staying in the lines" and "predigested activities that force youngsters into imitative behavior and inhibit their own creative expression" (Lowenfeld & Brittain, 1975, pp. 22–25).

POST IT PAGE 1–8

WAYS TO BOOST CREATIVE THINKING

◆ **Brainstorm:** (1) Go for quantity first. (2) List all ideas. Keep driving and don't brake! (3) Include way-out ideas. (4) Piggyback on each other's ideas. (5) Set a time limit. After finishing, ideas can be grouped. Then evaluation begins (Osborne, 1963). Some research supports doing individual before group brainstorming to produce *more* ideas. Giving evaluation criteria before brainstorming session will reduce the number of ideas, but may increase quality. *Variation: Reverse* brainstorming. Brainstorm nonexamples instead of examples.

◆ **Word association** (similar to brainstorming): List everything connected to a given word. Use to introduce a lesson [e.g. Use "courage" as the concept to introduce the book, *Mirette on the High Wire* (McCully, 1992). Ideas can be written by the teacher or students].

◆ **Use question frames as prompts:** "How might we . . . ," "What if . . . ," "What are all the ways . . . ," "An idea nobody would think of is . . ." Focus on a problem under study (e.g., how might we move if it was winter and we were marching from Valley Forge?).

◆ **Stumped or stymied?** Stop and do something else. Listen to music or do something physical (e.g., stretches and bends to music).

◆ **Turn mistakes into opportunities.** See *The Big Orange Splot* by D. M. Pinkwater (1993). Make lemonade!

◆ **Data gather.** Sometimes there just isn't enough of a knowledge or skill base. Stop and read, observe, talk.

◆ **Don't take the first idea.** The best idea may be the one right after you think you've run out.

◆ **Mind meld.** Open an encyclopedia, dictionary, or magazine and pick an idea (noun, verb). Combine this idea with the one you are trying to develop. Don't worry about weird ideas. Just stretch mentally because "An imagination once stretched will never again have the same dimensions." *Example:* I spotted scissors by my computer. I can meld the scissors with this chapter: I want to *cut out* drab teaching and can make *points* for why to use arts-based teaching. Scissors and the arts can be tools or weapons. There are different kinds of scissors (pinking, pruning, etc.), just as there should be a variety of arts-based programs.

◆ **Thinking Hats:** Get with four other people. Each of you "wears a hat" or takes a perspective on a problem: Hat 1 describes what is known, hat 2 gives feelings about the problem, hat 3 tells what is not known, hat 4 thinks of associations or images, and hat 5 lists ideas not at all related, i.e., nonexamples (adapted from deBono, 1991). This is similar to "cubing" (Neeld, 1986) in which a topic is explored in six ways: describe it and tell its parts, tell how it feels, what do you associate with it, what could you do with it, what is it like, and argue for or against it. This can be timed (e.g., spend 2 minutes on each "side" of the cube, or do one or two sides a day).

TAKE ACTION 6

PRACTICE THE **CPSP** PROCESS

Here are facts about the creative problem-solving process, followed by an "if–then." Consider the information as a proposition (if) and try to think of ways a classroom teacher might put the information into practice (then).

◆ CPSP can be an individual or group and may take minutes or years. When people become deeply involved, they attain the state Csikszentmihalyi called "flow" (1990). In decades of cross-cultural research on happiness—from Tokyo teens to Italian farmers—he found people who remembered being so engaged they lost all track of time. Flow is a highly motivating condition so people give enormous amounts of time and energy during flow. The sense of discovery and connections is like being transported to a new reality. Flow is a time of great enjoyment and is active, not passive, like TV watching. Blocks of time are needed to reach flow. The whole world seems closed out. It is an optimal experience during which a person feels focused, exhilarated, and satisfied. **If all this is true, then teachers should . . .**

◆ Creativity involves a leap that transcends logic, but is built on a base of knowledge and skills. Expertise is absolutely necessary to creativity. You cannot create without inputting ideas or skills. **If this is true, then teachers should . . .**

◆ Strategies for manipulating concepts and ideas (e.g., SCAMPER) in content areas, finding problems, and looking at content in new ways facilitate the creative process. **If this is true, then teachers should . . .**

◆ Motivation and positive attitude play a prominent role in creative problem solving. These mental states keep individuals committed to a task long enough for exploration, problem finding, and creative thinking to happen at all. **If this is true, then teachers should . . .**

◆ The creative process involves a struggle. Teachers who substitute following directions for creative thinking may think they are helping students by making it easy for them. Instead, such teachers are robbing students of opportunities to grow by overcoming obstacles. Feelings of accomplishment and pride stem from success-ful struggles. There is no creation without frustration; it involves bringing order to chaos, relating the unre-lated, connecting, discovering patterns, answering and raising questions—all of which are higher-order think-ing processes. (Note that, like creativity, humor does not come out of happiness, but out of conflicts and problems. Even a riddle is a problem to be solved—creatively.) **If this is true, then teachers should . . .**

◆ By looking carefully, observing, and discovering patterns, we can accumulate important data to fuel the fire of creativity. **If this is true, then teachers should . . .**

◆ We stand on the shoulders of our ancestors in our creative efforts, building bit by bit in a long, constantly evolving effort. **If this is true, then teachers should . . .**

◆ The process is goal oriented and focused. **If this is true, then teachers should . . .**

◆ There is a difference between problem solving and problem finding. The latter is as much needed as the for-mer. There are three problem types: (1) ones given to us and we are to apply a known formula (most school problems), (2) a problem is given but the solution is unknown, and (3) a problem is not presented, but must be found, and the solution is unknown (e.g., advertisers try to create markets for products we don't even know we need or want). **If this is true, then teachers should . . .**

◆ Creativity includes a variety of types of thinking, including metaphoric, divergent, and convergent, combining opposites (e.g., "dull sunshine"). **If this is true, then teachers should . . .**

Conditions for Learning: Basic Beliefs

This chapter has presented much information about research and theories that support the concept of arts integration. All of us can "stand on the shoulders of the greats" as we put theory into practice, but only in-dividual teachers can convert these ideas into class-room reality. Every teacher must use her or his own ex-periences, creativity, and desire to help children, as forces behind a workable philosophy or set of beliefs—a work forever in progress. Basic beliefs about what students need to be successful are best set out *before* beginning to teach. It is often easier to work from a draft, so here is one to use to synthesize a model for creating a classroom for student meaning making *with, about, in,* and *through* the arts. Try using statements starting with **"I believe in . . ."**

Immersion. Students need to be in a stimulat-ing, accepting classroom. This is shown in an esthetic physical environment full of books, posters, fine art, music, and opportunities to move and pretend. Students need to be around others who are in the process of creating mean-ing with, about, in, and through the arts.

Expectation. Students need to *expect* to be creative and successful. This expectation is made strong when teachers support student risk taking

through their comments and actions. Students also need to know what to expect, in terms of the schedule and basic routines. Predictable structures and schedules that use creative variations contribute to clarity.

Freedom to fail. All people experience failure; students need to learn how mistakes can be opportunities. The classroom environment, created mostly by teacher attitude, should encourage experimentation and allow students to feel comfortable learning from mistakes.

Meaningfulness. People want to be involved in important and purposeful work that contributes to their own happiness and the happiness of others. This means goals need to be clear. Learning is most successful when it is focused on solving life problems with life-centered materials and strategies, such as focus on *discovering patterns* in all disciplines. To paraphrase John Dewey, school is not preparation for life—it is life. Each person must *create* personal meaning using all meaning-making tools available, including reading, writing, speaking, listening, drama, music, art, literature, and dance.

Demonstration. We all need examples, not models, to copy. Demonstrating strategies and techniques is crucial to learning and gets learning started. (The *I do–we do–you do* process is credited to Wittenberg University Professor Chuck Novak.) Children do not need teachers to *do* tasks *for* them because this encourages dependency.

Active learning. People remember more, are more satisfied, and achieve mastery of ideas and skills sooner when they are mentally and/or physically engaged. Active learning includes starting with the known and building on that knowledge and skill base. Passive listening to a lecture or watching a video is not effective. Hands-on learning is powerful: If you don't act, you don't learn.

Application and practice. Repeated practice of what has been introduced helps students to own the new skill or idea. One of the greatest problems in our schools is not giving students adequate amounts and numbers of *meaningful* practices. Without practice, it is almost impossible to achieve competence, and it is competence that puts us in control of our own lives.

Independence. Human beings want to be in charge of themselves and need to learn how to work independently. We are proud of ourselves when we can function using our own resources. Teachers can move students toward independence by teaching independent problem-solving strategies and providing time to work independently. It is important to have role models of hardworking people who persist at overcoming obstacles to independence. Independence is gained only through hard work to obtain a knowledge and skill base in the areas in which we want to work.

Responsibility. People become responsible when they are taught how to make good choices and are given second chances. There is a story about how Thomas Edison had just finished an early prototype of his light bulb. He called a boy to take it to the factory, and the boy dropped it on the way. Edison had to start all over. When he had another light bulb made—many days later—he sent for the same boy. He told him to take it to the factory.

Progress and success. We progress when we have goals that are clear and can gauge improvement by self-evaluation and feedback from respected others (hopefully teachers). We all need concrete progress indicators to feel like we are getting better.

Motivation. People are motivated by the ABCs and Z: Achievement, Belonging to a group, Control/choice, and Z (intrinsic factors such as interest). External reinforcers such as stamps, stickers, and praise can decrease interest in doing something for its own sake. People are motivated by challenge, but if it is not appropriate, it will lead to frustration or boredom.

Creativity. People are born creative and can learn to intentionally use their creative capacities. The arts provide some of the richest arenas for developing creative capacities. Evaluation, certain time restraints, and close surveillance can inhibit creativity. Humor and play are essential to developing creative capacities.

Teachers. A teacher's own knowledge, strategy repertoire, enthusiasm, humor, creativity, and passion are forces so powerful they can change a child's universe, as well as the future we all share. A teacher's artistry can give hope and vision to tackle personal and world problems.

◆ Conclusion

. . .the basic problem gripping the American workplace is . . . the crisis of creativity. Ideas . . . are what built American business. Richard Gurin, president and CEO of Binney and Smith, Inc. and member of the National Alliance of Business.
(quoted in Bruce, 1996, p. 2)

the cutting-edge worker in the Information Age Economy is a . . . highly-adaptable learner who possesses a wide range of "higher order thinking skills." This employee is an imaginative thinker with high-level communication and interpersonal skills.
Bruce, 1996, p. 3

Arts integration creates a different classroom ethos. Much integrated arts instruction takes place in a project-centered curriculum that targets creative problem solving. Students are involved in specific content that is intellectually challenging and emotionally engaging. Risk taking is encouraged through the teacher's consistent support for thinking about possibilities using arts perspectives: Visual art provokes reflection and introspection while satisfying the need to produce and complete work. Dance uses the body to communicate feelings and ideas. Drama invites the suspension of disbelief and consideration of "what if." Music "soothes the soul" while giving insight into people and events. Concentrated work becomes punctuated with gleeful play. Curiosity is aroused and learning proceeds with a sense of wonder and mystery. Students learn there are multiple ways to understand and express themselves so learning potential is increased.

An education infused with the arts delivers precisely the kinds of thinking skills that the 21st century workplace demands: analysis, synthesis, evaluation, and critical judgment. It nourishes imagination and creativity while focusing deliberately on content and end products. Collaborative and teamwork skills, tech-nological competencies, flexible thinking, an appreciation for diversity and self-discipline become integral to learning. "The public's preoccupation with 'getting back to basics' is being reinforced by a new commitment to school restructuring, school-based decision-making, and standards . . . Too few Americans recognize, however, the breadth and depth of the contribution arts education can make, both to education reform and to the quality of the workforce" (Bruce, 1996, p. 3).

◆ BIBLIOGRAPHY AND REFERENCES

Books and Videos

Armstrong, T. (1994). *Multiple intelligences in the classroom.* Alexandria, VA: Association for Supervision and Curriculum Development

Armstrong, T. (2000). *Multiple intelligences in the classroom.* Alexandria, VA: Association for Supervision and Curriculum Development.

Arnheim, R. (1989). *Thoughts on art education.* Los Angeles: Getty Center for Education in the Arts.

Barron, F. (1969). *Creative person and creative thinking.* New York: Holt, Rinehart & Winston.

Chauvet, J., Deschamps, E., & Hilliare, C. (1996). *Dawn of art: The Chauvet Cave: The oldest known paintings in the world.* New York: Abrams.

Consortium of National Arts Education Associations. (1994). *National Standards for Arts Education: What every young American should know and be able to do in the arts.* Reston, VA: Music Educators National Conference.

Cornett, C. (2001). *Learning through laughter, again.* Bloomington, IN: Phi Delta Kappa (800-766-1156).

Dacey, J. S. (1989). *Fundamentals of creative thinking.* Lexington, MA: Lexington Books.

deBono, E. (1991). *Six thinking hats for schools: 3–5 resource book.* Logan, IA: Perfection Learning.

Dewey, J. (1920). *How we think.* Boston: Heath.

Eberle, R. (1971). *SCAMPER: Games for imagination development.* Buffalo, NY: DOK.

Erikson, E. (1950). *Childhood and society.* New York: Norton.

Fiske, E. (Ed.). (1999). *Champions of change.* Washington, DC: Arts Education Partnership and the President's Committee on the Arts and the Humanities.

Gardner, H. (1983). *Frames of mind.* New York: Basic Books.

Gardner, H. (1993). *Creating minds: An anatomy of creativity seen through the lives of Freud, Einstein, Picasso, Stravinsky, Eliot, Graham & Gandhi.* New York: Basic Books.

Getzels, J. W., & Jackson, P. W. (1962). *Creativity and intelligence.* New York: Wiley.

Ginsberg, H., & Opper, S. (1969). *Piaget's theory of intellectual development.* Upper Saddle River, NJ: Prentice Hall.

Goleman, D. (1995). *Emotional intelligence: Why it can matter more than IQ.* New York: Bantam.

Hubel, D. (1988). *Eye, brain, and vision.* New York: Freeman.

Isaksen, S. G., & Treffinger, D. J. (1985). *Creative problem solving: The basic course.* Buffalo, NY: Bearly Limited.

J. Paul Getty Trust. (1993). *The power of the arts to transform education.* Los Angeles: Author.

Larson, G. (1997). *American canvas.* Washington, DC: National Endowment for the Arts.

Lowenfeld, V., & Brittain, W. L. (1975). *Creative and mental growth.* New York: Macmillan.

MacKinnon, D. W. (1978). *In search of human effectiveness.* Buffalo, NY: Creative Education Foundation.

Maslow, A. (1970). *Motivation and personality.* New York: Harper & Row.

National Center for Education Statistics. (2000). *Champion of change.* Washington, DC: U.S. Department of Education.

National Endowment for the Arts. (1995, January). *The arts and education: Partners in achieving our national education goals.* Washington, DC: Author.

Neeld, E. C. (1986). *Writing* (2nd ed.). Glenview, IL: Scott, Foresman.

New York City Board of Education. (1992–1993). *Chapter I developer/demonstration program: Learning to read through the arts.* New York: Office of Educational Research.

Osborne, A. (1963). *Applied imagination* (3rd ed.). New York: Scribner's.

President's Commission on National Goals. (1960). *Goals for Americans.* New York: The American Assembly, Columbia University.

Piaget, J. (1950). *The psychology of intelligence.* New York: Harcourt Brace.

Piaget, J. (1952). *The child's conception of number.* New York: Humanities Press.

Piaget, J. (1954). *The construction of relativity in the child.* New York: Basic Books.

Piaget, J. (1980). *To understand is to invent.* New York: Penguin.

Remer, J. (1996). *Beyond enrichment.* New York: American Council for the Arts.

Starko, A. (1995). *Creativity in the classroom: Schools of curious delight.* White Plains, NY: Longman.

Sternberg, R. (1997). *Successful intelligence: How practical and creative intelligence determine success in life.* New York: Dutton/Plume.

Torrance, E. P. (1962). *Guiding creative talent.* Upper Saddle River, NJ: Prentice Hall.

Torrance, E. P. (1973). Is creativity teachable? Bloomington, IN: Phi Delta Kappa.

The truth about teachers (video, 45 minutes). Santa Monica, CA: Pyramid Film & Video.

Vygotsky, L. S. (1978). *Mind in society.* Cambridge, MA: Harvard University Press.

Vygotsky, L. S. (1986). *Thought and language.* Cambridge, MA: MIT Press.

Wallace, G. (1926). *The art of thought.* New York: Harcourt Brace.

Articles

Aschbacher, P., & Herman, J. (1991). The humanities program evaluation. In *The arts and education: Partners in achieving our national education goals* (1995). Washington, DC: National Endowment for the Arts.

Bahna-James, T. (1991). The relationship between mathematics and music: Secondary school student perspectives. *Journal of Negro Education, 60,* 477–485.

Begley, S. (1996, February 19). Your child's brain. *Newsweek.*

Bennett, W. (1987–1988, December/January). Why the arts are essential. *Educational Leadership,* pp. 4–5.

Blythe, T., & Gardner, H. (1990, April). A school for all intelligences. *Educational Leadership,* pp. 33–36.

Boston, B. (1996). *Educating for the workplace through the arts.* Reprinted from *Business Week,* October 28, 1996. Columbus, OH: McGraw-Hill.

Boston, B. O., (1996). *Educating for the workplace through the arts,* reprinted from *Business Week,* October 28, 1996.

Brownlee, S. (1996). What science says about those tender feelins. *U.S. News and World Report,* Feb. 17.

Catterall, J. (1995). *Different ways of knowing.* 1991–1994 National Longitudinal Study Final Report.

Catterall, J. S., Chapleau, R., & Iwanaga, J. (1999). *The Imagination Project at UCLA Graduate School of Education and Information Studies, University of California at Los Angeles, September.* In E. Fiske (Ed.), *Champions of change.* Washington, DC: Arts Education Partnership, and the President's Committee on the Arts and the Humanities.

Csikszentmihalyi, M. (1990). The domain of creativity. In M. A. Runco & R. S. Albert (Eds.), *Theories of creativity* (pp. 190–212). Newbury Park, CA: Sage.

Dean, J., & Gross, J. L. (1992, April). Teaching basic skills through art and music. *Kappan,* pp. 613–618.

Edwards, K. L. (1994). *North American Indian music instruction: Influences upon attitudes, cultural perceptions and achievement.* D.M.A. dissertation, Arizona State University, Tempe.

Eisner, E. (1992, April). The misunderstood role of the arts in human development. *Kappan,* pp. 591–595.

Ellison, L. (1992, October). Using multiple intelligence to set goals. *Educational Leadership,* pp. 69–72.

Gelman, R. (1979). Preschool thought. *American Psychologist, 34,* 900–905.

Greene, M. (1997, February). Why ignore forms of art? *Education Week.*

Gregorian, V. (1997, March 13). 10 things you can do to make our schools better. *Parade Magazine.*

Hanna, J. (1992, April), Connections: Arts, academics and productive citizens. *Kappan,* pp. 601–607.

Luftig, R. (1994). *The schooled mind: Do the arts make a difference? An empirical evaluation of the Hamilton Fairfield SPECTRA1 Program, 1992–1993.*

Murfee, E. (1995). *Eloquent evidence: Arts at the core of learning.* Washington, DC: The President's Committee on the Arts and the Humanities and the National Assembly of State Arts Agencies with the National Endowment for the Arts.

Nash, J. M. (1997, February 3). Fertile minds. *Time,* pp. 48–56.

Nash, O. (1975). Eels. In *I wouldn't have missed it.* Boston: Little Brown.

Oppenheimer, T. (1999, September). Schooling the imagination. *Atlantic Monthly, 284*(3), 71–83.

Oreck, B., Baum, S., & McCartney, H. (1999). Artistic talent development for urban youth: The promise and the challenge. In E. Fiske (Ed.), *Champions of change.* Washington, DC: Arts Education Partnership and the President's Committee on the Arts and the Humanities.

Perkins, D. N. (1987–1988, December/January). Art as an occasion of intelligence. *Educational Leadership,* pp. 36–42.

Perrin, S. (1994, February). Education in the arts is an education for life. *Kappan,* pp. 452–453.

Rauscher, F., Shaw, G., Levine, L., Wright, E., Dennis, W., & Newcomb, R. (1997). Music training causes long-term enhancement of preschool children's spatial–temporal reasoning. *Neurological Research, 19,* 208.

Sternberg, R. J., & Lubar, T. I. (1991). Creating creative minds. *Phi Delta Kappan, 72,* 608–614.

Tardif, T. Z., with Sternberg, R. J. (1988). What do we know about creativity? In R. J. Sternberg (Ed.), *The nature of creativity* (pp. 429–440). New York: Cambridge University Press.

Valliant, G. E., & Valliant, C. O. (1981). Natural history of male psychological health, X: Work as a predictor of positive mental health. *American Journal of Psychiatry, 138,* 1433–1440.

Welch, N. (1995). *Schools, communities, and the arts: A research compendium.* Washington, DC: National Endowment for the Arts and The Arizona Board of Regents.

Children's Literature

Krull, K. (1995). *Lives of the musicians: Good times, bad times, and what the neighbors thought.* San Diego: Harcourt Brace.

Lionni, L. (1987). *Frederick.* New York: Knopf.

McCully, E. A. (1992). *Mirette on the high wire.* New York: Putnam.

Paterson, K. (1979). *Bridge to Terabithia.* New York: Harper & Row.

Pinkwater, D. (1993). *The big orange splot.* New York: Scholastic.

Wisniewski, D. (1997). *Golem.* New York: Clarion.

Yashima, T. (1965). *Crow boy.* New York: Scholastic.

◆ TEACHER RESOURCES

See Appendix F: *Bibliography of Recommended Reading and Viewing* for additional resources. Here is a sampling of videos from that bibliography.

Arts for life (1990). The Getty Center for Education in the Arts. 15 min. (Gives rationale for arts integration and classroom examples.)

Teaching in and through the arts (1995). The Getty Center for Education in the Arts. 25 min. (Classroom examples at the elementary and high school levels are shown.)

The arts and children: A success story. Goals 2000 Arts Education Partnership. 15 min. (A motivational video on why the arts should be integrated. Gives classroom examples, student testimonies, and interviews with doctors and other professionals.)

2

Integrating the Arts
Throughout the Curriculum

In a world where soul is neglected, beauty is placed last on its list of priorities. In the intellect-oriented curricula of our schools, for instance, science and math are considered important studies, because they allow further advances in technology. If there is a slash in funding, the arts are the first to go,

even before athletics. The clear implication is that the arts are dispensable: we can't live without technology, but we can live without beauty.

Thomas Moore, *Care of the Soul* (1992, p. 277)

◆ **CLASSROOM SNAPSHOT**

Ms. Lucas's Class: The Art of Teaching and Teaching the Arts

On a long wall outside Ms. Lucas's room is a time line of artists' birthdays. It is at children's eye level. Comments about the artists and their work is written in "speech bubbles." To the left of the door is a large, framed watercolor mural painted by students, after a study of Monet's water lily series. Beside the mural is an invitation to walk through "Monet's Garden" planted outside.

The school has remnants of the 1920s era—a large closet is labeled Cloak Room. But the room is alive with the arts. Four wooden easels display framed prints by Monet, Van Gogh, da Vinci, and Rembrandt. More prints hang at eye level. In one corner is a learning center on Van Gogh with baskets of art materials on a table below a bulletin board of his portraits and landscapes. A stack of student journals with "Arts for Life" on the cover of each is on the bookshelf. A yellow crate holds books about art—some are biographies and informational books like *Painting with Children* and *Crayons*. In another corner the floor is carpeted with squares secured with doubled-sided tape. A sign says this area is the Book Nook. Pillows and a bean-bag chair look inviting, couched among the classroom library. A recipe box holds student recommendation cards with their comments and a "smiley face" rating for each book. A ficus tree fills a corner, philodendron tentacles crawl across the window sill.

The bell rings and Ms. Lucas hustles to her CD player. The room fills with Vivaldi. Smiling children burst in and one boy shouts *The Four Seasons!* A debate ensues about which season is playing as the kids hang up coats and greet Ms. Lucas with *bonjour* and *goedemorgan*. Ms. Lucas says she teaches a bit of the language of the focus artist. So far they know greetings in German, Italian, Russian, French, and now, Dutch, for Van Gogh. Students scurry to get their journals and sit at their desks or at learning centers around the room's perimeter. Ms. Lucas explains how some choose to do artwork in their journals, so the art center offers more media options. She hands me a blank wallpaper book with "Arts for Life Journal" on the front. We seem to be the only two not on task, so I find a spot to write, and so does she. Inside the cover there is a note that says, "The arts are what give heart to our lives. Imagine a day without literature, music, art, dance, drama. Write or do a piece of art about how the arts are a part of your life." I look around the room at 27 second graders. Vivaldi plays on. I can't help but feel excited, and relaxed, as I begin to write. After about 10 minutes, Ms. Lucas asks the students to "find a place to pause" and morning routines continue. The agenda on the board gives the order of events. The children seem to be well rehearsed to take their turns:

Composer of the day. Rae Lyn and Jacques give a one-minute biographical report on Vivaldi. They tell what they think was most interesting in his life.

Riddle of the day. Shi Ming has written on the board, "What did the artist say when his minibus stopped in the middle of the street?" There are cue blanks below: _V_ ___ ___   _G_ ___ ___ ___. Students are reminded to guess letters—not the answer. Soon thumbs are up as letters are guessed. Finally there is a chorus of "Van Gogh!" Shi Ming proudly tells the class she made it up herself.

Art docent. Tony takes a seat in a red chair and begins to talk about a piece of art he made. It is a portrait of himself. It was done on wet cloth with chalk, and he explains how he used Van Gogh's poses, lines, and colors as starter ideas as he attempted this first self-rendering.

Looking closely. Three children unveil a new print on an easel. This one isn't framed. They take turns explaining and questioning the class. "What do you see? How does that make you feel? Why do you think the artist did that?" It is obvious the class has been taught to ask "fat questions" and are at ease with giving many interpretations. The students are excited to have a new *White Iris* print by Van Gogh (they guessed the artist during the discussion) and appear touched by the story of the single white iris representing the artist, who felt alone and different.

Poem a day. Two children put up a transparency of Lillian Moore's poem of questions, "Yellow Weed." Missy points at the "Poetry Alive" poster while Douglas reviews the directions for "echoic" reading. Missy and Douglas then take turns reading each line of the poem, with the class echoing their volume, rate, tone, pitch, pauses, and stress. The class claps at the end. Ms. Lucas asks if anyone wants to talk about the poem. Several hands go up and a short discussion takes place.

Sing in. Ms. Lucas asks for song nominations, and there is agreement on "Oats, Peas, and Beans" and "The Green Grass Grew All Around." Song posters on a clothesline across the back of the room have the lyrics written large enough to read from a distance. Julian chooses a pink baton pointer and takes charge: "We'll start with the oats song. Everyone stand up and take a deep breath. Now, ready, 1–2–3–begin!" When they sing "The Green Grass Grew All Around," another student hands out cards with words (*ground, hole, root, tree, branch,* etc.) and corresponding pictures. Students put them in a pocket chart as they sing this cumulative song.

The arts routines take about 15 minutes. Ms. Lucas has organized the rest of the morning around a science unit from the required second-grade curriculum. The unit is built around questions "How do plants affect people?, What causes these effects?", and "What affects plants?", with the central concern being an exploration of causes and effects. Students work at centers, in student-led learning circles, independently work, and in guided instruction groups with Ms. Lucas. She explains how reading, writing, speaking, and listening skills are taught in science and social studies units. For example, in this unit students are reading informational books, like Sylvia Johnson's *Why Flowers Have Colors* and Barbara Cooney's *Miss Rumphius,* and writing observation reports, original poetry, and reader's theater scripts (from books they are reading). Every unit involves the use of literature, art, drama, dance, and music to introduce and respond to unit content.

Every unit also includes a focus on people (scientists, composers, poets) who have wrestled with the same questions that the unit addresses. Van Gogh is a part of the plant unit because of his expressive paintings of plants. The study of Van Gogh is not limited to his paintings, however. The goal is to find a meaningful connection, but to then delve into the connection by exploring why Van Gogh painted the *way* he did and *what* he did (causes). Science becomes the study of people who have discovered relationships among living and nonliving things, rather than just a study of things and isolated processes. Vivaldi's compositions on seasons are an obvious connection to plants and the effects of the seasons on plants and the effects of his music on people. What Vivaldi conveys about the seasons and their effects is very different from what the students glean from reading an expository passage about the cycle of seasons and plant life. Ms. Lucas explains she wants students to know and *feel things* about the ideas they are learning. Much thought has gone into the role of *emotional intelligence* in structuring these integrated units.

Each unit culminates in a *portfolio* of work—evidence of what has been learned. Basically, these are pocket folders. In each, the unit questions are followed by a table of contents:

I. Music and plants: songs and pieces

II. Art and plants: artists and their artwork

III. Drama and plants: reader's theater scripts and drama workshops

IV. Dance/movement and plants

V. Literature and plants: fiction and nonfiction

VI. Writing about plants: information and creative writing

Bulges in the pocket folders testify to the use of audio and video tape evidence. Ms. Lucas explains that shoe boxes are also often used as portfolios because art projects are sometimes three dimensional. Portfolio highlights are presented at the end of the unit. Each student can invite guests to the "portfolio performances." Guests can be parents or even friends from other classes.

In the afternoon Ms. Lucas uses similar strategies with a social studies unit. Sometimes the science and social studies units are combined, but combinations are not forced. For the same reason, math is integrated as appropriate. This means students get direct instruction in math skills or reading and language arts skills as needed, and teacher-directed lessons may be taught separate from the units. Ms. Lucas tries to tie skill-based lessons to units so that students see the relevance of skills; integration is not done just for its own sake, but only as there is a meaningful connection.

It would be hard to describe with words all that happens in Ms. Lucas's class. The day ended with another set of student-led routines. They sang and told about what they liked learning that day and there were "book talks" to advertise "must reads." The grand finale was a narrative pantomime: The whole class became seeds and grew into tall irises. The silent drama was interrupted by the bell of reality. The school day ended with calls of "arrivederci" and "bon soir!"

"You know so much about the arts, Ms. Lucas. Are you an artist?" I asked.

"I am learning a lot, just like my students. Am I an artist? Of course, aren't you?" Ms. Lucas raised her brows and cocked her head.

"I play the piano and love to dance. I paint a little, but call myself an artist—I don't know."

Would you say you aren't a reader or that you can't do math or write?" she demanded.

"Some teachers would say being an artist is different," I explained.

"Being an artist is a part of being human. To say you aren't an artist—not a creative being with unique ways to understand and express thoughts and feelings—is to say you're less than human. Teachers *must* be artists. Anything less than an artist–teacher is just not good enough for my children, your children, or anyone's children. Integrating the arts begins with a mind-set: we decide the arts are what make us alive and make life livable. We tell each other and our students that the arts are for life and that school is not just getting ready for life—it is life. In my "living room"—some call a "classroom"—every person is an artist. Every teacher should claim artist status. To do less is to harm your own potential and the hope we can give our children—some of whom are in pretty hopeless circumstances."

I looked into the face of a veteran teacher. The wrinkles around her eyes were a testimony to a lifetime of laughing. In her dark brown eyes was compassion and passion. I was stunned. What else could I say. . . .

"I *am* an artist. Thank you for reminding me!"

VISIT POSTSCRIPT

Ms. Lucas teaches in an inner-city school. Her students face poverty, drugs, violence, parent apathy, and abuse. The school district has struggled financially and felt forced to cut elementary arts specialists. Classroom teachers became responsible for implementing the standards for art and music, along with making progress in a new inclusion model. The district provided some staff development, but most K–5 teachers felt unprepared to teach art and music. Teachers were concerned about preparation time and getting materials for art projects and music experiences. Three years hence, there seems to be little likelihood the specialist positions will be restored by voters. The same concerns about quality arts experiences still exist, but many teachers, including Ms. Lucas, have viewed the loss as a chance to try research-based arts infusion strategies used throughout the United States. These programs view the arts as significant, separate disciplines *and* tools to learn content in science and social studies and skills in math and language arts.

INTRODUCTION

Knowing how to shift intellectual gears beats rigid thinking every time.

Bruce Boston (1996, p. 8)

In Chapter 1 the concept of arts integration was introduced using a leveled concept of teaching *with, about, in,* and *through* the arts. Three main questions that teachers need to answer were also presented: *WHAT* do we need to know and teach? *WHY* should we integrate the arts? and *HOW* can integration be accomplished? These ideas structure this chapter and other chapters, along with another organizer—a series of 10 arts integration principles called INTEGRATES.

WHY INTEGRATE THE ARTS THROUGHOUT THE SCHOOL DAY?

When children create they are making sense of the world.

Robert Alexander

Take a moment to skim Post It Page 2–1 about arts integration in schools across the country.

News Bulletin: Research on Arts Integration

Chicago. Thirty-seven schools that integrated the arts outscored non-CAPE (Chicago Arts Partnerships in Education) schools on teacher surveys of school climate, relationships with parents, professional development, instructional practices and community relationships. By 1998 the differences favoring CAPE students were significant for both the ITBS (reading and math) and the Illinois State IGAP test. By sixth grade, more than 60 percent of CAPE students were performing at grade level on the ITBS. This gain is sizeable and significant. By ninth grade CAPE students were a full grade level higher than non-CAPE students in reading (Fiske, 1999, pp. 51–55).

New York, Connecticut, Virginia, and South Carolina. In a study of 2000 public school children, grades 4–8, researchers found "significant relationships between rich in-school arts programs and creative, cognitive and personal competencies needed for academic success" (Burton, Horowitz, & Abeles, 1999, p. 36).

Bronx, New York. At St. Augustine School 98 percent of students were "at grade level" after participating in an arts-integrated curriculum (Hanna, 1992).

Milwaukee, Wisconsin. Elm Elementary is number 1 out of 103 schools in the district. In 1970 the school was in the bottom 10 percent for academic performance. What changed? They introduced a comprehensive arts program.

Charleston, South Carolina. More than 90 percent of students in grades 1–3 have met basic skills assessment standards in reading and math at Ashley River Creative Arts Elementary. Ninety-six percent meet basic skill standards in other subjects, as well. These rates are about 10 percent higher than achievement scores of students in other South Carolina schools. At Ashley River the arts are taught as discrete disciplines and are fully integrated into the general curriculum.

Augusta, Georgia. The arts boost academics: students in grades 1–5 at the Redcliffe Elementary Arts Infusion School showed gains on the Stanford Achievement Test for each year of the project (Greater Augusta Arts Council).

Dallas, Texas. Integrating the arts into curriculum can have a positive effect on students' academic performance reports the Partnership for Arts, Culture and Education, Inc. (PACE). Three urban elementary schools were studied. One provided community-based arts and cultural programs with curriculum integration. Another school had art programming without such integration, and the third group had no programming. After 4 years, students in the first school had higher average scores in language arts on standardized tests than students from the other schools (*Inside OSBA's Briefcase,* July 3, 1997, vol. 28, no. 27). For more information, call PACE at 214-823-7601.

Five Minutes a Day?

We had a few minutes left in our middle school class today—just enough time where it's too late to start something but we needed to "fill the gap." I dug out my Claude Monet book and had them guess the focus of the painting Winterscapes (without looking at the title). I couldn't believe it—middle schoolers who were joking with me one minute turned "serious!"—intently looking at the painting. Some even commented "I like the way he did that in the back." I responded by saying, "You mean the horizon in the background?" "Yeah, that!"

They were different people! When I first asked if they had heard of Claude Monet, they said they knew of "Jean Claude Van Damme." Anyway, it was such a fleeting but intense experience. Also, they beg me everyday to do drama from the novel we are reading. I feel I'm depriving them if I don't do it. Anyway, integrating the arts, I believe, even if it's just 5 minutes a day, is so incredible—especially to see it at the middle school."

Bethany Gray, special education major,
Wittenberg University

Bethany Gray is new to the concept of arts integration, but she is fortunate to start her teaching career with some background. As far back as 1967, a report to the

Rockefeller Foundation declared the role of classroom teachers crucial to the "arts-in-general-education" project of the foundation (Remer, 1996, p. 306). Unfortunately, today it is still rare for novice or even veteran teachers to have more than an integrated arts workshop or a one-shot staff development session by an arts specialist or guest artist. The Rockefeller report declared this level of preparation for arts integration "simply not adequate to the task if we are serious about effecting genuine long-range change" (Remer, 1996, p. 306). John Goodlad, author and education reformer, blames the lack of arts integration behind the classroom doors on a "macho society" that pressures students to be athletic rather than esthetic. He decries a prevailing societal view that the arts are a luxury, unrelated to economic advancement, and bemoans the lack of teacher preparation to create a "large and sympathetic army of educators ready and willing to march for the arts" (Remer, 1996, p. 67).

An Arts Integration Army?

Why should teachers join an arts integration army? On the practical side is the fact that there is just too much to know and not enough time to teach it all. Harvard's library has acquired more volumes in the last 5 years than in the previous 100 years altogether. Integration allows connections to be made, so instead of continuing to cram in more information, the focus is on bigger issues, questions, and problems. Time is simply used differently in integrated classrooms. Isolated and outdated information is dropped from the curriculum through a process of prioritizing and allocating time to learning deemed most essential in an integrated world.

Which leads to the next reason: The arts are integral in the world outside school. We get much of our entertainment and information from the arts and value arts-based goods for their esthetics and as status symbols. Consider the arts connection to the film industry, television shows, radio, designer clothes, cars, restaurants, and museums. The economic impact of the arts is staggering. For example, the 1996 Cezanne exhibit in Philadelphia generated over $100 million in revenue. I recently sat in on a Senate Education Committee meeting in Columbus, Ohio. The state capitol building had recently been given a multimillion dollar overhaul to preserve its stunning architectural features. Ironically, the hearing room, with newly regilded Corinthian columns and magnificently restored wall paintings, was the location for testimony for an amendment that would deter students from taking arts courses.

Presently, the school day is often organized around isolated skill teaching and fragmented into subjects; this is not how life is organized. Making school more lifelike is important to motivation to learn. Students learn better in a context—the whole-to-part concept of learning. Integration allows students to bring to bear information and meaning-making tools on interesting world problems. Many current world problems have never before been faced; solutions must be created, not remembered. Information from the past is needed but must be viewed from original perspectives and solutions. Content and skill teaching are thus combined for a meaningful purpose.

The track record for integrating the arts to effect academic gain has continued to grow stronger. This isn't surprising since arts integration involves intentionally developing everything from a larger vocabulary to analytic thinking, historical and cultural perspective, and self-discipline. In addition, studies of successful people show that persistence pays off; the arts engage students in a manner that causes them to want to persist. Often it isn't that students *can't* learn; it's that they *won't*. New York City's successful Learning to Read through the Arts program is an example of how the arts motivate children to want to learn. Other projects illuminate additional integration options, such as Kentucky's Different Ways of Knowing programs in which teachers "use the arts as a vehicle for teaching academic subjects beginning with social studies, history, literature and leading ultimately to a fully integrated day, including science and math." In another site, in New Rochelle, New York, teachers and artists collaborate to integrate the arts with the goal of seeing a transfer of learning, "from making or composing in the arts to critical thinking or problem-solving in one or more of the other academic domains" (Remer, 1996, p. 338). Often the *thematic* unit is the structure for integration, with units focusing on important questions or concepts having relevance across disciplines (e.g., shapes and forms, patterns and cycles, change and constancy, causes and effects).

WHAT SHOULD TEACHERS KNOW ABOUT INTEGRATION?

Recommendation for elementary schools: "that one hour per week be given over to nature study . . . and that all work be conducted without the aid of a textbook. In addition, every attempt should be made to correlate the science observations with work in language, drawing, and literature."

Committee of Ten, 1892

Integration is not a 21st century notion. A plethora of labels have been used over the decades: *interdisciplinary instruction, unit teaching, project approach,* and *whole language,* to name but a few. Under any name, integration involves combining diverse fragments into harmonious systems, which brings satisfaction and meaning. Gestalt psychologists tell us it is only natural to want to bring pieces and parts together to make comprehensible wholes. What is a buckle without its belt or a sleeve without a shirt? The part is not usable, nor even understandable, without the whole; in art terms it is figure with background, the particular in a context. Of course, learners need a balance of attention to wholes and parts as they develop; but, even when adults are novices at a task, they tend to proceed from the gross to the particular, dwelling first on the most obvious, such as larger shapes or intuited feelings. Psychologist Daniel Goleman explains the evolutionary significance of reacting first to the holistic experience and then to details by describing a jogger who spies a long slender dark curved *something* coming up along his path. "Snake!" screams the ancient emotional impulses and the jogger stops dead in his tracks. Saved from a poisonous bite by primitive instincts, the jogger now uses his newer (in evolutionary time) powers of logic to discern the details of the *something*. And this time it's just a stick. Think of the consequences if we stopped to analyze all the pieces before responding to the whole.

The arts can play an important role in integrating wholes and parts. Literature, visual art, drama, dance, and music can interact with science, social studies, math, and the language arts and support learning about important life skills, concepts, and themes. Traditional lines become muddied in integrating the arts. "Is it art or science as a child mixes colors and discovers that blue and yellow make green? The child notices curves and angles in letters and then makes them with his or her own body or draws them in the air; is this language arts or dance?" (Stinson, 1988, p. 95). The arts draw on the common concepts of shape, action, motion, pattern, and rhythm and can be tapped for their power to reveal these same aspects in other curricular areas. This way of teaching and learning that uses the arts as meaning-making tools begins with seeing the curriculum from the "what if" vantage point of an artist. For example, to integrate dance one must think about movement *possibilities* in lessons and units—not just *how* something moves, but how it *might* move under different circumstances, while maintaining a focus on targeted curricular concepts, skills, or themes. Arts integration is a different

vehicle for more students to achieve academic success and life satisfaction by using ways of knowing available only through the arts.

HOW CAN TEACHERS MEANINGFULLY INTEGRATE THE ARTS?

If you believe in great things, other people will too.
Oliver Wendell Holmes

Teaching *With, About, In,* and *Through* the Arts

It is not beyond the teacher's competence to talk with the children about the bark paintings of the Australian aborigines. Not everywhere, she will explain, do people have paper. On whatever material they can prepare, they tell of their concerns and beliefs . . . they describe what matters most about boating and hunting. . . . The kinship between the simply shaped but impressive and beautiful paintings of a distant race and the children's own artwork is established without effort.
Arnheim, 1989, p. 48

Henceforth, the term *integration* is used to denote a variety of ways and intensities with which classroom teachers include the arts. Integration of the arts can occur along a continuum from a small degree, at a surface level, to total arts infusion throughout the curriculum. The latter idea includes a respect for the arts as unique disciplines that use unique communication modes to study science, social studies, math, and the language arts. For example, learning or expressing ideas about "courage" through poetry is very different from examining this concept through painting, music, or sculpture—think of the ineffable messages about courage possible from Auguste Rodin's sculpture of *The Burghers of Calais* or the themes about how fear is necessary for courage in literature like *Call It Courage.* In a total integrated arts design, teachers present information and skills *from* arts disciplines and use the arts as teaching tools and learning processes. This requires classroom teachers to have basic arts knowledge, but does not necessitate one becoming bona fide artists or specialists. Consider the possible combinations of each of the following designs for classroom teachers.

Teaching **WITH:** The goals of teaching *with* the arts are for students to get pleasure from the arts and have chances to work creatively. At this level, the arts are casually used by teachers in isolated lessons, and students are given opportunities to explore materials or ideas with minimal teacher guidance. For example, teachers may include a visual art project with science, teach a song related to a holiday, or set up a classroom routine (e.g., an opening patriotic song). These activities may not be keyed to district or state standards nor related to units in science, social studies, math, or reading and language arts.

Teaching **ABOUT** *and* **IN:** When teachers use the *about* and *in* structures, they plan for students to learn *about* the arts and do work *in* the arts. The goal is to have students enjoy and develop both *creativity* and *artistry.* At this level, learning events focus on arts *content* and *skills.* The structure of the art form—its elements, history, special vocabulary, artists, techniques, and skills—are taught. Often general classroom teachers work with arts specialists or guest artists to construct substantive units around an artist or art form, with other curricular areas pulled in to support the focus. For example, a unit on Van Gogh's struggles and triumphs could involve learning about music and musicians at the turn of the century, historical events during his life, the use of maps and globes to pinpoint Van Gogh's life journey, reading biographies, and writing informational and creative pieces. At a modest level, teachers may give substance to casual routines, like opening songs, by adding short minilessons about the composer or musical elements. Most importantly, when teaching *about* and *in* the arts, there is a conscious effort to develop students' esthetic sensibilities through guided experiences. Students are involved in exploration, creation, response, performance, and evaluation. Experiences are tied to the school district's standards of what will be assessed.

Teaching **THROUGH** *the arts:* The arts are prominent through *focused* daily arts routines, an esthetic classroom environment, and as both *content* and *means* of learning in units specified by the school district's standards. Usually this model involves using content areas such as science and social studies as the center of units into which the arts, language arts, and math are used to explore the central topic, problem, or questions. Since the arts are content disciplines, as well as processes, any art can serve as a unit center or focus, too. Teaching *through* the arts involves creating a classroom in which students actually live and learn through the arts.

Jacobs's *disciplines*-focused integration can be used to think about the teaching *through* the arts con-

cept. She proposes using central concepts and particular disciplinary skills for a unit core and emphasizes student creative problem solving, active inquiry, and discovery about important issues (Jacobs, 1989). The process entails continuous questioning as integration progresses:

◆ Does the integrative structure reveal basic "secrets of the universe"? (patterns, truths)

◆ Does it fascinate, challenge, and interest students? (a sense of mystery or empowerment)

◆ Is it inclusive enough to pull in many disciplines in meaningful and natural ways?

◆ Is it worthy of time and attention?

◆ Is it appropriate at this time for these students? (interests, skill levels, cognitive development)

◆ Does the structure allow for students to use real methods to investigate? (primary source material, authentic strategies of researching and coming to know)

◆ Does the structure allow students to view an issue from the perspectives of the various disciplines? (How would an artist describe this picture? a scientist? a mathematician?)

◆ Is the integrity of each discipline maintained in integration? (Are the arts trivialized?)

In addition, teaching *through* the arts means developing high esthetic standards by involving students in significant arts experiences. Arts advocate Jane Remer (1996) warns:

> Producing 25 identical Kachina dolls from a pattern or slopping paint thoughtlessly on brown kraft paper to represent ancient cave drawings does not exemplify high aesthetic standards. Moreover, dancing in geometric patterns will not substitute for learning how to calculate area, perimeter, and volume. Spending a lot of time working on colonial artifacts is only going to be worthwhile if students also understand the meanings and know how these objects symbolize the cultural history and values of a particular time and place. (p. 339)

So, while the emphasis in teaching *through* the arts is the process of meaning making using the arts, the subject matter of each of the arts is still valued and taught. The end goal is to have students construct personal messages using the unique communication forms that the arts provide. In a manner, this can be thought of as *applied* arts because of its practical life goals.

More Than Entertainment

It is desirable and feasible for teachers to move in and out of the phases of teaching *with, about, in,* and *through* the arts during a school year. Each type of integration offers important avenues for arts integration and should be selected to fit student needs, curricular structures, available materials, time constraints, and the teaching personnel. Teachers need to feel comfortable drawing on and developing their backgrounds in the arts, so the type and pace of integration depends on the people involved. In addition, classroom teachers who wish to work with school arts specialists and visiting artists need to learn how to plan with specialists and must have the time to do so. Ineffective integration happens when arts specialists come for one-shot performances without pre- and postperformance lessons with students. A teacher may choose to integrate several disciplines or just a couple, work alone or with a group of colleagues, use a project approach or thematic units, set up learning centers or simply start ongoing arts routines, work with a schoolwide theme or try an integrated day in the classroom, target student interests or focus on essential "big questions," remain at school or emphasize field work. The goals are the same for all these integration models—to make natural and meaningful arts connections that add depth to learning, not adding more *things* to the already jam-packed school curriculum, and to ensure that the arts are not reduced to entertainment only.

Integration Principles and Strategies

What is now proved was once only imagined.

William Blake

While the concept of teaching *with, about, in,* and *through* the arts provides a general perspective on integration, teachers need specific ideas to make implementation successful. INTEGRATES includes 10 principles to help guide the move to an arts-based curriculum.

1. Immersion in an arts-based environment sets the stage.
2. Nitty-gritty arts concepts and skills provide the foundation for meaning making.
3. Teaching habits cause students to know what to expect.
4. Energizers and warm-ups increase creative problem solving.
5. Great children's literature should support each arts area.
6. Routines that organize the day maximize time for the arts.
7. Adaptations of curriculum and instruction models guide planning for integration.
8. Trips outside of school extend art-based learning.
9. Evidence to document student progress is necessary for assessment.
10. Specialists in the arts are important and necessary.

Principle 1: IMMERSION in an Arts-Based Environment

Eighteenth-century novelist Henri Beyle, who used the pseudonym Stendhal, observed how beauty had the power to stun people, to stir them emotionally and even physically. I experienced this "Stendhal effect" when I saw Michelangelo's sculpture of David in Florence, Italy. The arts can be a form of beauty that can uplift, give energy, and excite a passion for living. This power is underemployed in America's classrooms. Teachers can create classrooms that are more like living rooms—esthetically pleasing, comfortable, and full of sensory stimulation. Classrooms can be transformed into places that smell wonderful and are filled with beautiful music and provocative art. The goal is to create learning places that invite children in and make them want to come to school and enjoy learning. Here are a few inexpensive ways this can happen.

The Esthetic Environment. Think of spaces and places that cause good feelings. Furniture arrangement can suggest a pleasant openness—groups of desks versus rows. Air freshener, plants, flowers, special things to taste, textures to feel, artwork on easels, dramatic prop boxes, poems and songs on posters, centers with buckets of brushes and sponges for art, tapes and CDs to listen to and move with create changes in the feel of a room. I believe this is what Elliot Eisner (1997) means when he says the "subtle is significant." Small changes *can be* significant in a classroom, and an esthetic awareness is developed by stimulating the senses.

Art Displays and a Beauty Corner. Here are examples of ways to bring the arts into a classroom. *Beauty boxes* are simple student collections of pictures and objects that evoke pleasant responses. These can be used as writing prompts, for discussions, or displayed in a classroom Beauty Corner. An art print can be displayed at children's eye level to promote concentration on one piece of art for a day or a week using an art easel to suggest that the work is special. Post questions with the prints to stimulate close examination and critical creative responses: "What title would you give to this piece?" or "How many words can you list to describe how this art makes you feel? What catches your eye first? What do you see that you think no one else sees? What are some adjectives you'd use to describe how this feels? How would a mathematician describe this art?" Teachers may also show a title and then ask for predictions about color, line, and media before the art is revealed. Alternatively, show a painting and ask for title possibilities. The **Partial Picture Preview** strategy involves showing part of the picture and asking students to predict the remaining portion. A large magnifying glass is a motivating prop to use with the **I Spy** strategy. The teacher begins by saying, "I spy . . ." and gives a challenge related to art elements (e.g., "four geometric shapes" or "three primary colors"). Students look closely to try to meet the challenge, and volunteers come up and "show they know" with the magnifying glass. The student then takes over the "I spy . . ." and challenges the class. (Fine-art prints are available from companies such as Shorewood or the National Gallery. Many art posters cost as little as a dollar. Check out calendar art for up to 75 percent off in January and invite students to bring in art to display—prints, sculpture, and paintings.)

Background Music. Setting the right mood for learning is tricky, but more and more schools now play music in classrooms, halls, and the cafeteria to create a civilized school atmosphere. For example, at Hymera Elementary, in Indiana, music is used schoolwide throughout the day; a CD player sits right inside the front door. Music can uplift, calm, and even make time seem to go faster. We tend to be *entrained* to the rhythm and tempo of music, so it's not surprising to feel energetic after hearing a Sousa march or Dixieland jazz. We respond physically to the fast rhythms and even smile. Rock and roll makes us want to move, and classical music, like that of the Baroque period, can give a sense of grandeur; think of Bach or Vivaldi. Chopin and other Romantic music can trigger dreamy images, and Puccini's operas exude passion. Playing background music sets a tone, so music can be an important learning tool during sustained silent reading and writing times. Gardner's musical intelligence aspect of multiple intelligence (MI) theory and implications from brain research provide support for using music in this way. Music without lyrics, especially classical pieces such as Mozart, stimulate brain activity, particularly in the right hemisphere, so there is more

brain power for children to access during other work. This is evident from imaging devices that now give us pictures of the brain at rest, the brain on words, the brain listening to music, and the brain receiving words and music. These pictures show that entirely different areas of the brain are active when music is heard, and additional brain activity may boost learning capacity.

An Arts-for-Life Center. A special arts-based learning center can include inspirational quotes about the arts and artists. Students can be assigned the classroom job of writing Arts-for-Life quotes in a special corner of the chalkboard. Definitions of art can be included that are found or created by students as they explore the idea of using the arts as learning tools. An arts time line with birthdays of artists and other significant arts events, like the invention of the camera in 1839, can be located in the center, along with a map to pin the homes of artists. Don't forget informational books, biographies, poetry, and fiction about the arts. See the Arts-based Children's Literature bibliography in the appendix for books categorized by individual arts areas.

A Classroom That Celebrates the Arts. I have enjoyed the posters of Jean Luc Picard (Star Trek character) and other art that students bring to enrich the classroom; a part of a morning routine can include students explaining their arts contributions. Once children understand and experience the concept of creating an esthetically pleasing environment, they can become both creative and adventuresome in the joint effort. Get ready for fresh flowers, potpourri, and unique CDs. It was a student that introduced a class to pianist George Winston, which stimulated a run on solo instrumentals. We went on to Kenny G (saxophone) and Wynton Marsalis (trumpet) and then back to piano with Emile Pandolfi.

Principle 2: NITTY-GRITTY Arts Concepts and Skills

Freedom without tools is really no freedom at all; for example, asking children to discuss picture book art when no basic art elements have been taught can frustrate students and the teacher. Just teaching a few words and concepts, such as color, line, shape, and texture, can free students to tap thinking structures (brain schema) to talk about what they see. While the regular classroom teacher may not have the background to go into *depth* when teaching *about* or *in* each art form, it is feasible to teach basic knowledge for making sense (i.e., key concepts, elements, media, styles, genre, art forms, and artists). Since the arts are integral to functioning and understanding in our world, such basics need to be taught so that students have language to talk about, respond to, and create with the arts. Gardner (1989) expressed his concern about this issue when he visited schools and found that

> few teachers had artistic skills, and because those who did were skittish about exposing their works to students, the chief activity was simply giving children opportunities to paint, to pot, or to dance. This ploy was fine during the early years of childhood but made little sense in middle childhood and preadolescence when youngsters crave skills. The resulting works were either derivative from the mass media, or showed a vestige of a good idea but lacked the technical means to express it properly. In my terms, a creative spark, but no basic skills. (p. 141)

Basic background gives students the knowledge to ask questions, strategically pursue interests, make choices, give interpretations, express meaning, and identify worthiness of ideas. All these are higher-order thinking skills (HOTS) that can be developed through the arts and then used in other areas. In addition, using arts content to make meaning is a part of teaching the general process of understanding or comprehension, which the National Assessment of Educational Progress (NAEP) shows we do well at a *literal* level. Unfortunately, NAEP scores reveal how students have greater difficulty with implicit messages—*making* sense, rather than just *getting* an explicit main idea. This suggests they do not have the content or thinking skills to get beyond the obvious. Teaching basic nitty-gritty arts concepts and skills can help fill this gap.

Teachers find arts concepts valuable in forming provocative questions: "What colors does Eric Carle use? How would his books feel different if he used more pastels?" Basic knowledge enables teachers and students to be more creative because concepts can be combined in an infinite number of ways to create more art or diverse interpretations of art. For example, think about how much harder it is to use the *general* idea of "integrating art" than to plan ways to use a specific idea like collage or 3D art in a unit.

When teachers integrate core arts content (concepts and skills), they help students understand the adage "you can't break the rules until you've mastered them." Even Picasso and Michelangelo studied the great artist's techniques before striking out on their own. Indeed, knowledge of the components used to create meaning in the arts liberates and empowers children to make meaning from or with all

art forms. Here are other guidelines to use when teaching basic arts concepts and skills.

Age-stage Appropriateness and Teachable Moments. Suggested basic arts content teachers should know and teach in each of the art forms are presented in the **WHAT** sections in Chapters 3, 5, 7, 9, and 11. In addition, teachers should talk with arts specialists at their schools to coordinate efforts. Implications from the learning and teaching theories presented in Chapter 1 should be applied during the teaching of arts elements and skills, too. For example, the work of Piaget, Maslow, Vygotsky, and others support Arnheim's (1989) conclusion:

> At no level of development can either children or accomplished artists state, to their own satisfaction, what they want to say unless they have acquired the means of saying it. In the beginning, these means are simple . . . no attempts should be made to foist upon the learner technical tricks that go beyond his or her stage of conception. Nor should the means of visual expression be taught as isolated devices. The need to master them should naturally emerge from the demands of the task, and whenever possible the learner himself ought to be made to discover them by himself rather than have them supplied by the teacher. (p. 42)

Social learning theorists also suggest we keep in mind that students are usually most successful applying or practicing new learning in a group situation, before going it alone. To simply say "write a song" or "make a play" or "do art" or "make up a dance" is overwhelming, even for adults.

Teaching Students How Artists Work. Knowing that real artists take time to look and listen and study other artists' use of techniques, before adapting one another's ideas, helps students understand how to begin. From the research on creative individuals and the creative problem-solving process, it is clear we should encourage students to use strategies that have heretofore been considered problematic or even cheating. For example, we *should* suggest that students reread books and poems, write on the same topics, and study the same subject for extended times, just as Monet repeatedly painted water lilies and haystacks.

Charts, Word Walls, and Other Visual Aids. We learn what we live with and we remember what we see repeatedly. In each of the chapters there is a concise set of basic arts concepts, elements, and definitions that can be adapted and posted for students to use as references. In any one day the art in picture books may be discussed, as well as the illustrations in science and social studies texts. When key words in the arts are displayed on Word Walls or charts children are better able to talk about components of art or music, drama, dance, or literature. Banners and "big books" can also be made and used as visual reference tools. Arts concept reference charts serve the same function as "fix-up" charts posted to remind students of what to do when encountering unknown words while reading or how to edit writing.

Using the Arts to Learn Key Arts Content.   Nitty-gritty arts elements can be learned *through* arts strategies, too. For example, lyrics can be created to fit familiar tunes, or other mnemonics can be used to learn visual art elements: ROY G. BIV is a common acronym to remember the spectrum of the rainbow: red–orange–yellow–green–blue–indigo–violet. "Every good boy does fine" is a time-tested mnemonic for musical notes on the staff lines for the treble clef, just as do–re–mi–fa–so–la–ti–do is a tool to sing the scale, and STAB helps us remember the voices in a quartet.

Teaching "Why" Is Important.   Students need real-life reasons for what we are teaching to activate their motivation to learn. This is especially important when introducing a new idea like using the arts as learning tools. Teachers need to explain how impossible it is to understand a culture without having access to its music, art, drama and theater, dance, and literature, since people express what is most important to them through the arts. What's more, to understand the art of a culture, we need conceptual anchors that structure each art, be that the *rhythmic* (music element) differences between African music and Western music, or Picasso's concept of collage (media and technique). Teaching basic arts components lets students in on a "secret of the universe": Language liberates, and each of the arts has a language all its own. Learning the language of the arts increases literacy, not in the narrow sense of just reading words during language arts time, but understanding major concepts about people and the world we share. When teachers are explicit about such connections, students are more likely to feel there is purpose to learning.

Principle 3: TEACHING HABITS Cause Students to Know What to Expect

It seems only logical that encouraging [children to be] explorers and questioners rather than passive acceptors cannot help honing creativity, thinking and learning.
                                                         Starko, 1995, p. 114

Integrating the arts isn't a unit to do and be done with. It involves changing what is done on a daily ba-

sis. It includes how teachers view and present themselves to students and how they interact and react to classroom events. Here are general teaching habits that can profoundly influence the success of arts integration by promoting artistry, creativity, and meaning making.

Lesson Plan Frameworks for Arts Integration.   A lesson or series of lessons using the arts as teaching tools begins with planning the arts content to be integrated with another curricular area. This planning respects that important concepts and skills will be taught *about the arts,* as well as from other curricular areas. The goal is to use the arts, not abuse them. So, while there may be several integration *prongs,* there needs to be at least one significant arts focus and one focus in another discipline if integration is to be meaningful. This *pronged focus* should come out of the school district courses of study and be checked against other standards or goals such as the *National Standards for the Arts.* From the pronged focus, student objectives are written that explain what students should know and be able to do by the lesson conclusion. Because student progress will be assessed, it is important to write objectives in *assessable* ways (i.e., be clear and use observable verbs to describe the evidence for student learning).

Just as a good meal or a well-written paper has a beginning, middle, and end, so does an effective lesson. A short *introduction* prepares students for learning and allows teachers to assess students' background. The mood of the lesson is set, and the purposes or focus of the lesson should be made clear so that students feel the lesson is meaningful. Teachers may begin with a titillating question or the introduction of new vocabulary through a riddle or "mystery bag" holding things related to a key lesson concept. The introduction should be brief but, if skipped, students may never tune in and be lost for the remaining lesson segments.

In the *development* the teacher presents or demonstrates. A sense of the whole is developed, perhaps through storytelling, sharing artwork, or listening to a piece of music. A skill or strategy may be presented to use with a problem or question previously introduced. Students explore and discuss, practice, and apply skills, strategies, or media use in this stage.

Finally, there is the lesson *conclusion* in which students are expected to go beyond mere imitation of demonstrated skills and pull together problem solutions, showing they have learned and used personal creativity, artistry, and higher-order thinking skills. The conclusion provides the satisfaction of completion and is an important part of continuing learner motivation.

In general, most lessons proceed in a whole–part–whole manner, giving opportunities to experience art forms and ideas in esthetic ways before examining the parts and pieces. This allows the arts to work their motivational magic on students and shows respect for the arts. How this is accomplished is part of the art of teaching, but usually involves individual teacher variations on the lesson framework previously described. Post It Page 2–2 is a summary of a frame-work for integrated planning. Examples of integrated lesson plans are given in each integration chapter.

Teacher Enthusiasm and Passion. The etymology of the word *enthusiasm* is interesting. It originally meant to be "in god" (*theo*) or "in spirit." When students are around teachers who are possessed of the creative and artistic spirit, they are drawn to their enthusiasm. We can tell students what we feel passionate about and share personal stories of our own creative and artistic efforts, being sure to include stories of

---

POST IT PAGE 2–2   Post It

INTEGRATED LESSON PLAN

Pronged Focus: What specific skills and concepts are to be taught? Prongs include what to teach about/in the arts *and* concepts and skills from at least one other area (e.g., science concepts, reading skills).

Student Objectives: What important student behaviors will be developed, assessed, and evaluated at the lesson conclusion? These are tied to the focus prongs.

Teaching Procedure: How will the arts and other strategies be used to help students make meaning? (**I–D–C** organization.)

◆ **Introduction:** AIM-PRREE

— Get *attention* by eliminating distractions and using signals (see Post It Page 7–4).

— *Interest* by using questions, a riddle, or mystery or presenting a problem to solve.

— *Mood* set with voice, music, use of the lights.

— Set *purposes and reasons* so that students feel the lesson is meaningful. Discuss connections to life outside school.

— *Review prior knowledge* with prediction and anticipation activities, fat questions, brainstorming, or webbing (also yields assessment data). Make sure ground *rules and expectations* are clear. Some teachers post these.

— *Energizers* and warm-ups cause students to get mentally and physically ready.

— Basic *elements* or important concepts can be introduced at this time. A visual aid is very important to make these memorable and interesting.

◆ **Development:** Next the teacher presents or demonstrates. A sense of the whole is given by sharing a story or piece of artwork. A skill or strategy may be presented to use with a problem or question previously intro-duced. Students explore, discuss, experiment, practice, and apply skills, strategies, or media in this stage. Students may plan and rehearse as the teacher coaches and gives feedback while circulating around the classroom.

◆ **Conclusion:** This is when the students "show they know." Students are expected to go beyond mere imita-tion of a demonstrated skill or ideas. They are to pull together a problem solution, apply new knowledge and skills, and show they have learned, and used, personal creativity and artistry. This could include a perform-ance for peers. Self- and peer evaluation, as well as teacher evaluation, should occur through a debriefing activity. End with a calming activity (e.g., fantasy journey, journal entry).

Assessment: Return to the student objectives to gauge student progress. Items may be added to a portfolio and connect work to general goals in the portfolio.

struggle, to dispel the widely circulated misconception that artistic and creative individuals don't have to work hard. We can share personal arts experiences and remember how artists and authors persist: Dr. Seuss persisted in his efforts to publish even after being rejected some 80 times.

Teaching for Transfer.   All *meaningful* learning is essentially creative, since it is only when we *make or create* meaning for ourselves that we understand. What the word *dog* means to your friend is not the meaning you make. Your "dog" experiences are different so you even visualize "dogness" based on personal experiences. Reminders to use specific creative and artistic meaning-making strategies, like SCAMPER, in math, science, social studies, reading, and writing are helpful to students because this assists in establishing why they are learning them. In addition, being explicit about the need for students to *make the effort to create* can cause a transfer of creative thinking skills. Post the *creative problem-solving process* (Post It Page 1–6) and refer students to it as a resource. Better yet, model creative strategies during teaching so that they see you practice what you teach.

Motivating through Choice.   The power of choice in motivation was made clear in an experiment in a factory where buttons were provided to control noise level. One group had noise-level buttons and another group did not. The group with the buttons were found to like their work more, missed less work, and were more productive than the no-button group. Interestingly, no one in the button group ever *used* their buttons—they just had the choice. However, offering choice does not mean giving unrestricted options. For example, the choice could be among art media to use in a social studies response or writing a poem in one of the many *poem patterns* (Post it Page 3–5). *No* response should not be a choice since it is only through active interaction with ideas that we learn.

Structure and Limits.   Consider the difference between (1) "I'll give you time to be creative. Get ready. Go." and (2) "I'll give you one minute to think of all the ways we could use this pencil." The real world does not permit unlimited time and resources. Let's prepare children for the real world by appropriately structuring time and being clear about the necessary restrictions on materials, ideas, and how they are to be used. Criteria should be set in advance for creative work so students know if a response needs to include specific components (e.g., your dance needs a beginning, middle, and end).

Time and Materials

Individual Projects Students Care About.   It isn't difficult to set aside time, at least once a week, for interest work or to encourage students to develop personal collections (e.g., rocks, cards, pictures). Whatever students pursue during such project times becomes rich material to connect with the arts (e.g., writing poems about work, assuming the role of "expert" to do a class presentation).

Explore and Experiment.   Creative ideas don't pop out of nothingness. Students need to know this. Time needs to be spent playing with art media, observing the work of others for ideas to adapt, brainstorming, reading, and listening to songs or music for nuggets of ideas. Exploration time is not "doing nothing," but using specific strategies to get started—to get material to work with and the time needed to explore ele-

---

TAKE ACTION 1
INTEGRATED LESSON PLANS

Lesson planning is both an art and a skill. The skill part involves being clear about the generic structure of most plans, i.e., the framework on Post It Page 2–2. Take this quiz about the integrated plan related to dance in Chapter 9 in Post It Page 9–8:

1. What are the two basic areas (prongs) the students will learn about?
2. What are three parts used to organize the teaching procedure?
3. How do most of the objectives and teaching strategies in the IDC begin?
4. How will the teacher know if the students met the objectives?

Now for the art of teaching the plan! Take another few minutes and visualize yourself doing the plan with students. What does the room look like? How are you and the students dressed? What materials do you have and where are they? What do you do first? second? etc. How do you end the lesson? How do the students feel about the lesson?

Answers: (1) Health/science and dance;
(2) I–D–C; (3) verb; (4) observe with checklist and criteria.

ments, media, and techniques whenever something new is introduced. Have fun first and then, when students are feeling good, give directions and expectations. Students can also make an Idea Keeper folder for sketches, notes, pictures, words—anything to use later in a creative way. Stacks of old magazines can be kept to cut up for picture files to use as resources. Greeting cards, old calendars, clippings, wrapping paper, buttons, even objects work, too.

Real-World Materials and Methods.   Students want to play significant roles in the real world and are more likely to feel worthy when they use materials used outside school to learn. Primary source material such as diaries, autobiographies, actual paintings, and music, rather than textbooks or drill sheets, promote authentic learning. In addition, students can use the methodology of researchers, such as surveys and interviews, rather than passively reading *about* the work of others.

Alternative Views and New Perspectives.   Delight in and respect for diverse viewpoints are shown verbally and nonverbally with comments such as "I hear what you are saying" and "I never thought of that" and "What an unusual idea!" We need to *show* we value the unique and different by forming supportive, honest, and descriptive verbal habits. Saying "Marla has a new idea" or "Joe's idea is so different from anyone else's" and asking questions such as "What are some other answers? What's another way we could do this?" conveys potent values. Of course, it isn't just what is said, but *how* it is said, so it's a good idea to periodically self-assess *tone* by listening to a tape of a lesson.

Encourage the Unusual, Novel, and Curious.   If we are serious about promoting creative problem solving, we need to encourage unpredictable answers and products. "Question of the day" and "Answer of the day" are examples of routines teachers set up and then encourage students to assume. Begin by posting intriguing questions or answers. Children can even do research based on each others' questions; for example, one student wanted to know how much trash the school threw away, so a group interviewed custodians and cafeteria workers. Surveys were made to find out how much kids left on their plates. The result was colorful graphs and students in the role of "reporters" (drama) to present findings.

Develop Forms of Expression.   Students can never have enough tools, techniques, or different kinds of media. Each new form makes a contribution to ex-

---

pression and may be the one form that will liberate pent-up thoughts and feelings. We recently had an art exhibit at our local museum by a man who didn't begin painting until he was nearly 70. He had cerebral palsy, was wheelchair bound, and for most of his life was not able to express himself—he could not talk. One day an art therapist attached a stylus to a head band. A paint brush was attached and Ralph Bell proceeded to paint every day for the rest of his life—over 1,000 paintings. Students need to hear these kinds of stories so that they can realize that much is locked inside each of us waiting to be released through the arts.

Nix Context, Content-Free Lessons.   Stanford educator Elliot Eisner explains this point:

> to read a map meaningfully it must be perceived as a configuration, not simply as a collection of discrete units. Where a nation is situated within a continent and where a continent is situated on the globe are as important in understanding geographical space as where a city is located within a nation. The optimal development of mind requires attention not only to intellectual processes but to intuitive ones as well. Children . . . should be encouraged to see the whole, not only the parts . . . a part without a field is without an anchor. (Arnheim, 1989, p. 5)

Any of the creative thinking strategies discussed in Chapter 1 could be used as examples, but brainstorming is a good one to illustrate this point. Students need a real problem in science, social studies, or literature to brainstorm about if the process is to be meaningful. Brainstorming as an isolated skill is useless. Attention to the whole and to its components is one of the important lessons the arts can teach. Fragmenting learning into isolated skill or concept lessons does not yield a satisfied feeling and can lead to dissatisfaction with school and learning. Unhappily, too much of the teaching and curricula in our schools has a piecemeal character. To truly understand, students must be helped to perceive pictures, poems, and songs as wholes, while attending to the patterns and pieces that contribute to making the entirety possible.

Use Open or Fat Questions. Fat questions are open ended and ask for many responses. Even a bland question such as "Who was the first president of the United States?" can be made interesting when changed to "What do you know about the first president of the United States?" Better yet, try this one: "Show me what you know about the first president of the United States." (This can yield pantomimes of tree chopping, horse riding, posturing, and even lying flat out in a funeral pose.) Fat questions call for students to do more integrated thinking because they ask for ideas to be retrieved and synthesized from many areas of the brain. One way to start is to use questions beginning with *What if? Why? How?* Avoid yes–no questions beginning with *who, could, would, should,* and *when*. When fat questions are coupled with a wait time of at least 5 seconds, more students will have responses and the responses will be of better quality. Post It Page 2–3 on the *art of teacher questioning* includes more pointers on habits to increase student thinking.

Clear Purposes. From early childhood on people have a strong desire to know the reasons why. Purposes motivate. Students need examples of why strategies such as SCAMPER (Post It Page 1–6) should be used in art projects, in drama responses, or to solve problems in math. One study done in a public area with a copy machine demonstrated the power of purpose giving. Confederates approached people and asked to be allowed to "cut in" to copy. People often did allow cutters to do so. But when confederates gave a reason such as "I'm in a hurry because my boss is waiting and I'll get in trouble if I'm late!" the allowance percentages increased into the nineties. It is also effective to ask students to *figure out* the purposes, although this generally takes longer.

Grouping for Creative Work. Planning a pantomime is much more fun when done with a partner, in a triad, or quad, and there is the potential for pig-gybacking on each other's creative ideas. This teacher habit is drawn from Vygotsky's ideas about social interaction stimulating thinking. In addition, groups who take risks together feel better about sharing their efforts in public.

Creative Problem Solving and Thinking Focus. We can encourage students to have a "what if" approach to problems and show them the power of hope and imagination. When they complain about a short recess, ask, "What if there were no recesses or what if we only had recess and no school?" Ask them to generate as many "what ifs" as they can in one minute. Use strategies such as Eberle's SCAMPER (see Chapter 1) to help students learn to stretch and twist ideas. SCAMPER time can even be scheduled once a week and the verbs posted on a chart. Students can become expert at creative problem solving if they learn to use the process. Again, it is helpful to post the *creative problem-solving process* (Post It Page 1–6) for students to use as a reference.

Encourage Risk Taking to Develop Courage. We live in a world full of problems and danger, but hiding in a hole isn't an option. The classroom is an ideal safe setting for students to experiment and make mistakes, to "give it a try and see what happens." We can celebrate risk taking, even when the results don't work: "I'm glad you tried to write a poem that doesn't rhyme. I hear you saying you don't like the poem. Is there a part you do like? What could you do to make it suit you better?" Both teachers and students can collect stories about people who take risks and may have appeared foolish to others at the time. The newspaper is a good source. Another idea is to create a class add-on bulletin board to acknowledge risk takers entitled "Risk Taking Takes Courage."

Descriptive Feedback, Praise, and Extrinsic Rewards. If our goals are to enable students to think originally and be independent, we need to align our feedback with our goals. "Good! Great! Awesome!" are value-laden vague words that students may or may not believe are genuine, especially if overused. People tend to believe specifics. By truthfully commenting on a child's work, a teacher can provide valuable guidance and cause the child to feel important because time, honest thought, and attention were given to her. Consider the difference between "Good job!" and "Rudy, you really used a lot of different facial expressions in your pantomime. That showed you were really into your character." Imagine how you'd feel if a teacher told you you'd get an A or a certificate on Friday—if

ART OF TEACHER QUESTIONING

◆ Ask open or fat questions that require divergent thinking and answers of more than one word or yes–no answer. Limit use of "Do you . . .? Could you . . .? Would you . . .? Should you . . .?" Rephrase, instead.

◆ "What if . . .?" questions stimulate creative thinking at the *synthesis* level.

◆ Ask questions that call for use of both experiences and text evidence. Ask "What evidence or examples can you give?"

◆ Follow fat questions with wait time—at least 5 seconds. This yields longer, better answers and more will participate.

◆ Ask for an *every pupil response* (EPR) after questions. "When you have an idea, put your thumb up or turn the card over." More will *expect* to participate, and you can call on anyone who signals. Give wait time for all, or most, to signal.

◆ Offer a pass option for students to use when they are called on and go blank (or a "pass" coupon). Do private conferences with those who pass too often.

◆ Post Bloom's taxonomy or another set of thinking categories. Everyone can use the poster to formulate questions and do self-checks to ensure that not all questions are literal or memory level. (Bloom's levels: memory, interpretation, application, analysis, synthesis, and evaluation. See Chapter 4.)

◆ Not all literal questions are bad. Consider these two memory questions from "Little Red Riding Hood": "What did Red do that started her troubles?" versus "How many items were in Red's basket for Grandma?" Questions should lead toward meaning and, in the case of literature, toward themes.

◆ Get students to generate their own questions by posting examples of good questions (fat, related to important ideas). Do minilessons on good questions. Discuss the importance of asking questions that (1) you can't answer yourself and (2) you really *care* about. Another strategy: Ask all students to write down a question or point to discuss on a card before the discussion, or pair students to generate "All the questions they can think of about. . . ." Questions can be collected and drawn from a hat.

◆ Instead of taking volunteers, use a random method that ensures that all genders, races, and ability levels are included. Number students and draw out numbers, simply check off students called on or ask students to keep track.

◆ During discussions, offer ways for students to get a turn besides raising their hands. This can be distracting and turn into an attention competition. Use an "I have the floor" object (scarf, small box) that can be passed to responders.

◆ Model and teach students to paraphrase responses of others, piggyback on others' answers, and ask clarification questions. For example, "What do you mean by . . .?" Active listening creates a meaningful exchange of ideas.

you were good all week. I'd want to know exactly what the teacher meant by "good" first of all. Then I could decide whether I wanted to "be good" and whether I wanted to be good just to "be good" or be corrupted by a focus on what I'd *get* for being good. The point is that it is very helpful for teachers to have specific language to give descriptive feedback, in addition to praise, to liberate student thinking. In the arts the basic elements offer such focus to specifically describe what each child is doing or saying. In addition, by using each child's *name* and emphasizing positive progress, the feedback is made more potent in helping reach goals.

Give Examples, Not Models. Albert Schweitzer declared that examples weren't the important things, they're *everything* to understanding. There is a mountain of difference between examples and models,

TAKE ACTION 3
USE DESCRIPTIVE FEEDBACK

Find a partner and take turns giving each other descriptive feedback. Be honest and focus on the positive; e.g., "I see you are wearing your favorite T-shirt with the geometric shapes all over it." Remember, people like to hear their names used in a positive context. Here are some sentence stems to prime the pump: I see . . ., I feel . . ., I hear . . . , I liked. . . . You can also ask questions: e.g., "Jenny, why did you choose to write a diamante?" Or use a request: "Todd, tell me about your collage." As a challenge, try to make a comment related to LADDM; e.g., "You're sitting in a shape that has lots of angles" (dance/movement element 5 shape). Try to keep going for a set time, e.g., 3 minutes. Stop and then tell each other how it felt to give and receive descriptive feedback.

however. Think of a teacher who shows a collage as a model and presents a step-by-step collage-making process. If the model is left up, students are likely to try to copy it. The teacher who decides to use collage as a *meaning maker* may show several examples and describe some of the options for creation. But, by *removing* the examples, students are left to create their own meaning. Of course, it's all in the presentation. Teachers need to emphasize that copying is not the goal and encourage students to glean ideas from a variety of sources. This focus gives students tools without squashing individual creative capabilities.

Student Independence and Self-Discipline. It is time consuming, frustrating, sometimes even painful, to watch students struggle to do what we could do *for* them quickly. It is much easier to just draw a horse for the child who can't seem to get down an image that pleases him. The question is, what is the goal? If the goal is to end up with a great drawing of a horse, perhaps the teacher should do it. Usually, this is not the goal of arts-based school activities. The goal is engaging students in the process of learning all kinds of concepts and skills, including how pride only comes when you do the work yourself. If someone else does it, maybe you'll be grateful, but you can't be proud of yourself unless you struggle and have some sense of triumphing (note the "tri" in triumph). Many well-intentioned teachers and parents shield children from the necessary frustrations inherent in achieving inde-

pendence. The *learned helpless* syndrome is the result. We can tell children about the hard work we've attempted and about both the successful and unsuccessful results. We can share our efforts at creative production, showing that the focus is on effort, not necessarily the product. We also need to dispel the notion that great ideas just pop out—a balloon must be pumped full before it pops. So it is with people and creative problem solving. We need to input the knowledge and skills relevant to the task and then bright ideas will seem to pop out. Few artists hit the jackpot on the first or even second try, so they serve as pertinent biographical examples of how persistence pays off.

This doesn't mean teachers can't teach students self-help "fix ups" and other strategies to deal with problems. In fact, it is important to post problem-solving steps, arts elements charts, and book response choices. We can also directly teach strategies that students can use independently, such as "set work aside and come back later, stop and get input from another source, use music to relax, examine past work for ideas, make use of mistakes, brainstorm or web." A general classroom expectation is in order for students to "try *something*" before asking for help. Teachers can then attend to help signals (like a red flag stuck in a ball of clay on a desk) by asking, "What have you tried? What do you know? What could you try? What has worked before when you were having trouble?" How sad for children to have no way to cope except to sit passively waiting for someone to come and do it for them.

Process versus Product Focus. There are times when an art product, a piece of creative writing, or an actual dance performance is the expected outcome in a lesson. However, the rule of thumb for regular classroom arts integration is to emphasize the *processes of knowing* that the arts offer by giving time to explore techniques and materials. Students might perform a play for an audience each year, but drama can occur *daily* in a fully arts-integrated classroom. Artwork by children can be displayed in a class gallery that changes weekly, but discussing art in picture books and texts needs to happen every day. Using art as a prewriting or postwriting response or as an alternative way to keep a journal are daily teaching and learning strategies. Creative movement and dance, singing, hearing music— all are a part of the daily life in an integrated classroom. These are ways to make sense and express meaning, not merely to entertain parents or the principal. It is the inner audience that children need to learn to please.

No Dictated Art! Art educator Peggy Jenkins (1986) calls coloring books and other fill-in outlines and patterns "dictated art." She decries this adult habit and summarizes research on its effects: Children lose creativity, sensitivity, self-confidence, and independent thinking. In addition, children tend to become conformists and perfectionists and seek stereotypes when focused on dictated art, and it provides little outlet for individual expression and emotional release. Children can become confused and rigid as they struggle to "stay in the lines." Fill-in art is often "doing without thinking" and promotes mindless obedience to authority, rather than creative problem solving. The sense of achievement and pride that should come from art is lacking in dictated art. Where are the creative decision-making options that art should provide? Where is the thinking to prepare children to live in a democratic country whose citizenry values freedom, choice, and individuality? (pp. 27–28). "But children like it," some say, and "it keeps them quiet and busy." We must ask about the goals of arts integration to respond. At least, if such material is occasionally used, we need not call it *art* and can make creative modifications. For example, teachers can encourage adding lines, using unconventional colors, tearing off sections, pasting materials on, adding captions or titles, and scrunching the paper to give it texture.

Where to Start

Esthetic Responses First. It would be easy to drop into using the arts as meaning-making tools, while neglecting their power to stimulate esthetic sensibilities. One good way to ensure respect for the unique nature of the arts is to get into the habit of starting discussions with a focus on how students *feel*, rather than what they think. Instead of first using the art in picture books to predict problems, events, and characters, ask students to take time to look at the art and share how it feels. Volunteers can try to explain what the artist has done to create that feeling, but often the stimulus is as inexpressible as the feeling itself. The same is true for music, drama, dance, or literature. The arts have tremendous potential to engage emotions that cause us to be more sensitive and empathetic. As teachers, we can provide the time and the direction for children's emotional intelligence to be activated. "How does this make you feel? Why?" are powerful questions that acknowledge infinite individual responses residing in all of us.

Start with the Known. In our cynical, critical world it has become common to dwell on what students don't know and can't do. It's much more pleasant, and likely to encourage more risk taking, if we do the opposite. Arts lessons are natural contexts for practicing a habit of introducing lessons with an affirming question or strategy that serves as a model for students as they approach problems: "What do you know about shapes? colors? Mary Cassatt? jazz? Beethoven? Charlie Chaplin? pantomime? characters? mysteries?" By activating the known, we cause students to open schema that can subsequently be used to understand a lesson and finally store new information. If not a question, try small groups or partners to brainstorm or web a key idea. The KWL strategy (Ogle, 1986) is based on this idea. Students begin by listing what they know in one column, what they want to know in a second column, and, finally, after the lesson is finished, what they learned.

Look and Listen More Closely. To view meaning making through the prism of the arts is not a fast nor particularly efficient way of teaching. The artist in us will not be hurried. As teachers, we need to relax and begin to carefully observe children, ourselves, and special moments. Taking time for students to explore all the shapes they can make with their bodies and translate new-found shapes into messages about science or other cultures takes time. But using movement to show understanding of verbs such as "hunker down" or "slink" gives students the chance to do. During the joy of movement, teachers can take time to watch, listen, and give descriptive feedback, piggyback on students' ideas, and even assess. Integrating the arts requires habits of the heart and mind that help remove the "get it covered" guilt—it's just fine to stop a lesson to examine a spider web glistening with morning dew or listen to the principal whistle as she walks down the hall.

The Teacher's Personal Attributes. Who we are as teachers begins with who we are as persons. Teachers need the uplifting and provocative experiences that the arts provide to keep themselves alive with the energy and examples that all great teachers have in such immense quantity. This is a painless habit: Go to the museum, join the symphony, go dancing, sing in the choir, take up watercolor, or do cross stitch. Seek out the arts as a person and as a professional. Pretty soon you'll find you can't turn it off and you'll be taking lesson plan notes in the dark at *Les Miserables*.

No Personal Put-Downs. For a teacher to say "I can't sing" or "I'm not good at drawing" writes the arts off. It's as if the person is saying, so what—it's not important anyway. As Ms. Lucas reminded us, no teacher would claim he was poor at reading or math when talking with a class, the principal, or parents. A commitment to weaving the arts throughout the curriculum brings many benefits; it also brings the obligation for teachers to approach the arts with a can do, will do, want to do attitude. Sometimes that's scary. But we do it with a belief in what can be accomplished. So, no put-downs, please, especially arts self-deprecation.

Principle 4: ENERGIZERS and Warm-Ups Boost Creative Thinking

We wouldn't think of going to a fine restaurant and starting the meal with filet mignon; we shouldn't begin an arts-based lesson without a starter, either. Divergent thinking needs to be unlocked, muscles need to warm up, and voices need to be prepared. Energizers don't need to be lengthy, but are essential to activating the creative problem-solving process and giving focus. In each of the LADDM (literature, art, drama, dance, music) strategy seed chapters there are activities to warm up for creative and artistic work: See *Energizers and Warm-ups*. Many collections of energizers are also available, such as *Playfair, Serendipity,* and books by Viola Spolin and David Booth. See the bibliography in the appendix for more. Here are a few example energizers and warm-ups for creative problem solving:

Focus Ball.   This is a mirroring activity for concentration. A leader puts her hands together, as if holding an invisible ball. Students mirror the leader as the ball is slowly raised, lowered, and so on.

Tongue Twisters and Lip Blisters.   In addition to favorites such as "Bugs Black Blood" and "Swiss Wrist Watch," there are challenging new ones in books such as *Six Sick Sheep.* "Aluminum Linoleum" and "Zip zap zot" gets everyone puckered, giggling—relaxed and ready to be creative.

Games

1.   *The Bell Tolls* is a category game that requires fast thinking and movement. You need a half-inch piece of masking tape for each participant. Everyone stands in a circle with an IT in the center. Each person stands on a piece of tape. IT begins by saying "The bell tolls for all those who . . ." and plugs in a category (play an instrument, know Picasso's first name). Anyone who fits the category must move and try to get a new spot while IT tries to get a spot. Whoever doesn't have a tape spot is the new IT. At any point in

the game, IT can shout "tornado" and everyone must move to a new spot not right next door.

2.   *Name Sock* is an energizer that requires everyone to learn names. Make two balls by winding up old socks; use two per ball to make a big ball. First, stand in a circle and have everyone say his name. Next, the leader says her name and the name of another person to whom she throws a ball. That person says her own name, another person's, and throws to that person, etc. When things are going well, the leader throws a second sock ball and uses the same rules.

Variation: Use character names.

Rhythm Echo.   The leader creates a rhythm and the group echoes it. Keep going, getting increasingly complicated, with whistles, clicks, claps, slaps, slower and faster. At any point the leader can "pass it on" and another person becomes leader.

Chants, Action Poems, and Songs.   These warm up the voice and the body. Many good collections are available, such as Cole's *Miss Mary Mack* and Booth's *Dr. Knickerbocker.* Teach by asking students to echo line by line. Words can be displayed on a transparency and actions added. For example, with Dr. Knickerbocker the chant suggests actions: "Let's put the rhythm in our hands" (clap clap).

Word Play.   These are creative thinking and voice warm-ups such as "Uncle Charlie likes . . . but not . . .," which starts with the leader thinking of a category and giving clues. For example, "Uncle Charlie likes pepper but not salt." If someone wants to guess, the person responds by saying, "Uncle Charlie likes . . ." and gives an example that fits. The leader then says, "Yes, you can come in," meaning they are right or "No, you can't come in," meaning they are wrong. Here's another clue for the example: "Uncle Charlie likes butter but not bread." (If you responded "Uncle Charlie likes hammers but not saws," you can come in, because the category is "words with double consonants!"

Principle 5: GREAT CHILDREN'S LITERATURE about the Arts

One of the richest and most available resources that classroom teachers have for integrating the arts is our vast store of children's literature. In this book, literature is treated as an art form, and there is a separate chapter on how to integrate literature with skill and content areas. There is also an extensive arts-based bibliography, by art form, in the appendix. A bibliography of award-winning children's books such as the

Caldecott (the American Library Association's best picture book of the year) and the Newbery Award (best literature) is also in the appendix. Here are a few very important strategies teachers can use to integrate the arts using children's literature.

Sustained Silent Reading (SSR). Since its conception, this planned time for students and teachers to read choice materials, for pure enjoyment, has proved itself. Research confirms that time spent reading causes students to significantly increase vocabulary and comprehension. A variation of SSR involves giving students a choice *within a topic* (e.g., biographies or books related to music or dance). While it is important to have "free reading" every day, some days can be designated as "Arts Alive" SSR times. Generally, the period is 15 or 20 minutes, but for young children the time should be less and they won't be *completely* silent. For additional guidelines on SSR, see Chapter 3.

Expressive Daily Reading (EDR). EDR is a daily event when the teacher reads a piece of literature aloud TO and WITH children, focusing on providing an esthetic experience through student involvement in a story or poem. Like SSR, EDR can be based on children's literature related to the arts. The important feature of this strategy is that the teacher read *expressively*, using voice to convey mood and character so that the piece comes alive. EDR makes literature a lived-through experience memorable to students, often for the rest of their lives. It is a time to laugh together, experience danger vicariously, share beautiful art in picture books, and make mental images of places real and imaginary. Teachers who read expressively also show students how to use a dramatic vocal skill to share words with others.

Visual Literacy: Reading the Art of Picture Books. We are most fortunate to have fine art readily available in school and public libraries in the form of picture books. There are numerous awards for picture books (the most renowned is the Randolph Caldecott Award, given each year by the American Library Association) to aid teachers in selecting books for art study. Picture books are meant to be examined as art, but teachers often feel unprepared to teach children how to enjoy and understand the art. (See Post It Pages 5–9 and 5–12 for questioning strategies and picture book teaching ideas.) Teachers should take heart in that teaching about picture book art can begin with taking time to look closely and discussing the emotional impact of the composition. As mentioned before, using questions such as "How does this picture make you feel?" is a good start. Students can later learn to examine elements of color, line, shape, and texture to understand what the artist has done. Even primary students can see the effect of brushstrokes or how color can balance a composition, how a line can lead the eye and make the reader turn a page, how repeated shapes move the eye around and give a sense of rhythm. In addition, by doing a bit of research on picture book artists, teachers can build a repertoire of information about how these special people work. Reference books such as *Books Are by People* and the encyclopedic *Something about the Author* are valuable tools to obtain biographical and artistic information. Picture books have a story, but they are called *picture* books.

Literature Centers. Special areas for arts books and related activities can be established and offered as "choice" work, or students can be scheduled into the centers for a time each day or week. Centers can be set up for each arts area or changed to reflect units or projects (e.g., "Life Struggles of Artists, Authors, and Musicians" or "Exploring Space through the Arts"). Chapter 3 provides more guidelines for setting up and managing centers and stations.

Literature-Based Units. Just as units can be centered around science, social studies, or arts themes, they can be built around literature. Important structures for integrating the arts into literature include genre studies (a folk tale or mystery unit), author or artists studies (these focus on the person and his or her style, as well as the literature itself), and single or core book studies (an example is a unit on *Mirette on the High Wire*, which gives opportunity to study impressionism, turn of the century music and composers, and unusual art forms such as tight rope walking).

Principle 6: ROUTINES Make Learning Predictable and Structured

We all know the best way to diet, exercise, or learn is to set up an ongoing regular schedule. One of the most effective ways to ensure that the arts are a living part of the class is to establish daily arts routines in which students assume the roles of researchers and presenters. Ms. Lucas used this strategy in the opening vignette. Here are some possible choices. Generally, each takes a few minutes and occurs at the beginning of the day, end of the day, or at some other break point, like after lunch. Students can sign up or be selected, just as they would for classroom jobs.

Experts. Students find fascinating facts to share about a person or an artist's way of creating. Information can be presented on an overhead, which gives

On Monet's Lily Pond

experience using visuals and makes students more comfortable talking in front of a group. Students may work on these "minireports" in pairs. Presentations can become very creative by encouraging students to make them as songs, poems, or with accompanying art.

Docent Talks. The word *docent* simply means teacher and has long been used in the art world: art docents give museum tours to teach about art and artists. When students do docent talks, they present a piece of art (original or that of an artist they've researched) and teach about the work. Students can tell about the media used, aspects of the creative process tried, what they learned by experimenting and making mistakes, etc. Classmates then respond with descriptive feedback about what they see or how the piece makes them feel or they ask the docent questions.

Arts Riddle of the Day. Riddles have potential to trigger higher-order thinking skills, especially creative

problem solving, and contain attractive language for quick lessons on patterns (e.g., spelling–phonic patterns). Since riddles are basically a question and an answer, students can write their own about any topic and show they have learned important content. Here is a teaching sequence: (1) Write the riddle on the board in a special place for "Riddle of the Day." (2) Put blanks for the answer; fill in a few letters, especially consonants, to make sure students are successful. For example, "What do you call a boy that hangs on the wall?" ____ ____ ____ (3) Everyone chorally reads the riddle as one person points to the words. (4) Students guess letters, *not the answer!* (the goal is to engage everyone in the process, not just answer). Letters are written as guessed. (5) When all but a few letters are guessed, the class is asked to signal if they know the answer. If everyone does, the answer is said chorally; if not, more letters are contributed until everyone is "in the know." (6) Students then are given a pattern to find or asked to tell patterns of language or interesting language they notice (e.g., silent *ee*, double vowels and diphthongs, *r*-controlled, closed and open syllables, suffixes, homonyms, homophones, homographs, verbs). (The answer is ART.)

Word of the Day (WAD). WAD involves students or the teacher choosing a word (e.g., *baroque, scumbling, motif, onomatopoeia*) and displaying it. A one-minute lesson on the word is then presented. Effective word teaching involves saying the word, using it in context, explaining or showing examples, giving nonexamples, and then asking the class to think of sentences to use it. The class can be challenged to use the word throughout the day: play "Beat the Teacher" and tally the times the WAD words are used, meaningfully, on the chalkboard.

Poem a Day. This routine begins with displaying a poem, usually related to a unit, on the overhead or on a chart. The poem is expressively read so that all enjoy the sounds and images. A pointer can be used with primary students to connect the oral reading with the print. If the teacher wants to then engage the class in bringing the poem to life with choral reading, echoic reading, movement, music, and drama, there are about a dozen strategies to choose from in *Poetry Alive* (see Post It Page 4–4).

Pattern Finds. Any material can be used to engage students in finding high-frequency symbol patterns, both graphic–visual and aural–oral. Coming to recognize the importance of redundancy is a learning breakthrough that empowers students; once they realize that artists, authors, musicians, dancers, and actors use many of the same ideas over and over, they feel it's okay for them to do so in their creations. As an example, in the previous riddle students might find the phonic patterns of *r*-controlled vowels in *art* or the diphthong "-*oy*" in *boy*. Others might bring up the pattern writers use of creating visual images with words like "hangs on the wall." Students learn how words spelled the same may have different meanings and pronunciations in different contexts (*Art*). Repeated elements can be found in music (refrains), art (geometric shapes), dance (nonlocomotor moves), or drama (facial expressions). Patterns occur at note and letter levels and make up the large structures called genres (e.g., a literary genre such as science fiction or a musical genre such as jazz).

Storytelling Club. Clubs can be scheduled to meet for students to share original stories or ones found and prepared. Children get a sense of belonging in a club that represents their interests. By using puppets, music, and other props, students can develop oral expression dramatic skills so important in life in and outside of school. Rives Collins's (1996) *The Power of Story* is a great resource for teachers who'd like a short book on storytelling. Also see the special section in Chapter 8.

Sing In. During a sing-in routine, poems or songs are displayed on charts or on the overhead. (It is important for students to first *hear* a song all the way through before singing it—to enjoy it for its esthetic properties—but also so that they get a sense of the whole before attempting the parts.) Like music, songs set mood. Many songs are meant to stimulate movement and actions, and children do love to move. Songs can start and end a day, be sung during cleanup (create lyrics for "I've Been Working on the Railroad": "We've been working in this classroom, all the live long day. We've been working in this classroom—it's a mess now, wouldn't you say? Can't you see the clock a ticking. Soon the bell will ring. Let's get this place in order. Clean up as we sing"). Rhythmic words can be chanted as attention getters: "Mozart, Beethoven, Manalow, Bach. Get cleaned up and beat the clock." Even a name or word that has musical powers can be used as the attention getter of the day: "Rimsky-Korsakov." See Post It Page 11–9 and the appendix for more on teaching songs and song book titles.

Arts for Life Journals. By using a journal routine that focuses on the arts, students learn to reflect on how the arts are integral to life. Students can discover how pervasive and important the arts are—economically, spiritually, politically, culturally, and historically.

Principle 7: ADAPTATIONS of Curriculum and Instruction Frameworks Help with Planning for Arts Integration

Arts integration and the concept of teaching *with, about, in,* and *through* the arts are broad ideas that include several frameworks adjustable for the special needs of a school or classroom. For example, an entire elementary or middle school curriculum can be organized around important integrative themes and problems at the center of life. The goal is to plan around topics or problems that make a difference. Instead of a cute teddy bear unit, do a unit on inventions and discoveries resulting from happy accidents or the creative problem-solving process so that students get a sense of relevance from school. *Meaning construction by students* is a core concept in arts integration. Meaning comes from grappling with problems and questions of importance. Grappling is done when we apply ideas and skills to troublesome situations, which assumes we have key concepts, strategies, techniques, skills, and processes in our background and know when and why to use them. What follows are general principles for adapting curriculum and instruction for this kind of integration.

Surveying Interests.   Interest has astounding effects on learning and accounts for much of the variance in reading success. While it is delightful to watch the joy of curiosity young children display, it is equally disheartening to witness the lack of interest students as young as third and fourth grade may show. In the reading center at Wittenberg University we routinely inventoried students about their interests as they enrolled for tutoring for reading difficulties. More often than not students had trouble telling things they'd like to learn more about or about hobbies they had. This is a special population, and yet it provokes questions about the choices children are given in the early grades. Are students regularly given opportunities to study interests in which the arts and other meaning-making tools could be used? From interviews about memorable school experiences and projects, Starko (1995, p. 136) found that not a single eighth-grade student remembered ever being allowed to select to study a personal interest. While teachers may not be ready to make all lessons interest based, certainly we can shift the balance in that direction and still guide students through important traditional academic content. "Texture may be explored in the paintings of Seurat, in wooden masks, in stuffed toys, or in the costumes of 'grunge' musicians. Economic development can be studied through the activities of prospectors as well as pioneers, through the fate of the local mill as well as the growth of economic centers, or even through the potential economy of Tolkien's fantasy world" (Starko, 1995, p. 136). However, the quality of choice that teachers give is important, too. "If student selections are limited to Which Greek god will you study? or Which system of the body will you choose for your report? students are unlikely to view the process of selecting and investigating as a powerful, interest-driven experience" (Starko, 1995, p. 136).

It is human to return to areas with which we've had positive experiences, and we need not wait for students to just *get* interests; interests can be developed. A person develops a taste for chocolate chip cookies because he has eaten them. Teachers who expose students to the arts and teach them about the unique nature of each art form are providing experiences that students can pursue independently at school and at home, given time, materials, and encouragement. Students must be *taught* to care about content, to feel how a question can perplex and provoke, puzzle or intrigue, and to delight in insights discovered through getting involved in interest areas. (There is an example interest inventory in the appendix.) Or try this: Ask students to draw a line down the middle of a piece of paper. At the top of one column write *Interests and Talents* and at the top of the second, *Problems and Questions*. Turn the students loose for 5 minutes to list everything they can. This solves the problem of students not knowing what to write, read, and create and is a strategy that artists and authors use. (Students can keep this in an *Ideas* folder.)

Connections to Life.   The brain is a neural network system that works through connections. Learning depends on accessing and forging brain connections, so connections need to be made across grade levels and among disciplines so that students see how the arts fit into the big picture of life from a variety of angles. To begin with we need to connect the arts to symbol systems used in English, math, and science to help students find the common purposes of symbols and learn how the same concepts occur repeatedly in separate areas of life. For example, these concepts express meaning and emotion in many different arenas: *rhythm* is found in music, art, dance, and science; *composition* is equally important in writing and art; *shape* is critical to math, dance, and literature. Students need to be prodded to find how *mood* is created in stories, paintings, and pieces of music and helped to see that people involved in the arts are multifaceted and cross reference ideas: da Vinci studied plants, designed flying machines, studied anatomy, and painted; Paul Klee made puppets, painted, wrote poems, and played the violin. The richer a person's experiences, the more connections are possible, and when the arts are interwoven with life, additional dimensions of understanding and expression are made possible. A caveat is in order, however: It is important that natural and meaningful connections be developed; it is a stretch to consider counting the beans Jack bought in the folktale "Jack and the Beanstalk" as meaningful integration of math and literature.

Depth and Breadth.   Broad important ideas and processes, not just a tally of facts, dates, and isolated skills, cause a unit to fly rather than flounder. Every human being wants to know secrets and truths about people and the world, the ways to succeed and be happy. Themes from literature, generalizations in social studies, axioms of science, all offer paths to the se-

TAKE ACTION 4
LIFE-CENTERED TOPICS

Work with a partner or a small group. Take 5 minutes to brainstorm world problems and issues. Next, rank the list in high, middle, and lower priority as it would be viewed from the point of view of an elementary or middle school teacher. Take the top item on the high list and brainstorm again. This time list ideas under science, social studies, and math that connect to the problem. Branch off these three areas with LADDM connections. Remember, when brainstorming, go for quantity of ideas first. Don't stop to judge the quality.

crets. *Charlotte's Web* is not about a pig and a spider, nor is it simply about the topic of friendship. It is about *particular truths* about friendship that we understand as we mature—how good friends stick by each other during tough times, how good friends believe in you and see good in you that you may not have discovered, how friends live on in our hearts and minds because they positively alter our existence. Literature and the arts offer powerful material to explore big ideas about the spirit-honing quality of struggle, how wisdom is achieved and where beauty is found. Teachers can access this power by planning for focus on significant ideas and taking time to explore them in depth. One planning design is given next.

Essential Questions. Curriculum consultant Heidi Jacobs recommends beginning integration by mapping the curriculum: Make a big chart of what each teacher presently teaches, month by month and by grade level, for vertical and horizontal analysis. Teachers can then see what everyone is doing and where integration possibilities are easiest to implement. Unit possibilities are then developed around three to four essential questions to be explored in the unit.

Themes versus Topics. In the past teachers have worked hard to develop units around topics such as plants, quilts, and dinosaurs. These topics often served as content for integrating the arts: large papier-mâché dinosaur sculptures, plant dances, and cooperative quilt making. But are these truly thematic units or simply activities associated with a topic? Edelsky, Altwerger, and Flores (1991) distinguish between thematic units that are topic based and thematic cycles:

. . . theme cycles are a means for pursuing a line of inquiry. They consist of a chain—one task grows out of questions raised in the preceding tasks all connected to an original theme or initiating questions (e.g., Were there prehistoric people living where we live now? How do supermarkets really work? How can we get rid of drug dealers on the playground? . . . subjects and skills (science, math, reading, etc.) are used for investigating the topic. . . . Since thematic units are skills-driven, they are also full of exercises or strings of "activities" related to one topic. . . . Theme cycles, by contrast, are not loaded with exercises or "activities." Theme cycle centers that pull together resources in one location are not established to rev up lagging interests but to satisfy already heightened curiosity or to answer questions raised. (pp. 64–66)

The concept of the theme should take the topic focus a step further. In literature, a theme is a complete thought: "If you keep trying, you have a good chance of success," "Evil beings usually lose at the end," and "There are patterns and cycles that occur over and over in life." When teachers start with essential questions for students to explore and predict conclusions that students might draw from topics, they can build units to cause students to think more deeply about life issues and options. This does not mean students are to be led to derive only the themes the teacher identifies or that the teacher is the only creator of questions. On the contrary, using the arts and other learning tools to develop particular themes only ensures meaningfulness if students actively participate in searching for "big thoughts." This search assumes that students are asking questions and the teacher is listening. The teacher that intends to cause thinking about principles of living would also teach students that an infinite number of themes can be pulled from any given experience. Individual people make interpretations based on their peculiar prior experiences, and it is a time for celebration when students synthesize their own themes, and they do so, even in primary grades, when teachers ask questions such as, "What did you learn? What was this mostly about? What did this tell you about people or the world?" and "What will you remember forever from this book or song?"

Standards, Benchmarks, Courses of Study, and Curriculum Guides. Nearly every state now has standards of learning for each curricular area. Many districts also have designated "benchmark" behaviors that signal appropriate learning progress by grade level or by developmental stage. These documents are essential guides in planning units and lessons. They make clear what students should know and be able to do. Also, most states have aligned their achievement testing with standards so teachers need to teach to the standards if students are to reach them. In terms of organizing instruction, many districts have followed the lead of national professional organizations that advocate life-centered unit and project approaches. Often units and projects align with science and social studies, so it behooves teachers to consult documents that give such direction; for example, in Ohio there is a state arts education model to be used to guide local curriculum development. It features "life-centered learning" through the arts that helps "students develop understanding within their own human context in order for them to acquire a rich awareness of life's complexity" (Ohio Department of Education, 1996, p. 1). Write to the state department in any state for its courses of study.

The National Standards for the Arts. This document (Consortium of National Arts Education Associations [CNAEA], 1994) is a useful tool for classroom teachers in designing integrated learning. It specifies the knowledge base, skills, and affective achievements expected of students in each of the arts in grade groupings of K–4, 5–8, and 9–12. Teachers with minimal background in specific arts disciplines will find many questions clarified about what to teach. For example, the standards for K–4 dance call for students to "accurately demonstrate nonlocomotor/axial movements (such as bend, twist, stretch, and swing)," "create a sequence with a beginning, middle and end," and "create a dance project that reveals understanding of a concept or idea from another discipline (such as pattern in dance and science)" (CNAEA, 1994, pp. 23–25). Once teachers understand concepts such as nonlocomotor and three-part sequence, they can envision how movement can be used to convey meaning in math, literature, social studies, and science. Post It Page 9–2 summarizes dance elements.

Integrated Unit Structures. Units are often structured in the following four ways: (1) around life problems, topics or themes, or important questions that form the content of all disciplines (i.e., science, social studies, the arts, math, and language); (2) with an artist, author, or some person at the center of study; (3) focusing on a genre or form (e.g., poetry, historical fiction, symphonies, plays, sculpture); and (4) using a single or core book, a poem, song, or piece of art (e.g., a particular piece of literature might be studied

and used as the integration center). Books like *Sarah, Plain and Tall* offer plentiful opportunities to examine themes such as "Families can be structured in a variety of ways" or "The role of mother in a family is central," using music, art, drama, dance, poetry, and writing containing such themes or as tools to express thoughts and feelings about these themes.

The arts can be used to develop any unit, and the arts can be integrated with other arts, as happens in life: Beethoven used the poem "Ode to Joy" as inspiration for his Ninth Symphony. See Post It Page 2–4 for the four-body, nine-legged model, which is a variation of the curricular design options Jacobs (1989) recommends. Her model includes the following aspects: (1) *discipline based:* specific skills, concepts, and main ideas or themes of a subject area such as science or social studies; (2) *parallel:* two or more teachers plan so that units coincide (e.g., art teacher does masks while classroom teacher does Africa); the students may have to make the disciplinary connections if teachers do not make them explicit; (3) *multidisciplinary:* themes, topics, and concepts are the focus and several disciplines are used to explore the focus; (4) *interdisciplinary:* similar to multidisciplinary, but cuts across disciplines (e.g., the history of music or the art of science); (5) *integrated day:* student interests and problems are used throughout the day; and (6) *field based:* outside of class work (e.g., environmental lab).

Schoolwide Topics. Discoveries, patterns, cycles, problem solving, creativity, and dreams are topics to unite a school in a several-month or year-long integrated study. Each grade level or teacher team addresses the topic by developing questions and themes appropriate to the developmental levels of their students. Often these topics are recycled every 2 or 3 years.

Centers or Stations Related to Themes. Centers allow students to work independently with self-directed materials. In this book a *station* is a narrowly focused area (e.g., a computer station might have software to explore unit themes or topics). A *center* is a space that has independent learning options from several sources (e.g., art materials, CDs, props, game boards, and other activities all related to a unit topic, such as "Reoccurring Patterns and Cycles in Our World").

Multiple Intelligences Lesson Formats. By using a spreadsheet to graph the days of the week along one axis and the seven intelligences along the other, teachers can map out what music, art, dance or movement, drama, and literature (linguistic intelligence) is ad-

UNIT STRUCTURES AND NINE-LEGGED WEB

Directions: Choose one of the four "bodies" below; the legs stay the same.

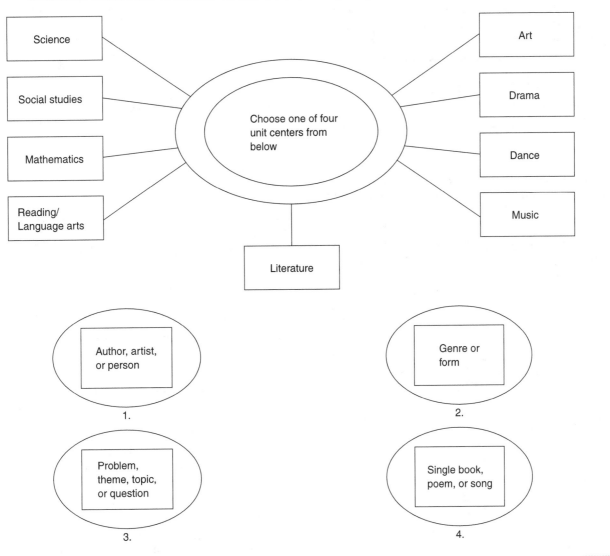

dressed on which days. This serves as a monitoring device to make sure no area is neglected to the detriment of another.

Arts with Arts Integration. Remember that aspects of each art discipline can serve as the focal point of study, and other arts areas can then be pulled in. A visual art unit on the "nature and effects of color" would be well served by children's literature that explores color such as Baylor's (1992) *Guess Who My Favorite Person Is*, the poetry in O'Neill's (1989) *Hail-* *stones and Halibut Bones*, creative movement in response to colors, and music that stimulates color imagery or songs about color. Chapter 13 is a compendium of strategy *seed* ideas for integrating the arts with the arts in 10 combinations.

Lesson Introductions, Developments, and Conclusions. As discussed under "Teaching Habits" these three lesson parts are the workhorses of planning and teaching (see the integrated lesson plan in Post It Page 2–2). The arts are natural motivators,

TAKE ACTION 5

WEBBING

Brainstorm a unit using one body in Post It Page 2–4. Try something familiar ("Little Miss Muffet," an example of a "single or core book or piece"). Use the nine legs to think of connections to the "body." As a teacher you would then sort the "web" of ideas according to a course of study objectives and decide the order for the lessons. An integrated lesson plan is used to write the lessons in the unit (Post It Page 2–2).

attention getters, and interest generators in the introduction to a lesson: Picasso's painting *Guernica* could provoke discussion before a lesson or unit dealing with war; drama activities, such as pantomime, put students in a role so that they become part of the learning and might introduce a unit dealing with cycles or patterns by involving students in the mime of everyday activities done in the morning, afternoon, and evening; "The Star Spangled Banner" could be studied as a source of feelings and messages before beginning a unit on American history. The arts are equally valuable as responses to learning in a lesson conclusion. By writing songs and poems, making art, and performing skits and dances, students show what they know. Fourth graders wrote this song after studying the chemical effects of humor on the body (to the tune of "Ghost Busters"):

> *When you're all alone and your smiles are gone, who ya' gonna' call? GRIMBUSTERS!*
>
> *When you're feelin' blue and you don't know what to do, who ya' gonna' call? GRIMBUSTERS.*
>
> *They'll make you laugh 'til you cry. Give you a natural high. So, who ya' gonna' call? GRIMBUSTERS!*

Principle 8: TRIPS Away from School

Field trips to an art museum or to hear a concert are not unusual in elementary and middle school. What is unusual is the *meaningful integration* of these trips. Without pretrip lessons to prepare students and follow-up assessment, field trips can become little more than social time.

Field trips should be directly connected to the school district's course of study or curriculum goals and objectives. If they are to be meaningful experiences, teachers need to plan teaching strategies for

before the trip, *during* the trip, and *after* the trip. Here are a few trip tips.

Pretrip Planning. Ask students to generate questions they want answered during the trip and role play how to act on the trip. Concept minilessons that focus on crucial ideas such as museum, sculpture, abstract, orchestra, conductor, and song versus musical piece can be presented to prepare students.

- *Behavior expectations need to be made clear to students.* This includes consequences. This means the teacher must know the expectations of the site being visited. For example, art museums do not allow people to touch works of art and run in the galleries. Teachers need to know these rules and convey them to students.

- *Obtain information from the arts organization about the nature of the visit.* Some museums, orchestras, and arts centers provide activity packets to use to prepare ahead of time.

- *Make a visit to the site prior to the field trip.* Check about coat racks, restrooms, seating, etc. At this time, try to generate questions or points to focus on in pretrip lessons, for example, concepts or questions related to special exhibits at an art museum. Pick up printed information at the site to share with students.

- *Students need guidelines about what they are expected to learn from the field trip and should be held accountable.* If students know there is to be an assessment after the trip, they are more focused on the trip's purpose and less on socializing with peers. This can be accomplished by reviewing specific study sheets or general questions before the trip that are to be used upon return from the trip: What was the most important thing you learned? What is one thing you could follow up on and find out more about? How did the experience make you feel? Why? What did the trip have to do with what we've been studying? Write about the trip and what you learned about. Show what you learned with art materials, drama, music, or dance and movement. Write a poem about the trip. Write a letter to the teacher convincing her that field trips like these are important in school. Write a thank you note to . . . .

During the Trip. It is important for teachers to participate as learners and as managers of their classes. Many times I've conducted student tours at our local museum only to have teachers stand with parents at the back of the group and talk. Teachers should be models of active learning.

Concluding the Trip.   Teachers may wish to debrief students before leaving the site and let hosts know some of what students gained. Students need to be made aware that the teacher will do this so that they can prepare during the visit and not embarrass themselves and their teachers with poor responses. Responses to field trips can be in many forms: journal entries, skits, or artwork. Whatever form responses take, they should be selected to reveal the quantity and quality of the meaning making that students did related to the visit.

Take Looking–Listening Walks or Discovery Trips. These can be field trips in and of themselves for students to find colors, textures, sounds, roles in which people are engaged, or ways people and things move. Field trips don't have to mean a bus trip. Students often get so excited about field trips they can't get *serious about learning*. We can take so few field trips. But short, close to school trips can be fun and great practice for larger trips.

Principle 9: EVIDENCE to Document Student Progress

Student progress toward lesson objectives, school goals, or even the *National Standards* can only be determined if there is assessment and evaluation—assessment to gather information and evaluation to place a value on the progress in relation to predetermined criteria. (See Chapter 14 for more about this assessment and see the "Exhibition" section of Chapters 3, 5, 7, 9, and 11.) Student progress can be shown in the arts through the following:

School Museums and Displays.   "If you build it, they will come!" Class museums and other displays are a visual means for students to show their work. A school museum can just as well be a class museum consisting of a special bulletin board. Mounting or framing student art shows it is valued. Museum information plaques should accompany work and contain the artist's name and birth date, the title of the work, the media used and surface, and the date the work was completed. Students can also prepare catalogs to go with exhibits for visitors to gain information about the works and the artists.

Designated tables or cases for completed projects are other ideal ways to make students' progress public. By expecting students to have three-dimensional results that others will want to see, we set up a way of thinking and planning for students. Meaningful displays also include titles with works "tagged" so that others understand their significance, much like a museum plaque.

Portfolios.   Portfolios of work have long been common in the arts. Students need large pocket folders to hold art (e.g., made from two pieces of poster board and attached ribbon or rope handles; boxes to hold audio and video tapes of drama and dance performances; divided notebooks to keep written materials—creative writing, learning logs, and journals). All work needs to be dated. Students can learn to do self-evaluation with much of the same criteria the teacher will use to evaluate work if they are given the means to do so. See the "Skills Checklist" example in Chapter 7. While not every piece of work needs to be kept, work that shows something important about the learning going on should be selected. Keeping just the good work does not allow students to view their progress over time and return to pieces to celebrate growth or past successes.

Audiences Are Motivational.   When students think others will hear their songs and poems or watch their dances and drama responses, they often become more concerned about quality. This doesn't mean arts activities should be done just for audiences. It does mean students can benefit from performing in front of a group, even if it's just the other half of the class. And students benefit from learning how to be an audience— how to be active listeners and show appreciation. Audience etiquette needs to be taught: when to applaud in a concert, when to stand, what an ovation means, what happens if you arrive late to a play. Consider offering a standing invitation to parents to come visit and not wait for the annual school play. Cooperate with teachers in lower grades to allow your students to perform for their classes. Seek out audiences from unconventional sources (e.g., custodian and cooks). Think about taking performances on the road to nearby nursing homes or senior service centers. The important idea is not to think that the yearly play or concert that students rehearse for weeks and weeks is the only time an audience is in order.

Morning announcements are another way to get an audience. Invitations for other classes to view a new exhibit can be extended or students can share song compositions over the school address system. One local elementary just spent the whole school year playing different genres of music each morning, followed by 2-minute genre reports done by students. Its amazing how much can be learned about jazz on the morning announcements on the 2-minute-a-day plan.

Teach How to Respond. This relates to audience etiquette but goes beyond into the area of giving feedback to peers. After drama presentations or art docent talks, students can be given structures to help them learn to articulate their thoughts and feelings. Let students know they can give feedback by simply telling what they saw or heard, that is, describing honestly—hopefully using new-found arts elements. They can also use sentence stems such as these to help express their feelings: I liked . . ., It made me feel . . . . A strategy called **Liked–Wonder–Learn** can be used after a presentation by giving students time to jot down responses in columns with these labels, or the teacher can scribe on the overhead as ideas are generated in each category. Finally, students should learn that asking questions of other students is a form of feedback. Because receiving feedback is hard for some students, it helps to take time to role play giving and receiving feedback. This also helps students realize how rude or thoughtless remarks can make a person feel. Sensitivity and empathy are important factors in giving feedback.

Speaking and Writing about the Creative Process. One way to help students describe growth in their uses of the creative process is to provide self-evaluation questions to guide sharing. Example questions for written or oral sharing include:

◆ How did you get your idea?

◆ Why did you do what you did?

◆ Where did you gather ideas?

◆ What were you trying to do?

◆ What did you try that you've never tried before?

◆ What did you learn most?

◆ How is this connected to other things you are learning?

◆ What ideas did you use from learning about the arts? (elements, skills, concepts)

All these questions help students think more deeply and facilitate success in expressing their ideas.

General Assignment Criteria to Guide Work. Rather than squelch the urge to create by using only grades and traditional forms of evaluation, teachers can give basic framework criteria, ahead of time, to facilitate success. For example, "Fill up your space, and use collage materials to create a response with a key idea from the fairy tale unit" leaves plenty of room to use the process of creative production but puts structure limitations to ensure thoughtful connections to

content and growth in the use of arts concepts. Boundaries focus mental energy and increase creative thinking.

Principle 10: SPECIALISTS in the Arts Are Important and Necessary

Licensed arts teachers, professional artists, and community arts organizations are crucial resources. It is part of every classroom teacher's role to seek out these specialists, who can show where connections between the arts and other disciplines exist and how to make them without damaging the integrity of the art form. Arts teachers in schools are often willing to plan with teachers, especially if the teacher expects integration to go both ways: The art or music teacher should be able to expect the classroom teacher to support a unit on a theme or topic in art or music.

Making It Easy for Arts Teachers. At a minimum, teachers can give specialists a month-by-month list of units, concepts, and skills to be presented in science, social studies, reading and language arts, and math and invite arts connections in special classes. At Duxberry Elementary in Columbus, Ohio, this is how collaboration is organized: Classroom teachers supply specialists with lesson topics, units, and goals for each coming grade period. But arts specialists should be invited to do the same for classroom teachers. Classroom teachers can solicit ways to follow up on arts classes to extend art, music, dance, and drama. In addition, it is important for classroom teachers to sit in on special classes to learn more about the arts and about students' arts intelligences.

School Talent Directory. Additional specialized help can be located by doing a school and community survey. Circulate a form to adults requesting names and contact information for persons who could be used as arts resources. Encourage people to list themselves. The teacher next door may own every piece of big band music ever written, and the principal just may play the African slit drum. Students can also be surveyed, as well as PTA members. Other sources are AAA, travel agents, and real estate brokers, who often have packets that detail cultural opportunities and organizations. Use the Internet to locate home pages of arts organizations in your state and community. See the appendix for starter addresses. Finally, ask the PTA to *assemble* the directory!

Arts Agency Collaborations. Under the auspices of The Kennedy Center, the J. Paul Getty Foundation, and other organizations, nationwide initiatives are helping schools across the country learn ways to integrate the arts. Contact local museums or arts councils to see if they are involved in such projects or interested in getting started. Use the appendix to contact organizations by mail, phone, e-mail, or fax. Teacher workshops conducted by artists and classroom teachers engaged in integrating the arts are becoming more common. For example, the focus of The Kennedy Center School Partnership program is on providing workshops for classroom teachers in their communities.

Plan for Artist Residencies. Arts specialists may be available through a local arts council or by contacting artists in the community. It is important to realize that artists often have little or no background in teaching or in child development. Before bringing an artist to the school or class, teachers need to meet with them to prepare. Both parties need to agree on and know the following:

- Goals of the visit (e.g., the objectives from your unit and course of study)
- Composition of the class (economic, social, developmental levels)
- Exact time limits
- Physical limitations of the classroom (materials you have and don't have)
- Special needs students
- Discipline system used and who will handle discipline during the visit
- Basic effective teaching strategies (e.g., use of proximity, questioning, eye contact, hands-on, pace, transitions, use of students' prior knowledge)
- How to prepare students for the visit
- How the classroom teacher can participate
- How to assess and evaluate what the students learn
- How the classroom teacher can follow up after the visit to extend learning

Post It Page 2–5 summarizes the 10 principles of arts integration.

☀ SPECIAL NEEDS STUDENTS: TEN WAYS TO ADAPT

Arts advocate Jane Remer has a motto: "All the arts, of all cultures, for all the children and youth, of all cultures." It's a beautiful dream. To make the dream a reality, educators can use the intrinsic power of the arts to engage students. Overriding the concept of integration, however, is a perspective that any model or strategy must be adjusted to differentiate for the range of student needs. Painting all children with the same brush will not create a masterpiece. The word, *individualization* itself holds a key for educators. It is made of the chunks: in = not, di = two, vid = see, ual = one, tion = process: *the process of not seeing or treating two people as if they are the same or one.* This viewpoint is particularly important as we address issues related to inclusion.

Here are general strategies to individualize or differentiate the curriculum. They were derived from the most common categories of possible areas of adjustment. The strategies are based on the belief that each child needs *particular* accommodations to ensure progress toward independence. Basically, teachers increase the likelihood of student success when they make adjustments for place, amount, rate, target objective, instruction, curriculum, utensils, levels of difficulty, assistance, and response. Post It Page 2–6 summarizes the 10 *particular* strategies and 2–7 gives adaptations.

1. Place (learning setting). Change the environment. Limit or expand the space. Use carrels and centers. Play music. Add or subtract visual stimuli. Use different desk arrangements. Have carpet squares available. Lower or brighten lighting. Provide headsets and classical music during independent work.

2. Amount (time and materials). Give more or less time (e.g., to explore materials). Simplify with more repetition and smaller steps. Reduce or increase the number of things to be learned. Alter the number of examples and amount of feedback given. Give additional practices. For example, focus on a few concepts or strategies, such as locomotor moves in dance, to convey interpretation of characters in literature or people in social studies ("Walk like . . ."). Teach one thing well, and make sure it is learned before proceeding.

3. Rate (oftenness). Change the pace—go faster or slower. Give more breaks. Create more or less time structure for the activity (e.g., intensity of teacher-directed lessons). For example, let students set their own time or give a short time to do a small amount. "As I count to five, make shapes to show *fear.*"

4. Target objectives. Make it clear what students are to know and be able to do. Write out goals or outcomes. Alter goals or means of reaching goals.

TEN PRINCIPLES FOR ARTS INTEGRATION: INTEGRATES MODEL

IMMERSION. Create an esthetic environment. Display art. Play music. Set up an Arts for Life center. Make the classroom a place that celebrates the arts.

NITTY-GRITTY arts concepts and skills. Make charts of elements, banners, and big books to use as reference tools. Compose songs and use other mnemonics. Explain *why* to learn elements and arts concepts.

TEACHING HABITS. Use the IDC lesson framework. Show an enthusiasm and passion for the arts. Tell students they are creative. Give choices. Use structure to increase creativity. Give time to experiment. Use the unusual, novel, and curious questions. Delight in new perspectives. Encourage a variety of forms of expression. Nix on context, content-free arts, or creative thinking activities. Ask fat questions. Give clear purposes. Use small group work. Plan regular time for projects. Focus on creative problem solving and thinking. Use more descriptive feedback. Encourage risk taking. Give more examples than models. Develop independence and self-discipline. Focus on process more than product. Avoid coloring book art! Start with esthetic response and ask for evidence. Start with the "known." "No put-downs." Look and listen more closely. Use real-world materials and methods.

ENERGIZERS and warm-ups. Use movement, tongue twisters, games, rhythms, chants, action poems and songs, and word play.

GREAT CHILDREN'S LITERATURE about the arts. Sustained silent reading and expressive daily reading can integrate arts-based literature. Use as centers and literature-based units. Teach how to "read" picture book art.

ROUTINES structure the school day. Short daily routines include artist of the day, docent talks, arts riddle of the day, word of the day, poem a day, pattern finds, and Arts for Life journals.

ADAPT CURRICULUM AND INSTRUCTION models. Survey students about interests and make connections to life. Teach for depth and breadth. Focus on essential questions. Distinguish between themes and topics. Sources of unit topics are district standards, especially for science and social studies and the *National Standards for the Arts.* Use the four integrated unit structures: core, genre, person, problem/topic/theme/question. Choose from six interdisciplinary design options, including schoolwide topics. Centers or stations should relate to themes. Multiple intelligences lesson formats focus on diverse ways to learn. Lesson introductions, developments, and conclusions need to be adapted. The arts can be integrated with one another.

TRIPS away from school. Tips for trips: pretrip–during–after guidelines.

EVIDENCE of student progress/assessment. Create a school museum to display student work. Use portfolios. Invite an audience! Teach how to respond and articulate the creative process. Give assignment criteria to guide work.

SPECIALISTS in the arts. Collaborate with arts teachers. Create a school talent directory and a community arts directory. Use arts agency collaborations. Attend teacher workshops. Plan for artist residencies with the artists.

Decide what a child can realistically achieve. Make objectives life centered and connected to student interests. For example, instead of "write a poem" permit adaptation of a poem (e.g., use a poem frame such as haiku).

5. Instruction (teaching strategies). Use more or less structure and direct/guided instruction (models, demonstration, examples, descriptive feedback, reassurance, scaffolding). Cause students to be mentally and physically active, engaged and involved with fat questions and Every Pupil Response techniques. Organize lessons in whole–part–whole fashion and use inductive as well as deductive methods. Set up routines and other structures to provide security but vary the order and content. Build choice into instruction. Consider Gardner's eight intelligences to plan the day and monitor the week. Use a multisensory approach: visual, auditory, kinesthetic, tactile, and humor (VAKTH).

6. Curriculum. Give easier materials to read or adapt materials (e.g., highlight important parts with pen, tape record, or rewrite). Give more or less choice. Use more hands-on materials such as games or art media. Use LADDM strategies adaptable throughout the curriculum. Use computer software. For example, read a piece of historical fiction about the Civil War (e.g., picture book *Pink and Say*) instead of using only the social studies text.

7. Utensils (media and tools). Use visual and auditory aids. Teach meaning-making tools and strategies (i.e., ways to learn or comprehend) such as fix ups, shortcuts, cue sheets, cue cards, and mnemonics (acronyms and acrostics). Focus on patterns and students making the meaning by using utensils. Teach strategies and *when* and *how* to use them. For example, post arts elements so that students can refer to them (e.g., concepts to use when making or discussing visual art). Demonstrate how to do a portrait by examining the subject in sections. Teach how to identify and make basic lines and shapes.

8. Level of difficulty. Make the lesson easier or harder to challenge appropriately. Alter complexity. Allow notes or cue cards during tests. Give more or less structure or surveillance.

9. Assistance (scaffolding). Set up peer tutoring, use small groups, and cues/prompts. Focus on building independence through teaching students

---

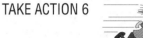

TAKE ACTION 6

PARTY! PARTY!

Here's an integrated idea to weave throughout the school year. The first step is to help students find an artist, author, or musician born on their birthdays. Use encyclopedias or references like *Something about the Author* or Krull's *Lives of Musicians* to do research.

Birthday Buddies: Artists, Authors, and Musicians

1. *Research* his or her life: basic biographical facts, unique artistic style, the time in which he or she lives or lived, the geographic area(s) in which he or she lives or lived, the country or area he or she is from, and the time period of the literary, artistic, or musical work.
2. *Collect* quotes from your birthday buddy, fascinating or funny facts about the person, and pictures or other information available from publishers.
3. *Make a time line of* the artist, author, or musician's life and works.
4. *Use a map* to locate where the artist, author, or musician lives or lived, the birthplace, the city where she or he worked, and where the person is buried, if deceased.
5. *Write* a newspaper story with headlines about the artist, author, or musician, a letter to the artist, author, and composer with whom you share a birthday, an article for the newspaper as if you were a critic. Write about the artistic, literary, or musical work by your birthday buddy, about your favorite artistic, literary, or musical work created by your birthday buddy, a tribute to your birth mate, a poem (couplet, diamante, haiku, etc.) about your artistic friend, a dialog between you and your birth mate if you were to meet, a scene about your birth mate visiting your town or school, or a list of questions to ask your birthday buddy.
6. *Create* a birthday card for your birth mate or riddles about your friend. Create a birthday present for your artistic birthday buddy (e.g., a piece of art, song, or poem), a time capsule of items your birthday buddy would want saved for the future, an exhibit of the artist, author, or musician's work, or a hat your birthday buddy would wear.
7. *Orally share* about birth mates with the class. Sit in a special birthday chair. Share an original work created by the birthday buddy: art, poem, or passage from a book. Pretend you are your birth mate and use props or costumes, and tell the class about yourself. Expect them to ask you questions.
8. *Watch* a video or listen to a tape about the life of your birth mate.
9. *Have a birthday party* for kids and their birthday buddies. For summer birthdays, pick a special day during the academic year for the celebration. For example, select a special date in the life of the birthday buddy such as first publication date or exhibit or concert date.

PARTICULAR: TEN WAYS TO ADAPT FOR SPECIAL NEEDS

Place (learning setting). Change the environment or amount of space. Use carrels, centers, music, different desk arrangements, carpet squares, lower or brighten lighting.

Amount (time and materials). Give more or less time (e.g., to explore materials). Use more repetition and break into smaller steps. Reduce or increase the number of things to be learned. Alter amount of examples and feedback given. Give additional practices.

Rate (oftenness). Change the pace. Give more breaks. Create more or less structure for the activity (e.g., intensity of teacher-directed lessons).

Target objectives. Make sure students are clear about goals or outcomes. Consider alternative goals or alternative means of reaching goals. Decide what a child can realistically achieve (know and be able to do). Make objectives life centered and connected to interests.

Instruction (teaching strategies). Use more or less direct instruction (models, demonstration, examples, descriptive feedback, reassurance, scaffolding). Cause students to be mentally and physically active, engaged and involved with fat questions, Every Pupil Response, etc. Organize lessons in whole–part–whole fashion and use inductive as well as deductive teaching. Set up class routines and other structures to provide security, with many possibilities within the structures. Use Gardner's intelligences to plan each day and monitor the week. Use multisensory approaches: visual, auditory, kinesthetic, tactile, and humor (VAKTH).

Curriculum. Give easier materials to read or adapt materials (e.g., highlight, tape record, rewrite). Give more or less choice. Use hands-on materials such as games or art media. Use LADDM strategies adaptable throughout the curriculum and computer software.

Utensils (media and tools). Use visual and auditory aids. Teach meaning-making tools and strategies, i.e., ways to learn or comprehend, like fix ups, shortcuts, cue sheets, cue cards, mnemonics (acronyms and acrostics). Focus on patterns and students making the meaning by using utensils. Don't just teach strategies, but teach *when* to use them and *how*.

Level of difficulty. Make the lesson easier or harder to challenge appropriately. Highlight text essentials. Allow notes during tests. Change amount of structure or supervision.

Assistance (scaffolding). Set up peer tutoring, grouping, structure changes, and prompts. Create independence through pattern finding and mnemonics use.

Response. Allow students to show that they know in a variety of ways. Use projects that call for a product or piece to perform. Distinguish between assessment, evaluation, and grading. Give exemptions (e.g., from oral reading).

---

how to find patterns and use mnemonics. For example, group students to do a drama response (e.g., a tableau to represent an important moment in a piece of literature). Ask students to think of ideas they've used successfully before in their art or writing if they are stymied in a search for a topic.

10. Response. Allow students to show that they know in many ways (e.g., perform what they know and can do). Connect responses to real life. Use projects that call for a product or piece to perform as a result of problem solving. Distinguish between assessment, evaluation, and grading by thinking of assessment as *getting information to inform instruction*, evaluation as *judgment of progress against criteria after lessons have taken place*, and grading as *a scale applied to responses*. Give exemptions (e.g., from oral reading) or pass options. Remember responsibility contains the concept *response*.

Post It Page 2–6 summarizes the 10 *particular* strategies to differentiate instruction for individual student needs.

Interventions for Diverse Populations

The subject of the arts is the subject of life. The arts provide avenues to understand ourselves, make meaning of the world, express talents in unique ways, and create empathy for others different from ourselves. Through the arts, children discover common bonds with people. This understanding and awareness are the essence of the arts and can build a feeling of kinship. In a world where quality of life depends on the quality of our relationships with others, the arts can lessen feelings of alienation and be great levelers among students, because no one is considered greater or lesser than another in his or her creative expressions or esthetic tastes. With this in mind, we can think about how diverse populations of students are more similar than different and stress commonalities, not just differences. We are all human and need to be respected, to belong, to achieve, and to communicate. Suggestions are given on Post It Page 2–7 to stimulate thinking about adaptations for students' needs. These ideas should be used in conjunction with the 10 ways to differentiate in the *particular* model for special needs.

POST IT PAGE 2–7

SPECIAL POPULATIONS

Children with Developmental Disabilities

◆ Give many concrete experiences. Pictures, props, labels, charts, name tags, and other similar aids help children understand information and concepts.

◆ Plan activities that move from simple to complex. Repeat activities more often and plan more time for exploration and practice.

◆ Plan lessons to make sure to teach all points clearly, especially abstract concepts and ideas that are not easily understood.

◆ For those with less advanced verbal skills, use lots of hands-on art and activities with rhythm instruments, creative movement, and pantomime.

◆ Seek the appropriate level of challenge so students feel successful. Children often surprise us with their insights when working in the arts. This different form of communication often liberates expression. Students may also show more concentration, focus, and involvement. Reinforce things students do well with descriptive feedback.

◆ All students notice their peers and need chances to participate in mixed groups.

Children with Physical Disabilities

◆ Limit the space to make it easier for them to manage.

◆ Use plenty of verbal activities for students with limited body movements.

◆ Match up with a "buddy" who can quietly explain points to children with hearing impairments, help move a wheelchair, or make an area accessible for those with limited mobility. With a sighted buddy, students with visual impairments can explore space gradually.

◆ Don't let a wheelchair act as a barrier. Use touch to calm, direct, and assist. Give tactile encouragement to students who use wheelchairs as often as you do to others.

◆ Focus on dance and pantomime that can be done with a child's most mobile part. Facial expressions can be used for those whose arms and legs are impaired or gestures can be emphasized if hands and arms are mobile.

◆ Paint word pictures and give clear details. Describe art materials, tools, pictures, and props and tell stories with great detail to create mental images for those with visual impairments.

◆ Let children with visual impairments explore through touch.

◆ Place students with hearing impairments close to the music source to feel the vibrations.

◆ Be sure children with hearing impairments can see your face, especially the lips, if they are lip readers. Don't stand against a window or a shadow will be cast on your face. Don't exaggerate speech because this distorts the sounds children are taught to observe.

◆ Repeat student comments if they are too soft to be heard by those with hearing loss.

◆ Use visual cues, pictures, props, gestures, and directions on cards.

Children with Emotional Disabilities

◆ Some children have difficulty controlling themselves, while others are very quiet and withdrawn.

◆ A secure, consistent, and supportive environment is important. These children need extra amounts of success to feel good. Start with short activities, such as energizers and warm-ups, so that they feel comfortable.

◆ Children with short attention spans need to move frequently from one task to another. Be alert to their responses, and be ready to cut an activity short and go to another.

◆ Move in slow increments to increase concentration. Select activities that increase attention span. See *Energizers and Warm-ups* in strategy seeds arts chapter of this book: Chapters 4, 6, 8, 10, 12, and 13.

◆ Body-movement activities, doing murals, and other large art and pantomime are particularly helpful. Movement involving large muscles is often successful.

Children from Diverse Language and Multicultural Backgrounds

◆ Bilingual children can participate easily in dance, art, and drama activities that call for nonverbal communication; the arts are universal languages used to communicate when words cannot or are inadequate for ideas and feelings.

◆ Infuse connections to special cultural holidays, customs, people, and experiences in arts activities. Invite students to share their rich multiethnic backgrounds and use this as a basis for artistic creations. Invite parents as guests to share multicultural art forms.

◆ Folk literature is a universal literary form, so it is one place to begin to integrate multicultural art. (Many plot lines, e.g., "Cinderella," occur in hundreds of cultures and are written in dozens of languages.) Include stories from students' language and cultural heritages. Encourage students to tell cultural stories from home. Use these for drama, dance, art, and music activities.

◆ Drama, art, dance, or music based on children's literature can be a good vehicle for learning English vocabulary. Songs familiar to students can be translated into English. Name tags or hats can be made for characters during drama, e.g., tags with *stepsister, mother, father, prince* in both English and the children's native language.

Children with Speech Difficulties

◆ Provide an open, relaxed atmosphere that encourages, rather than inhibits, children.

◆ When children are having fun, they tend to forget about speech difficulties, so get them involved *actively* through dance, art, and pantomime experiences.

◆ Being able to engage in oral activities that have a "play" feel to them is useful for children with speech impairments.

◆ Puppetry allows students to speak through a puppet and may give security.

◆ Give opportunities to sing, speak, and hear others use language.

◆ Rhythmic activities, singing, unison choral speaking, and character role playing can lessen stuttering.

Students with Academic Gifts and Talents

◆ Some students can bypass basics. Allow them to do so.

◆ Academically gifted children with high IQs are usually ahead of their peers in language development. They may excel in dialog, improvisation, and writing. Allow students to create their own materials by writing

Reader's Theater scripts, narrative pantomimes, and sound effects stories. Show students how to adapt poems and other pieces of literature or subject area material for use as subject matter for art, dance, and drama.

- ◆ Children may be able to be the leaders in a dance, drama, or music activity. They might narrate a pantomime or direct poetry sharing using *Poetry Alive* strategies (Post It Page 4–4). Encourage new ways to interpret stories into art and songs.

- ◆ Encourage play writing, creating puppet shows, and writing and binding their own books.

- ◆ Children may be interested in studying in more depth in areas. Find mentors for them.

- ◆ Gifted students often pursue interests alone and may have difficulty working in a group. Dance, drama, and music are often group arts and give opportunities to learn social skills, but be alert to the discomfort group work may cause at first.

◆ CONCLUSION

The spirit of Creative America has spurred us to say and write and draw what we think, feel and dream . . . to celebrate through dance, in songs, in paint and on paper, the story of America: of who we are, where we have been, and what we hope to be.

Hillary Rodham Clinton

Here are a few of the resource organizations to help start teaching *with, about, in,* and *through* the arts. See Appendix C for more information.

◆ TEACHER RESOURCES

See *Appendix C: Bibliography of Recommended Reading and Viewing* under "Integrating the Arts" for teacher resources. One useful video series on integration is the H. Jacobs (1993) video series, *Integrating the Curriculum* (Alexandria, VA: Association for Supervision and Curriculum Development).

Americans for the Arts. 1285 Avenue of the Americas, Floor 3, Area M, New York, NY 10022, 800-596-7437

One of the country's oldest arts agencies, ACA's goals focus on art advocacy, collection and dissemination of information, arts education, and partnership building. The National Arts Policy Clearinghouse is one resource for arts information. ArtsUSA is ACA's Internet site.

Getty Center for Education in the Arts. 1875 Century Park East, No. 2300, Los Angeles, CA 90067, 213-277-9188

The center seeks to improve arts education in grades K–12. The arts are viewed as the principal means of understanding human experiences and transmitting cultural values. The Getty Center promotes instruction in four disciplines: art production, art history, art criticism, and esthetics. This approach is known as DBAE (discipline-based art education). The center coordinates partnerships between arts agencies and schools and disseminates information about arts education. Its website,

ArtsEdNet, reviews trends, has lesson plans, curriculum resources, an idea exchange, and seminar information.

The Kennedy Center Partners in Education. Washington, DC 20566, 202-416-8800

This is a coalition of statewide, nonprofit organizations that supports policies, practices, and partnerships to ensure that the arts are woven into the "very fiber of American education." ArtsEdge is its website and is a source of curricular materials, general information, and personal and school contacts.

Leonard Bernstein Center for Education through the Arts. Scott Masey, president, 615-329-1813, Fax 615-321-2242

Its mission is to research, develop, and sustain school practices that are inspired by Bernstein's legacy and support a lifelong love of learning.

National Endowment for the Arts Artists-in-Education Program, Washington, DC 20506

The National Endowment for the Arts website is divided into (1) "arts.community," a hyperlinked periodical with news about the arts and regular features such as Focus on Community, Featured Artist, Arts Links, Writers Corner, and Endowment News; (2) Guide to the National Endowment for the Arts, an overview of the grant making programs and a hyperlinked list of state and regional arts organizations; (3) Arts Resource Center includes a catalog of publications, contact information for national arts organizations, and a library of online publications.

Lincoln Center Institute. Lincoln Center for the Performing Arts, Inc., 70 Lincoln Center Plaza, New York, NY 10023-6594, 212-875-5535, Fax 212-875-5539

The institute promotes esthetic education as an important part of learning through educational partnerships with schools. The focus is on developing perception through understanding of art forms, of how artists make choices, and how these understandings relate to life. The institute believes that perceiving and understanding esthetic qualities in art and in life are as basic

to enlightened citizenship as are understanding of math or social studies and that this kind of understanding has an important place in student learning. There are institutes in the United States and Australia. See Appendix C for member sites.

Very Special Arts. Kennedy Center for the Performing Arts, Washington, DC 20566, 202-662-8899

Very Special Arts promotes arts education and creative expression for children and adults with disabilities. Founded in 1974 by Jean Kennedy Smith, it is an affiliate of the John F. Kennedy Center for the Performing Arts. There are affiliates in all 50 states and 85 countries worldwide. *Start with the Arts* is a national curriculum initiative of Very Special Arts for young children.

◆ BIBLIOGRAPHY AND REFERENCES

Books and Articles

Arnheim, R. (1989). *Thoughts on art education.* Los Angeles: Getty Center for Education in the Arts.

Boston, B., (1996). *Educating for the workplace through the arts.* Reprinted from *Business Week,* October 28, 1996. Columbus, OH: McGraw-Hill.

Burton, J., Horowitz, R., & Abeles, H. (1999). Learning in and through the arts: Curriculum implications. In E. Fiske (Ed.), *Champions of change.* Washington, DC: Arts Education Partnership, and the President's Committee on the Arts and the Humanities.

Collins, R., & Cooper, P. (1996). *The power of story.* Upper Saddle River, NJ: Prentice Hall.

Consortium of National Arts Education Associations (CNAEA). (1994). *National standards for arts education: What every young person should know and be able to do in the arts.* Reston, VA: Music Educators National Conference.

Edelsky, C., Altwerger, A. B., & Flores, B. (1991). *Whole language: What's the difference?* Portsmouth, NH: Heinemann.

Eisner, E. (1997, November). Talk delivered at the Imagination Celebration Conference, Columbia University, New York City.

Fiske, E. (Ed.). (1999). *Champions of change.* Washington, DC: Arts Education Partnership and the President's Committee on the Arts and the Humanities.

Gardner, H. (1989, Winter). Zero-based arts education: an introduction to ARTS PROPEL. *Studies in Art Education,* pp. 71–83.

Hanna, J. L. (1992, April). Connections: Arts, academics, and productive citizens. *Kappan,* pp. 601–607.

Jacobs, H. (Ed.). (1989). *Interdisciplinary curriculum: Design and implementation* (videorecording). Alexandria, VA: Association for Supervision and Curriculum Development.

Jenkins, P. (1986). *Art for the fun of it.* New York: Simon & Schuster.

Moore, T. (1992). *Care of the soul: A guide for cultivating depth and sacredness in everyday life.* New York: HarperCollins.

Ogle, D. (1986). K-W-L: A teaching model that develops active reading of expository text. *Reading Teacher, 39,* 564–570.

Ohio Department of Education. (1996). *Ohio's model competency-based program: Comprehensive arts education.* Columbus: State Board of Education.

Remer, J. (1996). *Beyond enrichment.* New York: American Council for the Arts.

Starko, A. (1995). *Creativity in the classroom: Schools of curious delight.* White Plains, NY: Longman.

Stinson, S. (1988). *Dance for young children: Finding the magic in movement.* Reston, VA: American Alliance for Health, Physical Education, Recreation and Dance.

Children's Literature References

Baylor, B. (1992). *Guess who my favorite person is.* New York: Atheneum.

Booth, D. (1993). *Dr. Knickerbocker and other rhymes.* New York: Ticknor and Fields.

Cole, J. (1993). *Six sick sheep: 101 tongue twists.* Long Beach, CA: Beech Tree Books.

Cole, J., & Calmenson, S. (1990). *"Miss Mary Mack" and other children's street rhymes.* Long Beach, CA: Beech Tree Books.

McCully, E. A. (1992). *Mirette on the high wire.* New York: Putnam's.

O'Neill, M. (1989). *Hailstones and halibut bones—adventures in color.* New York: Doubleday.

Polacco, P. (1994). *Pink and say.* New York: Philomel.

Schwartz, A. (1972). *A twister of twists and a tangler of tongues.* New York: Harper & Row.

3

Integrating Literature Throughout the Curriculum

At one point, J.K. Rowling's first three Harry Potter novels occupied the top three spots on the New York Times *hardback fiction best-seller list. This caused such heartburn among the literati that a best-seller list of children's books was created so that Rowling's books could be banished to it. . .*

Columnist George F. Will, November 11, 2001

❖ Classroom Snapshot

Amy Weiss's Core Book Unit

Ms. Weiss's students are seated in learning circles on a well-worn oriental carpet in the center of the room. Red and blue cushions are stacked on the carpet.

"Diamond people can come and pick up four wallpaper books," she announces.

Six students rush to the cushions and rummage through blank books with wallpaper covers. There's momentary commotion as "diamonds" return to their groups and everyone picks a book.

"Do we get to keep these?" asks one girl.

"Yes! What do you think they're for?" Ms. Weiss asks mischievously. Hands go up. "Phil?"

"To write or draw in?" Phil asks.

"You are right on. These will be special lit logs for a core book unit we'll be doing. There's at least a page for each chapter I'm going to read to you, starting right now."

Ms. Weiss flips the overhead on. *"Write Right Away"* (WRA) is written on a transparency.

"We've done this kind of writing before. What do you remember?" Hands go up. "Rich?"

"Write Right Away means just write whatever you think about for a certain amount of time."

"Exactly. What else do you remember about this writing strategy? Just call out ideas."

"It gets your brain going," says a tiny girl with long, shiny black hair.

"It's just like a quick write," another girl adds.

"It helps you think because you start with what you know and then think about more after you write. We did it in social studies when we started the states and capitals unit."

"You are right, Shaena, we did use it in social studies," Ms. Weiss says. "Our WRA today is for the first chapter I'm going to read." Ms. Weiss pulls the transparency down. "Read this title with me." The students chorally read the title *"The Day I Was Born."*

"Think about anything your parents or grandparents have told you. Two people in here were adopted, so you might write about when you were first brought home," Ms. Weiss explains. "Open your lit logs and write today's date and the title—like I'm doing on the overhead. We'll write about five minutes. Questions?"

"Do we need to write in a paragraph or what?" a tall girl with glasses asks.

"Remember with WRA it doesn't matter. This is writing to get ideas out. Write in any form you wish, even a list. Other questions?"

Seeing none, Ms. Weiss begins to write. The children open their logs. Ms. Weiss uses the *public writing* strategy to show how to deal with spelling and mistakes—she crosses out words, circles others, and uses a caret to insert. Some students watch at first, but most start writing.

After 5 minutes she says, "Find a place to stop." She waits and then adds, "We'll use the *pairs share* strategy. In your groups, either read what you wrote or pick out ideas to tell."

Pairs form and begin to talk. One boy explains how he was a preemie baby and had remained in the hospital a month after birth. Some read what they wrote. Ms. Weiss circulates listening, smiling, questioning, and commenting. She seems genuinely interested in their experiences.

"Okay, let's come together. Who heard a story that should be shared with everyone?" she asks.

Hands go up and students volunteer their partners. One girl tells about the surprise of twins. A boy explains that he was born in Korea and his adopted parents were there at the hospital. After a few minutes of whole-group sharing, Ms. Weiss makes a transition.

"Would you think for a minute about what you think the core book I'll be reading might be about? Just think. Remember, good literature usually has problems at its core." After a wait time period, she nods and hands go up. She moves to the chart paper and picks up a marker. "Arman?"

"It could be about getting born and the problem of no one wanting you." Ms. Weiss writes Arman's idea on the chart.

"Tim?"

"Maybe it's about a family who has a new baby and the other children are jealous."

Several more predictions are accepted and Ms. Weiss records them. She then shows the cover of the book *Sarah, Plain and Tall*. A few children make "oo-oo" sounds.

"How many of you have read this book or seen the movie?"

Two children raise their hands. Both say they saw the video.

"Well, Sandy and Mechelle know the plot, so they may already know the connection to our Write Right Away. Get in a comfortable spot and I'll read Chapter 1. Try to make *different* connections. Afterward we'll discuss what is *important* in this first chapter."

Kids scurry to find a spot on the rug. Some stretch out. Others grab cushions. Ms. Weiss sits in a rocking chair and when all are settled begins to read. Her voice is soft at first, and she changes her pitch to distinguish the characters. Sometimes she reads slowly and pauses. At other points she reads quickly. It is almost like she is singing the words. When she gets to the point where the father says he has received a letter, she stops, lays the book down, and walks over to a message board.

"And I have received a response," Ms. Weiss says in the character of Jacob, the father. Ms. Weiss takes an envelope from the message board. It is a stamped letter. She opens it and reads the letter from Sarah Elizabeth Wheaton aloud—still in the character of Jacob. When she finishes she puts it back in the envelope and walks back to her chair. The class is totally quiet and seems expectant. Ms. Weiss picks up the book and finishes the chapter. The last line she reads, "Ask her if she . . ." (pause). The class chimes in "sings!"

Ms. Weiss returns to the prediction chart and students do thumbs up or down about whether each prediction was confirmed or rejected. The class then brainstorms important ideas in the chapter as Ms. Weiss acts as a scribe to record what the students say on the overhead: "Missing someone." "Grief." "Wanting to remember." "Being a family." "Loving each other." "Hope." Next, Ms. Weiss asks them to think about how to show "missing someone" with face and body. She reminds them about dance elements and points to a chart on the wall that lists body, energy, space, and time.

"Get a personal space. Reach out and make sure you have room around you. Okay, I'll count to three and on three freeze in a shape that shows "missing someone." Ms. Weiss counts and the room is filled with statues—many are bent over, some are curled in a ball on the floor. Ms. Weiss describes some different body shapes and levels students are using. "When I touch you come alive, look around, and describe body shapes and levels you see." She circulates and touches five children. They, in turn, describe curves, angles, and levels of peers.

"You really thought about the feelings, didn't you? How did doing the frozen shapes feel?"

"I felt the memory of losing somebody in my arms and my whole body!" a girl in a black T shirt says right out.

"What else?" Ms. Weiss asks.

"I saw how it made lots of us just ball up, almost like you have a stomach ache," a boy says.

"Yeah! I did feel like that," another boy piggybacks on the comment.

Ms. Weiss uses the "frozen shapes" dance strategy with ideas on the web and then leads the class to create a dance machine on the theme "Family members each have a different role." Students reflect on Chapter 1 and think of moves the characters made. One comes up and rolls dough. Another comes and sweeps. A third sits and writes. Eventually, all join the "dance machine."

"When I say 'family,' add a sound, and when I say 'stop,' just freeze," Ms. Weiss announces. "Ready, 'family.'" The room becomes a cacophony of giggles and noises. "I see people really involved in concentrating on body shape and moves," she comments. Giggles subside and the class seems to focus on being a family machine. Ms. Weiss calls "stop."

Students return to their lit logs to write about an important idea in Chapter 1 that means something to them personally. Ms. Weiss writes, too, but this time in her own wallpaper lit log.

By the end of the core book unit, students had a log of chapter responses. Examples of strategies that Ms. Weiss used in the unit are as follows (see the seed ideas chapters of this book for descriptions):

Chapter 1: *Prereading.* Write Right Away (WRA) "Day You Were Born" to activate past experiences. *After reading.* "Shape–move–shape" dances to explore important concepts related to theme; dance machine on "family" (topic related to unit theme).

Chapter 2: *Prereading.* "Pretend and Write" to Sarah as a character (point of view drama). *After reading.* Compare lists and letters with Sarah's and write back to Sarah. Start class museum.

Chapter 3: *Prereading.* "Chain 7" poem using one important idea so far (theme development). *After reading.* Play "Hot Sock" categories game about key concepts (drama energizer).

Chapter 4: *Prereading.* "Character Map" of Anna. *After reading.* Listen to tape of "Sumer Is Icumen In" and teach by rote to sing as a round.

Chapter 5: *Prereading.* Character "One liners" (drama). *After reading.* "Somebody–Wanted–But–So" plot map (Schmidt, in Macon, 1991).

Chapter 6: *Prereading.* Minilesson on poetic elements. *After reading.* Web and discuss assonance, consonance, imagery, rhyme, repetition, hyperbole, metaphor, and simile.

Chapter 7: *Prereading.* "Acrostic poem" about a character. *After reading.* Revise poem.

Chapter 8: *Prereading.* "CAP Prediction" using key words: "overalls, argument, strange clouds, tears, barn, wait, eerie, hail, drive, glass." *After reading.* Rainstorm (music energizer).

Chapter 9: *Prereading.* Colored pencil sketches of key book moment. *After reading.* Tableau of favorite book scene. View video and do Venn diagram (literary elements).

INTRODUCTION

I now enjoy Tolstoy and Jane Austin and Trollope as well as fairy tales and I call that growth; if I had had to lose the fairy tales in order to acquire the novelists, I would not say that I had grown but only that I had changed. A tree grows because it adds rings; a train doesn't grow by leaving one station behind and puffing on to the next.

C. S. Lewis, 1980, p. 11

A powerful and controversial aspect of art is its role as a vehicle for truth. This chapter includes a discussion of how authors are artists who share their truths through the creative art forms of story and poem. In Chapters 1 and 2, research about child development, creativity, multiple intelligences, and adapting instruction for special needs was used to build a model for integrating literature and other arts throughout the curriculum; those theories and the 10 INTEGRATES principles will now be applied to literature. Viewing literature as a discipline in its own right, as well as an art form to teach and learn, is a key chapter concept, too, as is the idea of using class time differently by tapping strengths of holistic approaches. The chapter is organized into sections: WHY teachers should integrate literature, WHAT to know to do so, and a HOW sec-

tion with the principles of INTEGRATES. Chapter 4 is a compendium of specific *seed* ideas to integrate literature throughout the curriculum. In addition, Chapter 13 has a collection of strategy seed ideas for integrating literature with the other arts.

WHY SHOULD TEACHERS INTEGRATE LITERATURE?

The book that made the greatest difference in my life was The Secret in the Daisy *by Carol Grace, Random House, published in 1955. . . . It took me from a miserable, unhappy wretch to a joyful, glad-to-be-alive human. I fell so in love with the book that I searched out and married the girl who wrote it.*

(Walter Matthau in *Books That Made the Difference* by Gordon and Patricia Sabine, 1983)

Reasons to Integrate Literature Throughout the Curriculum

1.   **Literature combats illiteracy and aliteracy.** Illiteracy renders people incapable of reading newspapers, food labels, and job applications; it afflicts

some 20–40 million people in the United States; the range depends on the level used to define literacy. Many others *can* read, but *don't;* these aliterates never develop a love of stories, poetry, or plays (what David Russell calls "belletristic reading"). These bookless individuals suffer a poverty of mind and spirit. Millions never read literature that could broaden their experiences, widen perspectives, stimulate imaginative thinking, and refine esthetic sensibilities. Educators have examined reasons *within* learners, as well as *outside* classroom variables, such as reading materials and approaches, to discover why. Findings? Where literature is integral to instruction, students read more, enjoy it, and perform as well or better on tests than control groups without trade books (see Post It Page 3–1). These experiments show good books do more than teach the *skill* of reading. The word and visual artistry of literature gives an esthetic experience that captures readers, personally. It is this experience that creates bibliophiles.

Students who read a *lot* get better at it, so it's disheartening that less than 1 percent of children read in their spare time and only about 5 percent of the population checks out library books. Many readers do buy books and read magazines or newspapers, rather than go to the library, but we cannot assume that by teaching a child *to* read, even with literature, she will automatically enjoy and use this skill. Good books must be used *wisely;* students must be guided to develop tastes for genres and authors and to view literature as an art to be savored. Literature integration can help with illiteracy and aliteracy problems; good books have the capacity to stimulate the senses, challenge the intellect, and touch the heart. A childhood spent in vicarious ex-

NEWS BULLETIN: LITERATURE RESEARCH YOU CAN USE

POST IT PAGE 3–1

Utah. Literature approaches, supplemented by short, special "decoding lessons," were favored over other approaches in a study using 50 classrooms and 1,000 second graders. Treatment groups were superior to control groups in achievement gains and attitudes toward reading (Eldredge & Butterfield, 1986).

New Zealand. A literature-based program for first graders had such impressive successes that the Department of Education began a nationwide staff development to prepare all teachers to use literature in this manner. Since then the staff development program has become widely popular in the United States under the title Reading Recovery (Holdaway, 1982; Pinnell, 1986).

Utah. Sixty-three first graders matched with more than 2,000 books yielded impressive results on a state proficiency test: Students scored 93 percent by January (13 points higher than the state standard and 4 months earlier than the normal testing time). Reading scores were in the 99th percentile for the group, and all but 4 children scored above grade level. Even a child with an IQ of 68 was on grade level (Reutzel & Cooter, 1992; Tunnell & Jacobs, 1989).

Lake Whitmore, Michigan. When boys at the W. J. Maxey Training School for Boys were given hundreds of paperback books to read and released of the assignment of making book reports, they showed significant gains over a control group on measures of self-esteem, attitudes toward reading, reading comprehension, verbal proficiency, and anxiety (Fader & McNeil, 1976).

Children in literature-based reading programs read as many as 100 books in a school year, as compared with programs without literature where students read an average of only seven minutes during reading class and only one or two reading *textbooks* during the year (Anderson, Hiebert, Scott, & Wilkinson, 1985; Hepler, 1982).

New York City. Second graders from low socioeconomic backgrounds, with a history of academic difficulties, were taught using trade books. Books were read aloud, time was given for free reading, and students were involved in responses about the books' meanings. At year's end they significantly outscored a control group taught with traditional reading materials. Comprehension and vocabulary were measured with standardized tests. This study was replicated with the same results (Cohen, 1968).

Students involved with multicultural literature showed less negative attitudes toward those different from themselves (Pate, 1988; also see summary of studies in *Social Education,* April/May, 1988).

periences with Pooh, Max, and Stellaluna increases the likelihood that books will be sought out for a lifetime.

2. Literature should provide the context for learning basic skills. It behooves us to make sure the next generation has literacy skills to survive and thrive in the 21st century. Tests will continue to be important gauges of student abilities to use English; standardized vocabulary and comprehension tests show that basic skills are learned well when literature is plentiful and times to write imaginatively are frequent. Gains of as much as 4 years occur when literature is the core of the reading program, and attitudes toward reading are more positive when trade books replace basals and workbooks (Five, 1986; Reutzel & Cooter, 1992; Tunnell & Jabobs, 1989). For those involved in special education, the results of using literature-based approaches with at-risk students are encouraging (see Allen, Michalove, & Shockley, 1991; D'Alessandro, 1990; Roser, Hofman, & Farest, 1990). Reading literature can also have a dramatic effect on writing. Students who read books, with well-developed literary elements, write with higher quality, use more complex sentences, use more variety of literary forms (genre), and include a greater range of poetic devices (rhythm, rhyme, repetition, alliteration) (Dressell, 1990). Many artists recall learning by "aping the greats"; when children write, they also need to believe that they are artists *creating art,* free to employ strategies used by other artists and authors. In addition, high correlation exists between the amount of experience with literature and linguistic development (Chomsky, 1972). Children who enter school having had hundreds of books read to them (successful readers have been read to some 5,000 hours) know how "book language" is different; people don't normally say things like "he sailed off through night and day and in and out of weeks and almost over a year to where the wild things are" (Sendak, 1963). Reading literature *to* children helps them learn about invisible people whose words speak through print. John Paul Sartre recalled grappling with the notion of "reading."

> Anne Marie sat me down opposite to her, on my little chair. She bent forward, lowered her eyelids, fell asleep. From that statue-like face came a plaster voice. I was bewildered: Who was telling what and to whom? My mother had gone off: not a smile, not a sign of complicity. I was in exile. And besides, I didn't recognize her speech . . . a moment later, I realized: it was a book that was speaking. Frightening sentences emerged from it: they were real centipedes . . . sometimes they disappeared before I was able to understand them; and other times I understood in advance; and they continued to roll nobly to their end without sparing me a single comma.

Sostarich (1974) found good readers usually had been read to from age 3, valued reading more, and planned to read throughout life. The rhyme, rhythm, and repetition in literature such as "Mother Goose" lays groundwork for enjoyment and attunes the ear to language sounds. Those rimes and onsets, vowels and consonant sounds, played with in the poetry of Dr. Seuss and others, introduce the musical aspects of language that delight and inform us about the feelings of words. In addition, when children are read to, they gain general vocabulary and assimilate sentence patterns they hear into speech and writing (Purcell-Gates, 1988). For example, 5-year-old Sarah heard Wanda Gag's *Millions of Cats* and was moved to write her own book about sister Liza going in search of a dog and returning with "billions and zillions and pavilions of dogs." Through "lap reading" children hear expressive language and develop the concept of story structure. They discover the universal patterns of plot, character, and theme, which become bedrock for understanding other books and for writing original stories. Even young children enjoy finding motifs—how fairy tales often have "threes" (three pigs or bears or tries) and there are very bad and very good characters. They learn to expect good to triumph over evil and may get quite annoyed with modern versions that spare evil doers.

3. Literature stimulates interest, gives enjoyment and respite.

On November 17, 2001 "Harry Potter and the Sorcerer's Stone" opened at theatres across the country. It set a record that weekend with over $93 million in tickets sales.
                                        (*Good Morning America*)

Interest is a mighty motivator. No amount of pizza coupons will ever match the force of interest in causing children to become voracious readers. People simply read more and better when materials are related to interests; interest accounts for more than 25 times the variance in reading comprehension (Barr, Kamil, & Mosenthal, 1996). Abundant fiction and nonfiction is now available in any area, from sports to fantasy to cooking, and source books such as *A to Zoo: A Subject Access to Children's Picture Books* and *The Bookfinder* can help match readers with interests. There is no excuse for not assessing interests and introducing books that allow students to develop and pursue independent reading (see the sample interest inventory in the appendix).

Reading books also offers children relaxation and a distance from scheduled stressful lives. Unlike television, books trigger greater imagination by allowing the personal creation of images, which is satisfying *and* stimulates brain activity, rather than passivity. It has been proposed that excessive television watching may cause brain atrophy and impair ability to visualize, an ability crucial to the enjoying and understanding of books. Until the facts are in, it is far safer to bank on reading for relaxation and doing other generative activities such as writing and drawing.

4.   Literature provides for the esthetic need for beauty, pleasure, awe, and joy. Children's literature should be viewed as an art form, primarily, and a tool for teaching, second. Just like all art forms, books can elicit the Stendhal effect (see Chapter 2 about the power of beauty), and it would be art abuse to see the instructional possibilities of literature as paramount. Children's literature grew out of an oral storytelling tradition that endured because words were used artfully. Children who have heard the music of poetry and experienced the thrill of folktale journeys seek out literature. In our efforts to milk literature's power to boost skills, we may destroy its potential to affect children esthetically. Rosenblatt's (1985) work on esthetic reading has made a great contribution in helping teachers think about attuning students to the beauty of books. She believes readers and writers are engaged esthetically when they are taught to attend and respond to sounds and images associated with words and to experience emotional, as well as denotational, properties of words. A word's sound makes us feel certain things, just as words give us information by labeling ideas. Children need time to experience how books make us laugh and sob, stir the imagination with "what if" questions, and give different perspectives on problems. In addition, picture books offer a visual art dimension of esthetic experience through the diverse styles and forms technology affords today's picture book artists.

Children do not automatically gain esthetic joy from books. Children with reading difficulties may have trouble suspending belief, which inhibits use of the imagination (Purcell-Gates, 1991). Children who missed the read aloud experience with caregivers may see only a troublesome decoding task ahead as they confront a page. A level of fluency is needed to enjoy reading; halting word identification does not make

Literature Response

reading fun. Supportive teaching strategies such as choral reading, taped books, and partner reading can be used so struggling readers can relax and share in the meaning-making focus of reading. Even fluent readers benefit from the use of strategies that release ideas, make connections, help draw conclusions, and evaluate judgments. Chapter 4 has examples such as EPC (Exciting–Puzzling–Connecting), Write Right Away, bridges, and student-led discussions.

5.   Literature experiences provoke higher-order thinking. Good books can move us from an egocentric, single perspective into complex abstract thinking (see Chapter 1 on Piaget). At the core of literature, and drama, is conflict—even in simple nursery rhymes conflict drives the story. It may be introduced and resolved quickly; in three lines Little Miss Muffet encounters the problem, a spider, and solves it—by running away. Children must use higher-order thinking skills (HOTS) to analyze and make sense of these problems. Techniques such as "put your thumb up when you find the problem" engage analytic thinking, and children can be guided through the creative problem-solving process to gather data and brainstorm solutions. (Also see the Moral Dilemma strategy under social studies in Chapter 8.) Such predictions increase active engagement and encourage the creative problem-solving skills necessary for family living and workplace success.

Other higher-order thinking triggered by literature includes considering alternative perspectives, evaluating character actions, and deriving personal meanings from themes; for example, when students retell a story from another character's point of view (e.g., Cinderella from the stepmother's point of view), they learn how problems have many sides. In addition, connections to life are made as students learn to use *point of view*, a key literary element. For example, after reading Jane Yolen's *Owl Moon* (1987), second graders discussed the problem of an endangered species, the spotted owl, from the point of view of loggers who feel they need to earn money to feed and clothe their families. Even young children can abstract generalized themes from literature, especially if this thinking is demonstrated for them (Lehr, 1991). The key is for teachers to "model literature as a way of learning about life, participate as learners rather than experts, and offer students choices in how they respond to literature; [then] students are more likely to make strong connections between literature and life" (Tompkins & McGee, 1993, p. 15).

6. Literature experiences build empathy and respect for others.

Literature is indispensable to the world. . . . The world changes according to the way people see it and if you alter, even by a millimeter, the way a person looks at reality, then you can change it.

James Baldwin, author

"For decades experienced educators have reported success stories about using children's literature to broaden attitudes toward people from a variety of cultures" (Hansen-Krening, 1992, p. 126). Literature is a potent weapon in the fight against xenophobia. Books can bring us close to characters of every nationality, racial, ethnic, and religious group, lessening the fear of the unknown. In literature, readers meet characters from every imaginable culture, country, and time period. Given the chance to "walk a mile in the moccasins of others" with contrasting beliefs and lifestyles, learners can develop empathy. Beyond sympathy, empathy involves using the senses to perceive and understand another's viewpoint. Empathy includes using emotions and intellect and is much needed in this

TAKE ACTION 1
BOOK RECOLLECTION

Before I read *Black Beauty* in second grade it had never occurred to me that someone would intentionally hurt an animal. For months the images haunted me and helped form a value for living things. Think back to a book that had a powerful effect on you. Why did the book affect you so much?

time when getting along is rated among the highest concerns of business and industry. Combining literature with drama strategies such as *empathy roles* allows students to *become* characters from other cultures and share about their lives.

Respect for diversity begins, however, with respect for self and personal background. Through literature, students can discover commonalities among peoples, as well as differences, and in so doing begin to think about positive aspects of their own background. For example, hard work is a value in all cultures and is a character trait that pays off in most stories. Thus, in the African trickster stories of the lazy spider Anansi, laziness gets him nowhere and ends up earning him a bad reputation among the other animals.

7. Literature is part of our cultural heritage.
History has long been passed on through story. The ancient art of storytelling grew from the need to make sense of existence and understand the natural world. Our world treasury of literature is the result of a continuous search for truth and celebration of the uniquely human need to create and consume art. So, on the surface Lewis Carroll's "Jabberwocky" is wonderfully alliterative nonsense. I smile and enjoy the pure sound of it. Then I find myself wondering at Carroll's creativity in showing how sense and nonsense collide. His feelings for words are illuminated, his command of his craft revealed, and I think differently about what makes sense.

Through poems and stories children also are privy to the bittersweet lessons of history. From the view of our ancestors' shoulders we learn that dreams can set life's course and good can surpass evil, often through the courage of a single individual. No history text will ever make the pain of the Civil War as real as *The Red Badge of Courage* or *Across Five Aprils*. No science book will ever reveal the poetry of the universe the way Seymour Simon's picture books do. No lectures nor character-building activities can teach moral lessons more effectively than the world's collection of folktales. And who has read Jules Vern's *Twenty Thousand Leagues under the Sea* and not marveled at how his imagined inventions became reality these many decades hence.

8. Literature reveals the grandeur of truth. Good literature deals with universal concerns—big questions about surmounting a multitude of obstacles. Sometimes the problems are with relationships; other times they grow out of conflict between nature and humans. Appealing literature parallels our interest in discovering what life is about, what author Katherine Paterson and psychiatrist Robert Coles have called finding the "secrets of the universe." From the early myths, which explained mysteries through memorable gods and goddesses, to one of the newest genres, science fiction, we have a literary bank to help us consider what we are and imagine what we might become. Through the artistic genius of storytellers, we find friends in characters who share our fears and heroes willing to confront fear and fight evil. We can travel back in time or forward to the future. Books take us places we may never physically go, and yet who has read *Charlotte's Web* (White, 1952) and not felt wrapped in the coziness of the barn, sitting on the stool, watching Charlotte, and or listening to the sounds E. B. White evokes with artful imagery.

What's more, good literature reveals truths, often beautifully, and in so doing satisfies our need to know. Through the creative writing form of literature we are persuaded to think about large life questions: What is good? right? wrong? What is my place in the world? What contribution can I make? How do I do what I am afraid to do? The themes of literature are meanings we derive from being engaged with this most thought-provoking, emotional art form. By integrating fine stories and poems throughout the curriculum, we provide students with tools to pleasurably gain information and to apply moral and ethical standards to problems that they are likely to confront.

9. Literature increases self-understanding through bibliotherapy.

You think your pain and your heartache are unprecedented in the history of the world, but then you read. It was books that taught me that the things that tormented me most were the very things that connected me with all the people who were alive, or had ever been alive.

James Baldwin

Just as the disciples asked Jesus why he spoke in parables, so we may ask why use the art forms of story or poem to teach. Perhaps from the words of a master teacher comes the answer. It is through stories that we are given a palatable way of understanding ourselves—to realize we are not unique nor alone in our suffering. Such insight gives solace. The process of reaching that point has been called *bibliotherapy*, book or story therapy, and involves using books to promote insight or comfort. Stories are thought to "heal the soul" when a person encounters just the right book at the right time (Cornett & Cornett, 1980); readers vicariously experience a character's joys and struggles and actually feel they *are* the characters. While teachers are cautioned not to begin bibliotherapy without careful study, anytime a book is used to give emotional comfort a degree of bibliotherapy is taking place. Teachers interested in the selection of appropriate books and strategies to involve students in the process are encouraged to consult references such as *The Bookfinder*. In the meantime, teachers who select fine literature to meet course of study goals will automatically set up opportunities, especially if they use approaches, such as Rosenblatt's reader response, that call for readers to make personal connections to stories and poems.

10. Literature stimulates moral thinking about values and issues of right and wrong. Teaching of values is a sensitive area, but no one denies that children must learn right from wrong and come to understand and behave using common standards for honesty, justice, responsibility, initiative, and so forth. It is hard to imagine how lessons can be value free. In the arts, this is virtually impossible since the content of the arts is expressing and understanding value-based opinions or perspectives. Indeed, literature is value laden, and literature integration offers a chance for students to use personal value systems to think about and respond to conflicts inherent in stories. From Aesop's fables to *Goosebumps*, authors write about what they believe is important. They cause characters to act in ways that reveal meaning. Great literature does this subtly and allows many interpretations, while plot-driven mediocre books leave us entertained, but without increased insight. The point is that values are natural and important, and we *can* respect the diverse values of students' families while integrating literature. For example, when students discuss stories with others of different backgrounds, they have a chance to sort out thoughts and feelings and reach conclusions based on additional points of view. When a variety of discussion strategies are used, students can learn to question and comment using supportive evidence in the story (text-based discussions), connect experiences others may not share, and do creative extrapolations of "what if?" In this chapter and the next, discussion and response strategies are described that target the idea of student-led discussions (see Censorship in Chapter 14 for concerns about objections to particular literature).

11. Literature gives both meaning and enjoyment. Like all art, good literature offers both information and entertainment. Think of the best book you've ever read. Did it not *teach* something—facts, main points, concepts? Did the author not also use words to build emotional bridges between real life and the book (you may have laughed or wept deeply)? Perhaps you had the experience I had reading Paterson's (1977) *Bridge to Terabithia*. Not only were the characters believable, the setting and the premise engaging, and the plot forceful, but her use of language left me envious—I caught my breath and grieved with Jess when Leslie died. When I closed the book, I felt different. So much had I learned about loss, I felt if I looked in a mirror I could not appear the same; surely my outside face would show the inside changes.

12. Through good books children learn concepts and skills related to all curricular areas. It cannot be by coincidence that within the word *history* is the word *story*. The most exciting history teacher I know now lives in the mountains of North Carolina where, in retirement, he continues to do what he did his whole teaching career—tell compelling stories about men and women who shaped the world. History would be a jumble of lifeless facts without its stories, and so would science, math, art, music, theater, and dance. Integrating literature throughout the curriculum literally means bringing in the stories and poems that give life to numbers and verbs and dates and names. The results can be phenomenal. For example, sixth graders that learned history by reading historical fiction recalled more history than those that used the social studies text (Levstik, 1986).

How can stories be integrated into the curriculum? Easily available source books categorize picture books on nearly every topic or skill. Other aids match fiction and informational books to social studies and science (see Post it Page 3–8). There is a math-based literature bibliography in Chapter 4, and the appendix includes an arts-based bibliography divided into art, drama, dance, and music.

What is the unique contribution of literature? It would be redundant to return to all the reasons just discussed. In sum, literature is a rich, engaging art form from which students can derive information and pleasure. In a time when teachers list "motivating students" as one of their greatest challenges, it would be irresponsible to neglect one of the most accessible arts.

WHAT SHOULD TEACHERS KNOW AND TEACH ABOUT LITERATURE TO INTEGRATE IT THROUGHOUT THE CURRICULUM?

When I was ten, I read fairy tales in secret and would have been ashamed if I had been found doing so. Now that I am fifty I read them openly. When I became a man I put away childish things, including the fear of childishness and the desire to be very grown up.

C. S. Lewis, 1980, p. 210

Much of what we call civilization and culture is stored in the art created by each generation. Some records of human history are left only in shadowy cave drawings and haunting stone sculptures. We prize these artifacts for their extraordinary beauty and the insight they offer about who we are and from whence we came. But art and culture have certain ephemeral qualities, and huge quantities of music, dance, and literature were lost because they were not recorded. Literature began as oral art; ancient stories survived only because of retelling. Early ancestors must have huddled around flickering campfires sharing stories about heroes on noble quests, adventures of clever animals, acts of foolish peasants, and the search for perfect love. Mixed with dance, mime, and song, all literature grew from these tales and became a vast *oral tradition* of fables, rhymes, parables, and proverbs used to both entertain and instruct in primitive societies.

Today *written* literature is taken for granted. Of the thousands of books published, more than 5,000 books published each year in the United States are considered *children's* literature. How did we come to have such a surfeit of this specialized literature? How did it take shape? All art reflects the milieu in which it was created, and so it is with children's literature. Attitudes toward children and schooling evolved in response to political, social, religious, and economic

---

TAKE ACTION 2

REASONS TO INTEGRATE LITERATURE

Take a few minutes to make a list of important reasons to integrate literature to use in discussions with parents, administrators, or community members.

forces. In between *Aesop's Fables* and *Harry Potter* lie centuries of changing beliefs about childhood and children's education, mirrored in stories and poems. Until "childhood" was recognized, there was no literature for children. Children's literature has a dual nature: *to offer enjoyment and to teach,* but during some periods the instructional or didactic purpose has overshadowed the esthetic. Authors and publishers still struggle to maintain balance—after all the audience is children, vulnerable to the power of art to shape thoughts, actions, and feelings. Then there are the children themselves, eavesdropping by ancient hearths to hear tales meant for adult ears—journeys plagued with horrific beasts with magical powers. Children appropriated the stories with animal characters, fast action, magic, and swift justice. Even Aesop's fables, now an important part of early literary experience, were not originally intended for children. Through the evolution of literature, in response to societal changes, fables eventually became the province of youth. Books, like orally conveyed stories, were assimilated by children. For example, *Robinson Crusoe* (1719) was written for the general public, but its captivating characters and adventure caused the young to usurp it, and we now think of it as children's literature. Nineteenth century children also gobbled up *Treasure Island,* and the story's realism stimulated an appetite for more books in this genre. Today we delight in new genres that creative authors devine, and it is odd to imagine a time when genres, such as science fiction, did not exist.

Definitions: Children's Literature— A Hopeful Idea?

When teachers integrate literature throughout curricular areas, they involve students in *discovering* truths about life from implicit and explicit themes. A major part of the elementary curriculum is now devoted to discussing, creating, sharing, and performing literature through approaches using daily time blocks to read, write, talk about, and listen to good stories and poems. But what distinguishes children's literature from other literature? One definition never seems to quite get it all, but two features seem to mark this special literature: (1) It is intended for a young audience and (2) unlike adult literature, it nearly always holds out a degree of hope. For example, there is hope even when Charlotte dies, because her children will continue her legacy. Winnie gives us hope in *Tuck Everlasting* when she courageously chooses not to live forever. Most art offers some hope, even if it's just

hope born of expanded perspective. Here are three other definitions to help clarify the nature of children's literature.

> [Literature is] an art form, as are painting, sculpture, architecture, and music. (Russell, 1994, p. 212)

> [Literature is] all instances in which language is used imaginatively. . . . Literature speaks of the mysteries of the human condition, although in books for children, treatment of these themes is adjusted according to the age-related interests and capacities of the audience. (Cullinan, 1989, p. 8)

> In both its meaning and in the words and images that convey that meaning, literature encourages a thoughtful, aesthetic response. . . . Literature for children differs from adult literature in degree rather than kind. The same themes or topics may be addressed and the same elements manipulated, but the experiences and understanding of children determine whether a book is "for" them . . . the main characters themselves are often children, and often more emphasis is placed on the actions than on the thoughts of the characters.. . . The book becomes a child's book when children read, enjoy, and understand it. (Glazer, 1997, pp. 5–7)

Goals for Literature Integration

While there are divergent opinions about what students should know and be able to do in the art domain of literature, there is agreement about (1) studying the historical, social, and cultural role of literature, (2) learning how people communicate through literature by reading, writing, performing, and responding to it, and (3) developing an esthetic sense by studying the roles of beauty and emotion in words and visual art in literature. To accomplish these goals, classroom teachers who integrate literature throughout the curriculum need to teach the following:

◆ *The history of children's literature,* including classic books that are part of a common culture

---

TAKE ACTION 3

A DEFINITION OF CHILDREN'S LITERATURE

Use ideas from the definitions above, and your experiences reading children's literature, to write your own definition. For more ideas, consult children's literature textbooks and specialized dictionaries.

- *Many good children's books,* found through using selection sources to evaluate and locate books for units (core book, author study, genre study, and topic or problem focused) and books for individual student interests and levels
- *The basic structure of literature:* literary elements, genre structures, and other types of writing authors use
- *Actual authors and artists,* including how and why children's authors and artists create literature and art
- *Many meaning-making strategies,* to teach students how to understand, create, and respond to literature

It is helpful to gather and organize information on literature integration. Here is a checklist of titles for folder tabs or computer files:

- *Literary elements* (to think about and write literature)
- *Styles, forms, or genres* of literature (include bibliographies of each)
- *Authors and artists* who create children's literature (include biographical information, quotes about and from authors and artists, book lists of their works)
- *Significant literature* and recommended lists of "ones everyone should know" (canon)
- *Bibliographies* of books for each curricular area (e.g., science fiction and science informational books, historical fiction, biography, books about language or parts of speech)
- *Bibliotherapy* aids (books that can be used to give perspective on problems)
- *Approaches* to teaching literature (e.g., reader response theory and the critical approach)
- *Other possibilities:* history of children's literature, science of bookmaking, the math of creating literature (e.g., Edgar Allen Poe's mathematical formulas for "The Raven"), process writing stages, economics (book selling, publishing, advertising)

National Standards Related to Literature

In 1996 the National Council for the Teachers of English Language Arts and the International Reading Association collaborated to develop goals for students in reading, writing, speaking, and listening. The result is

TAKE ACTION 4
CONNECT TO THE STANDARDS

Think about Mrs. Weiss's core book lesson at the start of the chapter. Select the IRA/NCTE *Standards* that you think were the goals of the lesson. Give your reasons. How would students be helped if lessons were more focused on goals or standards related to literature?

---

a set of broad statements of what students should be able to do by graduation. These standards can guide integration of literature throughout the curriculum by making clear the kinds of focuses possible in lessons. The standards are voluntary but are being used at both state and local levels to develop curriculum and construct assessments. The *Standards* are given in Post It Page 3–2.

Literary Elements

The elements of plot, theme, character, point of view, and style are the building blocks used to write and understand literature. Authors' decisions create the memorable writings of our literary tradition, as well as forgettable dull works. How can this be so? The elements are but tools in the creative process—it's artistry and imagination that make the magic. By giving students tools, techniques, and materials to work with, we provide them with the chance to read and write creatively. Literary elements are indispensable in understanding the unique attributes of literary genre and subgenre. For these reasons teachers need to know about and teach the following:

Theme *is the unifying truth or universal message in literature.* When we read and write stories and poems, private meanings are constructed as authors reach out to us to make public their messages. These messages are literary themes, value-laden statements that tie a story together. It helps to ask, "What is the story *really* about?" and go beyond just stating the topic. For example, *Charlotte's Web* is about the *topic* of "friendship." To pull a theme together, ask an additional question, "What *about* friendship?" One answer is "Good friends stick by you during tough times." This is a clear theme statement. There are two types or ways that themes occur in literature:

Explicit themes are directly stated. These are present as *morals* in fables. In other genres, authors may state themes, but often *imply* them. An explicit theme

STANDARDS FOR THE ENGLISH LANGUAGE ARTS

Overall focus: Literacy growth through experience and experimenting with literacy activities; reading and writing and associating spoken words with their graphic representations.

Students would:

1. **Read a wide range of print and nonprint texts:** fiction and nonfiction, classic and contemporary works, multicultural literature, genre characteristics and purposes.
2. **Read a wide range of literature from many periods in many genres:** understand philosophical, ethical, esthetic aspects of human experience, compare and contrast literature from different periods.
3. **Apply a wide range of strategies to comprehend, interpret, evaluate, and appreciate texts:** draw on their prior experience and interactions with others, use word meanings and their understanding of text features.
4. **Adjust use of spoken, written, and visual language:** vocabulary development, variety of audiences for a variety of purposes.
5. **Employ a wide range of strategies as they write:** writing process, patterns from books read, different audiences and purposes.
6. **Apply knowledge of language structure, language conventions, media techniques, figurative language, and genre to create, critique, discuss print and nonprint texts:** literary elements, art elements, patterns of writing, analyze literary devices used to create style.
7. **Conduct research on issues and interests by generating ideas and questions and by posing problems:** gather, evaluate, and synthesize data from a variety of sources; use literary experiences to solve problems; seeks out books for personal information.
8. **Use a variety of technological and informational resources:** libraries, databases, computer networks, video.
9. **Develop an understanding of and respect for diversity in language use, patterns, and dialects:** multicultural literature, including poetry sharing.
10. **Participate as knowledgeable, reflective, creative, and critical members of a variety of literacy communities:** literature discussions and conversations, oral sharing of poetry, author's chair, evaluate literary and artistic merit of a book.
11. **Use spoken, written, and visual language to accomplish their own purposes:** oral interpretation of poetry, writing in different genre, book making, connect life events to literature, respond to literature through other art forms, read literature for enjoyment, storytelling, develop literary preferences.

Source: Copyright 1996 by the International Reading Association and the National Council of Teachers of English. Adapted from *12 Standards,* as applicable to the concept of integrating the arts. Material following standards represents the author's interpretation of the standards.

---

from *Charlotte's Web* is "Life is always a rich and steady time when you are waiting for something to happen or to hatch" (White, 1952, p. 176).

Implicit themes are not directly stated but are truth statements inferred by reading between the lines. The theme statement above about the topic of friendship is an implied theme.

Themes can be further drawn out by asking, "What does the author seem to believe?" If he seems to say "We only show courage when we are afraid," then characters, plot, and other elements must unite around this idea. Theme is not a retelling of the story; it is a value-based conclusion.

Plot *is the order of events in a story.* The question "What happened?" gets at the plot. Plot is the sequence of events usually set in motion by a *problem* that begins the action or causes conflict. *Conflict* is tension between opposing forces; author Robert Newton Peck calls this the "two dogs and one bone" idea. Conflict motivates characters to act and keeps our interest. Four types are:

1. Between a character and nature (*Tornado* by Arnold Adoff)
2. Between a character and society (*Charlotte's Web:* Wilbur wants to live but societal forces dictate he should be bacon)

3. Between characters (Katherine Paterson's *Jacob Have I Loved:* between sisters)

4. Within a character (Evaline Ness's *Sam, Bangs and Moonshine:* lying child)

The *climax* is the high point of the plot. Tension breaks, the problem begins to be resolved, and conflict lessens. The *denouement* is the final pulling together or conclusion. All these plot aspects usually come together in patterns. (See plot lines strategy in Chapter 4.) Common plot structure patterns are:

Linear plot pattern: In the beginning section a *problem is introduced.* In the middle section the plot is developed by *rising or increased action,* and there may be several events and consequences. In the conclusion, or end, the action peaks (*climax*), and the *problem is resolved. Cinderella* is an example.

Cumulative plot patterns have repeated phrases, sentences, or events that keep adding up or accumulating, for example, *The House That Jack Built.*

Episodic plot patterns are like several ministories tied together. For each episode there is a complete linear plot development. Examples are: *George and Martha* or *Frog and Toad.*

Creative variations in the basic plot patterns can be made using *cliffhangers,* which consist of unresolved suspense, usually at the end of a chapter, and *flashbacks,* which create suspense and excite through use of look-backs at previous events or times. This complicates the plot and halts forward progression because events are out of the chronological time order of the main plot. *Foreshadowing* gives a clue or hint about something to come later. It is a way to make the reader feel involved and can add excitement because it heightens anticipation. For example, White foreshadows the conflict with the question "Where's Papa going with that ax?" (*Charlotte's Web*, White, 1952, p. 1).

Character *is a person, animal, or object taking on a role.* Through characters, children can begin to understand the many sides of being human, both the dark and the light. By reaching out imaginatively to characters, a child vicariously lives a slice of another's life and gains perspective on who she is and what she might become. Only with close friends do we share the kinds of secrets that we learn about literary characters. These are the Pooh bears and Cats in the Hat who become dear friends, who make us laugh and weep, who become heroes and heroines and inspire dreams for the future. And then there are horrid characters, like those in folktales, who show how a character's decision to behave bravely or badly is duly rewarded or punished. A realization that character choices create triumph or failure gives the growing child an important insight—the world is something over which she, as a character in life, has a measure of control. It is through the characters, their motives, actions, and dialog that the theme is uncovered. To help children unravel story characters and create their own characters, the following writing categories are helpful:

Characters are shown by: (1) *descriptions,* (2) *actions they take,* (3) *their speech and thoughts,* and (4) *what others think and say.*

- *Protagonist:* the main character (hero or heroine). This is the character who changes the most (e.g., Wilbur in *Charlotte's Web*).

- *Antagonist:* the character who opposes the protagonist by creating obstacles or problems; "between characters" conflict pattern (e.g., Mr. McGregor in Beatrix Potter's *Peter Rabbit*).

- *Round character:* well-developed character. Many traits are revealed, both positive and negative (e.g., Max in *Where the Wild Things Are*).

- *Flat or stock character:* has little or no development, is one sided (all good or all bad); author gives only a few traits (e.g., Prince in *Cinderella*).

- *Dynamic:* character that takes action, makes a substantial change during the story, and causes events to happen (e.g., Peter Rabbit).

- *Static character:* character who does *not* change; may be round or flat (e.g., Charlotte in *Charlotte's Web*).

- *Foil:* character with traits opposite to the main character. Foils help clarify the protagonist by contrast. Foils are usually flat (e.g., Beauty's sisters in *Beauty and the Beast*).

- *Stereotype:* character who exhibits only *expected* traits of a group. Stereotypes are destructive when they use narrow and negative images, such as depicting Native Americans as savages.

Setting *is the time and place: when and where.* Setting provides the backdrop or "scenery" for the characters to act out the plot. *When* the story happens may be a past or future time *period* or a certain month or day. *Where* it happens can be vague and unimportant, as in folktales ("a kingdom far away"), or specific and integral, such as the cabin on the Oklahoma prairie in *Out of the Dust* (1998). In fantasy, setting is especially important because the reader must believe in a whole new world. In realistic stories the setting can function as an antagonist, as in survival stories such as *Hatchet* (1989), where a young boy fights the Canadian wilderness. If the title of the story includes the setting, then it is probably more than a mere backdrop; for example, in *The Little House in the Big Woods* (1971) the setting helps create mood and adds plot tension. The big homey barn in *Charlotte's Web* creates a different mood than the bustling fair where Wilbur must perform to save himself. The setting can also be a *symbol* of what the story is about; for example, one setting of *Walk Two Moon* (1994) is a car that, like the main character, is controlled by others and on its way to a mysterious destination. The car with its hard exterior and comfortable interior is a safe place in a time within a "larger" time that is frightening. The car also foreshadows another important vehicle in the book—a bus.

- *Types of settings:* scenery backdrop or integral
- *Aspects of setting:* place or location, time or time period, weather

The ***primary world*** is a realistic world used as a setting for fiction (realism or fantasy). An example is the "real" world of Winnie in *Tuck Everlasting*. The ***secondary world*** is a "created" world used in fantasy. An example is the "living forever" time warp in which the Tuck family is trapped in *Tuck Everlasting*.

Point of view (POV) *is the vantage point from which a story is written.* The angle from which the action is viewed may be through the eyes of one character or many. When one character tells the story and uses "I," the POV is first person and allows the reader to identify with one character; it is used a lot in realistic fiction. Many children's books have an *outside* narrator who sees and hears all, including what's inside characters' minds. This is called the omniscient (all knowing) POV and allows the reader to know many characters; it is as if the author has a godlike power to be in on everything. White takes this POV in *Charlotte's Web*. An author may combine or alternate first person and a limited version of omniscient POV by using two or three characters.

- *First person point of view:* uses "I" to tell the story; one character's perspective.
- *Omniscient or third person:* an all-knowing point of view using the third person (he, she, it). The narrator tells the story from above the action and can tell about any character's thoughts.
- *Limited omniscient:* same as omniscient, but only a few characters are targeted.

- *Objective:* the third person is used by the narrator to tell the story, but there is no subjective interpretation of what characters feel or of events. The author is like a video camera recording action.

Stylistic or poetic elements *are the creative use of words for artistic effect.* Style is how an author crafts words to express ideas and feelings. In both prose and poetry, carefully selected words determine what we know and feel about character, theme, setting, and plot. When used with skill and artistry, the reader may not notice the poetic devices of rhyme, rhythm, repetition, or figurative language adding impact or beauty or the dialect in which a character speaks, but we feel the effect. An author may choose unemotional language and short sentences to create a controlled seriousness or may use flamboyant words, even nonsense, and defy conventional sentence structure to create humor. To understand style, examine how words are used in special ways:

Figurative language is the use of words to stand for other things:

Imagery appeals to the senses of smell, taste, feel or texture, vision, and hearing. Such language triggers concrete images that engage a reader or listener. For example, "The morning light shone through its ears, turning them pink" (*Charlotte's Web*, p. 4).

Personification: giving of human traits, such as feeling, actions, and the ability to speak, to animals or objects. For example, "The streams and ditches bubbled and chattered with rushing water" (*Charlotte's Web*, p. 176).

Metaphors are comparisons that create mental images because they connect something familiar with something less familiar. By comparing unlike things we see things in novel ways. Simile is a kind of metaphor using an explicit comparison and is set up in the pattern of _____ *is like* _____ or _____ *as* _____. For example, Charlotte is "about the size of a gumdrop" (p. 37).

Connotation and denotation: denotation is the dictionary definition, while connotation is the use of words in a way that has come to be understood, but nonliterally. For example, saying "the car was a real dog" is using the connotation of the word "dog" to give a feeling.

Motifs are recurring patterns and can be images or events, such as plot patterns. Openings and closings of folk tales are motifs: "Once upon a time" and "They lived happily." Huck, Hepler, and Hickman (2001) list six folktale motifs: (1) a long sleep or enchantment (*Rapunzel*), (2) magical powers (*Jack in the Beanstalk*), (3) magical transformations (*The Frog Prince*), (4) magical objects (*Anansi and the Moss-covered Rock*), (5) wishes (*The Three Wishes*), and (6) trickery (*The Three Little Pigs*). Common *plot* motifs are (1) a cyclical pattern of a young character leaving home, having a dangerous journey, and coming home with new wisdom (*Peter Rabbit*), (2) journeys with obstacles and confrontations with giants or monsters (*Jack and the Beanstalk*), (3) helpless characters (often female) rescued from dire circumstances (*Cinderella*), and (4) miraculous events that help a hero or heroine end up with a happy life (*Cinderella*). These motifs are frequent in traditional literature, but less so in modern genres.

Archetypes relate to motifs but go beyond being a pattern. They are universally understood symbols, centuries old. Archetypes trigger unconscious and conscious feelings and beliefs through images, situations, events, plot patterns, characters, and themes. Understood the world over, archetypes occur in myths, folktales, religious ritual, songs, dances, theater, and visual art forms. Common archetypes are (1) seasons (spring = rebirth and beginning, summer = celebration, autumn = tragedy, and winter = death and despair); (2) plot pattern of the hero on a quest (Odysseus) or hero rescues helpless maiden; (3) colors and shapes (circle = cycles, white = death or purity), (3) settings (forests = danger and the unknown, moving water = journey). Water is used to signal birth, baptism, and transformation. In *Tuck Everlasting* the archetypes of the forest, water, and seasons are all used as symbols, along with the archetype of the cycle of life pattern (see Carl Jung's work on the mandala) (Frye, 1957).

Symbols stand for or represent someone or something else. They are more recent and not as universally understood as archetypes. Companies use symbols as logos to trigger associations, for example, Wal-Mart's smiley face. In *Charlotte's Web*, the web is a symbol of the connectedness of things and how life and death are interwoven. Symbols are difficult to explain since they exist to fill in where words, alone and literally, are inadequate.

Allusions are indirect references to something well known or common knowledge; we allude to "building a house of straw" from *Three Little Pigs* to refer to foolish decisions.

Mood is a feeling created by many literary elements. Style contributes to mood when language signals the emotional state of the story (e.g., humorous or mysterious). Mood is related to the *tone,* which is the feeling infused by using style devices such as sounds of language and imagery.

Irony is deliberately saying the opposite of what is meant. It highlights the discrepancy between what is stated and what is known to be true. By juxtaposing opposite but balanced ideas, a story or poem can be made more interesting. For example, Wilbur says, "I'm less than two months old and I'm tired of living" (*Charlotte's Web*, p. 16).

Humor is the simultaneous juxtaposition of sense and nonsense to produce a surprising result. Events can be juxtaposed to create humor as when Jake and Alex talk about "woolly legs," "being fat," and being in Jake's coat, in Jukes's (1984) *Like Jake and Me*. Jake thinks they're talking about his wife, but Alex is talking about a spider. Homophones, homographs, and polysemous words (double meaning) can create puns, riddles, and witty remarks. Poetic language and surprising word use also create humor, like the goose's speech in *Charlotte's Web* ("poking-oking-oking") that makes humor through sound repetition, but make sense, too—if a goose *could* talk, it might sound just so.

Sound and musical features of style include the following:

- *Rhyme:* the repetition of phonograms (sound-spelling patterns that start with a vowel—ack, ick, eet); often at the ends of lines of poetry. (See rhyme patterns under genre of poetry.)
- *Rhythm:* a pattern of sounds. Includes beat and accent.
- *Repetition:* the repeated use of sounds, words, or patterns of words.
- *Alliteration:* the repetition of the same sound in a series (as in the phrase I just wrote) of words. It refers to beginning sounds.
- *Consonance:* the repetition of consonants any place in a series of words. For example, "slip slop slap" (p) or "little kitten knitting" (t).
- *Assonance:* the repetition of vowel sounds any place in a series of words. For example, note the vowel sounds in "soul" and "hole" in this quote from Sigmund Freud: "Concentrated is my soul in my molar hole when I have a toothache."
- *Onomatopoeia:* use of words that sound like their meanings, such as *whack* or *clap.*

Post It Page 3–3 summarizes the literary elements.

LITERARY ELEMENTS

◆ **Theme:** *the unifying truth or universal message in literature.*

Key question: What is the story or poem really about? (Go beyond a topic to a complete truth statement.)

Explicit themes: messages directly stated.

Implicit themes: indirectly stated truth statements.

◆ **Plot:** *the order of events in a story set in motion by a problem or conflict.*

Key question: What happened?

Four types of conflict: between (1) character and nature, (2) character and society, (3) character and another character, or (4) within a character.

Types of plot patterns: *Linear three part:* Introduction–Development–Conclusion (includes *climax* and *denouement*); *cumulative:* events build on one another; *episodic:* ministories tied together.

Techniques to vary plot patterns: *cliffhangers, flashbacks, foreshadowing.*

◆ **Character:** *person, animal, or object taking on a role.*

Key questions: Who is it about? Who wants something? Who has a problem? Who changes the most?

Ways characters revealed: (1) descriptions, (2) their actions, (3) their speech and thoughts, (4) what others think and say.

Types: protagonist/antagonist, round or flat/stock, dynamic or static, foil, stereotype.

◆ **Setting:** *the time and place.*

Key questions: When and where does the story take place?

Types of settings: scenery backdrop or integral.

Aspects of setting: place or location, time or time period, weather.

Primary world: real world.

Secondary world: a created world used in fantasy.

◆ **Point of View:** *the vantage point from which a story is written.*

Key question: Who is telling the story? How?

First person point of view: uses "I" to tell the story.

Omniscient or third person: all-knowing, using third person (he, she, it).

Limited omniscient: omniscient but only a few characters.

Objective: events reported with no interpretation.

◆ **Stylistic or poetic elements:** *creative use of words for artistic effect.*

Key question: How are words used in special ways?

Figurative language is the use of words to stand for other things: *imagery, personification, metaphors, connotation and denotation, motifs, archetypes, symbols,* and *allusions.*

Mood is the feeling created. Mood is related to the tone.

Irony is deliberately saying or doing the opposite of what is meant.

Humor is the simultaneous juxtaposition of sense and nonsense to produce a surprising result.

Sound and musical features of style include *rhyme, rhythm, repetition, alliteration, consonance, assonance,* and *onomatopoeia.*

Genre: A Category of Literature with Similar Traits

In human history, millions of pieces of art and music have been created—millions more stories and poems. To comprehend this vast creative storehouse, we need to separate it into piles, and that's what's been happening for centuries. Several ways to classify children's literature are by age of *intended audience* (baby books), *topic* (humor, travel), *problems* (disease, aging), and *length* (novella, short story). Each has a specific purpose useful in planning lessons and units. Source books, libraries, and bookstores organize by these groupings. Going further, however, we find divisions of a different sort. Poetry and prose represent distinct bodies of writing, with poetry being among the oldest valued writing and clearly a genre all its own with many divisions. Prose also covers a wide range of forms, subject matter, and style; it can be narrative or expository, fiction or nonfiction. Fiction can be subdivided into traditional literature, realistic fiction, fantastic fiction, historical and contemporary fiction. What is left is nonfiction, which includes informational books from alphabet books to biography. But literature is the creation of human beings who defy classification schemes. Many books fit into many groups and often in more than one genre; for example, picture books are published in every genre from fables to science fiction and are enjoyed by adults as well as children.

Because the goal of integrating literature is to give both meaning and information, as well as an enjoyable esthetic experience, knowledge of how literature works is crucial. In addition, teacher genre knowledge helps ensure that students receive breadth of exposure to books and is invaluable to children in understanding books and forms of writing, since the brain operates using categories. Genre are *literary categories*. Once students understand the characteristics of genre, they can enjoy greater comprehension and more freedom to write different genre. This is not to suggest that we subject children to lessons demanding formal, lifeless analysis of genre and elements. If taught effectively, literary knowledge helps us make richer interpretations by finding creative variations on writing patterns that have evolved over time. Once discovered, patterns become tools to adapt present genre and create new genre. Moreover, understanding how *particular* literary elements have significance within a genre helps classify literature and reveal the genre's composition. This knowledge (1) increases appreciation of literature, (2) establishes

generic expectations to aid comprehension by showing how a story is constructed and why characters act in predictable ways, and (3) helps writing by providing insight into how authors (and artists) use compositional elements to create books.

Each genre has evolved through the imaginative powers of storytellers and scribes and is further broken down into subgenres or more detailed classifications; for example, there are several different kinds of realistic fiction. There is a set of genre types in Post It Page 3–4. The discussion that follows includes examples of how literary elements are treated differently in each.

Poetry

Poetry *is a genre of literature with many forms and characteristics that include, but are not limited to, rhythm, rhyme, repetition, and meter.*

Every Friday is Poetree Day in Rebecca Hofmeister's fifth-grade class. Students write and find poetry, rehearse all week, and then perform it. They make it sing with their voices, and they dance their poems, too. Using performance techniques such as choral or antiphonal reading, character voices, and sound effects gives life to poetry. After each poem is shared, it is ceremoniously hung on a "poetree" made from a real tree branch set in plaster of Paris. After the weekly performance the class sings a song they wrote together:

> *Oh Poetree Oh Poetree*
> *How funny are your verses*
> *They make us laugh*
> *They make us grin*
> *They make us feel all good within*
> *Oh Poetree Oh Poetree*
> *Thank you for your verses.*

After a year-long poetry focus, Ms. Hofmeister's class is quick to talk about what they think makes poetry: (1) compact and emotional language, (2) rhythm and rhyme and other sound patterns created by alliteration

NINE GENRES AND EXAMPLE SUBGENRES

POST IT PAGE 3–4

Poetry	Couplet, limerick, concrete or shape, diamante, haiku, free verse
Traditional	Folktales, Mother Goose rhymes, proverbs and parables, fables, myths and legends, tall tales
Fantasy	Animal, toy and tiny-being tales, modern folk and fairy tales, science fiction, high fantasy, time fantasies, horror
Realistic fiction	Contemporary stories about sports, animals, survival, school, and family; also includes historical fiction, mystery; often occur in a series
Informational	Factual writing about art, music, dance, theater, ecology, psychology, sexuality, technology; also includes alphabet books, counting books, concept books, biography, and autobiography
Picture books	Combines art and text, but can be wordless stories (all art); available in all genre
Humor	Jokes, riddles, tongue twisters, spoonerisms, hink-pinks, Tom Swifties, palindromes, calindromes, echo bursts, chants
Predictable	Can be in any genre, but follow a highly repetitive pattern that makes them very appealing to young children
Multicultural	Can be any genre, but presently is dominated by folktales from diverse worldwide **and international** groups, with emphasis on Native Americans and those groups who have immigrated (by choice or force) in large numbers to the United States (Asians, Mexicans, Africans)

and repetition, and (3) metaphor and other figurative language. But these aspects of poetry were undoubtedly experienced by these fifth graders long before they were conscious of their impact. Through nursery rhymes, Dr. Seuss, and other forms of word play, infants and toddlers learn to enjoy language and hear poetic words that attract attention and give comfort. Poetry is a natural language of childhood that conveys the difficult concept that "to read well one must make music from print." Unfortunately, many children turn away from poetry. What happens to the joyous language play with rhyme, rhythm, and repetition of words and sounds of preschoolers? How can teachers involve children with poetry they do enjoy—usually poems that tell a story or use rhyme, rhythm, and humor—but also provide bridges from light verse to poetry that is more diverse? How can interest in reading and writing a range of poetry be broadened? These are important questions, and answers rest with teachers knowing the basics about this genre and knowing poets and poetry.

Poetry elements are used across genre and are included in the literary element of *style:* imagery, figurative language (personification, metaphors, connotation and denotation, motifs, archetypes, symbols, and allusions), mood and tone, irony, humor, sound, and musical features (rhyme, rhythm, repetition, alliteration, consonance, assonance, onomatopoeia). Then there are the many *structures* and forms that poets use to weave their word magic:

◆ *Verse* is a line of poetry or a stanza, particularly one with a refrain like the verse of a song. ("Verse" is also used to refer to poetry, in general, or light-hearted poetry as opposed to serious.)

◆ *Stanza* is a grouping of several lines together.

◆ *Meter* is related to repeated patterns of words, including the beat and accent.

◆ *Rhyme scheme* is a pattern of rhyming words in a line, stanza, or poem. Letters are used to code lines that rhyme. For example, *abab* is a four-line poem with lines 1 and 3 rhyming and lines 2 and 4 rhyming.

◆ *Blank verse* is unrhymed iambic pentameter (used a lot by Shakespeare). An iamb is the accent pattern "dah DAH," as in *"Do what?"* Iambic pentameter is five iambs, as in *"I like to eat my peas without a fork."*

◆ *Free verse* is free of the usual or formal traditional meter or stanza patterns.

◆ *Lyrical poetry* is flowing, descriptive, and personal, follows no form or pattern, and can be set to music—hence the word *lyric* in both music and poetry.

◆ *Narrative poetry* tells a story. It usually has no refrain. *Hiawatha* is an example.

◆ *Ballads* are narrative poems with short stanzas, with or without music.

◆ *Sonnets* are 14 lines long, often in iambic pentameter, and often with the rhyme scheme *abab cdcd efef gg.*

The different forms of poetry have recurring patterns that can serve as scaffolds as children experiment with recording ideas, feelings, and images. Post It

Page 3–5 summarizes some of the variety of poem patterns children can find and use for writing. By using creative problem-solving strategies such as data gathering and brainstorming, ideas can be generated *before* writing, and children can experiment with the feelings and images that words create. Poems can then be written as a whole class, in small groups, or individually. Students do need help learning what they can write poems *about* and the many *ways* in which poetry is written. Without guidance, student interest generally declines as they advance in school (Kutiper, 1985). Without exposure to many types of poems, children, and adults, think poetry must rhyme and be cute. We can broaden the poetry experience for children by sharing the breadth of poetry available so that they come to understand that poetry is about things a poet knows and feels strongly about and is made in many forms, which may or may not include rhyme.

Finding Good Poetry.   With the barrage of books published each year, it can be hard to know where to

---

Poem Patterns

POST IT PAGE 3–5

Strategies: Orally share poetry *before* showing it. Ask students to examine poems for discoveries. Brainstorm about personal and important ideas, images, and feelings in poems. Writing poetry: use varying repetition in lines and words. Use poetic elements such as alliteration, rhyme, onomatopoeia, imagery, and metaphor. See the special poetry section at the end of Chapter 4.

◆ **Repeated lines:** Write as many lines as desired using these frames.

I wish . . . *I wish the sky would stay red all day. I wish I could touch a cloud.*

Color poems: Yellow is . . . Red is . . . (see O'Neill's Hailstones and Halibut Bones, *1989, as an example).*

Is . . . *Thunder is . . . Happiness is . . .*

I used to (think or feel), but now I (think or feel) *I used to think poetry had to rhyme, but now I think I can just write my feelings and have a good time.*

Five senses: *Sounds like . . . Looks like . . . Tastes like . . . , etc.*

If I were . . . *If I were a light bulb/I would glow hot and bright / So people could read in bed*

◆ **Five-line poem:** Each line has a focus: (1) a thing, (2) a person, (3) special place, (4) a feeling, (5) a sound.

◆ **Riddle poems:** Give three clue lines, with the first most general and the third most specific.

Easy to carry. Full of words inside. Rhymes with cook. ____ ____ ____ ____

◆ **Lie poems:** Each line is something not true (do collaboratively).

◆ **Preposition poem:** *Within the drawer / In a desk / Inside the metal tray / Like a row of teeth* (staples in a stapler).

◆ **Concrete or shape:** Words of a poem are placed on the page to look like the poem's topic (e.g., a swing, tree, ocean, a kiss shape for a love poem).

◆ **Couplet:** Two lines that end in rhyming words. *What if trees / Had knobby knees?*

◆ **Triplet:** Three lines that rhyme.

◆ **Quartet:** Four lines with a variety of rhyme patterns: *aabb, abab, abcb, abca.*

◆ **Clerihew or bio poem:** Quartet about a person: *Pat Benne/Did marry Kenny/But they are poor/And want money more.*

◆ **Limerick:** Humorous five-lined rhymed verse with an *aabba* pattern. The rhythm pattern is important:

> *There once was a cat on a porch*
> *He sat in the sun 'til he scorched*
> *His paws and backside*
> *Were both nearly fried*
> *So his friends starting calling him "Torch."*

◆ ***Syllable and word count poems***

Haiku: Japanese lyric verse consisting of 3 unrhymed lines. The subject is nature and there are 17 syllables in the entire poem distributed by line as 5–7–5.

Tanka: Five lines with these syllables per line: 5–7–5–7–7.

Cinquain: Five-line poem that does not rhyme. Number of words per line: 2–4–6–8–2 (subject, adjectives, action, feeling or observation, adjective/synonym).

Diamante: Seven-line poem, shaped like a diamond. Pattern for each line: 1 noun, 2 adjectives, 3 ing words, 4 word phrases or 4 nouns, 3 ing words, 2 adjectives, 1 antonym. Note: The poem topic can be reversed in the middle to relate to the antonym. For example,

> *Halloween*
> *Spooky   Fun*
> *Running   Screaming   Eating*
> *Costumes   Candy   Bunny   Baskets*
> *Hunting   Coloring   Singing*
> *Happy   Pastel*
> *Easter*

◆ **Found poems:** Random phrases are cut from magazines, newspapers, or greeting cards. Phrases are arranged until any form of poem is created (need not rhyme).

◆ **Other pattern possibilities:** Tongue-twisters, jump-rope rhymes, and advertising jingles.

---

find poetry for a particular unit or a child's interests. Places to start are (1) lists of children's favorite poems and poets, (2) collections of particular poets and anthologies that contain the works of many poets, and (3) poetry awards. Kutiper and Wilson (1993) examined school library circulation records and found the humorous contemporary poetry of Shel Silverstein and Jack Prelutsky dominating children's choices in recent years. Children's poets that teachers should know include David McCord, Aileen Fisher, Myra C. Livingston, Eve Merriam, Lilian Moore, Arnold Adoff, Valerie Worth, John Ciardi, Eleanor Farjeon, Ann Hoberman, Langston Hughes, Edward Lear, Vachel Lindsay, Ogden Nash, Karla Kuskin, Irene

Rutherford McLeod, Laura E. Richards, Judith Viorst, Paul Janeczko, and Jane Yolan (Fisher & Natarella, 1979; Kutiper & Wilson, 1993). Post It Page 3–6 lists a *sampling of poets and poetry.* The following poems are common favorites:

Eleanor Farjeon's "Cat"

Ogden Nash's "Adventures of Isabel"

John Ciardi's "Mummy Slept Late and Daddy Fixed Breakfast" and "Why Nobody Pets the Lion at the Zoo"

Ann Hoberman's "A Bookworm of Curious Breed"

POST IT PAGE 3–6

Post It

POETS AND POETRY: A SAMPLING

Collections of Single Poets

Adoff, A. (1979). *Eats.* Lothrop, Lee & Shepard.

Carlson, L. (ed.) (1994). *Cool salsa: Bilingual poems on growing up Latino in the United States.* Holt.

Chertle, A. (1994). *How now, brown cow?* Browndeer.

Fleischman, P. (1988). *Joyful noise: Poems for two voices.* Harper & Row.

Florian, D. (1994). *Beast feast.* Harcourt Brace Jovanovich.

Greenfield, E. (1988). *Under the Sunday tree.* Harper & Row.

Grimes, N. (1994). *Meet Denitra Brown.* Lothrop.

Hughes, L. (1994). *Sweet and sour animal book.* Oxford University Press.

Koontz, D. (2001). *The paper doorway: Funny verse and nothing worse.* HarperCollins.

Livingston, M. C. (1986). *Earth songs.* Holiday House (see also *Sea songs* and *Space songs*).

Lobel, A. (1983). *The book of piggericks.* Harper & Row (limericks).

Moss, Jeff. (1989). *The butterfly jar.* Bantam.

Pomerantz, C. (1982). *If I had a paka: Poems in 11 languages.* Greenwillow.

Prelutsky, J. (1976). *Nightmares: Poems to trouble your sleep.* Greenwillow.

Prelutsky, J. (1984). *The new kid on the block.* Greenwillow.

Silverstein, S. (1974). *Where the sidewalk ends.* Harper & Row (also *A light in the attic* and *Falling up*).

Stepanek, M. (2001). *Heartsongs.* Vacation Spot Press.

Stepanek, M. (2001). *Journey through heartsongs.* Vacation Spot Press.

Yolen, J. (1990). *Bird watch: A book of poetry.* Philomel.

Whitehead, J. (2001). *Lunch box mail and other poems.* Henry Holt.

Anthologies (many poets under one cover)

A jar of tiny stars: Poems by NCTE award-winning poets (1995). Boyds Mills Press.

Bryan, A. (1997). *Ashley Bryan's ABC of African American poetry: A Jean Karl book.* Atheneum.

de Paola, T. (1988). *Tomie de Paola's book of poems.* Putnam.

de Regniers, B. S., Moore, E., White, M. M., & Carr, J. (1988). *Sing a song of popcorn: Every child's book of poems.* Scholastic.

Dunning, S., Leuders, E., & Smith, H. (1967). *Reflections on a gift of watermelon pickle, and other modern verse.* Lothrop, Lee & Shepard.

Kennedy, X. J., & Kennedy, D. M. (1982). *Knock at a star: A child's introduction to poetry.* Little, Brown.

Nye, N. (1992). *This same sky: A collection of poems from around the world.* Four Winds.

Prelutsky, J. (1999*) The 20th century children's poetry treasury,* Alfred A. Knopf.

Prelutsky, J. (1983). *The Random House book of poetry for children.* Random House.

Worth, V. (1994). *All the small poems and fourteen more.* Farrar, Straus & Giroux.

In Picture Book Form

Adoff, A. (1973). *Black is brown is tan.* Harper & Row.

Atwood, A. (1977). *Haiku vision.* New York: Scribner's.

Baylor, B. (1977). *Guess who my favorite person is.* New York: Scribner's.

Blake, W. (1993). *The tiger.* Harcourt Brace Jovanovich.

Frost, R. (1988) (Ill. by E. Young). *Birches.* Henry Holt.

Hopkins, L. (1993). *Poems of Halloween night: Ragged shadows.* Little, Brown.

Johnson, J. (1993). *Lift every voice and sing.* Walker.

Lobel, A. (1984). *A Rose in my garden.* Greenwillow.

Longfellow, H. W. (1990) (Ill. by T. Rand). *Paul Revere's ride.* Dutton.

Noyes, A. (1981) (Ill. by C. Keeping). *The highwayman.* Oxford University Press.

Pomerantz, C. (1974). *Piggy in the puddle.* New York: Aladdin.

Thayer, E. L. (1988) (Ill. by P. Polacco). *Casey at the bat: A ballad of the Republic, sung in the year 1888.* Putnam.

Westcott, N. B. (1988). *The lady with the alligator purse.* Little, Brown.

Award-winning Poets

Excellence in Poetry for Children Award (given by the National Council of Teachers of English) since 1977 for a body work). ***Recipients:*** David McCord, Aileen Fisher, Karla Kuskin, Myra Cohn Livingston, Eve Merriam, John Ciardi, Lilian Moore, Arnold Adoff, Valerie Worth, Barbara Juster Esbensen.

The Newbery Medal has gone to two poetry books: *A Visit to William Blake's Inn* (Willard, 1981) and *Joyful noise: Poems for two voices* (Fleischman, 1988).

Horn Book Magazine and the *Bulletin of the Center for Children's Books* regularly review poetry.

Karla Kuskin's "Hughbert and the Glue"

Irene McLeod's "Lone Dog"

Laura E. Richards's "Eletelephony"

Judith Viorst's "Mother Doesn't Want a Dog"

Shel Silverstein's "The Unicorn" and "Sick"

Jane Yolen's "Homework"

Langston Hughes's "Dreams"

Jack Prelutsky's "Willie Ate a Worm Today," "Oh, Teddy Bear," and "The Lurpp Is on the Loose"

Traditional Literature

Folktales . . . resonate with the truths of life across cultures and times.

The names of the creators of most traditional literature have been lost in time, since these anonymous rhymes, folktales and fairy stories, myths, legends, and tall tales mostly predate the printing press. But this "old stuff" has remained popular, along with modern versions with new twists, such as *The True Story of the 3 Little Pigs by A. Wolf* (Scieszka, 1991), "feminist" folktales such as Jane Yolen's *Sleeping Ugly,* and Munsch's *The Paper Bag Princess.*

Folktales *are stories passed down through the oral tradition.* (*Note:* Folk*lore* is the beliefs and customs of a society.) This subgenre includes fairy tales, cumulative stories, talking beasts, and noodlehead and fool stories. Point of view is omniscient and characterization is narrow and static and often includes archetypes: a wicked stepmother, a cunning animal, or trickster (Frye, 1957). Settings are vague, with time and place referred to as "long ago in a faraway land" or "in a land before time."

Fairy tales include magical objects, spells, wishes, and magical transformations as key plot events. Characters are either ordinary humans or humanlike animals transformed because of an extraordinary kindness or sacrifice. These are also tales of unfortunate heroines rescued by true love. The characters are often flat and static, and stories contain many stock characters such as witches, giants, and fairy godmothers. The themes relate to good overcoming evil or the importance of perseverance and hard work. The style of fairy tales includes the use of conventional openings and closings, repetition, and archetypes: the colors red, black; dark forests; types of water.

Cumulative tales have a unique plot structure because characters or objects are added in a chain of events. Animals occur often and sometimes rescue human friends. These tales frequently include food, such as large vegetables or fruit, as in *The Enormous Turnip* (2001).

Talking beast stories have characters who are anthropomorphized animals. There is usually a lesson at the end, much like a fable. The plot conflict involves a confrontation between two characters who are flat—portrayed as good or bad, stupid or clever.

Trickster tales have a character who outsmarts other characters. The trickster often takes animal form, such as B'rer Rabbit in the Uncle Remus stories or Anansi the Spider in African tales.

Noodlehead or *fool tales* involve characters that are stupid or clever, good or bad. Foolish decisions result in silly consequences, so these tales are full of absurdity that delight and surprise. When characters confront the problem, the story can be like a roller-coaster ride, but by the end everyone is happy.

Examples of folk and fairy tales are:

Aardema, V. (1975). *Why mosquitoes buzz in people's ears.* Dial.

Climo, S. (1989). *The Egyptian Cinderella.* Crowell.

Huck, C. (1989). *Princess Furball.* Greenwillow.

Louie, A. (1982). *Yeh-Shen: A Cinderella story from China.* Philomel.

Trivizas, E. (1993). *The three little wolves and the big bad pig.* Macmillan.

Wegman, W. (1993). *Little Red Riding Hood.* Hyperion.

Yolen, J. (1986). *The sleeping beauty.* Knopf.

Fables *are brief narratives with explicitly stated morals about behavior.* Main characters are one-dimensional personified animals that are strong or weak, wise or foolish. The plot centers on one event and the setting is a barely sketched backdrop. Conflict is between characters. Theme is stated as a moral at the end. Example collections are:

Lionni, L. (1985). *Frederick's fables.* Pantheon.

Lobel, A. (1980). *Fables.* Harper & Row.

Paxton, T. (1988). *Aesop's fables.* Morrow.

Nursery rhymes *include Mother Goose rhymes and other poetry, light verse, chants, laments, and songs.* They are usually short and full of action and memorable characters—Old King Cole, the crooked man, and pencil-thin Jack Sprat. Some are life stories in a few lines such as "Solomon Grundy." Themes have to do with concerns, happenings, and struggles of everyday people, who may be single parents with children to feed or worried about someone not getting home on time. Beautiful lines are contained in the treasure house of Mother Goose such as "Over the hills and far away" and "One misty moisty morning when cloudy was the weather." Like much original traditional literature, they are full of violence and death, from drowning to decapitation. Example collections of nursery rhymes are:

Ahlberg, J., and Ahlberg, A. (1978). *Each peach pear plum: An I spy story.* Viking.

De Angeli, M. (1954). *Margaret De Angeli's book of Mother Goose and nursery rhymes.* Doubleday.

de Paola, Tomie (1985). *Tomie de Paola's Mother Goose.* Putnam.

Opie, I., and Opie, P. (1992). *I saw Esau: A schoolchild's pocketbook.* Candlewick.

Myths *are stories in which gods and heroes have supernatural and magical powers.* Myths explain natural phenomena, such as the origin of the world, human beings, the seasons, and animal features, for example, *pourquoi* (French for *why*) tales about how the tiger got its tail or the elephant its trunk. Minimal information is given about the setting.

Legends *are tales usually based in historical fact and originating with a person who did something courageous or made an important contribution to society.* Over time the character becomes regarded as a hero or heroine, and the events related to the deed often become embellished and romanticized. *Epics* are long narratives or poems about legendary figures. The *Iliad* and *The Odyssey* are Greek epics, and *Beowulf* is a Norse epic.

Tall tales *are based on actual people and some exaggeration of fact is the distinguishing feature.* Tall tales are relative newcomers to the traditional literature genre, with the most well known finding their source in North America. Paul Bunyan, Pecos Bill, Johnny Appleseed, and John Henry are famous characters from this subgenre.

Examples of myths, legends, and tall tales are:

D'Aulaire, I., & D'Aulaire, E. P. (1967). *D'Aulaires' Norse gods and giants.* Doubleday.

de Paola, T. (1988). *The legend of the Indian paintbrush*. Putnam.

Dixon, A. (1993). *How raven brought light to people*. Macmillan.

Goble, P. (1968). *Iktomi and the boulder*. Orchard Books.

Highwater, J. (1977). *Anpao: An American Indian odyssey*. Lippincott.

Hodges, M. (1984). *Saint George and the dragon*. Little, Brown.

Houston, J. (1973). *Kiviok's magic journey: An Eskimo legend*. Atheneum.

Issacs, A. (1994). *Swamp angel*. Dutton.

San Souci, R. (1993). *Cut from the same cloth: American women of myth, legend, and tall tale*. Philomel.

Steptoe, J. (1984). *The story of jumping mouse*. Mulberry Books.

Fantasy: A Modern Genre with Impossible Elements

When I examine myself and my method of thought, I come to the conclusion that the gift of fantasy has meant more to me than my talent for absorbing knowledge.

Albert Einstein

The timeless quality of fantasy has provided us with such diverse classics as *Alice in Wonderland* and *Charlotte's Web*. Perhaps the things most real in life can best be understood through the distant perspective that fantasy offers. How does the creator of fantasy make it so believable? The overlap between traditional literature and fantasy may hold some clues.

In fantasy, reality is abstracted to make special imaginary worlds come to life. The reality-based world helps readers to believe that such worlds exist. For this reason, the setting is integral; time and place significantly affect plot action. For example, in the subgenre of science fiction, a spaceship may house an entire community as in *Star Trek*, where all character actions and thoughts are tied into the *Enterprise*. Themes in fantasy are lofty and have to do with an idealized world of truth and goodness and may evoke strong emotion. Good destroys evil in spite of great odds, but usually with struggle and suspense. Sometimes characters possess supernatural traits, and there are both good and bad characters; a few are round and dynamic, but most are flat and static, firmly on one side or the other of the "dark." Point of view is often omniscient to give readers the necessary background. All this is especially true of *high fantasy* and *science fiction*. The plot is often straightforward, or linear, with few digressions, but with impossible events and magical objects. Often the hero is forced to go on a quest and is pulled into another world that is threatening. There are usually trials to be endured to forge the hero's character, but often there is a protector to help out. When the spirit of the hero is finally honed, he is able to go home. (See Joseph Campbell, 1996, *Hero with a Thousand Faces*.)

Key differences in fantasy and realistic fiction are most obvious with characterization, which is more narrow and static in fantasy (and traditional literature). With the exception of a dynamic hero and a small number of round characters, high fantasy is full of flat characters, either good or evil. An idealized "other world," based on what we know to be true, reveals truths through a different dimension. Flat characters allow this abstraction to occur more easily.

The subgenres of fantasy often overlap and include the following:

Animal fantasy has the distinguishing feature of personified animals (e.g., *Charlotte's Web*, in which the magic object is a web and a spider is the protector of the hero pig). Other examples are:

Grahame, K. (1961). *The wind in the willows*. Scribner's.

Howe, D., & Howe, J. (1979). *Bunnicula: A rabbit-tale of mystery*. Atheneum.

Selden, G. (1960). *The cricket in Times Square*. Farrar, Strauss & Giroux.

Toy or tiny beings are the peculiarity of one subgenre: *Pinocchio* comes to life to grow a long nose, and inch-high borrowers live under the floor and snatch things in Norton's *The Borrowers*. Other examples are:

Banks, L. R. (1980). *The Indian in the cupboard*. Doubleday.

Lewis, N. (1992) *The steadfast tin soldier*. Gulliver.

Lionni, L. (1969). *Alexander and the wind-up mouse*. Knopf.

Van Allsburg, C. (1981). *Jumanji*. Houghton Mifflin.

Modern folk and fairy tales take up the tradition of oral tales in their elements, but are *written* works with identifiable authors. Examples are:

Calmenson, S. (1989). *The principal's new clothes*. Scholastic.

Ehrlich, A. (1982). *The snow queen*. Dial.

Thurber, J. (1943). *Many moons*. Harcourt Brace Jovanovich.

Yolen, J. (1972). *The girl who cried flowers*. Crowell.

Fantastic events, situations, or imaginary worlds use exaggeration, the ridiculous, and imagined settings. In Dahl's *James and the Giant Peach,* an unhappy child can travel inside a huge peach, and in Barrie's *Peter Pan,* Never Land is where one never grows up. Example books are:

Barrett, J. (1978). *Cloudy with a chance of meatballs*. Macmillan.

Brittain, B. (1983). *The wish giver*. Harper & Row.

Carroll, L. (1985). *Alice's adventures in Wonderland*. Holt.

Juster, N. (1961). *The phantom toll booth*. Random House.

Sendak, M. (1983). *Where the wild things are*. Harper & Row.

Van Allsburg, C. (1985). *The polar express*. Houghton Mifflin.

Time warp fantasy distorts time as we know it, so Tom can enter a special garden that existed in the past in Pearce's *Tom's Midnight Garden*. Other examples are:

Babbitt, N. (1975). *Tuck everlasting*. Farrar, Straus & Giroux.

Banks, L. (1981). *The Indian in the cupboard*. Doubleday.

Rohmann, E. (1994). *Times flies*. Crown.

Scieszka, J. (1994). *Your mother was a Neanderthal*. Viking.

Science-fiction fantasy is set in a future time and relies on fictional inventions, often extensions of modern technology and scientific fact, for example, L'Engle's *A Wrinkle in Time* and John Christopher's *The White Mountains*. Other examples are:

Norton, A. (1966). *Moon of three rings*. Viking.

O'Brien, R. C. (1971). *Mrs. Frisby and the rats of NIMH*. Atheneum.

Sleator, W. (1984). *Interstellar pig*. Dutton.

Yolen, J. (1990). *The devil's arithmetic*. Viking.

High fantasy is a subgenre that has the characteristics of a romance. The forces of good and evil collide in ultimate confrontations. Examples are:

Alexander, L. (1968). *The high king*. Henry Holt.

Cooper, S. (1973). *The dark is rising*. Atheneum.

L'Engle, M. (1962). *A wrinkle in time*. Farrar, Straus & Giroux.

Lewis, C. S. (1950). *The lion, the witch, and the wardrobe*. Macmillan (Narnia series).

McKinley, R. (1989). *The hero and the crown*. Ace Books.

Rowling, J.K. (1998). *Harry Potter* (series). Scholastic.

Horror stories speak to the human urge to be a little afraid—under safe circumstances. Wright's *The Ghost Comes Calling* is an example, as is the *Goosebumps* series. Other examples are:

Hahn, A. (1994). *Time for Andrew. A ghost story*. Clarion.

Mahy, M. (1982). *The haunting*. Atheneum.

McBratney, S. (1989). *The ghosts of Hungryhouse Lane*. Holt.

Westall, R. (1989). *Ghost abbey*. Scholastic.

Realistic Fiction: A Modern Genre in Which Stories Mirror Reality

Realistic fiction has had great success among modern children, perhaps because it is closer to life as they know it, a reason that gives pause in light of horrific fantasy being hard on the heels of realism in popularity. Recently, the content has included a range of alternative life-styles and views of society and has addressed sensitive issues such as homosexuality, AIDS, and gangs. Series books like Nancy Drew, the Hardy Boys, and newer series, such as the Babysitter's Club, still enjoy phenomenal appeal.

In terms of literary elements, realistic plots are structured using many patterns, but are more given to include flashbacks or other events that stretch out problem resolution. First-person child-narrator point of view is common in young adult realistic novels, which gives immediacy and facilitates reader identification, but a variety of points of view may be found. Themes are usually related to modern life, and the setting is generalized from reality. Characterization is realistic and fully developed, like ourselves and our friends, showing conflicting emotions and motives. This multidimensionality gives realistic fiction its power to cause reader identification with characters.

Contemporary realism is set in current times and places much like the settings of actual children's lives. Konigsburg's *View from Saturday* (1997 Newbery) is an example, as are:

Bauer, M. D. (1986). *On my honor.* Houghton Mifflin.

Bunting, E. (1991). *Fly away home.* Clarion.

Bunting, E. (1994). *Smoky nights.* Harcourt Brace Jovanovich.

Byars, B. (1977). *The pinballs.* Harper & Row.

Cleary, B. (1981). *Ramona Quimby, age 8.* Morrow.

Fox, M. (1988). *Wilfrid Gordon McDonald Partridge.* Kane Miller.

Gilson, J. (1981). *Do bananas chew gum?* Archway.

Jukes, M. (1984). *Like Jake and me.* Knopf.

Paterson, K. (1977). *Bridge to Terabithia.* Crowell.

Spinelli, J. (1990). *Maniac Magee.* Little, Brown.

Steptoe, J. (1980). *Daddy is a monster . . . sometimes.* Harper & Row.

Viorst, J. (1972). *Alexander and the terrible, horrible, no good, very bad day.* Atheneum.

Historical fiction is a subgenre of realistic fiction in which the setting is integral and in the past. Often set in specific regions of a country (the West, the South, Appalachia), these stories provide opportunities to live history. Well-crafted stories encourage attitudes about caring for and appreciation of others not like the reader and provide rich opportunity to make history memorable. For example, Polacco's *Pink and Say,* set in the Civil War, gives both information and emotional connection to real characters and events, but with fictional dialog. This is the line that separates informational books from realistic ones. The use of historical fiction to teach history should be contingent on (1) the book having an authentic setting and accurate historical details and (2) making clear to students that the book is *fiction,*

meaning that aspects of the plot, setting, and characters are invented. Historical fiction often reveals as much of the time in which it was written as of the time written about, so it provides this additional angle on life-styles, values, and perspectives on events. The 1998 Newbery, *Out of the Dust,* is a fine piece of historical fiction as are these:

Avi. (1990). *The true confessions of Charlotte Doyle.* Orchard Books.

Cohen, B. (1983). *Molly's pilgrim.* Lothrop.

Fleischman, S. (1986). *The whipping boy.* Greenwillow.

Forbes, E. (1970). *Johny Tremain.* Houghton Mifflin.

Fox, P. (1973). *The slave dancer.* Bradbury.

Greene, B. (1973). *Summer of my German soldier.* Dutton.

Hunt, I. (1966). *Across five Aprils.* Follett.

Lowry, L. (1989). *Number the stars.* Houghton Mifflin.

O'Dell, S. (1970). *Sing down the moon.* Houghton Mifflin.

Speare, E. G. (1958). *The witch of Blackbird Pond.* Houghton Mifflin.

Speare, E. G. (1983). *The sign of the beaver.* Houghton Mifflin.

Uchida, Y. (1971). *Journey to Topaz.* Creative Arts.

Informational Books

These books are fact-based writing about people and natural phenomena and include biography and autobiography. Informational stories are grounded in facts about people and the world, allowing children to learn about life literally and esthetically. An immense array of topics exists, from cookbooks to alphabet books. Since literature is for enjoyment *and* information, the narrative is important, as is the accuracy of the information and the clarity and accuracy of illustration. This genre can trigger a research focus for a child and is the place to look for resources on authors, artists, musicians, dancers, and actors as the arts are integrated. It will be interesting to see how informational books compete with CD-ROMs as information sources in the future.

General informational books are how-to and "all about it" stories that give an understanding of a process or topic in biology and physical sciences, social studies, the arts, crafts, cooking, experiments, and so forth. Examples are included in Chapter 4 with strategy seeds for curricular areas.

Concept books *are informational books in simple form.* They offer alphabet and number knowledge by showing relationships between objects and actions. Basic facts about colors, shapes, and sounds are presented in concept books, often with striking art and humor.

Biography *is a factual account of someone's life written by another person.* *Autobiography* *results when someone writes about his own life.* Modern media bring real-life characters into our homes and our lives, but these close-ups are by necessity fragmented (the exception being PBS ventures such as Ken Burns's series on Lewis and Clark). Literary biographies may also present only a slice of a person's life but can give more of a sense of wholeness or continuity within a particular time and place. Famous media stars, authors, inventors, artists, composers, dancers, and sports figures are the focus of this subgenre, usually with the plot centering on a person overcoming great odds to succeed. The best of the genre brings the person to life through stylistic devices and presents a balanced picture, rather than creating an unrealistic one-dimensional character. Text may be extended through illustrations and photos, for example, Freedman's (1987) *Lincoln, a Photobiography.* The book may be a part of a person's life or attempt a complete recounting. These real-life characters can be potent role models and give opportunities to "try on" various occupations or life-styles, but children do need honest representations of the faces of society in terms of race, gender, class, ethnicity, and religion. Current societal concerns influence the subjects of children's biographies; there are now more books about females and minorities. The potential for solid information giving makes biography an important way to introduce youth to people unlike themselves, and many videos and audiotapes of authors and artists are available with biographical works.

Biographical fiction *is both a realistic and fanciful story that includes some factual material.* Based on fact, it includes invented dialog or events. For a biography to be *authentic,* facts need to be documented and no characters, dialog, or scenes invented. Some degree of fictionalization occurs in most children's biography, so we must point out this aspect of the genre.

Picture Books

These books use art as well as text to convey meaning, with each playing an important role in telling the story. In some cases, the artwork may tell the whole story (wordless picture books).

In contrast to other genre, this one depends on *appearance,* not the content of the work. Picture books are available in every genre from poetry to information. For today's children, bombarded with myriad visual images, picture books can be an important introduction to *fine* art; we learn visual preferences based on what is seen, so if we expose children to diverse styles, media, and representations of people, children may form more generous and inclusive viewpoints.

Picture books are good tools to teach "book parts": *title and half title pages, borders* that may be used to even tell a side story, *gutters* that connect two pages and become important in *double-page spreads* of art over two pages. *Endpapers* are the sheets immediately inside the front and back covers of a book that can be used to set mood with art. Of course, the art styles and media used by the artist are crucial concepts. See the section in Chapter 5 for a discussion and Post It Pages 5–4, 5–5, 5–6 and 5–7 on the visual aspect of picture books. When selecting picture books, it is important to examine the art to see if it dates otherwise timely content and to determine how the media and techniques interface with the mood and tone of a literary work. Ask *to what degree does the art:*

1. *Extend or elaborate* on the setting, plot, characterization, and theme? How do the *art elements* of color, line, shape, texture, use of space, and perspective do so?

2. *Foreshadow* events *and* show *action?*

3. Show *detail?* Are the details *accurate* (historically, culturally, geographically) and nonstereotypical?

4. *Media* (collage, photography, paint, etc.) contribute to the development of setting, plot, characterization, and theme? How does the media do so?

5. *Style* affect the book? Is the mood created by the art style appropriate to the story?

6. *Interact* with the actual print on the page?

7. Play an *integral* role in the book? Does the art *conflict* in any way? (Adapted from Norton, 1995)

In the past, picture books have been regarded as the province of the young, but today picture books are available for all ages to enjoy. Even *wordless* picture books exist for all levels; for example, *The Silver Pony* is a wordless book. Here are other examples of popular wordless books:

Alexander, M. (1970). *Bobo's dream*. Dial.

Anno, M. (1983). *Anno's USA*. Philomel.

Briggs, R. (1980). *The snowman*. Random House.

Day, A. (1985). *Good dog, Carl*. Green Tiger.

de Paola, T. (1979). *Flicks*. Harcourt Brace Jovanovich.

de Paola, T. (1983). *Sing, Pierrot, sing*. Harcourt Brace Jovanovich.

Mayer, M. (1967). *A boy, a dog, and a frog*. Dial.

Monro, R. (1987). *The inside–outside book of Washington, D.C.* Dutton.

Turkle, B. (1976). *Deep in the forest*. Dutton (a Goldilocks variation).

Vast changes have occurred in the 20th century in using illustrations as a means of portraying positive multicultural images of childhood and in making art integral to the story, rather than a decoration. Baby board books, pop up, and other toy books continue to be popular. The Caldecott Award was created in 1936 to recognize this genre, and a bibliography is given in the appendix.

Humorous Literature

Since humorous books and poems top lists of children's favorite reads, this category cannot be ignored. When we give children opportunities to laugh at language and life, we give them an important coping device. The source of most humor is problems. When used appropriately, to uplift and elevate, not denigrate nor devastate, humor can enrich and energize (Cornett, 2001). Special bibliographies of humorous books and poems can be located by using the *Source Books* in Post It Page 3–8. Examples of special books of pure humor, such as word play, jokes, riddles, and tongue twisters, are *Too Hot to Hoot* (palindromes) (Terban, 1985); *A Twister of Twists, a Tangler of Tongues* (Schwartz, 1974); *Puniddles* (McMillan, 1982); and *Swine Lake: Music and Dance Riddles* (Keller, 1985).

Predictable Books

When research showed that children learn to read more easily with stories and poems with a repetitive structure, parents and teachers clamored for bibliographies of such literature. In addition, these books provide patterns usable as frames or scaffolds to help children write their own books (i.e., make a copycat book). Here are examples classified by unique features:

- ◆ **Repeated phrase, sentence, or refrain.** These stories often have a musical or poetic quality. In Martin's *Brown Bear, Brown Bear,* a rhythmic question is repeated, "Brown Bear Brown Bear, What do you see?" In Barrett's *Animals Should Definitely Not Wear Clothing,* the title repeats.

- ◆ **Word play and rhyme books** have predictable word patterns or poetry elements (e.g., couplets or internal rhymes) as in Cameron's *I Can't Said the Ant* and Gwynne's *The King Who Rained* (idiomatic and homophonic expressions with literal art from a child's point of view).

- ◆ **Predictable plots.** In Charlip's *Fortunately,* a boy has both fortunate and unfortunate events in his life in an alternating pattern.

- ◆ **Cumulative books** have a series of words and events that repeat and build on one another until a climax is reached. The process is then usually reversed, as in Wood's *The Napping House.*

- ◆ **Concept books** (alphabet, number, color, shape, days of the week) are informational books that often use a predictable structure (e.g., *Anno's Counting Book* and Elting's *Q is for Duck*).

Multicultural and International Literature

I recently saw a picture of a fourth-grade class in Los Angeles. The names and smiling faces reinforced the image of the United States as a nation of diverse cultures. When the term *multicultural* is used in the United States, it often refers to minorities outside the sociopolitical mainstream, usually people "of color"— African Americans, Asian Americans, Native Americans, and Hispanics (Bishop, 1992). But multicultural literature and art include works from all distinct cultural, regional, and religious groups (Jewish, Amish, Moslem, Appalachian) and all literary genre. Multicultural and international books (ones first published in other countries) exist in every genre and are increasingly well represented by stunning picture books, such as the 1997 Caldecott winner *The Golem* (a Jewish folktale). As a symbol of our growing national respect for the diverse language, customs, religions, music, art, and history of minority groups, it is important to recognize this area as a separate category of literature (Faltis, Hudelson, & Hudelson, 1997).

By integrating multicultural and international literature, we can influence children's views of people's differences, as well as create an understanding of what we share. Art has the power to break down walls of hate. Literature is no exception, and its value in fostering cognitive and affective development is well documented (Hansen-Krening, 1992; Pate, 1988). Literature for children from minority groups should not be limited to stories about any one group, any more than we should deprive students in the mainstream of the literature of diverse cultures; but for children sensitive to their own cultural differences, multicultural literature offers validation; a dearth of literature about a child's own culture can negatively affect development and learning. In addition, Gee (1989) reported how African American children (especially girls) used different narrative structures compared to white, middle-class children when telling stories, which showed how stories influence thinking.

Multicultural literature should be a part of the literary heritage of all American children and is available, in varying quantities, about most centers of civilization (Africa, Asia, Australia, Europe, North and South America, and Oceania). Presently, there are concerns about stereotypical language and images, inappropriate retellings, and the small number of books published. However, the past decade has witnessed a surge of interest in publishing multicultural and international literature. Picture books are increasingly common, but collections of stories for older readers remain scarce. In selecting books it is important to examine how well characters, situations, and culture are portrayed and to consider accuracy, amount of detail, and whether language or text perpetuate stereotypes. The International Board on Books for Young People publishes a quarterly journal, *Bookbird: World of Children's Books,* to help teachers find appropriate literature.

African American.   African American traditional literature has its roots in many distinct countries and cultures, such as Swahili, Mali, Zulu, and Ashanti. Many were stories brought by slaves to America and retold, some mixed with Caribbean stories, thus creating new variations. These tales flourished and evolved; for example, Anansi, the trickster spider from the Ashanti, became "Aunt Nancy" in some tellings. Brer Rabbit stories, collected by Joel Chandler Harris in the nineteenth century, were traced to the African tradition of cunning animal characters. African American literature is rich in themes about perseverance, beauty, and generosity and has engaging language; for example, Ashley Bryan uses chanted verse in his *Beat the Story Drum, Pum-Pum* (1980), a collection of pourquoi tales such as "How Animals Got Their Tails." Set in Zimbabwe, *Mufaro's Beautiful Daughters: An African Tale* (Steptoe, 1987) is a Cinderella tale of sibling rivalry. A Caldecott honor book, Steptoe's illustrations are a visual feast of the East African landscape. Other examples are:

Adoff, A. (1991). *In for winter, out for spring* (poetry). Harcourt Brace Jovanovich.

Greenfield, E. (1988). *Nathaniel talking* (poetry). Black Butterfly.

Hamilton, V. (1985). *The people could fly: American Black folktales* (folktales). Knopf.

Hoffman, M. (1991). *Amazing grace* (realistic fiction). Dial.

Hudson, W. (1993). *Pass it on: African-American poetry for children* (poetry). Scholastic.

McKissack, P. (1988). *Mirandy and Brother Wind* (fantasy). Knopf.

Native American.   Native American cultures are diverse (there are more than 300 tribes in North America), reflecting features of the plains, the eastern woodlands, and the southwestern deserts. Together with the Canadian Native American cultures, these groups have a vast store of art expressed in ritual and mythology. Despite distinct differences, common patterns occur: (1) *the creation myth* (how the world arose from chaos), as in Bruchac and London's 1992 *Thirteen Moons on a Turtle's Back,* (2) *family myths about kinship,* (3) *hero myths* (a young hero is a trickster until he gains virtue, usually through a quest), such as *Anpao: An American Indian Odyssey* (Highwater, 1977), a Newbery honor book, which is a collection of hero myths set in the Great Plains and Rocky Mountains, and (4) *rites of passage myths* (involve crossing a threshold in and out of a dream state of a parallel world) (Bierhorst, 1976). Other examples of Native American literature are:

Baylor, B. (1972). *When clay sings* (Southwest Indians). Macmillan.

Begay, S. (1992). *Ma'ii and Cousin Horned Toad: A traditional Navajo story.* Scholastic.

de Paola, T. (1988). *Legend of Indian paintbrush.* Putnam.

Esbensen, B. (1988). *The star maiden: An Ojibway tale*. Little, Brown.

Goble, P. (1990). *Iktomi and the ducks: A Plains Indian tale*. Orchard.

Hirshfelder, A., and Singer, B. *Rising voices: Writings of young Native Americans* (poetry). Scribner.

McDermott, G. (1993). *Raven: A trickster tale from the Pacific Northwest*. Harcourt Brace Jovanovich.

O'Dell, S. (1970). *Sing down the moon*. Houghton Mifflin.

Rafe, M. (1992). *Rough faced girl* (a Cinderella tale). Putnam.

Seattle, C. (1991). *Brother Eagle, Sister Sky: A message from Chief Seattle* (Suquamish). Dial.

Sneve, V. D. H. (1989). *Dancing teepees: Poems of American Indian youth*. Holiday House.

Hispanic American.   Faltis, Hudelson, and Hudelson (1997) reports that Spanish-speaking children are the largest and fastest-growing school group of second-language learners in the United States. Unfortunately, Hispanic literature is difficult to find. This stems from confusion over the many geographical and cultural settings to which the term *Hispanic* alludes: islands of Caribbean and Puerto Rico, South America, and Mexico. Hispanic is a nearly unmanageable term. Add to this the history of the ancient Mayan, Aztec, and Inca civilizations and the Roman Catholicism of the last five centuries, and it is clear that there is too much material from cultures much too diverse to continue to use one label. Some noteworthy books that *are* available are:

Aardema, V. (1979). *The riddle of the drum: A tale from Tizapan, Mexico* (impossible task). Four Winds Press.

Bryan, A. (1992). *Sing to the sun* (poetry). HarperCollins.

Carlson, L., & Ventura, C. (1990). *Where angels glide at dawn: New stories from Latin America*. Lippincott.

Clark, A. (1976). *Secret of the Andes* (Peruvian Indian). Puffin.

Colman, H. (1973). *The girl from Puerto Rico*. Morrow.

de Paola, T. (1980). *The Lady of Guadalupe* (Mexican Catholic faith story). Holiday House.

Dorros, A. (1991). *Abuela*. Dutton.

Joseph, L. (1992). *Coconut kind of day: Island poems*. Puffin.

Lessac, F. (comp.) (1992). *Caribbean carnival*. Tambourine.

O'Dell, S. (1979). *The captive* (Mayan Indian). Houghton Mifflin.

Soto, G. (1991). *A fire in my hands: A book of poems*. Scholastic.

Asian American.   This body of literature includes stories and poems from Japan, Vietnam, China, the Philippines, and other Pacific Rim countries. Examples are scarce and books may contain stereotypes showing characters without individual traits (e.g., *Five Chinese Brothers* 1989). Positive examples are *Yeh-Shen: A Cinderella Story from China* (Louie, 1982) and *The Rainbow People* (Yep, 1992), a collection of folk tales from Oakland, California's, Chinatown in the 1930s. *Many Lands, Many Stories: Asian Folktales for Children* (Conger, 1987) is a collection of folk tales. See also:

Demi, T.-S. H. (translator) (1994). *In the eyes of the cat: Japanese poetry for all seasons*. Holt.

Huffman, J. (translator) (1999). *The cat who lived a million lives*. University of Hawaii Press.

Mado, M. (1990). *The animals: Selected poems*. Margaret McElderry Books.

Say, A. (1993). *Grandfather's journey*. Houghton Mifflin.

Uchida, Y. (1981). *A jar of dreams*. Atheneum.

Yasima, T. (1955). *Crow boy*. Viking.

Yep, L. (1977). *Child of the owl*. Harper & Row.

Books Related to Other Areas of Diversity

Not to be ignored are the variety of **religious cultures** with which more and more children's books deal. Some examples are:

Ammon, R. (1989). *Growing up Amish*. Atheneum.

Cohen, B. (1983). *Molly's pilgrim*. Lothrop Lee & Shepard.

Cormier, R. (1990). *Other bells for us to ring* (Catholic). Delacorte.

Dickinson, P. (1979). *Tulku* (Buddhist). Dutton.

Highwater, J. (1994). *Rama: A legend* (Hindu). Holt.

Oppenheim, S. L. (1994). *Iblis: An Islamic tale.* Harcourt Brace Jovanovich.

Rylant, C. (1986). *A fine white dust* (Protestant). Bradbury.

International books are from or about other countries. Examples are:

Fox, M. (1987). *Possum magic* (Australia). Omnibus.

Lunn, J. (1987). *Shadow in Hawthorn Bay* (Canada). Scribner.

Morris, S. (1991). *One lonely Kakapo* (New Zealand).

Naidoo, B. (1990). *Chain of fire* (South Africa). Lippincott.

Newth, M. (1989). *The abduction* (Norway). Farrar, Straus & Giroux.

Rubinstein, G. (1990). *Beyond the labyrinth* (Australia). Orchard.

Sutcliff, R. (1990). *The shining company* (UK). Bodley Head.

And there is a growing group of fine books that have been **translated** from their original language. Several noteworthy ones are:

Bjork, C. (1987). *Linnea in Monet's garden* (Sweden). R & S.

Gallaz, C. (1985). *Rose Blanche* (France). Creative Education.

Maruki, T. (1982). *Hiroshima no Pika* (Japan). Lothrop, Lee and Shepard.

Orlev, U. (1995). *The man from the other side* (Israel). Puffin.

Richter, H. P. (1987). *Friedrich* (Germany). Puffin.

HOW CAN TEACHERS INTEGRATE LITERATURE THROUGHOUT THE CURRICULUM?

The study of children's literature is the study of childhood, of human aesthetic development, of human intellectual development, of social development. The purpose of children's literature and its study is to bring the advantages and the joys of reading to all children, for without reading the ideas of the

past would be lost forever, and we would be forced naked into the world. The more that we, as adults, know about children's literature, the better equipped will we be to help children discover these advantages and these joys.

David Russell, 1994, p. 16

Guidelines and Principles for Integrating Literature

In Chapter 2 a model for how the arts can be used as teaching tools throughout the curriculum was introduced. Each of the letters in the word INTEGRATES (Post It Page 2–5) represents a principle to guide *meaningful* arts integration and is applied to literature in the next section.

Principle 1: IMMERSE Students in Literature

A Literary Environment. Visualize a classroom with a carpeted book nook stocked with pillows, a sofa, a rocker, and books from every genre and reading level. Using the "classroom as living room" idea, teachers have brought in claw-foot bathtubs, telephone booths, and Conestoga wagons and have built lofts to give comfortable places to read. The chalk tray is a convenient display for "books of the week" with enticing advertising slogans or questions: "Why would anyone eat a worm? Read *How to Eat Fried Worms* to find out." Or "A dog with an attitude—*Officer Buckles and Gloria*." Special pages can be tabbed to give readers a quick look and displays can be connected to units. Poem charts are another way to display literature. Using a wire clothesline, poster-sized charts can be changed regularly. Daily poem sharing is an important routine, so charts make poems ready to go. A poetry wall can be a place to post favorites, and poem pockets can be made from library pockets or manila folders. Students can add art to poem pockets, fill with poems, and trade poems.

Centers and Stations. A center can be a transportable shoe box of activities or an elaborate bulletin board–table combination. By placing "reading and writing for life" hands-on centers and stations around the classroom perimeter or in corners, students can use books, writing, and art materials while instruction happens in the middle. A center may focus on literary genre, such as historical fiction or folktales, and have activities for students to explore genre characteristics, culminating in original writing in the genre. A block of time each day can be set aside to work at choice stations; time may be allotted for specific work, such as a listening station to hear poetry or stories read by authors that penned them or interviews on tape with authors and artists like Tomie de Paola. A listening station can also have music available to listen to during silent reading. A "real-life writing" center would have examples of common writing forms—invitations, friendly letters, notes of apology, lists, riddles, and job applications (see Post It Page 4–2 for different formats). An alphabetized set of file folders, tabbed with common writing forms, is useful in this type of center. Stocked with art supplies to mount, frame, bind, or suspend finished writing products, the center is a "must visit" for students each day. Center and station visits can be organized with a class chart of names down the left side and a symbol for each center across the top. Laminate the chart so that students can check off and the record can be erased for new use.

Literature Collections. Invitations for children to share well-loved books, poems, and stories from home, as well as posters and quotes that celebrate books, extend space ownership; we tend to "own" what we help create, so children need to participate in the design of the classroom. When children are encouraged to root out the writers and readers in their families and make public how literature is alive outside of school, everyone benefits. Children are proud to discover uncles and aunts and dads and cousins who write poetry or short stories. Even if the school has a wonderful book collection, the classroom is simply closer than the library. Availability of books is crucial to creating a love of literature. If the school doesn't provide several hundred "trade books" for each classroom, teachers can begin collecting in relatively inexpensive ways: send home a letter asking for used book donations, go to garage or tag sales, buy from book clubs like Scholastic and Trumpet (teachers get bonus books), or ask the PTA to conduct an old-fashioned book drive in the community (set limits on what can be contributed). Of particular importance is having multiple copies of books that will be used as core book studies. This means enough copies for small groups to form and read the same book (six to eight copies or class sets of books). In addition, teachers need to accumulate *text sets* of literature around unit plans for the year, for example, sets of books, stories, and poems around the topic of weather or text sets of fairy tales for a genre unit. No teacher starts off with such book wealth, but by targeting one or two units a year the collecting pays off.

Principle 2: NITTY-GRITTY Literary Concepts and Elements

Charts of Elements, Banners, and Big Books as Reference Tools. In Chapter 2 the idea of teaching the building blocks of the art forms was introduced. In the area of literature this includes the *literary elements* and the *traits of each genre* so that students have tools to read with more depth and write with greater variety. As mentioned previously, teaching the nitty-gritty can be dull and irrelevant if students don't understand how these ideas can be used; this is not information that stands alone in its worth—hence the principle of explaining *why* to learn the elements. In general, the process of teaching elements and other arts content begins with experiencing the art *first*. In literature, this means reading aloud stories and poetry, as well as providing daily time for "just plain reading." Once students have enjoyed poems, fables, or mysteries in an esthetic manner, they are ready to discover the inner workings and create their own. This kind of instruction can be summarized by thinking of a teaching sequence that goes *whole–part–whole*. It begins with reading and oral sharing of literature, moves to examining elements and traits, and returns to the whole literature again to generate new works or reread favorite familiar ones with new perspective.

A helpful way to teach literary elements and genre characteristics is to post them on charts or banners as they are introduced. Collaborative big books can be made by students, with individuals or groups working on specific pages designated for each idea (e.g., a page on characters, another on theme). Pages can include examples from literature, explanations, and artwork. Genre charts, with the traits of a genre down the left side and actual book, poem, or story titles across the top, are tools to help discover examples that support each genre trait. A pocket chart can be used to create a chart by asking students questions such as "What are the characters like in fables? What do you notice about the action (plot)? How do you know what the fable is really about? Not the topic but the theme?" List discoveries on cards and place cards down the left side to generate traits as a group, divide into small groups, jigsaw the chart by assigning each a trait, and go to work to ferret out actual examples from stories. (This is an important life thinking process since it teaches students to support ideas with evidence.)

Songs and other mnemonics can be written by students to transform elements and genre traits in ways that are creative and enjoyable and cause deep processing. Here is a second grade's song about literary elements to the tune of "Frère Jacques": *Plots and themes. Plots and themes. Make a story. Make a story. Add in characters. Add in characters. Play with words. That makes style.*

Minilessons.   Five to 10 minutes of direct instruction can target specific information or skills that students need to read and write literature with more artistry. In the strategy seed ideas chapters for each art, there are ideas for minilessons on literary elements, genre characteristics, and specifics about authors and illustrators. Here is an example strategy to explore the element of character: After reading a piece of literature, collaboratively complete the Character Report Card given below on one or more characters. (Do on the overhead with teacher guidance.) Ask students to justify grades.

Principle 3: TEACHING HABITS to Integrate Literature

Pre–During–Post.   A special literature lesson framework divides the teaching and learning sequence into *pre–during–post* stages based on the process that good readers and writers commonly use. Children who are taught about the complementary nature of reading and writing—both are *composing meaning* processes—and how both have three stages become more skilled and motivated, since this knowledge builds independence and fluency. The *pre* or before reading and writing stage is necessary to prepare the brain. This is a getting-ready stage much like the first stage in the creative problem-solving process (see Post It Page 1–6) and includes activating prior knowledge, making predictions, and data gathering. The *during* stage is the doing part, actually reading and writing. This should be a very active stage, with readers asking themselves questions to monitor understanding and using strategies to fix themselves up when they aren't understanding a word or passage. This is a time to *draft* in writing—to just get ideas down without worrying about spelling or grammar. In both reading and writing, the *during* stage focuses on attending to words—finding, appreciating, and using new ones. Finally comes the *post* stage of reading and writing, which involves pulling ideas together; it entails getting a piece of writing into a final form or responding to a piece of literature through a discussion or an art form that captures themes.

Pre–during–post are parts of an important learning principle about connecting school activities to life through clear *purposes and goals* linked to life, because to reach a goal a person must know it. For 10 years I listened to children with reading and writing difficulties in our reading clinic declare that they weren't good readers. What's more, they didn't know why they needed to be. It was disconcerting to realize that no one had taught them that reading was *not* equal to *sounding out words* and that writing was not the same as spelling and handwriting. Most of these children needed a clear goal as much or more than they needed phonics and sight words. What goal? An accurate description of what good readers and writers really do in real life: *pre–during–post*. Here is one well-known strategy using the *pre–during–post* process:

Character Report Card for _____

Characteristic	Grade	Comments
Talent		
Tact		
Poise		
Appearance		
Honesty		
Reliability		
Creativity		
Industry		
Punctuality		

TAKE ACTION 6
DARE TO COMPARE

Return to the creative problem-solving process (CPSP) in Post It Page 1–6. Construct a Venn diagram to show how the pre–during–post process for reading and writing are similar and different to the CPSP.

KWL. A chart is divided into three columns (Ogle, 1989). The first is entitled **K** for *What I Know,* the second is labeled **W** for *What I Need to Know,* and the final is labeled **L** for *What I Learned.* The first two columns are used for prereading and prewriting. Students list what they already *know* about a topic. Then they list what they *want* to learn. The class then reads to *learn* more and keeps track of important ideas in the third column. Writing products are then drafted or other arts responses are made based on what was learned. *Variation:* The acronym **AQUA** can also be used to stand for "already know," "questions to answer," and "answers found."

Encourage Risk Taking and Creative Thinking. When children are learning to respond or create literature, they are like any artist just starting out; they are afraid they won't get it right. But fresh new ideas do not flow from a mind fixed on right answers. If children are to interpret literature esthetically using genuine personal reactions to beauty and write with passion, it is necessary to form the habit of sharing *examples* of what stories and poems can mean, not giving answers in the attempt to model thinking. Parallel to this habit is being careful to give *examples* of types of writing, to clarify structural conventions, but to emphasize using personal ideas in poems and other writing (see Post It Page 4–2). Copying is not creating. This does not mean that teachers shouldn't use strategies such as *echoic reading* to expand children's use of their voices to interpret poems and stories; this is modeling and imitation to develop vocal skills that then can be used imaginatively.

Words have the power to give hope and a way to encourage risk taking and creativity: "That's an original interpretation of the story," "You took the idea of the fable and wrote one never written before" (flexible thinking), "You really took a key idea in the book and explained in detail to make us all think more about it" (elaboration) are comments that teach the creative process, are fun to give, and uplift students. Encourage risking and develop courage by giving encouraging messages and feedback. An encouraging message is "I think you're on the right track with writing a haiku on *Charlotte's Web.* It is a book about nature so you have a lot to work with."

Creativity is also encouraged by giving choices. Why must everyone write a sequel to a book or a letter to a character? Why should all students read the same stories at the same time all year long? Teachers need a repertoire of choices before they can offer them to students, and throughout this book there are such choices; see Post It Page 4–1, *A Hundred Plus Book Response Options,* options to use *instead of book reports,* and *Things to Write and Say from A to Z* (Post It Page 4–2). Writing literature can also be made more imaginative by using the creative problem-solving process. For example, brainstorming, data gathering, and SCAMPER work well to get ideas before writing. The process can be used to think about literature, too. For example, data can be gathered, through close examination of picture books, to discover the art media, style, and techniques used.

Flexible Small Groups. Writers talk with others to get feedback, generate directions, and get angles on ideas. In real life, people pair up to discuss books and join book clubs. At family gatherings, grandparents tell stories that embarrass grown aunts and uncles, but further bond the family together with laughter and memory. The social nature of literature and writing is a force to put to motivational use. By making it a habit to group students in different ways and allowing choice groups to form based on interests and needs, we can meet the basic need to belong, facilitate exchange of points of view, and develop cooperative skills. The key is *flexible* grouping, and the structure to avoid is keeping students in the same ability groups—a narrow-minded practice that rests on a false assumption that people need to have equal skill levels to learn or work together.

Focus on Process. This habit entails considering the thinking behind students' words, not just whether the words are spelled correctly or all the lines rhyme. What happens *during* the reading of a book or *during* a literature discussion is just as important, if not more so, than reading proficiency test results. If we emphasized how to be *actively engaged* during reading (make mental pictures in your head, stop and think how the story relates to life, jot down questions to discuss later) and during discussion, test scores would more likely take care of themselves.

Esthetic Response and Evidence.   The teaching habit of starting with esthetic responses is particularly important for literature discussions or when students are sharing writing. The habit acknowledges literature as an art form, first, and allows students to express feelings and attitudes from the emotional intelligence, which tends to overshadow other intelligences if not permitted expression. After the sharing of feelings, teachers can ask for evidence or reasons for the response. Here are example questions to initiate such discussions: *How did the story or poem make you feel? Why? What was the mood of the story? How did the author create the mood? What struck you about how the story was written? How were words and pictures used to create a feeling in the book?*

Start with the Known.   Anyone who begins a creative effort can be overwhelmed by an infinite number of possible directions to choose from. The same is true in thinking about the meanings of literature or expressing ideas through writing. One way to ease this stress is to use strategies such as timed writings—unstructured free writes to release what is already known. For example, suppose a child is to use some form of writing to respond to a book. A good place to begin is to make two lists: (1) possible types of writing to use and (2) important moments or ideas in the book. From these lists, students can then be helped to make more choices; if a student picks a letter form and wants to write about when Jack chose to go up the beanstalk the third time, then those two things can be squeezed for what is known about letter writing and that moment in the story.

Look and Listen More Closely.   When teachers meaningfully integrate the arts, class time use is changed. Examining art in a picture book to find how text and illustration mesh takes time. Teaching students to engage in significant literature discussions that go beyond plot retellings takes lots of time. Where is the time to come from? From many places, with two of the most important being discipline and motivational time hogs. There is no doubt that students who are taught to *take time* to look and listen more closely become more interested in books and writing. This is the path to the intrinsic rewards of literature. Coupons and stickers may be fast, but their effect does not last.

The poignant moments possible when time is taken to *really* discuss books are remembered and "re-member" students—make them members again—by drawing them into the human family, held together by common beliefs and history, both of which can be known through the vehicle of literature.

Student Independence and Self-Discipline.   Teachers can show ways to respond to and write literature, but they must then go one step more and expect these tools to be used. The teacher who asks "What have you tried?" when the student complains about not knowing what to write or can't decode an unknown word is setting an expectation for independence. Independence and self-discipline are not acquired easily or quickly, but they are two areas for which the arts hold much potential. Once students understand that the teacher is not going to do it *for them* or give them a "right answer," they are more likely to look inward—if they have been taught tools to help themselves. For example, students need specific strategies to cope with unknown words, besides sounding out, and need spelling fix ups to use when writing. A tool for independence to gauge the difficulty of a book is the *rule of thumb* or *five-finger method:* Children open to a page in the middle, read, and, for every unfamiliar word, raise one finger starting with the pinky. If they get to the thumb by the end of the page, then the book may be too hard. A caveat is in order, however; a book may be too difficult, but a child's interest can compensate for the reading level. *Variation:* Ohlhausen and Jepsen (1992) explain book selection by likening it to Goldilocks deciding whether the porridge was too hot, cold, or just right; students decide if a book is too hard, easy, or just right to read.

Time for Individual Projects.   When I announce in undergraduate classes "Book reports are not to be used below ninth grade!" the class usually cheers. Eighteen-year-olds have fresh memories about book reports and claim that they singlehandedly made many of them not want to read. One of the primary themes of this text is the need to implement multiple intelligences theory and other research on alternative ways of expressing and knowing. A strong implication from this work is using the many real-life writing structures, which form the genres we read, and choice options for literature response. Alternative meaningful options to the despised book report can be found in Post It Page 4–1, *A Hundred Plus Book Response Options.* Two sources for writing forms are Post It Pages 4–2 and 3–5.

Principle 4: ENERGIZERS and Warm-ups

Just as in other arts areas, we need to help students get ready to read literature and write about it. Chapter 4 includes energizers that have to do with word play and other creative language ideas. Check the energizers and warm-ups from all the arts chapters, since many work for literature and creative writing.

Principle 5: GREAT CHILDREN'S LITERATURE

What Makes Great Literature? So many books, genre, and literary elements mean many decisions about writing and reading. The decisions can't just hinge on finding books that match a genre unit planned or a topic of interest, either. The goal is to integrate *fine* literature so that students are immersed in the creative and artistic use of words. This leads to a consideration of what criteria can be used to determine *great* literature. What makes a piece of writing truly excellent? As with all art, this is a sensitive, difficult, and to some extent very personal decision. However, using standards to make wise judgments is crucial for teachers, who must select from thousands of available books. Equally important is for students to learn to present informed opinions derived from anchor ideas about quality. Here are three *anchor concepts* teachers can use.

Creativity. Are the elements used in original ways? Remember from Chapter 1 how a creative idea is not "entirely new," but a twist, stretch, or substitution of others' ideas. The key is whether the author makes a creative leap to mold and shape new characters, context, and plots from the literary clay. Is there energy or a spark to the work that makes it seem alive and leaves us with a sense of rejuvenation and hope? Are the basic and universal themes, motifs, and archetypes varied to create a story or poem that seems to be both a new invention and a comfortable friend? Or is the plot tired, the style clichè, and the characters dull?

Unity and Balance. Do the literary elements work in concert to make an integrated whole? Characters may be believable and fascinating, but they need a plot that intrigues the reader and a setting that is appropriate for the story to unfold. Beautiful words that go nowhere soon frustrate even the most poetic soul, and a well-drawn setting without characters to act in it is useless. Finally, as in all good art, we expect good literature to be provocative—a creative invention that will disturb our universe by unveiling enduring truths about people and the world, without ramming them down our throats. We must feel that the story has united the elements in an inviting way and allows readers to make discoveries about themes, rather than be victimized by didacticism.

Taste. A book can be judged high in creativity, unity, and balance (i.e., be a quality piece of literature) and still not be beloved. Judging art always includes personal taste, which has to do with what we like, relate to, feel comfortable with, and just plain suits us at a particular time. Many children's books, such as the series books like *Hardy Boys* and *Bobsey Twins,* are judged to be mediocre and formulaic by critics, but they are as popular in the late twentieth century as they were in the 1950s and are now joined by a host of children's favorites, including *The Babysitter's Club* and *Goosebumps* books. Adults risk alienating children by forcing books of quality on them. It's much like expecting everyone to want a Frank Lloyd Wright designed house because his is great architecture, without regard for the cost or personal taste of the buyer. One way to learn to recognize excellence is to practice using criteria. One tool for teachers to use appears in Post It Page 3–7.

Awards bibliographies provide another way to find books recommended based on certain criteria. *Children's Books: Awards and Prizes* from the Children's Book Council is a handy book that summarizes most awards, even ones given by other countries and individual states in the United States. For example, Ohio gives the Buckeye Book Award each year based on nominations by children and teachers. Also see the literature website addresses in the appendix. Here are some prominent awards that teachers should know. The ones with asterisks are listed in the appendix.

- ◆ * *Newbery Medal Award* (since 1922): Presented by the American Library Association to the U.S. author of the most distinguished contribution to children's literature published during the preceding year. An award winner and runner-up honor books are chosen.

- ◆ * *Caldecott Medal Award* (since 1936): The American Library Association awards this medal to the artist of the most distinguished picture book published in the United States in the preceding year and recognizes honor books as well. Only U.S. residents or citizens are eligible.

EVALUATING CHILDREN'S LITERATURE USING LITERARY ELEMENTS

Directions: Evaluate a piece of children's literature using these criteria. If an element is very evident, circle 1; not evident, circle 5. Indicate 2, 3, or 4 for ratings in between. Circle NA for not applicable.

Plot

1. Has sense of momentum based on the conflict.	1	2	3	4	5	NA
2. Conflict is clear and believable.	1	2	3	4	5	NA
3. Does not depend on coincidence.	1	2	3	4	5	NA
4. Original, not *dully* predictable.	1	2	3	4	5	NA
5. Suspense raised by withholding easy problem resolutions.	1	2	3	4	5	NA
6. Use of subplots and/or flashbacks to enhance without complicating.	1	2	3	4	5	NA
7. Has a climax of action or hints of conflict resolution.	1	2	3	4	5	NA

Theme

1. Universal truths can be understood on more than one level.	1	2	3	4	5	NA
2. Contains one or more subthemes to support main theme.	1	2	3	4	5	NA
3. Causes reader to confront a problem or see life as it might be.	1	2	3	4	5	NA
4. Avoids imposing values, prejudices, and opinions.	1	2	3	4	5	NA

Characters

1. Revealed through:						
a. Physical description	1	2	3	4	5	NA
b. Actions	1	2	3	4	5	NA
c. Speech and thoughts	1	2	3	4	5	NA
d. Others' thoughts and words	1	2	3	4	5	NA
2. Mostly developed through action rather than description.	1	2	3	4	5	NA
3. Believable, original, convincing, and consistent (i.e., age, background, ethnicity).	1	2	3	4	5	NA
4. Protagonist changes or grows.	1	2	3	4	5	NA
5. Foils and flat characters are used novelly.	1	2	3	4	5	NA
6. Avoids stereotypes.	1	2	3	4	5	NA

Setting

1. Sets stage for action with details and background.	1	2	3	4	5	NA
2. Time and place developed by references to well-known site or through language use.	1	2	3	4	5	NA
3. Details are appropriate to the time and place.	1	2	3	4	5	NA

Point of View

1. Strongly influences how characters are revealed.	1	2	3	4	5	NA
2. Contains objectivity appropriate to the reader's maturity level.	1	2	3	4	5	NA

Style

1. Language use matches characters and intended reader's age.	1	2	3	4	5	NA
2. Language is artistic and creative.	1	2	3	4	5	NA
3. Used effectively to create mood.	1	2	3	4	5	NA

Conclusion

Overall, how well written is this piece of literature?	1	2	3	4	5*	NA

---

*5 = well written to 1 = poorly written.

◆ *Coretta Scott King Awards,* founded in 1969 to commemorate Dr. Martin Luther King, Jr., and his wife, Coretta Scott King, for promoting peace and world brotherhood, are given to an African American author and an illustrator whose books, published in the preceding year, made outstanding inspirational and educational contributions to literature for young people (sponsored by the Social Responsibilities Round Table of the American Library Association).

◆ *Carnegie Medal* (since 1937), sponsored by the British Library Association, is given to the author of the most outstanding children's book first published in English in the United Kingdom.

◆ *Hans Christian Andersen Award* is an international award, given every two years, and is sponsored by the International Board on Books for Young People. A living author is honored and, since 1966, a living illustrator whose complete works are important contributions.

◆ *Mildred Batchelder Award* (since 1968) is sponsored by the American Library Association and goes to a book judged to be the most outstanding of books originally published outside the United States in a language other than English and then translated.

◆ *Orbis Pictus Award* is sponsored by the National Council for the Teachers of English and is given to an author for excellence in nonfiction for children published in the United States.

◆ *Children's Choices* are lists of "best books" selected by children. The list is published annually in the October *Reading Teacher,* a journal of the International Reading Association.

Source books are resources to help teachers and parents find books and information about books and authors. Post It Page 3–8 lists useful sources to find books for integrated arts units.

Classic literature is "news that stays news" (Ezra Pound) and includes books that have endured the test of time; they continue to delight and inform audiences. The significance of the theme, credibility of the characters, reality of the conflict, and a style that engages are why some books remain in circulation. This relates to the discussion about human needs in Chapter 1: We need to know, belong, feel safe, and have beauty in our lives. Horn Book, Inc., publishes a list of such children's classics, as do organizations such as the Children's Literature Association. (See the list of organizations in Appendix C.) On nearly every list are Aesop's fables, Andersen's fairy tales, Mother Goose rhymes, Perrault's fairy tales, *Charlotte's Web, Little Women, Winnie the Pooh, The Wizard of Oz,* and *The Adventures of Huckleberry Finn,* among others.

Principle 6: ROUTINES

Effective daily routines to make literature integration a way of life in the classroom include the following:

Expressive Daily Reading (EDR). The focus of this kind of teacher oral reading is on giving an esthetic experience—hearing good literature read interpretively. Through EDR, teachers engage children in making "mind pictures" from "word music," and they hear book language, very unlike normal talk. When a teacher reads a book such as *Tuck Everlasting* to a third grade, students hear words and think about ideas that may very well be above their *reading* level, but match their *interest* level. In addition, experiencing a book together bonds a group in the way that singing does. EDR should be scheduled each day and may include

SOURCE BOOKS TO LOCATE AND SELECT LITERATURE

Use to find bibliographies for genre studies, problem or topic studies, author and artists units, read alouds, bibliotherapy, and particular age groups. Also see Teacher Resources at the end of the chapter.

A to zoo: Subject access to children's picture books, 4th ed. (2001). Bowker.

Adventuring with books: A book list for pre-K and grade 6 (1997). National Council of Teachers of English.

Accept me as I am: Best books of juvenile nonfiction on impairments and disabilities (1985). Bowker.

Children's books: Awards and prizes. Children's Book Council (revised periodically).

Award-winning books for children and young adults. Scarecrow (annual publication).

Best books for children: Preschool through grade 6, 4th ed. (1990). Bowker.

Beyond picture books: A guide to first readers (1989). Bowker.

Books kids will sit still for: The complete read-aloud guide, 2nd ed. (1990). Bowker.

The bookfinder: A guide to children's literature about the needs and problems of youth aged 2–15 (1989). American Guidance.

Books to help children cope with separation and loss, 2nd ed. (1983). Bowker.

Children's books in print. Bowker (annual edition).

Choosing books for children, rev. ed. (1990). Delacorte.

The elementary school library collection: A guide to books and other media (1992). Brodart.

Exciting, funny, scary, short, different, and sad books kids like about animals, science, sports, families, songs, and other things (1984). American Library Association.

Hear no evil, see no evil, speak no evil: An annotated bibliography for the handicapped (1990). Libraries Unlimited.

A Hispanic heritage: A guide to juvenile books about Hispanic people and cultures (1991). Scarecrow.

Horn Book guide to children's and young adult books. Vol. 7, No. 2 (1996). Horn Books.

Notes for a different drummer: A guide to juvenile fiction portraying the handicapped (1977). Bowker.

More notes for a different drummer: A guide to juvenile fiction portraying the disabled (1984). Bowker.

The literature of delight: A critical guide to humorous books for children (1991). Bowker.

Pass the poetry please (1987). HarperCollins.

Science and technology in fact and fiction: A guide to children's books (1989). Bowker.

Author–Artist Studies

Books are by people (short biographies of authors and artists) (1969). Citation Press.

Contemporary authors: A biographical guide to current writers in fiction, general non-fiction, poetry, and journalism, drama, motion pictures, television, and other fields (122 volumes). Gale Research.

Something about the author: Facts and pictures about contemporary authors and illustrators of books for young people (1971+) (Vols. 1–50). Gale Research.

Dictionary of literary biography, Volume 140: American writers for children since 1960: Poets, illustrators, and nonfiction authors. (1993). Gale Research.

A state-by-state guide to children's and young adult authors and illustrators (1991). Libraries Unlimited.

An author a month (for pennies) (1991). Libraries Unlimited.

Bookpeople: A first album (1991). Libraries Unlimited.

Bookpeople: A second album (1991). Libraries Unlimited.

An author a month (for nickels) (1990). Libraries Unlimited.

Behind the covers: Interviews with authors and illustrators of books for children and young adults (1990) (Vol. 2). Libraries Unlimited.

Something about the author autobiography series (1986–1987) (Vols. 1–4). Gale Research.

Sixth book of junior authors and illustrators (1989). Wilson.

Twentieth century children's authors, 4th ed. (1995). St. James.

---

pre–during–post reading arts responses, such as those Mrs. Weiss used to prepare for and follow up *Sarah, Plain and Tall.* In addition, pausing to discuss words and inviting students to chime in with predictions increases involvement.

Just Plain Reading.   There are many names for the classroom routine involving silent reading of choice books each day. SSR stands for "sustained silent reading," SQUIRT is "silent quiet independent reading time," DEAR is "drop everything and read," and RIBET is "reading is bringing everybody together." Whatever it is called, it is essential for children to read and not just have lessons *about* reading. Crucial to the success of this routine is the full participation of everyone, including the teacher, who acts as a role model. Here are the basic guidelines to ensure success.

- Plan a regular time of 10–20 minutes (shorter at first and with younger children).
- Everyone needs a book ready and an extra book in case the book is finished during SSR; however, immature readers should be encouraged to do *repeated readings* of the same book to gain fluency. (This can be encouraged by planning regular times for students to tape themselves reading, listening to their own tapes, and graphing fluency—correct words per minute.)
- Everyone should be in a comfortable place and stay put. Teachers may allow buddy or partner reading, especially with young children who need to read aloud or have the support of a partner. Books on tape may also be used as a support.
- Background soft mood music may be played if all agree and it increases comfort.
- After reading, time can be planned to record responses in lit logs and discussed in small or whole group. Generic questions can be used: What was the most exciting or interesting part? What were some special words? How did the

pictures make you feel and why? What have you figured out about the characters? (See the *generic discussion questions* in Post It Page 3–9.)

Repeated Reading.   This routine is especially important for beginning readers who need regular practice with skills to become fluent. Fluency, in turn, increases enjoyment of literature. By reading the same story or poem several times, students become familiar with plot and characters and gain confidence and comprehension. Through repeated readings, beginners realize that words have meaning and can be said many ways to give personal interpretation. Thus vocabulary grows.

Literature Discussions.   Begin discussion routines by assuming that they are a rewarding human experience that all will *want* to participate in. Once students learn how to use the process, it holds excitement and unmatched potential to make meaning. There is no more powerful way to enhance comprehension than through building discussions into the daily classroom routine. It is through talking out thoughts and listening to others that students create a web of meanings, but discussions that promote interconnecting are not made of question-and-answer turn taking between teacher and students or of dull plot retellings. On the contrary, they are more like "grand conversations" (Eeds & Wells, 1989) among people who have all shared in the same experience (know the plot already) and wish to share. This implies a leadership shift away from the teacher. Students need to learn how to *prepare for* and *participate in* discussions among equals.

Student-Led Discussion.   The goal is to eventually have students hold their own small-group discussions in which all come away with new perspectives. This is a learned skill that becomes an art as students are guided through the process. To begin, develop discussion rules.

- Everyone who has read the book can participate. Come prepared.

GENERIC QUESTIONS TO DISCUSS LITERATURE

Guidelines: Ask think questions that have many answers that can be supported with text evidence. Ask students to read aloud sections that answer questions. Choose 1–2 questions to discuss in depth. Have students stop and write down ideas related to a question *before* the discussion; this causes reflection *before* and focus *during* the discussion. Comprehension is increased when text is connected to students' lives and students respond both cognitively and esthetically. To increase esthetic response, read *first for pleasure;* then reread to find information related to selected questions. Post questions for students to use as choices. Some examples follow.

◆ **Look at the title and a few pictures; then ask:**

What do you think this is about? Who? When and where? (characters/setting)

What might be the problems in a book with this title? (theme)

◆ **Read a bit; then ask:**

What did you notice so far?

What's the big question? How do you know? (theme)

What's the problem? How might it get solved? (conflict/plot)

What kind of person is this character? How do you know?

What should the character do? Why? (critical thinking)

What's happening? Why? What are the important things that have happened? (plot)

Whose story is this? (point of view)

What do you notice in the pictures? (art elements: color, texture, shape, line, perspective) How does this affect the story?

What will happen? Why? What would you like to find out?

◆ **Read more; then repeat from above or ask:**

What do you now know that you didn't know before?

What questions got answered? (confirm/reject predictions)

What is confusing? (clarification)

What events are important? How do you know? (critical thinking)

What words or language stands out? Why? (style)

What does this story make you feel? (illustrations, mood)

What does the dialog tell you about the main character?

◆ **After the entire reading ask:**

What happened? Why? (plot; cause/effect) What were the problems? How were they solved?

What did you like? What were your favorite parts? (critical thinking)

What was this story really about? (themes/key concepts)

What in this story was like something in your life? (connections)

Was it right that . . .? Why or why not? (critical thinking)

Was . . . a believable (seem real) character? Why? (evaluation)

What was special or important about . . .? (inference)

What did . . . believe/value? (inference)

What will you remember about this story next week? Next year?

How is this story like others you've read? (connections)

What was special or unusual about the illustrations?

What is special about how the author writes? How did the author make the story interesting? (style)

Why did the characters do what they did? What does the story tell you about people and behavior?

Did the story end the way you thought it would? Why or why not?

How did the characters change in the story? (characterization)

Why did the author write this story?

- Finding different interpretations is the goal.
- Opinions should be supported with examples or evidence.
- Restate the other person's idea before you present an opposite opinion.
- Try to learn something you didn't think of on your own.
- Show you are an active listener with "body talk" and by responding to the ideas of others with positive comments.

In addition, students need ways to organize thoughts so that they feel prepared to share. Even adults are reluctant to speak up if they don't feel prepared or feel their point of view will not be respected. There are several discussion strategies in Chapters 4, 5, 6, and 8. Here are a few to get started:

1. *Discussion cards.* Each student is given an index card to jot down interesting ideas she or he wants to discuss. The goal is to cause students to become engaged with reading and prepare for a student-led discussion. Some categories to give students to think about are important events, puzzling things, exciting parts, emotional parts, things characters say, and special words.

2. *EPC charts.* Students are given a frame with the categories of exciting part, puzzling part and connecting part (Cornett, 1997). (These can be three large circles or three columns.) During reading, students note sections that fit into these categories (*connecting* means parts that relate to your life) and jot down page numbers. Ask students to star the one or two that they want to discuss.

3. *Read alouds.* Students choose a part of the story or poem that they want to read aloud as a discussion focus. They should be able to tell why they chose it (e.g., important event, use of language, connected to their lives). Students rehearse the section so that the reading will be pleasant for all. Suggest to students that the section be a certain length and contain a whole idea.

Organizing the Discussion. After students read and prepare, it is time to begin: (1) Take a few minutes and role play the discussion rules. For example, "Show me you're being an active listener." "Use your face and body to make me believe." "Now show me being a poor listener." Practice giving each other descriptive feedback, paraphrasing ideas, and asking clarification questions with partners. (2) Sit in a circle so everyone can see. To create comfort when starting discussion routines, the *fishbowl* technique can be used: Volunteers come into an inner circle to discuss while an outer circle listens in. At stop points, the outer circle follows up on comments made by individuals or asks questions such as "I liked what Lisa said because I did not think that the boy might have died" (based on *The Giver*); "I would like to ask Tom why he thought the mother committed suicide" (based on *Walk Two Moon*). Next, the circles exchange positions. This helps all to learn to really listen, as well as speak. (3) Use the Write Right Away strategy with a good question—one the teacher cares about, but can't answer, and there are clues to many answers in the story.

During the discussion, students can be encouraged to participate by starting with volunteers or calling on students (all should have something prepared). The web of meaning is made stronger when student responses are woven together by questions such as "What do the rest of you think about Shannon's idea?" and "Did anyone have the same idea?" and "Is this a new idea for anyone?" or "Who has an opposite idea from Shannon's?" and "What in the story supports Shannon's idea?" Periodically stop and ask students to recap the most important ideas that have been shared so far.

To bring the discussion to a conclusion, ask students to share (1) the most important points made, (2) what made sense, (3) what someone said that was a new idea, and (4) how people had like ideas. The "tell one thing" strategy can be used, with a pass option to allow face-saving; usually this is "pass and come back," since by the full round all ideas have been expressed and it is acceptable to repeat ideas.

Post It Page 3–9 includes recommended *generic questions for discussing literature* to post so that students can choose questions to discuss and become skilled at creating their own questions, with the focus on asking about things that they really *care* about and for which they *don't have answers*.

Reading and Writing Workshops.   These are routines that include other routines such as free reading. Blocks of time are set aside to read and write, with a focus on trade books, poetry, and a variety of writing generated in the writing process (prewriting, during, and after writing strategies). During workshop times, students may write in *Arts for Life* journals, lit logs, *Look Back and Laugh* logs (journals on humor in their lives), do SSR, repeat readings, or work at learning centers.

Weekly or Daily Spotlight.   A few minutes can be spent regularly studying an author, artist, genre, or literary element. If the spotlight was on Ezra Jack Keats, students could take turns finding out something about him to report each day. Often teachers set this up as a classroom job with short spotlights as part of a morning routine. *Variations:* Use one of these spotlights: (1) *Humor of the Day* (write a joke, riddle, or hink pink on the board or share a cartoon on the overhead); (2) *WAD* is "word a day" and consists of students finding special and important words that can be worn as "buttons" or written on cards to post on a word wall; (3) *Poem a Day* (PAD) is daily poem sharing, usually using a chart or the overhead (see the *poetry alive* strategies Post It Page 4–4); and (4) *I Spy* is a routine in which a word pattern is targeted and students find examples in the room, a poem, song, and so forth. *I Spy* patterns might be onomatopoetic words, rhyming words, or alliterative words.

Docent Talks.   Allow students to "teach" the class by sharing original pieces they've written. The class can gather around a special chair in which one student sits to read. Listeners are directed to be active nonverbally and think of questions and comments to give the reader. Feedback is given, another student proceeds to read, and so on. This strategy helps children to feel that writing is more than an assignment because it becomes a way to share feelings, emotions, and ideas. For example, students write a fantasy during a genre unit using the genre characteristics learned. The author's chair is used

to share. *Variation:* Use a reader's chair to share favorite books or poems and an artist's chair to share artwork.

Book Ads or Talks.   The purpose is to interest others in a book and these are much like the ads done on *Reading Rainbow* or *Cover to Cover*. Weekly or daily times can be set for students to do book ads. Children have seen so many TV and radio ads that they can offer ideas for what makes a good ad, and the teacher can demonstrate how to do a 2 or 3 minute ad with an *introduction* (attention getter; tell book title and author, display a few pictures, read chapter titles or book blurb, or share author facts), *development* (read short excerpt; perhaps a section of dialog), and *conclusion* (ask for predictions about the book and invite the audience to read the book to find out if they are right). Students may choose to make a tape or a video or write a jingle or slogan, too. Ads are more interesting if props, visual aids, and music are used; for example, for *Beethoven Lives Upstairs*, the beginning of the Fifth Symphony can be played as a letter from the book is read aloud or a clip from the video viewed. Ads also function as book responses to show student comprehension.

Reader's Theatre Presentations.   Students can do *expressive* oral reading of their original scripts or those of others—sometimes even found in basal reading series. The focus is on using just the voice to create a "theatre of the mind" (see Reader's Theatre in Chapter 8).

Principle 7: ADAPTATION of Curriculum and Instructional Models

In Chapters 1 and 2, the concept of teaching *with, about, in,* and *through* the arts was introduced, and this can be applied to the integration of the art form of literature. The goal is to get beyond casual entertainment *with* books and narrow artificial writing assignments; students need to learn significant information *about* literature and its creators and how to use these ideas *in* writing and reading. Beyond the *about* and *in* is teaching *through* literature by connecting books and writing to science, social studies, math, music, art, drama, and dance so that all curricular areas are enhanced. The curriculum delivery models discussed in Chapter 2 can be adapted for literature integration.

National Standards for the English Language Arts. The *National Standards* appear on Post It Page 3–2 and are an important starting point when choosing goals for literature integration. State and local standards also give information about key concepts and skills expected of students in curricular areas, generally divided into grade groupings. It is important to plan with these documents in hand. Curriculum guides provide sources for integrated units, which should focus on life-centered issues and questions, be adapted to accommodate for student diversity, and be structured so that depth of learning happens. In integrated units, discipline-based methods, as well as content (facts, broad trends, and concepts that organize each discipline) are combined into a meaningful whole. How do students learn about justice, power, human rights, or interdependence? Textbooks offer explanations and definitions, but the arts, and in this case, literature, offer the *lives of people*. In a core book study, using a biography of Benjamin Franklin, we can understand the context of his discovery of electricity—what else he was doing at the time,

where he lived, what he was worried about, who his friends were. This puts a face and feelings to facts and allows us to go through the invention process with him. We are detectives, finding how things got to be the way they are today, through integrated literature units involving investigations rife with exciting adventure and the motives of people who are like us or like we might be.

Two-Pronged Integrated Lesson Plan. The concept of an integrated arts lesson, with at least a two-pronged focus (an art form and another curricular area) and a teaching sequence with the introduction, development, and conclusion (IDC) pattern was introduced in Chapter 2. This suggested structure can be used to plan and teach lessons that integrate literature with other curricular areas. An example plan appears on Post It Page 3–10.

POST IT PAGE 3–10

INTEGRATED PLAN FOR LITERATURE AND SOCIAL STUDIES (THIRD GRADE)

Two-pronged Focus: Literary elements and concepts: perspective or point of view (POV), informational genre (authentic biography versus fictionalized biography). Social studies main idea: The historical record depends on who is "telling the story."

Standards 3, 6, and 11 (See Post It 3–2)

Student Objectives: Students will be able to

1. Give the POV of books (first person, omniscient, etc.) and explain evidence.
2. Decide whether an informational book is authentic or fictionalized and explain why knowing about this is important.
3. Explain how perspective and point of view are important in life.
4. Use POV to write about an event from two different perspectives.

Materials Needed: Four copies of each of the following books:

Yolen's *Encounter* (1992) (Columbus's landing in 1492 reported from the point of view of a native islander)

Columbus's diary entries in *The Log of Christopher Columbus* (Lowe, 1992)

Dyson's (1971) *Westward with Columbus* (information book; third-person account)

Ocean music (any CD of waves), one copy of Hoban's (1971) *Look Again,* Evidence Chart

Teaching Procedure

◆ **Introduction**

1. Ask students to raise hands if they know the Cinderella story. Group and give each a role: mice, stepsister, stepmother, father, neighbor, king. Use teacher in role to interview each group, asking "What happened?" Afterward, ask students what they noticed about the stories. Why were they different?

2. Show transparency with "POV = point of view." Show a few pictures in *Look Again* and ask students to guess what the pictures are (all close-ups of ordinary objects). Ask them to relate this to POV. Ask volunteers to describe the classroom from the point of view, or perspective, of a bug on the ceiling, a kindergartner, the principal, an eighth grader.

3. Ask how POV and perspective make a difference in real life.

4. Tell students they'll be using POV and perspective to think about our social studies unit on "exploration and discovery" and that Writing Workshop will be about this the next week.

◆ **Development**

5. Ask what students know about Columbus. Record their comments on chart.

6. Show covers and a few pictures from the three books and ask to do Predict–Prove strategy; focus on POV or perspective that each might take. Show rest of POV transparency with the different types and examples.

7. Explain that the books are based on facts, but sometimes authors make up dialog or even characters to make a story interesting. Show "Informational genre: Authentic biography and fictionalized transparency" and explain. Tell students they will be buddy reading during sustained silent reading (SSR) using one of the books on Columbus. The goal is to find out the POV and any clues about whether the book is authentic or fictionalized. Number off in 2s. Number 1 comes and picks up book and gets with partner to do 15 minutes of buddy reading. Give Evidence Chart to pairs to record findings.

8. Pull together in three groups based on books for Evidence Chart sharing and elaboration. Circulate to give feedback and ask fat questions to prompt evidence given from books (actual details).

9. Assemble whole group and ask a person from each of three groups to report findings on POV and subgenre decisions. Compare with predictions on chart. Add new information about Columbus.

◆ **Conclusion and Informal Assessment**

10. Ask students to TOT (tell one thing) learned about POV and authentic versus fictionalized biography. Ask each student to write down something they think will happen in the book (the buddy reading will continue for several days) and a question they have about Columbus. Collect questions.

11. Tell them to begin thinking about a real event, at school, home, in the news, that they may want to write about using a different POV and that we'll web ideas together at the start of Writing Workshop. Point out display on chalk tray of books written from different perspectives (e.g., Scieszka's *The True Story of Three Little Pigs by A. Wolf*).

Four Integrated Unit Structures. Unit structures can be planned for time blocks ranging from several days to weeks, a month, or a year-long study for a schoolwide unit. Four-unit types center around (1) core or single literary work, (2) genre (focus on traits), (3) person, or (4) problem or topic or theme question. An excellent book, story, or poem can be the core work, any literary genre can be a focus, an author and/or artist of picture books can organize a unit on the person's life and works, or a unit can be designed around real-life issues (see Chapter 2 for examples). The nine-legged unit web is a planning device to integrate curricular areas with one of the four unit centers. An author–artist unit web is included in Post It Page 5–13. Information sources and guidelines for artist–author studies appear in Post It Page 3–8 and in Chapter 5, along with names of authors and artists for this kind of unit.

Special Needs and Developmental Stages. PARTICULAR is the model for 10 ways to differentiate curriculum and instruction presented in Chapter 2. It involves adapting place, amount, rate, target objective, instruction, curriculum materials, utensils, level of difficulty, assistance, and/or response possibilities (see Post It Pages 2–6 and 2–7). Lesson formats to track the use of multiple intelligences (see Chapter 1) in literature and writing instruction can be individualized to meet interest, age, and stage differences. In general, literary development proceeds along a continuum from sound to sense and simple to complex literary forms. Here are broad guidelines to assist in differentiating for children at different age levels:

Preschool: Rhyme, rhythm, and repetition (sounds of language) are important. Children enjoy and understand stories and rhymes with simple plots, short dialog, clear images, and action that builds quickly to a climax, followed by a satisfying ending. A blend of fantasy and reality is preferred. Humor and animal stories are popular (e.g., *The Mitten*).

Grades 1–2: Traditional literature, how and why stories, magic, and fantasy are popular. Predictable books empower children to read and write their own versions at this age.

Grades 3–4: More sophisticated folktales, with problems and decisions made by characters, are enjoyed, as well as stories about the use of reason and judgment, scary tales, myths, legends, tall tales, and fables. Chapter books are appealing because they seem more grown-up.

Grades 5–6: The search for personal identity has now begun and children question things more. They enjoy more elaborate tales (grandfather tales) and fables, fantasy, humor (e.g., Jack tales), myths (Greek and legends), informational books, biography, mysteries, and ghost stories.

Principle 8: TRIPS for Literature Integration

Tips for Trips: Before–During–After Guidelines. Literature-focused trips include visits to art museums to compare with picture book art styles, media, and art elements use; public libraries to hear stories or talks about special collections; and the newspaper to understand publishing; or to studios or artists or writers. Naturally, a field trip can connect to any unit focus, from fairy tales (e.g., a play based on Cinderella) to death rituals (e.g., cemetery field trip), but the key is making the trip meaningful by using the before, during, and after activities. (Also see Chapter 2.)

Principle 9: EVIDENCE to Document Student Progress

Create a School Museum with Ongoing Displays. Displays of books that students have made based on the different genre and of literature response projects are important items to include in a school museum. Many book response projects are arts activities, and the overlap between visual art and literature allows the "minigallery" for art projects to function as a way to share excitement about books. Displays of poetry anthologies that children write or collect are another example of a way to show off growth and make an event out of an assignment completion (e.g., have an opening for each new gallery display, with appetizers, beverages—the works!).

Class Library of Books Children Write. It is not unreasonable to expect all children to write and bind many books in a school year. These can be class collaborative books, co-authored books, and single-author

works. The project nature of writing and book-making motivates students and is a *concrete progress indicator.* Books can be pocketed and placed in a special class library. Autographing parties can mark the "publication" of each new book.

Portfolios. Portfolios of student writing have become a staple in elementary and middle schools. In addition to writing samples, students can show literary growth through logs of books read, charts that show the distribution of reading across genres, and lists of favorites (characters, words, books, authors). Literature log entries and other written responses to literature can be included to document growth toward specific goals and objectives (see Post It Page 3–2 for reading and writing goals). A way to make portfolios meaningful and manageable progress exhibitions is to organize the collecting with items connected to goals attached to the front of the portfolio.

Individual Conferences. Key assessment information is gathered during times when students "show they know" in a one-on-one setting. It is ideal to have at least a 5-minute conference weekly with each student to review the portfolio, discuss progress, and set goals (e.g., plan book responses or review a list of books each child wants to read). Conference time can be used to discuss books and listen to a child orally read to check fluency progress. It is helpful to keep a conference notebook, with a page for each child, to note goals and progress made toward each goal.

Principle 10: SPECIALISTS in Literature Are Important and Necessary

Many teachers and librarians are specialists who can work collaboratively to enrich literature integration. A good librarian can help find excellent trade books for a social studies unit or a genre study. Our local library offers a phone-order service; call up with your unit request and they'll pull out 30 books for you to pick up and keep a month. To find book specialists, use the idea of creating a directory, using computer technology to survey and list interests and talents. There are poets, novelists, authorities on genre, and artists among the faculty and staff of most schools.

Children's Authors and Artists. Today the writers and illustrators of children's literature are celebrities who travel to schools for residencies and draw admiring audiences at conferences. An author or artist visit is an exciting occasion, but, as with any art event, planning is critical. Here are tips for planning to work with children's book writers and artists through an in-school residency.

- Plan early, even a year in advance. Most authors and artists make school visits, but not all. Contact the publisher to make arrangements with an appearance coordinator.
- Plan a budget to cover the author's honorarium, travel, food, and so forth. (Many charge at least $500 a day plus expenses of traveling, eating, and staying overnight.)
- Phone interviews aren't usually free. Generally, $50–$75 for a half-hour is expected, and you need a speaker phone for the whole class to benefit.
- Decisions have to be made about the agenda for the day, what you want the author to do, how many presentations, how to handle autographs, and ordering books in advance.
- Request publicity materials from the publisher (e.g., biographies in quantity, black and white pictures, book lists, posters, bookmarks, and jackets).
- Prepare the students: Do an author–artist study, read lots of books, see videos and listen to tapes, respond to books through LADDM (literature, art, drama, dance, and music) and make lists of questions to ask the author.
- Have definite curricular objectives for the visit to get the most out of it. Expect students to get both enjoyment and information from the residency.
- Follow up visits with "what did you learn" activities and thank-you notes from students.

◆ CONCLUSION

Social, religious, and economic forces continue to influence human history and the evolution of children's books. The definition of childhood will no doubt change in the next era, with a distinct effect on literature for children. It is already apparent that children are expected to be independent earlier and, some say, are hurried into adolescence. With many over-scheduled and overstressed, we must ask questions about the roles literature can play in the lives of youth and how books, even e-books, can remain viable in our media-saturated world. How *can* entertainment and enjoyment be balanced with information and instruction as we integrate children's literature throughout the curriculum? Multicultural and feminist concerns about contemporary literature exist, but progress can be monitored on the websites of book publishers. Teachers will need to increase connections between student interests and books if we are to influence reading habits. Perhaps the nature and concerns of childhood will change so radically that some books will not be relevant. We need to consider this possibility in our integration efforts. We must also guard against potential abuses of literature, as we implement research on its power to motivate children to read, write, and learn in curricular areas. Literature needs to be primarily regarded for its esthetic nature, and not simply as a tool to achieve literacy. Finally, children will undoubtedly continue to cull from the book supply the literature that gives them information and enjoyment, just as they have for centuries. Informed adults can help them to not miss enduring classics whose artistry allows reflection on what it means to be human.

◆ TEACHER RESOURCES FOR INTEGRATING LITERATURE

Also see Bibliography of Recommended Reading and Viewing in the appendix.

Internet Site (see the appendix for additional addresses)

The Children's Literature Web Guide (bibliographies of banned books, "must reads," and more) *www.acs.ucalgary.ca/~dkbrown*

Audio Visual Sources for Children's Literature and Authors

Booklist (published by the American Library Association) reviews audio visuals (AVs) in each issue.

Elementary School Library Collection: A Guide to Books and Other Media (1978). Newark, NJ: Bro-dart.

American School Publishers, Box 408, Highstown, NJ 08520

Pied Piper, P.O. Box 320, Verdugo City, CA 91046

Houghton Mifflin, 2 Park Street, Boston, MA 02108

Weston Woods, Weston, CT 06883

Journals (Research, Articles, Reviews of Books)

Bookbird (International Board on Books for Young People)

Booklist (American Library Association)

Books Links (American Library Association)

Bulletin of the Center for Children's Books (University of Illinois Press)

Children's Book Review Index (Gale Research)

Children's Literature in Education (APS Publications)

Horn Book Magazine (Horn Book, Inc.)

Language Arts (National Council of the Teachers of English)

The New Advocate (Christopher–Gordon Publishers)

Reading Teacher (International Reading Association)

School Library Journal (Bowker)

◆ REFERENCES

Books

Anderson, R. C., Hiesert, E., Scott, J., & Wilkinson, I. (1985). *Becoming a nation of readers: The report of the Commission on Reading*. Washington, DC: National Institute of Education.

Barr, R., Kamil, M., & Mosenthal, P. (Eds.), (1996). *Handbook of reading research*. Vol. 2. Mahwah, NJ: Erlbaum.

The bookfinder: A guide to children's literature. Vol. 1. (1994). Circle Pines, MN: American Guidance.

Campbell, J. (1996). *Hero with a thousand faces*. New York: MJF Books.

Cornett, C. (2001). *Learning through laughter: Again*. Bloomington, IN: Phi Delta Kappa.

Cornett, C., & Cornett, C. (1980). *Bibliotherapy: The right book at the right time*. Bloomington, IN: Phi Delta Kappa.

Cullinan, B. (1989). *Literature and the child* (2nd ed.). New York: Harcourt Brace Jovanovich.

Fader, D., & McNeil, E. (1976). *The new hooked on books*. New York: Berkley.

Faltis, C., Hudelson, S., & Hudelson, S. (1997). *Bilingual education in elementary and secondary school communities: Toward understanding and caring*. New York: Allyn & Bacon.

Glazer, J. (1997). *Introduction to children's literature* (2nd ed.). Upper Saddle River, NJ: Prentice Hall.

Huck, C., Hepler, S., & Hickman, J. (2001). *Children's literature in the elementary school* (4th ed.). Dubuque, IA: McGraw-Hill.

Lehr, S. S. (1991). *The child's developing sense of theme: Responses to literature*. New York: Teachers College Press.

Lima, C. (2001). *A to zoo: Subject access to children's picture books*. Westport, CT: Bowker-Greenwood.

Macon, J. (1991). *Responses to literature*. Newark, DE: International Reading Association.

Norton, D. (1995). *Through the eyes of a child: An introduction to children's literature* (4th ed.). Upper Saddle River, NJ: Prentice Hall.

Reutzel, D., & Cooter, R. (1992). *Teaching children to read: From basals to books*. Upper Saddle River, NJ: Merrill/Prentice Hall.

Russell, D. (1994). *Literature for children: A short introduction* (2nd ed.). New York: Longman.

Sabine, G., & Sabine, P. (1983). *Books that made the difference: What people told us*. Hamden, CT: Library Professional Publications.

Starko, A. (1995). *Creativity in the classroom: Schools of curious delight*. White Plains, NY: Longman.

Stauffer, R. (1969). *Directing reading maturity as a cognitive process*. New York: Harper & Row.

Sutherland, Z., & Arbuthnot, M. (1986). *Children and books*. Glenview, IL: Scott Foresman.

Tompkins, G., & McGee, L. (1993). *Teaching reading with literature: Case studies to action plans*. New York: Merrill.

Articles

Allen, J., Michalove, B., & Shockley, B. (1991, March). I'm really worried about Joseph: reducing the risks of literacy learning. *Reading Teacher, 44,* 458–472.

Anderson, R. C., et al (1986). Interestingness of children's reading materials. In R. Snow & M. Farr (Eds.), *Aptitude, learning and instruction*. Hillsdale, NJ: Erlbaum.

Barone, D., & Lovell, J. (1990). Michael and the show-and-tell magician: A journey through literature to self. *Language Arts, 67,* 134–143.

Bierhorst, J. (1976). *The red swan: Myths & tales of the American Indian*. New York: Farrar, Straus & Giroux.

Bishop, R. (1992). Multicultural literature for children: Making informed choices. In V. Harris (Ed.), *Teaching multicultural literature in grades K–8*. Norwood, MA: Christopher-Gordon.

Chomsky, C. (1972). Stages in language development and reading exposure. *Harvard Educational Review, 42,* 1–33.

Cohen, D. (1968). The effect of literature on vocabulary and reading achievement. *Elementary English, 45,* 209–213, 217.

Cornett, C. (1997, March). Beyond plot retelling. *Reading Teacher,* pp. 527–528.

D'Alessandro, M. (1990). Accommodating emotionally handicapped children through a literature-based reading program. *Reading Teacher, 44,* 288–293.

Dressel, J. H. (1990). The effects of listening to and discussing different qualities of children's literature on the narrative writing of fifth graders. *Research in the Teaching of English, 24,* 397–414.

Eeds, M., & Wells, D. (1989). Grand conversations: An exploration of meaning construction in literature study groups. *Research in the Teaching of English, 23,* 4–29.

Eldredge, J. L., & Butterfield, D. (1986). Alternatives to traditional reading instruction. *Reading Teacher, 40,* 32–37.

Fisher, C. J., & Natarella, M. A. (1979). *Poetry preferences of primary, first, second, and third graders: Studies in language education*. Unpublished doctoral dissertation, University of Georgia, Athens.

Five, C. (1986). Fifth graders respond to a changed reading program. *Harvard Educational Review, 56,* 395–405.

Frye, N. (1957). Theory of symbol. In *Anatomy of criticism*. Princeton, NJ: Princeton University Press.

Gee, J. P. (1989). Commonalities and differences in narrative construction. *Discourse Process, 12,* 287–307.

Hansen-Krening, N. (1992). Authors of color: A multicultural perspective. *Journal of Reading, 26*(2), 124–129.

Hepler, S. (1982). *Patterns of response to literature: A one-year study of a fifth and sixth grade classroom*. Unpublished doctoral dissertation, The Ohio State University, Columbus.

Holdaway, D. (1982). Shared book experience: Teaching reading using favorite books. *Theory into Practice, 21,* 293–300.

Kutiper, K., & Wilson, P. (1993). Updating poetry preferences: A look at the poetry children really like. *Reading Teacher, 47*(1), 28–35.

Kutiper, K. S. (1985). *A survey of the adolescent poetry preferences of seventh, eighth, and ninth graders*. Unpublished doctoral dissertation, University of Houston, Houston.

Levstik, L. (1986). The relationship between historical response and narrative in a sixth-grade classroom. *Theory and Research in Social Education, 14,* 1–15.

Lewis, C. S. (1980). On three ways of writing for children. In S. Eghoff et al. (Eds.), *Only connect*. New York: Oxford University Press.

Ogle, D. (1989). The know, want to know, learn strategy. In K. Muth (Ed.), *Children's comprehension of text: Research into practice*. Newark, DE: International Reading Association.

Ohlhausen, M. M., & Jepsen, M. (1992). Lessons from Goldilocks: Somebody's been choosing my books but I can make my own choices now! *New Advocate, 5,* 31–46.

Pate, G. (1988). Research on reducing prejudice. *Social Education, 52*(4), 287–291.

Pinnell, G. (1986). *Reading recovery in Ohio, 1985–86: Final report*. Technical report. Columbus: The Ohio State University.

Purcell-Gates, V. (1988). Lexical and syntactic knowledge of written narrative held by well-read-to kindergartners and second graders. *Research in the Teaching of English, 22,* 128–160.

Purcell-Gates, V. (1991). On the outside looking in: A study of remedial readers' meaning-making while reading literature, *Journal of Reading Behavior, 23,* 235–253.

Rosenblatt, L. (1985). Viewpoints: Transaction versus interaction—a terminological rescue operation. *Research in the Teaching of English, 19,* 98–107.

Roser, N. L., Hofman, J. V., & Farest, C. (1990). Language, literature, and at-risk children. *Reading Teacher, 43,* 554–559.

Schmidt, B. (1991). Story map. In J. Macon (Ed.), *Responses to literature*. Newark, DE: International Reading Association.

Sostarich, J. (1974). *A study of the reading behavior of sixth graders: Comparisons of active and other readers*. Unpublished doctoral dissertation, The Ohio State University, Columbus.

Terry, C. A. (1972). *A national study of children's poetry preferences in the fourth, fifth, and sixth grades*. Unpublished doctoral dissertation, The Ohio State University, Columbus.

Tunnell, M. O., & Jacobs, J. S. (1989). Using "real" books: Research findings on literature-based reading instruction. *Reading Teacher, 42,* 470–477.

Children's Literature

Adoff, A. (1977). *Tornado*. New York: Delacorte.

Babbitt, N. (1986). *Tuck everlasting*. New York: Farrar, Straus & Giroux.

Babbitt, N. (1987). *Tuck everlasting*. Santa Barbara, CA: ABC-Clio.

Barrett, J. (1989). *Animals should definitely not wear clothing*. New York: Aladdin.

Bishop, C. (1989). *Five Chinese brothers*. New York: Coward-McCann.

Brett, J. (1989). *The Mitten: A Ukrainian folktale*. New York: Putnam.

Bruchac, J., & London, J. (1992). *Thirteen moons on a turtle's back*. New York: Philomel.

Bryan, A. (1987). *Beat the story drum, pum-pum*. New York: Aladdin.

Cameron, P. (1961). *I can't said the ant*. New York: Putnam.

Charlip, R. (1984). *Fortunately*. New York: Simon & Schuster.

Christopher, J. (1967). *The white mountains*. New York: Simon & Schuster.

Conger, D. (1987). *Many lands, many stories: Asian folktales for children*. Rutland, VT: Charles E. Tuttle.

Crane, S. (2002). *The red badge of courage*. New York: Atheneum.

Creech, S. (1994). *Walk Two Moons*. New York: HarperCollins.

Dahl, R. (1983). *James and the giant peach*. New York: Puffin.

Dyson, J. (1991). *Westward with Columbus*. New York: Scholastic.

Elting, M. (1980). *Q is for duck*. New York: Houghton Mifflin.

Fleischman, P. (1992). *Joyful noise: Poems for two voices*. New York: HarperCollins.

Freedman, R. (1987). *Lincoln: A photobiography*. New York: Clarion.

Gag, W. (1928). *Millions of cats*. New York: Coward-McCann.

Gwynne, F. (1970). *The king who rained*. New York: Trumpet Club.

Hesse, K. (1998). *Out of the dust*. New York: Classic Press.

Highwater, J. (1977). *Anpao: An American Indian odyssey*. Philadelphia: Lippincott.

Highwater, J., & Scholder, F. (1992). *Anpao: An American Indian odyssey*. New York: HarperCollins.

Hoban, T. (1971). *Look again*. New York: Macmillan.

Hunt, I. (1994). *Across five Aprils*. New York: Silver Burdett.

Jukes, M. (1987). *Like Jake and me*. New York: Knopf.

Keller, C. (1985). *Swine lake: Music and dance riddles*. Upper Saddle River, NJ: Prentice Hall.

L'Engle, M. (1962). *A wrinkle in time*. New York: Farrar, Straus & Giroux.

Lobel, A. (1979). *Frog and Toad together*. New York: Harper & Row.

Lowe, S. (1992). *The log of Christopher Columbus*. New York: Philomel.

Lowry, L. (1993). *The giver*. New York: Bantam Doubleday Dell.

Maclachlan, P. (1985). *Sarah, plain and tall*. Santa Barbara, CA: ABC-Clio.

Marshall, J. (1973). *George and Martha*. Boston: Houghton Mifflin.

Martin, B. (1992). *Brown bear, brown bear, what do you see?* New York. Henry Holt.

McMillan, B. (1982). *Puniddles*. Boston: Houghton Mifflin.

Munsch, R. (1980). *The paper bag princess*. Toronto: Annick.

Ness, E. (1971). *Sam, Bangs & moonshine*. New York: Henry Holt.

Norton, M. (1953). *The borrowers*. New York: Harcourt Brace.

O'Neill, M. (1989). *Hailstones and halibut bones*. New York: Doubleday.

Paterson, K. (1977). *Bridge to Terabithia*. New York: Crowell.

Paterson, K. (1980). *Jacob have I loved*. New York: Crowell.

Paulsen, G. (1999). *Hatchet*. New York: Aladdin.

Rathman, P. (1995). *Officer Buckles and Gloria*. New York: Putnam.

Rockwell, T. (1973). *How to eat fried worms*. New York: Franklin Watts.

Schwartz, A. (1974). *A twister of twists and a tangler of tongues*. London: Deutsch.

Scieszka, J. (1991). *The true story of the 3 little pigs*. New York: Viking.

Sendak, M. (1963). *Where the wild things are*. New York: Harper & Row.

Steptoe, J. (1987). *Mufaro's beautiful daughter: An African Tale*. New York: Lothrop, Lee and Shepard.

Terban, M. (1985). *Too hot to hoot*. New York: Clarion.

Tolstoy, L. (2002). *The enormous turnip*. San Diego: Harcourt Brace Jovanvich.

Van Allsburg, C. (1981). *Jumanji*. Boston: Houghton Mifflin.

Verne, J. (1997). *20,000 Leagues under the sea*. New York: Random House.

Ward, L. (1973). *The silver pony*. Boston: Houghton Mifflin.

White, E. B. (1952). *Charlotte's web*. New York: Harper & Row.

Wilder, L. E. (1971). *Little house in the big woods*. New York: Harper Trophy.

Willard, N. (1981). *A visit to William Blake's Inn: Poems for innocent and experienced travelers.* San Diego: Harcourt Brace.

Wisniewski, D. (1997). *The Golem.* New York: Clarion.

Wood, A. (1984). *The napping house.* New York: Harcourt Brace.

Wright, B. R. (1994). *The ghost comes calling.* New York: Scholastic Trade.

Yep, L. (1992). *The rainbow people.* HarperCollins.

Yolen, J. (1987). *Owl moon.* New York: Philomel.

Yolen, J. (1992). *Encounter.* San Diego: Harcourt Brace.

Yolen, J. (1997). *Sleeping ugly.* New York: Coward, McCann & Geoghegan.

4

Literature Seed Strategies

The students rewrote a section of James and the Giant Peach *in script form. We broke into 4 groups and each covered a certain set of pages so we could combine to make one play. As they were writing, they asked me if they could make it funny. I told them, "sure!" The results were the following lines: James: We need plenty of strong string. I don't think we can do it. Grasshopper: James, we have plenty of string. We can wake the silkworm up and made him spin. Spider: What about me, what am I chopped liver? Ladybug: (giggling) No, chopped spider.*

Ms. Smith, 5th grade, Lady's Island Elementary School

INTRODUCTION

This chapter includes specific ways to integrate literature throughout the curriculum. The strategies are intentionally in seed or kernel form. Most are adaptable for elementary and middle levels. Use the ideas to prompt thinking, not as recipes. The ideas should be considered flexible, and adaptations are encouraged as teachers use literature to reach curricular goals and do unit planning. The strategy seeds are organized into four sections, but many fit in more than one section. The sections on *energizers, elements,* and *genre traits* do *not* represent an integrated focus but are provided to ready students for creative problem solving and subsequent participation in integrated lessons. Note: *Meaningful* integration of the arts, with each other and other curricular areas, won't happen unless lessons have at least one focus on an art form and one in another curricular area. For ideas on integrating literature with the four other arts areas, see Chapter 13.

I. ENERGIZERS AND WARM-UPS

Energizers and warm-ups are used to get students ready for creative thinking. There are *energizers* and *warm-ups* in each strategy seeds chapter that can be adapted to literature.

Creative Problem-Solving Process. See Post It Page 1–6 for ideas adaptable to literature. For example, SCAMPER a character by telling students to close their eyes; then take them on a fantasy journey:

> Think about Wilbur. Imagine him turning into a little dog looking up at Charlotte's web. Now change him into a big dog. Now think of Wilbur as a pig with a dog body. Make this new Wilbur really small. He is trying to talk to Charlotte, but he gets littler and littler. Oops,

now he's growing, growing, growing. He is getting so big. Look at Charlotte's expression when she sees this giant Wilbur. Now he shrinks back and Charlotte starts to grow. She's bigger than Wilbur now.

Analogy Go Round. Base this activity on a book or story students all know (adapted from Starko, 1995). The idea is to stretch and twist thinking, so it often turns out funny. Sit in a circle and set up a *frame* for each to fill in when it comes to them. Oral frames to use are:

◆ *Opposites:* Pick opposite characters and force together: *Wilbur is like Templeton because____.* This can be done with any literary element: *The farm is like the fair because____.*

◆ *Random combinations:* Combine a random idea with a literary element: *Wilbur is like a pencil because____.* Plug in different ideas in the first blank and students give reasons in the second.

◆ *Personal analogies: I am like Charlotte because____.* (Students fill in a character and the blank or all use the same character.)

Minister's Cat. This is a memory and category game done to a rhythm, with all joining on "The minister's cat is a (fill in) cat." The play proceeds around the circle, with each person plugging in an adjective, in alphabetical order: "The minister's cat is an active cat. The minister's cat is a brave cat. . . ."

Who Stole the Cookies from the Cookie Jar? (Language Play). Leader begins by using a child's name and says, "John stole the cookies from the cookie jar," and then the child says, "Not I," and the group chants, "Then who?" and the child chooses another child and says, "Mary stole the cookies . . . .," and so on.

Prereading and Writing. Here are three *before* reading or writing energizers:

◆ *Webbing* is brainstorming on paper. Put a topic in the center and think of ideas connected to it. Draw out legs from the center and write ideas on them. Try to fill up the paper. Next, group ideas together by circling or coding like ideas with a symbol (diamond, heart, etc.). For example, to get ready to read *Jack in the Beanstalk*, web the word *greed. Variations:* Any literary element, genre, topic, person, and the like can be webbed.

◆ *Chaining* is like webbing but simpler in some ways. Decide on how many words to chain. Choose a topic and connect the first word to the topic, the second to the first, and so on. As an

Play: James and the Giant Peach

additional challenge, make the last word connect to the one before it *and* to the topic. For example, Chain 7 for *greed:* (1) hog, (2) fat, (3) grease, (4) slime, (5) green, (6) puce, and (7) ugly. (*Note:* This sounds like poetry when read aloud and can be used as a poem pattern.)

◆ *Cubing* (Neeld, 1986) is based on the idea that a cube has six sides and is a way to explore a topic from six angles. For example, Cube *greed:* (1) describe it, (2) analyze it (what are its parts), (3) associate feelings with it, (4) apply it (what can it be used for), (5) argue for it (pro), and (6) argue against it (con). *Variation:* Give a time limit (e.g., one minute on each side).

Predict–Prove. This is a teacher-directed strategy to guide prediction *before* reading and then confirm or reject predictions during and *after* reading (adapted from Stauffer, 1969). Predict–prove emphasizes active learning during the entire process of reading. The basic steps are:

1. Show the book cover, read aloud the title, and show a few pictures (if illustrated).

2. Ask students to predict in three areas: (1) Who will it be about? (2) When and where? (3) What problems might be in the story?

3. Record predictions on a chart or overhead, or in individual journals.

4. Students read or teacher reads to students.

5. Build in think stops for students to discuss predictions. Confirm or reject and tell why. Celebrate rejections as much as confirmations.

Mystery Bag. Students try to figure a connection as the teacher reveals one object at a time from a sack or box. For example, for *Little Red Riding Hood:* a stick (forest), red handkerchief, a Lone-Ranger-type half-mask, and a basket. Take out the easiest last, to draw out suspense. Ask students to not "call out" so that all have a chance to see everything before guesses are accepted. *Variation:* Students can make collections and present a mystery bag as a book response.

Story or Book Riddles. Show students how to write and share riddles about characters. Simple ones just give three clues, from broad to specific, but even first graders can learn to do a bit of punning by following these steps: (1) Choose a subject such as "cats"; (2) take a book title or character and brainstorm all the words that sound like the syllables in it: Wil-bur = Chill, hill, still, fill, jill, sill; bur = stir, were, her, purr, sir; (3) combine syllables to fit with the subject: Wil-purr; (4) make up a question: What did the *Charlotte's Web* fan name his cat? (Wilpurr)

Write Right Away (Quickwrites). Students write freely for a few minutes on a topic to either activate prior knowledge or pull together information (e.g., after a discussion). Often a time limit is set of about 5 minutes.

CAP Prediction. This is a prereading warm-up. List words from an upcoming book that relate to *characters, actions,* and *problems* (CAP). Have students sort the words into these categories by predicting how they would connect with C, A, or P. Word cards can be used or words can be coded with a letter.

Word Pairs. This can be used for prereading or as an energizer for creative thinking for writing. Select an even number of important words from an upcoming book or poem. Ask students to work in groups to pair the words any way that makes sense, as long as they have a good reason. Ask each group to explain their reasons and celebrate novel connections. For example, choose eight words that could make four pairs.

II. Teaching about Literature: Elements and Genre Characteristics

Venn Diagrams. Venn diagrams are used to compare and contrast different aspects of two books or stories: literary or art elements, genre traits, versions of the same story, or books by the same author. Two overlapping circles are drawn. Each separate circle is for the individual characteristics of the two things being compared. The overlap area is for commonalities.

Big Bingo (Literary Elements Review and Application). Use bulletin board paper cut into 4-foot lengths and folded in half three or four times to divide it into a giant bingo board. Divide students into learning circles of four to five and give a few minutes to write elements with markers on their blank giant bingo card (post elements to copy). Then play. Give a definition and have students cover the elements with index cards. When a learning circle wins, they read back the labels, paraphrase a definition, and give a book example.

Character: Web, Wheel, and Graph

◆ *Web.* A character's name is written in the center. Draw legs on the web to represent aspects of the character and label them: how the character talks, thoughts of the character, actions, appearance, what other's think or say about the character. (Other categories: the character's feelings, worries, hobbies, talents, skills, personality, etc.). *Adaptations:* For biographies, change the web legs to include fitting categories: obstacles faced, significant achievements, special life events.

◆ *Graph.* Make a graph with boxes at least one inch square and with enough spaces on the X and Y axes to write the names of the important characters in a story. List the characters' names twice: on the left side in a vertical column and then at the top across the row of squares. Where the two names intersect, students then write in how the characters interacted or related to one another in a story.

◆ *Sociowheel.* Put the name of a character in the center or hub of a wheel drawn on paper. Write the names of three or four other characters around the rim. Draw a spoke to connect the hub character to each of the rim characters. On each spoke, write how the hub character is connected or related to each rim character to show the relationships. *Suggestion:* Do on the overhead as a whole class or on a large chart. *Variation:* Students need two circles: make one about as big as a coffee can lid and the other an inch in diameter bigger. Fasten the circles in the center with a brad. Students then write the names of important story characters around the edges of both circles. When wheels are ready, students can line up character names and discuss the ways the characters relate. Turn the wheel and a new character pair lines up and discussion proceeds. *Adaptation:* Make one large character wheel for the class. Laminate it so that you can change the character names. Wheels can be made with overhead transparencies.

Character Inventories. Students fill out a personality inventory on a character. Possible items: Favorite foods? Likes? Dislikes? Favorite books? Films? Hobbies? Encourage students to think beyond literal information in the book to conjecture logically. Variation: Describe clothes, hands, eyes, body.

Character Poems.   Use any of the *Poem Patterns* on Post It Page 3–5 to write poems about characters.

Somebody–Wanted–But–So (Character, Motive, Problem, Plot).   Make a chart with the four words across the top (Macon, 1991). Students draw or write about the main character (*somebody*) in the first section, what the character *wanted* (second section), character's roadblocks or conflict *(but)*, and the story resolution in the *(so)*.

Plot Lines.   The linear mountainlike, circular, and episodic patterns of events in a story can be shown by *drawing the plot line* and writing events along it (Tomlinson & Brown, 1996). Roadblocks or obstacles are indicated by bumps in the line. For example:

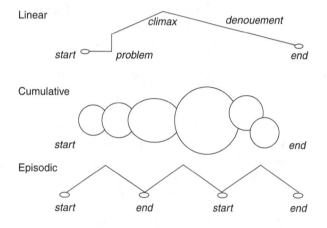

Episode Plot Cards.   Key events are brainstormed and each written individually on cards. Cards are then placed in order. *Variation:* Use a pocket chart or clothesline to order the ideas as a group.

Home–Adventure–Home Map.   This plot structure is also called the BME: beginning–middle–end (Tompkins & McGee, 1993) and the I–D–C (introduction, development, conclusion). It involves categorizing a story's plot into three main parts. This can be used as an *after* reading strategy or *during* reading to help structure comprehension. The objective is to learn how a *problem* sets the plot in motion in the beginning, the middle section is a series of events (the "adventure") that deals with the problem, and in the end events happen to resolve the problem. Students can map out original stories by dividing their papers into home–adventure–home parts and planning the events that will happen in each section they write. This can be used as a planning device for drama responses and to prepare for student-led discussions by asking students to star items they wish to talk about on their maps.

Circle or Pie Story Maps.   Diagram story events or the plot of the home–adventure–home pattern (stories begin and end in the same location) on a large circle divided into pie-shaped sections. At the top of the circle, a house can be drawn to show how stories often begin in a safe, homey place. Then characters have an adventure and return home again. The events of the story are written or drawn, one at a time, while moving clockwise around the circle. The pie slice below the house is where students begin to put down important events. When the circle is complete, the story ends in the same place it began. *Adaptations:* Make a large circle pie map on the board or on chart paper and do this together as a class. Use the completed maps to do retelling of stories.

Ladders to Accomplishment.   Ladders are especially good for biography and similar to a lifeline (Tompkins & McGee, 1993). Students keep track of important events in a character's life using the rungs. Events on each rung lead up to a climatic event. Earlier events (chronologically) are closer to the bottom of the ladder. The final and climactic event is the top rung.

Setting Sense Web.   The setting of a story is put in the center. Five legs extend with the labels *see, taste, smell, hear,* and *touch*. Students record what can be known about the setting using each of these senses. For example, *What would you see, hear, taste, smell, touch in the setting of* Peter Rabbit?

Get in Line (Themes).   After themes have been derived from a story (see questions in Post It Page 3–3), they are written out on the board or overhead and numbered. Students stand on a "strongly agree to strongly disagree" imaginary line to show their feelings about the theme. Teacher calls a theme number and students line up. Students can be interviewed along the line to get reasons for where they stand.

Genre Traits
◆   *Chart:* Write several story titles, from the same genre, in boxes across the top of a page. The

---

TAKE ACTION 1

ADAPT STRATEGIES

Choose a strategy seed from *Energizers* or *Literary Elements and Genre Traits* and adapt it for math, science, reading and language arts, or social studies. See examples in the next section.

characteristics of the genre are then written along the left-hand side. Examples from each book are then sought to go with each trait.

◆ *Web:* The title of a story is written in the center. Each of the legs extending from this center contains one of the traits of the genre to which the story belongs. For example, for a folktale (1) opening or closing language convention, such as "Once upon a time," (2) setting vague—could be anywhere, (3) plot is a simple order of chronological events, (4) flat or one-dimensional characters (good or evil, foolish or genius), (5) problem revolves around a journey from home to perform tasks and confrontation with obstacles, and (6) miraculous events, happy ending. *Variation:* Do as a whole class.

Bio Webs (for Biographies). A person's name is placed in the center and legs are drawn to important events in that person's life. Legs can be webbed off the main events to go into more detail. *Extension:* Students can use the webs to write biographical summaries.

III. CONNECTING LITERATURE TO OTHER CURRICULAR AREAS
Book Report Alternatives

To begin this section, Post It Page 4–1 lists book report alternatives.

Science Focus

◆ Natural world, systems of the body, seasons, weather, plants, animals, the environment, machines, electricity, magnets, space, gravity, and states of matter

◆ Finding out how and why things happen in the world through careful observation, hypothesis making, and prediction

Informational Books. Informational books allow students to make discoveries about the world and become involved in the scientific method. See Post It Page 3–8 for source books that list books by topic. Here are examples of books to integrate into science units:

Physical Sciences

Gallant, R. (1989). *Before the sun dies: The story of evolution.* Macmillan.

Gibbons, G. (1987). *Weather forecasting.* Four Winds.

Hartman, G. (1991). *As the crow flies: A first book of maps.* Bradbury.

Krementz, J. (1987). *A visit to Washington, D.C.* Scholastic.

Lauber, P. (1990). *Seeing the earth from space.* Orchard.

Lowry, L. (1991). *Earth day.* Carolrhoda.

Simon, S. (1979). *Danger from below: Earthquakes—past, present, and future.* Four Winds.

Waters, J. (1994). *Deep sea vents: Living worlds without sun.* Cobblehill.

Biology

Aliki. (1985). *Dinosaurs are different.* Harper & Row.

Cole, J. (1989). *The magic school bus inside the human body.* Scholastic.

Cole, J. (1991). *My puppy is born.* Morrow.

George, J. C. (1995). *Animals who have won our heart.* HarperCollins.

Heller, R. (1984). *Plants that never bloom.* Grosset & Dunlap.

Melter, M. (1992). *The amazing potato.* HarperCollins.

Smith, R. (1990). *Sea otter rescue.* Cobblehill.

Squire, A. (1991). *Understanding man's best friend: Why dogs look and act the way they do.* Macmillan.

Genre Study Connections. Certain genres have particular importance in science. General informational books are important, but biographies of scientists and inventors are also key literature. For example, Fox's *Women Astronauts: Aboard the Shuttle* (1987) tells the stories of eight women, including Sally Ride. In addition, a science fiction genre study can focus on verifying which science is "real" in a book. Poetry can be found to go with both informational books and science units, for example, the informational book *Monarch Butterfly* (Gibbons, 1989) and the poem "Chrysalis Diary" (*Joyful Noise*, Fleischman, 1988) would both enhance an insect unit.

Reading Engagement: Informational Books. To increase engagement, provide students with generic prompts for noting ideas as they read an informational

LITERATURE RESPONSE OPTIONS (INSTEAD OF BOOK REPORTS)

Overview: Students decide on projects to show understanding of a book and further investigate interests in a book. Intrinsic motivation is emphasized through arts-based response options.

Poetry

Poem match: Find a poem that complements the book. Place a copy in the book.

Poem patterns: Write a cinquain, diamante, or clerihew about the story, a main point, or a character.

Poetry alive: Share a poem using a *poetry alive* strategy (Post It Page 4–4): choral, antiphonal, cumulative.

Write a poem: Create a poem about the book. (See Poem Patterns on Post It Page 3–5).

Writing and Speaking

Author study: Research the author and give a report about the person and why he or she writes.

Best friend: Write to your best friend, telling why you did or did not like a book.

Biography: Write a biography of one of the characters.

Book critic: Find a part in a realistic book that could not happen. Defend your choice.

Book dedications: Dedicate a book to a character. Tell why the character should read the book.

Book improvement: The author writes to you and wants to know how the book could be improved. Write back.

Book reviews: Present oral reviews to a younger class to "sell" the book.

Bring a character home: Explain how your home would be changed if a character lived there.

Business letter: Request information from a company or organization on a topic in the book.

Call an author: Plan the questions and use a conference call setup.

Cliffhanger: Read aloud a part and stop at a suspenseful point. Ask for predictions from others.

Connecting: Write or tell about how the book connected to you or your life.

Copycat story: Write your own story using the same title, theme, or pattern of the book.

Crossword puzzles: Use clues about setting, characters, and plot.

Current events: Choose a situation in the news. Give a character's probable reaction to the event.

Decision making: Take a familiar story. At midpoint, stop and speculate on what would have happened if a character had made a different decision.

Demonstration: Show something you learned and tell about why it is important.

Diary: Write a few pages from a diary as if you were one of the characters.

Dictionary: Make a dictionary of special words in the books and their definitions.

Episode cards: Put all the plot events on individual cards and arrange them in order to tell the story.

Episode or sequel: What happened next after the story ended?

Exciting happening: Write or tell about the most exciting event.

Facts: Make a list of facts you learned from reading a nonfiction book.

Famous person: Write to a celebrity as if you are a character in a book.

Fan mail: Write a letter of appreciation to an author. Ask questions and share thoughts.

Favorite part: Write or tell about your favorite part.

Friendship: Tell why you would or would not like to have a character for a friend.

Grocery list or menu: Create a menu of what the characters might eat.

Heinz 57: Describe the main character in 57 words.

Humorous event: Write or tell about the funniest part.

Important part: Write or tell about the most important part of the book. Use a sentence frame.

Interesting character: Describe a character, making him or her come alive.

Interesting event: Write or tell about the most interesting event.

Interview: Interview someone who is knowledgeable about a topic related to the book.

Interview: Write an interview between a character and the author or between you and the author.

Letter: Write a letter about the book to a friend.

Library recommendation: Write a recommendation to the librarian to buy a book you have read.

Lifeline: Put all the events in a character's life along a line.

Literature logs: Use a spiral notebook to make notes as you read: special words, ideas, feelings.

Mob book: Find a group to write a "book about the book" together.

Movie: Write or tell why a book could (or could not) become a movie.

Newspaper: Write news stories, advertisements based on characters and episodes from the book.

Next-door neighbor: Pick a character. Tell why you would or would not like to have her as a neighbor.

Object talk: Give an oral summary of the story. Use a box of objects as props.

Past to present: Bring a book character from past to present. How would the character act today?

President's address: The president wants to know what you have read that all Americans should read.

Principal: Would you recommend this book to your school principal? Why or why not?

Puzzling: Write or tell about the most confusing or puzzling event in the story.

Research a topic: Pick an interesting idea in the book. Present the information in a report.

Scrapbook about the book. Collect and label all items. Write a short description of the most interesting.

Sentence list: Make a list of the five most interesting or important sentences in the book.

Simplify: Rewrite an incident for a younger reader.

Summarization: Get the plot down to one paragraph.

Telegram: Summarize the book in 15–50 words.

Time line: Make a time line of the events in the book.

Venn diagram: Compare this book to another. Diagram common literary or art elements.

Word hunt: Think of 10 words to describe the book. Explain why you chose them.

Word sharing: Make a list of unusual, difficult, or exciting words from the book.

Write: Write a letter to a favorite character.

Music and Dance

Dance moves: List movements in the story. Show them with different body parts: head, hand, fingers.

Dancing characters: List the kinds of dance the main character might like to learn and why.

Favorites list: Make a list of songs and music that the main character would like.

Make a mix: Collect music that goes with aspects of the book (special scenes, overall mood or theme).

Music mesh: List ways music connects to the book: songs, music, rhythm, melody, instruments, and so forth.

Rap: Write one about the book or read aloud a favorite part to a rap beat.

Slow motion: Demonstrate how a character moved at three points in the story. Show in slow motion.

Songwriting: Write a song with lyrics that represents the book, its characters, or the setting.

Tape recording: Tape part of the story for the class with appropriate musical background.

Three-part dance: Choreograph a shape–moves–shape dance about a feeling or main idea in the story.

Art

Book jacket: Create a book jacket for the book or story to advertise it. Place it on the book.

Bookmarks: Include book quotes and a blurb to advertise the book on a bookmark you make.

Bulletin board: Make a bulletin board about the book, showing the main characters, setting, and so forth.

Can do: Use a can or a cereal box to create book scenes. Fill with characters quotes or book objects.

Cartoon characters: Draw cartoons of the characters in important scenes.

Cartoon strips: Sequence the main points of the book with cartoons.

Clay model: Use clay to model a character, setting, or special object in the book.

Clothesline props: Make props and picture cards to pin up as you retell the story.

Collage: Use found objects, torn paper, and wallpaper to assemble a collage about the theme.

Cooking: Prepare and serve a related food from the book.

Diorama: Create a diorama that illustrates the setting of the book.

Flannel board pieces: Cut pieces and glue on sandpaper backs. Use to retell the story.

Greeting card: Create a greeting card using the theme, characters, or setting of your book.

Literary cartoons: Collect cartoons that use literary allusions found in books you have read.

Lost and found: Make up a lost or found ad for an object or character.

Map: Make a map of the country or imaginary land in the book.

Map or relief map: Create a map of the setting using a dough recipe.

Media and style: Experiment with the techniques in the book.

Mobile: Make a mobile from drawings of people or objects in the book. Organize by literary elements.

Model: Make a model of something in the story: house, log cabin, rocket, and the like.

Movie time: Make a hand-rolled movie of your book using shelf paper.

Mural: Create a mural about the book. Use charcoals, crayons, cut paper, or watercolors.

Paper dolls: Create paper dolls of the main characters.

Peep show: Make a peep box of an important scene or event.

Photography: Photograph people, settings, events, and the like that illustrate your book.

Photography: Take pictures related to the themes or places that could be settings in the book.

Postcard: Create a postcard that describes your book.

Poster ad: Create a poster that sells the book. Try cutting block letters or using calligraphy.

Puppets: See 10 types of puppets to make in Chapter 6.

Routes: Make a map showing routes taken in the story.

Scrapbook: Prepare a scrapbook illustrating the book.

Scroll: Create a scroll to unroll and show important things about the book.

Sculpture, diagram, or model: Make 3D art about an important idea in the book.

Seed, button, cut paper mosaic: Make a mosaic to illustrate a setting or event.

Sketch a sequence: Draw an action sequence. Make into a flip book to make characters move.

Soap carving: Make a soap carving of a character or important object in the book.

Stage: Use a box to design a miniature stage setting for a portion of the story.

Story map: Draw a map that illustrates the main events of the story.

Travelog: Create a travelog using pictures, postcards, magazine clips to show the settings.

Wordless book: Make a book about the story and use no words. Use any media or techniques.

Drama

Author: Become the author and tell why you wrote this story. Use a prop.

Author's prerogative: Tell how you would change the story if you wrote it.

Be the book: Pretend to be a book and tell what you hold within your pages. Advertise yourself.

Be the character: Imagine you are a character. Tell what you think of the author.

Book review: Read example book reviews and then write your own about the book and its art.

Book talk: Write or tell what the book would say about itself if it could talk.

Chalk talk: Give a chalk talk by drawing on the board as you tell the main story events.

Character interview: Write an interview between two characters in the book.

Charades: Develop a game of charades based on the characters in the book.

Commercial: Do a one-minute advertisement for a book.

Dinner date: Invite a character to dinner. Create a menu.

Doll clothes: Dress a doll as one of the book's characters.

Dress up: Create a character costume from the book and answer questions in character.

Flannel board: Make flannel board characters and tell the story (or part of it).

Minor character: Become a minor character and tell the story.

Movie producer: Be a movie producer. Evaluate the book as a possible film.

Movie version: Compare the movie or television version with the book. You could use a Venn diagram.

Panel discussion: Organize a pro and con panel and debate an issue. One person can be the author.

Pantomime: Do a slow-motion pantomime of a character or scene and ask the class to guess.

Persuasive speech: Persuade the audience why they should (or should not) read the book.

Pretend and write: Be a character and write to another character or keep a journal.

Puppets: Make a puppet or puppets of the characters. Set up dialog or retell the story.

Radio announcements: Broadcast an advertisement for the book. Use the morning announcements.

Readers' theater: Write a script and present the book.

Reporter: Be a TV reporter and report on the book. Choose an exciting part for "Live on the scene . . . ."

Sales talk: Make a sales talk. Pretend your audience is bookstore clerks. You want to push the book.

Skit: Pantomime or use dialog in a skit about an important event.

Stump the expert: Have classmates try to stump you with questions about the book.

Television show: Create one based on the book, for example, game show, news show.

Unpopular position: Choose a character and defend why his or her role in a story should be made different.

Literature

Biography imagination: Pretend you visited the person. Tell or write about your visit.

Character web: Web what the main character looks like, acts like, feels like, and says.

Comparison chart: Compare with another version or with the film version.

Critical reading: Evaluate the book using literary elements.

Experiment: Do a scientific experiment associated with an informational book about science.

Fairy tales: Read several fairy tales and list the common elements of the stories.

Fairy tales: Read several fairy tales and create your own tale using the common elements.

Folktales: Mix the characters of several familiar folktales and write the story that results.

Genre change: Make a case for how a certain book could be used in another genre. Write it.

Historical fiction: Find music that was popular during the same period as the book.

Mystery: Put an object from the story inside a box. Give clues to guess the book.

Plot diagram: Draw how the plot is organized in the book (linear, episodic, cumulative).

Plot graph: List the events and then graph them on a scale of good news to bad news events.

Point of view: Rewrite the story from the perspective of a different character.

Read another book: Same author, same illustrator, same theme, same genre, or with same character.

---

book. Brozo (1998) lists these types of questions: *What is:*

1. The most interesting or exciting word, phrase, sentence, or picture?

2. An idea, detail, issue, or concept you feel strongly about?

3. A feeling about this idea, detail, issue, or concept? Why?

4. A connection between your own experiences and the ideas, details, issues, and concepts?

5. A place in the book that made you think of something you have experienced, seen, or know about? Why?

Things to Write and Say.   See Post It Page 4–2. Any of the 75 writing forms can be used in science. For example, write a *letter* to a character about what you are learning in science.

Poem Patterns.   See Post It Page 3–5. These patterns can be used to write about science topics or processes. For example, write a five-sense poem about the circulatory system.

Five Ws and H Webs.   After reading an informational book or story, students web who, what, when, where, how, and why to summarize learning. Add details to answer the five Ws and H questions.

Social Studies Focus

- Relationships among human beings, occupations, transportation, communities, governments, customs, cultures, holidays, and use of natural resources

- History, geography (use of maps), civics (citizenship and government), or political science, economics, anthropology, and sociology

- Investigations into cultural diversity and global understanding

- Special questions: How did it used to be and why? Why is it like it is today? What can I do about it? Thinking processes: cause and effect, sequence, gather data, discover relationships, make judgments, draw conclusions, and problem solve about community issues, for example, economic issues such as school funding or values conflicts related to free speech

- Use of primary source material such as newspapers, art, music, diaries, letters, journals, books, and artifacts, rather than use of textbooks, and gathering data through interviews, surveys, and other investigatory strategies that historians and other social scientists use

In the long history of man, countless empires and nations have come and gone. Those which created no lasting works of art are reduced today to short footnotes in history's catalog. Art is a nation's most precious heritage, for it is in our works of art that we reveal to ourselves, and to others, the inner vision which guides us as a Nation. And where there is no vision, the people perish.

President Lyndon B. Johnson
at the signing ceremony for the
National Foundation on the
Arts and Humanities Act of 1965

Informational Books for Social Studies

There are now excellent informational books available on many topics in the social studies. Use Post It Page 3–8 to locate ones for units. Here is a sampling:

Social Studies—Related Informational Books

Fritz, J. (1987). *Shy! We're writing the Constitution.* Putnam.

Goon, R., & Goon, N. (1986). *Pompeii: Exploring a Roman ghost town.* Harper & Row.

THINGS TO WRITE AND SAY FROM A TO Z

Directions: Use this list of forms as a reference for responding to any work of art (literature, song, dance, drama) or to generate writing. Any can also be done "in character" as drama.

Acceptance speech	Fable	Paradox
Advertisement	Funny word list	Poem (see Post It Page 3–5)
Advice column (Dear Abby)	Greeting card	Postcard
Announcement	Haiku	Poster
Apology	Headline	Propaganda (e.g., card stacking,
Award presentation	Holler (see call or yell)	glittering generalities, etc.)
Brief biography	Horoscopes	Ransom note
Bumper sticker	Insult	Remedy
Call or holler	Introduction	Report
Campaign speech	Invitation	Résumé
Certificate	Irony	Slogan
Chant	Jingle	Stinky pinky or wordy gurdy
Cheer	Journal, log, or diary	Telegram
Cinquain	Jump-rope rhyme	Thank you note
Command	Letter (business or friendly)	Title (e.g., book, TV program)
Commercial	Lie	Tom Swifty
Complaint	Limerick	Tongue twister
Compliment	List (to-do, grocery, wishes, etc.)	Tribute
Contract	Love note	Triplet or tercet
Curse	Magic spell	Understatement
Definitions (of unusual words,	Marquee notice	Wanted poster
e.g., *tuffet*)	Menu	Warning
Diamante	Mixed metaphor	Weather forecast or report
Editorial	Nominating speech	Will
Encyclopedia entry	Note	Wish
Epilog	Obituary	Yell (see call or holler)
Excuse	Ode	

Green, R. (1992). *Women in American Indian society*. Schloss House.

Hamanaka, S. (1990). *The Journey: Japanese Americans, racism, and renewal*. Orchard Books.

Langford, M. (1994). *Quinceanero, a Latino's journey to womanhood*. Millbrook.

Macaulay, D. (1975). *Pyramid*. Houghton Mifflin.

Monroe, R. (1985). *The inside outside book of Washington, D.C.* Dodd, Mead.

Murphy, J. (1995). *A young patriot: The American revolution as experienced by one boy*. Clarion.

Provensen, A. (1990). *The buck stops here: The presidents of the United States*. Harper & Row.

Biography Samples

Aliki. (1988). *The many lives of Benjamin Franklin*. Simon & Schuster.

Bray, R. (1995). *Martin Luther King*. Greenwillow.

Corer, E. (1993). *Sadako*. Putnam. (Hiroshima victim folds 1,000 paper cranes)

Davis, Ooze (1982). *Langston: A play*. Delacorte. (Langston Hughes)

Ferris, J. (1988). *Walking the road to freedom: A story about Sojourner Truth*. Carolrhoda.

Freedman, R. (1987). *Lincoln: A photo biography*. Clarion.

Freedman, R. (1991). *The Wright brothers: How they invented the airplane*. Holiday House.

Fritz, J. (1983). *The double life of Pocahontas*. Putnam.

Lauber, P. (1988). *Lost star: The story of Amelia Earhart*. Scholastic.

Provenson, A., & Provenson, M. (1983). *The glorious flight across the Channel with Louis Bleriot*. Viking.

Quackenbush, R. (1989). *Pass the quill, I'll write a draft: A story of Thomas Jefferson*. Pippin.

Say, A. (1990). *El Chino*. Houghton Mifflin.

Genre Studies in Social Studies.   While any genre has potential connection to social studies, general informational books, biography, and historical fiction have particular value because each can elaborate on a unit from a different angle. With historical fiction, students can use informational books and their texts to verify which details are accurate and which are fictionalized. In addition, poetry can be found on unit topics and paired with informational books. For example, the narrative poem "The Midnight Ride of Paul Revere" by Longfellow can be paired with a Revolutionary War study.

Culture Unit Maps and Webs.   One way to structure a culture unit is to "map" findings as students read a variety of literature. Here are important category legs to map or web: (1) *language:* dialect or actual words used in a book, (2) *values:* contrast with mainstream America, (3) *art, music, drama or dance in the book* and what they reveal, (4) *historical information,* (5) *customs and traditions,* (6) *contributions the culture has made,* and (7) *events and issues* associated with the culture.

What-If Writing.   In *Jokes to Tell Your Worst Enemy* (Corbett, 1984), there is a section on "History Rewritten Mother's Way" (e.g., Paul Revere's mother will not let him go out for his midnight ride) that can be used to prompt other "what-if" writing about historical events. Discuss the humor and possible serious side effects.

Joke Books.   There is now a collection of jokes and riddles about nearly all our presidents. Start a Joke of the Day routine with students by finding ones about or by presidents to share. *The Abraham Lincoln Joke Book* (DeRegniers, 1978) is a gem because most of the stories and jokes are ones Lincoln actually told.

Mystery Person.   After reading a piece of historical fiction or a biography, students choose a book character and find three objects that represent him or her. Objects are then revealed to the class one at a time, with the most obvious one (in its connection to the character) coming last. Students try to guess who the person is by connecting the three items.

Biography Boxes.   Students fill boxes with objects, pictures, and poems that may have been important to a person's life. Boxes can then be shared. Students learn that things used or seen each day are also things famous individuals might use. *Variation:* Use with any book character or an artist or author.

Folktale Detectives.   Students (1) read folktales from a culture to find out what is *valued* or (2) explore how the literature of the world's cultures has common *motifs* or *patterns.* For example, compare Snow White and the Queen: young vs. old; happy vs. bitter; inner strength vs. focus on magic and spells. *Suggestions:* Contrast characters and settings in folktales—high vs. low place, young vs. old, bad vs. good, strong vs. weak (Levi-Straus, 1967).

Book Map Making.   A biography or piece of historical fiction is used (Johnson & Louis, 1987). The setting or a portion of it is drawn to show where and what story events take place. Johnson and Louis suggest three steps:

1. *Demonstrate map making.* Read aloud a story with simple events and setting, and keep track of characters on a setting drawing.

2. *Guide students in map making.* Read aloud another story with simple events and settings with the students tracking where the characters are and the events of the story. Each decides what he or she would like to include in the map and how.

3. *Encourage map making during independent reading.*

Time Lines.   Time lines are visual representations of historical events and can be used to summarize an informational book or historical fiction. Use a horizontal line and make hash marks vertically to write chronologically important dates and events.

Point-of-View Guide.   Before reading a historical or informational book, students pair up to interview one another about characters that will appear in the book (e.g., settlers, explorers, or any personages). Interviewers ask five Ws and H questions and write down responses. After reading, students review interviews and compare and contrast with information in the book. To further develop comparisons, students can role play a press conference or TV talk show.

Lifelines. The goal is to record important events in a person's life by doing careful rereading to choose important and specific information (Tompkins, 1990). Long shelf paper or a piece of large paper is cut. A line is drawn down the middle. Dates of important events are put chronologically on the line, marked by a hash mark. Beside, above, or under each date a title, description, and/or picture of that event are shown. Photocopied pictures can be used or students may create their own illustrations and descriptions.

Reading and Language Arts Focus

◆ Reading, listening, speaking, written composition (including handwriting and spelling, grammar, usage, capitalization, and punctuation), since reading and language arts are processes they must be connected to a subject to have meaning, that is, something to read and write about

◆ Goal: *Create* meaning and enjoyment using print through thinking, at every level from memory to critical thinking or evaluation

◆ The printed word and its components (letters, syllables, spelling patterns), how words combine to make phrases and sentences and sentences combine to make paragraphs and other forms of discourse from tongue twisters to novels

◆ Types of words: antonyms and synonyms, parts of speech and figurative language (metaphor, idiomatic expressions)

Lit Logs. Literature logs (wallpaper books, composition books, or a section in a notebook) can be used along with free reading. Students make dated entries, note the stories they are reading (titles and pages), and write reactions or questions about the plot, characters, and style. They may also retell plot events, make predictions, write a poem about what they have read, and/or free write about feelings. *Variation:* Logs may be exchanged to share written reactions or the teacher may collect logs and write comments. If students write in each others' logs, they should be taught how to re-

spond positively. This can be modeled using an example log entry on the overhead.

Prequels and Sequels. After reading a story, students write about what may have happened *before* the book was written or after the end. Students attend to details and literary elements to use the same style, characters, and a fitting plot. Emphasize consistency with characters and style, as well as probability in the plot.

Class Newspaper. News articles, weather forecasts, advertisements, articles, interviews, police reports, classifieds, comics, and obituaries can be written by students about literature they are reading. For example, a newspaper could be constructed around *Charlotte's Web* so that students learn about the parts of a newspaper, the five Ws and H structure of news articles, and so on. The newspaper could be a culmination of a core book unit or developed chapter by chapter (e.g., do cartoons for one chapter, classifieds for another, and obituaries at the end).

Real-Life Writing. Post It Page 4–2 shows many of the forms that people write in. Students can use these forms to write about any topic or book they have read.

Word Walls. Word walls make visible a basic part of literature and writing—words. Students can be on the lookout for interesting and important words to put up (recycled cards can be used for students to write on). A word wall soon becomes a source for writing ideas and an aid for unknown words. A variation is to web the words, individually or as a class, to expand them by adding affixes. This can become a classroom routine that celebrates word possibilities; for example, the word *range* can be webbed or expanded into *ranger, arrange, arrangement, arranging, deranged,* and *rearrange.*

Word Sorts. Students list interesting words they find as they read a book, story, or poem (use index cards). Afterward, students pair up and categorize the words. Possible categories are characters or people, setting, time, problems or conflict, main idea or themes, plot or action. *Adaptations:* (1) Present a list of words from the story or poem *before* the students read it. Students group the words as a prediction exercise. This can be done as a whole group on the overhead or in small groups; (2) give students a chart listing literary elements. Students jot down a key word for each element as they read.

Partner or Buddy Reading. Use this as an alternative to sustained silent reading. Students pair up and share a book. They may take turns reading aloud, read chorally, or read silently. They should agree to stop at certain points to discuss *exciting* or *puzzling* parts. They may also discuss how the story or information connects to their lives. Students enjoy questioning each other using the five Ws and H questions or using questioning strategies they've learned (e.g., fat questions, textually explicit, textually implicit, or scripturally implicit). See Post It Page 3–9 for questions to post for students to choose from. For older students, pair to discuss parts they've read silently using strategies such as EPC (see "discussions" under the principle of ROUTINES in Chapter 3).

Partner Writing. Students read a story and then write to a friend about it. Possible written entries are a letter, a note about what they liked or didn't like and why, or a minibook review (appropriate for intermediate students who've read book reviews; consult *Book Review Digest* in a library or get reviews from journals such as *Horn Book* or *School Library Journal* to use as examples). For example:

> *Dear Jenny,*
>
>   *I want to recommend* Walk Two Moon *to you. The book really makes you think because there are lots of flashbacks. It is sort of like a mystery because you only get clues to what is going on and then you find out the truth at the very end.*
>
>   *I think you would want to read this book because the author makes you love the characters—especially the grandparents. It is a book that made me cry, but I felt like it all made sense at the end. This book made me treasure my parents and grandparents.*
>
>   *Your buddy, Lou*

Bridges. A line is drawn down the middle of a page (based on Barone & Lovell, 1980; Berthoff, 1981). The line represents a bridge. The left-hand side is used to write down words, phrases, sentences, or passages students find interesting or important as they read a book. On the right-hand side, students *bridge* the ideas from the left column to their own experiences (i.e., they write connections). *Variation:* Use to help students prepare for discussion by asking them to write questions, as well as connections, in the right column. These can then be prioritized by starring the ones that are most important to raise. Follow discussions with time for students to write about how the discussion changed their ideas about things noted.

Anticipation Guides. This is a prereading strategy (Head & Readence, 1986). Students are given several statements related to a book they will read. They rate their degree of agreement or disagree. Time can be taken for students to discuss reasons for ratings. They then read and decide whether each rating was confirmed or should be rejected. *Adaptation:* Do as a follow-up reaction rating and use to stimulate discussion of the book (e.g., based on *Like Jake and Me*).

Directions. Rate your agreement from 1 to 5 with 1 = Strongly Agree and 5 = Strongly Disagree.

1. Everyone is afraid of something.
2. It is important for people to feel they are needed by other people.
3. Boys should not do things like dance because that is a girl thing.
4. If two people talk together about something, they will understand each other.

Variation: Use an alternative rating system: True, Sometimes True, False, Sometimes False.

Storymap Yourself. Teach students the grammar or structure of stories by having them create a map or web of their own lives. Map sections are *Who?* (main character is the student), *When and where?* (setting), *Problems? Goals? Plot* (key events so far to reach goals), *Plot resolution* (what the student hopes will happen). *Variations:* A variety of map forms can be used to make visuals: (1) web with three legs labeled beginning, middle, and end, (2) bubbles for each literary element, (3) E-shaped charts with the theme along the vertical line, key events on the beginning, middle, and end on the horizontal lines, and characters in the open spaces of the E.

Sentence Frames. Sentence frames are prompts to help students respond verbally to a book or topic. The structure gets them started, which is the hardest part for many children. They can be used after any book or lesson and for writing, as well. These are mostly taken from children's books. Repeat the frame as many times as desired (e.g., three fortunately–unfortunately statements).

1. *Fortunately . . . Unfortunately . . .*
2. *Someday . . .*
3. *Why . . . ? Because . . .*

4. *. . . is the hardest when . . . and is the easiest when . . .*

5. *I used to (think or feel) . . . But now I (think or feel) . . .*

6. *When I . . . I look or feel like . . . Because . . .*

7. *I seem to be . . . But really I am . . .*

8. *The important thing about . . . is that . . . It's . . ., It's . . ., And it's . . . But the most important thing about . . . is that it . . .*

9. *I am . . . I saw . . . I heard . . . I smelled . . . I tasted . . . I felt . . .*

Letters. (Tierney, Soter, O'Flahavan, & McGinley, 1989). (1) Use Beverly Cleary's *Dear Mr. Henshaw* as an introduction to writing letters to an author or book artist. In the letter include questions about how particular characters were created, ideas or feelings about books, and why the artist chose to use a specific art medium or style. (Explain that they may not receive a personal reply from the artist.) (2) Letter to the editor: Present an issue to the class that will appear in an upcoming book. Students take a stance on the issue and think of ways to defend it. They then write a letter to the editor, share letters, and defend opinions with evidence. Next, they read the book. *Note:* A fascinating book in which actual letters are delivered to fairy tale characters is *The Jolly Postman's or Other People's Letters* (Ahlberg, 1986). The letters can form the basis of drama or many writing possibilities (e.g., writing letters to other characters).

Writing Take-offs or Copycatting. Take-off or copycat writing is adapting a book pattern to make a new story. The degree of adaptation depends on the writer. Predictable books like Williams and Chorao's *Kevin's Grandma* provide a framework in which to write. For example, Zolotow's *Someday* is a series of episodes that all begin with the word *someday*. Books can then be illustrated and bound using options in the art chapter.

Word Collections. Everyone lists interesting words found during reading. Small groups decide whether each word describes or relates to the main character and, if so, how. This provides a student-led discussion vehicle. For example, use words from Lindbergh's *View from the Air: nature, season, pasture, nestled, transformed, perspective. Discussion connections:* What does nature have to do with Charles Lindbergh?

Math Focus

◆ Daily living situations involving counting, measuring, probability, statistics, geometry, logic, patterns, functions, and numbers.

◆ Problem solving through the use of skills (raising questions and answering them, finding relationships and patterns).

◆ Concepts about numbers, operations, and concepts such as bigger, longer, greater than, less, three, four, even and odd.

◆ The National Council of the Teachers of Mathematics encourages teachers to have children solve problems in many ways, focus on explaining and thinking, rather than just correctness, and using a hands-on approach.

Teachers often feel that math is harder to integrate with literature and writing than other areas. But there really are many delightful pieces of literature that are math based, such as:

Anno, M. (1983). *Anno's mysterious multiplying jar.* Philomel. (estimation, multiplication and division, number relationships)

Capie, K. (1985). *The biggest nose.* Houghton Mifflin. (length, capacity, area, and volume)

Lionni, L. (1960). *Inch by inch.* Astor-Honor. (length, capacity, area, and volume)

Schwartz, D. (1989). *If you made a million.* Lothrop, Lee & Shepard. (money, numbers.)

Scieszka, J., & Smith, L. (1995). *Math curse.* Viking. (many aspects of math)

Tompert, A. (1990). *Grandfather Tang's story.* Crown. (geometry, shapes, tangrams)

Post It Page 4–3 is a bibliography of math-based literature from all genre to make it easier to introduce or reinforce math concepts. A recommended source book, published by the National Council of Teachers of Mathematics, is *The Wonderful World of Mathematics: A Critically Annotated List of Children's Books in Mathematics* (Thiessen, & Matthias, 1998).

Math Poetry. Many types of poetry depend on math concepts for their construction (e.g., counting syllables, words, and numbers of lines in haiku, diamante, and limericks). Show students Post It Page 3–5 and then write poems about math (e.g., a haiku about

MATH-BASED CHILDREN'S LITERATURE

Addition and Subtraction

Galdone, P. (1986). *Over in the meadow.* Prentice Hall.

Hoban, T. (1985). *Is it larger? Is it smaller?* Greenwillow.

Attributes

Hoban, T. (1978). *Is it red? Is it yellow? Is it blue?* Greenwillow.

Attributes and Measurement

Horenstein, H. (1993). *How are sneakers made?* Simon & Schuster.

Estimation

Clement, R. (1991). *Counting on Frank.* Gareth Stevens.

Heller, R. (1987). *A cache of jewels.* Grosset & Dunlap.

Fractions

Shotwell, L. (1963). *Roosevelt Grady.* World.

Geometry and Shapes

Bang, M. (1985). *The paper crane.* Greenwillow.

Flournoy, V. (1993). *The patchwork quilt.* Lee & Low.

Hopkins, D. (1993). *Sweet Clara and the Freedom Quilt.* Knopf.

Geometry, Shapes, Sequence, Pattern

Jonas, A. (1983). *Round trip.* Greenwillow.

Graphing

Wildsmith, B. (1982). *Red is best.* Annick.

Large Numbers

Estes, E. (1971). *The hundred dresses.* Harcourt Brace, Jovanovich.

Gag, W. (1988). *Millions of cats.* Random House.

McKissack, P. (1992). *A million fish, more or less.* Knopf.

Petie, H. (1975). *Billions of bugs.* Prentice Hall.

Schwartz, D. (1985). *How much is a million?* Lothrop, Lee & Shepard.

Logic

Anno, M. (1985). *Anno's hat tricks.* Philomel.

Guarino, D. (1989). *Is your mama a llama?* Scholastic.

Measurement and Size

Briggs, R. (1970). *Jim and the beanstalk.* Hamilton.

Carle, E. (1987). *The tiny seed.* Picture Book Studio.

Krauss, R. (1973). *The carrot seed.* HarperCollins.

Money

Axelrod, A. (1994). *Pigs will be pigs.* Simon & Schuster.

Mathis, S. B. (1975). *The hundred penny box.* Viking.

Viorst, J. (1978). *Alexander, who used to be rich last Sunday.* Atheneum.

Multiplication and Division

Dubanevich, A. (1983). *Pigs in hiding.* Four Winds.

Mahy, M. (1987). *17 Kings and 42 elephants.* Dent.

Number Relationships

Larrick, N. (1988). *Cats are cats.* Philomel.

Lottridge, C. (1986). *One watermelon seed.* Oxford University Press.

Ormerod, J. (1983). *101 Things to do with a baby.* Lothrop, Lee & Shepard.

Numbers and Counting

Archambault, J. (1989). *Counting sheep.* Henry Holt.

Crews, D. (1986). *Ten black dots.* Greenwillow.

Dee, R. (1988). *Two ways to count to ten.* Henry Holt.

Haskins, J. (1989). *Count your way through Africa.* Carolrhoda.

Martin, B. (1987). *Knots on a counting rope.* Henry Holt.

Numbers, Counting, Sequence, Patterns

Anno, M. (1992). *Anno's counting book.* HarperCollins.

Probability

Lobel, A. (1972). *Mouse tales.* HarperCollins.

Problem Solving

Hutchins, P. (1967). *Rosie's walk.* Macmillan.

Jonas, A. (1987). *Reflections.* Greenwillow.

Thurber, J. (1990). *Many moons.* Harcourt Brace Jovanovich.

Sequence and Pattern

de Paola, T. (1978). *Pancakes for breakfast.* Harcourt Brace, Jovanovich.

Friedman, A. (1994). *A cloak for the dreamer.* Scholastic Day.

Sorting and Classifying

Hoberman, M. A. (1988). *A house is a house for me.* Viking Penguin.

Sorting, Classifying, and Graphing

Freeman, D. (1978). *Corduroy.* Puffin.

Spatial Relations

Berenstain, S. (1968). *Inside outside upside down.* Random House.
Maestro, B. (1976). *Where is my friend?* Crown.

Time

Anno, M. (1986). *All in a day.* Philomel.
Carle, E. (1977). *The very grouchy ladybug.* Crowell.
Lionni, L. (1967). *Frederick.* Pantheon.

Miscellaneous Math

Anno, M. (1987). *Anno's math games.* Philomel.

---

numbers in nature: *A two-eyed giraffe/Uses four legs to reach high/And eat with one mouth*).

Write Story Problems. Use math-based literature to create story problems. For example, in Carle's *The Very Hungry Caterpillar* the caterpillar eats a certain number of things each day. How many total items did he eat?

Chapter Books. Students create a math character and write a story with several chapters. In each chapter the character solves another math problem. The problems can be related to skills and concepts being taught each week (D. Smith, Teacher, Lody's Island Elementary School, Beaufort, SC).

Graphing Plots. Students can learn the concept of graphing by measuring the excitement level or "good news–bad news" event in a story (Johnson & Louis, 1987). Here's how:

1. *Prepare a graph.* The vertical axis is labeled "excitement level," with the top line "high," and its bottom labeled "low" (or use "good news to bad news"). The horizontal axis is labeled using numbers to represent the different events.

2. *Present the graph.* Use the overhead to explain how graphs work. The class should then brainstorm events in the story. These should be written down.

3. *Complete the graph.* The event list is numbered in chronological order. Event numbers are then placed along the horizontal axis and "rated" by placing a dot at the level decided. Dots are then connected.

4. *Students' graph.* Pairs create their own graphs for another story.

Variation. List favorite books and graph how much students like them.

Math Shape or Concept Books. Students choose a geometric shape or a concept (addition, fractions, etc.). They write stories in which their shapes or concepts are characters or create an information book with pages that describe facts about the math concept. Books can be illustrated and bound. *Variation:* Show the video *Dot and the Line,* a romance between these two shapes (also art elements).

Math Copycat Books. Use math-based children's books as frames for students to write a copycat book of their own. For example, McMillan's *Counting Wildflowers,* Carle's *The Very Hungry Caterpillar,* or Sendak's *Chicken Soup with Rice* can all be used as frames.

Picture Book Math. Give groups stacks of picture books and ask them to find the math necessary to make a book by filling in facts for these categories: number of pages (usually 32), size of pages, words per page (or in whole book), and so forth.

Sequence Story. Write or tell a story with each line beginning with a number, in consecutive order. For example,

One day Mary was sleeping when the doorbell rang. Two men were at the door. Three fingers were missing on one man's hand. Four minutes passed before Mary decided what to do.

Variation. Teams can work to try to get as far as possible.

IV. SPECIAL FOCUS: POETRY SHARING AND WRITING

Poetry is sound and sense and singing words.

This is a brief overview of how to make poetry a *daily* part of arts integration. Why? Poetry has particular importance in reading and language arts because it is through poetry that children are usually introduced to the music of print (Mother Goose rhymes, Dr. Seuss). Fortunately, there is poetry about science, social studies, and math that can be shared using the *poetry alive* strategies in Post It Page 4–4, and children can use poetry writing strategies to transform subject matter. Poetry and the other arts of art, drama, dance, and music can also be connected using strategies such as poem prints (art strategy) and setting poetry to music. See Chapter 13 on integrating the arts with the arts for

---

POST IT PAGE 4–4

POETRY ALIVE STRATEGIES

Directions: Here are ways to orally share poetry throughout the curriculum.

Choral or unison. Do all together.

Cumulative. One or two start and gradually more voices come in; all together on last line.

Antiphonal. Two opposing groups, for example, high and low, loud and soft.

Line-a-child. One line per person.

Refrain with groups. Repeated lines are done by a chorus.

Character voices. Assume a character and use dialect or idiolect, for example, southern.

Narrative pantomime. Do actions that poem suggests as narrator reads or recites.

Sign language. Use finger spelling or American Sign Language to perform.

Background music or art. Play or show as poem is read, for example, transparencies, CDs.

Cloze. Use Post-its and cover predictable words; students then orally guess them.

Reader–responder. Reader reads one line and responder orally improves. For example, *Mary had a little lamb.* Responder: *I bet her husband was surprised.*

Reader's theater. Set up poem like a script with names and parts to be read.

Use props. Add musical instruments, puppets, objects.

Sound effects. Assign sounds to be made when certain words are read.

Question and answer. Find poems that are set up in question and answer form. For example, Q = Who has seen the wind? A = Neither I nor you (Christina Rossetti). Everyone gets a Q or A and reads when it makes sense. *Note:* Students can then write their own Q & A poems.

Actions. Children do an action for certain words or phrases, that is, dance or mime.

Memorize and recite. Add volume, pitch, tone, rate, pause, stress, and emphasis to give your special oral interpretation Q–U (cue you); you read your line on your cue card after you hear your cue. For example,

Q: Mary had a little lamb.

U: Its fleece was white as snow.

Q: Its fleece was white as snow.

U: And everywhere that Mary went . . . .

Call and response (echoic). Students echo leader's oral interpretation line by line.

Canon or round. Read like a round in which different groups start at different times.

Ostinatoes. Repeat a word or phrase that is important, for example, "Who has seen the wind?" (Repeat *Wind–Wind* or chant throughout poetry reading.)

ideas and consult Post it Pages 3–5 and 3–6 on recommended poets and poems. The WHAT? Literary Elements section of Chapter 3 includes a discussion of *poetic elements*.

General Principles for Poetry Integration

As with any arts area, the emphasis in poetry integration is on the process of sharing and creating poetry, not perfect performance or product. Here are other general principles:

Poetry is sound. Nothing is as important as sharing poems *orally*, using a variety of strategies to make it live.

Poetry is sense. Share poetry *first* and discuss afterward. No one knows what a poem really means, so encourage many types of student response and go light on interpreting *for* students.

Creating and sharing poems gives children a sense of control over language. This confidence leads directly to both reading and writing growth.

Encourage children to take risks. The strange, the silly, or the far-fetched can be freely explored when reading and writing poetry. Rules about correct grammar, punctuation, and capitalization don't apply to poetry.

Help students discover what makes poetry. For example, it usually is *compact, emotionally intense, full of sound patterns* (rhythm and rhyme, onomatopoeia, alliteration) and *figurative language* (metaphor, imagery).

Teach about the musical qualities of poetry. Rhyme, rhythm, repetition, onomatopoeia, and alliteration are what make poetry often seem like songs. Knowing this helps students understand the difference between prose and poetry.

Set Up Ongoing Poetry Routines

- *PAD* (poem a day) is the routine of sharing poetry using *poetry alive* strategies (Post It Page 4–4). It is coupled with *poem charts* that are enlargements of poems on posters so that all can see the poem.

- *Poetree:* A tree or just a branch is in a pot in the classroom. From the limbs, students hang copies of poems they have read, adapted, or written. If a

unit is being used, the class finds poems to connect (Hopkins, 1987).

- *Poetry anthologies:* Students create their own collections of favorite poetry by writing their own, trading, and copying poems from source books. Personal anthologies can be made into books or organized in recipe boxes under common categories such as animals, humor, weather, people, places, holidays, and feelings.

Pointers for Poetry Sharing

- Warm up the face and voice. See *energizers and warm-ups* in Chapters 8 and 10.

- Repeated sharing of the same poems increases enjoyment and attunes the ear to the special uses of words in poems.

- Choral reading allows the power and support of the group to be used, especially when you first start doing poetry. Teach choral reading through lessons on musical dynamics: sing together; do rounds; group the class into twos, threes, or fours and give each a musical phrase, ostinato, or refrain.

- Use signals for *start, stop, slow, fast, loud,* and *soft.* Conduct poems like an orchestra conductor (see Chapter 12).

- Teach students to use rhythm and beat by encouraging clapping, snapping, and tapping of feet, or divide the class in half, with one group chanting a phrase or refrain while the other claps out the beat. Challenge by giving the second group a different, syncopated refrain to the same simple beat.

- Coach a child out of shyness. Focus on thinking about the images in the poem, add simple gestures and movements, try the poem in different voices, or try reading louder and slower.

- Asks students to give each other feedback on what worked.

Pointers for Memorizing Poetry

- Memorizing is an important, ongoing class activity. Make sure students choose their own poems, and there are many options for doing recitations (e.g., partners, tape recordings, use of visual aids, props, or puppets).

◆ Warm up memory and imaging skills. Build in daily routines such as *The Minister's Cat, I'm Going on a Trip,* and *Who Stole the Cookies from the Cookie Jar,* that require students to remember and repeat all the ideas previous children have said. Memory lists also can be used by having a category each day. For example, list all the red things in your house.

◆ Start simple. For example, give each child one line to memorize. Class recites the poem with everyone doing only their line. Use a longer poem with a refrain and have students practice learning just the refrain. They can then do it chorally, while the teacher reads the rest.

◆ Use the build-it-up method: Teach the first line of a poem, then recite it and add the second line, then add the third, and so on until the whole poem is memorized.

Composing Poetry: Written and Oral

◆ Start with oral sharing: Children learn to speak before they learn to write. See Post It Page 4–4.

◆ Coach children to write about concrete things, use specific details (especially the five senses).

◆ Sharpen the powers of observation:

Ask students to describe an object in the room, then one not in the room; go for details.

Ask students to describe an object in the room using only three words.

Offer a series of nouns, such as *cat, tree,* and *sky.* Ask students to list possible varieties using adjectives. Coach to go beyond the obvious.

Provide a line. Challenge students to expand using details. For example, *The man walked down the street.* (Expand and elaborate by inserting words and adding phrases.)

◆ Teach about imagery:

Use categories, such as places, feelings, animals, colors, flowers, noises, smells, vehicles, weather, and so forth and develop lists to keep in an idea book for writing.

◆ Teach metaphor:

Ask students to look at a familiar object or out the window at the sky. Ask what it looks like. What it is like. What it reminds them of. Use cubing (see Energizers).

Make two lists of nouns and compare something from one list to something on another.

Offer a choice of several objects; then ask students to write an accurate, detailed, objective description of it. Then have students write a poem made up of one-line comparisons to something. For example, A____ is like a ____ because ____.

◆ Use *poem patterns* (Post It Page 3–5) to give structures to adapt. For example, for the "I wish . . ." pattern, have each child write a line that includes a color. The class shares the poem using line-a-child. Another example: Select an object or person. Each child says one line about it. Students can be encouraged to use the five senses (e.g., I see, I hear, It feels, . . .).

◆ Teach the concepts of line, syllable, and counting syllables:

Cut up a poem into lines. Have students reassemble it.

Put separate lines in a pocket chart or have students each hold a sentence strip with a line as the class reads or it is read by the teacher.

Count lines in a poem.

Count syllables by feeling the vibration in the Adam's apple as words are said. Exaggerate and stretch syllables for emphasis.

◆ Teach about rhyme:

Read a poem, leaving out the rhyme words. Pause for students to provide (cloze strategy).

Contests: Groups try to recite the longest list of rhymes.

Challenge: Write a silly poem using as many rhyming words as possible.

Pick a word and ask for three to five rhymes. Write a poem using those as end words. Repeat with three pairs of different rhymes.

Orally compose a poem in rhymed couplets. Give the first line, and the students supply the second, back and forth.

Memorize four-line nursery rhymes. Take out the familiar rhyme words and ask for new ones. Explore combinations. What happens?

Write quatrains in different patterns: *aabb, abab, abcb, abca.*

◆ Teach rhythm and beat:

Start with songs, keeping time with hands, feet or rhythm instruments.

Overemphasize the beat in choral recitations.

Replace the words with numbers or scat phrases such as "doo-wop."

◆ REFERENCES

See Appendix: Recommended Reading and Viewing for additional resources.

Books and Articles

Barone, D., & Lovell, J. (1990). Michael and the show-and-tell magician: A journey through literature to self. *Language Arts, 67,* 134–143.

Berthoff, A. E. (1981). *The making of meaning.* Montclair, NJ: Boynton/Cook.

Bierhorst, J. (1976). *The Red Swan: Myths and tales of the American Indian.* New York: Farrar, Straus & Giroux.

Brozo, W. (1998). *Readers, teachers and learners: Expanding literacy across the content areas.* Upper Saddle River, NJ: Merrill/Prentice Hall.

Head, M., & Readence, J. (1986). Anticipation guides: Enhancing meaning through prediction. In E. Dishner, T. Bean, & J. Readence, (Eds.), *Reading in the content areas: Improving classroom instruction,* (2nd ed.). Dubuque, IA: Kendall/Hunt.

Hopkins, L. (1969). *Books are by people.* New York: Citation.

Hopkins, L. B. (1987). *Pass the poetry please.* New York: Harper & Row.

Johnson, T., & Louis, D. (1987). *Literacy through literature.* Portsmouth, NH: Heinemann.

Levi-Straus, C. (1967). *Scope of anthropology* (S. Paul & R. Paul, trans). London: Cape.

Macon, J. (1991). *Responses to literature.* Newark, DE: International Reading Association.

Neeld, E. C. (1986). *Writing.* Glenview, IL: Scott, Foresman.

Starko, A. (1995). *Creativity in the classroom schools of curious delight.* White Plains, NY: Longman.

Stauffer, R. (1969). *Directing reading maturity and cognitive process.* New York: Harper & Row.

Thiessen, D., Matthias, M., & Smith, J. (Eds). (1998). *The wonderful world of mathematics: A critically annotated list of children's books in mathematics.* Reston, VA: National Council of Teachers of Mathematics.

Tierney, R., Soter, A., & O'Flahavan, J. (1989). The effects of reading and writing upon thinking critically. *Reading Research Quarterly, 24,* 134–173.

Tomlinson, C., & Brown, C. (1996). *Essentials of children's literature* (2nd ed.). Boston: Allyn & Bacon.

Tompkins, G. (1990). *Teaching writing: Balancing process and product.* Upper Saddle River, NJ: Merrill/Prentice Hall.

Tompkins, G., & McGee, L. (1993). *Teaching reading with literature: Case studies to action plans.* New York: Merrill.

Wood, K. (1988). Guiding students through informational text. *Reading Teacher, 41,* 912–920.

Children's Literature

Ahlberg, J. (1986). *The jolly postman's or other people's letters.* Boston: Little, Brown.

Aliki. (1986). *How a book is made.* New York: Harper & Row.

Anno, M. (1977). *Anno's counting book.* New York: Crowell.

Bruchac, J., & London, J. (1992). *Thirteen moons on turtle's back.* New York: Philomel.

Carle, E. (1984). *The very hungry caterpillar.* New York: Putnam.

Cleary, B. (1996). *Dear Mr. Henshaw.* New York: Avon.

Corbett, S. (1984). *Jokes to tell your worst enemy.* New York: Dutton.

DeRegniers, B. S. (1978). *The Abraham Lincoln joke book.* New York: Random Library.

Fleischman, P. (1988). *Joyful noise: Poems for two voices.* New York: Harper & Row.

Fox, M. (1987). *Women astronauts: Aboard the shuttle.* New York: Messner.

Fox, M. V. (1984). *Women astronauts: Aboard the shuttle.* New York: Julian Messner.

Gibbons, G. (1989). *Monarch butterfly.* New York: Holiday House.

Highwater, J. (1977). *Anpao: An American Indian Odyssey.* New York: Lippincott.

Keller, C. (1985). *Swine lake: Music and dance riddles.* Upper Saddle River, NJ: Prentice Hall.

Krull, K. (1995). *Lives of the artists.* San Diego: Harcourt Brace.

Lindbergh, R. (1996). *View from the air: Charles Lindbergh's earth and sky.* New York: Puffin.

Lionni, L. (1963). *Swimmy*. New York: Pantheon.

Louie, A. (1982). *Yeh-shen: A Cinderella story from China*. New York: Philomel.

Lowe, S., & Sabuda, R. (1992). *The log of Christopher Columbus*. New York: Philomel.

McCully, E. (1992). *Mirette on the high wire*. New York: Putnam.

McKissack, P. (1988). *Mirandy and brother wind*. New York: Knopf.

McMillan, B. (1982). *Puniddles*. Boston: Houghton Mifflin.

McMillan, B. (1986). *Counting wildflowers*. New York: William Morrow.

Palocco, P. (1994). *Pink and Say*. New York: Philomel.

Rockwell, T. (1959). *How to eat fried worms*. Yearling.

Schwartz, A. (1972). *A twister of twists, a tangler of tongues*. New York: Harper & Row.

Sendak, M. (1962). *Chicken soup with rice*. New York: Harpercrest.

Terban, M. (1985). *Too hot to hoot*. New York: Clarion.

White, E. B. (1952). *Charlotte's web*. New York: HarperTrophy.

Williams, B., & Chorao, K. (1991). *Kevin's grandma*. New York: Dutton.

Yolen, J. (1992). *Encounter*. New York: Harcourt Brace.

Yolen, J. (1997). *Sleeping Ugly*. New York: Coward, McCann & Geoghegan.

Zolotow, C. (1989). *Someday*. New York: HarperTrophy

5

Integrating Visual Art Throughout the Curriculum

Every genuine work of art has as much reason for being
as the earth and the sun.

Ralph Waldo Emerson

CLASSROOM SNAPSHOT

Mr. Novak's Multiage Class: Fantasy Unit with Chagall's *I and the Village*

Every child is an artist. The problem is how to remain an artist once he grows up.

Pablo Picasso

The artist easel at the front of the room is draped with a black cloth. Mr. Novak is sitting on a low chair in front of his class of fourth and fifth graders. This is the language arts block scheduled each morning around a *reading–writing workshop* approach designed to let students read a variety of genres and do many kinds of real-life writing during the 2 hours.

"What is this?" Mr. Novak begins.

"It's your mystery bag," the class chorally responds.

"Right. You know the routine. First item." Mr. Novak pulls a yellow rubber duck from the bag. He places it on the table next to him. Students giggle.

"Look closely. Think about what it is, the colors, what it means, how it makes you feel." He pauses. "Next item." He reaches into the brown sack and slowly reveals a yellow plastic ball.

"Oh, oh," one boy raises his hand, "I know."

"Keep looking. We have two more items. Charles, glad you are making connections. Next item." Mr. Novak theatrically struggles to reveal a furry, floppy teddy bear. Charles looks puzzled.

"Last item. Think about how all these items are related." Mr. Novak pulls out a well-worn child's tutu and places it on the table. There are giggles, but students now put their thumbs up.

"I see several thumbs up. I'll give everyone a few more seconds. Look closely. Make associations. Okay, Michael, don't tell us the category—just give us a clue."

Michael pauses, "I think they're all things from our past."

"Great clue. Why do you say that?"

"Because, they are kids' stuff. They are all soft, too, though—and man-made."

"Yes. You're right. Who else? Sonya?"

"I think they are all happy things. They remind me of playing and just having fun when I didn't have to go to school so much." The class laughs and so does Mr. Novak.

"What do you think of Sonya's idea about how these things make you feel? Aspen?"

"I agree about how they make you feel happy and I agree with Michael about the past. I think it can all go together. Soft toys in our past remind us of good pleasant memories." Several children shake their heads to agree with Aspen.

"Charles, you had an idea early on. What were you thinking?"

"I thought you were just doing 'yellow' or 'plastic.' Then you brought out the teddy bear. But at least the yellow part fits because yellow is such an uplifting color in its feeling."

The discussion continues for a few more minutes. Mr. Novak then ceremoniously unveils the bottom half of the shrouded print.

"Cool," one boy says.

"What is it?" someone else says.

"Look closely. What do you see?" asks Mr. Novak.

"Really weird stuff. Is that a tree?"

"I see two people and one is green with white lips."

"Look, a cross. He has on a ring, too."

"The nuts or flowers are exploding or something. See the splattered paint!"

"Wow, those are strange shapes, like a moon eclipse or something. But it's red. Look there's a ring with an apple on it. Maybe this artist didn't have a lot of toys and had to play with this stuff."

"It's not a person on the right. Look. It's more the shape of a snout or something. Maybe he played with a pig!" The class laughs again.

"You are really noticing colors, shapes, and images. What else? How does this make you feel?"

"It has bright yellow so it's happy. There is the cross. Maybe he's really religious."

"But the guy is green. Of course, when you're a kid, colors don't matter so much. Maybe a kid painted this?" Kristen asks.

The class continues a few more minutes with many more discoveries until Mr. Novak asks them to get ready to see the rest of the work. The whole class gets still and many lean forward.

Slowly Mr. Novak pulls the black cloth up. Little by little the print is revealed. The kids gasp.

"Make some connections," Mr. Novak urges them.

"This is crazy. Look the people and houses are upside down and the woman is milking a cow in the head of a horse!"

"But the colors are really interesting. It's like a dream or something. You know, things can be anything in your dreams," a red-haired girl who hasn't spoken before is quite passionate.

The class discussion becomes animated, with students finding more and more things in the print. Comments seem to converge on ideas about dreams, toys, happy memories, and childhood. One child actually uses the term "abstract" and another mentions "collage."

About 15 minutes into the lesson, Mr. Novak finally tells them the painting was made by a Russian Jew named Marc Chagall in 1911. He takes about 5 minutes to explain how Chagall was inspired to paint pleasant childhood memories—his experiences and things from folktales he had been told. He then spends a few minutes asking them about their memories of stories from childhood, and they share lots of fairy tale titles and Disney films.

The lesson introduction ends and Mr. Novak moves into the development by asking what makes fantasy, and as students call out characteristics, such as "something not real," "dreamlike places and events," he writes them on the overhead. He then explains they are starting a genre unit on fantasy and asks them why they think Chagall might have painted fantastic images such as those in *I and the Village*. The students return to the "good feelings and freedom" ideas generated earlier. He then asks them about the book *Charlotte's Web* (White, 1952) and how it might relate to the discussion. Students comment on the elements of fantasy in the story (e.g., animals talking) and also how it was a book most of them heard a teacher read aloud in second grade; it was a good memory from their childhood.

The lesson is brought to a conclusion when Mr. Novak asks them why people might write or read or paint fantasy, and there are many responses: for entertainment, relaxation, to make money, to be creative, to get ideas out, to feel good. He then shows them five fantasy books, *Tuck Everlasting* (Babbitt, 1975), *Able's Island* (Steig, 1976), *The Borrowers* (Norton, 1991), *Bunnicula* (Howe & Howe, 1999), and *The Indian in the Cupboard* (Banks, 1980) from which they'll be able to choose as they study fantasy and try to find out more of its characteristics. He tells them he'll put them on the chalk tray for browsing and ask them to rate their choices by the end of the day. Five book circles will then form to read together. He also explains that the unit will involve them in the creation of fantasy because they'll be doing their own fantasy art responses.

Postscript: Mr. Novak spent a month on the fantasy unit, and students met daily to discuss their books. He displayed and held "What do you see?" discussions of other fantasy paintings, Henri Rousseau's *The Dream* and Marcel Duchamp's *Nude Descending a Staircase,* and students explored the artists' motives and means for creating these works. The unit culminated in a fantasy museum display of student paintings. All the paintings were framed, in some sense. One special day students acted as docent guides for small groups of students and adults who came to tour the museum (a converted area of the hall) and find out about the paintings and the painters. The unit had indeed integrated art with the language arts of reading, writing, speaking, and listening.

Introduction

The arts—literature, visual art, music, drama, and dance—are our culture's most powerful means for making life in its particulars vivid. In this way the arts escalate consciousness.
Elliot Eisner

Stop to See Details

Mr. Novak is like more and more teachers who use art to cause students to notice details and patterns, remember past experiences, and come to see the world as an intriguing place. Unfortunately, according to art educator Rudolf Arnheim, schools still often emphasize commonality, generalization, and classification, rather than concentration on one special thing—such as in-depth study of a single work of art that connects to a science or social studies unit. Uniqueness and commonality are both important and can be treated simultaneously in a lesson, as Mr. Novak did. The point is, however, in visual art meaning comes mostly from details and specifics, in the same way we know a person by particular features. Art study involves examining how a work is made special by an artist's different use of light or line, such as the line that creates Mona Lisa's smile. How different the impact would be if da Vinci had painted her with a broad grin. Elliot Eisner (in Arnheim, 1989) urges a focus on details. He even sees a cause–effect relationship between development of acute visual perception and student abilities to write well. "Attention to the sensibilities and to the distinctive is not attention to educational ornamentation, but attention to the core of education" (p. 7).

Visual Art Literacy

Art is the imposing of a pattern on experience, and our aesthetic enjoyment in recognition of the patterns.
Alfred North Whitehead

In this chapter the concept of art and visual literacy will be examined as related to general student goals for the development of higher-order thinking skills and creative problem solving. This is not a new idea. Visual art has long been associated with literacy. For example, historically, religious frescoes and paintings in churches throughout the world were intended to not just adorn but to educate illiterate people about powerful events. Educators are newly reawakening to these abandoned learning tools, and there is a growing respect for how creating art involves more than simple use of the hands. Indeed, the use of the senses in art is "a cognitive event . . . the eye is part of the mind" (Eisner, in Arnheim, 1989, p. 4). Consider how a piece of art is a reflection of an artist's experiences in a particular time and culture; each work is a "dramatic puzzle cast in a beautiful form." Students who learn to "read" art become literate in profound ways as they learn to decode the symbol systems to interpret or make meaning from visual images. By peeling away layers and unwinding bits of the message, people develop the esthetic sense to make judgments, like a subject of psychologist Abraham Maslow's (1968), who observed how "a first-rate soup is more creative than a second-rate painting" (p. 136).

Through art making and art discussions, children can experience the joy of discovery and learn how much of life is ineffable—the search for meaning does not always end in the finding, but in a satisfying journey. Students learn to go beyond mere literal thinking and gain new ways to make meaning. For example, teachers can explain how cubism, and other nonrepresentational art styles, is an artist's effort to say, without words, something strongly felt. Abstract art is not meant to "be" anything. Art can come to be seen as a tool to create for myriad reasons and in many ways. Unfortunately, art is unduly viewed as a way to entertain or decorate. Our cultural bias for verbal communication, particularly in school, persists despite the intensely visual nature of contemporary society. Visual images in the forms of signs and billboards and on television are pervasive. This school preference for words over visual-spatial "intelligence" leads to minimal attention to pictorial *details* during teaching, even by those who include picture books in the literacy program. The scarce instruction in visual literacy is evident in children's stereotyped use of symbols, when research shows they are capable of more mature perceptions. For example, middle school students often depict the sun as a mandala—a circle with sticks coming off it—or birds as joined commas; they are capable of seeing and representing using much more representative details if given time and guided to look more closely.

WHY SHOULD TEACHERS INTEGRATE ART?

A painter takes the sun and makes it into a yellow spot. An artist takes a yellow spot and makes it into a sun.

Pablo Picasso

What's so special about learning through visual art? The research on integrating art provides implementation rationale and is summarized in Post It Page 5–1.

Visual Art: Effects on Learning and Motivation

1. Art activates emotions and motivates.

At the start of the 21st century we seem to have a new respect for the centrality of intuition in understanding. The author of *Emotional Intelligence*, Daniel Goleman (1995), claims "A view of human nature that ignores the power of emotions is sadly shortsighted . . . intelligence can come to nothing when the emotions hold sway" (p. 4). The roots of both the words *emotion* and *motivate* have to do with motion or movement. Emotions and motivation cause us to take action that can result in positive or negative consequences. While art involves the intellect, it also activates *affective* ways of knowing. It is an outlet for ideas and feelings—a release, a safety valve—and can give an emotional catharsis. Jenkins (1986) calls this "externalizing" what we feel and know (p. 15). Both *viewing* and *doing* art can give emotional release or response. This is evident in art therapy sessions when clients report feelings of relaxation or a joyous high. There is delight in making a line that curves in a special way and pleasure in seeing an artist's new view on a subject.

2. Art is a way of communicating through visual and spatial symbols.

The most fundamental fact to be understood about art is that whatever it shows is presented as a symbol. A human figure carved in wood is never just a human figure, a painted apple is never just an apple. Images point to the nature of the human condition.

Arnheim, 1989, p. 26

POST IT PAGE 5–1

NEWS BULLETIN: ART RESEARCH YOU CAN USE

Visual arts students scored an average of 47 points higher on the math and 31 points higher on the verbal section of the SAT (College Board, 1999–2000).*

Reading and math scores were significantly higher for 96 students in eight visual-art-enriched first grades. The students scored an average of 77 percent at grade level, as compared to 55 percent for the control group (Gardiner, 1996).

Studies support that visual thinking using color tools increases the cognitive processes of problem solving, organizing, and memory (Longo, 1999).

Needham, Massachusetts: Since integrating art into the curriculum in 1983, test scores for average third-grade students in Eliot Elementary, a racially mixed school, have increased to the 99th percentile.

Rocky Mountains: Writing skills showed significant improvement when drawing and drama strategies were used in the primary grades (Moore & Caldwell, 1993).

CBS This Morning, February 28, 1997: Teacher Mrs. Fodero said her students with learning disabilities gained 1–2 years in developmental levels after 8 weeks of special drawing instruction that focuses on attending to five elements of shapes: circles, dots, straight lines, curved, and angle lines. The program has been found to increase reading, writing, math, and language skills up to 20 percent in other schools. "[I]f you draw what you are learning about, you will learn it much faster and retain the information longer," claims the program developer, Mona Brookes (Brookes, 1996, p. xx).

---

*See more information about SAT scores and college bound seniors for 1999–2000 at *http://www.collegeboard.org/prof/*. Click the "search" button and enter "national report."

Imagery and metaphor are used from early childhood to think and learn. A child sees a "fingernail" in the night sky by comparing a known image with something inexplicable. There is little teaching and learning in any discipline that doesn't include concrete images. Think of drawings in the dictionary, photographs in history texts, plastic models in science. Often these images are not realistic; a map is an abstraction, as are charts and diagrams. Arnheim (1989) points out, "images produced for practical purposes have more sophisticated functions than that of supplying faithful duplicates . . . what an illustration needs to show is not an object as such but some of its *significant properties*" (p. 30, emphasis added).

When we teach for visual literacy, we involve children in thinking about and expressing in images what is often beyond *linguistic* capabilities. This can be as simple as asking students to look closely and observe repeated elements that make patterns in fabrics or plant leaves. Children are attuned to metaphoric thinking so this taps into a strength and stimulates the use of *multiple* schemata—understanding from logical analysis *and* affective response. A common way to develop imaging is a strategy called *guided visualization trips:* Students are asked to relax and make pictures in their heads as a story is read or told about an imaginary journey. For example, before a plant unit, students might visualize a trip through a plant and hear vocabulary used that will be read later. Vivid and accurate adjectives activate the brain to make personal pictures or meanings. This is a powerful motivator to read and learn more.

3. Art is a means of thinking through the senses.

It is more than likely that if men were ever to lose the appetite for meaning, which we call thinking, they would lose the ability to produce those thought-things we call works of art.
                                                                Hannah Arendt

"At the root of knowledge is a sensible world, something we can experience" (Arnheim, 1989, p. 7). Art is hands-on and tangible. We touch materials to make art and manipulate color, line, and shape to create it. When we *view* a piece of art, kinesthetic and tactile senses are activated by the artist's brushstrokes that go up or down or are heavy or light. Visual perception is a cognitive event because interpretation and meaning are indivisible parts of seeing. What we see is a function of intellect—a painting can evoke the sounds and smells of a summer boat ride or a raucous party. As the senses are stimulated, we experience mental, physical, and emotional responses. So the symbols used in art are also thinking tools. These sensory-rich symbols form a special language that beckons us to consider a new perspective and use prior knowledge to interpret, apply, analyze, synthesize, and evaluate what we are creating or viewing.

4. Art develops esthetic sensitivity.

For the soul, beauty is not defined as pleasantness of form but rather as the quality in things that invites absorption and contemplation . . . beauty is a source of imagination . . . that never dries up. A thing so attractive and absorbing may not be pretty or pleasant. It could be ugly, in fact, and yet seize the soul as beautiful in this special sense. James Hillman defines beauty for the soul as things displaying themselves in their individuality. . . . Some pieces of art are not pleasing to look at, and yet their content and form are arresting and lure the heart into profound imagination.
                            Thomas Moore, *Care of the Soul*, 1992, p. 278

It is puzzling that esthetic awareness does not get more attention from educators. According to educational philosopher, Harry Broudy (1979), esthetic sensitivity is the "primary source of experience" and that esthetic experiences are vital to every child's education (p. 636). Esthetic responses lie at the heart of much of daily living. Aromas, sounds, colors, tastes, and textures fill our environment and stimulate esthetic response. Esthetic response involves a sharpening of

---

TAKE ACTION 1
GUIDED VISUALIZATION

Pick a topic in science or social studies. (Check courses of study or textbooks.) Write a one-page guided imagination trip with a "you are there" feel to it. Use the pronoun "you" to direct the listener. Try it out and ask for feedback. Do a piece of art or writing after the imagination trip.

TAKE ACTION 2
WHAT IS ART?

Use an ordinary object (eraser, paper, safety pin). Discuss the steps and thought processes an artist uses to create, produce, and market it. Decide whether you think such an object is art.

the senses—an awareness or appreciation of pleasant experiences (Feeney & Moravcik, 1987). Lowenfeld and Brittain (1975) explain esthetic sensitivity as perceptual process, "an interaction between a person and an object (natural or man made) that gives a stimulating and harmonious experience." While children may not have language to express esthetic awareness, they often are at a higher level of esthetic development than adults might think. Think of the expressions of wonder and delight at beautiful flowers, birds, butterflies, or pictures—gasps and sighs that show heightened sensory responses. Eventually, this sensitivity can grow into an ability to critically evaluate artwork using criteria for beauty defined by each culture. Michael Parson's research on the *stages of esthetic development* is summarized in Post It Page 5–2 and is presented to show a progression of esthetic development and gives teachers a basis for making appropriate instructional decisions.

5. Art develops higher-order thinking and creative problem-solving capabilities.

Artistic and creative problem solving begins early. As children draw people and trees, they show they can shrewdly analyze and translate observations into basic shape patterns. This is not mechanical imitation of reality but an expression of the *essence* of things—young children often make the head the largest part of a person because it is the most relevant feature. When given materials and tools to create art, children will experiment and use imagination. When *taught* how to use the materials and tools, they work with greater satisfaction. This can be as simple as showing possibilities for painting with different strokes, amounts of paint, or the effects of splattering and dripping. After such demonstrations it is appropriate for students to have time to explore with tools and media—to create a product or just experiment, period. In addition, when teachers expect students to think for themselves, to generate rather than imitate, more personal involvement occurs. In contrast, teachers who give black line pages to color in or oral directions that mimic painting by number, distort art. It's no surprise when the result is a series of look-alike products—students are not engaged in higher-order thinking or using creative problem-solving capabilities.

Esthetic development is nurtured by personal confrontation with words and images. Artists and authors give us cues, but we must arrive at our own con-

---

POST IT PAGE 5–2

STAGES OF ESTHETIC DEVELOPMENT

Stage 1: Favorites. Children delight in virtually all paintings, especially the colors. They like to pick favorites and talk about personal connections.

Stage 2: Subject matter. Focus on representational art; it's better if it is more realistic. The artist's skill is admired.

Stage 3: Emotions. Concern is for emotional stimulation, the more intense the better. Now the person has more than a personal preference and has developed an appreciation for how an artist causes the viewer to respond with emotion.

Stage 4: Style and form. The viewer now understands that art is socially and culturally influenced and is important because of its meaning-making capabilities. Art is viewed as an important communication vehicle, with its power to give meaning being primary. Color, texture, space, and form are analyzed as the person judges the competence of the artist to create new perspectives.

Stage 5: Autonomy. Judgments are made on a personal and social basis. Art is viewed now as an important means of helping humans consider the human condition and life itself through the questions it raises and the ideas and feelings it evokes. The work is used to seek truth and shared meaning with others in a kind of "conversation about life."

Source: Adapted from Parsons, Michael, J. (1987). Talk about a painting: A cognitive developmental analysis. *Journal of Aesthetic Education, 21*(1), 37–55.

TAKE ACTION 3
ESTHETIC DEVELOPMENT

Do a self-assessment with Parsons' model (see Post It Page 5–2). List ways to stimulate students to progress through the stages: Classroom arrangement? An esthetic environment? What questions might you ask to increase esthetic awareness? How can you respond as students notice esthetic properties of things (texture of chicks that hatch, brilliant colors of trees)?

TAKE ACTION 4
STIMULATING HOTS

Use an art print or a book illustration to write questions with Bloom's (1956) taxonomy. Literal questions can be used because HOTS are grounded in a knowledge. Avoid trivial literal questions not related to main concepts and themes: asking how many sticks or bricks a pig used to build his house in the *Three Little Pigs* is questionable. "What materials did each pig use?" is a literal question that leads to facts about the theme of building a strong foundation.

clusions. While pedagogy abandoned copying at the turn of the century, unfortunately there still are some art specialists and classroom teachers who either do not understand problems with dictated art or who are professionally irresponsible. Teaching can both advance and thwart development. In no area is this more obvious than when teachers damage students' concepts about what art is and how it comes to be. When students are taught that art must be representational, or look like something, children can lose faith in their abilities to make art. Some begin to refuse to even try for fear their art will not look like a "real" artist's or the teacher's. Arnheim reminds us that realism may be needed for *technical* purposes but is *not even appropriate* under some circumstances. For example, representing the pharaohs, *realistically,* conveys a kind of humanity incongruous with early Egyptian religious views because no pharaoh believed himself or herself to be a mere mortal.

One way to stretch thinking during art creation and response is to use Benjamin Bloom's taxonomy of thinking to construct questions. Bloom (1956) divided cognition into levels:

- *Memory:* just the facts, literal thinking. Example: *What are the primary colors?*

- *Interpretation:* reading between the lines, adding your own experiences to make an inference. Example: *How could you explain in your own words how to create shades and tints?*

- *Application:* putting a skill you've learned to use. Example: *Use what we've been learning about mixing colors to make different skin tones.*

- *Analysis:* examining the parts or pieces to come to understanding. Example: *Look closely to discover all the repeated elements in this piece of art.*

- *Synthesis:* putting parts or pieces together to make a creative whole; requires invention and imagination. Example: *What can you make with these collage materials that shows what you have learned about the environment?*

- *Evaluation:* making a judgment based on the goodness or badness, rightness or wrongness of something using some criteria. Example: *What do you think about this piece of art and why do you think what you do?*

Both teachers and students can use Bloom's model to generate questions and to respond to work in any art form. For example, a synthesis-level art project could demonstrate what was learned from a science unit on ecology. The goal is to make sure students think above the memory or literal level and use more higher-order thinking skills (HOTS).

Ways to expand the use of the creative problem-solving process (CPSP) were presented in Chapter 1. Take time to review the CPSP process and strategies such as SCAMPER on Post It Page 1–6.

6. Art strengthens self-understanding and confidence about being unique.

Art is an extension of a person, an expression of who I am and what I am.

Sabe and Harrison

Through the inventive and imaginative processes of art, students are empowered to make personal discoveries. Promoting personal investigation should be central to teaching, and students are often more willing to experiment in the art arena where creativity is often more openly valued by adults. When art is coupled with other areas of study (science, social studies, math), students can associate positive feelings and powerful thinking processes from art with these subjects. Art also offers ways to control emotions, images, and even the environment, which yields a sense of confidence. There is a Jewish folktale about a tailor who continually makes "something from nothing" and brings joy to himself and his family in the doing. (See Gilman's [1992] picture book version, *Something from Nothing.*) Self-expression is a primary goal of integrating art and expression is linked to understanding. When students explore interpretations of a work of art, it is their *different* perspectives, not coming to one answer, that is the goal. This focus on novel thinking and the noncompetitive nature of art allows students to vie only with internal standards.

7. Art promotes respect for diversity.

If you walk around the world with black and white film in your camera, you are not especially inclined to look for color on your travels.

Elliot Eisner in Arnheim, 1989, p. 7

To see the world from an artist's viewpoint is to look for what is special and different. The aphorism "The devil is in the details" reminds us how much small things can matter. Art reflects culture, so it is an ideal source for information about the diverse values and customs of the world's peoples. A cultural print or artifact can be an effective lesson tool to show how similar problems, such as how people have dressed in different times and places to protect ourselves from the elements, are addressed in myriad ways. Visual images and objects grab attention when used in lesson introductions. Students can be motivated to find out more when shown portraits, landscapes, still lifes, sculptures, or architecture that illuminates the past, especially if asked what each shows about the people who created it.

In a classroom infused with the visual arts, students also have the opportunity to learn to respect the variety of products fellow classmates create. As students share work, during times like art docent talks, all come to realize how no one's work is the same and that differences are exciting.

8. Art develops responsibility, focus, concentration, and self-discipline.

For those parents and teachers that decry the inability of children to stay on task and complete work with pride, art offers a viable means of developing important social and character habits. Students soon learn that nothing can be created without learning to use materials and tools and sticking with work to completion. As peers admire the work of those who are self-disciplined, all get insight into what it takes to be successful, and students see that those who handle materials responsibly are given privileges not available to those who do not.

9. Art reflects life, so it naturally integrates all curricular areas.

Art is to society as dreams are to a person.

Laliberte and Kehl

Art more than reflects life—it is life. Look around and find the art of life. Chairs and cups mirror the world of their creators. The common plastic drinking cup implies values and suggests a way of life that invented it. Its composition, size, shape, color, and texture comment on the Western custom of use and dispose. Different kinds of chairs—from the regal throne to the bean bag chair—show how we devise ways of sitting that signal relationships, scientific advances, and economic situations. Art shows how we create to survive and thrive. This life-centeredness invites students to transfer the meaning-making processes of art to other curricular areas. The parallels between the written composition process and art making are good examples. The pre–during–post stages of the writing process can be introduced first by comparing it to creating a painting or sculpture. The lessons of art have to do with exploring, experimenting, and learning to use tools and materials—the same thinking necessary to produce good writing. Essential properties of a writing topic may even best be captured through art making first, offering an insightful means of getting over writer's block. Artists do rough drafts, such as sketches for paintings, and refine products through revision and editing, just as writers do.

Looking at topics through the lens of an esthetic perspective develops multiple viewpoints. Examining visual art about plants, animals, historical events, and people yields insights into science and social studies and can be an introduction to, or an elaboration of, knowledge gained through reading expository material in science or social studies texts. Information gathered in such investigations changes frames of understanding, much as a piece of art is changed by its frame. The esthetic *feeling* frame of reference liberates beauty and richness embedded in the subject matter of any discipline. Students who learn to savor learning, by taking time to reflect, explore, and respond emotionally, develop new perspectives and sensitivities. Broudy (1979) contends this form of esthetic interaction is a "primary form of experience on which all cognition, judgment, and action depend. It is the fundamental and distinctive power of image making by the imagination. It furnishes the raw material for concepts and ideals" (p. 63). Art also links curricular areas to life, in which cognitive, affective, and psychomotor (physical–mental coordination) aspects are rarely separated. Art is an alternative way of knowing—an intelligence that promotes learning in and across domains. For example, it is impossible to ever think of an iris in the same way after seeing Georgia O'Keefe's paintings, nor could the horror of war ever be made more poignant than through Picasso's magnificent *Guernica*. Heart, head, and hands are used in creating, evaluating, understanding, and responding to art. It is dreary to imagine studying a discipline without art—books without photos, illustrations, diagrams, or maps; math, social studies, and science without models to show the human body, the atom, or the world. Students need to be alerted to the significant role of art in making the invisible visible.

10. Art is a way to assess.

Art is a private feeling made into a public form.

Judith Rubin

A child's art gives a peek inside a private world of thoughts and feelings. Teachers must be cautious, however, in inferring meanings from a student's art—an excessive use of black may occur because the black crayon is the most convenient. Given that caveat, it is appropriate to examine artwork for signs of conceptual and motor development. For example, when (circle, vertical, horizontal, and diagonal lines appear in children's art this indicates that they are ready for formal handwriting instruction. In addition, just as a child's writing gives clues to thinking and learning, a student's artwork provides evidence of cognitive development. In fact, children who lack verbal fluency may be able to express ideas with paint or clay or may have their words released through art. Stories told through art are often passionate tales of events that capture children's imaginations. Here is 6-year-old Liza's story based on a drawing she did of an erupting volcano.

All the town was afraid. They could hear the insides making growling sounds. Then it happened. The lava broke out and ran all over the people. It was blood red because it was hot rock. Hot hot rock. So hot it burned up the people. But see here. This is a people bird. The people were burned to ashes but the ashes molded into lava birds that could fly so high no volcano could ever touch them again. The end.

National Standards for Art and Other Curriculum Frameworks

The *National Standards for Visual Art* are summarized in Post It Page 5–8 and provide another reason for classroom art integration. These goals are difficult to achieve without collaboration among generalists and specialists. Teachers need to have district, state, and national standards in hand as they write lesson plans that prepare students to meet standards. Like most standards documents, the Visual Art Standards help teachers know *what* to teach; they do not explain *how* to teach. Districts hire teachers with the expectation they bring a professional repertoire of strategies, materials ideas, and discipline/management tools to the job. *Note:* The HOW sections of chapters and the Strategy Seeds chapters (4, 6, 8, 10, 12, and 13) focus on how to teach.

Contact your state department of education and the curriculum director in your school district for guidelines that have been developed from the *National Standards for Visual Art* document to meet local needs. For examples of arts standards developed at the state level, contact the Ohio Department of Education (Columbus, OH). Kentucky also has state standards for the arts that have been widely implemented. Wisconsin's Model Academic Standards for the Arts can be ordered online: *http://www.dpl.state.wi.us/dpl/dltcl/els/pubsales/arts.html.*

TAKE ACTION 5
CONNECT TO THE STANDARDS

Think about Mr. Novak's lesson using the Chagall print. Select the *Standards* from Post It Page 5–8 that you think were the goals of his lesson. Give reasons.

WHAT DO TEACHERS NEED TO KNOW AND TEACH TO INTEGRATE ART?

Every artist dips his brush into his own soul.

Henry Ward Beecher

The integration process occurs when two or more ideas are combined. All parts retain their worth, but a synergism is created in which "the sum is greater than the parts" and time use is maximized. Teachers must know *about* visual art to integrate it or teach *through* it. In elementary and middle school, basic visual art content and skills includes studying: (1) the historical, social, and cultural role of each art in our lives, (2) communication through art forms by *creating* and *responding* to art, and (3) valuing art and developing esthetic sensitivity (understanding the roles of beauty and emotion in life). Classroom teachers who integrate visual art into other curricular areas will need to teach about art elements, artists, pieces of art, art forms, styles, history of art, artistic tastes, art making through a variety of media, the role of art in personal life and society, the art of other cultures, and how to learn in a museum setting. Here is a checklist of titles for file folder tabs or computer folders to assist teachers in collecting and organizing resources needed for visual art integration:

- Basic art elements and concepts used to create and think about art
- Artist information (biographies, styles, and techniques used)
- Styles of art, such as impressionism, expressionism, and cubism
- Forms, types of art, and media such as collage, sculpture, painting
- Subject matter (portrait, landscape, abstract, still life)
- Actual pieces of art (calendar art, prints, art postcards, sculpture)
- Cultural artifacts such as masks and pots
- Other possibilities: art history, science of art (pigment making), math of art (perspective), sociology of art, economics (museum shows, selling art), psychology (art therapy)

Art and Child Development: Cognitive, Affective, and Psychomotor

Children who are encouraged to draw and scribble stories at an early age will later learn to compose more easily, more effectively, and with greater confidence than children who do not have this encouragement.

What Works: Research about Teaching and Learning (1986), U.S. Department of Education, Washington, DC, p. 14

Thanks to researchers such as Rhonda Kellogg, Victor Lowenfeld, and Howard Gardner, we no longer look on children's early drawings as poor attempts at art making. It is clear that art shows evidence of brain growth and development. For example, drawing is a natural type of human communication that develops the world over, and children's drawings reveal how they think (cognition), their emotional state (affective domain), and fine and gross motor development. By observing efforts to control drawing tools and examining what drawings say about thoughts and feelings, much assessment information can be acquired.

Scribbles Have Meaning. Symbolic drawing development grows in stages, similar to growth in verbal communication: Small steps lead to giant leaps, general abilities become increasingly particular. Post It Page 5–3 shows basic scribbling stages through which children progress. Beginning with the basic art element of *line*, art development can be seen in toddlers who discover how art tools extend their fingers to make marks, sometimes to the chagrin of fastidious parents. Kellogg (1969) broke the ground in recording children's art development. She spent 20 years collecting over a million samples of children's drawings that unveiled the universal artistic journey from scribbling to enclosed shapes to use of graphic symbols. Analysis of research samples outlines patterns of growth Kellogg grouped into stages beginning with 20 basic scribbles. Her developmental sequence describes movement from random scribbles to more controlled scribbling and then to formation of enclosed shapes that indicate increased understanding of spatial relationships. Shapes evolve into symbols, like mandalas and suns, used to create people shapes. Lowenfeld and Brittain (1987) took this line of research through the adolescent years and theorized that children made advances naturally, without being taught to draw. By age 9, base lines and skylines appear, and "x-ray drawings" show

BASIC SCRIBBLES AND EVOLUTION OF PICTURES FROM SCRIBBLING

Post It

Note: Children's drawings reflect growth in thinking (cognition) and in physical control (gross and fine motor) over materials and art tools.

Ages	Benchmarks
1–2 years	*Random scribbling.* Exploration of tools and materials, showing increasing fine and gross motor control. Single and multiple dots and lines (vertical, horizontal, diagonal, and wavy) produce some 20 basic scribbles that eventually include loops, spirals, and circles. Examples:

2–7 years	*Shape making.* Scribbles begin to be intentionally used to make basic shapes or diagrams. Children combine shapes and use overlapping. Eventually, the shapes form aggregates (three or more diagrams together). Examples:

3–5 years	*Symbol making.* Lopsided geometric shapes are made. Mandalas and suns are drawn and evolve into human figures. At first, arms and legs stretch from the head. Eventually, torsos emerge and human figures are drawn with more and more completeness. Examples:

Source: Based on Kellogg (1969) and Lowenfeld and Brittain (1987).

understandings developed about the unseen. Unfortunately, by age 12 many children begin to abandon spontaneous drawing.

Art educator Mona Brookes (1996) offers an explanation for why youngsters often stop drawing. She thinks *symbolic* and *realistic* drawing are two distinct types of drawing and should not be compared. She sees symbolic drawing as natural drawing that children produce. It develops in a predictable progression like all human communication; it is *nonverbal* communication used for self-expression. During this time children create symbols for animals, people, houses, and trees and even talk to themselves as they draw, often telling a story. For example, "Here is my dad shaving. He has lots of cream on his face. It makes him look funny." Symbolic drawing usually culminates in abstract stick-figure images.

About age 8 or 9, children give up symbolic drawing and want to draw realistically, to record an image artistically so that it is recognizable by others. But Brookes (p. 15) argues that this skill doesn't usually happen without instruction, just as children don't naturally use conventional spelling or handwriting without instruction. (*Note:* Spelling development begins with scribbles and "pretend writing." It proceeds from gross approximations using just beginning and ending sounds to represent words, to more and more accurate spelling. Details of words, such as the spelling of the *schwa* sound and use of vowel digraphs, are the last to develop. Educators recognize the need for instruction to cause children to use correct spelling.) Realistic drawing demands attention to detail, a degree and kind of focus and concentration that Brookes thinks can be taught. She gives examples of drawings done from prompts to "draw a person," which produced simple stick-figure images, and drawings done after *one* lesson on analyzing elements of shape and attending to detail. The two sets of drawings show dramatic differences caused by explicit instruction. They demonstrate how most children are capable of sophisticated *realistic* drawing. Brookes uses a *drawing alphabet* to provide the "basis for seeing with an educated eye" and teaches five elements of shape to "analyze and break down what is seen" (p. xxx). While Brookes shows that children can be taught to do realistic work, she emphasizes that they should be encouraged to do free symbolic drawing (1996, pictures throughout).

Waves of Development.   Gardner's (1990) research on art development led him to postulate growth in *waves*, rather than stages. His theory depicts waves of knowledge rising higher and higher in a specific intelligence area and then spilling over into another intelligence. For example, children begin to draw animals and make the sounds of the animals as they draw, which he thought showed that they pull from their musical intelligences into the visual-spatial. By age 5, children begin *digital mapping,* which entails careful representation of numbers of fingers, legs, and arms in drawings. By age 7, children begin to invent original notation systems to catalog belongings and experiences.

To summarize, artistic growth proceeds from the gross to the particular, from uncontrolled to controlled, from exploration of media and tools to skilled use of lines to represent ideas. As more and more detail emerges, we can infer the child has keenly observed lines, shapes, colors, and textures in the world. Each piece of art is tangible evidence of connections forged in the child's brain. While art development begins with drawing, drawing is much more than entertainment for children. By examining samples of children's art and writing over time, it is possible to track developmental patterns that parallel the process our early human ancestors used to move from pictograph (early written human language) to alphabetic code to written language. Children's drawings contain symbols to represent objects and actions important in their lives, and show how drawing is a communication tool closely linked to linguistic growth. Artistic growth signals the cognitive and physical growth necessary to write, so teachers should

view drawing tools as writing tools, too. Moreover, children can return to artwork to revise it and use art as a source for new ideas, the same thinking skills needed in written composition. Finally, when we encourage children to draw and engage them in dialogs about their work, we acknowledge that marks have meaning. Thus, children's art can record experiences, ideas, and feelings related to curricular studies.

Teaching Students to *Do* and *View* Art

My own guess is that the fear of being disturbed by external direction occurs in individuals in whom the intuitive impulse and control are weak . . . and who therefore, in fact, cannot afford any distraction . . . it should serve as a warning to us educators. The growth of the young mind is at best a delicate process, easily disturbed by the wrong input at the wrong time. In the arts as well as elsewhere in education the best teacher is not the one who deals out all he knows or who withholds all he could give, but the one, with the wisdom of a good gardener, who watches, judges, and helps out when the help is needed.
Arnheim, 1989, p. 37

Children may indeed be distracted, at first, when they are made aware of what they have been doing unconsciously. This consciousness is necessary, however, if they are to grow and develop. Arnheim calls this discomfort an "intermediate phase of frustration." Students need to know that language and tools of art are conceptual anchors and give them expanded skills to create, discuss, understand, and make judgments in the visual domain. Those who are dubious about giving children explicit art instruction, fearing it may conflict with "natural" art development, should read the work of Mona Brookes (1996), founder of the teaching philosophy *Monart.* She makes a convincing argument that symbolic art development and the ability to create representational art are two *different* entities. Further she shows evidence of how explicit direct instruction in realistic drawing does not hinder symbolic natural expression. Without direct instruction, she believes most children do not automatically discover how to make realistic drawings and will abandon drawing in the teen years. (See more discussion about Monart in Chapter 6.) Indeed, most adults claim they can't draw—meaning they think they can't represent an image realistically. As a society we seem to accept this perceived inability, in contrast to how shocked we are by statistics that show levels of adult illiteracy in verbal communication.

The need for visual literacy, however, is increasingly recognized, and visual literacy skills are now included in literacy standards in most school districts. To become visually literate students need to be taught how to understand visual images and intentionally use art media to make meaning. Teachers also need to know and teach basic art concepts to *meaningfully* integrate art. Such focus ensures that art is not simply an amusement added to curricular areas. As with other arts, teachers should remember, however, that visual art needs to be experienced as a *whole* before it is broken down into component parts—children need to view and do art, before intensive explicit instruction in art elements or art styles begins. Looking at prints and exploring art materials, first develops moti-vation—a desire to learn more. Elements can be introduced informally, using labels *as* natural opportunities arise—teachers can point out lines, shapes, textures, and colors in picture book art, in illustrations of texts, or in nature. Classroom displays of visual art elements on posters and charts are important references to do so. (See Chapter 6 for ideas to teach art elements). What's more, instruction in art basics may counter the tendency children have to abandon art as a form of expression. Essential art information that teachers need to integrate is summarized in the Post It Pages 5–4 through 5–7.

POST IT PAGE 5–4

VISUAL ART ELEMENTS AND DESIGN CONCEPTS

Color: primary and secondary hues, tints, and shades created by light and pigments

Line: a horizontal, vertical, angled, or curved mark made by a tool across a surface

Shape: the two dimensions of height and width arranged geometrically (e.g., circles, triangles), organically (natural shapes), symbolically (e.g., letters)

Texture: the way something feels or looks like it would feel

Form: three-dimensional quality (height, width, and depth), for example, sphere, pyramid, cube

Pattern: something that is repeated (e.g., shapes, lines)

Space: the areas objects take up (positive space) and that surround shapes and forms (negative space)

Contrast: created by lighter colors next to darker ones

Light: illusion created with lighter colors such as white

Composition: arrangement of the masses and spaces

Perspective: illusion of distance and point of view created by techniques such as size, overlapping, atmosphere, sharpness or blurriness, and angles

Foreground, middle, and background: the areas in a piece of art that appear closest to the viewer, next closest, and farthest away

Other concepts: **balance, symmetry, asymmetry**

POST IT PAGE 5–5

MEDIA TECHNIQUES TO USE THROUGHOUT THE CURRICULUM

Directions: Use these ideas to integrate art making throughout the curriculum, including art responses to any topic.

Bookmaking: pop-up, accordion, big books, minibooks, sewn book, and so forth

Calligraphy and block lettering: embellished lettering or letters simply cut from standard-sized blocks (e.g., construction paper)

Collage: design made by pasting or gluing nonpainterly assembled materials on a surface

Craft: handcrafted item such as pottery, weaving, quilt square, or whole quilt

Diorama: shadow box, often made with shoe box to create a scene

Display or bulletin board: arrangements around a concept or theme

Drawing: linear art made with pencil, charcoal, marker, pen and ink, or crayon

Enlargement: use overhead projector to make images larger

Fiber art: fabrics, yarn, string, and so forth used to create art

Fresco: paint on wet plaster

Intaglio: process of engraving used in the production of early picture books

Lithography: printing method in which pictures are drawn with oil-based chalk or paint on a limestone plate. Then the plate is submerged in water. The ink adheres to the chalk or paint. Heavy pressure on the paper causes the design to print.

Mask: paper bag, tag board, balloon with papier mâché

Mixed media: paper, wire, paint, fabric all used in one artwork

Mobile: three-dimensional art that moves, usually suspended in space

Montage: combination of several distinct pictures to make a composite picture

Mural: large wall art

Painting: tempera (pigments in egg base), acrylic (made from polymer), watercolor, oil (pigments in oil base)

Pastel: chalk art

Poster: an advertisement for the artists, the style or a piece of artwork

Print: pull a print or "stamp" with found object, woodcut, linoleum

Puppet: bag, hand, stick

Rubbing: paper is placed over objects and crayons or markers are used to bring up images

Scratchboard: black crayon or ink is placed over another color such as silver or multiple colors; sharp tool is used to scratch surface and reveal color

Sculpture: three-dimensional art made from wood, clay, metal, found objects, plaster, papier mâché

Wash: translucent watercolor used over another medium

Art Materials and Techniques

Teachers with a repertoire of strategies beyond "draw a picture" can offer students media and techniques that enliven learning throughout the curriculum. Media use changes the content or message—the same idea captured in a cartoon comes across differently in a collage. Students simply learn a broader range of communication tools from a knowledgeable skilled teacher. Flexible use of many media and tools give alternative means of expressing and understanding students. Motivation and interest are also increased with the addition of more choices for how ideas and feelings can be shared. Post It Pages 5–5 and 5–6 summarize basic art materials and techniques.

Subject Matter: What Art Is About

The source of art is not visual reality, but the dreams, hopes, and aspirations which lie deep in every human.

Arthur Zaidenberg

Basic art subject matter groupings help students understand art and give more options for original art making. For example, a response to a piece of literature focused on characterization might be a portrait. Here are the most common classifications:

Portrait: person(s)

Cityscape: city view

Painted Ceiling Tiles at Lady's Island Elementary School

POST IT PAGE 5–6

ART MEDIA USED IN CHILDREN'S LITERATURE

Directions: Use these books to show examples of artwork in a medium or to teach about a medium.
Bang, M. (2000). *Picture this: How pictures work.* SeaStar.

Collage

Baker, J. (1987). *Where the forest meets the sea.* Greenwillow.

Brown, M. (1982). *Shadow.* Scribner.

Bunting, E. (1994) (Ill. by D. Diaz). *Smoky night.* Harcourt Brace Jovanovich.

Day, N. R. (1995). *The lion's whiskers. An Ethiopian folk tale.* Scholastic.

Desimini, L. (1994). *My house.* Henry Holt.

Dobrin, A. (1973). *Josephine's imagination.* Scholastic.

Ehlert, L. (1991). *Red leaf yellow leaf.* Harcourt Brace.

Gilman, P. (1992). *Something from nothing.* Scholastic.

Hughes, L. (1995). *The block.* Metropolitan Museum of Art.

Lionni, L. (1959). *Little blue and little yellow.* Mulberry Books.

Crayons and Colored Pencils

Brown, M. (1982). *The bun. A tale from Russia.* Harcourt Brace Jovanovich.

Lionni, L. (1970). *Fish is fish.* Knopf.

Peet, B. (1961). *Huge Harold.* Houghton Mifflin.

Van Allsburg, C. (1986). *The stranger.* Houghton Mifflin.

Drawing

Barrett, P., & Barrett, S. (1972). *The line Sophie drew.* Schroll.

Bush, T. (1995). *Grunt, the primitive cave boy.* Crown.

Charlstrom, N. W. (1992). *Northern lullaby.* Philomel.

Cohen, J. (1995). *Why did it happen?* William Morrow.

de Paola, T. (1989). *The art lesson.* Trumpet Club.

Johnson, C. (1955). *Harold and the purple crayon.* Harper & Row.

McCloskey, R. (1942). *Make way for ducklings.* Viking.

Munsch, R. (1992). *Purple, green and yellow.* Annick.

Schinck, E. (1987). *Art lessons.* Greenwillow.

Fiber Art

Hall, D. (1980). *The ox-cart man.* Viking.

Kroll, V. (1992). *Wood-Hoopoe Willie.* Charles Bridge.

Roessel, M. (1995). *Songs from the loom.* Lerner.

Mixed Media

Burningham, J. (1989). *Hey! Get off our train.* Crown.

Crews, D. (1982). *Carousel.* Greenwillow.

Most, B. (1978). *If the dinosaurs came back.* Harcourt Brace Jovanovich.

Wildsmith, B. (1963). *The lion and the rat.* Oxford University Press.

Young, E. (1989). *Lon po po. A Red Riding Hood story from China.* Philomel.

Mural

Gerstein, M. (1984). *The room.* Harper & Row.

Winters, J. (1991). *Diego.* Random House.

Painting

Agee, J. (1988). *The incredible painting of Felix Clousseau.* Farrar, Straus & Giroux.

Baker, A. (1994). *White rabbit's color book.* Larouse Kingfisher.

Collins, P. L. (1992). *I am an artist.* Millbrook.

Cooney, B. (1982). *Miss Rumphius.* Viking. (acrylics)

Demi, T. (1980). *Liang and the magic paintbrush.* Henry Holt.

de Paola, T. (1988). *The legend of the Indian paintbrush.* Putnam's.

Dunrea, O. (1995). *The painter who loved chickens.* Farrar, Straus & Giroux.

Lessac, F. (1989). *Caribbean alphabet.* Tambourine.

Locker, T. (1984). *Where the river begins.* Dial. (oil paints)

Locker, T. (1987). *The boy who held back the sea.* Dial. (oil paints)

Myers, W. D. (1995). *The story of the three kings.* HarperCollins.

Porte, B. A. (1995). *Chickens chickens.* Orchard.

Price, L. (1990) (Ill. by L. & D. Dillon). *Aida.* Harcourt Brace Jovanovich. (acrylics)

Pastels (Chalk)

Dewey, A. (1995). *The sky.* Green Tiger.

Howe, J. (1987) (Ill. by E. Young). *I wish I were a butterfly.* Harcourt Brace Jovanovich.

Jukes, M. (1984) (Ill. by L. Bloom). *Like Jake and me.* Knopf.

Van Allsburg, C. (1985). *The polar express.* Houghton Mifflin.

Pen and Pencil/Ink

Gag, W. (1956). *Millions of cats.* Coward, McCean & Geoghegan.

Lionni, L. (1961). *On my beach there are many pebbles.* Mulberry.

Macaulay, D. (1977). *Castle.* Houghton Mifflin.

Mayer, M. (1974). *Frog goes to dinner.* Dial.

Van Allsburg, C. (1981). *Jumanji.* Houghton Mifflin.

Viorst, J. (1972) (Ill. by R. Cruz). *Alexander and the terrible, horrible, no good, very bad day.* Atheneum.

Photography

Angelou, M. (1994). *My painted house, my friendly chicken.* Clarkson-Potter.

Brown, L. K., & Brown, M. (1996). *Visiting the art museum.* Dutton.

Desalvo J., Stanley, C. & Olive, J. (Photographers) (2001). *CowParade Houston.* Workman.

Johnson, N. (2001). *National Geographic photography guide for kids.* National Geographic Society.

Freedman, R. (1987). *Lincoln. A photobiography.* Clarion.

Hoban, T. (1990). *Shadows and reflections.* Greenwillow.

Kissinger, K. (1994). *All the colors we are.* Redleaf.

Lauber, P. (1990). *Seeing earth from space.* Orchard.

Patterson, F. (1985) (Ill. by R. H. Cohn). *Koko's kitten.* Scholastic.

Roalf, P. (1993). *Looking at painting. Children.* Hyperion.

Walter, M. P. (1995). *Darkness.* Simon & Schuster.

Printmaking

Brown, M. (1961). *Once a mouse.* Aladdin.

Carl, E. (1987). *The tiny seed.* Picture Book Studio.

Emberley, E., & Emberley, B. (1967). *Drummer Hoff.* Prentice-Hall.

Haley, G. E. (1970). *A story, a story.* Atheneum.

Lionni, L. (1963). *Swimmy.* Random House.

Tajima. (1987). *Owl lake.* Philomel.

Waber, B. (1996). *"You look ridiculous," said the rhinoceros to the hippopotamus.* Houghton-Mifflin.

Sculpture (Three-Dimensional Art)

de Paola, T. (1982). *Giorgio's village.* Putnam. (paper sculpture)

Feelings, M. (1974). *Jambo means hello: Swahili alphabet book.* Dial.

Haskins, J. (1989). *Count your way through Mexico.* Carolrhoda. (papier mâché)

Hawkinson, J. (1974). *A ball of clay.* Albert Whitman. (firing clay)

Hoyt-Goldsmith, D. (1990). *Totem pole.* Scholastic. (wood carving)

Miller, J. (1983). *The human body.* Viking. (paper sculpture)

Price, C. (1975). *Dancing masks of Africa.* Scribner. (masks)

Prokofiev, S. (1985) (Ill. by B. Cooney). *Peter and the wolf.* Viking. (paper sculpture)

Watercolor

Asch, F. (1995). *Water.* Harcourt Brace.

Bunting, E. (1990) (Ill. by R. Himler). *The wall.* Clarion.

Le Ford, B. (1995). *A blue butterfly. A story about Claude Monet.* Doubleday.

Potter, B. (1902). *The tale of Peter Rabbit.* Warne.

Say, A. (1990). *El chino.* Houghton Mifflin.

Yolen, J. (1987) (Ill. by J. Schoenherr). *Owl moon.* Philomel.

Weaving

Allen, C. (1991). *The rug makers.* Steck-Vaughn.

Castaneda, O. S. (1993). *Abuela's weave.* Lee & Low.

Miles, M. (1971). *Annie and the Old One.* Little, Brown.

TAKE ACTION 6

VISUAL LITERACY . . .
READING PICTURE BOOK ART

Directions: Use an expanded view of literacy that focuses on constructing meaning from more than the print. Examine a Caldecott book from the appendix or a book in Post It Page 5–5 to find how art elements and media are used. Create questions and strategies to help students interact with the art elements: line, space, shape, color, texture, composition, perspective, unity, style(s), and media. Include a *general art response* that would cause students to construct meaning or a bridge and extend their experiences. (See Chapter 6 for examples and ideas.)

Landscape: outdoor scene

Seascape: view of a body of water

Interior: inside view of a room or building

Still life: arrangement of nonliving objects

Abstract: color, shape, line, texture is the focus

The People of Art: Artists and Their Styles

Another important area of art integration is the study of the people of art and the unique styles they have created. Children find the childhoods of famous artists interesting, and studying artists is a natural connection to the literary genre of biography. Time lines about artists' lives emerge in classrooms where teachers provoke students' interests about the period of history when the person lived. Maps and globes become important tools to locate places where men and women created the world's art treasury. Since styles of art reflect the society in which they are created, students discuss economic and social circumstances under which new styles were born. For example, the chaotic turn into the 20th century was the context for the birth of abstract art, cubism, and dada. Higher-order thinking skills are honed when students analyze and evaluate style attributes as they learn to discriminate and appreciate art styles. Finally, students have robust role models in real people. They can learn ways to experiment and gain the courage to take more risks when they study the personal struggles of artists that resulted in revolutionary styles. Children come to understand that being creative doesn't mean starting with nothing

Artistic Styles in Children's Literature

Cartoon Style: Simple Lines and Use of Primary Colors

Cole, J. (1989) (Ill. by B. Degen). *The magic school bus inside the human body.* Scholastic.

Schulz, C. (2001). *Peanuts: The art of Charles M. Schulz.* Pantheon.

Schwartz, D. M. (1985) (Ill. by S. Kellogg). *How much is a million?* Scholastic.

Seuss, Dr. (1957). *Cat in the hat.* Random House.

Spier, P. (1980). *People.* Doubleday.

Westcott, N. B. (1984). *The emperor's new clothes.* Little, Brown.

Expressionism: Leans Toward Abstract Style, Focuses on Showing Emotions

Bemelmans, L. (1939). *Madeline.* Viking.

Carle, E. (1984). *The very busy spider.* Philomel.

Ehlert, L. (1989). *Color zoo.* Lippincott.

Le Tord, B. (1999). *A bird or two: A story about Henri Matisse.* William B. Eerdmans.

Livingston, M. C. (1985) (Ill. by L. E. Fisher). *A circle of seasons.* Holiday House.

Martin, B., Jr., & Archambault, J. (1989) (Ill. by L. Ehlert). *Chick chicka boom.* Simon & Schuster.

Williams, V. B. (1982). *A chair for my mother.* Mulberry.

Folk Art: Nontraditional Media Used by Untrained Artists

Aardema, V. (1975) (Ill. by L. Dillon & D. Dillon). *Why mosquitoes buzz in people's ears.* Dial.

Hall, D. (1979) (Ill. by B. Cooney). *The ox-cart man.* Viking.

Lindbergh, R. (1990). *Johnny Appleseed.* Little, Brown.

O'Kelley, M. L. (1986). *Circus!* Little, Brown.

Polacco, P. (1988). *Rechenska's eggs.* Philomel.

Provenson, A. (1990). *The buck stops here: The presidents of the United States.* Harper & Row.

Xiong, B. (1989) (Ill. by N. Hom). *Nine-in-one. Grr! Grr!* Children's Book Press.

Impressionism: Dreamlike Quality, Relies on Play of Light

Baker, O. (1981) (Ill. by S. Gammell). *Where the buffaloes begin.* Warne.

Bjork, C. (1985) (Ill. by L. Anderson). *Linnea in Monet's garden.* R&S Books.

Howe, J. (1987) (Ill. by E. Young). *I wish I were a butterfly.* Harcourt Brace Jovanovich.

Wildsmith, B. (1966). *The hare and the tortoise.* Oxford University Press.

Zolotow, C. (1962) (Ill. by M. Sendak). *Mr. Rabbit and the lovely present.* Harper & Row.

Realism: Represents Reality in Shape, Color, Proportion

Holling, H. C. (1969). *Paddle-to-the-sea.* Houghton Mifflin.

McCloskey, R. (1969). *Make way for ducklings.* Viking.

Turkle, B. (1976). *Deep in the forest.* Dutton.

(continued)

Viorst, J. (1972) (Ill. by R. Cruz). *Alexander and the terrible, horrible, no good, very bad day.* Atheneum.

Ziefert, H. (1986) (Ill. by A. Lobel). *A new coat for Anna.* Knopf.

Surrealism: Distorts and Plays with Images; Fantastic Quality

Bang, M. (1980). *The grey lady and the strawberry snatcher.* Four Winds.

Burningham, J. (1977). *Come away from the water, Shirley.* Harper & Row.

Sciezka, J. (1989) (Ill. by L. Smith). *The true story of the three little pigs.* Viking.

Van Allsberg, C. (1981). *Jumanji.* Houghton Mifflin.

Winter, J. (1988). *Follow the drinking gourd.* Knopf.

as they see how artists often copy other artists to learn how to use certain media or techniques: Picasso copied styles of African masks and Degas worked from photographs, but each adapted, twisted, combined, reshaped, stretched, or expanded others' work. Post It Page 5–7 lists art styles to assist in understanding art and as a resource for their art making. *Note:* The bibliography of arts-based literature in the appendix has books about artists and styles. There are also video and software resources. For example, see the book of interviews with children's book illustrators entitled *Talking with Artists* by Pat Cummings (1992).

TAKE ACTION 7
TRY DIFFERENT STYLES

Different artists use the same medium in different ways and portray the same content in diverse manners. Differences in how color, line, space, and shape are used create style. Style is as individual as a person's signature or smile. Try creating the same image in several styles (e.g., an apple in realistic, impressionistic, and cartoon style). Reflect on the differences.

Special Arts Integration Projects

Discipline-Based Art Education. Walling (2001) writes, "For much of the 20th century visual arts education centered on one overriding goal, helping students realize 'creative self-expression.' This self-limiting philoso-

phy, which eventually helped to push art away from the core curriculum, held increasing sway from the advent of modernism until the 1960s, when the post-Sputnik wave of reform washed ashore some new ideas." (p. 626). In the 1980s, the Getty Center for Education in the Arts, part of the J. Paul Getty Trust, created a curricular model that recommended decreased emphasis on art making and increased focus on teaching art history, esthetics, and art criticism. The model retained hands-on art as a focus but stressed discussion of art as a discipline of inquiry. The rationale was grounded in the belief that an art program, based entirely on creating art, does not give a sense of the place of art in life and the world, and art making does not prepare children to respond to the work of others or to develop a visual esthetic sense important in our highly visual world. The Getty curriculum proposal raised questions about how children were being educated as whole persons in schools that treated art as hands-on construction only. The curriculum developers expressed concern about the lack of visual and artistic literacy among students who could complete 13 years of education and have little opportunity to reflect on the vast treasury of art that is their cultural heritage. On the other hand, *discipline-based art education* (DBAE) has been criticized, especially by early childhood educators, who believe art making should remain the focus. For the most part, it has come to be accepted that a balanced program of art experiences is needed. While children's cognitive growth (e.g., language and conceptual development) is greatly facilitated by exploration through drawing and other artwork, even young children benefit from opportunities to examine and discuss their art and that of others. Classroom teachers interested in DBAE can visit the Getty Internet site ArtsEdNet (Alexander and Michael,

SIX *NATIONAL STANDARDS FOR VISUAL ARTS* (K–8)

Overall focus: Create, express, and respond through visual media, expression of feelings and emotions, new ways of communicating and thinking, application of knowledge to world problems, historical and cultural investigation, and evaluation and interpretation of the visual world.

1. **Understanding and applying media, techniques, and processes.** Example activities: Communicate ideas and experiences through visual art. Use materials safely.
2. **Using knowledge of structures and functions.** Example activities: Explain messages art conveys and what an artist does to convey messages.
3. **Choosing and evaluating a range of subject matter, symbols, and ideas.** Example activities: Explain possible content for artwork and ways to show meaning in different ways.
4. **Understanding the visual arts in relation to history and cultures.** Example activities: Examine how aspects of culture and history are expressed in works of art.
5. **Reflecting upon and assessing the characteristics and merits of their work and the work of others.** Example activities: Explain purposes for art and how people's experiences influence their art.
6. **Making connections between visual arts and other disciplines.** Example activities: Find similarities and differences between visual art and other disciplines. Use visual art throughout the curriculum to make meaning.

Source: Content Standards (material in bold type) excerpted from the *National Standards for Arts Education,* published by Music Educators National Conference (MENC). Copyright © 1994 by MENC. Reprinted with permission. The complete *National Standards* and additional materials relating to the *Standards* are available from MENC: The National Association for Music Education, 1806 Robert Fulton Drive, Reston, VA 20191 (telephone 800-336-3768).

1991; Eisner, 1983; Gardner, 1990; McWinnie, 1992; Winner et al., 1983).

Lincoln Center and Kennedy Center Projects. As discussed in Chapters 1 and 2, there are numerous initiatives across the country concerned with meaningful art integration and balanced art instruction. The Lincoln Center project in New York City and the Kennedy Center Partners in Education in Washington, D.C., are examples of programs focused on classroom teacher development. See the appendix for more information about how to contact these organizations.

National Standards for Art

Teachers should use the visual arts standards in the *National Standards for the Arts* to plan lessons and units that are directed toward learning *about* art and using art as a teaching and learning tool. The *Visual Arts Standards* are summarized on Post It Page 5–8.

HOW CAN CLASSROOM TEACHERS USE ART TO ENHANCE CURRICULAR AREAS?

Good work in biology or mathematics is done when the student's natural curiosity is awakened, when the desire to solve problems and to explain mysterious facts is enlisted, when the imagination is challenged to come up with new possibilities. In this sense, scientific work or the probing of history or the handling of a language is every bit as "artistic" as drawing and painting.

Rudolf Arnheim, 1989, p. 33

General Integration Principles

In Chapter 2 a framework for arts integration was described using the levels: teaching *with, about, in,* and *through* the arts. The 10 INTEGRATES principles are grounded in this framework and are ways to achieve curricular goals and standards, while maintaining the integrity of each art form. In examining the following principles, keep in mind how important it is to balance using art as a teaching and learning tool with respecting art as a special discipline itself.

Principle 1: IMMERSION in Visual Art

Though we travel the world over to find the beautiful, we must carry it with us or we find it not.

Ralph Waldo Emerson

The Esthetic Class Environment. Children may learn what they live, but they also learn best in good environments to live in. We create a home environment to satisfy individual taste and comfort needs; the same consideration needs to be given to the design of a classroom. Children feel and behave better in environments that please the senses. Broken blinds, dirty floors, mismatched furniture, and peeling paint indicate apathy and imply a low priority for esthetics. What makes a pleasing classroom? Cleanliness is a given. Color schemes need to complement one another. Light should be soft, not glaring white, to relax and make learning pleasant. Storage areas are needed to organize tools and materials. Framed art, live plants, music, pleasant smells, fresh air, and art displays all contribute to heightened sensory awareness. Such an environment inspires positive attitudes and uplifts spirits. While there is no one *best* esthetic environment, consider these questions when planning or evaluating a classroom (Jensen 2001; Koster, 1997):

◈ Is there plenty of soft, natural light?

◈ Are there carpeted and uncarpeted areas that are visually pleasing, inviting, and functional?

◈ Are there designated learning station nooks and centers balanced with open areas?

◈ Are walls and furniture neutral in color so that they give the illusion of space and wear well over time? Note that bold primary colors may inhibit the learning of some children.

◈ Are walls a neutral backdrop for displayed art?

◈ Does there seem to be planning in the displays or do they look like a chaotic hodgepodge?

◈ Are there easels on which art prints are displayed? Are they changed regularly?

◈ Are displays at students' eye levels?

◈ Are bulletin boards teacher made, using cutesy commercial art cutouts that limit esthetic development and reinforce stereotypes?

◈ Are holiday decorations stereotypical? Is cultural art trivialized by displaying it only for particular holidays?

◈ Are there focused displays of artifacts, a few select items at a time?

◈ Is there a sense of organization and order for supplies and books?

Children enjoy what is comfortable and familiar and may shrink from the strange. If they are to become accepting of dimensions of beauty, they need immersion in all its variations. Classrooms should contain art in many styles showing people of different ages, races, ethnic backgrounds, sexes, and skin colors. Students need to see art from different places and time periods—images of people going about life in ways that may be foreign to them, and yet show how basic needs for food, clothing, shelter, knowledge, love, and beauty are universal. Respect for diverse peoples is encouraged by seeing works where people are shown in dignified contemporary situations, not just historical garb. Care must be taken to not demean groups—to just show Native Americans half-naked, wearing skins and feathers, is inaccurate, to say the least. Commercial cutouts, cute cardboard pin-ups, and coloring book art should be avoided because they stultify thinking. Just as damaging are traceable patterns or punch outs of ethnic groups and races *only* in historical traditional clothing, suggesting they are less advanced and still live this way—we would think it absurd to shows "Americans" in Pilgrim outfits as a "typical" image, and yet, may not realize the parallel with showing Japanese only in kimonos or Eskimos only living in igloos. Original art sculptures, fine art prints, postcard prints, and art books are ways to show authentic cultural images. Most schools and public libraries have children's literature in every style and media, and students should be invited to bring artifacts from home (pottery, quilts, photographs), as well. Students often see the contributions of peers as stunning sources of esthetic stimulation and family heritage. Esthetic sensibilities can be cultivated by planning quiet times to pass around objects for close examination or taking time to listen to nature sounds and sound patterns created as people and machines go about their work. A "beauty center" stocked with student finds can include shells, leaves, and rocks and serve as a discussion starter about the special "magic" feelings possible when you see a field of sunflowers or touch a new baby's velvety hand (Koster, 1997).

Balancing Creation and Appreciation. Integrating art experiences means balancing *impression* and *expression*, *viewing* and *doing art*. Balance can be achieved through:

1. *Discovery or studio situations* during which materials and tools are provided for children to explore. Adults naturally begin new experiences by gravitating to the stage of "messing around"—most of us scribbled with computer drawing tools before trying to create shapes. Children need to have permission to do the same. Once students gain confidence in using tools and materials, they will want to do actual art making during studio times.

2. *Discipline-based study* where children's original art is discussed, artists and their work are introduced, art is placed in historical and social contexts, and there is opportunity to reflect and refine esthetic criteria. Copying adult art is *not* the goal, but children need time to examine others' art for ideas and learn artistic terms to describe esthetic qualities (e.g., color, texture). The teacher's role is to scaffold or support efforts to acquire language and concepts. Art integration involves looking and understanding, as well as making.

3. *Art-enriched contexts* in which students are surrounded by art and invited to examine artworks and use materials. This is what was previously discussed as the esthetic classroom environment, but can include areas beyond the classroom, such as a classroom garden—the outdoors possess rich opportunities to investigate color, texture, line, and shape.

4. *Meaningful art integration* with other arts and curricular areas. Meaningful integration entails the use of lessons with two or more prongs: art and math focus, art and language arts focus, art and dance, and so forth (see examples of two-pronged lessons in Post It Pages 3–10, 5–14, 7–8, 9–8, and 11–12). Integration should maintain the integrity of each discipline being integrated. Suggesting that children just draw pictures after reading something, when time has never been spent teaching anything about possible materials or drawing tools, does not do justice to art as a discipline and limits children's use of art for communication. A critical integration question is "What did my students *learn* about each discipline being integrated?" *not* "What subjects were *used* in the lesson?" This does not

mean the classroom teacher must be able to draw well. It does mean the teacher needs basic knowledge and skills to use language and present examples of possibilities. This also does not mean students shouldn't have *free* time to make art, without instruction (see item 1). This is analogous to giving children free reading time as a part of teaching them *to* read.

Basic Visual Art Materials. Architect Frank Lloyd Wright said that he "could feel in the palms of his hands the Froebel blocks." He recalled that it was in early childhood when these shapes "had become instinctive to him, giving him his first strong perception of the meanings of volume and form" (Bill, 1988, p. 29). No teacher's words or any book can ever substitute for giving students actual tools and materials of art. Kinesthetic– tactile intelligence is activated in these encounters and may indeed trigger the beginnings of a magnificent life devotion. What is considered *basic* for a regular classroom? At minimum, each classroom needs:

◆ An assortment of brushes, chalk, pencils, water-based markers, crayons, and paints (including tempera, watercolors, and paint crayons)

◆ Different kinds, sizes, and colors of paper, including everything from brown kraft paper to sketch pads to construction paper

◆ Clays and doughs to use for sculpting and modeling

◆ Glues and pastes, especially white glue

◆ Scissors

◆ Collage materials such as shells, buttons, pebbles, lace, ribbon, and fabric

◆ All shapes and sizes of boxes and tubes for construction and for papier mâché bases

◆ Cleanup supplies

◆ Work space (e.g., painting easels and tables that can be covered with old sheets or shower curtains for messy work)

In addition, art prints, children's literature about art and artists, quotes, cartoons, facts about artists, songs, photographs, and artifacts are important components. Begin a collection of basic materials by surveying what you have and then think of ways to get needed materials without undue time and money. Give friends, other teachers, the school staff, and parents a list of materials to save that are normally thrown out (e.g., paper towel and toilet paper tubes to use for "looking closely"). Stores that sell wallpaper may give away old wallpaper books that make perfect quick book binders for children's writing. Paper and photography companies often give paper products. Ask the principal about purchases, but don't despair if the budget is small and don't feel all materials are needed on the first day of school.

Picture files are invaluable and practically free. Collect pictures from magazines and calendars, save postcards, greeting cards, old photographs, and even restaurant place mats to use as sources for art study. Students enjoy discussing and sorting pictures by subject matter (landscape, portrait, etc.), media, style, artist, and art elements—in doing so they are using vocabulary and practicing important thinking skills such as classification, comparing, and contrasting. Pictures can be prompts for creating art or written compositions. Picture files can also become actual art-making materials (e.g., for collage) or be used for drama, storytelling. Start by collecting lots of pictures. Cut out interesting words and phrases that provoke images, too, such as headlines and advertisements. *Sort them into categories:* words and phrases, art styles, art subject matter, other cultures, people, holidays, emotions, places, toys, dance, and movement. Mount pictures and words or use plastic sleeves so that they are ready to use. It is useful to write drama/oral expression ideas and writing uses on each picture's file folder (see Post It Page 4–2, discussion questions for the art in Post It Page 2–3, and art discussions in Post It Page 5–9). Tab category sections and make a table of contents.

Another resource is collections of poems, quotes, and cartoons about art and artists to use in routines and bulletin boards, or as inspiration for students to make poem or quote books. Once the scavenging begins, you and your students will find something about art every day.

Principle 2: NITTY-GRITTY *Visual Art Concepts and Skills*

The acquisition of appropriate techniques and the insistence on acceptable results are as necessary in the arts as they are in the other areas of study.

Arnheim, 1989, p. 57

Arnheim (1989) denounced the Western notion that art could not be taught and that teaching art endan-

gers creative invention. He justifies teaching the tools because "at no level of development can either children or accomplished artists state, to their own satisfaction, what they want to say unless they have acquired the means of saying it" (p. 57). The intention of explicitly teaching basic art concepts and skills is not to foist technical tricks on children that are beyond their ability to use or understand, nor is the goal to teach visual expression in isolation. Ideally, tools and techniques should emerge from task demands. If taught at the wrong time, concepts and skills are meaningless to children, and it is preferable for them to *discover* as much as possible, rather than depend on the teacher.

Teach What Art Is. The concept of "art" is abstract, but students can be guided to discover characteristics of what makes something art. For example, ask students to think of an item they believe is art and then tell why they think so. Art elements, forms, styles, and media used to make art can be taught explicitly by displaying elements charts, teaching minilessons on elements, and using art concepts as categories for games and questions. (Post It Pages 5–4, 5–5, 5–6, and 5–7 summarize elements, forms, and media.) In Chapter 6 there are strategy seeds for teaching color, line, shape, texture, and so forth, including sorts, games, and questioning strategies.

Principle 3: TEACHING HABITS *for Integrating Visual Art*

Dictated art is not art but a contradiction of it.

Blanche Jefferson

Think Artistically. Teachers need not be able to draw realistically or sculpt *well* to help children do so. Artistic teachers are ones that set up an *esthetic* classroom, ask provocative questions, respond with descriptive comments, and are models of how to listen, look, and feel the world's beauty. Here are four examples of habits to develop students' esthetic senses.

Look Closely. Walt Whitman knew little about the brain, compared to what we know today. And yet, when he wrote about a child that went forth each day and became the object he looked upon, he poetically expressed what research now confirms: The images that enter the brain become the basis for the images we create and the people we become. We must work to guarantee that children see beautiful images. Make it a habit to show students that by taking time to notice details new discoveries can be made about everyday things. Offer paper towel tubes and magnifying glasses to examine fabrics and art prints for details. Colored overhead transparencies and cardboard transparency frames make interesting "windows" to focus attention. Books such as Hoban's (1971) *Look Again* can be inspirations to analyze the visual world by looking at parts of plants, animals, and clothes. Hoban overlays shape frames over photographs to cause the viewer to see only a tiny piece of a whole, such as a seed, a tail, a body part. A similar effect can be achieved using note cards or Post-its to mask part of a picture or object (e.g., half of a print could be masked for a guessing game to predict images, colors, shapes). Teachers can model use of descriptive language such as "I see rounded shapes or a muddy brown color" and ask students to describe using the "I see . . . and . . . structure."

Esthetic Aromas. The perfume industry knows well the power of smell to affect behavior. We avoid nasty smells and seek out wonderful aromas. A classroom with fresh flowers, potpourri, and fresh air provides for esthetic sensing and creating. Encourage students to share discoveries about good smells through discussions, journals, and on group-made charts. Give descriptive feedback to stretch language and encourage use of descriptive words; for example, "You like the lemony clean smell of this soap!"

Esthetic Sounds. Easy rhythm instruments can be made to explore the differences in sounds. For example, put beans in a butter tub or make sand blocks by gluing sand paper to old cassette tape cases. Tape record environmental sounds and create art to go with the sounds. At times, play music as students make art. Discuss a print or other art in terms of the sounds associated with it (e.g., a seascape or landscape). Write sound poems about art, like this *onomatopoeia poem* about sounds of a place and time: "Schoolday—Ring/ha ha ha/patter patter/slam/creak/ring ring/achoo/gobble crunch slurp/scribble/sigh/whew/ring/trip-trap, trip-trap/honk toot roar."

Texture and Touch Esthetics. To develop tactile perception so that students can express texture in artwork, (1) ask students to describe feelings as they finger paint, use collage materials, or experiment with different pressure of chalk and crayon. Model this, if needed. For example, "When I press hard the line is darker and thicker." (2) Make feely bags of textured items. Put them at a station to explore or use in circle times; students reach in to feel an object and either describe its nature or use it in an add-on storytelling. For example: "There was once a thin, soft bendy creature (stick of gum) who lived in a cave. One day he inched out to look for food and met a long, thin, soft creature with a rough, stringy tongue (tapered candle)." (3) Ask students to bring items for topical displays on rough, soft, silky, cold, or hard. (4) Go on texture walks to find items in categories (thin, thick, heavy). The items can be used for nature or "found things" collages or table displays. (5) Involve students in making texture books (e.g., fabrics, foils, papers) by gluing items to card stock and fastening with brads or make big books with text dictated or written by students.

Guide or Director. Classroom teachers often lack confidence about their own art abilities and may have limited personal experiences. Lack of confidence manifests itself in rigidity: using precut assembling activities, painting by number, coloring in the lines, cutting out black line masters, and tracing activities. These are no more than direction-following exercises—not art making. The goals of art integration do not focus on student-made art that "looks like something." Hopefully, this book will give enough basic philosophy, research, and knowledge for readers to reject destructive notions of art that focus on convenience, tradition (that's the way it's always been done), and entertainment. These reasons are not grounded in contemporary child development research and not what most educators choose for their own sons and daughters. Activities that squelch creativity, risk taking, and independent thinking cannot give students substantial experiences to grow into capable contributing adults. We lay the foundation in the elementary school. That foundation must be strong. Here are signs that the foundation is made of *straw:*

Teachers should NOT . . .

- Model step-by-step directions to copy rather than create.
- Use commercial bulletin board materials that are cute and convenient (e.g., bunnies and kittens).
- Use stencils to trace or punch out letters for displays.
- Make most of the bulletin boards, rather than having students plan and create them or using space to simply display student work.

◆ Use coloring-book-type activities in which staying in the lines and stereotyped use of color is stressed (color the sky blue and the grass green).

◆ Intervene to do parts of art projects *for* students or having "artistic" students do work for other students.

Other danger signs include students saying, "I can't do it" or "I can't draw" when art activities are introduced. These comments indicate students have little confidence in their own creativity and don't understand that the focus is on the process, not the product. When students know few ways to express themselves, for example, only drawing, it is clear the teacher has not done his job in teaching options for materials, techniques, and tools. Finally, when students say that they hate certain styles, like abstract art, without ever studying them, it is clear teachers have not taught students to *understand* before they judge.

Creative Problem Solving and Authentic Art.
Teachers who are committed to arts integration often have a "what if" perspective. Their teaching habits invite students to experiment, investigate, gather ideas, pose potential solutions, speculate, reflect, evaluate, and feel the joy of discovery. (See the creative problem-solving process on Post It Page 1–6.) But pressing students to deal with the dissonance created during creative problem solving can be exasperating, even for master artists. Georgia O'Keefe spent her early years teaching in Amarillo, Texas, and started teaching college in Canyon, Texas, about 1916. There is a story about how frustrated she became one day when she tried to get her students to think for themselves. She went to the board and wrote, "Would all the fools in this class please leave!" One student immediately asked, "Then who will teach us?" To her credit, Miss O'Keefe had a good laugh at her own expense. Children's author Katherine Paterson (1973) reminds us in *Sign of the Chrysanthemum,* that "it is only through fire that the spirit is forged." We should not back away from posing creative problem-solving situations to students, even though this will undoubtedly cause them to struggle. We can teach how to massage the process to make ideas more forthcoming. See Post It Page 1–8 for Ways to Jump Start).

Guidelines for *Making* Art. Here are key teaching ideas to help students "do" art successfully:

◆ Teach *how* to use a variety of media, tools, and techniques: printing, collage, watercolor, chalk, tempera, original stenciling, mobiles, sculpting, rubbings, papier mâché, and use different surfaces (e.g., fabric, wood). Students will not discover these things on their own. See the Chapter 6 strategy seed ideas for ideas on each of these.

◆ Provide several examples, *not* models, and then remove them so that students can't copy.

◆ Use an *explore–practice–express* lesson sequence. Exploration often causes students to want to learn more about how to use a tool or material, too. Give time to try, first, so that they develop a *need to know,* which builds readiness for direct instruction. Consider a teaching sequence of (1) time to explore, (2) time for practice with teacher feedback, as needed, and (3) actual use of materials. It is important to demonstrate key ways to use materials and tools before giving time to explore and experiment—especially if there are safety issues with particular materials. At times materials and tools can be put out without an introduction for students to discover possibilities—we want doers, not just viewers. Repeated use of the same materials and media gives practice, which leads to confidence and skill. Always the focus remains on involving students in actual use and practice with materials so that they learn how to *use them to communicate.*

◆ Limit direction giving. Even adults get impatient with long explanations.

◆ Give more descriptive feedback ("You have used four different shapes.") than praise ("Good shapes!") as students work. Describe what a student is doing. Use an *artistic vocabulary* to teach words and concepts. Focus on what is being learned. "Good job!" and "Great!" are too vague and really teach nothing. *Note:* Try not to interrupt with your comments when students are actively engaged in art making.

◆ Do not ask, "What is it?" This may insult a student. Instead, offer comments or ask about art elements or the process ("How did you do this? I see you are trying to put the wash over the candle drawing."), artistic decisions ("Why did you do it this way?"), or predictions ("What do you think will happen if. . . ? or How could you. . . ?").

◆ Create an atmosphere and expectation for appropriate behavior. Art making should be a time for focus and concentration. Play music, without lyrics, and make rules about quiet. Brookes (1996) believes children must be taught the pleasures of silence because they so rarely experience it. She has found it takes time for children to be comfortable with quiet, but stresses that it is necessary to truly concentrate. She offers strategies to teach the value of silence in her book.

◆ After students finish, invite them to do docent talks about their work to explain their creative problem-solving process.

◆ Invite students to write or tell stories about their art, find music that goes with the art, and even create original musical compositions for the art.

◆ Instead of writing on student art—it is common to ask children to give a sentence about the art or a title and the teacher writes it—have students write for themselves, even if it is in developmental spelling. This builds independence. Instead of anyone writing on a child's art, it is better to write on a separate piece of paper. Artists usually don't write anything except their signatures on their art.

◆ Connect art to the students' lives—a part without a whole is a "field without an anchor" (Eisner in Arnheim, 1989, p. 5). Instead of isolated art activities or art used only as a reward for finishing work, integrate art by using the *with, about, in,* and *through* model, discussed in Chapter 2, that includes meaning making through art in routines and content units in science and social studies.

◆ Refrain from using paint by numbers, coloring books, and dittos that are not art at all. This teaches conformity and discourages creativity and problem solving.

Stations and Centers.   Centers and stations provide opportunities for independent work that extend a lesson or a personal interest. A center does not have to be elaborate. Here are important *continuous* centers or stations (a station is a place with a single focused activity while a center has many activities around a topic):

◆ *Book-making station* with wallpaper, fabric, and other materials to bind student-made books

TAKE ACTION 8
DESCRIPTIVE FEEDBACK SCENARIO

Students are doing *fairy tale* paintings. You walk around and *give descriptive feedback* on art elements and the creative process. What do you say? Choose one or write your own. Careful!

1. You guys are doing a great job! This is really cute! Awesome!
2. You are staying right in the lines when you are coloring!
3. I love the way you are making yours like my model! I'm so glad you remembered to make the pumpkins orange and the trees green.

◆ *Puppet-making station* with examples of different types of puppets and materials to make them (see the types in Post It Page 6–4)

◆ Books about art and artists in a *book nook center* with shelves or areas with children's literature related to other arts areas, too

◆ *Art-making center* with collage materials (feathers, buttons, variety of papers), watercolors, pastels, markers, watercolor crayons, different papers, and a posted list of ideas to try in an art response to a book or unit under study. See art response possibilities in Post It Page 5–5. A few books that show how artists use different media and styles are important resources for data gathering to have at this center.

◆ *Multicultural arts center* with many examples of different kinds of art and actual artifacts. This is the place to include a picture file of art to examine for different styles or media use.

HOTS: Evaluative Judgments.   Students don't automatically know how to make good judgments, especially when looking at art. Without instruction, they tend to want to stop at loving or hating a work. These kinds of reactions halt thinking. Children need to be taught to take time and just describe what they see and the feelings a picture or object evokes. Then they can be guided to give reasons *why* they like or dislike a piece or think it is good or bad. Teachers can "think aloud" to model responses and form the habit of asking students for evidence for their opinions. Another strategy is to rate judgments of "goodness," or how much a work is liked, using a 1 to 5 scale. Ratings can then be discussed. These teaching habits create an expectation for reflection, first. A respect for considered thinking can be taught. Breezy conclusions are soon seen as just that. Ultimately, students need to grasp the concept that to *appreciate* art means to understand it—not that you have to like it.

Teach How to Decode Art. Students who know basic art elements and concepts that artists use will be able to talk more fluently about art. This increases individual and group understanding and enjoyment.

"What do you see?" and "Take time and look closely" discussion strategies help students learn to concentrate, take time (most people average less than 10 seconds looking at individual works in museums), and move from merely identifying and describing to becoming storytellers about art. Use of open questions and directed viewing (e.g., "Notice the use of overlapping") causes students to think at higher levels and do creative problem solving. Eventually, students see how artwork, done by others, gives insight. Group discussions move into meaningful areas. Student begin to feel free to express concerns about life issues when there are safe structured opportunities. Post It Page 5–9 has ideas to help implement these kinds of discussions.

POST IT PAGE 5–9

ART DISCUSSIONS: QUESTIONING AND OTHER STRATEGIES

Directions: Use these strategies to teach students to decode artwork and engage them in personal connections and storytelling. In a video called, *"What do you see?"* (Chicago Art Institute) Phillip Yenawine uses many of these strategies with elementary and high school students.

◆ **Concrete to abstract development.** Young children have difficulty with questions like "Why might the artist have painted this?" (motives or intentions) and understanding visual symbols such as colors or objects to represent seasons. Primary students can interpret art, however, so try these types of questions. If they still have trouble, use more concrete ones. *Note:* Young children need time to examine abstract art and often prefer it to detailed realism.

◆ **Plan questions ahead of time** that form a *line of questioning* that leads to a point. Help students see something they would not have seen otherwise. Go for the "Ahhh" response.

◆ **Ask open or fat questions:** *"What do you see? What's this about? What does this tell us about people? What story does this tell?"* These require higher-order thinking skills (HOTS). See Bloom's taxonomy in the text. Assure children there is no single interpretation of a work of art, and honest responses are welcome.

◆ **Give sufficient time to LOOK before questioning.** Encourage curiosity and commitment by guiding children to "look closely and take time." Set an amount of time for all to look and not talk.

◆ **Speak at children's level, but don't paternalize.** Relate to their experiences and try to include each child, at least with eye contact. Vary voice and smile to sustain interest.

◆ **Use wait time and every pupil response (EPR) signals.** More students will respond with longer and more meaningful answers if you ask, wait 3 to 5 seconds, and then ask for a response signal such as "thumbs up." Wait for everyone to think of a response for certain questions so that all feel "expected" to be active. Then call on selected students as time permits.

◆ **If your question doesn't work, rephrase it.** Keep trying!

◆ **Be sensitive to interests** and take advantage of unexpected teachable moments to follow through on an expressed curiosity.

◆ **Respond to children's answers.** Use active listening behaviors. Don't rush. Give them time to think and speak.

◆ **Compliment honest and appropriate answers.**

- ◆ **If a wrong or inaccurate response is given,** don't embarrass the student, but respond "That's an interesting idea. Who has a different idea?" Use "dignifying" techniques: Ask the student to explain why he thinks this; ask for the ideas of others; try to cue students toward accurate answers, but allow responders to save face. *Note:* This only is necessary in obvious situations such as a student says the painting is by Degas when it is actually by Rembrandt. Find ways to dignify any honest response. In this case you might say, "This was done by a Dutch artist but not van Gogh. Do you know another Dutch artist that might be the artist for this?"

- ◆ **When an answer is partly correct,** rephrase the question, using the correct information to create another question. "Yes it is true that . . . but let's look again and see if we can find. . . ."

- ◆ **Follow through on responses:** Ask for evidence for ideas. An example sequence is: *Question:* "What season of the year is it?" *Answer:* "Winter." *Follow-up:* "How does the artist show this?" *Question:* "How does this painting make you feel?" *Answer:* "Sad." *Follow-up:* "Why? What makes you feel that way?" or "Why do you think that?" Ask them to "tell more" about their thinking. Paraphrase or repeat responses and ask if you've done so accurately. Ask other students to respond or piggyback on a student's idea (e.g., "What do the rest of you think about Joan's point?").

- ◆ **Encourage student questions** with requests such as "What questions do you have?" or invite students to all write out questions. Put them in a hat and draw out to help students feel safe.

- ◆ **Plan small-group discussion.** Start with pairs or trios with immature students and work up to groups of four to six. Give a few minutes to discuss a question among themselves: "Find a partner and talk about what choices this artist had to make to create this work (materials), how it was arranged." This allows shy students to participate and prepares all for a large-group discussion.

- ◆ **End the discussion.** Ask students to tell something they learned, what someone said that made sense, something that was surprising, or just repeat an idea they heard that was interesting.

Additional Pointers about Art Discussions. Because detail is so important in art, it is helpful to have a large magnifying glass to examine brush strokes and other art aspects. Children are intrigued by details that emerge when magnified—details that were insignificant or invisible before. A flashlight can also be used to highlight areas during discussions. Start by asking students to describe art. Next, ask for interpretations (e.g., "What does this mean? Why do you think the artist did that?") Finally, ask students to create stories about the art, as soon as feasible because interpretive and creative discussion are more engaging than ones that focus on identification or description. Another effective strategy is to cover half of a painting or ask groups to choose a section on which to focus (e.g., foreground, background). Small groups can then serve as "experts" on their sections and report back. Another strategy that can be a teaching habit is to ask students to imagine what happened one minute *after* an art piece was finished. This can evolve into a writing or drama activity.

TAKE ACTION 9

QUESTIONING

Choose a piece of art and practice writing questions for it. Ask at least one question in each of these categories: about the story the art tells, the process the artist used, the elements, feelings the art evokes, curriculum connections, and movement responses (e.g., "how might you show . . .").

Principle 4: ENERGIZERS and Warm-ups

Energizers and warm-ups prepare students to make meaning through art. They get them ready to think like an artist and activate the senses. These and other examples are described in Chapter 6:

- ◆ Listening and looking walks
- ◆ Collections

- ◆ Displays
- ◆ Mystery bag
- ◆ Brainstorming
- ◆ Twenty questions
- ◆ Sense stations
- ◆ Browsing picture file and books
- ◆ Exploring and messing around

Principle 5: GREAT CHILDREN'S LITERATURE about Visual Art and Artists

We are fortunate to have technology to make exquisite literature containing visual art. In addition to the genre of picture books, there are hundreds of books whose themes make powerful statements about art's central place in life. In the appendix there is a bibliography of award-winning art-based children's literature, including Caldecott Award winners. (The Caldecott is presented yearly by the American Library Association for excellence in picture books—books that contain pictures that are more than illustrations, pictures that make esthetic statements.) Post It Page 5–10 has a few annotated books that show the variety of art topics in books, making them an important teaching resource. Included are notes about media, art elements and concepts, and culture.

POST IT PAGE 5–10

CHILDREN'S LITERATURE AND ART CONCEPTS

Adoff, A. (1973). *Black is brown is tan.* HarperCollins. (Art elements: color. Describes the skin colors in an interracial family.)

Allington, R. (1979). *Colors.* Raintree. (Art elements: color. Twelve base colors and how to mix them.)

Blizzard, G. S. (1992). *Come look with me: Exploring landscape art with children.* Thomason-Grant. (Art concept: landscape. Twelve landscape paintings are shown, with information on the artists. Part of a series: *World of Play, Animals in Art, and Enjoying Art with Children.*)

Brown, M. (1979). *Listen to a shape.* F. Watts. (Art elements: shape. Basic shapes of square, circle, and more are introduced using poetry and nature.)

Cheltenham Elementary School, Kindergarten (1994). *We are all alike . . . We are all different.* Scholastic. (Art concepts: portraits. Also in big book.)

Crews, D. (1995). *Sail away.* Greenwillow. (Art elements = color, pattern, shape. Air-brushed shapes provide a way to show the concept of pattern through repeated images of objects.)

Crosbie, M. J., & Rosenthal, S. (1993). *Architecture COLORS.* Preservation. (Art concept = architecture. Art elements: color, form. Each color is illustrated with a photograph of an architectural feature opposite the word for the color. Series by the National Trust for Historic Preservation includes *Architecture SHAPES* and *Architecture COUNTS.*)

Ehlert, L. (1994). *Color zoo.* HarperCollins. (Art concept: using your senses. Art elements = space. Wordless book. Layered holes form abstract animals that change shape.)

Everett, G. (1991). *Li'l sis and Uncle Willie.* Hyperion. (Culture: African American. African American artist William H. Johnson's art is used to create this story of his life.)

Heller, R. (1995). *Color! Color! Color!* Grosset & Dunlap. (Art elements: color. Art concepts: mixing colors. With rhythmic language, Ruth Heller presents concepts about color with color acetates that overlap to show mixing.)

Jonas, A. (1989). *Color dance.* Greenwillow. (Art elements: color. Children dance with transparent cloth that overlaps to create new colors.)

Lepschy, I. (1992). *Pablo Picasso.* Baron's Education Series. (Art as a career. This biography of Picasso as a child focuses on his difficulties. Recommended for teachers. Part of a series called *Children of Genius.* Also in the series is *Leonardo da Vinci* [1984].)

Lewis, S. (1991). *African American art for young people.* Davis. (Culture: African American. Twelve African American artists are the topic of the book. Example artwork is reproduced: Powers [quilting], Barthe and Lewis [sculpture], Tanner, Hunter, Hayden, Johnson, Jones, Bearden, Lawrence, and Catlett [painting], and Butler [found art constructions] are presented.)

Lionni, L. (1991). *Matthew's dream.* Knopf. (Art as a career. Art concepts: museums. A young mouse is inspired to become a painter.)

Locker, T. (1994). *Miranda's smile.* Dial. (Art concepts: portrait. Art as a career. Media: painting. An artist tries to paint his daughter's portrait.)

Lord, S. (1995). *The story of the dreamcatcher and other Native American crafts.* Scholastic. (Media: beadwork, masks, photographs. Culture: Native American. Tells about several Native American crafts, including the dreamcatcher, beadwork, and mask making.)

McDermott, G. (1993). *Raven: A trickster tale from the Pacific Northwest.* Harcourt Brace. (Art elements: shape, pattern. Culture: Native American. Pictures are based on the traditional art forms and patterns of the Northwest coastal tribes.)

McGovern, A. (1969). *Black is beautiful.* Scholastic. (Art elements: color. Celebrates the color black.)

McLerran, A. (1991). *Roxaboxen.* Lothrop, Lee & Shepard. (Art concept: architecture. Media: construction. Children build "houses" from stones, old pottery, and crates.)

Micklethwait, L. (1994). *I spy a lion: Animals in art.* Greenwillow. (Find animals and details in famous artworks.)

Paul, A. W. (1991). *Eight hands round.* HarperCollins. (Art elements: pattern. Media: quilting. Traditional American quilt patterns are shown along with explanations for their origins.)

Pfister, M. (1992). *The rainbow fish.* North-South Books. (Art element: color. The most beautiful fish in the ocean discovers how to find happiness. The scales are made with real reflective foil.)

Pinkwater, D. M. (1977). *The big orange splat.* Scholastic. (Art element: color. Story about a creative man who paints his house his own unique way.)

Polacco, P. (1988). *Rechenko's eggs.* Philomel. (Art elements: pattern. Culture: Ukrainian. Patterns are everywhere in this story of a magic goose and beautiful Pysanky eggs.)

Polacco, P. (1990). *Thunder cake.* Putnam. (Art elements: pattern. Clothing and quilts are full of patterns. Story of a grandmother who teaches her granddaughter about bravery.)

*Ringgold, F. (1991). *Tar beach.* Random House. (Culture: African American. Media: quilting. Autobiography about growing up in Harlem. Painted and quilted fabrics.)

Rodari, F. (1991). *A weekend with Picasso.* Rizzoli. (Uses facts from Picasso's life to create a fictional weekend spent with the artist. Illustrated with photographs and Picasso's artwork.)

*Sendak, M. (1964). *Where the wild things are.* Harper & Row. (Art elements: line. A little boy does not want to eat supper. Sendak uses expressive lines to add detail to his drawings.)

Shalom, V. (1995). *The color of things.* Rizzoli International. (Art elements: color. Colors are drained from a town and children paint them back again. Helps children see how important color is.)

Shaw, C. G. (1988). *It looked like spilt milk.* Harper Trophy. (Art element: shape. Free-form shapes turn into ordinary objects. Also in big book.)

Turner, R. M. (1993). *Faith Ringgold.* Little, Brown. (Media: quiltmaking. Biography of African American quilt maker Faith Ringgold. Provides background for Ringgold's *Tar Beach*.)

Venezia, M. (1991). *Paul Klee.* Children's Book. (Biography of Klee starting in childhood. Illustrated with reproductions of his artwork. One of a series called *Getting to Know the World's Greatest Artists.* Other books include *Rembrandt* [1988], *Monet* [1989], *Cassatt* [1990], *Michelangelo* [1991], *Botticelli* [1992], *Bruegel* [1992], *Pollock* [1992], *Goya* [1993], and *O'Keefe* [1993[.)

Wilson, F. (1969, 1988). *What it feels like to be a building.* Preservation. (Art concept: architecture. People shapes illustrate an analogy of how buildings are constructed. Beside each architectural feature, such as a column or arch, the illustrations show how the stress and strains would feel if the structure were built out of people.)

Yenawine, P., & the Museum of Modern Art (1991). *Colors.* Delacorte. (Art elements: Artwork from MOMA illustrates this art concept book. Series includes *Lines, Shapes,* and *Stories.*)

*Yolen, J. (1988). *Owl moon.* Philomel. (Art elements: color/white. Art concept: perspective. Media = painting. A boy and his father go for a walk on a snowy moonlit night.)

Young, E. (1991). *Seven blind mice.* Philomel. (Based on the tale of the blind men and the elephant, seven blind mice use their senses to investigate an elephant. Available as a big book.)

---

*Caldecott Award books.

Author–Artist Studies.   One of the basic types of integrated units used is the author–artist study. The purpose of this unit type is to learn about the creators of books. Students learn biographical information, the process of creation, and the artist's style, and other arts, skills, and subject areas are used to explore the person being studied. *Source books* for information on artist–authors appear in Post It Page 3–8. Post It Page 5–13 depicts a web for a study. Here are guidelines to plan an artist–author unit, and Post It Page 5–11 has a list of author–artists to focus this type of unit.

Artist–Author Study Unit Guidelines and Ideas

◆ Start by collecting material about authors and artists in a file. Use source books such as *Something about the Author* (Hedblad, 1998), filmstrips, and audio and videotapes to find biographical information, quotes, and interesting facts. (See Post It Pages 3–8 and 5–11.) Organize information on an author–artist "map" with these categories: name and vital statistics, books written and/or illustrated, awards, information about the books (genre, problems, themes, style), childhood, hobbies, interests and favorites, how and why the person writes or creates, idiosyncracies about the person, and special quotes about or from the person.

◆ Read a biography or autobiography of the author or artist.

◆ Locate where the person lives on a map.

◆ Collect and read all the works by the author or artist.

◆ Experiment with art media and styles of an artist. Invite a local artist to demonstrate or visit an artist's studio.

◆ Find other art and trade books in the same media and style. Read *If You Were a Writer* (Nixon & Degen, 1988) to learn how a writer works.

◆ Arrange a conference telephone call with the author or artist (check with the publisher).

◆ Write a letter to the author or artist.

◆ Do a presentation about the person and his or her work (biographical information, style; share examples by showing art and reading aloud sections). Do a drama presentation in which you become the author or artist.

◆ Make a bulletin board, display, posters, booklet, or brochure on the person and his or her work.

◆ Read Aliki's (1986) *How a Book Is Made* to learn how books are created.

◆ Write and bind a book about the author or artist.

◆ Interview a local author about the writing process.

◆ Create author and artist blurbs to include in books in the classroom so that future readers have this information.

◆ Visit a local publishing company or newspaper to see the publishing process.

Finding Art-Based Literature.   Locate information about authors and artists in source books such as Hedblad's (1998) *Something about the Author. A to Zoo* is a particularly helpful reference because it is a bibliography of *just* picture books, categorized by author, title, and subject or topic. Post It Page 3–8 lists other materials for units.

Picture Books Related to Curricular Areas.   Picture books are now available on nearly every curricular topic and are fine additions to science, social studies, and math collections. For example, during a Civil War unit, picture books such as Polacco's *Pink and Say* can be enjoyed, and they also provide significant factual information. *Mirandy and Brother Wind* is a beautiful picture book about a special dance in the African American culture and includes dialect. Seymour

Artist–Author Study Information*

Andersen, Hans Christian

Meet the Author: Hans Christian Andersen. American School Publishers (SF or V).

Greene, C. (1991). *Hans Christian Andersen: Prince of Storytellers.* Children's.

Brown, Marcia

Brown, M. (1983). Caldecott Medal Acceptance. *Horn Book Magazine, 59,* 414–422.

Carle, Eric

Eric Carle, Picturewriter. Searchlight Film (V).

Dahl, Roald

The Author's Eye: Roald Dahl. American School Publishers (V).

de Paola, Tomie

de Paola, T. (1989). *The Art Lesson.* Putnam.

"Tomie de Paola," (1986). Authors on Tape. *Trumpet* (audiotape).

Dillon, Leo, and Diane

Preiss, B. (1981). *The Art of Leo and Diane Dillon.* Ballantine.

Dr. Seuss

Who's Dr. Seuss?: Meet Ted Geisel. American School Publishers (SF).

Roth, R. (1989). On Beyond Zebra with Dr. Seuss. *New Advocate, 2,* 213–226.

Fox, Mem

Manning, M., & Manning, G. (March 1990). Mem Fox: Mem's the Word in Down Under? *Teaching PreK–8, 20,* 29–31.

Hamilton, Virginia

First Choice: Authors and Books—Virginia Hamilton. Pied Piper (SF).

Meet the Newbery Author: Virginia Hamilton. American School (SF).

Highwater, Jamake

Meet the Newbery Author: Jamake Highwater. American School (SF).

Keats, Ezra Jack

Ezra Jack Keats. Weston Woods (film).

Lanes, S. G. (1984). Ezra Jack Keats: In Memoriam. *Horn Book Magazine, 60,* 551–558.

Pope, M. (1990). Ezra Jack Keats: A Childhood Revisited. *New Advocate, 3,* 13–24.

Kellogg, Steven

How a Picture Book Is Made. Weston Woods (V).

Konigsburg, E. L.

First choice: Authors and books—E. L. Konigsburg. Pied Piper (SF).

Jones, L. T. (1986). Profile: Elaine Konigsburg. *Language Arts, 63,* 177–184.

L'Engle, Madeline

Meet the Newbery Author: Madeline L'Engle. American School (SF).

Raymond, A. (1991). Madeline L'Engle: Getting the Last Laugh. *Teaching PreK–8, 21,* 34–36.

Livingston, Myra Cohn

First Choice: Poets and poetry—Myra Cohn Livingston. Pied Piper (SF).

Porter, E. J. (1980). Profile: Myra Cohn Livingston. *Language Arts, 57,* 901–905.

Lobel, Arnold

Meet the Newbery Author: Arnold Lobel. American School (SF).

Lobel, A. (1981). Caldecott Medal Acceptance. *Horn Book Magazine, 57,* 400–404.

Lobel, A. (1981). Arnold at Home. *Horn Book Magazine, 57,* 405–410.

Macaulay, David

David Macaulay in His Studio. Houghton Mifflin (V).

Ammon, R. (1982). Profile: David Macaulay. *Language Arts, 59,* 374–378.

MacLachlan, Patricia

Babbitt, N. (1986). Patricia MacLachlan: The biography. *Horn Book Magazine, 62,* 414–416.

Langu Courtney, A. (1985). Profile: Patricia MacLachlan. *Language Arts, 62,* 783–787.

MacLachlan, P. (1986). A Newbery Medal Acceptance. *Horn Book Magazine, 62,* 407–413.

Raymond, A. (May 1989). Patricia MacLachlan: An advocate of "bare boning." *Teaching PreK–8, 19,* 46–48.

McDermott, Gerald

Evolution of a Graphic Concept: The Stonecutter. Weston Woods (SF).

McDermott, G. (1988). Sky Father, Earth Mother: An artist interprets myth. *New Advocate, 1,* 1–7.

Merriam, Eve

First choice: Poets and poetry—Eve Merriam. Pied Piper (SF).

Cox, S. T. (1989). A Word or Two with Eve Merriam: Talking about poetry. *New Advocate, 2,* 139–150.

Sloan, G. (1981). Profile: Eve Merriam. *Language Arts, 58,* 957–964.

Milne, A. A.

Meet the Author: A. A. Milne (and Pooh). American School (SF or V).

O'Dell, Scott

Meet the Newbery Author: Scott O'Dell, American School (SF).

A Visit with Scott O'Dell. Houghton Mifflin (V).

Roop, P. (1984). Profile: Scott O'Dell. *Language Arts, 61,* 750–752.

Paterson, Katherine

The Author's Eye: Katherine Paterson, American School (V).

Meet the Newbery Author: Katherine Paterson. American School (SF).

Jones, L. T. (1981). Profile: Katherine Paterson. *Language Arts, 58,* 189–196.

Namovic, G. I. (1981). Katherine Paterson. *Horn Book Magazine, 57,* 394–399.

Peet, Bill

Bill Peet in His Studio. Houghton Mifflin (V).

Peet, B. (1989). *Bill Peet: An autobiography.* Houghton Mifflin.

Polacco, Patricia

Babushka's Doll (1995). Audio cassette. Scholastic.

Patricia Polacco: Dream Keeper (1996). Philomel (V).

Vandergrift, Kay E. (1995). Patricia Polacco. In L. Berger (Ed.), *Twentieth-Century Children's Writers* (4th ed., pp. 759–760). St. James.

Potter, Beatrix

Beatrix Potter Had a Pet Named Peter. American School (SF or V).

Aldis, D. (1969). *Nothing is impossible: The story of Beatrix Potter.* Atheneum.

Collins, D. R. (1989). *The Country Artist: A story about Beatrix Potter.* Carolrhoda.

Prelutsky, Jack

Raymond, A. (Nov./Dec. 1986). Jack Prelutsky . . . Man of many talents. *Teaching PreK–8, 17,* 38–42.

Vardell, S. (1991). An Interview with Jack Prelutsky. *New Advocate, 4,* 101–112.

Rylant, Cynthia

Meet the Newbery Author: Cynthia Rylant. American School (SF or V).

Meet the Picture Book Author: Cynthia Rylant. American School (V).

Silvey, A. (1987). An Interview with Cynthia Rylant. *Horn Book Magazine, 63,* 695–702.

Sendak, Maurice

Max Made Mischief: An Approach to Literature (1977). Pennsylvania State University (V).

Sendak. Weston Woods (F).

Sendak, M. (1983). Laura Ingalls Wilder Award Acceptance. *Horn Book Magazine, 59,* 474–477.

Van Allsburg, Chris

Keifer, B. (1987). Profile: Chris Van Allsburg in Three Dimensions. *Language Arts, 64,* 664–671.

McKee, B. (1986). Van Allsburg: From a different perspective. *Horn Book Magazine, 62,* 566–571.

Van Allsburg, C. (1986). Caldecott Medal Acceptance. *Horn Book Magazine, 62,* 420–424.

White, E. B.

Meet the Newbery Author: E. B. White. American School (SF).

L. B. (1986). Profile in Memoriam: E. B. White. *Language Arts, 63,* 491–494.

Newmeyer, P. F. (1987). E. B. White: Aspects of Style. *Horn Book Magazine, 63,* 586–591.

Yolen, Jane

White, D. E. (1983). Profile: Jane Yolen. *Language Arts, 60,* 652–660.

Yolen, J. (1989). On Silent Wings: The making of Owl Moon. *New Advocate, 2,* 199–212.

Yolen, J. (1991). The Route to Story. *New Advocate, 4,* 143–149.

---

*Also see Post It Page 3–8. V = video; SF = sound filmstrip; F = film.

Simon's books contain wonderful examples of photography and science. Any fine picture book can serve as material to develop language arts and visual literacy skills by asking students to tell what they see (see Post It Page 5–9). Art strategies for picture book art exploration are given in Post It Page 5–12.

Principle 6: ROUTINES

Daily Art Routines and Rituals. Two examples of short routines to integrate visual art are (1) "artist of the day" or daily "art concept" (an art form, element, or style) and (2) art book ads to promote art-based literature. Invite students to become "experts" to present routines, as a means of developing speaking and listening. For shy students, use a puppet (named "Art" with a smock and beret?) to speak in front of the group. Daily riddles, poems, and songs about art and artists that you find or are written by the students are other possible routines. (Barbara Streisand's song "Putting It Together" is about making art.) Also see Chapter 6 for seed ideas.

Masterpiece Corner. Art prints are easy to obtain and inexpensive (see sources at the end of the chapter).

Calendars in every art style are available at huge savings in January and February. (Explain that prints are photographs of original art so that students understand the real thing may be much larger and look different. Students are interested in the dimensions of original art and locations where they might travel to see it in a gallery.) Display prints at children's eye level on easels, which adds a feeling of importance because they are special furniture, just for art. They can be found at flea markets for as little as a dollar. Provoke thought about the art by displaying the title and asking students to predict colors, mood, and the like before showing a print; asking students to compose a title, after viewing the print and taking time to discuss it; or displaying a question with a print as a journal stimulus. For example, "Why do you think the artist chose to paint this?" or "What do you see in this print that you don't think anyone else will see?" Postcards, matching the large print, can be used to make comparisons or to set up as a matching station. Another idea is to buy two copies of the same print and cut one up so that students can attend to art details by matching pieces with the whole. Students also enjoy playing "I spy" with prints with a large magnifying glass. The teacher begins

ART STRATEGIES FOR PICTURE BOOKS

1. **Ape the greats.** Explore picture book styles and media using Post It Page 5–9. Invite experimentation with an artist's media and styles. Adapt ideas using SCAMPER (Post It Page 1–6).

2. **Predict from art.** Activate thinking before reading a picture book by showing one or two pictures and giving time to look closely. Ask for predictions about the (1) Who? *characters,* (2) When and Where? *setting/time,* and (3) What might be the problems? from pictures. Ask students to support predictions with evidence from the art. Record ideas on a chart divided into three columns so they can return to predictions to confirm or reject them during and after the book.

3. **Clothesline art prediction.** You need two copies of the same book. One is taken apart and the text is cut off. Display the pictures, before reading the book. Ask students to arrange them in the order they think they will occur. Students must come to an agreement about the most probable order. Use a clothesline to pin them up in order or a pocket chart. Next, read the book and check picture order. Rearrange as necessary. *Variation:* Ask students to write stories to go with the pictures before reading the book.

4. **Experts.** Each child or group selects a picture for which they will become experts. The goal is to notice everything by looking closely. Small magnifying glasses make this more fun or use toilet paper tubes. Prepare cue sheets that give categories to observe: elements, media, style, decisions the artist made, composition (arrangement). Experts report back to entire group.

5. **Blow up art.** Many books are available as big books. This size enables a group to see the art more easily. Use the *art discussion strategies* in Post It Page 5–9 with any picture. Another option is to make color transparencies of selected pages to examine. Stewig's series called *Reading Pictures* (1988) has lesson plans and poster-sized art from picture books that work well, too.

6. **Partial picture preview.** This uses the idea that insight is gained and attention is focused if we view objects from different perspectives. Cover a portion of the picture and ask students to examine the remaining part. Use "What do you see?" and other open questions. Ask students to predict what is in the covered portion. *Variation:* Look at pictures in a mirror (reverse image), upside down, or from far away to discover colors and shapes not previously noticed. Composition can be studied by squinting to see the "masses," instead of the details, and students can hypothesize why the artist did what she did.

7. **Prints style match.** Find other art done in the same style as the book: impressionistic, folk art (see Post It Page 5–7). Compare, for example, the work of Monet and Emily McCully's art in *Mirette on the High Wire* to find how each treated light, color, shapes, and edges.

8. **Scavenger hunts.** Media, style, borders, perspective (within and among books). Students enjoy searching picture books to find specific items. Set up in a format, like a bingo board, and play in groups or individually. Make sure students have access to many books and they know the meanings of the elements for which they are looking. This can last a day or a week or turn into an ongoing routine.

9. **Wordless books and LEA.** Language experience approach (LEA) is a classic strategy to teach reading and writing. Use it with wordless books by asking students to dictate a story that goes with the pictures or write their own in groups or individually. Finished stories can then become the material for reading lessons (e.g., play "I Spy" to locate high-frequency spelling or phonic patterns, parts of speech, etc.) or for important daily free reading. *Suggestion:* To build independence, ask students to do the spelling when taking dictation from them. This also helps keep attention. At least ask students to give beginning and ending sounds.

10. **Book parts.** Teach students about the parts of books, for example, endpapers set the mood of the book, gutters should not break up pictures that run across double-page spreads. Examine the effects of borders on pages. Teach about title page, half-title page, and credits to increase visual literacy.

11. **Compare–contrast two books by different artists.** Use a Venn diagram to record likenesses and differences between the same story written and illustrated by two different picture book artists. This provides an opportunity to work on the higher-order thinking skills (HOTS) of analysis.

12. **Create characters.** Use body, head, and legs from different characters in picture books and combine these to make new characters. Either cut up tattered picture books or use the art as an inspiration for drawing (not copying). Write a story to go with the new creatures.

13. **Make a picture book.** Students should have opportunities to write and illustrate their own picture books based on inspirations from a variety of genre: alphabet books, concepts books, pattern or predictable books, fairy tales, and the like. Encourage the use of a variety of media and styles.

14. **Frame favorite pictures.** Treat picture book art as art. Cut books apart, make color copies, write to publishers for posters or prints, or use publishers' catalog pictures to create framed art. Create a favorites gallery.

15. **Play concentration or memory.** Use artists' photographs and book art. Use publishers' catalogs to find pictures of the artists and book covers or interiors. Write to publishers for photos and examples of book art. To play concentration, make 6 to10 pairs of cards with the artist's photo and one example of his or her art. Paste all on same-sized cards and turn upside down to play. The goal is to remember the location and pick up pairs.

16. **Set the scene.** Re-create a scene in a book using tableau (see drama). Students may want to use props, costumes, and so forth. *Example:* Make whole classroom into a water scene from *Swimmy.*

17. **Puzzles.** Cut up pictures and give each child a piece. Each person is to study the piece to try to tell as much as possible about it. Then assemble to see the whole picture. Can be done in groups, with each group getting a different or the same picture. Do before or after reading a book.

18. **Special days.** Everyone brings a certain kind of picture book (e.g., pop-up, alphabet, one with special endpapers, borders). Each child should have studied the book so that she or he can present the focus in a minute or less.

19. **Storytelling.** Cut up several different picture books and have students combine the mixed-up art to make a new story. Make sure there are pictures of characters and settings. The storytelling can be done in a circle, with each student picking a picture and adding on to the story, or groups can tell with "picture packs" or write or tape their stories. An alternative recording idea is to ask students to storymap stories they told or will tell.

20. **Collages.** Use old picture books as source material for picture collages (e.g., by media [cartoons, watercolor], subject matter [portraits, landscape], or topics [plants, animals]).

---

by saying "I spy . . . (a cat, triangle, the color puce, etc.)", and the first student or team to see it signals and is given the magnifying glass to prove the find. Provide students with information about artists and share books about artists when displaying a work of art. Krull's *Lives of Artists* is a source, and others are given in the appendix under Arts-Based Children's Literature.

Principle 7: ADAPT CURRICULUM MODELS to Integrate Art and Meet Student Needs

Units and Projects for Art Integration. Visual art can be the body/center of a unit or one of the legs. Any of the four unit types presented in Chapter 2 can be used to integrate visual art. When planning any unit, remember to web ideas, align activities with standards, including the *National Standards,* plan initiating or starting events, a sequence of lessons to de-

velop the unit, and a culminating event to wrap it up. An example author–artist unit web appears in Post It Page 5–13.

Projects are highly motivating for students and often are a part of unit study. Projects offer concrete assessment information about student learning, as well. They are usually interest based and may be done in small groups. They involve students in discovery learning and creative problem solving. Projects begin with exploration of an idea followed by planning. Students are encouraged to take on decision making, as appropriate for their age and stage. Schools like Reggio Emilia in Italy have formed the entire curriculum based on hands-on projects that result in student products to be shared or displayed. A project could involve the construction of a mural in science or social studies or the making of papier mâché sculptures of characters in a core book unit.

Art Connections to Math, Science, Social Studies, and Language Arts

Art is the lie that enables us to realize the truth.

Pablo Picasso

By the end of the 20th century the focus of schools had dramatically changed. Space exploration and the revolution in computer technology pushed math and science to the top of the list. The arts, previously justified for their potential to liberate creative self-expression, were pushed to the fringes of the curriculum. "Ironically, now science—coupled with high standards, an altered world view, and new understandings about teaching and learning—is pushing visual art back to the heart of the curriculum" (Walling, 2001).

What does art have to do with science or social studies or math? How does art show what we know about people or places? Consider these connections:

◆ **Social studies** can center around the lives of particular artists, artworks, styles, societal influences, cultures, and careers in art.

◆ **Science** and art were interchangeable in Leonardo da Vinci's world. He wrote about art and drew science—often on the same page of his notebooks. Then "the printing press drove a five-hundred-year wedge between science and art, pushing the latter to the brink of extinction in the curriculum. It is the new bits-and-pixels technology of the computer that will at last reunite science and art." (Walling, 2001, p. 631). Science depends on creative problem solving. In addition, specific science and art concept connections include the study of pigments, how color is made, the chemistry of art materials, the physics of art forms such as sculpture and mobiles, the creation of optical illusions, and the photographic process.

◆ **The language arts** of listening, speaking, reading, and writing are developed when students learn the special vocabulary associated with visual art and learn to write about art in both creative forms (stories, poems) or using art criticism. A special kind of integrated art and language arts lesson is the *guided art and language lesson*. See Post It Page 6–6 for an example of this engaging way to use art for reading and writing.

◆ **Literature and art** are naturally connected through picture books, but pre- and postreading art strategies enrich both art form by stimulating imaging and imagery (e.g., authors such as Natalie Babbitt use a lot of verbal imagery that can be transformed into a visual form).

◆ **Math and art** are integrally related. For example, linear perspective is math based, and both art and math include a focus on geometric shapes. Post It Page 5–14 is an example of a math and art integrated lesson using the plan format from Chapter 2.

◆ **Music and art** share many of the same elements, for example, rhythm and pattern. Think of looking at art and imagining what you hear. Music can inspire art, and vice versa.

◆ **Theater** includes art in the sets and costumes of the actors.

◆ **Dance and art** share elements such as lines that move and shapes that create a composition. Dancers have been an inspiration for art making (e.g., Degas's ballerinas).

Special Needs Students: Differentiating Instruction. In Chapter 2 (Post It Page 2–6), a set of 10 strategies to differentiate instruction called PARTICULAR was presented. Here are some ways to meet stage and age needs using PARTICULAR:

Place: Set up work areas where children who are distractible have few distractions.

Amount: Use projects that require just a few simple steps for children who need success.

Rate: Go more slowly when giving directions and allow more time to finish.

Target objectives: Make the goals clearer by showing more examples.

Instruction: Give more explicit instruction with clear art language; build more repetition into lessons through questioning and asking for choral responses.

Curriculum materials: Use more visual aids (e.g., color wheel, elements chart with symbols, and personal elements charts for each desk to help remember all the things to try).

UNIT WEB: AUTHOR–ARTIST STUDY

EXAMPLE LESSON PLAN: INTEGRATED ART–MATH

Two-Pronged Focus: Art elements of shape, pattern and repetition, abstract, and asymmetrical. Math concepts of pattern and geometric shapes.

Standards: 1, 2, 3 and 5 (See Post It Page 5–4)

Objectives: By the end of the lesson students will be able to:

1. Use five elements of shape and repetition to create a pattern.
2. Orally label geometric shapes (rectangle, circle, triangle, square).
3. Write examples of how shapes are a part of life and why pattern is important.

◈ **Teaching Procedure:** The teacher will . . .

◈ **Introduction**

Post ground rules (for discussions, about looking closely, use of art materials).

Tell students we'll do two silent activities. They are to figure out how they are related. (1) *Mystery bag:* draw out fabrics in three different patterns (dots, plaid, stripes) and tell them to look closely to find what they have in common. (2) Without talking, put five "elements of shape" word cards in pocket chart (Brookes, 1996): circle, dot, straight line, curved line, and angled line.

Gesture for students to draw these. Circulate, smile, and nod as students follow directions. Repeat with eight word cards that have a series of elements to make a pattern (dot, dot, horizontal line, horizontal line, curved down line, curved up line, triangle, triangle).

◈ **Development**

Ask: How were the mystery bag and the drawing activities related? If necessary, scaffold by holding fabric up to cards. What did both have?

Tell students the goal is to learn the five elements and use them to create an abstract work of art.

Show two prints: Kadinsky's *The White Dot* and Jamie Wyeth's *Due North.* Explain the difference between a reproduction print and an original work of art.

Ask: How are these two artworks alike and different? Probe for five elements. When they are named, write them on the board.

Tell students that Wyeth's work is called "realistic" because we recognize what it is and Kadinsky's work is called "abstract" because the focus is on color and elements of shape, not on representing things in a real way—the feel is more important. Clip cards with "abstract" and "realistic" on each work.

Divide into small groups and tell them to find examples of elements of shape, geometric shapes, and patterns (repeated elements). Give each group a clipboard to record. Allow 10 minutes.

Assemble group and take reports by randomly calling on students.

Ask: Why did you find so many examples? Where are there shapes outside of school? Why are patterns made? Used? How do patterns affect people?

Tell about making abstract art: How it is important to experiment, fill up the space with elements, shapes, patterns. Give paper, markers, and about 10 minutes to explore. Play tranquil New Age background music.

Reassemble group and ask students to TOT (tell one thing) they discovered about materials, elements, and patterns. Ask if these drawings are realistic or abstract and why?

Do *directed abstract* activity: Say (1) draw two lines that go to the edges of the paper, (2) draw three dots, (3) draw four curved lines, and (4) draw a circle that touches another line. Fill in all the spaces with colors or collage materials.

◈ **Conclusion/Assessment:** Circulate and give descriptive feedback about elements and concepts as students work. Do art docent talks in fishbowl arrangement, with docents telling elements, shapes, pattern, and how they got ideas. Audience members each need to ask one question or give a comment. Use a writing frame to wrap up: The five elements of shape are ____. Five geometric shapes are ____. When elements are repeated, they form ____. Patterns in my life are (1) ____ and (2) ____. Frame art and put up in class gallery.

Utensils

◈ Use a children's rotary cutter for those who cannot handle scissors.

◈ Tape paper to the table so that it won't move around.

◈ Use scented paint and markers for those who are color blind or have limited sight. Scents can be added (vanilla, lemon, etc.).

◈ Attach drawing and painting tools to head gear or tape to a hand to improve control.

◈ Thicken paint and use shorter and larger brushes.

◈ Use collage materials that can be arranged and rearranged. Start with larger pieces or objects that are easy to grasp.

◈ Wrap crayons and markers with masking tape or foam curlers to provide better grips.

Level of difficulty: Build in more time to explore materials so that students feel more in control.

Assistance: Use the "guided hand technique" to help students get the feel of drawing or painting (put your hand over theirs or theirs over yours); allow students to work with a partner.

Response: Consider different ways students can respond besides the project selected. For example, give materials choices, rather than all make a paper bag puppet from collage materials.

In general, consider ages, stages, and interests when designing art-making or art-looking lessons. Remember, young children are more concrete and less product oriented. They like bright colors and may prefer abstract art or simplified representational art. With intermediate and middle school students, use frequent small-group discussions and give direction; for example, discuss why they think the artist did this piece and how; tell them you expect all group members to be prepared to report back to the whole group so that everyone will be actively engaged during small-group times.

Principle 8: TRIPS with a Visual Art Focus

Opportunities for art-related field trips abound, including virtual trips on the Internet (see websites at the end of this chapter). Art connections can be made to most field trips; for example, connect art such as Picasso's "Paul as Harlequin" or Chagall's "The Blue Circus" to a circus visit. Walking trips to examine local architecture of churches, monuments, or cemeteries are chances to build art vocabulary, gather data for an art project, and develop community pride. Just a trip around the block can provide rich images to categorize by colors, lines, shapes, and textures. See Tips for Field Trips in Chapter 2 for a discussion of pretrip, during trip, and posttrip suggestions. Museum visits are the most common art field trip, so here are guidelines to make sure students get the most out of the trip:

Plan museum visits:

◈ *Before the visit:* Study art elements, practice looking at paintings, study artists and forms you'll see, and make a list of what you want to find out together.

◈ *During the visit:* Give students specific things to look for and do.

◈ *After the visit:* Follow up with activities to find out what students learned. Ask them to write about favorite paintings or do art response projects (media, styles, forms, etc.).

See the books in the arts-based bibliography in the appendix about museum visits (e.g., Lionni's *Matthew's Dream* and Brown's *Visiting the Art Museum*). Post It Page 5–15 has strategies for museum visits.

MUSEUM SCAVENGER HUNT AND GENERAL STRATEGIES

Directions: Use this information *before* the trip and to prepare guides for *during* the visit.

Ask students to find examples of . . .

◆ Striking use of colors (e.g., complementary)

◆ Art where use of line is important

◆ How artists create texture

◆ Art where light is important (use of white?)

◆ Art with different moods

◆ Shapes and masses in art (e.g., geometric, organic)

◆ Subject matter: still life, landscape, portrait, abstract, seascape, cityscape, interior

◆ Examples of perspective: atmospheric, linear, overlapping, and the like

◆ Paintings with lots of detail and ones without

◆ How unity is achieved

◆ Patterns or motifs or repeated elements

◆ Different arrangements or compositions

◆ Media examples: sculpture (materials), water color, acrylic, oil, tempera, collage, fabric art

◆ Different time periods

◆ Different ways art is framed (e.g., oval, fancy gold frame) and the effect

Things to look for . . .

◆ What's in the background?

◆ Eyes: Where do they look? Do they follow you?

◆ Hands: details? where, why, and how placed? folded?

◆ Brushstrokes, for example, scumbling (dry brush painting)

◆ Edges: lost and found, contours and shadows

Questions and Directives: Things to say and do.

◆ "Take a few minutes to look around and I'll meet you in the next gallery."

◆ "Look up close, middle, and far away . . . find the magic viewing spot."

◆ "Look closely, study for 20 seconds, go beyond the obvious, look at details."

◆ "What is going on in the art?"

◆ "What is the mood? How does it make you feel?"

◆ "What do you see? Colors? Shapes? Images?"

◆ "Where does the artist want you to enter the work? What is the focal point?"

◆ "Where does your eye go first? Why? Next?"

◆ "Decode or read the painting. Squint. See the shapes, colors, what stands out/pops out?"

◆ "Use your senses: see? feel? smell? hear? music? taste?"

◆ "What do you notice about the brush strokes? Why did the artist do this?"

◆ "What story did the artist want to tell?"

- "Find examples of 'beauty of the masses.'"
- "What is the subject matter: landscape, seascape?"
- Portraits: "What about the background? effect? essence of the person? hair? hands? eyes?"
- "What adjectives or nouns can be connected to the art?"
- "What is the time of day?"
- Nudity: "Why is it used?" (shows timelessness, e.g., no clothes to date the work; symbol of superiority or shows person has nothing to hide; beauty of human curves)
- "What about edges? hard? lost?"
- "What did the artist choose to do? arrangement? what purposes?"
- "What does the title have to do with the work?"
- "How does the artist use color to move your eyes around?"
- "What did the artist want you to think or feel?"
- "How are . . . and . . . alike and different?"
- "What if . . . changed?" (size, color, materials)

TAKE ACTION 10
MUSEUM TRIP: QUESTIONS

You are planning a field trip to a local art museum. Prepare a list of three questions to ask students about the paintings. Make two of them related to *specific art elements or art forms* (e.g., landscape). What is the reason for asking these kinds of questions?

Principle 9: EVIDENCE to Document and Assess Student Progress

Task Completion. It is difficult to judge results unless work is completed. The satisfaction of success is withheld if effort is not made to reach closure, and students cannot improve without opportunity to understand failures. Self-discipline is developed by working through problems and frustrations with the support of others. Therefore, it is valuable to insist an art project, once undertaken, be carried as far as possible, provided it is self-chosen. Such a discipline is not an unwarranted imposition. Anybody who has watched children "spend long periods of time on some challenging piece of construction or deconstruction knows that there is no end to patience, once the goal is sufficiently attractive. . . . The discipline needed for the completion of the tasks of life must be trained from the beginning" (Arnheim, 1989, p. 34).

Student Portfolios. Student growth, both artistic and cognitive, can be documented by setting up portfolios that are organized around a few basic goals attached to the front of the container (folder, box). Goals may include using many types of media, experimenting with styles of different artists, using art to respond to science, social studies, and math, writing stories and poems about art, learning about art in another culture, and finding out about specific artists and their work. Large art portfolios can be made using packing tape to bind together two large pieces of cardboard and connecting strings to tie it shut. Items placed in the collection should be dated and titled; include a note about the media and the assignment and how it is connected to one or more of the goals.

See examples of arts assessment tools in Appendix D. Chapter 14 begins with an overview of the assessment process.

Principle 10: SPECIALISTS in Visual Art

Collaboration between classroom teachers, art teachers, guest artists, and artists in residence is only fruitful if all participants feel they have an important role. While the classroom teacher will know the students better, the specialist knows more about doing art or a particular artist, which brings expertise and depth to art integration efforts. A successful collaboration begins with planning together. Questions that need to be asked and discussed include:

1. What are specific things students should know and do by the end of the lesson or unit?

2. How is art to be *meaningfully* integrated? What is to be the art content of the lesson and to what is it to be connected?

3. What are the children like? (interests, developmental levels, amount of structure needed)

4. Specialists, outside schools, may not be aware of safety concerns related to toxicity of materials and fumes from markers and sprays. This needs to be discussed.

5. How should the space be arranged? What materials are needed? What about time?

6. Should the specialist work with the whole group or should small groups be rotated?

7. Specialists may not have a wide range of teaching strategies and need to understand that children need active involvement through questions, visual aids, and demonstrations, rather than a lecture. Discuss a lesson introduction that begins with questions or a demonstration.

8. What is the discipline and management system in the classroom? How should problems be handled if they arise and who will handle them?

A number of community-based programs are available that offer trained volunteers to teach lessons about artists and subject matter or to do art projects. **Arts Go to School** is often based in a museum and volunteers are trained as docents to go into classrooms. An example in operation is at the Ella Sharp Museum in Jackson, Michigan (517-787-2320). **ArtReach** is a similar program run by the Springfield Museum of Art in Springfield, Ohio (937-324-3629). Contact museums nearby about school programs or discuss starting one of the above with education curators.

◆ CONCLUSION

Life is a great big canvas and you should throw all the paint you can on it!

Danny Kaye

This chapter presents an introduction to visual art integration throughout the curriculum for general classroom teachers. Of particular importance are the rationale for integrating art (WHY), basic information teachers need to know and teach to accomplish art integration meaningfully (WHAT), and general principles for doing art integration (HOW). The next chapter is a categorized collection of strategy starter ideas that extend the focus of HOW to a more specific level in an effort to help teachers plan units and lessons with a strong visual art component.

◆ RESOURCES AND ART SUPPLY SOURCES

See the appendixes for more resources like these:

Braman, A. (1999). *Kids around the world create! The best crafts and activities from many lands.* New York: Wiley.

Evans, J., & Moore, J. E. (1985). *How to make books with children.* Monterey, CA: Evan Moore.

Kohl, M., & Potter, J. (1998). *Global art: Activities, projects, and inventions from around the world.* Beltsville, MD: Gryphon House.

Le Tord, B. (1999). *A Bird or two: A story about Henri Matisse.* Grand Rapids, MI: William B. Eerdmans.

Terzian, A. (1993). *The kids' multicultural art book: Art & craft experiences from around the world.* Charlotte, VT: Williamson.

Videos

Art's place (1994). Princeton, NJ: Films for the Humanities (series of children's videos on art).

Artscape (1994). Princeton, NJ: Films for the Humanities (series of children's videos on art).

Traditional expressions. Santa Cruz, CA: Multi-Cultural Communications (cultural art projects).

What do you see? Art Institute of Chicago (how to discuss art with children).

World Wide Web

Virtual tours of museums around the world are now available on the Internet. Tour the Louvre in several different languages, visit the Exploratorium in San Francisco or the Museum of Modern Art in New York. Websites of galleries, museum, and libraries are continually updated. Download the material in advance to save class time to receive graphic images. Here are examples of places to visit. See the appendix for more addresses.

Andy Warhol Museum (http://www.warhol.org)

LibrarySpot (http://www.libraryspot.com); gateway to websites of 2,500 libraries

Smithsonian (ftp://photo1.si.edu)

Virtual Museums (http://www.icom.org/vlmp)

World Wide Arts Resources (http://www.wwar.com); more than 500 types of resources and links to 1,000 websites

World Wide Web Virtual Library, the museum pages (http://www.icom.org/vlmp)

Multicultural Art Sources: Artifacts

Art Institute of Chicago (yarn painting, beadwork, weaving) (800-621-9337)

Christian Children's Fund (global crafts) (800-366-5896)

Great Alaska Catalog (Eskimo carvings) (800-326-2197)

Jas. Townsend & Son, Inc. (Colonial American items) (800-338-1665)

Marketplace (fabric from India) (800-726-8905)

Mola Lady (Molas made by Panamanians) (800-880-6677)

Museum of Modern Art (Chinese brush paintings) (800-447-6662)

Oxfam America (handmade items from India, Africa, Indonesia, South and Central America), P.O. Box 821, Lewiston ME 04240

Pueblo to People (baskets, weavings, pottery, beadwork, bark paper from Mexico, Guatemala, and Peru) (713-956-1172)

Save the Children (handmade artifacts from Africa and Asia) (800-833-3154)

Southwest Indian Foundation (Native American artifacts) (505-863-4037)

Sources of Prints and Posters

Art Institute of Chicago, The Museum Shop (800-621-9337)

National Gallery of Art, Washington, DC

Print Finders (914-725-2332)

Sax Visual Arts Resources (800-558-6696)

S & S (800-243-9232)

Shorewood Prints (203-426-8100)

UNICEF (800-553-1200)

Art and Computer Supplies

Crystal Publications (800-913-8555)

Educational Resources (800-624-2926)

Quality Computers (800-777-3642)

Sax Arts and Crafts (800-522-4278)

Sunburst (800-321-5711)

Touch Window, APL/MAC: Art tool; attaches to screen to draw with your finger

Software examples:

Art Explorer by Adobe

ClarisDraw by Claris: MAC Plus or better

Color Me by SVE: APL/IBM

Crayola Art Studio 2, Micrografx (800-326-3576)

Dabbler by Fractal Design: MAC/Power MAC/Power-MAC/WIN

Delta Drawing Today by Power Industries: APL

Flying Colors by Davidson (800-545-7677)

Incredible Coloring Kit (800-653-8298)

Kid-Pix 2 by Broderbund

Kids Riffs; IBM (800-426-7235)

Kindercomp Draw by Spinnaker

MacPaint by Claris: MAC

CD-ROM

Electronic library of art (Sony)

Exploring modern art: Tate Gallery (Microsoft)

History and cultures of Africa (Queue)

History through art series (available through Quality Computers, 1 [800]777-3642)

Le Louvre, the palace and its paintings (Montparnasses Multimedia)

Look what I see! (Metropolitan Museum of Art)

Microsoft art gallery (Microsoft)

With open eyes: Art works from the Chicago Institute of Art (Chicago Institute)

Videodiscs

(Allow access to individual pieces of art and information. All are available from Crystal Publications; 1[800]913-8555)

American art from the national gallery

Art of the Western world series

Great artist series

The National Gallery of Art

With open eyes: Art works from the Chicago Institute of Art

◆ REFERENCES

Books

Alexander, K., and Michael, D. (Eds.). (1991). *Discipline-based art education: A curriculum sample*. Santa Monica, CA: Getty Center for Education in the Arts.

Arnheim, R. (1989). *Thoughts on art education*. Santa Monica, CA: Getty Center for Education in the Arts.

Bill, B. (1988). *Many manys: A life of Frank Lloyd Wright*. London: Heinemann.

Bloom, B. (1956). *Taxonomy of educational objectives*. New York: Longman.

Brookes, M. (1996). *Drawing with children*. New York: Putnam.

Eisner, E. (1983). *Beyond creating*. Los Angeles: Getty Center for Education in Art.

Gardner, H. (1990). *Art education and human development*. Los Angeles: Getty Center for Education in the Arts.

Goleman, D. (1995). *Emotional intelligence: Why it can matter more than IQ*. New York: Bantam.

Hedblad, A. (1998). *Something about the author*. Detroit: Gale.

Jenkins, P. (1986). *Art for the fun of it*. New York: Simon & Schuster.

Jensen, E. (2001). *Arts with the brain in mind*. Alexandria, VA: Association for Supervision and Curriculum Development.

Kellogg, R. (1969). *Analyzing children's art*. Palo Alto, CA: Mayfield.

Koster, J. (1997). *Growing artists*. Albany, NY: Delmar.

Lima, C. (2001). *A to zoo: Subject access to children's picture books*. Westport, CT: Bowker-Greenwood.

Lowenfeld, V., & Brittain, W. L. (1987). *Creative and mental growth*. New York: Macmillan.

Maslow, A. (1968). *Toward a psychology of being*. Princeton, NJ: Van Nostrand.

Moore, T. (1993). *Care of the soul*. New York: Walker.

Stewig, J. (1988). *Reading pictures*. New Berlin, WI: Jenson.

Articles

Broudy, H. S. (1979). How basic is aesthetic education? or is it the fourth *r*? *Language Arts, 54*, 631–637.

Feeney, S., & Moravcik, E. (1987). A thing of beauty: Aesthetic development in young children. *Young Children, 42*(6), 7–15.

Gardiner, M. (1996). Learning improved by arts training. *Scientific Correspondence in Nature, 381*(580), 284.

Longo, P. (1999, November 8). *Distributed knowledge in the brain: Using visual thinking networking to improve students' learning*. Boston: Talk given at the Learning and the Brain Conference.

McWinnie, H. J. (1992). Art in early childhood education. In C. Seefeldt (Ed.), *The early childhood curriculum*. New York: Teachers College Press.

Moore, B., & Caldwell, H. (1993). Drama and drawing for narrative writing in primary grades. *Journal of Educational Research, 8*(2), 100–110.

Walling, D. (2001, April). Rethinking visual arts education: A convergence of Influences. *Phi Delta Kappan*, pp. 626–631.

Winner, E. et al. (1983). Children's sensitivity to aesthetic properties in line drawings. In D. R. Rogers & J. A. Sloboda (Eds.), *The acquisition of symbolic skills*. London: Plenum.

Children's Literature

Babbitt, N. (1975). *Tuck everlasting*. NY: Farrar, Straus & Giroux.

Banks, L. (1980). *The Indian in the cupboard*. Garden City, NJ: Doubleday.

Brown, L. K., & Brown, M. (1992). *Visiting the art museum*. New York: Dutton.

Cummings, P. (1992). *Talking with artists*. New York: Bradbury.

Gilman, P. (1992). *Something from nothing*. New York: Scholastic.

Heller, R. (1995). *Color! Color! Color!* New York: Grosset & Dunlap.

Hoban, T. (1971). *Look again*. New York: Macmillan.

Howe, D. & Howe, J. (1999). *Bunnicula*. New York: Atheneum.

Lionni, L. (1995). *Matthew's dream*. New York: Knopf.

McKissack, P. (1998). *Mirandy and Brother Wind*. New York: Knopf.

Nixon, J., & Degen, B. (1988). *If you were a writer*. New York: Four Winds.

Norton, M. (1991). *The borrowers*. San Diego: Harcourt Brace Jovanovich.

O'Neill, M. (1989). *Hailstones and halibut bones—Adventures in color*. New York: Doubleday.

Paterson, K. (1973). *Sign of the chrysanthemum*. NY: Crowell.

Polacco, P. (1994). *Pink and say*. New York: Philomel.

Steig, W. (1976). *Able's Island*. NY: Farrar, Straus & Giroux.

White, E. B. (1952). *Charlotte's web*. NY: Harper & Row.

Art Seed Strategies

◆ **CLASSROOM SNAPSHOT:**

Ms. Smith's Fifth Grade

Pyramids, cathedrals and rockets exist not because of geometry, theories of structures or thermodynamics, but because they were first a picture—literally a vision—in the minds of those who built them.

Eugene Ferguson (historian)

This is my first year in an arts-infused school. I have conscientiously thought about tying art and the standards together. I am seeing a huge difference in the students' retention of information and their interest level is much higher.

In science we made two group collages classifying animals as vertebrates and invertebrates. The students learned the art form of collage and gained a higher understanding of the different animals in the two groups. We also made camouflaged butterflies and hid them in the classroom. The ones with the best camouflage were not found at all. Those students got extra points. This was a wonderful demonstration of their understanding of camouflage. The students also invented their own animals and drew special adaptations for survival.

In social studies students researched Indian tribes and used authentic techniques to make crafts. We've done a lot with drawing historical events, too. Recently, we studied cartooning and the students drew their own political cartoons. Some of them were better than what you see in the newspaper! One child drew a Pilgrim shooting airplane-shaped bullets at a turkey who had the head of Osama bin Laden. We have an ongoing thing with kindergarten buddies and we do multicultural units on a country together.

In math students made drawings to show their understanding of square numbers. They really had to internalize the concept to depict their number. They also created "measurement monsters" to learn about equivalencies of measurement—such as 2 cups equal 1 pint. Students wrote number sentences that described themselves and included self-portraits.

In English/language arts students wrote and illustrated four framed comic strips, each with a different type of sentence: declarative, interrogative, exclamatory, and imperative. The process was amazing. Not only did they have to write each type of sentence, but it had to be creative and funny! We've also illustrated poems (me, too, actually) and made simple masks to act out stories for the kindergarten children.

It has been an amazing year and it is just October!

INTRODUCTION

This chapter includes specific seed or kernel ideas to help create lessons and units that integrate visual art throughout the curriculum. The seed strategies are generic—they are not geared to particular ages or stage. Most can be adapted for students in grades K–8 by using the 10 PARTICULAR ideas in Post It 2–6. The strategies are organized into the sections, but many fit in more than one section. The separate sections on *energizers* and *elements and concepts* do *not* represent integration but are provided to help teach these concepts so that students can meaningfully participate in art integration throughout curricular areas.

I. ENERGIZERS AND WARM-UPS

Creation begins with a vision.

Henry Matisse

SCAMPER. Eberle's (1971) SCAMPER verbs are a way to stretch students' thinking before starting an art project. Brainstorm how to Substitute, Combine, Adapt (change), Modify (minify or magnify), Put to other uses, Eliminate, or Rearrange or reverse any idea. For example, *What surfaces can be painted on besides paper? What if you made the image upside down? What if you took a part of the picture and made it huge? tiny?* Practice using an object or a picture, and show examples of how artists have used SCAMPER (e.g., Picasso's bull's head made from a bicycle seat and handle bars).

Walks. Go on walks to find art and beauty in nature. Return to the same spots to find differences during a year. Look for color, texture, and shapes. Use blindfolds on a listening walk. During walks, collect natural items to use in displays or collages. After walks, draw or paint the experience.

Eye Relaxation. Students warm hands by rubbing them together and then place them lightly over their eyes. *Variation:* Students close eyes and imagine colors and shapes as they are mentioned by the teacher.

Scribble and Doodle.   Tell students to make lines, dots, and circles of all shapes and sizes to fill up their paper. Encourage overlapping and working both rapidly and freely.

Drawing Fantasy Journey.   Teacher gives students a series of images to draw or imagine in their minds: angles, curves, dots, circles, triangles, ovals, and so forth.

Elements of Shape.   Give teams one minute to find all the circles, dots, straight lines, angled lines, and curved lines they can in the room. *Variation:* Do one element of shape for one minute.

Mirror Image.   Give students a line drawing and ask them to draw the mirror image. The drawing can be an abstract scribble (e.g., a curved line or a jagged line).

Elements of Shape Match.   Each child gets a set of cards containing aspects of shape: circles, dots, lines (can use pictures, and/or words). Show a print and ask each to find an example for each card.

Collections.   Start scrapbooks, photo wallets, and albums or use clear shoe bags to help students save and organize items that grab their esthetic attention. Even beans, sand, or pebbles can be layered in jars to study the effects of pattern on our eyes. Collections can be shared and written about to involve students in meaningful talk and writing about things they know about.

Displays.   Students can learn about organizing ideas and composing from arranging flowers, furniture, or collected nature items. Labeling of displays involves students in the use of the language arts.

Ceiling Tile Art (To Create a More Esthetic Environment).   Get permission to remove the ceiling tiles in a drop ceiling. Use acrylic or tempera paint and allow students to work in groups on a tile. Use masking tape to divide off sections for each person; make the sections different shapes. Plan by examining other art from books or prints: plants, flowers, geometric shapes, or some theme. Paint, replace in ceiling when dry, and voila!

Art Songs and Chants.   Compose art songs together to familiar tunes. For example, "There was an artist had some paints—red and yellow and blue. And with the paints he made his art—red and yellow and blue. Here a red, there a blue, now its purple—what a hue!"

Art Poems.   Students can collect poems about art or poems that could inspire art making. A classic collection on color to be used as a starter is O'Neill's *Hailstones and Halibut Bones.*

Art Riddles.   Find or create riddles about art, artists, styles, particular works, and so forth. It's easy to write your own. Start with an *answer* such as "Picasso." Take each syllable in the word and think of other sound alikes. Make up a question: "What pig artist liked to make abstract paintings?" Answer: Pigasso. Or "What did the art loving horse say?" Answer = mon neigh!

Make a Mess.   Give time to explore new materials and techniques *before* asking students to create a product. During exploration they'll make discoveries and gain confidence and control. Take time to share discoveries.

Tell One Thing (TOT).   Start lessons by asking students to think of one thing they already know about the lesson topic. Do a quick sharing.

Brain Squeeze.   Before doing a piece of art or individual art interpretation, take time to squeeze out all the ideas from the group. For example, "What are all the things we can look for in art?" Ideas can be recorded in web form or on a list.

Mystery Bag Collection.   Introduce a piece of art or an art project by finding three to five objects that connect to it in some way. Pull each out of a bag and ask students to connect the objects to solve the mystery. This is the strategy Mr. Novak used in the case at the beginning of Chapter 5.

Twenty Questions.   Think of an art concept or put an object in a bag that represents an idea (e.g., texture). Students get 10 or 20 questions to discover it. All questions must be able to be answered with a yes or no, for example, "Is it something about landscape?" "Is it something you mix?"

Five Senses Stations.   Stimulate the senses before doing or viewing art by setting up centers for students to:

Taste: Close eyes and taste salt, sugar, lemon. Use popsicle sticks for individual dips.

Touch: Feely boxes with sandpaper, silk, foil.

Sight: Magnifying glasses, tubes, kaleidoscopes.

Smell: Perfumes, potpourri, oils, candles.

Hear: Tapes with environment sounds, boxes and bags to shake, conch shells to listen to.

Look Back. When students have trouble coming up with ideas, suggest they look through past art for ideas, something to redo in a different way. A part of a past piece can become a whole piece; a tree or shape in the background can be the full subject of a new work. If students have a picture file, or the teacher does, browsing through it can spark ideas (see Chapter 5 for picture file categories).

Picture Book Starters. Picture books are rich sources for ideas about how to use different media, styles, and subject matter. For example, Bunting's *Smoky Night* is an example for variety in collage materials and many Eric Carle books are collages made from "painted papers" he paints and cuts up.

Doodle Log. Instead of writing in journals, give students a prompt to doodle about favorite words, their day, or what they want to be when they grow up. These can also be used when sutdents finish projects early (Ohio art teacher Misty Kaplafka).

II. TEACHING ART CONCEPTS AND ELEMENTS

Questions. Use open or fat questions to stimulate thinking about art: *What is special about. . .? What is happening? What does this make you think about? How did the artist make this? How do you think the artist felt when she created this? Why? Find–trace–point to (elements or concepts, e.g., biggest, brightest . . .).* Post It Page 6–1 has example *questions and activities for art elements.*

Compare and Contrast. Use a Venn diagram to find likenesses and differences between two paintings. For example, compare and contrast the elements, media, style, and subject matter of reproductions of two paintings both called *First Steps*—one is by van Gogh and the other by Picasso.

Game Boards. Make all-purpose game boards using file folders or pizza cardboard. Laminate and use manuscript to write any information needed. Make separate cards to practice content; for example, use art question cards or concept cards (colors, shapes, lines, styles). Students play by naming as many ideas in a category to move spaces as designated by a spinner or roll of dice.

Food Alternatives. Food, such as potatoes for printing, are commonly used in school projects. However, it is important that children distinguish art materials from food—for safety reasons and for esthetic purposes. Instead of using pasta, consider using buttons, shells, or pebbles in collages or cut up drinking straws for stringing. Sponges or Styrofoam can be cut in creative shapes for printing (precut sponges are not recommended because this makes dictated art).

Postcard Activities

Card Sorts. Students hone observational skills by categorizing art postcards according to classifications. For example, sort by color, style, artist, type of art, or subject matter. Students can work in groups to place cards in the categories designated (a closed sort), or students can be given a stack of postcards and asked to create their own categories (an open sort). Art postcards also make wonderful cards to remember children's special days or as note cards to send home to parents. If the teacher is enthusiastic about collecting the cards, children often catch the spirit and want to collect them, just as kids collect baseball cards. Students can make art postcards with index cards and original art or magazine art (e.g., ads for fine art sales appear in magazines such as *Architectural Digest*).

Concentration. This favorite memory game can be played with art postcards. You need about 10 pairs of matching cards or related cards (e.g., two pieces by Renoir that students know). The game is played by laying out cards face down or using a pocket chart for group play. Each person gets a turn at turning over two cards to try to make a match. If successful, the player keeps the two cards and plays again. If not, she must turn the cards down and the play passes to the next person, who tries to remember cards that have been turned over. To reinforce learning during the game, make a rule that students must name the artist or style or "say something true" about each card turned over.

Art Element Drawings. Give a grid (paper divided into 8 to 10 sections). Label each box with an art element: color, line, shape. Students then do a drawing that serves as a mnemonic for each element and its aspects.

One-Minute Element Find. Call an art element category and give groups of students one minute to find as many examples as they can (e.g., kinds of lines in the classroom).

QUESTIONS AND ACTIVITIES FOR ART ELEMENTS

Line: What kinds of lines do you see? Straight, curved, and so on? How do the lines make you feel? Tired, busy, angry, relaxed, peaceful? Which are repeated? Why, do you think? Which lines are strong? Which are faster? *Activities:* Ask students to pick a line and follow its movement with their hand or draw in the air the predominant line in the painting or sculpture. Use a flashlight to "trace" a line or kids can make light lines on the wall or floor to get the feel of all sorts of lines. Use lines as a stimulus for dance or movement: shape your body in angles, move in a zigzag pattern, make curves with different body parts (e.g., arms, fingers).

Shape: What kind of shapes do you see in the painting? How do the shapes create a pattern? Which are organic? geometric? *Activities:* Students make a particular shape with their arms, fingers, or bodies. Ask them to look for a shape around the room. Then find that same shape in a painting or a sculpture. Paint or draw as many different kinds of lines as you can think of (e.g., wavy, zigzag). Go on a shape walk around the school to find all the shapes within shapes (e.g., windows, roofs, cars).

Texture: If you were able to touch the objects in the painting, how would they feel? How has the artist made the textures appear real? *Activities:* Ask the children to touch the floor, face, hands, a bench and describe how each feels. Have them cup their hands and use them as telescopes or cameras to isolate an area of a painting and ask them what kinds of brush strokes the artist used?

Color: How has the artist used color? How does it make you feel? Why? How would the painting be different if . . . was changed to. . .? Name all the colors. What colors are used the most? What are some unusual uses of color? What happens when white is used? What happens when colors are put next to each other, for example, red and green? *Activities:* Close your eyes and think of a color in the painting. Imagine yourself turning that color. How do you feel? Find complementary colors, primary colors, and examples of hues, tints, and shades. Get paint chips from paint stores to show hues and enjoy naming colors similar to those companies use.

Space and composition: Why and how has the artist established foreground, middle ground, and background? (Introduce perspective.) How is the space broken up? Where do you think the artist was standing? Why? Where does your eye go next in the painting? Why? Squint and look at a picture. What masses stand out? Why are some things smaller, blurrier, overlapping? How did the artist do that? *Activities:* Choose a small part of a picture and use paint or markers to enlarge it, that is magnify. Children create a tableau (frozen picture) of a painting, placing themselves in the proper perspective. Have the children become different things in the painting: a tree, pond, hills, and so forth.

Light and shadow: What is the light source? From what direction is it coming? How has the artist created volume (modeling—gradations of light and dark)? *Activities:* Have the children imagine the painting in a different kind of light. Ask how their response to the painting would change. Use a flashlight and shine it in different directions on a person or object and ask what the children notice.

Perspective: How does the artist show that some things are closer and others are far away? *Activities:* Look at objects from different angles and distances (e.g., stand on a chair and look down); use microscopes or magnifying glass.

Emotion and mood: How does the painting make you feel? Why (use of color, expressions)? How do you think the artist felt about his or her subject? What do you hear? taste? smell? How does this make you feel differently about the painting? *Activities:* Show with face and body shape how the art feels.

Big Book or Poster Elements. Books or posters of art elements and concepts are useful references during art viewing and doing. Class or individual big books or posters with titles such as *The Facts about Color* or *What to Know about Shape* can be made as a class. Poster board can be used for the front and back covers of big books; bulletin board paper can be folded and stapled with a long-arm stapler for pages.

Partial Picture Preview. See this idea in Post It Page 5–12.

Word Charts. The goal is to find unusual and descriptive words to expand the concepts of each of the elements and add words to charts, for example, for the category of *textures*. Student then chart words such as *rough, smooth, silky, bumpy*. For *pattern*, these words might be used: *checked, striped, borders, dotted*.

Hot Sock. This game develops verbal fluency and classification thinking. Use the word charts generated in the previous activity to play this category game. You need an old sock tied in a knot. Put each category on a card. Kids sit in a circle with one person in the center, who is IT. Center person closes his eyes and throws the sock, which is a "hot potato" no one wants. IT can call "stop" at any time. The person caught with the sock then passes it to the person on the right, who holds it while IT reads one category card title. The caught person must then name a set number of items in the category (four to six items) while the sock is passed around the circle. The goal is to finish before the sock gets back around; otherwise a new IT goes to the center. *Variation:* Use with categories (drama elements, dance elements) from any area. Even alphabet cards can be used.

Elements Exploration with Paint. Start with lots of newsprint and one color of paint. Invite students to bring in brushes from home (e.g., sponge, baster, dish-washing sponge, bottle washer). Give a series of directed explorations: Paint different lines: straight, angled, curved, lying down, angry, happy, calm, excited, thick, thin. Create different shapes: dots, circles, squares, triangles, uneven, loose, happy, sad. Take one shape and paint it different sizes. Group the same shapes together. Group shapes that are the same size. Change colors and color code "same" shapes or same sizes. Outline shapes in a lighter color. Try outlining in a darker color. Try painting very slowly. Try using very little paint to dab. Smear a lot of paint on. Give feedback as students work. Afterward, ask students what they discovered about the elements and use of paint with different tools. *Adaptation:* Ask students for ideas to try.

Bubbles. Explore shape and color with bubbles: Mix 1 tablespoon of dish detergent, 5 tablespoons of water, and 1 tablespoon of glycerine. Catch bubble mixture, with tempera added, with paper to make bubble art or just explore organic and geometric shapes with bubbles made through straws, pipe cleaner wands, plastic berry baskets, funnels and plastic from soda six packs.

Subject Matter: Questions and Activities. Post It Page 6–2 lists ways to involve students with the art concept of subject matter.

Parent Tips. Parents often don't know how to respond to children's art and don't know why and how to encourage art making. Here are suggestions to share with them:

POST IT PAGE 6–2

READING ART SUBJECT MATTER: QUESTIONS AND ACTIVITIES

Tell students to take time to stop and look carefully, first. Teacher questions come after this time. Meaningful art experience depends on learning to look longer, notice details, respond personally, ask own questions, and think about the meanings of what is seen. All art reflects the time period and culture that produced it. Art of the 20th century reflects values about originality and the importance of individuality in a world of mass production and imitation.

Landscapes *are about the land.*

◆ What is the mood? Season? How do you know? If you were there, how would you feel?

◆ Where do you enter the work of art? Why did the artist create this position for you?

◆ What did the artist do to make you feel a part of the scene?—OR—

◆ Do you feel like an onlooker? If so, how did the artist keep you at a distance?

◆ Look closely to see if there are any people. If so, how are they related to the landscape?

◆ Does the landscape seem real or imaginary? Why? Does it describe or capture the real look of a place or does it give more of the feeling of a place (expressive)? Why?

◆ What title would you give this work? Why?

❖ Walk into the painting. What do you see, hear, feel? What can you do there?

❖ Think of a special place you have been. What made it memorable? If you could artistically re-create this setting, what medium would you use (oil paint, watercolor, pastels, charcoal, pencil, collage)? What would you emphasize? Why?

Portraits *are of people but show more than what a person looks like. Artists use a "visual vocabulary" to communicate this. Consider this special artistic vocabulary as you look at a portrait.*

❖ What does the artist tell you about this person? How does this person feel?

❖ *Clothing:* What clues does the person's dress give about the person?

❖ *Facial expression, posture, and gestures:* What does the person's body language say about attitude and personality? What do the eyes, eyebrows, mouth, throat, forehead, and angle of head seem to tell? Where is the person looking? How does this affect you? How is the person positioned? Why? What is he or she doing with his or her hands? Take the position yourself. How do you feel? Would you want to meet the person in this portrait? Why or why not?

❖ *Background and accessories:* Where is the person? What clues does the environment provide about the person? What might the specific objects in the setting mean?

❖ *Size and medium:* Is the portrait life size or is it smaller? How does the size of the portrait change how you feel? What media and materials do you think the artist used? What if the materials were different? For example, how would marble give a different feeling than paint?

❖ Look closely. Start at the head and slowly observe everything. Pretend you are the person and walk, sit, and stand in role. Be the person and say one thing.

❖ Look at real people through a tube or frame to see shapes of eyes, lips, and head. Observe groups of people: How close are they? How are they grouped (line, circle, random)?

Still lifes *are paintings of inanimate (nonliving) objects.*

❖ What attracts your eye? What do you discover that you didn't notice at first glance?

❖ What is the most important part of the painting?

❖ How does the artist makes it seem like there is light on surfaces?

❖ What kind of life-style do the objects represent? Why might the artist have chosen these objects? What might the objects represent (symbols)?

❖ What objects could you use to make a still life (e.g., toys, fruit, school items)? Why? How would you arrange them? What would you want to say in a still life?

Abstract art *goes beyond showing the visible world to allow expression through color, line, and shape.*

❖ What is your first reaction? How did the artist cause you to react like this?

❖ What are you curious about? Why do you think the artist chose to create an abstract work?

❖ How does the work's abstractness change how it makes you feel?

❖ How would you describe the personality of the art? What contributes to it? How does it cause you to stop and think?

❖ What meaning or feelings do you think the artist intended? What does it mean to you?

Art Minipage for Parents

❖ Tell what you see in your child's art (e.g., colors, shapes, lines).

❖ Explain how the art makes you feel or what it makes you think of.

❖ Ask your child to "tell about the art."

❖ Don't ask "what is it?" because that's insulting.

❖ Ask how the art was made. Emphasize the process and the effort.

❖ Make art projects with your child.

- Keep a folder of your child's art and date the pieces.
- Set up a special place or table to do art.
- Visit museums and other special art displays and stop to talk about what you see and feel.
- Share what you think is beautiful and tell why.

Art Bags. Use large zip lock bags to send home a piece of art, a book related to it, and a related artifact or object. Invite students to check these out and share with their families. For example, prints or postcards of Monet's garden art, the book *Linnea in Monet's Garden*, and a packet of flower seeds to be planted at home in the spring is a popular take-home bag.

III. USING DIFFERENT MEDIA

Cleanup and Organization Tips

Before doing art projects, be sure to prepare for contingencies and think about these tips:

1. Make student cleanup a routine part of any art project. Make this clear in advance.
2. Stain removal: To remove crayon from clothing, try toothpaste on spots.
3. Collect egg cartons or ice cube trays and use half for different paint colors and the other half for mixing. *Alternative:* Use washed juice cans, cut them in half, and set in student milk cartons for stability. *Note:* Don't try to give students all possible colors. They need to explore mixing their own.
4. Q-tips are paint tools that can be used to make "dot art" similar to Seurat's style. Students can also paint with rolled newspaper "brushes" if tools are in short supply.
5. A ball of clay the size of a baseball can be used to store markers: poke holes so that it looks like a multiholed bowling ball with the markers and let clay harden.
6. Use clear plastic shoe boxes and clear shoe bags to store materials.
7. String a clothesline and use clothespins to hang art. Hang up straw beach mats and use drapery hooks to hang anything on them that you can punch a hole in and put over the hook. Use plastic drying racks that have clothespins on each arm as a way to display or as mobiles.

8. Old shirts can be used to cover clothes. Cut off long sleeves and button them on children backward. Garbage bags can also be used: slit and then cut arm holes and neck holes. Be careful about young children putting bags over their heads.
9. Trim brushes with scissors to keep them fresh.
10. A warm iron flattens curled art.
11. Mount or frame children's art to give it a finished look. Use transparency frames for quick framing. Save the tabs off soda cans to tape on the back of pictures for picture hangers.
12. If the teacher has to do too much preparation, it is probably not an appropriate art activity for kids. Students should do most of the work to learn (e.g., cutting out of shapes by the teacher is inappropriate).

Mixing Colors: Color Triangles

To show the primary colors and the secondary colors made from them, make a triangle with the three points being *red* (top point), *yellow* (next point moving clockwise), and *blue*. Draw an upside down triangle over the first triangle to create a star shape. Label these three points (moving clockwise from top right) *orange*, *green*, and *purple* (the last is also called indigo-violet). By combining two adjacent points on the star you get the color in between them (e.g., red and yellow make orange). Students can make color triangles for their desks.

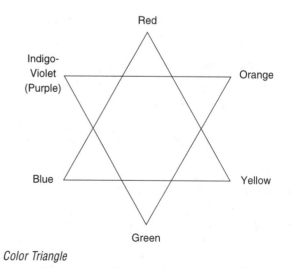

Color Triangle

Other Mixing Hints. (1) White paint *tints* or makes lighter. It makes colors pastel. White is used so much, so buy extra—double the amount of other colors. To tint, start with white and add color to it, a bit at a time. (Always start with the lighter color and add the darker when mixing.) (2) Black *shades* or makes darker or duller. Add a small amount of black to a color (e.g., black to white makes gray and black to red makes brown). Remember to *add to* the lighter color. (3) Skin colors can be made with black, brown, yellow, red, and white. Start with lighter and add darker colors to create desired shades; for example, blend white chalk with orange crayon to create a skin tone. (4) Use a clear pie pan on the overhead projector to drop in food coloring and show changes from mixing colors. (Turn out the lights and let the colors fill the room.) (5) Color sugar with food coloring and layer in jars. (6) Show how to mix colors on a color wheel. (These can be purchased at any art supply store.) (7) See children's literature in the annotated bibliography in Post It Page 5–10 for books about mixing colors (e.g., *Color! Color! Color!* [Heller, 1995] and *Colors* [Felix, 1993]).

Drawing and Rubbing

To draw you must close your eyes and sing.

Pablo Picasso

Human beings seem born to draw. *Drawing* is linear art made with any tool that will make a mark; it is also a precursor to writing. *Rubbings* are made by placing paper over objects such as coins, shells, wire, or any texture and then using crayon, marker, and so forth to bring up the lines from the objects or textured surfaces underneath. *Scratch art* or *etching* is scraping away a surface to reveal a lighter color. *Resist* consists of using a wash of paint over something that resists it (e.g., crayon).

Tools and Media. Fingers, sticks, toothpicks, and straws can be used, along with pencil, charcoal, marker, pen and ink, crayon, pastels or chalk, and shaving cream. Children can draw *on* a blank surface or *in* paint or a medium, such as glass wax sprayed on windows. (Color glass wax with tempera paint or add food coloring to hand lotion or toothpaste as a drawing medium. *Note:* Food color stains.)

Computer Technology. Computers have revolutionized the making of both commercial and fine art. Computers are now used for art in two ways: (1) to create and manipulate images (art making, including planning and producing virtual objects, e.g. two dimensional). A sketch can be scanned and then, using Adobe Photoshop, the image manipulated. (2) To investigate visual art (art history criticism, ethetics). Interactive CD-ROMs and the Internet (almost 100 percent of schools are now connected) offer text and images, virtual tours of art collections—often with sound and video clips that elaborate on the historical period with music and interviews with famous people. See websites at the conclusion of Chapter 5.

Surfaces. Experiment with a variety of papers, cloth, sandpaper, bags, towels, wrapping paper, paper doilies, graph paper, or chalk board. T-shirts can be drawn on with fabric markers or crayons (cover with a paper bag and iron on warm to fix crayon). Scratch board (light color goes under and dark color is over it; the latter is usually black) can be purchased or made by using light crayons first and then covering entire surface with heavy black or dark crayon. Scratch board can also be purchased with silver on top and black underneath. Use a nail or sticks to etch drawings.

Drawing Ideas

Lifelike images are still popular. It is a preference commonly found together with a materialistic interest in tangible things.

Arnheim, 1989, p. 180

Buy or make sketchbooks for students to capture ideas. Encourage "looking closely" and sectioning off an area (e.g., if it's a portrait, try thinking of the face in fourths). A squiggle on a paper, traced hands, and feet and thumb prints can be starters to create animals, objects, people, or abstract art. Try drawing to music or drawing something without looking down as a "model" is studied. Some artists have success drawing upside down.

Crosshatching is a technique in which artists draw fine black lines parallel to one another and then cross them. Crosshatching can be light or heavy and is used to add depth and texture.

Brookes (1996) suggests these "five elements of shape" (p. 59) be taught directly and used to analyze any image and assembled to produce a realistic drawing of most anything:

1. Dots in different shapes (oval, round, elliptical, and kidney)

2. Circles in different shapes (oval, round, elliptical, and kidney) and that are "empty" rather than "colored in" like dots

3. Straight lines
4. Curved lines
5. Angled lines

Drawing Figures.   Start with a focal point: eye, hole, center, and the like. Look closely and analyze. Notice dots, circles, straight lines, angled lines, and curved lines. For overlapping, draw things in the front, first, and then draw things farther away. If a mistake happens, make something out of it by repeating it, adding to it, or transforming it. Break people down into circles and tube shapes—the head is an egg shape and the neck is a tube. Grid off faces to position eyes, nose, and so on.

Crayon Ideas.   Peel and break crayons, use them on their sides, or even tape several together. Encourage mixing of colors and creation of hues of one color by using different amounts of pressure. Blend white chalk with orange crayon to create a skin tone, and rub crayon drawings with a cloth to give them a gloss. For crayon resist, try painting over crayon drawings with tempera, watercolor, or food color. Try using black construction paper for the background and painting over crayon drawing with white paint; or use a white crayon or candle to draw on white paper and then wash over with paint to reveal the image. The kids will think it's magic!

Chalk Ideas.   It's cleaner to use chalk if tape is put on one end. Encourage children to break the chalk, try using it on its side, or dipping it in water (once dipped it is ruined for regular chalk use, however). Try wetting the paper with a little sugar water and then using chalk. Of course, the chalkboard and sidewalks are surfaces not to be missed because of their size and texture.

Painting and Painting Tools

You paint what you are.

Andrew Wyeth

Types of Paint.   Acrylic, oils, tempera (comes in liquid, powder, and blocks), watercolors, watercolor crayons, and even melted crayons can be used to paint. (Turpentine melts crayons. Check about safety issues before using this with children. Always ventilate.) Refillable paint markers with felt tips can be an alternative way to use tempera. Paints can also be created by combining food color and egg or adding food color to shaving cream, liquid starch, hair gel, or even Vaseline. Explore stains and other paints made from tea, mustard, berries, bleach, shoe polish, or just water.

Tools.   Use a variety of brushes: toothbrushes, hair brushes, combs, and brush curlers. Fingers, feet, hands, feathers, rags, old deodorant rollers, sponges, squeeze bottles, sticks, Q-tips, cotton balls, and straws can be used as paint tools. Newspaper can be rolled into tubes and used as a throwaway brush. Chalk can be dipped into tempera to create interesting effects.

Painting Surfaces.   Paint can be applied to wood, paper, canvas, fabric, paper plates, windows, doilies, transparencies, plastic sheets, cookie sheets, or wallpaper. (Many stores are glad to donate old wallpaper books to schools.) Rocks can be painted on, too; just add liquid white glue to the paint to help it stick. Frescoes are created by using paint on wet plaster.

Techniques.   Have a brush for each color, but encourage experimentation with mixing colors (e.g., add white to tint and black to shade, and use the color wheel to mix secondary and tertiary colors from the primary colors of red, yellow, and blue). Introduce *scumbling* by showing how to use thicknesses of paint over dried paint (i.e., dry brush). Explore dabbing, spatter painting (use a ruler to flip paint from a brush), blot painting (place blob on paper and fold paper), and straw painting (blow blobs of paint by using a straw to direct the air and move the paint). Add salt, Epsom salts, flour, oatmeal, sand, sawdust, or soap flakes to paint to give it texture or make it thicker. (Salt gives a bubbly effect.) Liquid starch, corn syrup, or detergent can be added to change how paint spreads. Soap helps tempera adhere to glossy surfaces.

Hand painting can include pounding and dabbing with the fingers, fist, or side of hand. When *sponge painting*, it helps to clip a clothespin to the sponge as a handle. Bleach can be applied to construction paper or bright cotton fabric. To tie dye, fold cloth or knot and then dip in bleach or dye. For *marbling*, mix linseed oil and tempera powder (children should not breathe this) to a thick cream. Put a half-inch of water on a cookie sheet and drop the mixture on to it. Carefully lay a sheet of paper on top and lift up. Dry. Flatten with warm iron.

Tips.   Watercolors can stain clothing. Keep a bucket of soapy water and paper towels handy for kids to clean up. Never have children mix dry tempera powder because it is easily inhaled.

Printmaking

Prints are made with techniques to produce many copies (e.g., woodcut, linoleum, silk screen). *Monoprints* produce only one print. Prints can be pulled from a surface (e.g., a table on which students have fingerpainted) or stamped with found objects: vegetables such as carrots or potatoes, woodcuts, linoleum cuts, or any form that is raised and will make a printing tool. Real flowers can even be pounded into paper to make a monoprint.

Tools. Collect objects to use for printing: pieces of carpet, wire, mesh, bubble wrap, corrugated cardboard, fingers (use watercolors), feet, hands, sponges, erasers, corks, wood block, checkers, nature (leaf prints), and other gadgets. Cut print shapes from clean Styrofoam meat trays, rubber-tire inner tubes, or shoe insoles and glue to blocks for a handle to hold when printing. Vegetables and fruits can also be used but take care that kids don't confuse food and art materials. *Note:* Soles of feet can be painted and used to print animal bodies. Knuckles can be used to print rows and patterns, for example, a border of small pumpkins (A. Wirz, teacher, Lady's Island Elementary School).

Surfaces. Use paper, fabric, wood, clay, or even paper towels to print on.

Techniques. It is a good idea to place folded newspaper under your printing surface to give it a cushion. Put paint in shallow tray (e.g., cookie sheet or paper plates) and have a separate container for each color. Use a brayer (roller) to roll paint onto the item with which you will print. If there is too much paint, the image will smear. Make repeated patterns: vertical or horizontal prints, and overlap, twirl, and swirl to create designs. A print can also be made by outlining an image in white glue. Let it dry and the raised glue can be rolled with paint and used to print images. By gluing raised items or yarn on paper towel tubes and then coating the items with paint, you can *roll print*. Any carved item (see discussion on three-dimensional art) can be used for printmaking.

Children can make their own gift wrap, greeting cards, T-shirts, and stationery by printing or stenciling. *Stencils* can be cut from plastic or paper (e.g., fold paper in half, cut out a shape, open and use as a paint stencil—not much paint is needed). When stenciling, use a sponge or round brush to dab on paint. Use a variety of thicknesses to create a more interesting image.

Collage

The word *collage* derives from the French word *coller,* which simply means to paste on. Pablo Picasso and George Braque invented collage and used it in their abstract cubist works in the early 1900s. Collage consists of assembling materials and ordering this often chaotic assemblage. Children enjoy the tactile nature of collage, and this medium invites an experimental attitude because realism is not the goal. A collage can be stimulated by any topic or theme (e.g., winter, plants, nature, humor, school, etc.). Encourage the use of a variety of shapes and sizes, both torn and cut. Cover desks with newspaper or old magazines to protect them.

Materials. Just about anything can be used, from stones, sticks, and other found objects in nature to every sort of string, yarn, ribbon, or button to make a collage. There are thousands of types of paper, and collage can be made from sandpaper, foil, construction paper, cardboard, newspaper, tissue paper, wallpaper, greeting cards, and magazines. Wetting crepe paper and colored paper can produce interesting effects, but the bleeding may stain clothes. Children's own old paintings can be torn and cut up into collage material. Paper doilies offer wonderful possibilities for adding texture. Broken and shaved crayon pieces can be used to create a mosaic effect, as can small squares of other construction paper shapes. Sprinkle shavings on paper, fabric, T-shirts, or old sheets; then cover with newsprint and press with a warm iron. Look in reference books for examples of mosaics before beginning. Bits of fabric can be used, as well as pasta. For colored pasta, just combine food color and ¼ cup alcohol. Put in a covered container and shake (don't have children do this!). Colored rice, sawdust, or sand can be made by using tempera paint; don't let students use dry paint because it is too easily inhaled. The teacher should do the mixing. Collages can be sprinkled with sugar or salt to increase the texture and sparkle. Make sure you sprinkle over wet glue!

Backgrounds. Use roof shingles, cardboard, poster board, plastic lids, Styrofoam, and sandpaper as surfaces on which to arrange and glue. Leaves, crayons, and colored tissue paper can be pressed between wax paper using a warm iron (cover with newsprint so you don't get a sticky iron). For a thicker base and more texture, a collage dough can be made by combining half salt and half flour and adding water to make a thick dough. Objects can then be pressed into the dough and coated with thinned white glue. Use a shoe box lid, egg carton lid, or Styrofoam tray to hold the pressed-out dough. Plaster of Paris can also be used. Just mix according to the directions on the package and press objects such as shells or buttons into it. Food coloring can also be added to the plaster. It does set up fast—about 15 minutes.

Collage Glue. White glue is usually best. It can be thinned with water when working with colored tissue paper or used as an overall coating for a finished work, as in decoupage. Paste can be made from flour and water. Add oil of peppermint or wintergreen to keep it from spoiling. Have popsicle sticks or Q-tips available for students who don't want to use their fingers. Have a wet sponge or wet paper towels available to wipe off glue.

Techniques: Enlarge, Simplify, Crop

Many artists make small things very large or simplify a subject down to basic geometric forms (e.g., triangle or circle). Georgia O'Keefe is an example. She also *crops* pictures (cuts them off so only a part of a flower is showing. Show examples of these techniques and allow students to experiment with enlarging, simplifying, or cropping objects, plants, flowers, animals, and so forth. To enlarge, make a transparency of anything and enlarge it with the overhead projector. Pull the projector back to make the image bigger. For example, basic fairy tale character shapes can be traced by taping large paper to the wall and projecting the transparency for students to use. Outlines can then be painted or used in original ways—don't turn this into a big coloring book activity! Students can trace around each other's bodies to get basic outlines for large-people paintings.

Displays and Bulletin Boards

Students can create displays or bulletin boards about artists and their work. Interactive displays can be made by adding question cards or flip cards to lift for answers. Calligraphy and block lettering are ways students can label. See the appendix for books on calligraphy. An easy form of block lettering is based on the idea that any letter can be made from a block of paper by cutting straight lines. Begin by cutting as many blocks as letters needed; blocks can be as large or as small as you wish. Then imagine the letter and the cutting begins. Don't worry about "hole" letters like B

and R. Just cut through the joining areas because they'll be glued or stapled down.

To frame or finish off a bulletin board, make a creative border with ribbons or leaves or by cutting a border the old-fashioned way that strips of paper dolls were cut: First, pull off about 3 feet of large paper from a roll (bulletin board paper works). Roll into a tube and cut slices about 2 to 3 inches thick using a paper cutter. Creatively cut a pattern along one of the longer edges (zig-zag or scallops). Open the strip and staple onto the bulletin board. Make as many strips as needed.

Posters and signs can be made to advertise artists, the style, or a piece of artwork. Students should take time to examine ads for ideas they can adapt through creative problem solving like that used in SCAMPER (see Post It Page 1–6).

Murals

Murals are large wall paintings, but in schools murals can be any large composition and are usually created by groups. They can be made from a variety of media, from crayons to collage. Murals help children learn to cooperate and take pride in group work because group planning and sharing are essential aspects of mural making. The easiest murals are ones in which students each add an item (e.g., a nature collage mural or a print of a foot or hand). Students can learn how to develop full scenes relevant for science, social studies, or literature.

Mixed Media

Use paper, wire, paint, fabric, and any other materials in one artwork. Banners, murals, and even portraits, landscapes, or abstracts can be made with any imaginable combinations. See children's books such as Bunting's *Smoky Nights* and Ringold's *Tar Beach* for examples.

Fiber Art. Cloths and yarns are great for creating art with texture and pattern. Fabric art connects well with social studies: clothing of cultures and time periods and careers (knitter, weaver, quilter, tailor, seamstress). There are wonderful pieces of children's literature that deal with the fiber arts, for example, *Annie and the Old One* (weaving). For a science connection, explore the use of natural dyes, for example, carrot tops for a green–yellow, onion skins for an orange dye, and tea for brown or orange; colored drink mixes can serve as dyes. An ordinary crock pot can be used to heat. Be sure to use rubber gloves and rinse with cold water to set the dye.

Crafts. Crafts include handcrafted traditional art such as pottery, weaving, and quiltmaking.

Color Window Quilt or Banner. Give each child a zip lock bag and colored tissue paper and cellophane. Children cut, tear, and arrange their piece and then the bags are taped together with clear, wide tape. Make into window banners or quilts. (Source for clear wide tape: National Bag Inc., 800-247-6000.)

Class Quilt. Each child uses origami paper and other media to create a piece of art that represents him. Everyone making a quilt piece should use the same size piece. Focus on how to communicate important things about yourself through this piece of art. Experiment with printing, lettering, and collage. Encourage students to not do the obvious. (This need not be representational art; it can be abstract.) Glue all quilt pieces on a large piece of black bulletin board roll paper. Put a border on the quilt by cutting rolled bulletin board paper into 3- to 4-inch slices and then cutting designs into each rolled slice, like cutting out a string of paper dolls. Glue the border strips to the quilt. Students can make "speech bubbles" telling about their creation process to post with the finished quilt. Quilts are particularly adaptable as art responses for units. For example, students can each make a square about a favorite book to create a book quilt or a square about any unit topic. In math, quilts are used to explore geometric shapes (squares, triangles) and for counting.

Self-Portrait Banner. *Materials:* white paper, white fabric (12 by 12 inches), pencil, chalk, water, mirror, permanent black marker, and masking tape. *Directions:* (1) Look in a mirror and examine your face closely. Sketch each half, really thinking of shapes and line. Outline in black marker. Add whatever you want to represent you (e.g., hat or symbols). (2) Put fabric over paper and tape down. Trace black outline with marker. Wet fabric, do not soak. (3) Use chalk to put in color. When dry, spray with nonaerosol hair spray. (4) Sew or glue all portraits into banners or a quilt.

Photography

Creation begins with vision.

Matisse

Now that disposable cameras are readily available, classroom photography is doable. Students can learn some important aspects of composition by trying a series of tasks (Cecil & Lauritzen, 1994) and then discussing their results: (1) Take the same person or object close up and far away. (2) Take a person or object with a lot of light and then with shadows or less light. (3) Take pictures of different subject matters: people, places (land, water, interiors of houses), animals, and action shots. (4) Create a still-life arrangement and photograph it. (5) Photograph the same person or object in the center of the picture and then off center (more to the left, right, top, or bottom). Have students sort pictures into groups depending on what they believe worked best. Display their "best efforts" with captions created by students on poster board. *Variation:* Students can take a series of pictures of people, places, and events and then write a story that pulls all the photographs together. The story and the pictures can then be made into a book.

Three-Dimensional Art

Three-dimensional (3D) art can be made from many materials including found objects, papier mâché, paraffin, and soap through add or subtract methods. Three-dimensional art projects give tactile stimulation and provide an emotional outlet through touch because of the versatility of the materials.

Materials. Clays and doughs (see recipes in Post It Page 6–3) and firing clay (from earth used for pottery) can be used. See Baylor's (1987) *When Clay Sings* for clay examples. Wood, paraffin, and soap can be used for carving, as well as materials from recipes (Post It Page 6–3). Papier mâché is also inexpensive and versatile (see Post It Page 6–3). See the instructions that follow.

Tools. Fingers, spoons, nails, sticks, cutouts (not cookie cutters), rolling pins, and things to press in to give textures (e.g., potato masher) are all possibilities.

Techniques. Use each of these methods to sculpt: add, subtract, punch, slap, pound, pinch, and stack. Children will naturally use clays and doughs to make cylinders and then balls and then pancake shapes. Modeling and plasticine clays hold their shape well but need to be warmed to make them pliable. Let children know they must knead the clay to warm it, which provides exercise to develop finger strength.

Papier Mâché. This is a molding and sculpting material that is inexpensive and yields delightful shapes that can be painted or collaged. Simply cut or tear up newspaper into 2-inch-long strips. Use thinned white glue or wheat (wallpaper) plaster and dip strips in paste. Run strips between fingers to remove excess. Let dry. A base such as a Styrofoam tray, box, or tube is needed. Start by using boxes as bases and move to more difficult curved and rounded shapes such as balloons and cardboard tubes. It is easier to have one small group at a time work on papier mâché because of the mess. Begin with a project in mind, rather than explore as you would in other media. Be sure to do cleanup immediately because the mix becomes hard and is very slippery on floors. An old shower curtain is useful to cover work surfaces. Puppet heads can be made by starting with a base as simple as a wad of newspaper on top of a toilet paper tube reinforced with masking tape. Spaghetti or candy boxes can be covered with papier mâché, painted, and used for puppets (make sure children can get fingers or hands inside). Papier mâché can be bought from sources such as Dick Blick (800-447-8192) or J. L. Hammet Co. (800-333-4600).

Mobiles. These are 3D art that moves. Use sticks, hangers, or old picture frames to suspend items from wire, yarn, cord, or ribbon. Mobiles can be made from found objects or by attaching any created items. Students need to experiment with balancing the weights of objects.

Other Sculptures. *Stick sculptures* can be made by using a clay ball as a base and pushing in toothpicks, buttons, shells, and other similar objects.

Sand molds can be made by pressing objects into damp sand (lids, pencils, buttons, shells). Pour a thin mix of plaster of Paris (the thickness of salad dressing) about ½-inch deep into the depression. Put a pop-can tab or paper clip in the mixture to make a hanger.

To make *soap clay* for carving, mix ¾ cup soap powder and a tablespoon of water. Whip until stiff. This can be used to coat projects to create a snow effect or molded (with wet hands). It dries hard and can be painted.

Crepe paper sculptures can be made by tearing up the paper, soaking 1 to 2 hours, pouring off the water, and adding wheat paste. It dries hard and can be sanded. *Yarn sculptures* can be made by soaking yarn in white glue and then wrapping it around a balloon, as sparsely or densely as desired. When dry, break the balloon.

Vermiculite carvings can be made by combining vermiculite (get at a plant store) and plaster. Add water and stir until thick. Pour into a mold or small box. Tear the box away when dry and carve with a table knife, nail, or blunt scissors.

Diorama or shadow boxes are scenes made by using a shoe box or other container to create a stage-like setting with 3D objects that are made or found.

Architecture. Teach basic shapes such as the cube, arch, sphere, cone cylinder, pyramid, rectangular solid, and triangular solid. Then take a neighborhood walk to find examples in buildings. Books like McLerran's (1992) *Roxaboxen* can be used to motivate students to think about construction as art making. Arches can be made with boxes and blocks, and cardboard tubes make a base to construct columns that can become corinthian, doric, or ionic with some papier mâché, glue, and paint. This is a particularly relevant art connection to studies of countries (e.g., Greece or even students' own community). There's probably a post office or government building with columns in nearly every American city. Terms that relate to architecture such as arch, beam, column, post, and lintel can be taught to give students conceptual anchors.

Recipes. Post It Page 6–3 contains common easy recipes for clays, doughs, and pastes.

Puppets and Masks. Post It Page 6–4 describes ways to make puppets and masks with readily available materials.

Bookmaking

Pop-up, accordion, big books, minibooks, sewn book, and shape books can be made to bind up the writing and art of students. There are many books available on easy binding (staple on a wallpaper cover or "sew" with yarn through hole punches). See, for example, Irvine and Reid (1987).

Animal Flip Books and Grids. Both of these encourage play with visual images by combining different parts of animals to create new creatures. For the flip books, students draw or find magazine pictures of animals and insects that have distinct heads, bodies, and legs. Pictures should be similar in size for best results. Each animal is a page in a book that needs to be fastened together so that the body parts are in approximately the same place on each page. Each page is then cut into thirds: head, body, legs. By turning the different page parts, new animals are created and can

RECIPES: CLAYS, DOUGHS, AND PASTES

Clays and Doughs

Soft Dough (stays soft for a long time if stored in a plastic bag or closed container)

    1 cup water
    ¼ cup salt
    1 tablespoon vegetable oil
    1 tablespoon alum
    1 cup flour (nonrising)
    food coloring (optional)

Bring water to a boil. Add salt and food coloring. Remove from heat and add the oil, alum, and flour. While it is still hot, mix and knead for 5 minutes. *Note:* If you choose to add food coloring, it is best to do so at the beginning or add to dough after mixing by using a few drops at a time and folding dough over color to mix. Food coloring will stain skin and clothing. To change the texture, add cornmeal, sawdust, coffee grounds, sand, or other grainy items.

Goop: Mix one part cornstarch and one part cold water.

Baker's Clay (makes one cup): often used to make ornaments or jewelry

    4 cups flour
    1 cup salt
    ½ cup warm water
    food coloring (optional)

Mix all ingredients and then knead until smooth (about 5 minutes). Add more flour as needed. *Note:* If you choose to add food coloring, do so a few drops at a time and fold dough over coloring to mix. Food coloring will stain skin and clothing. This dough should be used the day it is made. Add one teaspoon alum and put in plastic bag to keep it longer. The dough can be baked at 300°F until hard, approximately 20 to 60 minutes depending on the thickness of the pieces. For Christmas ornaments, make holes for hanging before baking. This clay can be painted with felt tips on enamel or use half tempera and half white glue. Spray with fixative when done.

Soda–Starch Clay (makes one cup)

    1 cup baking soda
    ½ cup corn starch
    ⅔ cup warm water
    food coloring or tempera paint (optional)

Mix ingredients in pan until thickness of mashed potatoes. Stir to boiling. Pour on a cool surface and knead when cool. Add coloring during kneading. Store in plastic bag until ready to use. Shape beads by using a drinking straw to make holes. To speed dry, bake 10 minutes at lowest oven setting or 30 seconds on medium in a microwave. *Note:* Make a day or two ahead of time. Make batches in different colors. You can use crayons, paint, or marker to paint this clay. Set with clear nail polish or shellac.

Salt–Starch Clay

> 1 cup cornstarch
>
> ½ cup salt
>
> ½ cup water

Mix and cook over low heat until it hardens. Salad oil delays drying.

Sawdust Clay

> 2 cups fine sawdust
>
> 1 cup wheat paste (wallpaper)
>
> ½ to 1 cup water
>
> 1 teaspoon alum to keep from spoiling

Mix to bread dough consistency. Needs to dry slowly. Keeps in plastic bag or refrigerator. *Note:* Good for making puppet heads and relief maps. Can be painted with tempera.

Pastes

Corn Starch Paste (makes ½ pint)

> ¼ cup corn starch
>
> ¾ cup water
>
> 2 tablespoons sugar
>
> 1 tablespoon vinegar

Mix corn starch and cold water in a saucepan. Add sugar and vinegar. Stir constantly and slowly heat the mixture until it clears and thickens. Cool before using. Paste can be stored in the refrigerator several weeks if kept in a tightly sealed container. *Notes:* Corn starch paste has a pleasant smell and texture. It is not too sticky and is a safe, almost colorless paste—it dries clear. It forms a stronger bond than flour paste and can be used for lightweight items such as fabric, yarn, ribbon, rice, and thin cardboard. This is one of the stronger homemade pastes, but it must be cooked ahead of time. It is also hard to remove from surfaces when dry; it requires soaking and scrubbing.

Flour Paste

Add water to flour until it is thick but spreadable. *Notes:* Children can make this for themselves. This works well on most kinds of paper, and it is safe and does not stain clothes. The texture is different from school paste, so it makes an interesting change for the children. It wrinkles thinner papers and makes a relatively weak bond, so it is not recommended for collage. It washes off easily when wet, but requires soaking and scrubbing if allowed to dry. It cannot be stored and should be used when it is first made. Add oil of wintergreen or peppermint to help resist spoiling.

---

be named. This can evolve into creative writing by setting up categories for students to use to invent a description of their new creature: habitat, food, habits, and movements. For younger students, body parts can be placed on cards and assembled on a table. *Variation:* For older students, use a grid listing or depicting animal or insect heads across the top of a page and bodies down the left side. By finding the intersection of the X and Y axes, students can create new visual combinations (e.g., X (heads) = goat, cow, llama, cat, and Y (bodies/legs) = dolphin, turtle, snake, duck.

Big Books. Big books are enlarged copies of favorite books, poems, or chants about the size of posterboard. To construct a big book as a response to a book, poem, lesson or unit of study:

1. *Paper:* 18- by 30-inch white chart paper and 12- by 18-inch white construction paper will be needed, plus two pieces of poster board at least 18 by 30 inches, and clips, metal rings, or cord to secure the cover.

2. *Art materials:* Glue, markers, crayons, glue, wallpaper sample, and other collage materials.

3. *Type of book:* Replica or new version? To make this decision, select a predictable story or poem with obvious patterns or rhyme (see example list of predictable books in Chapter 3 under Genre). Reading the book or poem several times invites children to chime in. Prepare for writing by brainstorming and webbing ideas. Students then dictate a rough draft, which the teacher writes on a large chart or older students write independently. Then the story or poem is reread and revised.

4. *Text:* Words are printed on white construction paper and glued on the larger sheets of paper. The text should be divided evenly across the pages of the book so that there is plenty of room left for artwork.

5. *Illustrations:* Students can use materials, styles, and techniques. They may want to experiment with the style of a particular artist.

6. *Title page with the copyright year and the names of authors and artists:* Design a title page and, if the book is a replica, a statement such as "Retold and illustrated by Mr. Walker's class" should be added. If the big book is an adapted version, a statement such as "Based on Majorie Sharmat's book *Someday*" can be added. A dedication page can be made for the beginning of the book, and a page about the authors and even a reader comment page can be added at the back.

7. *Cover:* Students design a front and back cover, and it is glued to the poster board.

8. *Page sequence:* Have students order the pages, and put book together with front cover, title page, copyright page, dedication page, story, page about the authors, comment page, and back cover. Use rings, cord, or metal clips to bind the book.

POST IT PAGE 6–4

PUPPET- AND MASK-MAKING IDEAS

Finger puppets: Cut off fingers of cheap work gloves to make individual puppets students can develop by gluing on materials or using fabric paints. *Alternatives:* Use small candy boxes (like Halloween-sized Milk Duds boxes) as the base on which to create the puppet. Students can also create their own figures from paper or cardboard and attach "finger rings" to slip the puppets on.

Glove puppets: Each child needs one glove. Each finger becomes one character to be created from a story. Five characters are possible and some fingers can be objects in the story.

Stick puppets: Attach a popsicle stick, tongue depressor, ruler, or wooden dowel to a character made of paper, papier mâché, cloth, and so on. *Variation:* Find sticks from trees that can be used as a base to make a puppet.

Shadow puppets: Cut character body parts from construction paper and hinge arms, legs, and so forth together with brads. Lay on overhead projector and move body parts to tell story.

Paper bag puppets and masks: Use small paper bags to create a character's face or body using paint, collage, markers, and so on. The puppet's mouth can be placed at the fold of the paper bag so that it will look as if the character is talking. Yarn, grass, and twigs can be added for hair and paper or cloth used for clothes. Grocery bags can be used to make puppet masks that students wear on their heads with eyes, mouth, and nose holes.

Sock puppets: Students sew or glue scraps of fabric, yarn, and pipe cleaners on socks. The sock can also be cut at the toe to create a mouth or held so that a mouth is created by a fold.

Paper plate puppets: Paper plates can be used for puppets as well as for masks. Students add materials to create a character and then tape sticks or rulers to the back of the plates for handles. *Variation:* Use plastic coffee can lids instead of paper plates.

Papier mâché puppet heads and masks: Use the recipe for papier mâché and apply to a ball of newspaper with an attached toilet paper tube (secure with masking tape). When dry, paint and attach other materials to create a character. A fabric body can be glued or sewn using a generic body pattern made from two pieces of cloth or paper. To make a mask, papier mâché over a large balloon. When dry, paint and cut holes for eyes, nose, and mouth. Mask can be a full head cover or just cover the face.

Object puppets: Find and adapt objects that relate to a story and lay them on top of a box (used as a stage) or table as the story is told, for example: a covered thread spool (tuffet), a plastic spider, a tiny doll (Miss Muffet), or a toy spoon. Check craft stores and departments for a variety of these tiny objects, often in packages with multiples. *Variation:* Painted rock puppets: collect rocks and paint to represent characters and display and manipulate as story is told.

Clothespin puppets: Use old-fashioned clothespins as the base to create characters. Clip to a ruler to give extra height.

Envelope puppets: Use large or small envelopes as the character base. Combine several envelopes for a different effect.

Pipe cleaner puppets: Bend, cut, and combine pipe cleaners to form puppets. Create a handle from one pipe cleaner.

Paper cup puppets: Use Styrofoam or paper cups as the creation base. Use cups of different sizes and combine cups for creative effects, for example: create taller puppets with several cups.

Card puppets: Use index cards as bases. Cards can be attached to sticks or used on a flannel board if coarse sand paper or felt is glued to the back. Card puppets can be placed in a pocket chart as a story is told.

Tagboard masks: Cut tagboard into ovals big enough to cover a face. Make four 1-inch slits, one on each "corner" so that the mask can be given contour. Use masking tape to secure. Draw ovals for the eyes and a space to cut out a mouth. Paint and use collage materials to decorate according to a variety of cultures (display books with pictures of masks for data gathering).

Plaster gauze masks: The face is covered with Vaseline and then gauze, soaked in plaster, is applied and allowed to set up. (Keep nose, mouth, and eye areas clear.) Mask is removed and painted with acrylics or tempera.

TAKE ACTION 1

ADAPT STRATEGIES

Choose a strategy seed idea from *energizers* or *elements and concepts* and adapt it for science, math, reading and language arts, or social studies. See examples under each curricular area that follows.

IV. CONNECTING ART TO OTHER CURRICULAR AREAS

Science Focus

◆ Natural world, systems of the body, seasons, weather, plants, animals, the environment, machines, electricity, magnets, space, gravity, and states of matter

◆ Finding out how and why things happen in the world through careful observation, hypothesis making, and prediction

Art and Reality. Students can examine how a single object is shown realistically in many different ways by artists. For example, show five different pieces of art about an animal. Ask how each gives different information and feels different. Picture books can be used, for example (for cats), Gag's *Millions of Cats*, Pinkwater and dePaola's cat in *The Wuggie Norple Story*.

Fish and Bird Art. Students choose a fish or bird to find out (1) where it lives, (2) what it eats, and (3) how it moves. This information is then connected to how the fish or bird looks (color, shape, size of body parts). Students then create a new fish or bird by thinking of answers to the previous three questions and using a variety of art media. Name the new animal, do oral presentations, and display.

Food Mural. Students work in teams to research a food's origin step by step. Use paint and collage materials to construct a mural to show how it ends up on the dinner table. For example, show how wheat is planted, harvested, processed, baked, wrapped, and delivered to grocery stores.

Invisible Animals. Examine water under a microscope or with hand lenses and sketch living organisms. Show students how to do quick sketches with pencils to capture important details of what they see. Emphasize close looking to capture specifics. Sketches can be enlarged into full paintings. *Note:* In the video *The Lively Art of Picture Books* (Schindel, Weston Woods), Robert McCloskey sketches ducks.

Habitat 3D. Use boxes to create dioramas of an animal's habitat (land or water). Add clay sculptures, tempera paint, found objects, and papier mâché in construction. Emphasize the importance of showing how the habitat would enable the animal to survive (food, shelter, etc.).

Habitat Hat. Students research different habitats to discover unique characteristics. See www.fi.edu/tifi/units/life/habitat/habitat/html for more information. Students then bring in magazine pictures (wildlife magazines are a good source) and "found" objects (shells, sticks, etc.) to affix to hats. Use old hats or paper hats as a base. Provide Raffia, construction paper, tempera paint and glue (C. Kotarsky, teacher, Lady's Island Elementary School).

Museum Scavenger Hunt. Give student pairs or teams a scavenger hunt form on which to record "finds" in these categories: animals, plants, and other images related to space and land forms during a museum visit. Make spaces to note title, artist, date, and media for each piece of art.

Pound Flowers. Do this in the spring. Collect a variety of fresh flowers and discuss their names and how they are similar and different. Students then place the flowers on construction paper and cover them with clear plastic wrap. Pound each flower with a hammer until the color is embedded in the paper. Frame and display.

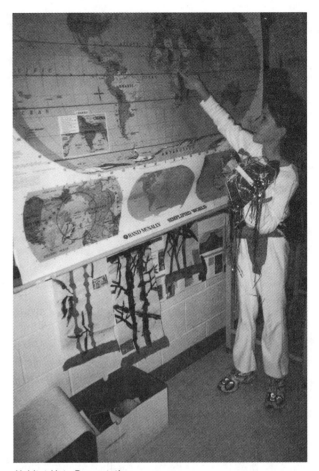
Habitat Hats Presentation

Scientific Drawings. Examine the drawings of Beatrix Potter and Robert McCloskey, both of whom studied animals and plants carefully to render their images. Students can then choose to do a careful scientific drawing, focusing on important details. Use photos or actual plants for close looking.

Nature Sculptures. Use types of clouds to inspire soft sculptures: stratus, cumulus, and so on. See the recipes in Post It Page 6–3.

Science of Color. Each group of students needs a prism to investigate color. Paint or use crayons to record observations and discover the pattern (ROYGBIV: Red Orange Yellow Green Blue Indigo Violet).

Nature Collections and Displays. Students can create collages and displays from "found" nature, for example, a fall collage using leaves, twigs, stones, and dried flowers.

Catch a Spider Web. Slide a piece of black construction paper behind a web and bring it forward so that the web clings to the paper. Dust with flour or dusting powder. Spray with fixative or nonaerosol hair spray. Discuss the patterns of lines created by the web. Look closely to compare and contrast.

Rock Paintings. Students select rocks about fist sized to paint. Add white glue to tempera paint or use acrylics to make it stick. The paintings can be abstract or students can carefully study the rock shape to see what representational images are suggested (e.g., mouse, cat).

Step into the Painting. Tell students to think like scientists and tell or write their observations as they look at a piece of art (e.g., a landscape). Focus on how the painting might have been made and the content.

Grow a Head. Use pantyhose feet to make living heads. Fill hose with a teaspoon of grass seed and then a mixture of soil and sawdust. Tie snugly with a string. Paint on face with fabric paint. Put head in a shallow dish and pour water over it. Place in a sunny area and watch the grass "hair" grow.

Garbage Art. Use clean trash that students have collected to make collages that promote looking at throwaways in a different way. Emphasize experimenting with how to group items on cardboard and the use of patterns. Encourage tearing, scrunching, and even using pieces of plastic and glass for mosaic effects (take care about sharp edges). *Variation:* Combine with painting, fabrics, and nature materials.

Social Studies Focus

◆ Relationships among human beings, occupations, transportation, communities, governments, customs, cultures, holidays, and use of natural resources.

◆ History, geography (use of maps), civics (citizenship and government) or political science, economics, anthropology, and sociology.

◆ Investigations into cultural diversity and global understanding.

◆ Special questions: How did it used to be and why? Why is it like it is today? What can I do about it? Thinking processes: cause and effect, sequence, gather data, discover relationships, make judgments, draw conclusions, and problem solve about community issues, for example, economic issues such as school funding or value conflicts related to free speech.

◆ Use of primary source material such as newspapers, art, music, diaries, letters, journals, books, and artifacts, rather than use of textbooks and gathering data through interviews, surveys, and other investigatory strategies that historians and other social scientists use.

Make Me a World. Papier mâché used over a balloon provides a base to create personal globes or planets that can accompany individual research projects that will be presented to the class. (See papier mâché directions given earlier.)

Signature Art. Part of social studies involves coming to respect individual differences. Show a facsimile of signatures (e.g., Declaration of Independence). Give students paper and choices of tools and media. Allow time to write signatures many different ways. Display products and discuss differences in size, color, lines, and shapes. Focus on what makes each name so different and the effect on a viewer.

Group Composition. Since learning cooperative behavior is a key goal of social studies, any art project on which students have individual responsibilities and come together to create a whole work is appropriate, for example, murals, class quilts on a topic (transportation, state, city, etc.), group sculptures such as totem poles, or constructing with cardboard boxes, tubes, or papier mâché around a topic such as inventions. Emphasize that the art need not be representational.

Multicultural Art. Any country or culture can be studied through its art forms. Assemble prints, pictures, and artifacts and then discuss the details and patterns. Ask about what the figures are doing and why. Students can research the background of pieces of art (media, techniques) and then experiment with these. Emphasize the values that are portrayed in each art form by asking, "What does this show about the people?" *Note:* See how to mix different skin tones described earlier. *Variation:* Each child begins a personal collection of art from different culture and ethnic groups using magazines, advertisements, and postcards.

Artifacts. Artifacts are another type of art students can learn about and, in doing so, come to new understandings about different cultures. These handmade art forms are usually three dimensional and are related to the everyday life of a people. Baskets, carvings, quilts, pots, and jewelry give us hints about the artist's values and needs. Invite students to bring in artifacts and create displays with written "museum tags" about each piece. Artifacts can be coordinated with social studies units and used for writing and discussion. For example, write or tell the 5Ws and H about a family artifact.

Holidays. There are many complaints today about the "holiday curriculum" overtaking the curriculum. The problem lies in the superficial ways in which holidays are studied and the lack of connections to courses of study. Stereotypical and dictated art abound and need to be avoided. Instead of tracing hand turkeys and coloring Pilgrim and Indian heads at Thanksgiving, it is more substantial to engage students in using a variety of art media to express ideas and feelings about major themes. For example, (1) meals are rituals used to celebrate events in many cultures, (2) people offer food as a gift to show appreciation and love, and (3) there are many ways to give thanks.

Mandalas. The mandala is a circular shape that has been used in all cultures for eons. The circle is thought to be a satisfying and comforting shape to make in all sizes. First, get students to search out examples of circles or compositions arranged in circular patterns in the art of a variety of cultures and in contemporary art, even in advertisements such as the Coke sign. Brainstorm all the circular things in nature, such as the sun and moon or the cycle of seasons. Students can then make their own mandalas by creating a piece of art that has the concept of the circle. This is a broad idea that can be interpreted any way students like, from round abstract artworks to poster-sized realistic works containing many circular-shaped images. Any material may be used, and young children especially enjoy collage mandalas.

Update Art. Do a modern-day version of an artist's work, one that reflects the current time rather than the time in which it was created. Change the background or dress of portraits (e.g., *Mona Lisa*).

Class Flag. Examine the flags and symbols of countries. Discuss how and why they use the colors, shapes, designs, materials, and lines that they do. Divide into groups to create a class flag to represent what's important about the class. Make fabric, paper, paint, and collage materials available for design.

Famous People Sculptures. Students choose a person they wish to study who has made a significant con-

tribution to history (explorer, president, artist, musician, activist). Brainstorm what students would like to know. They then find details about how the person looked, moved, talked, and dressed, what she or he ate, valued, achieved, and so forth. Students then construct sculptures from papier mâché or make a puppet (use paper bags, papier mâché heads, stuffed hose, or stuffed plastic bags to make heads; see Post It Page 6–4). (*Note:* Papier mâché is used over a balloon for a base.) Students use sculptures or puppets to role play and do a presentation to the class. Allow time for questions.

Reading and Language Arts Focus

◈ Reading, listening, speaking, written composition (including handwriting, spelling, grammar, usage, capitalization, and punctuation). Since reading and language arts are processes, they must be connected to a subject to have meaning, that is, something to read and write about.

◈ Goal: *Create* meaning and enjoyment using print through thinking at every level from memory to critical thinking or evaluation.

◈ The printed word and its components (letters, syllables, spelling patterns), how words combine to make phrases and sentences and sentences combine to make paragraphs and other forms of discourse from tongue twisters to novels.

◈ Types of words: antonyms and synonyms, parts of speech, and figurative language (metaphor, idiomatic expressions).

Guided Art and Language Lesson: LPR-SWAP. Visual art and listening, speaking, reading, and writing are integrated in guided art and language lessons led by the teacher using an adaptation of the introduction, development, and conclusion procedure. Students can learn to guide these lessons if the steps are posted for them to practice. See Post It Page 6–5.

Artist Birth Mates. These are described in Take Action 6 in Chapter 2.

Artists Like Me. After studying an artist, have students write about all the ways the artist was like them (Misty Kaplafka, Ohio art teacher).

Art Print Story. Choose any art print(s) to write group or individual stories. Use portraits for the characters, a landscape for the setting, and an abstract or

POST IT PAGE 6–5

GUIDED ART AND LANGUAGE LESSON: LPR-SWAP

Introduction

L   **Look Closely and Think.** Students examine a work of art for a set period of time to see and feel everything it is about. No talking at this stage. *Example:* Look at *I and the Village* by Chagall.

P   **Predict.** Students write predictions about what the artist is trying to communicate. With younger children the teacher can scribe on a chart or the overhead. *Example:* The artist has everything going in different directions, so he may be trying to say he is confused.

Development

R   **Read.** Read about the artist and/or the work of art. Teachers may read to the students. *Example:* Read Greenfield's *Marc Chagall.*

S   **Share.** Students share their predictions about the work of art, whether they were confirmed or rejected in the reading material. This can be done in pairs, small groups, or whole group. *Example:* Prediction above is rejected because Chagall was being playful and childlike. He focused on dream qualities.

Conclusion

W   **Write.** Students do a writing response (see Post It Page 4–2). *Example:* Write a letter to Chagall or a story about his dream. The story could start at the top of the picture and move to the bottom.

A   **Art.** Students do an art response (see Post It Page 5–5). *Example:* Watercolor paintings of children's dreams or a class mural of good memories done in Chagall's style.

P   **Publish.** Students responses are made public through displays, oral sharing, and bookmaking (e.g., class big book).

---

nonfigurative work for the problem. Establish the problem quickly and be descriptive about the setting and the characters.

Talking Art.   Each child writes something a person in the print might be saying on a speech bubble. Bubbles are displayed around the art.

Cinco Strategy.   Look closely at a piece of fine art. Number your paper 1 to 5. Beside 1, put all the nouns you see; by 2, verbs and actions; by 3, what it is a kind of or adjectives; by 4, adverbs; by 5, a sentence using the ideas you've generated. *Note:* Abstract art works well with this.

Learn–Wonder–Like.   Students pretend they are going to meet the artist of the work and generate a list of comments and questions about what they learned, wondered, and liked about the work.

Fine Art Storytelling.   Show or review the literary elements (plot with a problem, setting, characters, themes, style). Use an art print as a stimulus to tell a story. Pass

the print around a circle with each student adding on to the tale. *Variation:* Use several portraits and a landscape (or seascape or cityscape) to set up the characters and setting.

Parts of Speech.   Put parts of speech categories on the board or on a chart. Under each category, ask students to find verbs, adjectives, and the like related to a piece of art. This can be done in small groups, with each group taking a part of speech.

Word Squeeze.   Look closely at a piece of fine art to find all the colors, shapes, places, textures, lines, feelings, actions, things, and so forth. Make columns on a piece of paper and try to get as many words as you can in each. Tell the students to squeeze it like you would a sponge and try to find things no one else sees. *Variation:* Use a magnifying glass or cardboard tube to focus on or examine picture in halves.

Name a Color.   Make a list of all the color names the students know. Divide into groups to find new words for the colors (e.g., cerise for red). Follow with doing a piece of art to experiment with making new colors through mixing.

Walk into the Painting.   Students pretend to actually enter a landscape, seascape, or cityscape and write or tell how they feel and what they see. Use all five senses.

Art Ads.   Use propaganda devices to sell a painting, for example, bandwagon, glittering generalities, celebrity endorsement, common folks, everybody's doing it. Break students into groups to create a one-minute ad to sell a piece of art using the techniques. These can be in writing or presented orally.

Artist Interview.   Ask students to list questions to ask an artist about a particular piece of art (sculpture, collage, painting). Example question categories are puzzlements? wonderings? time? culture? Actually set up partners to take turns interviewing each other. Take turns using questions by alternating being the artist and interviewer.

Poetry Art.   Students examine a piece of art to note how it feels, the mood, use of media, style, and art elements. Give students examples of types of poetry patterns (diamante, cinquain, haiku, limerick, quatrain, triplet; see Post It Page 3–5 for a list and examples). Write some collaborative pattern poems together and then try writing individual ones based on art. *Alternative:* Students write poems and then create art to go with them, for example, print over the poem, collages, or watercolors.

I Spy (Visual Discrimination).   Set this up as a game as in the *Where's Waldo* books. Say "I spy . . ." and start the game; ask students to find things that are special to finish the phrase. Encourage students to *look closely* for big shapes, little shapes, curvy lines, light, and dark and to try to find action and details. Use with abstract art to stretch thinking. See the *I Spy* art series for children in which focus is on finding something in masterpieces, for example, letters, animals, and toys.

Match.   Show students shapes and colors on separate cards (construction paper shapes and colors). Ask students to find the same shape or color in a piece of art as many times as they can. Ask about the patterns created by repeated shapes and colors. Ask students to name the shapes and colors to encourage oral expression.

Memory Game.   Tell the students to study a piece of art carefully for a specified period of time and then cover it up. Ask them to then list everything they re-

member. They could do this individually or in groups, orally or in writing. Uncover the painting and check for the accuracy of their observations.

Word Walls and Webs: Vocabulary Development. Designate a space to put up art words. They can be alphabetized or grouped by color, shape, media, and style. Large word webs can be made: Put each art category in the center of a large sheet of paper. Students add to the webs by finding examples of art categories in artwork, drawing a line from the category, writing the example, and putting their initials beneath the idea. For example, a "line" web would be filled with these kinds of words: *zagged, straight, curved, pointed,* or *thin.*

Read about Artists.   Here is a list of possible things to read and find out about an artist:

- Life of the artist: biographical information such as birth, death, marriage, children, friends
- Who and what most influenced the artist
- Time period in which the artist lived
- Country or countries where the artist lived
- Style in which the artist worked or school of art to which the artist belonged
- Influence the artist had on the world of art (for what the artist is known)
- Other artists of that period
- Medium(s) the artist used
- A particular work of art the artist did, for example, the most famous or controversial
- Art criticism about the artist and his or her work

Write about Art and Artists.   Here are writing about art/artist connections:

- Letters: to artists or someone in the picture; to museum curator to request information about a work of art
- Biographical sketches of artists
- Story about a great artwork (See *Girl in Hyacinth Blue*—adult example)
- Story about how the work of art came to be
- Menu that might have been served during the time the art was created
- Report on the customs of the time of the artist
- Report on the clothing styles of the time of the artist

- Description or criticism of a piece of art
- Report about the period of art
- Paragraph hypothesizing what the artist would do if he or she were alive today
- Script for play or scene about the artist's life
- Comparison of the work of two artists; Venn diagram
- Time line of the artist's work
- Book for children about an artist, medium, or style (see bookmaking ideas in this chapter).

Artist Expert. Students pick an artist and do any number of the following activities to become an expert on the person and his or her work. Any of these can culminate in class oral presentations.

- *Collection:* Start finding and saving works of art by the artist (e.g., prints, calendar art, postcards).
- *Ape the greats:* Use the colors, mood, style, and techniques of the artist to create adapted works of art.
- *Update:* Make a modern-day version of the artist's work (e.g., change the costumes).
- *Vary it:* Do another version of the art (e.g. van Gogh's, *Starry Night*—do Sunny Day, Rainy Day, Stormy Night, Foggy Night, or Snowy Night).
- *Guests and experts:* Invite a local artist, museum curator, or college professor to speak about the artist or interview them.
- *Art gallery:* Visit a museum and see the real thing.
- *Artist's studio:* Visit the place where an artist works; ask to shadow the person for a day.
- *Video:* Watch a video of the artist's life (e.g., *Lust for Life* about van Gogh).
- *Art show:* Have an event to display the artist's work and students' work together.
- *Mini art gallery:* In the hall, classroom, or a special place in the school; include works by famous artists and students' works of art.
- *Painting of the week:* Students select a favorite from among several works of art and display it, with "speech bubbles" around it telling things they know or what they think or feel about it.

Creative Process Reflection. Teach the creative problem-solving process (CPSP) from Post It Page 1–6. After making art, ask students to write or tell about the parts of the CPSP used. The paper can be divided into particular CPSP sections: attitude, problem definition, data gathering, experimenting, SCAMPER, and so forth.

Journals and Logs. These could be done individually, as dialogs between two students, or as team journals. Topics to write about: What do you think about the painting? How does it make you feel? What does it make you think about? What mood do you think the artist was in when he or she created this work of art? Why did the artist entitle the work of art as he or she did?

Compare and Contrast. Different messages are conveyed through the use of different media (e.g., sculpture, poetry, dance). Compare and contrast two pieces of art that evoke similar feelings and messages. How does each artist create the response? What do both artists do that is similar? For example, look at art about courage, love, family, war, suffering, or nature.

Math Focus

- Daily living situations involving counting, measuring, probability, statistics, geometry, logic, patterns, functions, and numbers.
- Problem solving through the use of skills (raising questions and answering them, finding relationships and patterns).
- Concepts about numbers, operations, and ideas such as bigger, longer, greater than, less, three, four, even, and odd.
- The National Council of the Teachers of Mathematics encourages teachers to have children solve problems in many ways, focus on explaining and thinking, rather than just correctness, and using a hands-on approach.

Quilts. Create class geometric quilts using traditional patterns found in folk art collections or by observing patterns in the environment that could be used on pieces (dots, checkerboard, and stripes). Each student uses a square of paper (about 10 by 10 inches) to plan a pattern. Patterns can be painted or made from cut paper, fabric, newspaper, or thin plastic. Squares are completed and then glued on to a large piece of bulletin roll paper (black makes an excellent background). A border can then be added. *Variations:* Students can be limited to just one shape so that they can experiment with variations on it (e.g., triangle combinations).

Origami Art. Japanese paper folding art involves the study of shape, line, symmetry, and angle. Special origami paper in a variety of colors works best and is available from any art supply store. There are many resource books on simple origami shapes, such as bird shapes, and the children's book *Sadako and the Thousand Paper Cranes* would be a wonderful story addition to this art–math project.

Color Recipes (Measurement). Each pair of students needs an eyedropper and three small cups of tempera (red, yellow, and blue; use ice cube trays broken in half). Students experiment to create colors. They record the number of drops to create each color. Ask pairs to name their new color creations. *Variation:* Give students one primary color and a cup of white and black. Experiment with recipes for shapes and tints (numbers of drops).

Story Problem Art. Students create art to go with particular story problems that they are given or write. Problems can then be exchanged.

SCAMPER. Students are given a shape to manipulate using Eberle's steps: substitute, combine, adapt, minify or magnify, put to other uses, eliminate, and reverse or rearrange. They create a piece of art to show all the things they did with a triangle, square, or circle, using SCAMPER. Use any media.

Count Me In. Groups are given a piece of art to examine for numbers of things. Give a time limit and then share as a group (e.g., 11 curved lines, 8 right angles, 14 red flowers).

I Spy. Find all the math in any piece of art (print, collage, sculpture) or picture book. List geometric shapes, patterns (anything that is repeated), types of lines, and use of symmetry. Discuss any parts that give a feeling of infinity and how it is accomplished. Use a large magnifying glass.

Symmetry. Each student gets one-half of a picture from a magazine or print. By carefully studying the half, the student tries to duplicate it on the opposite side.

Making Math Art. Use art that is very geometric, such as Mondrian's, and ask students to discuss how the artist might have made it and why. Have students try their own geometric math art by repeating shape patterns.

Step into the Painting. Be mathematicians and tell or write all your observations based on your math point of view. Comment on how the painting might have been made and the content of the work.

Infinity Art. Show examples of George Seurat's dot art (pointillism) and ask student to look closely to discover how the images are all made. Discuss how the dots make up sets to create a whole image. Students can make their own dot art using Q-tips to paint.

◆ BIBLIOGRAPHY AND REFERENCES

Books

Annheim, R. (1989). *Thoughts on art education:* Los Angeles: Getty Center for Education in the arts.

Brookes, M. (1996). *Drawing with children.* New York: Putnam.

Cecil, N., & Lauritzen, P. (1994). *Literature and the arts for the integrated classroom.* White Plains, NY: Longman.

Eberle, R. (1971). *SCAMPER: Game for imagination development.* Buffalo, NY: DOK.

Children's Literature

Ahlberg, J., & Ahlberg, A. (1986). *The jolly postman.* Boston: Little, Brown.

Ai-Lang, L. (1982). *Yen Sen: A Chinese Cinderella story.* New York: Philomel.

Baylor, B. (1987). *When clay sings.* New York: Macmillan.

Bjork, C. (1987). *Linnea in Monet's garden.* New York: R&S Books.

Bruchac, J., & London, J. (1992). *Thirteen moons on a turtle's back.* New York: Philomel.

Bunting, E. (1994). *Smoky night.* San Diego: Harcourt Brace.

Coerr, E. (1977). *Sadako and the thousand paper cranes.* New York: Putnam.

Felix, M. (1993). *The colors.* Mankato, MN: Creative Education.

Gag, W. (1928). *Millions of cats.* New York: Coward, McCann.

Greenfield, H. (1991). *Marc Chagall.* New York: Abrams.

Irvine, J., & Reid, B. (1987). *How to make popups.* New York: Morrow.

McLerran, A. (1992). *Roxaboxen.* New York: Puffin.

Miles, M. (1971). *Annie and the Old One*. Boston: Little, Brown.

O'Neill, M. (1989). *Hailstones and halibut bones*. New York: Doubleday.

Pinkwater, D., & de Paola, T. (1988). *The Wuggie Norple story*. Palmer, AK: Aladdin.

Ringgold, F. (1991). *Tar Beach*. New York: Crown.

Willard, N. (1981). *A visit to William Blake's inn*. New York: Harcourt Brace Jovanovich.

Zolotow, C. (1989). *Someday*. New York: Harper & Row.

7

Integrating Drama Throughout the Curriculum

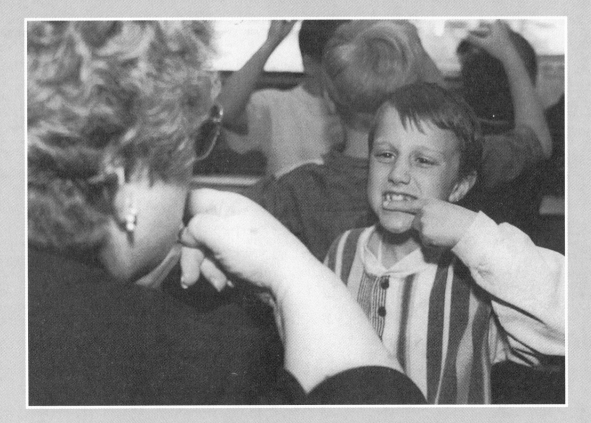

Drama is life with the dull bits cut out.

Alfred Hitchcock

◆ **CLASSROOM SNAPSHOT**

Ms. Tran's Sixth-Grade Social Studies Class

I think that an art gives shape and stability to the valued materials of life, in order that they may be stressed, attended to and preserved.

Josephine Miles

Ms. Tran has been teaching sixth grade for 5 years. She became interested in integrating drama during a special staff development project on arts integration 2 years ago. She is a young, vivacious teacher with a contagious sense of humor, and she seems very comfortable using drama on a daily basis. Today's lesson takes place during social studies time, and the students are in the middle of an environmental issues unit focusing on the question of how humans have changed the environment. They have been reading about the problems with the coral reef in the Bahamas.

Ms. Tran holds up a yellowish red piece of coral. "I'm going to pass this around and you can each say a one liner about it. Remember, you can pass and we'll come back to you, if you wish."

The students are seated in learning circle groups, and she starts with a student in a group to her left. The boy takes it and grins as he explores the surface.

"I'm hard but I'm dead," he says and passes it to a boy next to him.

"They're killing all of us by polluting our home," the next boy says and passes the coral on.

A small girl with large, dark eyes takes the coral and says, "I pass." She passes it on to the last person in the first group.

"I could make a lot of money if I could just find a way to get around the authorities and get more of this," the last boy in the group says.

It takes about 10 minutes to go around the room. When everyone has had a chance to speak, Ms. Tran nods to the girl who has passed earlier and the girl reaches for the coral.

"Without the coral reef, our country will not survive. When we kill it, we kill ourselves," she says softly.

"It was really interesting how you took on so many different roles," Ms. Tran remarks. "Shana, I could tell you were a very concerned Bahamian citizen by the sadness in your voice and how sincere you looked. What did some of the rest of you notice?"

Several hands go up and Ms. Tran calls on students.

"Some people spoke as if they were the piece of coral. That was really cool. I'd never have thought of doing that," a girl in the far right group says.

Other students make comments about how their classmates made clear who they were and how they felt with their words and even how the coral was held.

Ms. Tran then moves farther into her planned lesson and summarizes the main topics they've been studying: the Bahamian economy, life-style, and its relationship to the reef. She asks the students what she has left out, and several children add comments about the destruction of the reef and the tourist trade.

"Today we're going to go into more depth based on what you read in your assignment and what we've been studying. We want to really go into detail about the interaction between people and the environment. We'll be continuing our work on learning through being different characters and using your voice and body to make us all believe in your ideas. Let's get started."

Ms. Tran picks up a yellow Mr. Mike from the table. "Imagine you are a Bahamian citizen who has a specific interest in the reef—think of all the points of view you read about. We are just getting ready to have a live telecast to inform everyone in the Bahamas about the issues."

Half of you can be the audience and half of you can be the panel. All of you will have a chance to speak. Let's set up. Just five minutes to show time. Panel members take these chairs. Audience, arrange yourselves in two rows."

It seems like chaos for a few minutes, but students decide and soon all but two chairs on the 10-seat panel are taken.

"Great work. Okay. Only two minutes to show time. I'll be asking the panel members to introduce themselves and make a short statement about their position. Audience members, you'll be able to respond to the panel with remarks and questions."

Ms. Tran moves to a CD player and pushes a button. She flips the lights out and stands ready. Jazz music begins and she flips the lights on and holds up the mike.

"Welcome to *Bahama Today*. I'm Tina Tran and I'd like to welcome our panel of guests and audience members who are here today to discuss the issues surrounding the coral reef. We'll begin with our panel members. Please introduce yourselves and tell us why you have come."

Ms. Tran hands the mike to the panel member nearest her. The panel proves to be a diverse group ranging from fishermen to a politician. Some are vehemently opposed to government interference and others are passionate about the destruction of the reef.

After the opening remarks, Ms. Tran opens the discussion up to the audience.

"Please stand and give your name and why you have come," she tells them. The audience offers comments to specific panelists and asks questions. All but two students participate.

After about 15 minutes, Ms. Tran sums up remarks made during the show and ends with, "I'd like to thank all our guests for coming today and remind you to watch every day at this time to learn more about current issues on *Bahama Today*."

She starts the music again and flips out the lights. She lets the music play a bit and then stops it and turns on the lights.

"Okay, let's talk about what just happened," she tells the class. They seem reticent.

After a full half-minute, Ms. Tran backs up. "I think you all are still processing all this. Let's do a Write Right Away to debrief. Just use the next page in your journal and let's go for two minutes."

Students hustle to their desks for pencils and journals. Ms. Tran moves to an overhead projector and begins to jot down her observations in full view of the students. At first a few students just watch her. She jots down sentence fragments and key words. Gradually, all students begin to write. She actually gives them nearly 5 minutes and then asks them to find a place to stop (almost everyone is still writing).

"Please form groups of three or four people with the people nearest to you and take a few minutes to share what you wrote. You can read it if you like or just tell it."

Students turn to form groups and Ms. Tran waits until everyone is in a group. When the stragglers have finally joined a group, Ms. Tran circulates as students share.

"You think that you made the politician too stereotyped? Why do you say that?" she asks a boy who has critiqued his own performance.

As she moves from group to group, she comments and asks clarification questions such as "What do you mean by . . . ?" and "Are you saying that . . . ?"

The room is full of discussion. After about 10 minutes, Ms. Tran brings them back together.

"I could really tell you understood the importance of using details and examples to create believable characters. It sounds like many of you are planning to find out even more specifics before I spring another drama session on you!"

The students laugh and it is apparent they like Ms. Tran's enthusiasm.

"We're going to do some more group work to extend your thinking about the issues and what just happened on the TV program. I'm going to ask you to break into small groups of family, friends, or neighbors that live in the Bahamas and viewed the telecast. I want you to assume a role in this group and discuss the show. I think we'll count off in fives for this one."

After they count off, Ms. Tran directs each number to a certain area of the room. Because the room is carpeted, many choose to sit on the floor. There is a general commotion.

Ms. Tran rings a push bell and announces, "When I ring the bell again, I want you to begin to visit in your group. Ready," she dings the bell.

Another 10 minutes pass before Ms. Tran rings the bell and says, "Freeze." She then goes over to a group and knocks on a desk nearby. She is back in role, this time as a "newcomer."

"Hi everybody. Sorry I'm late. I just watched the TV show on the reef. What are you doing?"

A boy in the group tells her what they were just talking about, and he summarizes the gist of their discussion so far. It turns out they are a group of fishermen sitting on a wharf. Ms. Tran becomes a fisherman, too, and they commiserate about the hardships that may be placed on them by the government. A girl in the group brings up the long-term survival of the reef concerns.

This takes about 5 minutes. Then Ms. Tran steps out of role and compliments the groups on the diversity of roles they have chosen. She concludes the lesson by making an assignment, due at the end of the week. Students are to do a piece of writing, in a role, to show different perspectives on the reef issue. It can be a letter, newspaper article, editorial, or even a diary entry or a song.

The students seem excited about the writing and ask questions about whether they will get to share what they write, for example, if it is a song. Ms. Tran seems genuinely delighted with the prospect.

TAKE ACTION 1

WHAT? WHY? HOW?

Think about Ms. Tran's lesson. What did she teach about both social studies and drama? Why did she do what she did? How did she cause student engagement?

INTRODUCTION

Theater and drama have a long history of relationships with human behavior and education. Aristotle thought theater gave audiences a catharsis to release emotions, medieval priests used theater to explain Christianity to the masses, and primitive societies pantomimed and danced in rituals to cast out demons. *Creative drama,* however, had its beginnings in the early 20th century. In the 1920s progressive education emphasized having students *do,* rather than read about or memorize. Progressive educators, such as John Dewey, looked to the arts as learning tools; drama proved a natural. During this period Winifred Ward, who came to be called the "mother of creative drama," started a program in the Evanston Illinois Public Schools that used children's literature as the main stimulus for drama. By 1930, the field of creative drama was officially formed.

During the next decades, creative drama in the United States was significantly shaped by practitioners, scholars, and researchers in America and in the United Kingdom. Here is a brief look at ideas from influential people in the field.

Winifred Ward: Her goals were individual and social development. She used movement, pantomime, characterization activities, dialog, and story dramas that moved from simple to complex. She believed *performance* was a vital aspect of drama and that a teacher–leader should guide students.

Brian Way: His focus is on the drama process, not a performance. He used student personal experiences to lead them to self-discovery and encouraged teachers to "sneak" drama into the classroom, even for 5 minutes each day. His approach opposes teacher demonstration because he believes acting skills are unnecessary for drama participation. Life events are used as the drama stimulus, with few student performances and little focus on evaluation.

Dorothy Heathcote: Emphasizes using life experiences to reflect, analyze, and test out conclusions. Students are thrust into a sink or swim situation, with the teacher–leader as a significant participant. Heathcote sees four faces of dramatic activity: (1) making plays for audiences, (2) knowing the craft, history, and place of theater in our lives, (3) learning through making plays, and (4) using "as if it were" drama to motivate study.

Viola Spolin: Her approach emphasizes getting participants to *see* and *do*, not imagine or feel. The goals are to have students lose all inhibition and learn intuitively. Her books of theater games, originally used in actor training, have been tremendously popular and are used in a workshop format. Performance is a major objective.

Geraldine Siks: Her major focus is on students' creative and expressive skills. She placed drama in the categories of *art* and *language art*. Students learn to be audience members, players, and playmakers.

Among these approaches there is diversity in the goals, roles of the teacher, stimulus for drama, and the activities in which students are engaged. In this book, ideas from all the approaches have been culled for their appropriateness to the general classroom.

Successful drama integration starts small with a few minutes a day for drama. Eventually, drama can be used effectively in science, social studies, language arts, and math. Gradual, thoughtful implementation ensures that justice is done to both drama/theater (as an art) and the basic content and skills in core curricular areas. At points teachers may have the luxury of being able to do drama lessons for a full hour or longer; others prefer to do drama connected to units over several days, spending 15 to 20 minutes each day. In any case, it is important to design lessons that are more than just a series of isolated activities.

WHY SHOULD TEACHERS INTEGRATE DRAMA?

I am concerned . . . with the difference . . . between the real world . . . and the "as if" world where we can exist at will. Brecht calls this "visiting another room." . . . actions in the two rooms are to do with: 1. The freedom to experiment without the burden of future repercussions. 2. The absence of the "chance elements" of real life. If we needed a reasonable reason for including the arts in schools, surely it is here in these two rooms.
Dorothy Heathcote (in Robinson, 1990, p. 8)

Teachers who have incorporated drama into daily learning report increased enjoyment and substantial effects on skill and content achievement in science, social studies, math, and language arts. Post It Page 7–1 summarizes the results of drama integration in schools across the country.

POST IT PAGE 7–1

NEWS BULLETIN: DRAMA RESEARCH YOU CAN USE

The pattern in the reading proficiency data is clear. Drama-involved students outscored noninvolved students as of eighth grade. The difference favoring drama/theater students grows steadily so that by twelfth grade nearly 20% more are reading at high proficiency (Fiske, 1999, p. 14).

Fifth-grade remedial readers who were taught to use drama as a learning strategy consistently scored higher on the Metropolitan Reading Comprehension Test and outperformed a control group who did vocabulary lessons and discussed the stories (Dupont, 1992).

New Jersey. An Arts Alternatives program involving drama activities, including role playing, improvisation, and writing stories enabled elementary students to achieve significant gains in vocabulary and reading comprehension. Students also reported significantly improved attitudes relating to self-expression, trust, self-acceptance, and acceptance of others (Gourgey, Bousseau, & Delgado, 1985).

Sixteen studies of students in grades K–12 showed that drama positively affects the ability of students to take on the roles or perspectives of others, that is, increases empathy (Kardash & Wright, 1987).

Use of creative drama activities positively affected elementary student achievement in a variety of areas, such as reading, oral and written communication, and interpersonal and drama skills (Kardash and Wright, 1987).

Positive relationships were found between oral language growth (speaking) and use of creative drama in fourth, fifth, and seventh graders (Stewig & McKee, 1980; Stewig & Young, 1978).

When drama was used as a rehearsal for writing, letter writing and narrative writing were significantly improved for second, third, fourth, and eighth graders (Moore & Caldwell, 1993; Wagner, 1988).

ESL (English as a second language) students who were involved in drama exhibited significantly greater verbal improvement than a control group not involved in drama (Vitz, 1983).

Economically disadvantaged African American and Hispanic students in the fourth to sixth grades who participated in a dramatics program showed improved reading achievement and more positive self-concepts (Gourgey et al., 1985).

Drama increased interaction among students with and without mental handicaps in a study comparing fifth graders who either were involved in drama or noncompetitive games (Miller, Rynders, & Schleien, 1993).

About 40% more of the "no-drama" students felt that making such a (racist) remark would be acceptable. Only about 12% of high-theater students thought the same. The advantage favoring high-theater students is statistically significant ($p < .05$) (Fiske, 1999, p. 15).

---

1. Drama deals with real-life problems

The best drama uses as much truth as possible.

Dorothy Heathcote

Drama gives insight by allowing students to rehearse roles in which they will make life decisions—son, friend, boss, parent. This rehearsal for life deals with universal questions based on the powerful themes that comprise great literature: *What happens when someone is greedy and causes many others to suffer? How do true friends respond when times are tough? How do humans respond when they are given success, rather than earning it? What is the nature of real happiness? How should evil be dealt with in our world?* During drama, children examine different perspectives and try them on for size. In a safe and accepting atmosphere, they are free to sort out beliefs and values. In this way, drama helps give shape to ideas and feelings students naturally experience and thus helps children make sense out of concerns.

Drama capitalizes on children's natural desire to pretend and take roles during play. Through drama, the number of roles students can assume is expanded, so perspectives are stretched as well. In science, students may do research and assume the role of experts in debates about real-life problems, like the growing resistance of certain bacteria to antibiotics, or can pantomime aspects of careers they have investigated during a career education unit. During these drama activities, the seeds are sown for students to grow into people who look at problems more flexibly—from alternative viewpoints and with respect for diverse thinking. They begin to realize there are many solutions for all problems.

2. Drama provokes creative problem solving and decision making

You can't depend on your judgment when your imagination is out of focus.

Mark Twain

Conflict is the basis for drama. Consider the difference between pantomiming a squirrel gathering nuts versus miming a squirrel gathering nuts with something sticky on its paws. The first mime might be fun, but the second demands that the actor think of problem solutions. It is not surprising that students involved in rich drama experiences increase their problem-solving skills. When drama is integrated, school is changed from a place where students are told what to think into active experiences in thinking. Karioth (1967) found drama boosted creative thinking in disadvantaged fourth graders, and kindergarten students involved in drama scored significantly higher than a control group on verbal and visual creativity tests (Schmidt, Goforth, & Drew, 1975). Why? During drama, students must imagine, make hypotheses, test out solutions, evaluate ideas, and redefine problems. *What are all the ways to show how Jack felt as he climbed the beanstalk each time? How can we show the meanings of words such as* love, hate, disconcerted, *or* contrite *with bodies, faces, and one spoken word or line? What if Cinderella didn't want to marry the prince and fell in love with the doorman instead?*

3. Drama develops verbal and nonverbal communication. When students become a character and talk about ways to solve a story problem, *in character*, verbal skills are engaged. For example, *What should the father and the boys do to get the mother to come home in Brown's* The Piggybook? is a question with no one answer. It can be discussed using a moral problem-solving process and then played out in a scene (see Moral Dilemmas under social studies strategies in Chapter 8). Students involved in drama activities develop fluency in language and nonverbal communication skills—use of the body, face, and voice to communicate. It is essential for students to learn to match words and actions as they move through life, as in the old adage, "I hear what you say but I believe what you do." Through drama, students learn how a look, a gesture, body posture, and how a person walks communicate hesitancy, excitement, or fear. We become skilled at what we practice thoughtfully. Drama is a pleasurable and powerful practice for self-expression through speaking and listening.

4. Drama can enhance psychological well-being

Improvisation is a way of achieving identity.

Alfred Nieman

Drama allows students to express feelings and emotions under the protection of being in a "what if" role. This safety permits them to experience the therapeutic effects of release of emotions and tension. In addition, personal development occurs as students learn to control their bodies and their words to express ideas and feelings. Self-confidence and positive self-image emerge from repeated successes in drama problem-solving situations.

Through drama, students learn that people feel a range of emotions that need not always be suppressed and should be expressed *appropriately*. It is liberating for a child to realize she is not the first person to dislike another and that negative feelings can be worked out in positive ways. Drama can develop tolerance and acceptance and combat felt needs to confront and destroy those who behave, think, or feel differently.

5. Drama develops empathy. Taking on a role involves using the senses of smell, taste, touch, vision, hearing, movement, and even humor to understand. During a Civil War study, students who became comfortable with "I statements" from different people's perspectives showed they were really involved: "I saw smoke puff out of cannons so thick it looked like the cannons were belching dragons." "I heard the nurse crying and I knew the man in the cot next to me had died of his gut wound." "I smelled burning grass as we torched the town." "I felt the stiffness in my good leg as I hobbled the final mile on the stick I'd been given to use as a crutch." "I was so happy I couldn't stop laughing when I saw my wife come out on the porch as I walked up the dirt road of our farm. I was finally home."

Empathy goes beyond sympathy. Empathy involves "becoming" another person—feeling what another feels, thinking what another thinks. This is a lived-through experience that gives perspective in a way that facts or logic cannot because emotional intelligence is activated.

6. Drama builds cooperation and other social skills. Drama allows children to find appropriate roles and develop social awareness because it has an ensemble focus—drama is a group art. As students work in groups to plan drama, they learn to give and take. I've heard teachers say, "I just can't use groups because my students can't work in groups!" Yet, no teacher would ever argue that his students can't read so they won't be taught to read. Students learn cooperation and active listening by being taught how to do group work—there is no other way. Cooperation cannot be taught through a lecture or tested with a paper-and-pencil assessment. To learn to live together, we must work together. In addition, awareness of social problems grows as students research topics such as violence, hunger, poverty, and homelessness in preparation for drama presentations. Finally, as audience members for theater performances, students gain social awareness when actors engage them in expanded thinking about the problem-centered issues of plays.

7. Drama increases concentration and comprehension. Because drama involves all the senses, stimulates emotions, and focuses on the use of creative problem solving, it should not be surprising it boosts attention. When children are actively engaged and concentrating on a task, it is more likely they will understand the material being read. This is borne out in studies that show children who dramatize stories have higher reading comprehension scores than those who only read the story (DuPont, 1992; Henderson & Shanker, 1978). Textbooks are given life when teachers involve students in dramatizing important concepts and main ideas in science and social studies. Students who dislike reading see a purpose for reading that changes attitudes about putting forth effort. If students know they will be pantomiming significant actions of the main character after reading a basal story, they have a point of concentration: They are reading so they will be able to *do*.

In sum, drama fills a basic need for activity or engagement. It activates many intelligences including verbal and body-kinesthetic. When used to introduce or preview a lesson, drama causes students to think at higher levels, tap into feelings, and want to learn more. A problem from an upcoming lesson can be explored through pantomime or verbal drama, causing interest to develop and prediction thinking to be activated.

8.   Drama causes reflection on moral issues and values. While educators should not *impose* religious points of view on their students, lessons are rarely *valueless*. Teachers can't teach without revealing what they value. Religious issues and religion can be topics of study—and should be. Understanding cultures, such as that of Afghanistan, would be incomplete without information about the religions of its people. Drama permits students to become conscious of their values and form additional values as they work through curricular and social problems presented as drama content. In this way, drama helps bring closure through self-discovery.

The conflict core of drama causes values and attitudes to emerge as students struggle to solve the problem. Values can be the end products of dissonance

and problem resolutions; beliefs arise from these experiences. Indeed, values should not be imposed by the teacher but be discussed as students confront issues about rightness, wrongness, goodness, and badness in literature, math, science, and social studies. This doesn't mean a teacher need be value neutral; on the contrary, all teachers should make clear their support of universal values such as honesty, truth, hard work, courage, integrity, and respect for others.

9.   Drama can be used to assess. Concepts and facts, such as the structure of a cell or the movement of electrons, are abstract and are better understood when made concrete. During drama, students grapple with how to make ideas and feelings concrete by selecting words and using the body to "externalize," or make visible, what they know. Drama can be used to preview or review a lesson, and during this time teachers can observe student performance for assessment purposes to determine what students already know and have learned.

Assessment needs to be authentic—to really give accurate information about what students know and can do. Drama makes learning observable. Material learned in any subject area can be demonstrated through pantomime and verbal activities. Once externalized, the teacher and students can both assess growth, using criteria based on curricular goals. For example, students can be asked to write to a friend, in the role

Drama Props

of Charles Drew, to explain scientific work. Such a verbal drama causes students to achieve depth of understanding through personal involvement and yields a document that shows the degree of knowledge acquired about scientific concepts.

10. Drama is entertaining. It can't be by chance that the word *play* is so linked to theater and drama. In theater "the play is the thing." In drama, play is a verb that results in fun. Over the door of a school in Richmond, Virginia, there is a stone carving that reads, "Thou Shalt Have Fun." While many educators feel uncomfortable justifying inclusion of anything in a curriculum just because it is fun, we can never forget that fun is *fun*damental to happiness. One goal of education has to be to help students be happy. Fun and entertainment can help us forget, enable us to cope by giving respite from problems, and provide enjoyment—a state of elation, upliftedness or joy that gives energy and hope. We should not simply dismiss the importance of fun in learning and drama is definitely fun. Students have fun taking roles, solving problems, doing interesting things, learning new skills, working with people, meeting challenges, moving around, and making discoveries. Compare these aspects of *fun* with what we want to happen each day at school. There isn't much difference between *good* education and fun.

11. Drama contributes to esthetic development

Reason can answer questions but imagination has to ask them.

Albert Einstein

Drama integrates all the arts (music, art, dance, and literature), so it draws on the beauty-making power of each. Drama is also the key component of theater, and one area of the *National Standards for the Arts* is understanding of the art of theater. Through drama, students learn about dramatic structure involving conflict and characters, deepen sensory awareness, and learn to express themselves through the artistic use of pantomime, dialog, and improvisation.

12. Drama is a learning avenue to other areas of the curriculum. Drama helps students understand why they need to know about the bones of the body or the circulatory system. They can learn who needs to know about these topics and under what circumstances as they take roles as nurses, medics, parents, and scientists. Students can explore characters and their relationships to one another and to problems as-

TAKE ACTION 2
WHY INTEGRATE DRAMA?

Pretend a principal or parent asked you for three good reasons to use drama as a learning tool. What would you say? Justify your reasons.

---

sociated with issues in health, science, and social studies. From language arts to science, drama can be used as a tool to help students see relevance in a sea of skills and facts. It is a learning tool grounded in exploration and discovery. It draws on innate abilities and desires to assume roles and pretend. We associate actors and acting with drama and theater, and it is the action of drama that makes it so captivating. Children want to *do*. We should welcome student action. We do *not* need a nation of passive citizens. But we don't want our children to grow up taking action without information and reflection. Drama gives students a chance to act, but with a safety net to catch them when their decisions are not wise. This safety net includes the conscientious planful teacher who is knowledgeable about drama strategies and willling to adapt them for specific student needs.

WHAT DO TEACHERS NEED TO KNOW TO USE DRAMA AS A TEACHING TOOL?

I believe that every child I meet understands deep, basic matters worthy of exploration but they may as yet have no language for them. One of the languages they may develop is through dramatic work.

Dorothy Heathcote (in Robinson, 1990, p. 8)

Successful arts integration with any discipline depends on teacher knowledge and skill base. In addition, teachers need a repertoire of strategies to teach students how to interact and respond. The knowledge base for drama includes *elements or components* of drama, *kinds* of drama, and the *skills used to make drama* (use of voice and body). Drama and theater study also includes learning about actors and acting, plays, playwriting, theater history, drama, and theater in our lives and in other cultures.

Here are titles for computer folders or file folders to organize a resource collection for drama integration:

◆ Drama elements, skills, and concepts used to create and think about drama and theater

◆ Biographical and style information about actors, playwrights, directors, critics

◆ Styles, forms, and genres of drama and theater, for example, one acts, musical theater

◆ Particular examples, for example, plays such as *Les Miserables* and reader's theater scripts

◆ Approaches, teaching strategies, and activity ideas

◆ Other: career information, history of theater and drama, science and math of theater (stage construction, makeup, etc.), writing plays, sociology of theater and drama, economics and theater and drama, and psychology of dance (e.g., drama therapy)

Creative Drama Defined

Putting on rehearsed plays a few times a year and the *daily* use of drama are very different in purpose and process. Plays are more product oriented than drama is, and memorized scripts are rarely used as a teaching tool. This chapter dwells on a kind of drama that is easy for classroom teachers to use. It is called *creative drama*. According to drama educator Ruth Heinig (1993), creative drama is the term most widely used in the United States to describe drama integration. Creative drama is more structured than the dramatic play in which children naturally engage. Other terms such as *improvisation, role playing, informal drama, drama in education (DIE), process drama,* and *educational drama* are used in Great Britain and other countries, some of which identify teaching frameworks with a particular emphasis. For example, DIE strategies focus on causing students to project themselves into a "moment in time"; they learn more about a topic after first exploring it through their drama (Heinig, 1993, p. 4).

The American Alliance for Theater and Education (AATE) defines creative drama as "an improvisational, nonexhibitional, process-centered form of drama in which participants are guided by a leader to imagine, enact and reflect upon human experiences." In contrast, *theater* is focused on performance—the emphasis is on a spectacle for the audience to see. Drama

and theater share basic structures but "the process of drama is in sharp opposition to the theater product . . . theater is concerned with communication between actors and audience; drama is concerned with the experience of the participants, irrespective of the audience" (Way in Rosenberg, 1987, p. 31). Way even argues that young children should not view formal theater because "such theater attendance can only undermine creativity."

So, creative drama is participant and process centered, with a teacher or leader guiding students though explorations of personal experiences, social issues, or pieces of literature. In creative drama, children improvise action and dialog and use drama elements to structure the process. They creatively use voice, body, and space to make others believe in a mood, idea, or message. They assume "pretend" roles to generate creative problem solutions. Unlike role playing for therapeutic reasons, creative drama's purposes are artistic, emotional, social, and academic.

Drama Components

Imagination is more important than knowledge.

Albert Einstein

People create drama using both their outsides and insides. What is shown during drama with the body, face, gestures, and words reflects thoughts and feelings taken in through the senses. To make drama, a person must concentrate, sense, perceive, imagine, and think; the physical body and speech communicate these inner processes.

Life involves a constant struggle to fulfill basic needs met and deal with conflict. Drama is a slice of this struggle in the form of (1) characters who encounter problems, (2) in a specific setting, and (3) who take action to resolve the problems. Actors become characters who seem real as they convince, convert, coax, sell, feud, and bargain for their own motives. This structure with specific components is the same for both drama and literature: There must be a conflict or problem that motivates characters to make decisions and face the consequences of their actions (plot); all this occurs in a particular time and place (setting). Post It Page 7–2 summarizes the skills and elements of drama.

Drama Process.   During creative drama the teacher's role is to guide students, through questioning and coaching, to define problems, improvise solutions, try out ideas, reflect, and evaluate. While creative drama is

DRAMA ELEMENTS AND SKILLS

Elements

Conflict: Sets the plot in motion and should create suspension and tension. There are five types:

1. Between a character and nature
2. Between a character and societal rules or institutions
3. Between a character and another character
4. Within a character (internal conflict with self)
5. Between a character and technology

Characters initiate and carry out the plot (action). They must be believable and care about what happens. The main character is the hero or protagonist, who must face life, make decisions, and accept consequences. *Created through* actions, words, and what others say or how they react. When characters talk with each other they use ***dialog. Pantomime*** is free, creative, and mindful movement to express specific ideas and feelings with the face and body. There is no talking during pantomime.

Plot is the sequence of events set in motion by a problem or conflict. The simplest plot structure is beginning, middle, and end.

Setting consists of a time and place or context for action.

Mood is created by the setting (time, lighting, music, description of the place), pace, characters' use of word and body, and so forth. This is the *feel* of the piece.

Dramatic Skills

Use of body: ability to coordinate and control body, use of appropriate energy, display of sensory awareness and expression, use of gestures and facial expressions, communication through pantomime, interpretation of nonverbal communication of others.

Verbal expression: speaking clearly and using appropriate variety in volume, rate, tone and pitch, pause, stress and emphasis, inflection, fluency, and ability to improvise dialog.

Focus: concentration and staying involved, making others believe in the realness of the character, following directions.

Imagination: flexible creative thinking, contribution of unique ideas and elaboration on ideas, spontaneity.

Evaluation: giving constructive feedback, using suggestions of others, self-evaluation and adaptation of own behavior.

Social skills: working cooperatively with groups, listening and responding to others.

Audience etiquette: attending, listening, and responding appropriately to others.

---

not focused on performing for an audience, teachers can justify group sharing, at times, within the class or for other audiences. Creative drama can be simple or complex; Spolin's theater games and simple pantomimes are accepted as valuable drama work, as is Ward's story drama and Heathcote's in-depth explorations for personal meaning and perspective.

Dramatic Structure. Drama and literature share many structural components. These are the elements that create drama.

Conflict is described by author Robert Peck as "two dogs and one bone." Conflict sets plot in motion and should create suspension and tension. There are four types of conflict: (1) between a character and nature—the weather in *Island of the Blue*

Dolphins, (2) between a character and societal rules or institutions—the farm rule that runt pigs are slaughtered in *Charlotte's Web,* (3) between a character and another character—the other girls against a poor Polish girl in *The Hundred Dresses,* and (4) internal conflict within a character—Ramona constantly struggles against her proclivity for misunderstanding situations. A fifth type of conflict may also occur, especially in science fiction, between a character and technology as in *The Wretched Stone,* a tale about problems created by a mesmerizing rock with a blue glow, like a TV screen.

Characters initiate and carry out the plot (action). The main character must be believable and care about what happens. This is the hero or protagonist who must face life, make decisions, and accept consequences. In drama, characters are created through (1) actions, (2) words, and (3) what others say or how they react. When characters talk with each other, they use *dialog.* *Pantomime* is free, creative, and mindful movement with NO talking. It is used to express ideas and feelings through actions using the face and body.

Plot is the sequence of events set in motion by a problem or conflict. The simplest plot structure has a beginning, middle, and end.

Setting consists of a time and place that provide a context for action.

Mood is created by the setting (time, lighting, music, description of the place), pace, and characters' use of word and body. This is the *feel* of the piece.

Dramatic Skills. Students need to learn certain skills to become adept at creating drama. Remember from Chapter 1 how important it is to present a structure for creative and artistic work that includes (1) freedom with limits and (2) empowering students by teaching them the tools and elements of each art form. When students are taught these skills, they are given the tools to make meaning through drama.

Use of body: ability to coordinate and control body, use of appropriate energy, display of sensory awareness and expression, use of gestures and facial expressions, communication through pantomime, interpretation of nonverbal communication of others

Verbal expression: speaking clearly and using appropriate variety in volume, rate, tone and pitch, pause, stress and emphasis, inflection, fluency, and ability to improvise dialog

Focus: concentration and staying involved, making others believe in the realness of the character, following directions

Imagination: flexible creative thinking, contribution of unique ideas and elaboration on ideas, spontaneity

Evaluation: giving constructive feedback, using suggestions of others, self-reflection/evaluation and adaptation of own behavior

Social skills: working cooperatively with groups, listening and responding to others

Audience etiquette: attending, listening, and responding appropriately to others

The *National Standards for Theater:* American Goals

While drama and theater are not the same concepts, theater draws on dramatics. The *National Standards* include drama concepts and skills under the category of *theater.* Teachers can use these *Standards* as guidelines in planning lessons that have a drama prong.

Recall that the *National Standards for the Arts* are voluntary content and achievement goals being used across the country by schools to frame state and local standards. They served as references in the construction of the arts section of the National Assessment for Educational Progress (NAEP) and grew out of the *Goals 2000* legislation.

Standards, goals, objectives, and outcomes in curriculum frameworks help teachers know *what* to teach, but do not explain *how* to teach. When a teacher signs a contract in a school district, he is agreeing to teach to standards and goals adopted by the board of education. The teacher is hired with the expectation that he is competent to use current instruction methodology for assessment, planning and teaching, materials selection and use, and ways to discipline and manage a class. All teachers are expected to structure teaching so that students will achieve what the school district has set as performance goals. Teachers need to have in hand these goals or standards as they write lesson plans. Most districts expect teachers to specify connections between lesson activities and standards (see examples in lesson plans throughout this book). In addition, it is just good teaching to make lesson goals and objectives clear to students at the lesson outset; it is wise to communicate goals/standards to parents, too.

Post It Page 7–3 lists eight standards, related to drama, that students are expected to meet. All the

POST IT PAGE 7–3

NATIONAL STANDARDS FOR THEATER (K–8)

Overall focus: Learn about life, pretend and assume roles, social development, interact with peers, bring stories to life, direct one another, improvisation, writing, acting, designing, comparing forms, analyzing, evaluating, understanding the world (history, cultures).

1. **Script writing by planning and recording improvisations based on personal experience and heritage, imagination, literature and history (K–4), and by creation of improvisations and scripted scenes based on personal experience and heritage, imagination, literature, and history (5–8).** Example activities: Create classroom dramatizations. Improvise dialogues to tell a story.

2. **Acting by assuming roles and interacting in improvisations (K–4) and by developing basic acting skills to portray characters who interact in improvised and scripted scenes (5–8).** Example activities: Clearly describe characters. Use concentration and body and vocal elements to express characters. Dramatize personal stories.

3. **Designing by visualizing and arranging environments for classroom dramatizations (K–4) and by developing environments for improvised and scripted scenes (5–8).** Example activities: Use art media and techniques to make settings. Organize materials for dramatic play.

4. **Directing by planning classroom dramatizations (K–4) and by organizing rehearsals for improvised and scripted scenes (5–8).** Example activities: Plan a class play. Use drama elements and skills. Play the roles of director, writer, designer, and actor.

5. **Researching by finding information to support classroom dramatizations (K–4) and by using cultural and historical information to support improvised and scripted scenes (5–8).** Example activities: Find literature to adapt for classroom drama (books, poems, songs, any material usable for plays). Research time periods and cultures for dramatic material.

6. **Comparing and connecting art forms by describing theater, dramatic media (such as film, television, and electronic media), and other art forms (K–4). Comparing and incorporating art forms by analyzing methods of presentation and audience response for theater, dramatic media (such as film, television, and electronic media), and other art forms (5–8).** Example activities: Compare how the different arts communicate ideas. Describe visual, aural, oral, and kinetic elements of theater.

7. **Analyzing and explaining personal preferences and constructing meanings from classroom dramatizations and from theater, film, television, and electronic media productions (K–4). Analyzing, evaluating, and constructing meanings from improvised and scripted scenes and from theater, film, television, and electronic media productions (5–8).** Example activities: Evaluate performances using specific criteria. Explain characters' wants and needs.

8. **Understanding context by recognizing the role of theater, film, television, and electronic media in daily life (K–4). Understanding context by analyzing the role of theater, film, television, and electronic media in the community and other cultures (5–8).** Example activities: Web ideas for why theater is created. Attend performances and discuss what is learned about culture, history, and life from theater.

Source: Content Standards (material printed in bold type) excerpted from the *National Standards for Arts Education*, published by Music Educators National Conference (MENC). Copyright © 1994 by MENC. Reprinted with permission. The complete *National Standards* and related materials are available from MENC: The National Association for Music Education, 1806 Robert Fulton Drive, Reston, VA 20191 (800-336-3768).

---

drama strategies and activities in this book relate to one or more of these standards. For examples of state-level arts standards, contact the Ohio Department of Education (Columbus, OH). Kentucky also has a state standards for the arts that have been widely implemented. Wisconsin's Model Academic Standards for the Arts can be ordered online: (http://www.dpl.state.wi.us/dpl/dltcl/els/pubsales/arts.html).

TAKE ACTION 3
CONNECT TO THE STANDARDS

Think about Ms. Tran's lesson using drama to teach science. Select the *standards* you think were the goals of her lesson and give your reasons.

HOW CAN TEACHERS USE DRAMA AS A TEACHING TOOL?

Good teaching is one-fourth preparation and three-fourths theatre.

Gail Godwin, 1937 (*The Old Woman*)

General Integration Principles

Here are 10 principles for drama based on the INTE-GRATES framework introduced in Chapter 2. The ideas are grounded in the concept of teaching *with*, *about*, *in*, and *through* drama.

Principle 1: IMMERSION in Drama

In a classroom where the teacher creates a climate for risk taking and values creative thinking, students are more comfortable doing drama. The esthetic environment discussed in Chapter 2 lays a foundation for dramatic work to emerge. In addition, students who have a teacher who is always ready to think of "what if" and encourages "let's pretend" have a drama advantage. You may wish to review Post It Page 2–5 at this time.

Principle 2: NITTY-GRITTY Drama Concepts

Austrian writer Gustav Meyrink's (1994) fable *The Curse of the Toad* is about a millipede who loved to dance. It challenges us to consider the effect of bringing to a conscious level what we do unconsciously. An old toad, who hates the millipede, tests this effect by asking the millipede,

> Tell me then, oh most honorable one, when you walk, how do you know which foot to lift first: which is the second, and the third, which comes next as fourth, fifth, sixth—whether the next is the tenth or the hun-

dredth; what meanwhile the second is doing, and the seventh: is it standing, or moving; when you get to the 917th, whether you should lift the 700th, put down the 39th, bend the 1000th or stretch the fourth? . . . But the millipede was glued to the ground, paralyzed, unable to move one single joint. He had forgotten which leg to lift first, and the more he thought about it the less he could work it out (p. 54).

Children readily engage in "let's pretend." It may concern teachers that this joy will be disturbed by instructing them in specific elements and tools of drama. Might we not paralyze them as the toad did the millipede by imposing cognition on intuition? Indeed, most of us are awkward when learning a new skill and may initially resist the learning needed to become adept. Think of the baby's clumsy attempt to learn to walk. Parents intuitively support toddlers when they show the desire to stand and step. We demonstrate, encourage, coach, and label: "That's one step. Now step again. Look Joey took three steps by himself!"

Children enter school with a love for role playing and pretend. We can build on these innate dispositions by teaching them how to use drama to learn academic material. This involves both explicit or direct instruction (in what drama is and what we can use to make drama) and providing time for discovery learning. Explicit instruction includes demonstration, coaching, giving feedback, and teaching the vocabulary of theater and drama. Of special importance is teaching ways to identify conflict and tension (the core of drama) in literature, songs, paintings, and in life. For example, ask students to think about what decisions must be made to solve a problem. This gets at the heart of the drama. This is the nitty-gritty that gives children tools to use drama as a way to making meaning.

Special note: Most children understand the difference between pretend and reality, but it is useful to periodically tell or ask students about the difference. Students need to see drama as "pretend" time that allows practice of skills needed in real life. See Post It Page 7–2.

Principle 3: TEACHING HABITS for Integrating Drama

Creative Problem Solving. Drama relies heavily on creative problem solving, so it is important for teachers to understand the process and influences on this higher-order type of thinking. Use these resources in

Chapter 1 to help adapt creativity principles to drama: Post It Page 1–6, Take Action 6, and Post It Page 1–8.

Teacher Characteristics

[S]ome of the best work with children is done by experienced teachers who really understand what they are doing and yet, strangely enough, have very little knowledge of drama.
McCaslin, 1990, p. 443

Drama educator Nellie McCaslin (1990) believes the attributes of any good teacher are the characteristics most needed to integrate drama: sense of humor, high standards, good discipline, sympathetic leadership, imagination, respect for the ideas of others, sensitivity to individuals, ability to guide rather than direct, and a focus on sharing, rather than showing. In the end, the imaginative teacher creates his or her own methods by adapting ideas such as the strategy seeds in the next chapter. Teachers with a background in music and dance have the advantage of being able to combine these art forms with drama more readily. (pp. 441–442).

Teacher Participation in Drama. It is helpful for teachers to model enthusiasm and commitment by demonstrating drama elements such a verbal expression and use of the face and body throughout instruction. Teachers may assume a role, as well, and have students respond. For example, the teacher may become a bystander in the scene and ask for clarification about what's happening. She may take the roles of next-door neighbor or a town official. Heinig (1993) explains that teachers who assume roles extend belief, stimulate thinking, provoke discussion, direct problem solving, and break down barriers between themselves and students (pp. 265–280). When teachers engage students while "in role," the goal is to be low key and not overplay or stereotype a role. Teachers can become helpless characters: "I don't know and need help," authority figures [challenger], messengers, one of the crowd, devil's advocates [boss, expert, chief], or antagonists (p. 277). Simple props may be used but are not necessary.

Role taking also allows the teacher to control drama. Time management and direction of the action can be guided by the character the teacher assumes. The teacher can go into more depth by questioning students. Relationships are forged as the teacher is seen as a fellow risk taker, a "player" who is a part of the drama. A sense of mystery or urgency, belief, and

---

TAKE ACTION 4
TEACHER IN ROLE

Try your hand at planning a drama in which you will take a role. Practice on a fable or Mother Goose piece. Use these five steps. An example is given for each.

1. Analyze the story for problems and themes. What is this really about? What is the conflict? Who has the problem? (Jack in the Beanstalk *is about how goods are not equally distributed and how people are never satisfied with what they have.*)
2. List groups or individuals that may be affected by the problem. (*The giant's family who now has no income; Jack's mother, wife, and friends, who see a changed Jack; neighbors who don't like having a thief around.*)
3. Under what circumstances might these individuals come together (e.g., some kind of meeting)? (*Counseling session for Jack's materialistic addictions.*)
4. Choose a role and plan a short introduction speech about who you are and why you are there (*counselor*).
5. Plan the roles that the children can become. (*Children choose to be any of the characters affected by Jack's greed.*)

---

commitment can be engendered by the teacher's attitude and involvement. (Note: Young children, if they have difficulty differentiating between fantasy and reality, may be confused when teachers take a role. Teachers need to tell students when they are in role, so that children will not become confused. Some teachers put on a hat or nametag as a prop to signal they are in character.)

Signals to Manage Drama. Signals are valuable teaching habits to provide students with cues to organize their work. For example, say "places," "curtain," "stop–go," "home" to start and stop drama. Lights, sounds, music, a drum, bell, or tambourine are effective signals, too. EPR (every pupil response) signals after questions or directions teach students to control their own actions, as well as learn to direct others. Post It Page 7–4 has a list of attention-getting signals used by teachers for drama and other activities.

ATTENTION GETTERS AND SIGNALS

This list was generated by classroom teachers in Ohio.

1. Whisper directions.
2. Flick lights.
3. Play a favorite tape or CD.
4. Use tambourine, chimes, piano chord, or any pleasant sound.
5. Have children echo what you say. *Examples:* "Jambo Jambo" ("Hello Hello" in Swahili) or use a tongue twister (aluminum linoleum).
6. Ask children to mimic a rhythm pattern, sign, or movement.
7. Start a chain reaction: Say to one student "Would you tell the person next to you to. . . ."
8. Say, "I'm looking for someone who is . . . (fill in a behavior like 'in a curved shape')."
9. Write a message in large letters on the chalkboard.
10. Write directions on large cards. *Example:* "Look at me and smile."
11. Say, "Let's listen . . . to hear grass grow, clock tick, or snow fall."
12. Say, "I'd like to see . . . the color of everyone's eyes or everyone smile."
13. Have a secret code word. *Examples:* foreign language, special vocabulary, or interesting phrases such as "chicka boom chicka rucka."
14. Tell students to close their eyes.
15. Say, "Think what is stopping you from listening right now."
16. Count aloud backward from 10 (invite students to join in).
17. Agree on a class signal to get everyone's attention if . . . the ceiling was about to fall in, there was a fire in the wastebasket, and so forth.
18. Tell a joke or riddle. Knock knocks work.
19. Call students' names who are ready to listen.
20. Have a nonverbal signal. *Examples:* touch pocket or ear, hold up two fingers, thumb up.
21. Give a direction with universal appeal. *Example:* "Sit down if you ever wanted a two-hour recess," or "Freeze if you like money," or "Raise your hand if you'd like some ice cream."
22. Give points to students who are listening. Use a clipboard, board, or overhead.
23. Write on the board the names of the first five students who are ready.
24. Sit in a particular place or use a particular stance to signal.
25. Be creative! Do something different. Attire can attract attention, for example, "Did you notice that _____ is wearing _____?"
26. Say, "If you can hear my voice, _____ (behavior)"
27. Call and response sequences: T = Good Morning; S = Rice Krispies; T = Guaca Guaca, S = Agua Agua. (T = teacher and S = student.)
28. Use a group reinforcer. *Example:* Use cloze blanks on the chalkboard and say, "I need to see people ready to earn another letter in '_____' (letters spell out a goal like 'extra recess')."
29. Make up a class chant: "We're ready, we're ready as ready can be. In just five seconds, chicka rucka chicka bees."
30. Use actual sign language for directions such as sit down and line up. See *Joy of Signing* (Riekehof, 1987).
31. Ask students to close their eyes and imagine, for example, the sun setting or the ripples moving out from a stone in a pond.

Planning for Discipline and Management

Inexperienced leaders are often not sure they should plan, direct, or even incorporate discipline attitudes into creative drama lessons for fear of stifling their own and the children's imagination. But groups need organization, people need limits, and creativity needs discipline structure.

Heinig, 1993, pp. 25–26

Getting attention, giving directions, dealing with disruptions, handling rule breakers, rearranging desks, and keeping order require planning ahead. Here are basic pointers. (Also see Discipline, Prevention, and Intervention Strategies in the appendix and Discipline and Management in Chapter 9, especially the discussion on personal space, time limits, and touching restrictions.)

Set ground rules and expectations. We need to know the rules and limits at home, at work, and even in the stores where we shop. When a rule is broken, it is effective to acknowledge the student's feelings (to help the child save face) and then restate the rule. Next, implement a logical consequence, not an unrelated punishment. Consequences should be made clear at the lesson start, along with a review of basic ground rules. Chapter 9 has rule examples.

Control space, time, group size, and speed. For example, "Stay at your desk or in your personal spot, walk in place, I'll count to five, do this in slow motion." Larger groups and larger spaces require more planning and controls. Start with smaller amounts of time and space. Have students work in pairs, before trying larger groups. Asking students to pantomime in slow motion teaches self-control and calms students.

Give clear directions. Expectations should be stated in straightforward language without sugar coating or paternalism. Is is helpful to use cue words: *first, second, before, finally,* and so forth. After stating directions, ask "What questions do you have?" and then signal to begin work.

Remove distractions. Before beginning, desk tops should be cleared as should any area where the drama will happen. Props should be introduced, as needed, and not put out until that time. Props should be kept to a minimum or not used at all.

Make transitions by calling groups or rows or by creative categories such as eye color, patterns of clothes, or birthdays. It is helpful to cue students that a transition is coming up by announcing the time left: "You have one minute to finish planning."

Complaints and negative behaviors. Not everyone can be made happy by all circumstances. Children who whine usually stop if ignored. Each small infraction isn't worth the teacher's attention, and some behaviors are actually done to get attention. Watch for signs of need for attention, and give it frequently to those students when they show *positive* behaviors. *Note:* Drama is fun and interesting—don't cajole into participating. Start with those who want to participate and the rest will usually follow.

Mistakes happen. It is best to acknowledge failures and be honest about associated feelings. This helps model for children how to handle problems, too. It is appropriate to start over with a revised procedure. Students need to see drama as a creative experiment. It is not predictable—that's what makes it fun.

Proximity and eye contact. Veteran teachers know that "giving the eye" and being physically close are often enough to get students back on task. Circulate as students work and look them directly in the eye.

Follow through with consequences. Don't threaten, don't hesitate. Stop the activity to get the attention of the group. Don't keep going if only part of the class is involved. Note: consequences should have been discussed at the lesson outset or in previous lessons. They need to be reviewed periodically, however, and some teachers post them, along with the rules.

Private conferences. Repeat offenders and difficult children should be dealt with privately as soon after the lesson as possible. Public humiliation is unethical. If offenders must be removed, return them to the activity ASAP. Often a 2-minute time out is as effective as removing the child for a whole lesson. Of course, admission back into the group should be contingent upon agreeing to follow the rules.

Use drama to teach rules. Ask students to create improvised scenes (see the seed ideas in Chapter 8) that show cooperation, active listening, compromise, respect for alternative opinions, and other desirable behaviors. Direct them to make sure their scenes have a beginning, middle, and end. Scenes can be set up by first identifying characters, a setting, and a problem situation. Challenge them to think about "what if . . ." situations: What if students read each other's private journals or what if there was a group project and some people didn't do their share of the work? Encourage students to generate lists of ways to settle arguments and encourage everyone to participate and cooperate. Make this into a verbal activity in which students create a pledge based on the Golden Rule: Use a frame to help structure thinking: "Because I like to ____, I will ____. Because I don't like ____, I will ____. Because I want ____, I will ____." Here is a sixth-grade example: *We, the sixth grade class of Overlook Elementary, want to have our opinions heard, so we promise to listen to the opinions of others. We like to be treated with respect, so we will not disrespect each other in this class. We do not like to be touched in unfriendly ways, so we will not touch anyone with fighting on our minds. We want to work in groups with our friends, so we will cooperate and get work done while in groups. We hereby so promise all the above on this day in September, 2002.*

Involve All Students. A way to reach this goal is to use the *unison* strategy. Unison means simultaneous "all-at-once" participation. Time is used effectively and no one is waiting for a turn (waiting creates boredom and mischief making). When all the class participates at the same time, students feel the comfort created by safety in numbers. Maximum participation and involvement is achieved through double casting (have two or more children perform the same role). For example, have three wolves in "The Three Little Pigs."

Focus on *involvement* and *concentration* directly and by asking what helps students to concentrate and what distracts them. Practice *showing* involvement with words and body and verbally reinforce students who show they are involved through their behaviors. Say "Fred looks like he is really concentrating. He is remembering to keep his body bent like an old man." *Note:* Children can reach the state of creative flow in which they are totally involved (see discussion in Chapter 1). Signs of flow include feeling time goes quickly, spontaneously adding details to drama, and asking to repeat activities. For example, a class of third graders so enjoyed a narrative pantomime of *The Wretched Stone* they asked to do it again instead of having recess. When students ham it up or show off, they are not genuinely involved. Let them know this in a kind way before it happens. There are several activities in the energizers and warm-ups strategies section of Chapters 8 and 10 to help with concentration and focus.

Role of the Audience. When children are proud of their work, they want to share with the whole class. It is a learning opportunity for all when students see how groups treat the same drama problem differently. A good strategy is to divide the class in half. One half then performs while the other half views, interprets, and responds. Then reverse roles. With small groups, take turns presenting. For example, two groups can present a pantomime at the same time while the rest of the class is the audience.

Before students perform, the audience needs to be clear about its role. Discuss with students how it is polite to listen attentively, not talk during the performance, be respectful and responsive, and applaud at the end. Additional audience engagement happens when the teachers let the audience know they'll be expected to give feedback to the actors. Display questions they can choose from to respond at the end. For example, What worked? What made the characters believable? (Be sure to keep feedback focused on the positive.)

To firm up the role of the audience, it is a good idea to take a few minutes and have everyone role play the audience. For example, narrate as students pantomime: "You take your seats. You show that you are excited to see the performance. The curtain opens and you examine the set to see what you can. The scene is a sad one. Then a character does something that is meant to be funny. A character does something wonderful and you applaud. The scene ends and you applaud. The scene has been particularly good, so you stand and applaud. Now you take your seat and think about several things you'd like to tell the actors about their fine performance."

Volunteers and Small Groups. When drama is first introduced, it is best to invite volunteers and not force students to participate. Forced participation can increase reluctance and be contagious. We usually want to know what we are volunteering for, so explain the general idea. For example, "I need three people who know how to walk in place."

There is not as much teacher control when students work in pairs and small groups, but group work is a crucial part of dramatic development. Learning to cooperate is also an essential workplace and family skill. However, students can only learn to work in groups by working in groups. Create pairs, trios, and quads by counting off. At times students can be given a choice based on interests or ability to work together. Instead of "Find a partner," say "Find a partner that is your same height or find two people you can cooperate with." Students need to learn to distinguish between friends and those they can best work with. Avoid cliques by rotating groups. Learning circles can also be the basis for group work. Another option is to give each child a color or symbol (circle, heart, square, star) and group by having the same symbols work together. Group decision making is developed by asking students for their ideas and suggestions. Once they understand the variety of choices in drama, ask them to set time and space limits. Suggest the amount of rehearsal needed and discuss whether to present to an audience or not.

Discussions and Questioning Strategies. In nearly all the chapters, there are post it pages on questioning, with example questions and general guidelines for discussions. These ideas are relevant to discussions before and after drama in a lesson. Discussions may take place to clarify key concepts or special language or words or to stretch thinking. While yes–no, "closed" or "skinny" questions have a place, it is generally preferable to ask open, or fat, questions that require more thought and more than a one-word answer. Questions that get at universal themes are most likely to engage students in significant ways. For example, "What causes people to resent those who are different like Frederick?" "Why do characters disobey their parents as in Peter Rabbit or Little Red Riding Hood?" Frames can be used to extend thinking as well. For example, ask students to complete these sentence stems related to the subject matter under study: "I wonder . . ." or "What if. . . ."

Whole Group Before Individual and Small Group. To make sure students understand what is to be done in a small group or individually, it is important to practice an example or two with the whole group. This goes for any teaching, not just drama.

Examples Instead of Models. Just as in art or dance, students need to understand that there are many ways to express feelings and ideas through drama. For example, "Think of all the ways to use pantomime to show a feeling like greed or shyness. What are all the body parts that could be used and in what ways (use the BEST dance elements, Post It 9–2, to help stretch and twist thinking)? What are all the facial expressions that could be used? How could these feelings be shown in pairs or trios?" Teachers can form a habit of asking for examples, rather than giving them, and help students do their own thinking.

Descriptive Feedback. It is especially important to note unique and different ideas that students devise. Do so by infusing "I statements" and other teaching habits (see Teacher Habits in Chapters 2 and 5) and refrain from phony praise. Students can be asked to isolate part of a drama, such as just one movement in a pantomime, and give peer feedback, too. For example, ask a student to repeat just the part where she was grasping the beanstalk before beginning to climb it.

Ask other students what they see. This habit of *doing* (showing with hands, face, posture) and then asking for student observations uses a discovery or inductive method that promotes reflective thinking.

Coaching: The Power of Suggestion. Coaching can be used to remind about directions and goals, talk students through an activity, maintain control, help the audience understand what a group is doing, and fill in awkward silences. Coaching does *not* mean giving lots of directions. It involves offering suggestions and questions as scaffolds to drama. It is a way to stretch or challenge students to use their bodies and voices in new ways. (See BEST in Post It Page 9–2 for movement possibilities.) Coaching also is a supportive measure to boost success and satisfaction. For example, ask students questions during the drama such as: "What could you do to show the character's age or how the character feels? When coaching, ask "What if . . ." questions to stretch and direct. For example, "What if the weather changed?" "What if someone got sick?" "What if things got out of control and you couldn't stop the process?" "What if the world stopped rotating? What if dinosaurs still lived?"

To help students prepare scenes, ask:

◈ What does your character want? How can you show this?

◈ Tell me more about . . . (explore the emotion or thinking of the character).

◈ What does the place have to do with how the character feels or acts?

◈ What else might you try?

◈ How could this problem be solved?

◈ What do you want the audience to see and feel?

◈ How could props, lighting, or music be used?

It is worth the extra time to cue carefully and coach as students work. The effects are clear in their development of skill and confidence.

Teach How to Organize and Structure. Once students have explored the elements of drama, they are ready to use a three-part, beginning–middle–end (BME) format. This begins with teaching students to construct scenes that have these same three parts that stories have. Another structure for planning is: *Who? Where? What problems, conflicts, or obstacles? What actions or feelings?* A planning sheet with BME or the questions just listed can focus student work.

TAKE ACTION 5

TEACHING HABITS

Choose three of the teaching habits in the previous section you want to remember to use in planning drama. Put them on a cue card for yourself, and it is a good idea to write them in your lesson plan.

Lesson Introductions. The purpose of the lesson introduction is to motivate and ready students for learning. Here are common introduction strategies:

- Remove visual or auditory distractions and get attention. See Post It Page 7–4.

- Establish mood and set a climate for creative exploration (see Chapter 1 for ideas for stimulating a creative attitude).

- Build on prior knowledge—what they have studied and experienced.

- Direct students to concentrate and focus, to "make us believe," and not be a ham.

- Stimulate interest. Interest can account for 30 times the variance in understanding. Web, ask questions, and do warm-ups to build interest.

- Make sure students know the content. If they are to do a drama about pollution, they need background from a variety of experiences; they need knowledge to inform the drama.

- Make sure students understand that drama is an enjoyable art form used for serious learning purposes. At first they may not see why social studies time is used for drama; they may not connect the arts with content. Through discussions and reaching the point in drama where empathy and insight are experienced, students will start to value this art form. For example, students who were unfamiliar with drama acted silly when first pantomiming the *Trail of Tears March of the Cherokees.* In time, with drama coaching and more information about the dire circumstances of the migration, students were able to feel how hopeless, tired, and discouraged the Indians were after walking day after day through bad weather, starving and sick. See the generic lesson plan in Post It Page 2–2 for more ideas.

Principle 4: ENERGIZERS and Warm-ups

Energizers and warm-ups relax students so that they are more likely to use the creative thinking essential to drama. These short activities create a climate for risk taking, give focus, facilitate concentration, imagination, cooperation, and self-control. Here are sample warm-ups for the body: (1) make circle or jerky movements that slowly travel head to toe, (2) walk across the room in different ways, at different levels, or in a variety of "as if . . ." situations, and (3) direct students to pretend they are balloons blowing up and then collapsing (add sound effects, if you like). See the energizers and warms-ups in Chapter 8 and in all strategy seed chapters.

Principle 5: GREAT CHILDREN'S LITERATURE

Drama and literature share a focus on tension or conflict to propel the story forward so there is a natural compatibility. Every genre of children's literature offers potential material for drama. Biography can be particularly useful because the characters are real people in conflict-filled situations—dilemmas of life and death. In the appendix there is a bibliography of books about drama and theater, as well as children's literature, recommended for pantomime and verbal activities. An annotated sampling appears in Post It Page 7–5.

Principle 6: ROUTINES and Rituals

Routines and rituals establish habits of mind and body. Here are ways to get students in the habit of thinking using drama:

- Use energizers and warm-ups to start the day and/or lessons.

- Use humor strategies to relax students so that they feel comfortable taking risks to be creative.

- Make special times to discuss drama and theater in student lives. Ask, *What have you noticed?* (roles people play, actors on TV and why were they effective?).

- Announce special films or plays.

- Share your own theater experiences.

- Do morning charades to review yesterday's learning.

- Sing action songs and do poems to start the day (See Poetry Alive in Post It 4–4).

- Use signals for drama time: lights, desk arrangement routine.

Children's Literature for Drama

How to Books

Caruso, S., & Kosoff, S. (1998). *The young actor's book of improvisation: Dramatic situations from Shakespeare to Spielberg, Vol. 1.* Heinemann.

Friedman, L. (2001). *Break a leg!: The kid's guide to acting and stagecraft.* Workman.

Kohl, M. (1999). *Making make-believe: Fun props, costumes and creative play ideas.* Gryphon House.

Stevens, C. (1999). *Magnificent monologues for kids.* Sandcastle.

Literature for Pantomime

Adoff, A. (1981). *Outside/inside poems.* Lothrop, Lee & Shepard. (poems about feelings)

Berger, B. (1984). *Grandfather Twilight.* Philomel. (old man raises the moon in the sky)

Bunting, E. (1992). *The wall.* Clarion. (a boy and father visit the Vietnam War Memorial)

Carle, E. (1969). *The very hungry caterpillar.* Philomel/Putnam. (caterpillar becomes a butterfly; challenge to use a variety of actions to eat the foods; good for flannel board or puppet)

Carroll, L. (1989). *Jabberwocky.* Abrams. (good for imagining ways to move, e.g., gyre)

Chaconas, D. (1970). *The way the tiger walked.* Simon & Schuster. (animals imitate tiger's walk)

Charlip, R. (1980). *Fortunately.* Four Winds. (use for narrative pantomime)

Cole, J. (1987). *The magic school bus inside the earth.* Scholastic. (field trips in a microscopic bus. See other books in *The magic school bus* series)

de Paola, T. (1975). *Strega Nona.* Prentice Hall. (Strega Nona has a magic pasta pot that Big Anthony misuses; a town is flooded with pasta; good crowd scenes)

Emberley, B. (1967). *Drummer Hoff.* Prentice Hall. (cumulative story of a cannon being fired off; good for mechanical movements)

Gerstein, M. (1984). *Roll over!* Crown. (10 animals in bed roll out one at a time)

Giff, P. R. (1980). *Today was a terrible day.* Penguin. (boy has many problems at school)

Johnson, C. (1955). *Harold and the purple crayon.* Harper & Row. (boy has drawing adventures)

Kahl, V. (1955). *The duchess bakes a cake.* Scribner's. (many characters to mime)

Keats, E. J. (1962). *The snowy day.* Viking. (boy explores things to do on a snowy day)

Kuskin, K. (1982). *The philharmonic gets dressed.* Harper & Row. (members of an orchestra are shown getting ready; follow with a symphonic piece and let students conduct)

Maruki, T. (1980). *Hiroshima no pika.* Lothrop, Lee & Shepard. (a survivor's view of the bombing)

McCully, Emily (1992). *Mirette on the high wire.* Putnam. (girl learns to walk the highwire)

McDermott, G. (1975). *The stonecutter.* Viking Penguin. (Japanese folktale; no dialog)

Mendoza, G. (1989). The Hairy Toe. In G. Mendoza (Ed.), *Hairticklers.* Berkeley, CA: Ten Speed. (weird tale with a line to do chorally at the end)

Parish, P. (1963). *Amelia Bedelia.* Harper & Row. (a maid takes instructions literally; many sequels about misunderstanding idiomatic expressions)

Paulsen, G. (1987). *Hatchet.* Bradbury. (boy survives 54 days in the wilderness)

Pinkwater, D. (1993). *The big orange splat.* Scholastic Trade. (opportunities for interviews, as well as pantomimes in this tale about creativity and inspiration)

Ringgold, F. (1991). *Tar beach.* Crown. (girl imagines she can fly)

Rossetti, C. (1991). Who has seen the wind? In K. Sky-Pock (Ed.). *Who has seen the wind?* Rizzoli. (this poem offers pantomime opportunities through the leaf movements of blowing, trembling, and hanging)

Rounds, G. (1990). *Lizard in the sun.* William Morrow. (life from the animal's perspective)

Rylant, C. (1988). *All I see.* Orchard. (boy makes friend with a painter; pretends to paint many things)

Seuss, Dr. (1940). *Horton hatches the egg.* Random House. (Horton is "faithful, 100 percent," and hatches an egg for lazy Maizie bird. Everyone can chorally chant Horton's motto)

Seuss, Dr. (1961). *The Sneetches.* Random House. (sneetches with stars on their bellies feel superior to those without. Students can mime the machine)

Small, D. (1985). *Imogene's antlers.* Crown. (Imogene grows antlers and family tries to cope)

Spurdens, D. (1984). *BMX.* Sterling. (bicycle motorcross; pantomime stunts, riding, maintenance)

Tolstoy, A. (1968). *The great big enormous turnip.* Franklin Watts. (cumulative tale about characters trying to pull up a huge vegetable)

Ungerer, T. (1986). *Crictor.* Harper & Row. (Madame Bodot's pet boa protects her from burglars)

Van Allsburg, C. (1988). *Two bad ants.* Houghton Mifflin. (two ants have adventures)

Wood, A. (1984). *The napping house.* Harcourt Brace. (cumulative tale)

Zemach, M. (1976). *It could always be worse.* Farrar, Straus & Giroux. (a rabbi tells a crowded family to bring animals into their house)

Literature for Verbal Activities

Aardema, V. (1975). *Why mosquitoes buzz in people's ears.* Dial. (African tale shows the domino effect from a misunderstanding)

Aardema, V. (1981). *Bringing the rain to Kapiti Plain.* Dial. (African Nandi tale, in the cumulative form of "The House That Jack Built," about how a herdsman helps end drought)

Bayer, J. (1984). *My name is Alice.* Dial. (animals introduce themselves and the things they sell; do as a sequence drama)

Bemelmens, L. (1939). *Madeline.* Viking Penguin. (Madeline lives in a Paris convent)

Bennett, J. (Ed.). (1987). *Noisy poems.* Oxford University Press. (many sounds)

Bodecker, N. M. (1974). *"Let's marry," said the cherry.* Atheneum. (short, rhymed couplets)

Brown, M. (1947). *Stone soup.* Scribner's. (three soldiers teach some villagers how to make soup out of stones; follow with actual cooking)

Cameron, P. (1961). *"I can't," said the ant.* Coward-McCann. (a broken teapot creates a problem for inhabitants of a kitchen)

Chess, V. (1979). *Alfred's alphabet walk.* Greenwillow. (Alfred takes an alliterative walk to see many things such as a "herd of hungry hogs hurrying home")

Day, A. (1985). *Good dog, Carl.* Green Tiger. (a humorous story of an intelligent dog who babysits a squirmy small child; almost wordless; several sequels)

de Paola, T. (1983). *Legend of the bluebonnet.* Putnam. (a Comanche Indian tribe is saved by the sacrifice of a young girl's warrior doll)

Gag, W. (1928). *Millions of cats.* Coward-McCann. (old man goes to find a pet for his wife and gets more than he bargained for; there is repeated chant)

Galdone, P. (1968). *The Bremen town musicians.* McGraw-Hill. (four animals encounter a band of robbers and gain wealth to keep them happy)

Haley, G. (1970). *A story—A story.* Atheneum. (African tale about Anansi, who must capture and give to the sky god a leopard, hornets, and a dancing fairy in order to own all the stories)

Heide, F. P. (1971). *The shrinking of Treehorn.* Holiday House. (boy notices he is shrinking, but can't get the attention of adults)

Isaacs, A. (1994). *Swamp angel.* Dutton. (modern tall tale about a very big girl)

Kellogg, S. (1971). *Can I keep him?* Dial. (boy has a conversation with his mother about a pet)

Marshall, J. (1972). *George and Martha.* Houghton Mifflin. (delightful stories work well for QU (cue-you) readings and interviews; several sequels)

McDermott, B. (1976). *The Golem: A Jewish legend.* Lippincott. (a rabbi in Prague creates a clay figure to stop an uprising; good for debates and interviews)

McGovern, A. (1967). *Too much noise.* Houghton Mifflin. (an old man tries to find the solution to too much noise in his house; use for expert panels)

Munsch, R. (1980). *The paper bag princess.* Annick. (a princess rescues a prince but decides not to marry him; use for interviews)

Rathmann, P. (1995). *Officer Buckle and Gloria.* Putnam. (dog does a variety of tricks)

San Souci, R. (1989). *The talking eggs.* Dial. (girl gets riches while greedy sister is punished)

Say, A. (1993). *Grandfather's journey.* Houghton Mifflin. (good for interviews about home)

Scieszka, J. (1989). *The true story of the 3 little pigs by A. Wolf.* Viking. (wolf tells the story from his point of view; use to stimulate point of view storytelling of other tales)

Slepian, J., & Seidler, A. (1990). *The hungry thing.* Scholastic. (a beast's sign reads "Feed Me")

Steptoe, J. (1987). *Mufaro's beautiful daughters.* Lothrop, Lee & Shepard. (African Cinderella tale)

Tresslet, A. (1964). *The mitten.* Lothrop, Lee & Shepard. (a lost mitten is a haven for animals)

Turkle, B. (1976). *Deep in the forest.* Dutton. (a three bears story with a twist)

Van Allsburg, C. (1984). *The mysteries of Harris Burdick.* Houghton Mifflin. (black-and-white surrealistic pictures, each with its own caption; great material for storytelling)

Van Allsburg, C. (1986). *The stranger.* Houghton Mifflin. (a stranger is injured in an accident, suffers from amnesia, and stays with a family until he realizes his identity)

Viorst, J. (1972). *Alexander and the terrible, horrible, no good, very bad day.* Atheneum. (a boy details everything that goes wrong for him in one day; repeated lines)

Wiesner, D. (1991). *Tuesday.* Clarion. (almost wordless picture book about flying frogs)

Winter, P. (1976). *The bear and the fly.* Crown. (a bear family has a nagging fly)

Wood, A. (1985). *King Bidgood's in the bathtub.* Harcourt Brace Jovanovich. (the king loves his bath and invites everyone in the kingdom to come in; a page boy is forced to pull the plug)

Young, E. (1989). *Lon Po Po: A Red-Riding Hood story from China.* Philomel. (sisters outwit a wolf)

Principle 7: ADAPT Curriculum and Instruction Models to Meet Diverse Needs

Drama . . . can be a mirror, a magnifying glass, a microscope or a searchlight.

Cecily O'Neill (in McCaslin, 1990, p. 294)

The controversy regarding drama as a means or end is not settled and perhaps never will be. Compelling arguments on both sides press for a curriculum in which there is a place for each. Leading educators have declared drama and speech to be central to a language curriculum. They believe that drama can motivate writing and improve oral skills; they believe that it stimulates reading. Some insist it can be used to teach any subject effectively. (McCaslin, 1990, p. 301)

Since the progressive education movement began in the early twentieth century, integration of drama with other curricular areas has been popular. While drama and theater are disciplines worthy of study in their own right, they are also effective learning mediums. One of the best known advocates of using drama as a learning tool throughout the curriculum is Britain's Dorothy Heathcote.

The Center of Drama: Real-Life Science and Social Studies Issues. In lieu of putting on plays with memorized lines, Dorothy Heathcote helps children make sense of their world by causing them to reflect on life experiences. She has demonstrated how learning can be given depth and breadth through drama integration with every area of the curriculum, but with science and social studies, in particular. (See, for example, *Dorothy Heathcote Talks to Teachers—Parts I and II*, each about 30 minutes, Northwestern University Film Library, 1735 Benson Ave, Evanston, Il. 60201.) At the core of her approach is identifying a point of great interest, tension, or conflict in any unit under study. To get this point, Heathcote begins with discussions to elicit students' ideas, which yields a lesson focus. She then usually takes the role of a character, herself, and engages students in roles, although she frequently steps out of role to clarify directions or redirect thinking. Current events, moral and ethical problems, universal themes and questions, and the cognitive and affective domains become grist for the drama mill.

Cecily O'Neill shares Heathcote's philosophy and has extended it for American educators during her tenure at The Ohio State University in Columbus. "Drama lessons that rely on games and exercises to the neglect of the creation of dramatic roles and context are lacking what is, for me, the essential activity of drama. . . . We create a fictional world not to escape from the real world, but to reflect on it. . . . We are trying to release students into finding their own questions" (O'Neill in McCaslin, 1990, pp. 293–294). See the appendix and references at the end of this chapter for further reading.

Curriculum Standards and Goals. The first step in planning for units and lessons is to examine local, state, and national standards documents, including the *National Standards for the Arts.* These provide sources for content for drama and guide teachers in deciding drama skills to teach during integrated lessons.

Any of the four integrated unit centers or bodies (see Post It 2–4) can be used to teach school district requirements in math, reading and language arts, science, and social studies, as well as in the arts of music, art, drama, dance, and literature. Integrated drama lessons and units can be centered around one or more of the traditional subject areas—a literature-based unit study of an author and illustrator like Bryd Baylor can use drama and the other arts, as well as math, science, social studies, and reading/language arts as "legs" to support the center—the focus on Baylor. Drama would be a learning tool in such a unit, just as any other leg. An adaptation of this common idea is to envision a unit with drama as the body with the focus on (1) a person (actor, playwright, director, author, artist), (2) a particular genre or form (improvisation, reader's theater, comedy), (3) a problem,

theme, topic, or question (e.g., how has drama or theater been used to educate people about the effects of war), or (4) a particular book, poem, song, or play (e.g., "Amazing Grace"), with major concepts and skills in math, science, social studies, reading and language arts, and the other art forms used as support legs. Of course, in any integrated lesson or unit, all bodies and legs should be correlated with standards to ensure substantive and focused study. See Post It Page 5–13 for an example of a unit web. Post It Page 7–6 shows drama strategies planned during a literature-based unit on Patricia Polacco and her books.

Adjusting for Diverse Needs. In addition to considering information about developmental stages from Chapter 1, teachers can use the basic principles for adapting instruction for at-risk and special needs students presented in Chapter 2. Post It Pages 2–6, 2–7, and 7–7 give examples of such adaptations for drama. Drawing on students' abilities, rather than focusing just on disabilities, is a key idea when considering instructional modifications.

Drama is unique in its ensemble focus: The emphasis is on partner or group work. Group work can be particularly enjoyable for special needs students. Reluctant or shy children are not forced to participate in uncomfortable ways and soon want to be involved as they see peers having fun. Puppets and props help children feel safe. In general, nonverbal (pantomime) activities are easier than verbal activities. Solo or individual drama strategies done in unison are recommended before small group work. (The exception is older students who have body concerns that make an introduction to drama through pantomime awkward for some.) It works well to start with common ways pantomime is used in daily life—nonverbal communication to show how something is too hot or cold, to greet others, or to show excitement. Space should be managed, as appropriate to student needs, by beginning with limiting students to small areas, like their desks, and then moving to large arenas as they show readiness to handle more. Large areas such as cafeterias, gyms, or playgrounds may have echoes, signal a recess attitude, and cause chaos if students are not properly prepared.

As with any creative problem solving, it is productive to use whole-group teacher-directed drama strategies before breaking students into small groups. This helps set expectations about the kinds of thinking and behaving that will be expected in the small groups. The rule of thumb is to order activities from

DRAMA STRATEGIES: PATRICIA POLACCO BOOKS

Pink and Say

Pantomime

Tableau or frozen pictures: After reading *Pink and Say,* group students. Give each an important scene to depict and freeze in position. For example, create a tableau of Pinkus helping Sheldon to safety or when the boys were being pulled apart after the Confederate soldiers discovered them. These are tension-filled moments. The "audience" can then ask characters about how they feel. Frozen characters "come alive," stay in character, and answer questions or just say a one liner. For example, "We are very scared and don't know if we will live or die." Adaptation: Do frozen pictures behind a white sheet with a bright light to make body language more dramatic.

Verbal

Television show: Different members of the class portray characters on a discussion panel for a television show. The audience questions them about what happened and how they felt. For example, "How did it feel serving your country during the Civil War?"

Newsbreaks: Students become newscasters and do short news break interruptions to update the class on what is going on in the Civil War. Interviews from characters in the book can be included. This is easy to connect with a social studies lesson, with students sharing feelings of people during the war, as well as factual information about events.

The Bee Tree

Pantomime

Narrative pantomime (students mime as narrator reads): "You are a bee. Show how you fly to a flower and land. Show how you begin to gather pollen. Show how the pollen is sticky. Fly back to your bee hive. Put down the pollen and go to sleep for the night."

Verbal

Character interviews: Students pair up with one as the interviewer and the other as a character from the story. Students focus on becoming a character by using a character's language and style of speaking. The interviewer asks questions using Who, What, When, Where, How, and Why. Partners can switch roles and repeat.

My Ol' Man

Pantomime

Comic strip: Break into small groups of three or four and give each group one scene. Choose four scenes that sum up the story. A comic strip will be created with four frames by each group making frozen pictures or tableaux. Give groups 5 minutes to plan. Group 1 poses for the first frame, holds 10 seconds, and then moves to the next scene, and so on. When finished, say "Curtain."

Verbal

Interview: Pair off with an A partner and a B. Partner B becomes a newspaper reporter who just heard about this amazing man who is out of a job but keeps his hopes alive with the help of a magic rock. Partner A is the extraordinary man. Partner B interviews A to find out information to write a good news story. (Use five W's and H questions.) Switch roles. Variation: Students actually write the news stories.

My Rotten Redheaded Older Brother

Pantomime

Creative pantomime: Read the story until right after Teresa makes her wish to be better than her brother in something. Stop and ask the students to pantomime what they think will happen next. Coach students to explore many possibilities.

Verbal Strategies

One liners: Ask the students to look at an illustration and become a character or an object in the picture. Students then say a sentence to describe feelings, using their voices to make the audience believe in the character. Coach to use volume, rate, tone, and pitch.

Show time: Divide into small groups and choose whether to do a commercial, news update, song, or other broadcast about the story. Tell students to present the most important aspects of the story.

POST IT PAGE 7–7

PARTICULAR: STRATEGIES TO DIFFERENTIATE DRAMA FOR SPECIAL NEEDS

Place: Limit and define the space for doing drama (e.g., desk area).

Amount: Do fewer activities or shorter ones.

Rate: Go slower or faster to meet student needs.

Target Objectives: Change the goals or make them clearer to students.

Instruction: Use more teacher direction. For example, use narrative pantomime to start off in drama and consider taking a role, yourself, in the drama.

Curriculum Materials: Use familiar stories or student experiences for drama activities.

Utensils: Use visual aids such as name tags or headbands to help students understand the roles.

Levels of Difficulty: Generally, pantomime is easier than verbal improvisation, and individual drama activities directed by the teacher are easier than group work. Perhaps the material is too conceptually difficult and needs to be altered. If students act silly, it may be they don't know what to do or feel they can't do what is expected. Humor is often used to cover embarrassment. Consider adapting the level of difficulty.

Assistance: For example, children with hearing impairments need to see your face and mouth as you speak. Ask students what to do to help themselves. Don't force shy children to participate because this may increase reluctance. If students don't seem to be able to end the drama, tell them to plan an ending before presenting, ask the audience for ideas, or you take a role and end it.

Response: Alter what you expect in the conclusion. For example, you may have planned for students to present small-group work to the whole group, but group work has been satisfying enough.

---

easy to more difficult and from low content to more content dense (e.g., move from personal interests to subject area concepts and ideas application). Humor used at the start of a lesson relaxes students and activates creative thinking for serious work (the tension and conflict in drama) later in the lesson. Finally, stu-

dents often see adaptations that teachers don't, so it is important to invite their ideas.

Structuring Lessons. The two-pronged integrated arts lesson framework introduced in Chapter 2 is a predictable structure. It can be used creatively to help students gain skills and learn concepts related to drama and other curricular areas. As discussed previously, integrated arts lessons need to include at least one arts concept—drama in this case—to ensure that the integrity of the art form is not lost when drama is integrated with another curricular area. By choosing to teach a few concepts, students are able to go into some depth and become comfortable with the possibilities of each skill or element (e.g., pantomime). Direct or explicit instruction using the introduction, development, and conclusion structure is used in the example plan that follows in Post It Page 7–8. *Note:* After doing a drama, take time to comment on things you saw or heard during the lesson. No names are necessary, since the focus of drama is on the group working together. The conclusion should be a time for students to reflect and do self-evaluation: What worked? didn't work? why? what you liked? what did you learn? new ideas? do differently? Teachers may also wish to invite students to repeat activities with a novel twist, even two or three times, if interest in this kind of exploration is shown during the concluding discussion.

Principle 8: TRIPS That Are Drama Connected

I am certain that human dignity has its roots in the quality of young people's experience.

Dr. Lee Salk

Theater Going. Attending plays is an experience with countless values, not the least of which is the opportunity for children to be introduced to a form of entertainment that can last a lifetime. Without school trips to see live performances, many children experience only in-house assemblies. Field trips to see children's theater have the potential to develop esthetic sensibilities, promote educational aims, and offer chances for social awareness and skill development. Just as with other field trips, theater experiences should be carefully selected to align with curricular goals and become an integral part of a unit through lessons that *prepare for* the trip and *follow up* the play. See Trips section of Chapter 2 for a review of what to do before, during, and after trips. With regards to theater and drama, students need to understand:

◆ Live performances are different from video or television dramas, largely because the audience shares in the event and there is a feeling of spontaneity. The more the audience gives to the

actors, the more the actors can give back to the audience.

◆ General aspects of the theater experience (e.g., expected audience etiquette so that everyone can enjoy the performance and the actors are respected).

◆ Topics and themes the play will deal with, as well as special language.

◆ The setup of the theater and the style of the production.

◆ *Note:* cue sheets or "look fors" help students know ahead of time what is coming. They can then experience a sense of discovery about the set, costumes, characters, and so forth.

After the play, it is helpful to have a discussion, and, just as in good literature discussions, it is important to encourage a variety of points of view. Some useful questions include "What did you see? How did it make you feel? What in the play made you feel that way? What was important in the play? What was it really about? What was missing? What was the playwright trying to say?"

Simulated or "Mind Trips." Students can use the power of pretending to create vivid virtual trip experiences in their minds. Just as radio and storytelling are able to trigger mental images of places, characters, and events, so can the teacher's voice. These fantasy journeys allow students to visit other countries, ecosystems, and even different time periods. Students' imaginations and creative thinking are stretched as they conjure up mental pictures. Simulated field trips can be used to introduce a unit or lesson or as a follow up. Here are guidelines to construct simulated field trips.

◆ Write, tell, or choose trip stories that provoke rich sensory imagery. Use science, social studies, or literature that is a part of your curriculum to obtain ideas for suitable topics.

◆ Have students clear away distractions from their desks, close their eyes, and be comfortable.

◆ Use your voice to calm students; speak slowly and softly and use pauses. Read or speak at a steady pace.

◆ Give students time to create the images in their heads using their senses of sight, hearing, smell, taste, touch or feel, and movement.

◆ Keep the trip to about 10 to 15 minutes.

LESSON PLAN: INTEGRATED DRAMA AND SCIENCE (SECOND GRADE)

Narrative pantomime is used in this lesson during a unit on habitats that began a week ago.

Two-pronged Focus: Drama elements and skills: *pantomime* with focus on control, display of sensory awareness, use of gestures and face, and responding to nonverbal communications of others; focus and concentration; following directions. Science concepts: components of habitat and effects on animals.

Theater Standards: 2, 5, and 7 (see Post It Page 7–3)

Student Objectives: Student will be able to:

1. Use body and face to show specific components of habitats (food, water, shelter, and space).
2. Concentrate and focus to control body and respond to others; follow oral directions (cues).
3. Predict responses of animals who are missing basic habitat components.

Teaching Procedure: The teacher will:

◆ Introduction

1. Use the focus ball strategy to help students focus and concentrate for the lesson.
2. Ask students to list names of animals and places they live—from previous lessons. Record their ideas on a chart (language experience strategy and ask them to spell chorally to help with phonics development). Ask what *habitat* means and clarify, as needed.
3. Tell them today's lesson is about parts of habitats and what happens when a part is missing. Explain narrative pantomime will be used to show animals in their habitats. Ask what makes drama. (Students can use drama elements chart up in room.) Ask about which kind of drama uses no words (pantomime).
4. Do a series of "Show Me" pantomimes with focus on use of face: happy, thinking, worried, hungry, angry. Repeat with whole body (at desk area). Divide class in half for demos and give time for each half to give the other half feedback on what they did that showed concentration and focus.

◆ Development

5. Put first habitat card in pocket chart: food. Read chorally and ask about foods in different habitats. Use a few student examples to stop and pantomime different animals eating those foods. Give descriptive feedback to those who show descriptive use of body and face (shapes, movements, sizes) to show the animal. Repeat with water, shelter, and space components.
6. Explain that narrative pantomime is when someone tells a story while others use their faces and bodies to show the story. Review rules about following start and stop signals. Tell everyone to find a personal space in the center of the room.
7. Give each a card with an animal name on it. No one knows it but there are duplicates. Say "When I say 'start' everyone is to explore ways to show their animal in a variety of ways (e.g., shape, moves, size). Stay in your personal spot. At the 'freeze' signal everyone should stop. Start." Give feedback on focus, concentration, unusual ideas. Repeat in *slow motion.*
8. Use start and stop signals for the *narrative pantomime* (read slowly and give time):

    You are hungry. You begin to look for *food* in your habitat. You find the kind of food you eat. Slowly you eat your meal. After a while you start to get full and begin to slow down. In an area nearby you hear a sound and you become afraid. Your body shows you are scared. You look for *shelter* and move there. You watch carefully and you wait, being very still, until you know you are safe. The coast seems to be clear. You are feeling good because you are safe and full of food. You move around your habitat *space* showing you are satisfied. Because you ate so much you are thirsty. You see *water* nearby and move there and begin to drink. The water is very cold. After a long cool drink, you begin to feel lonely and you look for another animal like you. You move around noticing how other animals move to see if you can find another of your species. You greet your fellow animal when you find him or her. It has been a long day and you are getting tired. You move slowly to a place of shelter. You begin to get ready to rest. Slowly you drift off to sleep.

◆ Conclusion/Assessment

9. Ask students what they thought about, what worked? what problems? How did they find another similar animal? Collect cards and repeat with new animals.
10. Brainstorm what might happen if a habitat part is limited—like space. Ask what information students need to show the parts of habitat and animal behavior better. List ideas on the chart.
11. Let students choose an animal to read more about habitat needs (library books on display). Tell them we'll do a drama Tuesday using what they find; this time the animals will have inadequate habitat components, so there will be problems (conflict).

◆ After the trip, have students mentally review the high points. Ask students to share what they experienced in small groups or have them do a 5-minute Write Right Away response or even an art response.

◆ Come together as a whole group to synthesize what was learned (e.g., in social studies, science, or literature) from the trip.

Principle 9: EVIDENCE of Student Progress/Assessment

Student progress in using drama as a learning medium can be demonstrated and celebrated using portfolios, videotapes, displays, and by sharing with audiences, as described in the Exhibit Progress section of Chapter 2. However, goals may be difficult to pinpoint, despite the new *Standards*, and measurement in drama is sometimes tricky because teachable moments emerge *during* drama. One of the best forms of assessment and evaluation is specific teacher observations of what students *show they know* in lessons. Teachers can use rubrics and checklists to assess progress and students can be involved in self-evaluation and peer feedback. (See example drama skills checklist below, Chapter 14, and Appendix D).

Rather than squelch creativity with grades or traditional tests, teachers can give general assignment criteria before work is done, which gives students guidance as they work. Here is a simple evaluation checklist that teachers and students can use to consider progress in drama use.

Response Options. Response relates to audience etiquette but goes beyond into the area of giving peer feedback. After drama presentations, students can use

---

Drama Skills Progress Checklist

Name _____ Date _____

Directions: Evaluate using 1, 2, 3, 4, 5, with 1 indicating no evidence and 5 indicating very evident. Add notes and discuss.

_____ **Use of body:** ability to coordinate and control body, use of appropriate energy, display of sensory awareness and expression, use of gestures and facial expressions, communication through pantomime, interpretation of nonverbal communication of others

_____ **Verbal expression:** speaking clearly and using appropriate variety in volume, rate, tone and pitch, pause, stress, emphasis, and inflection, fluency, and ability to improvise dialog

_____ **Focus:** concentration and staying involved, making others believe in the realness of the character, following directions

_____ **Imagination:** flexible creative thinking, contribution of unique ideas and elaboration on ideas, spontaneity

_____ **Evaluation:** giving constructive feedback, using suggestions of others, self-evaluation and adaptation of own behavior

_____ **Social skills:** working cooperatively with groups, listening and responding to others

_____ **Audience etiquette:** attending, listening, and responding appropriately to others' performances

structures to help them articulate thoughts and feelings. For example, students can simply tell what they saw or heard, describing honestly, using new-found vocabulary for drama elements. They can also use sentence stems to express their feelings: *I'd liked . . . It made me feel . . .* The *liked–wonder–learned* strategy described in Chapter 2 can be used after a drama to record responses in three columns. Students also need to learn to ask questions of others as a form of feedback. Because receiving feedback is hard for some, it helps to role play giving and receiving feedback. This also shows students how rude or thoughtless remarks can make a person feel; sensitivity and empathy are important to constructive feedback.

To help teach students discuss and write about their drama work, Post It Page 7–9 has questions for students to use as guides.

Principle 10: SPECIALISTS in Drama and Theater

Drama teachers, professional actors, playwrights, and community theater organizations are valuable classroom resources. Teachers need to seek out specialists who can help find connections between drama and other disciplines and show how to make them without damaging the integrity of the art form.

It is the lucky classroom teacher who has a drama specialist in the school. Specialists usually welcome invitations to plan with teachers, especially if integration is viewed as going both ways; at times the drama teacher should be able to ask for support for her unit focus on a theme or topic. Classroom teachers can make it easy for a specialist to assist in integration by providing a month by month listing of units and lessons in science, social studies, reading and language arts, and math so specialists can make suggestions. In addition, teachers can invite specialists to do the same with a list of topics they plan to develop. Classroom teachers can also ask for ways to follow up on drama classes or extend drama work. It is highly recommended that generalists sit in on drama classes to learn more about drama and about ways students can make meaning using drama.

POST IT PAGE 7–9

ALL-PURPOSE FAT QUESTIONS

Directions: Post question examples so students learn to use different kinds to discuss and reflect on their work. Teachers should model use of open/fat questions and show how they provoke more discussion than skinny/closed ones. These questions help students think more deeply and facilitate oral expression.

- What worked?
- What did you enjoy?
- What would you change?
- How was the ending? What was the best moment? Why?
- How did you work with others?
- How did you show involvement?
- How did you get your idea? Where did you gather ideas?
- Why did you do what you did?
- What were you trying to do?
- What did you try that you've never tried before?
- What did you learn most?
- How is this connected to other things you are learning?
- What ideas did you use from what we've been learning about drama (elements, skills, concepts)?
- What did you learn? What was this mostly about? What did this tell you about people or the world? What will you remember forever?"

When There Is No Drama Specialist. By starting a school directory of persons with drama background and skills, teachers have found drama expertise in nearby places—the teacher next door may have had courses in children's drama or the principal might write plays. A parent may be willing to conduct a workshop on nonverbal communication. Circulate a form to all adults in the school requesting names and contact information for people who could be used as drama or theater resources. Encourage people to list themselves. Students, parents, and community groups can also be tapped for potential skills. Use the Internet to locate home pages of drama and theater organizations at the local and state levels. Selected Internet websites are listed in the appendix for starters. Don't forget to contact the theater department in nearby colleges to find out about student internships or other ways college students might serve as drama resources.

Arts Agency Collaborations. Collaborations among a variety of arts organizations are helping schools in communities across the country learn ways to integrate drama and other arts under the auspices of the Kennedy Center Partners in Education and the Getty Education Institute. Shakespeare & Company, out of Lenox, Massachusetts, has been working with public schools for 20 years. Many organizations provide workshops for teachers on a low or no-charge basis. Contact local museums or arts council to see if they are involved in partnership projects or interested in getting started. Use the appendix to contact organizations by mail, phone, e-mail, or fax. Local workshops conducted by artists and classroom teachers engaged in integrating the arts are becoming more common so keep an eye out for advertisements of these, as well.

Artist Residencies. Drama and theater specialists may be available through a local arts council, college, or by contacting artists in your community. Not only are there children's theater groups that may be willing to be involved in your classroom, but Theater in Education projects are another dimension worth investigating. It is important to realize that artists often have little or no background in teaching or child development. Before bringing an artist into a school or class, it is important to meet ahead of time to prepare. Everyone needs to agree on and know:

- Goals of the visit, including the objectives from the unit and course of study related to the residency
- Composition of the class: economic, social, and developmental levels
- Exact time limits
- Physical limitations of your classroom (materials you have and don't have)
- Special needs students
- Disciplinary system in use and who will handle discipline during the visit
- Basic effective teaching strategies related to use of proximity, questioning, eye contact, hands on, pace, transitions, and use of students' prior knowledge
- How to prepare students for the visit
- How the classroom teacher will participate
- How to assess and evaluate what the students learn
- How to follow up after the visit to extend learning

◆ CONCLUSION

In this chapter the reasons *why* drama should be integrated, *what* a classroom teacher needs to know and be able to do to integrate drama, and the basic principles for *how* to use drama were discussed. The next chapter consists of specific strategy seed ideas that teachers can use to: (1) get students ready for creative problem solving using drama, (2) teach students the elements and skills to use drama as a learning tool, and (3) examples of ways to use drama throughout curricular areas.

◆ TEACHER RESOURCES

See the appendix for drama integration resources. Here is a sampling of what's available:

Creative dramatics: The first steps (video, 29 minutes). Northwestern Film Library, 614 Davis St., Evanston, Il. 60201. (drama in a fourth grade)

Dorothy Heathcote talks to teachers—part I and part II (videos, about 30 minutes). Northwestern University Film Library, 1735 Benson Ave, Evanston, Il. 60201.

Erior, P. (2000). *Drama in the classroom: Creative activities for teachers, parents and friends.* Fort Bragg, CA: Lost Coast Press.

Heinig, R. B. (1987). *Creative drama resource book for grades 4 through 6.* Upper Saddle River, NJ: Prentice Hall. (K–3 book also available)

Heinig, R. B. (1992). *Improvisation with favorite fairy tales.* Portsmouth, NH: Heinemann.

Introduction to creative drama and improvisation (1990). (110-minute video). Design Video, Communications, P.O. Box 40227, Indianapolis, IN 46240. (Rives Collins teaches college students about drama.)

Mahlmann, L. (1980). *Folk tale plays for puppets: 13 royalty-free plays for hand puppets, rod puppets, or marionettes.* Boston: Plays, Inc.

Max makes mischief (1977) (video). University Park: Pennsylvania State University. (core book drama unit for third grade using *Where the Wild Things Are*)

Merrion, M. (1996). *Creative drama and music methods: Introductory activities for children.* North Haven, CT: Linnet Professional.

Peterson, L. (1997). *Kids take the stage: Helping young people discover the creative outlet of theater.* New York: Back Stage Books.

Pollock, J. (1997). *Side by side: Twelve multicultural puppet plays.* School Library Media No. 13. Lanham, MD: Scarecrow.

Rooyackers, P. (1997). *101 Drama games for children: Fun and learning with acting and make-believe.* Alameda, CA: Hunter House.

Schafer, L. (1994). *Plays around the year: More than 20 thematic plays for the classroom.* New York: Scholastic Professional Books.

Walker, L. (1996). *Readers theater strategies development through Readers Theater, storytelling, writing and dramatizing!* Colorado Springs, CO: Meriwether.

Winters, L. (1997). *On stage: Theater games and activities for kids.* Chicago: Review Press.

◆ BIBLIOGRAPHY AND REFERENCES

Books

Fiske, E. (ed.). (1999). *Champions of change.* Washington, DC: Arts Education Partnership, and Washington, DC: President's Committee on the Arts and the Humanities.

Heinig, R. B. (1993). *Creative drama for the classroom teacher.* Upper Saddle River, NJ: Prentice Hall.

McCaslin, N. (1990). *Creative drama in the classroom* (5th ed.). New York: Longman.

Meyrink, G. (1994). The curse of the toad. In *The opal and other stories.* Riverside, CA: Ariadne.

Peck, R. (1988). *Secrets of successful fiction.* Seattle: Romar.

Riekehof, L. (1987). *Joy of signing.* Springfield, MO: Gospel Publishing.

Robinson, K. (Ed.). (1990). *Exploring theater and education.* London: Heinemann.

Rosenberg, H. (1987). *Creative drama and imagination: Transforming ideas into action.* New York: Holt, Rinehart & Winston.

Articles

Dupont, S. (1992). The effectiveness of creative drama as an instructional strategy to enhance reading comprehension skill of fifth-grade remedial readers. *Reading Research and Instruction, 31*(3), 41–52.

Gourgey, A., Bousseau, J., & Delgado, J. (1985). The impact of an improvisational dramatics program on student attitudes and achievement. *Children's Theater Review, 34*(3), 9–14.

Henderson, L. C., & Shanker, L. C. (1978). The use of interpretive dramatics versus basal reader workbooks. *Reading World, 17,* 239–243.

Kardash, C., & Wright, L. (Winter 1987). Does creative drama benefit elementary school students: A meta-analysis. *Youth Theater Journal,* pp. 11–18.

Karioth, E. (1967). *Creative dramatics as an aid to developing creative thinking abilities.* Unpublished doctoral dissertation, University of Minnesota.

Miller, H., Rynders, J., & Schleien, S. (1993). Drama: A medium to enhance social interaction between students with and without mental retardation. *Mental Retardation, 31*(4), 228–233.

Moore, B., & Caldwell, H. (1993). Drama and drawing for narrative writing in primary grades. *Journal of Educational Research, 8*(2), 100–110.

Schmidt, T., Goforth, E., & Drew, K. (1975, March 27). Creative dramatics and creativity: An experimental study. *Educational Theater Journal,* pp. 111–114.

Stewig, J., & McKee, J. (1980). Drama and language growth: A replication study. *Children's Theater Review, 29*(3), 1.

Stewig, J., & Young, L. (1978). An exploration of the relations between creative drama and language growth. *Children's Theater Review, 27*(2), 10–12.

Vitz, K. (1983). A review of empirical research in drama and language. *Children's Theater Review, 32*(4), 17–25.

Wagner, B. J. (1979, March). Using drama to create an environment for language development. *Language Arts, 56*(3), 268–274.

Wagner, B. J. (1988). A review of empirical research in drama and language. *Language Arts, 65*(1), 46–55.

Children's Literature

Brown, A. (1990). *The piggybook.* New York: Knopf.

Estes, E. (1994). *The hundred dresses,* New York: Harcourt Brace Jovanovich.

Hoffman, M. (1991). *Amazing grace.* New York: Dial.

O'Dell, S. (1960). *Island of the blue dolphins.* Boston: Houghton Mifflin.

Polacco, P. (1994). *Babushka's doll.* New York: Simon & Schuster.

Van Allsburg, C. (1991). *The wretched stone.* Boston: Houghton Mifflin.

White, E. B. (1952). *Charlotte's web.* New York: HarperTrophy.

8

Drama Seed Strategies

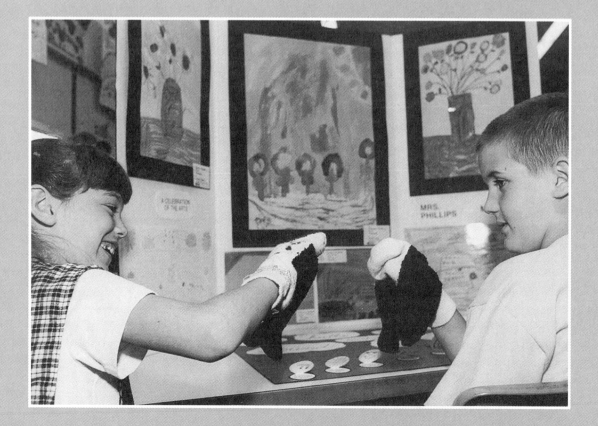

Introduction

This chapter includes starter ideas to integrate drama throughout the curriculum. The ideas are in seed or kernel form. They are brief prompts to help think creatively and need to be tailored to student needs and curricular standards. Most are adaptable for students in primary and intermediate grades. Seed strategies need to be selected, adapted, and expanded as appropriate to particular classrooms. The seeds are organized into five sections, but many could be placed in more than one section. The sections on energizers, pantomime, and verbal strategies do *not* represent integration, by themselves, but are provided to teach these drama forms so that students can then use drama to make meaning throughout curricular areas.

I. Energizers and Warm-ups

Energizers and warm-ups are used to relax students, give focus, and get them ready for creative thinking. Also see energizers from other chapters, especially for dance, for concentration activities.

Line Up Different Ways. Tell students to line up alphabetically, by birthday, by height, and so forth. Once in line, they then interview those around them to find out three things not known before.

Hand Study. Partner students and have them take turns examining each other's hands. Tell them to try to see and feel everything about the hand that makes it unique. This can be used as a "get to know you" activity: *This is Joe and he has very thick hands with short fingernails. His hands are tan as if he works outside a lot.*

Play Ball. Form a circle. Leader holds an imaginary ball (show size with hands) and calls someone's name as it is thrown, saying, "Sue, basketball." The receiver then says, "Thank you, basketball." Play continues, with receiver calling a name and throwing the pretend basketball. After a few rounds the leader introduces a second ball, saying, "Joe, beachball." and Joe responds, "Thank you beachball." Continue to add more balls as appropriate. At the end, call stop and ask everyone with a ball to hold it, and the audience guesses the kind of ball.

Tongue Twisters and Tanglers. Use as vocal warm-ups. Say them as a group and then practice in pairs or go around a circle (make into a game where play be-

gins over if a person mispronounces). Examples are: *A hot cup of coffee from a proper copper coffee pot. Aluminum linoleum. Bugs black blood. Six sick sheep. Rubber baby buggy bumpers. Toy boat. Unique New York.* One collection is *Six Sick Sheep* by Joanna Cole. Follow up: Ask students to collect and create twisters. Organize alphabetically in a recipe box. Put up a Twister Master chart for students to keep track of ones they learn to say three times without error. Many students will want to memorize longer twisters such as "Peter Piper" (see Schwartz's *A Twister of Twists: A Tangler of Tongues* for history of this one).

Finger Plays. Traditional finger plays such as "The Itsy Bitsy Spider" can be taught, and there are special collections that include other favorites. Here is an untraditional one to calm and focus. Seat everyone on the floor and say:

> *I relax and focus* (point to self with thumb and lay hands in lap)
> *I gather in the good* (gather with hands brought in)
> *I push out the bad* (push outward with both hands)
> *I celebrate the joy all around me* (raise hands, spread fingers, and do silent cheer)

Sound and Action Stories. "Going on a Bear Hunt" is an example of this kind of energizer in which a narrator tells a story while children echo lines and do actions. Narration is accompanied by a steady walking rhythm. Between sections of the story, give time to mime the motions. When the bear is seen, actions are reversed—double time.

Scavenger Hunts. Give groups items to find and a time limit. For example, "In five minutes try to find a silky item, a book with an r-controlled word in the title, something that moves, and something that can be used to create." *Variation:* Use the five senses to organize searches: "Find something that . . . looks like . . . , sounds like . . . , feels like . . . , etc."

Concentration. Make a tray of items. Students study them and then the tray is covered. Students try to list all they remember. *Variation:* Students close their eyes and an item is removed. Others try to figure out missing item. Try with a group using wipe-off boards so that all can write missing item and then simultaneously show boards.

Word Change. This is a creative thinking verbal exercise. Sit in a circle. First person gives a sentence (e.g., "Mary had a little lamb"). Next person repeats the sentence, but changes one word: "Mary had a little goat." Keep going all the way around. *Challenge:* Repeat and return the sentence to its original form.

Partner Search.   Make sets of cards with sounds or song titles and pass them out. The goal is to have groups form by finding those who are singing the same song or making the same sound (e.g., animal sound), for example, 5 different song titles on 5 sets of cards for 25 students to break into groups of 5.

Three Truths and a Lie.   Students write down a list of truths about themselves. One item should be false. Students read aloud items including the false one. The audience applauds to show which one they believe is the lie. *Note:* It is important to discuss how to use creative ideas without being obvious.

Animal–Car–Flower.   This creative-thinking activity helps students get to know one another. Students write down the three categories and an example that applies to them. For example, *My name is . . . and I identify with a cat because . . . , a Jeep because . . . , and roses because. . . .*

Reverse Web.   This is a creative-thinking team builder. Students get into groups of four or five. Use large paper and have everyone write, or use 8½ by 11 paper with one recorder. A circle is drawn in the center. A leg is drawn coming out of the circle for each person (five students equals five lines radiating out). Names are written on the legs. In the center, students put things the group has in common—the more unusual the better (e.g., all are left handed or all have traveled to Mexico).

Pass and Pretend.   Sit in a circle and pass around an ordinary object (pencil or scarf). Students then use it in a creative way by imagining what it can become. For example, a scarf could be rocked like a baby. Encourage focus on details of action. (See **Invisible Object** mime suggestions given later in this chapter.) *Variation:* Do this without a prop and ask students to imagine an object and pantomime using it and passing it to the next person, who must use the same object and transform it into something else. To increase difficulty, do with several objects. *Variation:* Use a verbal frame: Pass straw and say, "This is not a straw, it's a . . ." and then demonstrate what it has transformed into.

Voice Change.   This activity helps students use volume, rate, tone, pitch, pause, stress, and emphasis to convey a character or person. Make a set of character or person cards. Then make a list of random sentences:

"Hi, how are you?" "Can you tell me how to get to the nearest hospital?" "We've really been having bad weather lately." "I'm so tired." Students each draw a card and say one of the sentences, in character. Others tell what they heard (message, feelings) and who they think it is. For example, Santa might "ho-ho-ho" in between his words or phrases.

Laugh Contest.   A panel of students must try to resist laughing as one classmate has a crack at making them laugh by telling jokes, making faces, and the like. Discuss school-appropriate humor before doing this!

Belly Laughs.   Everyone lies on the floor with his or her head on someone else's belly. At a signal, one person says "ha" and the "ha" travels around the circle. When it gets around, another person starts another laugh (e.g., "he he").

Noiseless Sounds.   This is a great classroom management tool. Ask students to think of ways to pantomime sounds without making any noise: laugh, applause, choke, sneeze. *Variation:* Ask students to divide the sound into three consecutive pantomime actions (e.g., steps in a sneeze). Groups can practice and present to the whole class.

What's Different? (for Concentration).   Students partner with one being A and the other B. A studies B concentrating on details of appearance. Leader signals and they turn back to back. A makes a change. Pairs turn around and B gets three guesses to figure out "what's different." Then it's B's turn.

Hot Sock.   See Chapter 6 for this game, which develops verbal fluency and categorization.

Voice Stunts.   Form groups of four. Give groups a phrase. For example, "To be or not to be," "Zig-zag-zog," or "Slip-slap-slop." Each person only says one word in the phrase and play goes around a circle, or IT can pass by eye contact or pointing.

Stunts and Magic Tricks (Builds Pride and Confidence).   Students can learn stunts and tricks to perform, for example, rub stomach and pat head at same time, balance balloon or pencil on the end of your nose, stand with left shoulder and side of left foot snug against a wall and try to raise right leg. See Goodman's *Magic and the Educated Rabbit* and Randi's *The Magic World of the Amazing Randi* for more ideas.

Boring Words.   Brainstorm a list of boring words (e.g., *cardboard, the, board, box*). Practice saying them changing volume, rate, tone, pitch, pause, stress, and emphasis to make them interesting. *Variation:* Do the same with boring phrases or sentences. Collect phrases from reading and listening.

II. PANTOMIME STRATEGIES

Pantomime is acting without words. It often is used to show something in the process of "becoming," for example, a seed becoming a plant or a character becoming frustrated as he tries to whistle. It is helpful for shy students or those with limited oral expression skills because it is the kind of communication used before a child learns to speak. Movement and facial expression are used to show shape, size, weight, texture, and temperature—the things experienced through the senses. Through mime, students can imagine and experience places, events, and things beyond firsthand experiences (e.g., walking on the moon), and in so doing engage thinking, emotions, and body in learning. Mime can be as simple as showing the difference between water and ice, using only the body, or it can be as complex as a performance of Columbus's travails on his voyage to the New World.

The teacher's role is to set up pantomimes that focus on action related to children's lives and curricular areas, plus structure the drama for success. For example, a teacher might use narrative pantomime and comment and coach children as they mime by saying "I see . . ." or asking "What do you see?" to encourage students to develop skills at observing details. Teachers learn to deal with common problems that frequently arise by anticipating difficulties, such as children wanting to make all pantomimes into guessing games. (This can be handled by limiting guesses, focusing attention on details that *show*, or asking for evidence to support guesses.) This section includes types of pantomimes adaptable for use throughout curricular areas. It begins with Post It Page 8–1 to stimulate thinking about how *actions* can be connected to concepts in science, social studies, or math, thereby making learning through pantomime possible.

Invisible Objects. Use a mystery bag or basket. Each student pretends to pull out an item and *shows* its shape, size, weight, texture, and temperature and how it can be used. Guessers put thumbs up and IT calls on selected peers. To become IT, a student must tell the items and the details the mime used to make the idea clear. To make an object look real, coach students to take time to:

- Slowly study it (size, shape, texture, temperature).
- Reach out as if to touch it (move toward it to show how you will take hold).
- Take hold (imagine your hands on it, then feel it).

Pantomime Pairs

A-to-Z Pantomime Possibilities

Directions: Brainstorm with students things to mime about a topic. Use this list to give examples and to create original pantomimes in any curricular area. For example, pantomime verbs (action words) in language arts to have students *show* word meanings.

Actions: clean, travel, construct, eat, drink, ignore, cough, nudge, videotape

Animals: moving, eating, sleeping; different categories (e.g., insect, bird, mammal)

Book chapters: actions in each chapter

Book characters: spider writing in web, Jack climbing beanstalk

Emotions or feelings: happy, sad, angry, disgusted, surprised, sick, embarrassed

Foods: being prepared, eaten

Getting ready: to go to school, to go to the beach, to play ball

Hobbies and vacation activities: juggling, jumping rope, playing tennis

Holidays and festivals: dances at weddings, parties

Jobs, occupations, careers: bricklayer, janitor, carpenter

Machines: computers, mixers, vacuum, lawn mower

Musical instruments: being played, carried, cleaned

Objects: a shoe being made, types of Greek columns, holding and placing objects (fruit, animals, food)

Pairs: folding a sheet, playing tennis, tug of war, Ping-Pong

People: famous celebrities, inventors, politicians

Pets: how to care for

Places: beach, cave, closet, rooftop, edge of cliff, bodies of water, mountains, beach, city, farm

Plants: changing, growing, blooming, dying

Processes: nesting, cooking, building, manufacturing

Rituals and customs: greetings, farewells

Sensory responses to items: what if . . .?

Sports: how to dress for, actually playing, waiting for your turn

Things you: like to do; don't like to do

Tools: use of, cleaning, carrying

Toys: using, storing

Vehicles: scooter, inline skates, tricycle

Walking: under different circumstances, in different moods, to different locations, at different levels, taking different pathways, as different characters

Weather: response to different weather conditions or pretending to be a kind of weather

Wise sayings: for example, "you can lead a horse to water but you can't make him drink"

Word categories: antonyms, homophones, three syllable, silent *e,* three letter

---

◆ Use it as you would if it were really there.

◆ Stop and slowly replace it.

◆ Let go slowly and move away.

Afterward, tell students to isolate a part they did the best and demonstrate to the group, or ask them to give each other feedback on which steps looked most real and why. *Variation:* Objects could come from any curricular area of study (e.g., a butter churn from colonial times).

Number Freeze. Students number off in fives. Give them a setting (e.g., a circus). Teacher calls a number and these students pantomime an action done in the designated setting. The next number is then called and this group mimes while the others observe.

Quick Change. Give a series of *Show me with your face and body* directions. For example, *Show me . . . mad, upset because you dropped your ice cream cone, happy because you got an A on your test.* *Variation:* Use examples from science, social studies, or literature.

Mirrors (to Build Concentration). Partners face each other. Partner A pretends to look into a mirror and B becomes the mirror. The goal is to align actions so that an observer can't tell the "real" from the "reflection." Start in slow motion. *Variation:* Do in small groups and give a context such as a beauty salon. One person is the stylist and the rest are mirrors. Do in two facing lines. *Suggestion:* Start with slow movements.

Pantomime Solo. In pantomime solos, children work individually but can mime in unison, each in her or his personal space (Heinig, 1993). For example, *You are Little Miss Muffet looking for a place to sit and eat. Remember, you've been frightened by a spider in this garden before.* Give signals to start and end, such as flick lights or use drum, tambourine, or bell. Counting can also signal the playing: *5–4–3–2–1.* If students are to do multiple pantomimes, say "Think of three things Goldilocks might have done while going through the woods and number them, one, two, and three in your mind. As I say one of the numbers, you mime your idea." This kind of cuing keeps all on task and working together.

Pair Pantomime. Brainstorm actions requiring two people (e.g., teeter totter, dance, lift a long table, play checkers). Partner students. At a count, or with a time limit, students mime as many as they can. *Example connection to literature:* Prince putting the slipper on Cinderella or Cinderella and the Prince dancing. *Variations:* Do one action in slow, regular, and then in quick time. Add conflict (e.g., Cinderella's feet smell). Famous pairs can also be mimed (e.g., Wright brothers), and this pantomime can be adapted to focus on group effort by brainstorming actions it takes a group to do (e.g., carry a bathtub). Groups form and pantomime. Add conflict in repeat playing (e.g., your hands get sweaty).

Break It Down (Analysis and Sequencing). Students think of a series of movements associated with an event or a place (e.g., washing a pet, picking fruit). Break each into three to five parts to pantomime in order, for example, empty hamper. Carry basket down stairs. Sort clothes. Put clothes in washer. Set knobs. Close lid. Start washer. *Variation:* Add conflict (e.g., can't get all the clothes in the washer).

Think Back Pantomime. Ask students to remember actions they did in the past. Tell them to choose one and when you say "begin" repeat it in place until the signal to stop. Use the BEST (dance) elements to ask students to creatively manipulate the actions. Replay several times. For example, brush teeth with different body parts. *Variation:* Students recall actions from lessons in math or science.

Emotion Pantomimes. Give students a situation with an emotion. For example, *you are alone at home and you hear strange noises in different parts of the house.* Give start signal and feedback about ways students use details to show action. Split the class into presenters and audience to share. Reverse so that all have a chance to observe and discuss what works. *Variation:* Ask students to list emotions and give situations in which each might be felt. Add a problem or conflict to increase interest and pantomime.

Obstacle Pantomimes. Students brainstorm actions (e.g., walking to school, driving a car). Do a group unison pantomime of the ideas. Next, divide into small groups and ask groups to add a problem, obstacle, or conflict to one action. Small groups then pantomime (e.g., dancing, but with a broken toe).

Kalamazoo. Divide students into two groups to decide on a pantomime category (e.g., jobs, animals, toys) (adapted from Heinig, 1993). Then have them line up facing each other. Group 1 says "Here we come," and group 2 responds, "Where are you from?" Group 1, "Kalamazoo." Group 2, "What do you do?" Group 1, "Here's a clue." Group 1 then pantomimes while group 2 guesses. A time limit can be set.

Chain Pantomime. One person starts a pantomime and others become involved as they guess (guessers can whisper answers to the teacher or mime), for example, a giraffe walking and eating. Correct guessers can become additional giraffes and can interact with each other.

Categories Pantomime. Brainstorm words in categories (e.g., B words, rhyming words, silent *e* words).

Group students and give a list of numbered items. Half pantomimes while the other half numbers their papers and writes what they think is mimed, in order. Use a new list for the second half to mime.

Pantomime Category Ideas

Image: Things that move or are: Examples

vertical	elevator
horizontal	dust a table
high	clouds
low	caterpillar
fast	electric fan
slow	melting ice
circle	merry-go-round
twisted	pretzel

Five Senses Pantomimes.   Brainstorm things to do in the sense categories: smell, see, taste, touch, and hear. Students pantomime. *Variation:* Add a problem. For example, you are eating a chicken sandwich, but you bite into something hard, or you are zipping up your jacket, but it gets stuck.

Fights.   Drama is made from conflict, and most literature useful for drama involves conflict, so it is a good idea to practice pantomiming fights. Ask students to practice showing different moves in personal spaces *without touching anyone* (e.g., punch, stab, claw, slap). Do in slow motion or to a count. Get into pairs. In slow motion, practice with one person responding. Emphasize *no touching or falling down* (unless you also teach falling). Use start and stop signals.

Action Pantomime.   Brainstorm ways to move or actions. (See BEST dance elements in Post It Page 9–3 and Locomotor and Nonlocomotor Action Bingo in Chapter 10.) Put action words in a basket. Each person picks one and "becomes the move," while others guess its name. This can be done in partners (e.g., all A people "twist" while B's observe and switch).

Sequence QU Pantomime.   Students observe others to know when to mime their part (adapted from Heinig, 1993). Cue cards are made that have a Q (cue) and U (you) so that students know what to look for and what to mime. Teacher needs to keep a full copy of the QU sheet and cut another one apart so that she has a way to keep track of the action. Double or triple cast so everyone is involved. Here is an example based on *Charlotte's Web:*

Q: The leader says, "A Day in the Barn"

U: Pretend to be Charlotte spinning her web

Q: When Charlotte spins her web

U: Mime Wilbur eating out of his trough

Q: Wilbur eating out of his trough

U: Pretend to be Fern and come in and sit on a stool to watch

Q: Fern comes in and sits on her stool

U: Pretend to be Templeton sneaking around

Q: Templeton sneaking around

U: Applaud

Variation: Use to review material students have been studying (e.g., science experiments).

Charades.   This is an old favorite pantomime guessing game. Form two teams. Each takes a turn. Traditional pantomime categories are book, song, television show, film, and famous person, but any category can be used: one-, two-, or three-syllable words, rhyme pairs (hink pinks such as "sad dad"), synonyms, antonyms, words beginning with a letter or sound, homophones (sum–some, red–read), quotes, proverbs, famous pairs (e.g., peanut butter and jelly), states, countries, and so forth. Students enjoy creating cues to start the game: sounds like (pull ear), short word (show size with fingers), long word (show with two hands moving apart), syllable numbers (show with fingers), movie (pretend to roll film), book (use hands to show open book).

Imaginary Place.   The goal is to create a setting or place by stocking it with appropriate items (Heinig, 1993). Mark off space with masking tape. Students pantomime bringing in items and placing them. Pairs work together for big items. Audience can guess what is mimed. Challenge students to use items they add, plus a previous item, in some way, to fix visual images. For example, two students bring a stove into a restaurant, so the next player brings in a refrigerator. After placing the fridge, the student may check the oven temperature before exiting. Periodically, review all items and their placement. *Variations:* Use settings and places from history and literature.

Count–Freeze.   Give students a category to pantomime (see Post It Page 8–1). Tell students you will count to 10 as they pantomime. They are to freeze on 10. *Variation:* Do in pairs or trios, and count at different speeds. Examples are things you do at school or things you do in threes or twos. Here is a literature example from "The Mouse at the Seashore" fable: things the mouse might have done on his journey in the morning, afternoon, evening (teacher says each time of day and then students mime).

Time Mime (Focus on Self-Control). Students mime at different speeds from slow to fast. For example, slow = move as if you are under water or walking in thick mud. Play slow mood music or a piece such as "Clair de Lune." Fast motion pantomime = move like a fast motion movie. Play Scott Joplin songs or a fast piece such as the "Spinning Song." Use this idea to vary any pantomime, replaying at different speeds.

Transformations. Brainstorm characters or things that change (e.g., young to old, seed to plant). Ask students to break down phases and do in slow motion. Add music. For example, *Become a fairy tale character and change, on a slow count of 10, into another character* (e.g., beast into a prince).

Tableau (Frozen Picture). Pairs or small groups are given a scene to depict and asked to freeze in appropriate positions (e.g., a tension-filled moment in a story). Students can then be "tapped" to speak aloud and give a one liner of their thoughts. Audience may be asked to *describe* what they see, what it means, and what makes them believe in the picture. They may also wish to *ask questions* of members of the tableau, especially ones about their feelings and motives. Children may select their own scenes from science or social studies to portray and be guessed by peers as a unit review. *Variation:* Ask students to create three different tableaux to a count. For example, "Remain as the same character but move into three different positions as I count 5–4–3–2–1." Ask students to freeze, then move, and then freeze on cue to set the tableau to life for a few seconds. Give audience members a role to respond (e.g., if the scene was Wilbur winning the blue ribbon, ask the audience to tell what they see as if they are farmers, Templeton, Charlotte, or the owner of the local slaughterhouse. This increases thinking from a variety of perspectives). *Variation:* Frozen scenes may be performed as shadow pictures or silhouettes by using a light behind a taut sheet. Stand close to the sheet to present a clear image and turn lights off. Colored gels on the light create interesting effects.

Tableau Captions. Use book titles, newspaper headlines, current events, advertisement slogans, quotes from famous people, or phrases from units as prompts for frozen picture tableaus. For example, "Why does she always get to sit up front?" or "Mars Lander Hits Hard." *Variation:* Create three different frames.

Sound Motion Machines. Choose a category to pantomime (e.g., a chapter in MacLachlan's *Sarah Plain and Tall* has these movements: rolling a marble, sweeping, riding a horse). Each student chooses a repeatable movement related to the category. One person starts the pantomime and others join in until all are moving in a space. On signal, everyone adds a sound. *Variation:* All members of a machine must be touching to show that they are a connected whole.

Creative Pantomimes. Technically, all pantomimes should be creative, but creative pantomime offers greater room for improvisation. Instead of interpreting actions, these pantomimes involve thinking more about "what if." For example, stop reading a story at a poignant point and ask students to pantomime predictions of what might happen next. Emphasize "What are all the possibilities of what might happen." For example, "Let's see three things Cinderella might do after she gets home after the first night at the ball. I'll count to signal. Let's begin. One." *Variation:* Do half of an experiment or stop part way through a video and ask students to make predictions by miming an event they anticipate.

Improvised Pantomime Scene. Pick a scene from a story with two or more characters to pantomime or dialog can be added. Simple plot outlines may be suggested. For example, "Let's see the scene when Miss Muffet gets together all the things she needs to eat and then finally sits down on her tuffet." Use coaching as needed (e.g., "And then she had to find something to carry it all in"). Remind students to use start and stop signals for scenes. *Variation:* Give groups a scene to plan. Each group presents a different scene from the beginning, middle, or end of a story. Provide rehearsal time.

Narrative Pantomime. In narrative pantomime, someone reads or tells a story with lots of action as others mime. Narrative pantomime gives security to students because it is teacher directed and usually based on familiar material. Narrative pantomime can also introduce basic story structure (beginning, middle, end) and literary elements (plot, setting, characters, conflict, resolution).

Many children's stories can be used for narrative pantomime with slight modification. Just by casting the story in the second person, "you," children feel more like the character. Select stories with much action, a clear climax, and quiet ending. Stories of journeys, trips, or cycles of events (e.g., caterpillar turning into a butterfly or "day in the life of . . ." structures) work well. Van Allsburg's *The Z Was Zapped*, Van Laan's *Possum Come a-Knockin'*, Berger's *Grandfather Twilight*, Keat's *A Snowy Day*, and Chaconas' *The Way the Tiger Walked* are stories that need only minor changes to be used for narrative pantomime. Post It Page 7–5 provides an annotated bibliography of children's literature for narrative pantomime, and there are more in the bibliography in the appendix.

Edit stories for pantomime by eliminating dialog and extraneous description. Action can be added by expanding a line of description (e.g., instead of reading "It was a hot hazy day" change to "You wipe your brow and squint as you look across the hazy horizon"). In some stories there is a repeated sound, word, or a refrain that is hard to resist, so verbal activity can be added. For example, in Robert Munsch's *Thomas' Snowsuit* there is plenty of action, plus the repetition of the word, "No!" A pause for students to add the word in unison adds spice to this book, which can be converted to a solo narrative pantomime that all students do in unison. For chapter books or long stories, isolate one event to mime. For example, do a chapter in *Junie B. Jones and the Stupid Smelly Bus* (Park, 1992) and convert it to "you" while reading, rather than use the first person.

Narrative pantomimes can be written by the teacher or students. Good stories have a beginning, middle, end structure and conflict or tension increases interest. Just as with literature selection, beware of too much description and literary devices such as flashback. Be sure to keep events in order because it is difficult to mime a nonsequential narrative such as "You wake up. You get up and brush your teeth. First you turn on the water and then you put paste on your toothbrush." Use the BEST dance elements in Chapter 9 to put variety into the actions of a story.

When introducing a story for narrative pantomime, read the story through first, asking students to listen for actions as well as to enjoy the story. During the pantomime, the reader needs to read expressively and give the class time to mime. If time is short, students can mime a story they haven't heard, but make sure to anticipate problems.

Props, costumes, and scenery are not necessary, which is an advantage for teachers concerned about time. Imagination can supply all that is needed, along with music, if students are excited about developing the pantomimes further. In addition, teachers and students can make creative additions of characters or actions for group narrative pantomimes through imagining others who might enter the story. There is an example of a narrative pantomime written by a teacher in the lesson plan in Post It Page 7–8. Components of habitat were taught in a previous lesson.

Group Stories. *Strega Nona* (dePaola, 1989), *Clown of God* (dePaola, 1986), and *Lentil* (McCloskey, 1978) are examples of children's literature with crowd or group scenes. These stories can be used for narrative pantomime and for easing students into dialog by freezing scenes and asking members to give a one liner about who they are or what they are feeling at the moment. From there students can move into writing dialog for groups.

III. VERBAL STRATEGIES

Improvisation involves creating ideas spontaneously by "thinking on your feet." It can be done using pantomime or, as discussed in this section, using words. Verbal improvisation can be used to review any lesson, to make predictions at a stop point in a lesson, and to encourage in-depth analysis of material. The following strategies are organized from easy to more difficult.

Sound Effects Stories. Students can add simple sound effects with their voices or music (e.g., rhythm instruments) as the teacher reads or tells a story such as *Too Much Noise* (McGovern, 1966) or *Night Noises* (Fox, 1989). Read the story once and ask students what sounds they heard. Plan how and who will make the sounds. Specific groups can be responsible for certain parts with the whole group involved at other points. *Suggestion:* Use an imaginary volume-control knob and practice controlling loudness before doing the story.

Sound Stories. Find or write a story or poem that contains repeated words (e.g., character names) (Heinig, 1993). Each time the repeated word is read aloud, students do actions or sounds. To prepare for the reading, have students practice the sounds or actions that go with each cue word. For example, Jack = "oops" and sad face, Jill = giggle and play with curl. Many stories and poems are set up to use sounds, e.g.,

"Laughing Time" in William Jay's book by the same title, has animal names to elicit a variety of laughs such as hee-hee, ho-ho, hee-haw. McGovern's book, *Too Much Noise*, and Murphy's *Peace at Last* are other good ones. *Variation:* Select stories with refrains or repeated lines that students can contribute (e.g., Viorst's *Alexander and the Terrible, Horrible, No Good, Very Bad Day*, Peck's *Hamilton*, and Hutchins' *Don't Forget the Bacon*). There is an example sound story in Post It Page 8–2.

Volume Control. Group brainstorms sound categories (e.g., short vowels, city sounds, kitchen sounds). IT stands in front, calls a sound category for the group to make, and can "turn up" the volume by moving closer or "turn it down" by backing up. This can be done in pairs.

Don't Laugh at the Cop. Form groups of six. One is the cop, who points at someone and asks a question. Person *to the right of person questioned* must answer. Everyone tries not to laugh. Go fast.

Pair Sound Effects. Partners choose to be A or B. A makes sounds and B must try to coordinate actions with A's sounds. *Variation:* A's sounds could be coordinated with B's actions.

One Liners (with Props and Pictures). Students use their voices (volume, rate, tone, pitch, pause, stress, and emphasis) to become a character and respond to a picture or object. If a picture is used, students may choose to become characters or objects in it. If an object is used, students choose to be a person who would use the object. Each student says a related one liner. Others guess their identity and tell how the actor let the audience know who she or he was. For example, pass around a red cape after reading *Little Red Riding Hood* and each uses the cape and says a line to reveal who she or he is. *Variation:* Conflicting messages: Say a one liner differently from what the words seem to convey (e.g., "I am happy" said with great sadness). *Note:* Collect interesting pictures and unusual props for one liners. See Chapter 4 for art integration for picture file categories.

POST IT PAGE 8–2

SOUND STORY EXAMPLE

"Stolen Tarts"

Directions: Rehearse the sounds and actions the audience is to contribute before beginning. Pause after underlined words to give students time to respond.

    Heart: thump thump on chest with fist
    Queen: "Oh me!" and throw up hands
    King: "Find him!" and point finger
    Knave: "Tee hee!" while smiling and shaking head
    Tarts: "Yum" and rub tummy

Long ago in the Land of <u>Hearts</u> there was a terrible theft. It was on St. Valentine's Day that the <u>Queen</u> of <u>Hearts</u> baked some <u>tarts</u> to celebrate their national holiday. She had baked raspberry, lemon, and custard <u>tarts</u> as a gift for the man to whom she had given her <u>heart</u>—the <u>King</u> of <u>Hearts</u>. The <u>Queen</u> placed her <u>tarts</u> on the window sill to cool. While the <u>Queen</u> straightened up the royal kitchen, the <u>Knave</u> of <u>Hearts</u> sneaked up to the window. The <u>Knave</u> grabbed all the raspberry <u>tarts</u>. When the <u>Queen</u> saw the <u>tarts</u> were gone, she cried, "What <u>heart</u>less fellow has taken my <u>tarts</u>?"

    The <u>Queen</u> of <u>Hearts</u> went to the <u>King</u> of <u>Hearts</u> for help. Quickly he dispatched his soldiers to find the thief and the missing <u>tarts</u>, saying, "Find him!"

    It wasn't anytime before the soldiers returned with the <u>Knave</u> and what was left of the raspberry <u>tarts</u>. The <u>King</u> ordered that the <u>Knave</u> have no <u>tarts</u> to eat for a whole year. The <u>Knave</u> of <u>Hearts</u> knelt before the <u>Queen</u>, asked for forgiveness, and crossed his <u>heart</u> in promise he would never steal her <u>tarts</u> again. It was a <u>heart</u>warming ending.

Say It Your Way Sentences. Students say a sentence as a character in a role or in a mood. Others try to guess their identity. Students can be given roles by putting choices on cards for them to draw and should rehearse reading the sentence many ways (e.g., in a role, or a mood, angry, sad). Different words can be emphasized to change meanings: *Who* is my friend? Who *is* my friend? Who is *my* friend? Who is my *friend?* Here are example sentences:

> I don't like his attitude.
>
> I will pay the bill if you take a check.
>
> We had a good time at the party.
>
> Can I have another helping of dessert?
>
> Everyone just left.
>
> How much money have you got?
>
> She has an awful headache.
>
> We only have five left.
>
> Remember to check each answer.
>
> He's one person I won't do business with.
>
> Where do you think you are going?
>
> Who did you meet?
>
> Where are you going?
>
> Close the door.

Sentence Frames. Each person orally completes this sentence frame: "I am . . . and I want. . . ." The goal is to not give their names but roles they play in life and their life goals. Go around the group and have each person say the frame. The rest of the group can then echo, "She is . . . and she wants. . . ." This exercise can focus on the use of vocal elements of volume, rate, pause, pitch, stress, and emphasis in the echo. *Variation:* Be a book character or famous person. See more **sentence frames** under Reading and Language Arts in Chapter 4.

QU (Cue–You) Reading. Sequence readings can be made from a variety of literature, poetry, or subject matter. Jokes and riddles are perfect because of the reader–response or question–answer format. Prepare a set of cards that each have a Q (*cue*) statement and a U (*you*) statement. Students rehearse their U (can be highlighted) with as much expression as possible, and study the Q (the listen for). For example, *Q = Mary had a little lamb. U = Its fleece was white as snow.* The teacher should prepare a master copy until students become adept at listening for cues. *Suggestion:* Photocopy the original and cut it apart, rather than make

separate cards. Try adapting stories such as *If You Give a Mouse a Cookie, Pierre: A Cautionary Tale,* or *The True Story of the Three Little Pigs by A. Wolf.* Poetry written in the first person, like Silverstein's "Sick," also works well. See Post It Page 8–3.

Conflicting Motives. Ask for two volunteers. One leaves the room and the remaining one is given a motive (e.g., to have partner sit down). Other partner is secretly told a conflicting motive (e.g., to not sit down but to get partner to do so). Both partners are brought back and they improvise a scene. Neither partner can verbally give away his or her motive. *Suggestion:* Brainstorm a list of possible motives (e.g., to sell, heal, forgive, eat, make money to give, get, or win, grow, surprise).

Dialog Cards. Collect words, phrases, sentences, and headlines from magazines, newspapers, or even greeting cards. Ads are a good source. Paste each on a card. Give each student a card face down. Pair students and tell them to choose to be A or B. Turn over cards and A begins the dialog using his card. B must respond and incorporate his or her card. *Variation 1:* Do a chain activity. Everyone lines up and (1) just reads card expressively or (2) goes in order but improvises verbal response that connects to previous person by using what is on your card. *Variation 2:* Separate question and answer cards (make sure there is an equal number of each). Distribute randomly. Number questioners, who then read in numerical order. Whoever believes they can answer using their card has a go at it.

Emotion Conversation. Two people or characters start a conversation. Add freeze point and have audience tell the emotions of the characters. Then continue the conversation. *Variation:* Freeze and audience suggests a new emotion that characters must assume when they start again (e.g., angry, surprised, elated).

Character Monologs. Be a character and make an announcement, a wish, and the like. See Post It Page 4–2.

Car Wash. Make two facing lines. Two end people walk between the lines. As they pass, people say positive things to them. Then the next two go and so forth. *Variation:* Everyone prepares a one liner about a topic or in a role and shares in the same manner. For example, everyone thinks of good things about the dog in *Officer Buckles and Gloria.* Stop at the point where Officer Buckles feels like a fool. Walkers become Officer Buckles and pass through the car wash hearing the "voices" about his friend.

POST IT PAGE 8–3

Post It

Example QU Sequence Reading

Directions: Cut apart QU (cue-you) statements for each person or group. Distribute and give rehearsal time. The leader starts by reading the first Q. A person with U reads next, and it continues as readers hear their cues.

Q: Bellini's story.

U: I was a man in hiding—hiding from myself.

Q: I was a man in hiding—hiding from myself.

U: I just needed to rest.

Q: I just needed to rest.

U: Gateau's boardinghouse on English Street seemed as good a place as any.

Q: Gateau's boardinghouse on English Street seemed as good a place as any.

U: I did worry about the other guests seeing me.

Q: I did worry about the other guests seeing me.

U: It never occurred to me that I was being watched by much brighter eyes.

Q: It never occurred to me that I was being watched by much brighter eyes.

U: Mirette! the spunky redheaded daughter of Madame! Mais oui!

Q: Mirette! the spunky redheaded daughter of Madame! Mais oui!

U: She was not to be denied once the enchantment of the wire overtook her.

Q: She was not to be denied once the enchantment of the wire overtook her.

U: I saw her take her falls. I thought she'd give up.

Q: I saw her take her falls. I thought she'd give up.

U: But Mirette had the courage a young heart and a new dream give.

Q: But Mirette had the courage a young heart and a new dream give.

U: I did not want to be her teacher because I did not want her to discover my secret.

Q: I did not want to be her teacher because I did not want her to discover my secret.

U: I recognized the agent when he checked in.

Q: I recognized the agent when he checked in.

U: It was inevitable Mirette would learn my hidden fear.

Q: It was inevitable Mirette would learn my hidden fear.

U: Mirette's belief in me was greater than my fear of myself.

Q: Mirette's belief in me was greater than my fear of myself.

U: I bought the length of hemp and went to work. I worked automatically preparing for the walk.

Q: I bought the length of hemp and went to work. I worked automatically preparing for the walk.

U: But I could not move when I felt the wire touch my feet.

Q: But I could not move when I felt the wire touch my feet.

U: That child's face shattered the cage around my heart. Dear Mirette.

Q: That child's face shattered the cage around my heart. Dear Mirette.

U: Bravo for the children! They make us remember what it means to be alive.

Source: Based on *Mirette on the High Wire* (McCully, 1992).

Television Shows. Adapt past and current game and talk shows for classroom use: *I've Got a Secret, Jeopardy, Wheel of Fortune, Concentration, Password, Oprah,* or *Phil Donahue.* The show adaptations work best after a unit of study (e.g., the Oprah format on endangered species).

Discussions. A discussion becomes a dramatic encounter when students take on roles during the discussion (e.g., characters, famous persons, objects). Use the generic literature discussion questions in Post It Page 3–9, as well as suggestions for questioning on post it pages throughout the book, for drama experiences. Students can also brainstorm in the role. See Chapter 1 for guidelines.

Empathy Roles. Each student takes the role of a character in a story or book everyone knows. The teacher begins a discussion or interview with an open question concerning a key moment, problem, or question about a theme. It works best if the discussion is focused on an important question (e.g., moral dilemma). Each child enters the discussion in character and remains in character throughout the discussion. If some don't participate, the teacher can specifically call on them for their ideas. For example, "We're here to discuss the issue of advertising in the newspaper for a husband or a wife. I'd like to find out what the group is thinking about this. Please introduce yourself and give your opinion" (based on *Sarah, Plain and Tall*). See Post It Page 3–9. *Variation:* Students write down who they are, what they want, and how they act and feel.

Character Panels. Everyone is the same character and presents views on a topic. The audience can question the panel. *Variation:* Take the roles of consultants or advisers on a topic. For science or social studies students can do research to become experts who will then serve on a panel.

The Chair. This is an improvisation in which a volunteer sits in a chair. Another volunteer assumes a role and begins a conversation with the person in the chair. The seated person must figure out who the other character is and respond accordingly. For example, volunteer is a mother and the one in chair must figure out that she is the daughter. This is easily adaptable for literature, social studies, and science.

Back-to-Back Improvisation. Pairs each decide on who they are (take the role of a book character, an occupation, or family role). On signal, they face each other and the first to talk sets the situation. The second person must figure out who his partner is and respond in an appropriate role.

Traffic Jam. Students are in small groups. The place is a traffic jam in which all movement has stopped. They are to think about who they are, what problems they are having, and how they feel. Each person can then be spotlighted to do a monolog or one liner that will reveal their characters. *Variation:* Do the same with waiting in a grocery store line or any public waiting place. Students can be book characters, persons from paintings, scientists, historical figures, and the like.

Interviews. Teacher assumes the role of interviewer and students take a character role. Students are questioned, in talk show style, and use voice and body to convey who they are. This can be done in pairs with one being the interviewer. For example, the teacher is a radio talk show host interviewing characters in (1) *Charlotte's Web* right after the first word appears in the web, (2) Arnold Lobel's fable "The Mouse at the Seashore": cat, bird, and dog are panel members, or (3) unpopular book characters, such as Templeton, who present a point of view. If a panel is used, they can be questioned by the class, who can also be in a role (e.g., mother mouse, news reporter). *Note:* It's a good idea for interviewers to introduce themselves (e.g., "I am . . . and I want to know. . ."). The teacher can coach students or play a role. *Variations:* Audience can interview tableau members. Touch each with a magic wand to come alive to speak. (See tableau pantomime strategy.) Use microphone prop.

Show Time. This is a review drama for after a unit of study. Groups write and present commercials, news updates, songs, and the like to present important information from a unit. Limit time to 3 to 5 minutes. For example:

> *Newsbreak. We interrupt this program to let you know that animals have now been found to have four components in their habitats. Without water, shelter, food, and adequate space, animals cannot survive. We learned today that habitats are shrinking and our world may soon lose valued animal populations. More on this breaking story on News at Six.*
>
> *Commercial Break. High bad cholesterol? Stressed? Negative attitude? Lethargic? You need the Laughter Prescription! With only fifteen laughs a day you can get your minimum daily requirement and be on the road to an energetic happy life. No more insurmountable problems when you learn to laugh your way through life. Call 1-800-JOKE. Variation:*

An item can be advertised (e.g., cotton gin for social studies or a graphing calculator in math). Remind students to include important points and not empty glitz. This provides a good opportunity to teach propaganda devices such as bandwagon or glittering generalities.

Book Ads. Individuals, pairs, or small groups set up a scene with a problem from a book they are advertising to the class. The scene is to end before the problem is solved. It is fun to end each commercial with "If you want to know what happened, you have to get this book." *Variations:* Students can create book commercials with music, slogans, and props to sell books. Limit time to one minute—TV time is expensive!

Debate. Divide class in half and assign each a side in an argument. Give time to plan. At signal, begin debate with a person from each side giving a reason. Alternate back and forth until all reasons have been heard. Rebuttal time can then be given to each side. Teacher can (1) moderate and assume a role (e.g., become a policeman who was called to the scene of the crime in *Little Red Riding Hood*) and (2) comment, question each side, and open it up for audience questions. This drama strategy can be done in pairs, too. For example, one side says Little Red should be taken away from her parents because of negligence, and then the other side takes the opposing position. *Variation:* Do as expert panels (e.g., experts on wolf behavior).

Improvised Scenes. Begin by giving students short scenes to play. Tell students to plan a beginning, middle, and end and signals to start and stop the scene. Emphasize the need to build in tension or conflict through a problem that is resolved by the end. Examples are (1) stepsisters and stepmother in the coach, going to the ball on the second night, worried about mysterious girl who seems to have charmed the prince; and (2) animals who saw the transformations of other animals are talking after Cinderella leaves for the ball. They want to get transformed, too. Eventually, students should begin to think of their own creative scenes. Direct them to focus on the most important moments or emotions in the story. In the case of science or social studies, consider significant events (e.g., when Philo Farnsworth gets the first television picture).

Sources for improvised scenes include children's literature, wordless picture books, and famous last words; use events, processes, and procedures from science, social studies, and math. Focus on "let's suppose" and "what if" (e.g., switch characters, settings,

or circumstances of any story or historical event). Create separate card sets for settings, characters, problems, and props for an infinite number of combinations or *characters, problems,* and *place cards.* For example:

1. Flying frogs. Hungry and lost. In New York City.
2. Hurried shoppers. Grocery. A robbery happens.
3. Family on vacation. Hotel. Stuck in elevator.
4. Hungry mosquitoes. On the beach when Columbus first lands.
5. Five young children. On the porch on a hot summer day. Dad brings out two double popsicles.

Start with discussion questions to develop characters, the setting, plan of action concerning the problem or conflict, and resolution. In other words, students need to be clear about who, where, what problems, what to do or actions, solutions, and resolutions. Eventually, students should be able to discuss in small groups.

Structure scenes with a beginning, middle, and end. Remember, conflict is essential, as is resolution. Make students feel the importance and the tension by giving time limits or telling them to have their characters persuade, argue, obstruct, or bargain. What the characters *want* needs to be emphasized. Use signals to add clear structure (e.g., to begin and end the scene) and music to create mood.

Coach during drama. See coaching ideas under **Teacher Habits** in Chapter 7.

Follow up with a discussion and replay with a twist (e.g., teacher may take a role or students may be engaged in a writing response such as a 5-minute Quickwrite).

Role Play. Role playing involves considering a situation from the viewpoint of another. Because of the added perspective that role playing provides, it can greatly enhance understanding of any subject. In general, teachers use role playing to put students in problem situations so that feelings, values, and viewpoints can be explored. A particular kind of role playing, called sociodrama, focuses on real-world problems of the present and future.

To create a role play:

- Choose problems or topics students know something about.

- Define the specific situation that requires the characters to take some action (e.g., factory owner whose factory is polluting a river and an EPA agent who must enforce the regulations about river pollution are brought together by a government agent).

◆ Give the audience a role (e.g., they can become questioners at a break point or evaluators of the different positions taken).

TAKE ACTION 1

IMPROVISED SCENE SOURCE MATERIAL

Directions: Add to the following lists to create a resource idea bank for scenes. If you have access to students, do it with them.

Characters: lizard, baker, potter, wise woman, fortune teller

Places: island, beach, cave, treehouse, barn, boarding house, jungle

Character conflict ideas: argue, convince, persuade, defend, plot, debate, tease, deny, confess, accuse, beg, forgive, gossip, lie, disagree, demand, complain

Rituals: graduation, inauguration, parade, eulogy, pledge, dinner, award, recognition, wedding, ship christening, ribbon-cutting dedication, nomination, greetings, farewells

Actions: eat, clean, drink, work, bathe, run, cook, swim, dance, drive, throw

Conditions or problems: illness, dark, nervous, hot, cold, embarrassed, odor, anger, stress, excited, hate, pressured, hungry, tired, wet, lost, lonely, noisy

---

TAKE ACTION 2

ADAPT STRATEGIES

Choose a seed idea from energizers, pantomime, or verbal strategies and adapt it for science, math, reading and language arts, or social studies.

◆ Plan an introduction to set up the scene.

◆ Play several times with different groups to get a variety of versions.

◆ Discuss the drama aspects, as well as the content of the scenes.

IV. CONNECTING DRAMA TO OTHER CURRICULAR AREAS

In this section there are examples of pantomime and verbal activities that have been further adapted to show how drama can be used as a teaching tool to enhance academic learning.

Science Focus

◆ Natural world, systems of the body, seasons, weather, plants, animals, the environment, machines, electricity, magnets, space, gravity, and states of matter

◆ Finding out how and why things happen in the world through careful observation, hypothesis making, and prediction

Project Wild. *Project Wild* has hands-on, activity-oriented lesson plans for science. In addition to drama, there are music, art, and literature and creative writing activities related to science. *Project Wild* is available from 5430 Grosvenor Lane, Bethesda, MD, 301-493-5447. *Project Wet* is also available.

Animal Sounds. IT makes the sound of an animal and group must make shapes and moves related to the animal. *Variation:* IT makes sounds from everyday world (e.g., clock ticking or phone ringing) and group must become the sound.

Nature One Liners. Use pictures of natural forms: mountain, tree, stream. Each student says a sentence, in role as the object, to show specific known facts. For example, "I can feel my stalactites growing today" (cave).

Whales Debate. Divide students into two teams to research a side to an environmental issue. For example, "Should whales be hunted?" Each side presents an opening statement and then gives pros or cons in a time limit. After each side presents, give time for rebuttal and a summary statement.

Famous Science Scenes. Break into groups to do tableaux (frozen scenes) of special moments in science, such as Alexander G. Bell's first telephone call, the Wright's flight at Kitty Hawk, or Armstrong's walking on the moon.

Animal Charades. Students brainstorm (after or before a unit) ways to classify animals (wild, domesticated, herbivores, carnivores, insects, mammals, aquatic, land based). Small groups list animals in each category. (Record on a large chart for younger children.) Each student then picks an animal to pantomime. Coach to think of how the animal sleeps, moves, eats, where it lives. Set up pantomimes to be presented in this order: start frozen, move, and then freeze. Teams write animal or category guess on a wipe-off board and display on a signal. The mime confirms correct guesses. Emphasize science content by asking *why* the animal belongs in a category. To emphasize the drama aspect, ask students to give feedback on what the mime did to make them believe in the animal. *Variation:* Limit categories to two for less mature learners. Do with other categories in science: land forms, states of water. Mimes can be planned and presented in small groups, too.

Watch, Then Nature Mime. Take time to observe mammals, insects, or fish on a video or in real life. Discuss observations about how they moved and why (e.g., to get food, to avoid predators). If animals are in groups, ask how they are organized. Student groups then decide what they will pantomime, based on observations. Give time to rehearse how to best show what was observed individually or in groups. Present the pantomimes to the whole group. Audience describes what they see, not just guesses.

Special Props. Challenge students to use simple props to really feel as animals do. For example, try to actually eat rice with your mouth as birds do or try to drink like a cat or dog from a tub of water. What could students use to get the feel of snakes shedding their skins or birds in a nest?

Animal Panels. Groups choose an animal to research. Each group forms a panel, all in the role of their animal, and tells about themselves. Audience questions them about their lives, problems, and the like.

Social Studies Focus

◆ Relationships among human beings, occupations, transportation, communities, governments, customs, cultures, holidays, and use of natural resources

◆ History, geography (use of maps), civics (citizenship and government) or political science, economics, anthropology, and sociology

◆ Investigations into cultural diversity and global understanding

◆ Special questions: How did it used to be and why? Why is it like it is today? What can I do about it? Thinking processes: cause and effect, sequence, gather data, discover relationships, make judgments, draw conclusions, and problem solve about community issues, for example, economic issues such as school funding or value conflicts related to free speech

◆ Use of primary source material such as newspapers, art, music, diaries, letters, journals, books, and artifacts, rather than use of textbooks, and gathering data through interviews, surveys, and other investigatory strategies that historians and other social scientists use

Moral Dilemmas (Use with Historical Fiction or Biography). Everyone stops reading at a point where a character has to make a decision. Groups talk about the dilemma and use the information from the story to make decisions in the role of the character. Groups reassemble to tell or dramatize what was decided. *Note:* The dilemma should *not* have a clear right answer so that students are forced to take a stand. For example, Avi's *Night Journeys* has many points where a stop would be appropriate.

Stop when the problem has been found in the story. Then:

1. Figure out the problem:
   ◆ What is it?
   ◆ Who has the problem?
   ◆ What are the general circumstances of the problem?
   ◆ What is the goal for solving the problem?
2. Brainstorm problem solutions:
   ◆ What possibilities are there that would be legal and safe for all?
   ◆ What is the best solution (consider cost, safety, length of time, legal, moral, and practical issues)?
3. Try out the solution:
   ◆ Role play . . . did the problem get solved?
   ◆ What does this say to you for the future?

4. Read the rest of the story and compare your solution with the one in the book (based on the work of Lawrence Kohlberg and adapted from Johnson & Louis, 1987).

Portrait Conversations. Pair students and have them create a conversation between two portraits of famous historical figures that might hang side by side in a gallery. Look closely to examine the works for clues about time period, values, cultural aspects, message, and the like that would give ideas for dialog. These can be written or oral.

Famous People Portraits. Use portraits of famous figures. Students can become persons in the art and talk about the times, values, economics, and customs.

What's My Line? Based on the television show from the 1950s, this game focuses on finding out the occupations or careers of panel members. Panel members can all be the same occupation or have the same role (e.g., all might be signers of the Declaration of Independence). The audience can only ask yes or no questions and is given a time limit or a limit to number of questions (e.g., 5 minutes or 20 questions). The teacher acts as moderator and allows audience members to take turns questioning. To deal with monopolizers, use the rule that if the panel answers *no* someone else takes a turn to question.

Biography Drama. Students read a biography and find actions they can pantomime, special events, an important scene, and special lines of dialog. For example, improvise dialog for the scene leading up to Patrick Henry saying "Give me liberty or give me death." Find the actual words the person used and conflicting positions the person took (e.g., Jefferson owned slaves).

Reading and Language Arts Focus

◆ Reading, listening, speaking, written composition (including handwriting and spelling, grammar, usage, capitalization, and punctuation); since reading and language arts are processes, they must be connected to a subject to have meaning, that is, something to read and write about.

◆ Goal: *Create* meaning and enjoyment using print through thinking at every level, from memory to critical thinking or evaluation.

◆ The printed word and its components (letters, syllables, spelling, patterns), how words combine to make phrases and sentences and sentences combine to make paragraphs and other forms of discourse, from tongue twisters to novels.

◆ Types of words: antonyms and synonyms, parts of speech and figurative language (metaphor, idiomatic expressions).

Theater and drama are language rich and actively engage students in language use and other communication skills, for example, nonverbal communication. Students involved in theater and drama spend time writing scripts, reading and learning lines, and doing research on characters and settings. Most drama involves the language arts of listening, speaking, reading, or writing, and nearly all pantomime and verbal strategies can be adapted for language-based lessons.

Emotional Vowels. Form a circle. IT goes in the center and chooses an emotion or feeling. IT then expresses the emotion, but can only make a vowel sound (A, E, I, O, or U). (Teacher can designate short vowels, long, etc.) Group listens and tries to echo perfectly. Students can then signal if they know the emotion and vowel sound. IT calls on people until a correct answer is found and that person becomes IT.

Pretend and Write: Journals. Students assume the role of a character and keep a daily journal. The point is not to write about what really happened in the character's life, but about what could have happened, as well as about feelings. In the case of historical fiction or biography, students can extend the journal's authenticity by doing research on characters. *Variation:* For chapter books, students make entries after each chapter to document how a character's thoughts and emotions change through experiences. Students can pair up and read each other's journals to get different perspectives.

Pretend and Write: Letters. This strategy focuses on using conventional letter-writing form, the writing process, grammar, and spelling. Students take a role of a character and write a friendly or business letter and choose to write to another character or real person, so the contents and purposes vary.

Point of View Roles. Students are given a role of a character in a story. They then read the story and answer questions in the role in writing or orally, for example, *Mirette on the High Wire* (McCully, 1992).

Imagine that you are a touring artist staying at the rooming house. Answer these questions (before the high wire act at the end):

1. What have you noticed about the man? How does he make you feel?
2. What do you think about his friendship with Mirette?
3. Why do you think he stays to himself so much?

Reader's Theater. Reader's Theater (RT) is "theater of the mind" and is like a radio play. Readers sit or stand while doing oral interpretive reading from a script and try to create the illusion of dramatic action in the minds of the audience. The focus is on using the voice; props are usually not employed. RT is particularly suitable for intermediate students, but can be adapted for younger children by choosing shorter scripts and reading to them as they follow along on the first go-through. Poems can also be used. For example, see Wolf's *It's Show Time!: Poetry from the Page to the Stage* (poem scripts).

Reader's Theater is an appropriate use of oral reading because it is audience oriented and students practice for the presentation versus cold round-robin reading deemed detrimental to children. Other values of RT are that (1) it integrates listening, speaking, and reading and can include writing by involving students in creating their own scripts. They can begin by adapting pieces of literature and move on to writing original pieces. Biographical information such as letters, diaries, or speeches can also be adapted to script form; (2) because of the ensemble or group project nature of RT, cooperation and other social skills are developed; (3) when readers assume roles of characters they have a chance to empathize and identify with a variety of feelings and viewpoints, which can yield valuable insights about people and the world; (4) self-confidence is increased as students share exciting stories with the support of a script—no lines are memorized. *To use Reader's Theater:*

◆ *Find or create scripts* appropriate to students' interests and abilities. Several companies publish scripts, and basal readers often contain stories converted to script form. See the bibliography. The Institute for Readers Theatre in California also has a script service. See the bookstore list of more than 40 titles at the website *www.amazon.com* (everything from holiday scripts to fractured folktale scripts).

◆ *The script can be read to students* for the first reading, read silently by students, or orally read by students in small groups.

◆ *Groups are formed* according to the characters outlined in the scripts. Groups can prepare different scripts or perform the same script and then discuss their different interpretations.

◆ *Students need time to rehearse their parts.* Emphasize the need to use volume, rate, tone and pitch, pause, and stress and emphasis to convey meaning. Students can highlight their parts and mark words to stress. Nonverbal communication with the face, some gestures, and even body posture can be added—the focus still remains on oral interpretation, however.

◆ *When students do their presentations,* they need to have their scripts in folders or binders so that they can hold them without distracting the audience with page turning. Students may sit on high stools or stand. By using stools of varying heights, character relationships can be suggested.

◆ *When setting up the staging,* it can be effective to have readers start with their backs to the audience and then turn around as each part is introduced. Characters with major roles might stand to the far left and right, if they don't need to interact with one another. Characters with similar ideas might be grouped together. With younger students it may help the audience to use hatbands or name tags on the characters. Lights can be used to signal scenes.

◆ *The point of Reader's Theater is not to create a "spectacle,"* but students may shift position on stage (e.g., to indicate joining a group). Readers may stand when they speak and then sit, or spotlights might be used. Props should be used, only if essential, because it is awkward to handle a script and a prop. Sound effects and music can also be added. Be open to students' creative ideas.

◆ *It is desirable for the narrator to make eye contact with the audience.* Other characters may look up when not reading or when they can during reading.

◆ *Make sure the audience is aware of its important role* in being active listeners. Review appropriate audience responses before the presentations. After the presentations, invite readers and audience members to discuss what worked, what they learned, what they noticed about the use of voice to establish character, what the most important parts were, and so forth.

◆ *Follow up presentations* with invitations for students to write different script endings, trade scripts with other groups, videotape, or even perform for other groups (e.g., a touring troupe to visit other classes) (Georges & Cornett, 1986).

There is an example Reader's Theater script, converted from an old tale, in Post It Page 8–4.

Antonym Pantomimes. Make a set of cards with two antonyms on each card. A student draws a card and pantomimes one word. The audience must guess the opposite. This can be done in small groups with a set of cards for each group. *Suggestion:* Instead of students calling out guesses, all should wait until the pantomime is done, write out a guess, and, on signal, hold it up. *Variation:* Do with synonyms, homonyms, and homophones.

POST IT PAGE 8–4

EXAMPLE READER'S THEATER SCRIPT

Cast: Narrator, Girl, Old Man

Narrator: A girl once went to the fair to hire herself out as a servant. A funny looking old gentleman finally agreed to engage her and took her home to his house. When she got there, he said he had some things to teach her, for in his house he had his own names for things.

Old Man: What will you call me?

Girl: Why master, or mister, or whatever else you please, sir.

Old Man: No, you must call me "master of all masters." And what would you call this?

Narrator: The old man pointed to his bed.

Girl: Why bed or couch, or whatever you please, sir.

Old Man: No, that's my "barnacle." And what do you call those?

Narrator: He pointed to his pantaloons.

Girl: By breeches, or trousers, or whatever else you please, sir.

Old Man: No, you must call them "squibs and crackers." And what do you call her?

Narrator: The old man pointed at his cat.

Girl: Cat or kit, or whatever you please, sir.

Old Man: No, you must call her "white-faced simminy." And now this, what would you call this?

Girl: Fire or flame, or whatever you please, sir.

Old Man: No, no. You must call it "hot cockalorum." And what is this?

Narrator: He went on, pointing to the water.

Girl: Water or wet, or whatever you please, sir.

Old Man: No, "pondalorum" is its name. And what do you call this?

Narrator: Asked the man as he pointed to his house.

Girl: House or cottage, or whatever you please, sir.

Old Man: You must call it "high topper mountain."

Narrator: That very night the servant girl woke her master up in a fright.

Girl: Master of all masters, get out of your barnacle and put on your squibs and crackers. For white-faced simminy has got a spark of hot cockalorum on his tail, and unless you get some pondalorum, high topper mountain will be all on hot cockalorum!

Source: Adapted from the English folktale "Master of All Masters" (Weil, 1973).

Daffynitions. Teams of four to five students find or are given unusual vocabulary. Each team member writes a definition for the word, but only *one* member writes the correct definition. (Students can use the dictionary.) Each team stands and orally reads their definitions, trying to convince the audience that each of them has the correct one. Audience applauds to vote on which they believe is correct. *Variation:* Use objects instead of words.

Rhyme Change. Nursery rhymes and other chants and poems are adaptable to word play activities that serve as verbal warm-ups and stimulate creative thinking. Here is an example: "Hickory Dickory Dock, A mouse ran up my . . ." (students supply rhyme). You can do all the vowel sounds for phonemic awareness development: Hickory Dickory Dack, Hickory Dickory Deck, and so forth.

Spelling Drama. Pantomime the letters or something that starts with each letter in a word. For example; CAT = *cup* plus *apple* plus *typing*.

Pretend and Write. Either assign students roles or let them choose a role from a piece of literature, song, or painting. They are then to write in role (see Post It Page 4–2; e.g., letters, wills, chants, lists). An example is to choose to be one of the family members (Anna, Caleb, or Jacob) in *Sarah, Plain and Tall* (after Chapter 2). Write a letter to Sarah introducing yourself and asking her questions. Students then switch letters and become Sarah to write a reply. *Variation:* Do this as a guessing game. Don't sign the letters and be sure to discuss clues to give about who you are, without coming right out and saying your name or family role.

Pretend and Write: Dear Abby. Show examples of the newspaper column "Dear Abby." Students then write a "Dear Abby" letter using a problem from a piece of literature. Partners then exchange and, in the role of Abby, write a reply. For example (after the first chapter of *Sarah, Plain and Tall*),

> *Dear Abby,*
>
> *My father is a widower and I think he really needs a wife. My brother and I also need a mother. What should we do? Worried daughter*

> *Dear Worried Daughter,*
>
> *Why don't you talk to your dad about how you feel? Be honest. This will let him know you think it is okay to look around. Your friend, Abby*

Math Focus

- Daily living situations involving counting, measuring, probability, statistics, geometry, logic, patterns, functions, and numbers

- Problem solving through the use of skills (raising questions and answering them, finding relationships and patterns)

- Concepts about numbers, operations, and concepts such as bigger, longer, greater than, less, three, four, even, and odd

- The National Council of the Teachers of Mathematics encourages teachers to have children solve problems in many ways, focusing on explaining and thinking, rather than just correctness, and using a hands-on approach.

Fraction Mime. After introducing fractions, use an open space to have the whole group practice dividing themselves up to solve problems that are given: Divide in half, fourths, thirds. When numbers are uneven, ask how this can be shown.

Break It Down. Give pairs an "answer." They plan how to mime combinations to show the "answer." For example, 36 5 9 3 4 or 3 3 10 1 6 or 6 3 6.

Talking Math. Children choose to become a math concept. They form expert panels to present themselves, and the audience can question them using the five Ws and H questions (e.g., panel of squares or the number 1).

Math Commercials. Students prepare ads to sell particular math concepts and skills: fractions, time, division. The goal is to convince the audience they need this math item.

Math Improvisation. Make a set of cards with math-related situations. Give each group three cards. They plan a scene using ideas on all three cards. Scenes should have a beginning, middle, and end. Example cards are (1) 3 men, (2) a quart of milk, and (3) a 10-story building on fire.

V. STORYTELLING'S SPECIAL RELATIONSHIP WITH DRAMA

You are the vessel for the tale.

Heather Forrest, storyteller

There once was a rabbi who was a gifted storyteller. Everyone who heard his stories felt the rabbi gave the story just to him. So special were the stories one man finally asked the rabbi, "How is it we all hear the same story but you touch each of our individual hearts?"

In response, the rabbi told a story of a girl who shot arrows. Wherever an arrow stuck, she pulled it out and painted a bright bull's eye around it. "It is you that paints the target around these stories," the rabbi said, "inviting them into your heart." (Collins, 1994)

The first written accounts of storytelling are thousands of years old. Four thousand years ago the sons of the Great Pyramid builder, Cheops, told stories to him that were preserved on papyri. Storyteller Rives Collins believes human beings are the "storytelling animals" and that storytelling is a natural and common human activity. Across cultures, people love to tell and listen to stories. The griots of Africa tell stories, as do the Irish shanachies and the Navajo shaman. The bards of medieval Europe, norse skalds, German minnesingers, and French troubadours all are storytellers who preserve our history and educate, enlighten, and enliven our lives. We tell stories to ourselves and each other. *"How was your day?" "What did you do at school?" "What do you think will happen?"* We tell stories to prepare and reassure ourselves. We invent fantasy stories to amuse others, to make sense of the world, and to build relationships.

Drama and storytelling share many of the same characteristics. Perhaps, most importantly, they both rely on conflict to develop characters and plot and reveal themes. To be a storyteller is to take on a role, to use your voice, face, and body to communicate. In essence, storytelling is a dramatic vehicle. It was Winifred Ward's course in storytelling in the 1920s that led to the evolution of creative drama. Storytelling was at the center of her work in which she created drama opportunities for children based on stories. "[S]torytelling [is] at the roots of drama/theatre education . . ." (Collins, 1997, p. 6).

Why Storytelling?

If teachers should succeed in developing the state of mind that would cause the pupils to go to the printed page as they would go to the feet of one who has a story to tell, we should be willing to ask nothing else of them as a results of all their teaching.
S. H. Clark,
How to Teach Reading in the Public Schools, 1899

We put much store in the power of stories. From biblical parables, to creation myths and tall tales, stories engage us as no other words can. For example, someone commenting, "We learn from our mistakes"

has a very different impact than hearing this story with a similar theme:

A young man who wished to be wise went to a sage high on the mountain.

"How can I become wise?" the young man asked respectfully.

The old man looked thoughtful and replied, "Have wisdom."

"But how do I get wisdom?" asked the young man.

"Develop good judgment," the sage answered.

"But how can I get good judgment?" the young man cried.

"Experience," said the sage wisely.

"And how do I get experience?" said the young man in frustration.

"Bad judgment," said the sage.

Storytelling Is Valuable Because It . . .

◈ Brings us together. It introduces listeners to an array of cultures, including relevant symbols and traditions.

◈ Exposes listeners to fine literature. Many tales are too difficult for children to read independently, but are appropriate for their interest and cognitive levels.

◈ Whets the appetite for further literary experiences because it creates an interest in reading and writing.

◈ Gives listeners characters with whom they can identify.

◈ Creates a special bond between listeners and tellers. Reading aloud and storytelling are very different experiences mainly because storytelling seems much more intimate.

◈ Develops listening and speaking vocabularies by sensitizing children to language from diverse sources.

◈ Improves listening comprehension, which is the foundation for reading comprehension.

◈ Stimulates interest in creative writing and other creative activities.

◈ Helps the listener learn in a way that doesn't feel like a "taught" lesson. Everyone loves to learn, but we resist didactic teaching.

◈ Helps the listener to better understand life, to try to make sense of conflict and see that there are patterns, for example, the relationship between good and evil.

- Provides information, opinions, new perspectives, and knowledge.
- Increases oral communication skills, especially when listeners become tellers.
- Is a holistic activity involving both thinking and feeling.
- Encourages higher-order thinking skills such as prediction, analysis, synthesis, and evaluation.
- Stimulates creative problem solving and decision making.
- Stimulates the use of the imagination and imagery.
- Is powerful entertainment.

Where can you get good stories to tell? There are plenty available, and there are even stories about stories, such as this African Anansi tale: "After playing many tricks on them, the trickster, Anansi, got the box of stories from the sky people. He threw open the lid and the stories flew out. Some of them he grabbed and put in his pocket. The others flew to the four corners of the earth."

Post It Page 8–5 is Pointers for Storytellers and 8–6 is an Example Story Plot Skeleton. Use these to find stories, learn to tell them, and involve students in storytelling.

POINTERS FOR STORYTELLERS

POST IT PAGE 8–5

Like love, knowledge, and fairy dust, stories are best when shared. From *The Woman Who Flummoxed the Fairies*

Choose Stories

- You like, ones you care about and are important to you—ones you feel compelled to tell—we are the stories we tell.
- That appeal to the better part of our natures, for example, ones about courage, love, laughter—ones that stimulate our emotions and leave the audience enriched.
- That reveal an aspect of the human condition.
- That evoke emotions.
- That fit your personality.
- That have the force of language—words that evoke images, are beautiful, and specific.
- That are fair to the cultures they came from.
- That are appropriate for the audience that will hear them. Consider your audience—age, stage, time, place, occasion, interests.
- That have a strong beginning and a satisfying ending. Try to end with a "punch."
- That are short; work up to longer ones.

Note: Plan to read 10 to find 1 that suits you.

Know the Story

- Be prepared. Visualize each event and character in relation to the story climax. Rerun the story in your mind's eye like it is a movie.
- Learn to use a whole-to-part process in which you read or listen to the whole story several times before beginning to learn the parts.
- Learn the plot first. Focus on getting a clear sequence of images and events, that is, the story line. Don't memorize the story. Stories have a general structure that answers the questions who? what? where? why? and how? Organize events into beginning, middle, and end to help your thinking. Some tellers make a plot

skeleton using a map, chart, notecards for events, or an outline. Storyteller Heather Forrest uses a series of connected circles she calls "steppingstones." Another option is to make a series of stick cartoon drawings of plot events as a rehearsal device. See Post It Page 8–6.

◆ Memorize your opening and your ending to give yourself a frame in which to work. Also memorize any special phrases or refrains. The rest of the story should be rehearsed but not memorized. Just as we use improvisation to give directions, engage in conversation, or give excuses, storytelling relies on improvisation. This gives each telling a spontaneity.

◆ Practice telling the story out loud. Use a tape recorder. Listen to yourself. Tell it to the mirror. Videotape. Practice telling it to a friend and then to a group. A story becomes your own the more times you tell it to others.

◆ Try exaggerating gestures and the use of voice during practice to extend yourself. For example, open your mouth and increase volume, show the "back row" your gestures, go into great detail, count to five during a pause, say some parts very fast. Later you can tone down and select what you want to keep.

◆ Focus on developing the characters. Imagine what they would wear, what their hands would look like, their posture, voices. Create interesting characters with detail (verbal and nonverbal).

◆ Select a powerful first sentence to capture your audience.

◆ Select words to paint pictures and describe feelings, elaborate on details, add sound effects where appropriate.

◆ If you are going to use puppets or props, plan how you will keep them out of sight until they are needed.

Telling the Story

◆ Dress appropriately for the telling. Choose a location without distractions. Sit in a circle to establish an intimate warm climate.

Introduction Ideas

◆ Use poetry, rhymes, games, sayings, riddles, and tongue twisters to get attention.

◆ Empower the audience to imagine, to participate, to be together in a mind space.

◆ Relax the audience, for example, with a smile or humor; knock-knocks build rapport.

◆ Make the introduction short.

◆ Establish mood with your demeanor.

◆ Use a ritual, for example, light a candle, close your eyes, touch fingers of both hands together as if you are holding a ball and bow your head, use an opener, for example, a call or response such as "When I say HI you say HO. HI (you) HO (audience)" or "When I say CRICK you say CRACK." (The latter is an opening ritual from the West Indies.)

◆ Pass around an object or picture and probe with questions, for example, what does this make you think of or feel?

◆ Use eye contact with audience members in different locations so that all feel you are telling to them.

◆ Be as physically close to your audience as possible.

◆ Look for opportunities to personalize the story to the people and place.

◆ Motivate the audience to listen, use a hook, make them eager.

Throughout

◆ Show enthusiasm with your voice, eyes, body, gestures, and tempo.

◆ Share the power with your audience by involving them; for example, *pause* to let them image and predict, to savor a moment. "The pause is like the big space that makes the beauty in Japanese paintings" (Heather Forrest). Pause is waiting with a purpose.

◆ See the story in your own head so that you can make it live for your audience.

- Remember, there is elegance in simplicity. Use only what you need.
- Give the audience a sense of the place and the mood with your voice, body, and actual descriptive words.
- Give each telling a sense of the spontaneous.
- Imagine being your own audience and think about your telling from this perspective.
- Create vivid images by using language that evokes all five senses. Help the audience savor language by using words that are special for the story. Make word pictures for them. For example, when telling *The Baker's Scent,* storyteller Heather Forrest says, "The smell rose up like a hand and went down the street collecting noses" (Jackson, MI, "Storyfest," 1994).
- Use your voice to enrich the telling: vary volume, rate, tone and pitch, pause, stress and emphasis. Use pauses and change tempo: whisper, yell, change voices for characters.
- Articulate and enunciate clearly.
- Refrain from using fillers such as "uh" and "um."
- Ignore interruptions.
- Use gestures, facial expressions, and movement to help define characters, create the setting, and set mood.
- Build suspense.

Conclusion

The last sentence should have a finality to it so that listeners feel satisfied and understand the tale is completed. You may want to use a closing ritual, for example, "Snip, Snap, Snout, This tale is told out."

POST IT PAGE 8–6

EXAMPLE STORY PLOT SKELETON

Fable of the Farmer and Mule

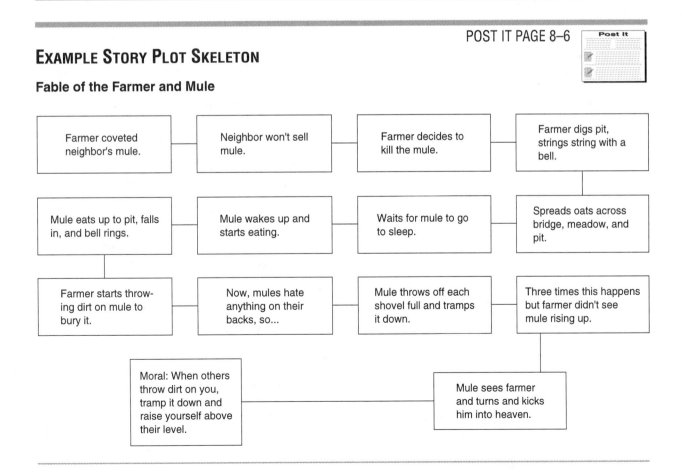

| Farmer coveted neighbor's mule. | → | Neighbor won't sell mule. | → | Farmer decides to kill the mule. | → | Farmer digs pit, strings string with a bell. |

Mule eats up to pit, falls in, and bell rings. ← Mule wakes up and starts eating. ← Waits for mule to go to sleep. ← Spreads oats across bridge, meadow, and pit.

Farmer starts throwing dirt on mule to bury it. — Now, mules hate anything on their backs, so... — Mule throws off each shovel full and tramps it down. — Three times this happens but farmer didn't see mule rising up.

Moral: When others throw dirt on you, tramp it down and raise yourself above their level. — Mule sees farmer and turns and kicks him into heaven.

Opening Rituals. Collect and create opening rituals from stories. For example (T: teller and A: audience):

◆ *Call and response:*

   T: Knock knock.
   A: Who's there?
   T: A story.
   A: A story who?
   T: A story for you.

◆ *African ritual:*

   T: A story. A story.
   A: Let it come, let it go.

◆ *From the Sudan:*

   T: This story is the truth.
   A: Right.
   T: This story is a lie.
   A: Right.
   T: This story is both truth and lie.
   A: Right.

   Candle lighting: "By the flame of the story candle we are freed to travel in our minds to other time and places."

   Beginnings: A long time ago back before yesterday and use-to-bes.

Adding Audience Participation. Storytelling is always participatory, as the audience is part of the co-creation of the story through their imaginations. Audience involvement can be extended with some of the following:

◆ Stop and ask the audience for ideas, for example, "What kind of fabric might the tailor use?"

◆ Increase curiosity and "what if . . ." thinking using the *pause* (e.g., "Nothing I'm going to tell you is true (pause) all the time").

◆ Use a cloze-pause during which the audience supplies refrain, phrase, or word (e.g., and the witch sang, "Bubble bubble pasta pot, boil me some pasta nice and hot," from Tomie dePaola's *Strega Nona*). Or "Once upon a time there were three bears who got up one morning and made some . . . ."

◆ Sound effects: audience supplies these creatively or "as rehearsed" before telling.

◆ Add sign language to stories that audience can mimic. *Joy of Signing* (Riekehof, 1987) is a clear reference.

◆ Cumulative stories: ones such as *This Is the House That Jack Built* (Taback, 2002) that involve lists that repeat and build. The audience joins in.

◆ Story stops: audience is invited to simultaneously mime or improvise dialog with a partner. For example (from *Little Red Riding Hood*), stop at point where Red first meets wolf and ask audience to show how she felt with face and body. Stop and pair a wolf and a Red and ask to have a conversation. Stop and ask audience to give Red advice about what she should do after meeting the wolf. Stop and interview the audience as if they are story characters.

◆ Questioning: Stop and ask the audience, "What do you know so far?" after the conflict in the story has been introduced. After the story, ask, "What images do you have in your head from the story?" (less judgmental than "What did you like best?").

◆ Whisper a line to one person, who passes it on until it circulates around the room. This works for special surprises (e.g., "And when he woke up on the end of his nose was a . . ." ([huge bologna]).

Voices. Brainstorm with students all the different ways they can use their voices as they tell stories, for example, talk slowly, very fast, high pitch, scared, giggly, use regional accents, dialects. Choose a paragraph or sentence out of the newspaper or a book. Have each student read or say it aloud using three different voices.

Talk with Your Body. Practice ways to talk with your body. Ask students to show each of the following: *I'm tired. I'm bored. I'm afraid. Go away. It's freezing in here.* Then ask students to think of sentences and pantomime for others to guess. Do as partners to get maximum participation. *Variation:* Try to show emotions without using the face (cover with a mask or paper bag).

Follow the Leader. This activity encourages students to think about using their bodies to communicate. This can be done in a circle. IT is the leader who mimes going on a walk (in place) and encountering a variety of obstacles (e.g., a crack in the sidewalk, a short wall, a fence with a gate, a puddle). The rest of the class imitates all actions. Limit the obstacles to five or less, and then everyone can guess what they were and a new IT can be chosen. *Variation:* Give students a variety of actions to mime (e.g., opening, reading, and closing a book, throwing many different types of balls, peeling and eating a banana). Invite students to find actions in stories to mime.

Painting Word Pictures. This helps students to learn to use interesting details in storytelling. Sit in a circle. Give students a simple sentence. Go around the circle, with each person repeating the sentence, but with added description. For example, *The woman walked down the road. The bent old woman walked down the narrow road. The spry old woman walked frantically down the long hot road.*

Riddle Stories. Riddles are a comfortable way for students to break into storytelling because they are short. There are hundreds of joke and riddle books available on nearly every topic from computers to insects. Here's a favorite:

Two legs was sitting on three legs with one leg in his lap.
In comes four legs and snatches one leg.
Up jumps two legs and picks up three legs and throws it at four legs and gets one leg back.

Note: Ask audience for guesses and then repeat more slowly so they "get it." (Answer: 1 = chicken leg, 2 = man, 3 = stool, 4 = dog)

Food Stories. Food and stories go together. Each person or group learns a story with a food connection. Stories are told and then everyone feasts. This works well with ethnic stories and folktales.

Circle Stories. Sit in circle and use an opener, for example, "Once upon a time. . . ." Each person adds just one word or how ever many you want. The goal is to introduce a problem and resolve it after a designated number of rounds. *Variation:* Use to review a subject under study. For example, "In science we've been studying about Mars and. . . ."

Story Challenge. Give three words, phrases, objects, or pictures that must be used (could be a circle story, partner, individual, etc.). Example phrases are a thorny rose, lightning strikes, one lost sneaker. Remind students that stories have a beginning, middle, and end and involve a problem to solve. *Variation:* Open a phone book and point to names for characters, spin a globe to find a setting, and draw from a "problem box" (collection of problems that children generate).

Jigsaw Stories. Cut up a story into parts so that each person has a section. Individuals learn parts and then the group assembles to tell the whole story. Number the sections the first time you try this.

Alphabet Stories. This is a challenging way to retell a story. Sit in a circle. Person 1 must begin the retelling and start her sentence with a word that starts with the letter A. The next person picks up the story, but must use the letter B at the start of his sentence, and so on. For example, *A family of three bears lived in a dark wood. Bears need special furniture and these three bears had chairs and beds to fit them. Chair Maximum was for Papa Bear, Chair Medium was for Mama Bear, and Chair Mini was for Baby Bear.* (Thanks to second graders in Springfield, Ohio, for this example.)

Literature Frames. Use a piece of children's literature that has a predictable structure as a verbal frame (e.g., *When I Was Young in the Mountains*). Partner students and have them tell about when they were young, using the stem "When I was young. . . ." *Variation:* Do this in a kind of Ping-Pong manner, with each person telling one line, and then the other, and so on.

Retell Favorite Stories. Students choose to paraphrase a family story. For shy students, invite them to use objects, props, or puppets. *Variation:* Each child makes a prop box of items to draw out as the story is told. This also helps students remember the story.

Partner Retelling. Students pair off and tell a favorite story. Partners must remember each other's stories. At a signal, all change partners and tell the story they just heard. This is excellent for increasing listening skills. *Variation:* All students hear the same story and then partner to tell it to each other. Partner A begins and, at a signal, stops and B must pick up the story line.

Personal Story Prompts. Have students choose or draw randomly a stem to use as a starter (e.g., "The funniest thing that ever happened to me was . . ." or "The most embarrassing moment I've ever had was the time . . ." or "The most memorable person in my family . . .").

I Am Stories. Brainstorm with students all the roles they play, for example, brother, sister, friend. In partners or small-group circles, ask students to use the stem "I am . . ." and tell all the roles they play. They should feel free to add interesting details (e.g., "I am the shortest person in a family of six people, three of whom are my brothers") (Collins, 1997).

Story Responses. After a story has been told, invite students to rerun the story in their heads. They may then do an art, music, drama, dance, or creative writing response. Students can also do a partner retelling (described previously).

Round-Robin Retelling. This is a kind of circle story. Students can retell picture books, fairy tales, and so forth by having one person start and pass the story line on. A ball of yarn with knots about every yard can be passed and used as a cue. *Variation:* Students retell from a different point of view than original story, for example, *Little Red Riding Hood* from Grandmother's viewpoint. Use in science or social studies to retell events.

Prop Stories. Many stories have an object that can be used as a puppet or visual aid as the story is told. Young children especially love this, and older children are more comfortable telling stories if they can use a prop to focus the audience's attention. Here are example titles of stories/books: Albert Lamorisse's (1967) *The Red Balloon,* Ruth Orbach's (1981) *Apple Pigs,* Robert Kraus's (1971) *The Tail Who Wagged the Dog,* Byrd Baylor's (1974) *Everybody Needs a Rock,* and Eric Carle's (1984) *The Very Hungry Caterpillar.*

Storytelling Sources and Resources

Western culture emphasizes happy endings, and folktales have often been sanitized to take out violence or darkness. Many scholars feel this lessens the impact of the story and denies the need to cope with the "shadow" (see, e.g., Bruno Bettleheim's [1977] classic book, *The Uses of Enchantment*). It is nearly impossible to explore multiculturality without controversy (e.g., many cultures use devils and witchcraft as a part of a belief system).

Printed versions of multicultural folktales and fables can be found in the 398.2 section of the public library. Check both the children's and adult areas. Simplified versions are an excellent source from which students can explore improvisation with storytelling.

Here are some places to start to find stories to tell:

- Children's literature, especially picture books
- Fables (Aesop, Lobel, Thurber)
- Folktales
- Your own ethnic traditions (like Patricia Polacco does)

◆ REFERENCES

Books and Articles

Bettleheim, B. (1977). *The uses of enchantment.* New York: Vintage.

Collins, R. (1994). Story told at Storyfest, Jackson, MI.

- Family stories
- Retellings of stories you've heard others tell
- Bible stories
- Historical events
- Contemporary news
- Stories from childhood
- Anthology examples:

Chase, R. (1948). *Grandfather tales.* Boston: Houghton Mifflin.

Chase, R. (1943). *The Jack tales.* Boston: Houghton Mifflin.

Gross, L., & Barnes, M. (1989). *Talk that talk: An anthology of African-American stories.* New York: Simon & Schuster.

Hamilton, V. (1985). *The people could fly: American black folktales.* New York: Knopf.

San Souci, R. (1987). *Short and shivery: Thirty chilling tales.* New York: Doubleday.

Schram, P. (1987). *Jewish stories one generation tells another.* Dunmore, PA: Aronson.

Schwartz, A. (1984). *More scary stories to tell in the dark.* New York: Harper & Row.

Yolen, J. (1986). *Favorite folktales from around the world.* New York: Pantheon.

NAPPS, the National Association f or the Preservation and Perpetuation of Storytelling, Box 309, Jonesboro, Tennessee 37659 (615-753-2171) has workshops, periodicals, and a directory of storytellers.

TAKE ACTION 3
ROUND-ROBIN STORYTELLING

Use the pointers about storytelling to prepare and do a round-robin telling with a group. Try telling the story from a different perspective (e.g., one of the stepsisters in Cinderella).

Collins, R. (1997). "Storytelling: Water from another time." *Drama Theatre Teacher, 5*(2), 6.

Georges, C., & Cornett, C. (1986). *Reader's theater.* Aurora, NY: DOK.

Heinig, R. (1993). *Creative drama for the classroom teacher.* Upper Saddle River, NJ: Prentice Hall.

Johnson, T., & Louis, D. (1987). *Literacy through literature.* Portsmouth, NH: Heinemann.

Riekehof, L. (1987). *The joy of signing.* Springfield, MO: Gospel.

Children's Literature

Avi. (1994). *Night journeys.* New York: Beech Tree.

Baylor, B. (1974). *Everybody needs a rock.* New York: Scribner.

Berger, B. (1984). *Grandfather twilight.* New York: Putnam.

Carle, E. (1984). *The very hungry caterpillar.* New York: Putnam.

Chaconas, D. (1970). *The way the tiger walked.* New York: Simon & Schuster.

Cole, J. (1993). *Six sick sheep: 101 tongue twists.* New York: Beech Tree.

dePaola, T. (1986). *The clown of God.* New York: Harcourt Brace.

dePaola, T. (1989). *Strega Nona.* New York: Harcourt Brace.

Forest, H. (1990). *The woman who flummoxed the fairies.* San Diego: Harcourt Brace Jovanovich.

Fox, M. (1989). *Night noises.* San Diego: Harcourt Brace Jovanovich.

Goodman, J. (1981). *Magic and the educated rabbit.* Paoli, PA: Instructo/McGraw-Hill.

Hutchins, P. (1978). *Don't forget the bacon.* New York: Puffin.

Jay, W. (1990). *Laughing time.* New York: Farrar, Straus & Giroux.

Keats, E. J. (1962). *A snowy day.* New York: Viking.

Kraus, R. (1971). *The tail who wagged the dog.* New York: Windmill.

Lamorisse, A. (1967). *The red balloon.* New York: Doubleday.

MacLachlan, P. (1985). *Sarah, plain and tall.* New York: Trumpet Club.

McCloskey, R. (1978). *Lentil.* New York: Viking.

McCully, E. (1992). *Mirette on the high wire.* New York: Putnam.

McGovern, A. (1966). *Too much noise.* Boston: Houghton Mifflin.

Munsch, R. (1988). *Thomas' snowsuit.* Toronto, Canada: Annick.

Murphy, J. (1992). *Peace at last.* New York: Dial.

Numeroff, L. J. (1985). *If you give a mouse a cookie.* New York: HarperCollins.

Orbach, R. (1981). *Apple pigs.* New York: Putnam.

Park, B. (1992). *Junie B. Jones and the stupid smelly bus.* New York: Random Library.

Peck, R. (1976). *Hamilton.* Boston: Little, Brown.

Randi, J. (1989). *The magic world of the Amazing Randi.* Holbrook, MA: Adams.

Rathmann, P. (1995). *Officer Buckles and Gloria.* New York: Scholastic.

Rylant, C. (1992). *When I was young in the mountains.* New York: Dutton.

Schwartz, A. (1974). *A twister of twists, a tangler of tongues.* London: Deutsch.

Scieszka, J. (1991). *The true story of the 3 little pigs.* New York: Viking.

Sendak, M. (1962). *Pierre: A cautionary tale.* New York: Harpercrest.

Taback, S. (2002). *This is the house that Jack built.* New York: Putman.

Van Allsburg, C. (1987). *The z was zapped.* Boston: Houghton Mifflin.

Van Laan, N. (1992). *Possum come a-knockin'.* New York: Knopf.

Viorst, J. (1972). *Alexander and the terrible, horrible, no good, very bad day.* New York: Atheneum.

Weil, L. (1973). *Master of all masters, a folktale.* New York: Scholastic.

Wolf, A. (1993). *It's show time!: Poetry from the page to the stage.* Asheville, NC: Poetry Alive!

9

Integrating Dance and Movement Throughout the Curriculum

When we teach a child to draw, we teach him how to see. When we teach a child to play a musical instrument, we teach her how to listen. When we teach a child how to dance, we teach him how to move through life with grace. When we *teach a child to read or write, we teach her how to think. When we nurture imagination, we create a better world, one child at a time.*

Jane Alexander, chair for the National Endowment for the Arts (*imagine!*, Donohue, 1997)

◆ **CLASSROOM SNAPSHOT**

Mr. Moore Uses Dance to Teach Fourth-Grade Science

Nothing is more revealing than movement.
　　　　　　　　Anonymous

The desks are pushed back and 27 students are standing in "personal spaces."

"Okay, everyone. Stretch out your arms to make sure you have enough room and won't be touching anyone during the warm-up."

Mr. Moore is a balding man in his forties who told me he'd been teaching for 18 years. He has a reputation for always being in a good humor, but being a "hard teacher."

In the background soft music is playing. It is a CD with sounds of water rushing and waves crashing on the beach. Nature sounds. No obvious rhythm. Mr. Moore's voice is easily heard as he begins his warm-up.

"Stretches. Reach your arms over your head. Now one arm higher and alternate back and forth. Let's go for eight counts: 1–2–3–4–5–6–7–8. Both arms up and drop to your sides. Relax. Reach up with both arms, now out in front of you. Let your hips tilt so your back and arms are flat and parallel to the floor. Now relax your back and curve it so you can dangle your head and hands toward the floor. Let's slowly roll up with your head coming up last. I'll count down from 8–7–6–5–4–3–2–1."

Students sigh in unison, and there are smiles across the room. Next, Mr. Moore takes the class through warm-ups especially for specific body parts, working from top to bottom: head, neck, torso (shoulders, hips, back, abdomen), arms and elbows, hands, fingers, and wrists, legs and knees, and feet and ankles.

"Ready, shake out! Right arm. Left arm. Shake your whole body out. Take a deep breath now and slowly let it out. Take another. Hold it. Very slowly release it without letting your body slump. I see straight bodies out there. Good concentration. Now, sit in your space, eyes up here."

The warm-ups take about 5 minutes.

Mr. Moore introduces the content portion of the lesson with a question, "Put your thumb up if you can tell me something about the water cycle we've been studying in science."

Almost everyone responds. The students are anxious to tell about where water is found on Earth, how much water there is, pollution problems, and what makes water. When someone tells the forms of water (ice, liquid, and steam), Mr. Moore asks the class the causes of the various states. There seems to be some uncertainty about this.

"It's fine if you're not sure about what causes water to be solid, liquid, or in a vapor or gas form because that's our lesson focus today. Let's start with what you know. In your space, when I say "three," show me a body shape that feels like water in its solid form. Ready 1–2–3. Yes! I see lots of stiff bodies and straight lines. Without losing your shape, try to look around. What do you notice?"

"People look hard."

"Everyone is compact."

"I see angles."

"Sarah, what do you mean by angles?"

"Like James has his arms and legs bent in straight. I think forty-five degree angles, aren't they?"

"Good observation!"

"I'll count again. This time, every time I say "three" change your solid shape in some way. Try a different level or direction. Look at the Elements Chart. Okay, ready? 1–2–3. 1–2–3. 1–2–3. Wow! You really thought of lots of hard shapes. What made you do what you did?"

Lots of thumbs go up.

"I wanted to do what you said and be different, so I tried to feel really solid, but change to a high level and use different body parts."

"I tried to really think about how it feels inside a piece of ice. I used more energy this time to try to hold my molecules together."

"Hey, I'm getting cold. B-R-R-R." The class laughs.

"But why is ice cold?" Mr. Moore asks.

The class discusses what they know about temperature and its effects on states of water. He then takes the student comment about molecules and asks students about what they think the distance is among the molecules in ice. They concur that they "felt" close together.

Mr. Moore takes the students through similar explorations of liquid water and finally water vapor. He increasingly focuses his questions and descriptive comments on the molecular structure of the three states and how each feels as they make their individual shapes.

After about 10 minutes, he tells the students to get into their small groups. Students seem to have been previously assigned and know where their group space is.

"Your group assignment is to create a dance using movements related to all three forms of water. Remember, you're not pretending to *be* the water, but trying to communicate about the states by showing all the possible movements. What do you remember the dance must have?"

"A beginning, middle, and end."

"A starting shape, then our movements, and an ending shape frozen."

"Creative ideas!"

"Thanks for reminding us Liza! Yes, the idea is to think differently about these water states. In your groups, begin by brainstorming ways water gets from one form to another and movements related to these changes. I'll come around as you work."

The students huddle up in groups of about four. Mr. Moore waits as students get started. After a few minutes, he begins to circulate and listen in.

"Let's see. Ice melts when it gets warmer—above thirty-two degrees. We could show melting by starting high and slowly getting lower and spreading out."

"Yeah. We could all be part of a rigid ice sculpture with lots of angles. We need to be really close together." Everyone giggles.

"What about when we melt and spread out. We'd be liquid, then. Somehow we need to show getting hotter so we can evaporate."

"We could be being cooked to boiling. Wow. You'd really have to move fast and jump around. Look at my fingers boiling!" Liza demonstrates with fast wild finger movements and the others join in.

"Look, my foot is boiling!"

Mr. Moore moves to another group that is discussing cloud movements and how to show water moving from a gas to precipitation (liquid). He pauses to ask what the difference is between precipitation and condensation, and they spend a few minutes discussing the terms.

Another group is working on water appearing as frost and is experimenting with "quick-freeze" movements.

After about 10 minutes, Mr. Moore announces they have 5 minutes to decide their starting shapes, how to include movements related to the three states of water, and their ending shapes. He coaches them to think about how to use the space in the room. He tells them to sit in their groups when they are ready.

The students finish planning, and he then has each of the four groups perform their dances as the rest of the class takes the part of the audience. Each performance takes about 3 or 4 minutes. After each performance Mr. Moore asks the audience to "tell what they saw," and he compliments students who give really specific observations about shapes, movements, and connections to the states of water.

The lesson ends with a debriefing in which Mr. Moore asks them what they learned about the states of water. Finally, students rearrange their desks and take out Science Learning Logs to write for about 5 minutes on the states of matter lesson. There is a reading assignment on the board about the water cycle in their science book, and students begin to read as they finish their logs. Mr. Moore explains that there is little in the reading that hasn't already come up in the lesson. He is sure many students need the visual or print reinforcement, and he claims he's too traditional to do away with the textbook, completely.

"I'll never forget the three water states and where the molecules are" one girl wrote in her Learning Log. "I like to learn this way because you just remember science better and it is fun."

The lesson has lasted about 40 minutes.

INTRODUCTION

The most creative ideas come from people who are not bound by conventional models of thinking . . . Knute Rockne patterned backfield formations for Notre Dame's famed "Four Horsemen" after watching a dance performance, and military designers borrowed Picasso's cubist art to create more effective camouflage patterns.

Bruce Boston (1996) p. 9

Relax! You Need Not Be a Dancer Yourself

Our bodies and how we move them intentionally and unintentionally say so much about us. So much, in fact, that muggers can choose victims by watching how people move—tentative irregular walking not directed toward a destination is what they look for. Movement is a powerful communicator that fascinates and repels us, delights, and disgusts. And yet, unlike the use of words, movement is not a communication form usually considered part of the core curriculum in schools. This reticence about dance is interesting, since our society is riveted on one particular area of movement—sports. Perhaps movement is so basic we take for granted that students know how to use it effectively. But most don't.

Dance and creative movement are frequently the art forms teachers feel least prepared to integrate. In the United States the look of one's body is very important; beautiful, intimidating body images bombard us daily through the media. We have become very sensitive about our bodies. It is not surprising teachers are sometimes uncomfortable using creative movement, especially if they're not sure exactly what that means. Teachers do not want to appear awkward or have their

TAKE ACTION 1

WHAT? WHY? HOW?

Think about Mr. Moore's lesson. What did he teach about both dance and science? Why did he use the strategies he used? How did he cause the students to become engaged in the lesson?

bodies examined for possible ridicule. Those who feel uncomfortable need to know that students, especially after the primary grades, often feel the same way.

It is unproductive to spend time wringing our hands about the lack of value for artistic movement. It is more useful to acknowledge ways movement is important in daily life and move on to finding strategies to put kinesthetic ways of knowing into action in creative and artistic ways. Most important is to start with a foundational truth—we all love to move. It feels good to walk, run, stretch, wiggle, and shake. It is also worthwhile to remember that what we *do* is remembered more easily than what is told to us or what we read about.

It is important for teachers to be actively engaged in their own lessons, but it is not necessary for teachers to demonstrate specific dances when integrating dance throughout the curriculum. The intent of this chapter is to present strategies classroom teachers can use to cause students to problem solve through movement. When and if teachers decide to include structured dances (e.g., folk dancing in social studies), they can choose to demonstrate such dances or invite guests to do so, perhaps in collaboration with the physical education teacher. If the school has created an arts resource directory, like the one described in Chapter 2, persons may be located through this resource who are willing to teach specific dances.

Morning Routine, Lady's Island Elementary School

WHY SHOULD TEACHERS INTEGRATE MOVEMENT AND DANCE?

I dance because it brings me closer to my creator.
                        Morgan Grant (Saginaw dancer)

Post It Page 9–1 shows the results of dance integration in schools.

Eleven Reasons to Integrate Dance

1. Dance increases sensitivity, respect, and cooperation. When a class is engaged in group or partner problem solving through movement, students begin to see how everyone has a different view of a situation. There are numerous ways to express thoughts and feelings about the cycle of life and death through movement; no one body shape or locomotor movement is right or wrong. The emphasis is on finding original ways to think and feel about what is being learned. Students soon see that other students think of things they wouldn't have come to know working alone—two bodies and heads are better than one. Students delight in the artistry of fellow classmates as they witness the inventiveness of peers; a graceful slide or a

humorous foot dab executed at the right moment can provide a moment of insight—oohs and ahs, laughter, and even awe. In a more structured vein, partner and circle dances require students to help each other in an enjoyable context. Students feel the intrinsic motivation to learn under these circumstances.

2. Dance gives joy.

The place of the dance is within the heart.

                                            Tom Robbins

Imagine a group of people dancing. Eyes sparkle. They smile and laugh as energy explodes in whirls and wiggles. People constantly surprise themselves as they discover ways bodies can be made to move—to a musical beat or an internal rhythm. It is hard to be still. Dance and creative movement are entertaining to both do and view. Nothing is more interesting than people-watching. What is it that attracts attention? The way people walk, their posture, how they get from one point to the next, the ways they move to music—all these images captivate us because they say so much about each person. Perhaps that's part of why generations have been influenced by Elvis Presley's hip and leg moves and Michael Jackson's moon walking. Elizabeth Wall, a Richmond, Virginia, school principal, recalled how students responded when dance was integrated at her school.

News Bulletin: Dance Research You Can Use

My heart lifted my feet, and I danced.
                          Nathan of Nemirov

The College Board reports that for the 1999 school year students with 4 or more years of dance background scored 27 points higher on the averaged math and verbal scores.*

Students with disabilities who participated in a 12-week dance program showed significantly higher scores for creativity (fluency, originality, and imagination) than those participating in an adaptive physical education program (Jay, 1991).

Third-grade science scores on tests about the water cycle were raised to 97 percent when dance was used as the meaning maker. Previous year's students scored below average on the test (Barron, 1997).

New York. Batoto Yetu is a Harlem children's dance company that teaches African music and dance to pass on cultural history. They say dance bridges generations and teaches discipline, respect, and hope ("This Morning" CBS, April 11, 1997).

Golden Valley, Minnesota. At the Minnesota Arts High School, physics and dance are combined in lessons that focus on the principles of momentum, velocity, force, and energy.

Seattle, Washington. Third graders who studied language arts through dance increased Metropolitan Achievement Test scores by 13 percent in 6 months. (Gilbert, 1977)

---

*For more information about SAT scores and college bound seniors for 1999–2000 go to (*http://www.collegeboard.org/prof/*). Click the Search button and enter "national report."

The teachers also seemed to feel that as children use their bodies they become different and that no other previous programs had accomplished this . . . [children expressed] a sense of humor and as attitudes and values changed, self-control developed. . . . They looked forward to school. (Fleming, 1990, p. 32)

3. Dance increases self-regulation. Students involved in solving movement problems or exploring movement have to focus on making their bodies work. They must focus to control body parts and energy. Teachers who use dance as a learning tool stress the growth of concentration by starting with small and easy movement problems and increasing the difficulty over time. They cause students to focus by structuring dances with beginning, middle, and end segments. They give positive descriptive feedback to those who show they can stay on task and show involvement. Dance integration includes teaching students to appreciate pleasant feelings that come from being quiet and still. They learn to feel sensations of inner peace and pride in controlling body parts and shapes. Self-discipline develops as they learn to manage movement, gradually at first and then for increasing lengths of time and with more variety. Eventually students learn to express ideas and emotions through dance in original ways as they become more self-regulated and can make their bodies respond as desired.

Dance often involves group work. Students develop responsibility when they are a part of a group in which their ideas and cooperation are *needed* and when they are taught how to be responsible. But they need to be taught *how* to respond in a group and to group members. Responsibility means "having the ability to respond." Teachers should model active listening behaviors such as paraphrasing another's ideas, asking for clarification, and nonverbals such as nodding and use of eye contact.

Students involved in *formal* dance study learn the rigor required to develop skills in ballet or tap or jazz. Any dance demands concentration on the body, energy, space, and time elements. Students who choose such study must commit to a regimen of regular practice. They quickly see that struggle and hard work is needed to master new ideas. Why do they choose pain and hard work? One students put it this way, "It was mind over movement for me. I really liked the challenge to get my body to do what I wanted. I was inspired by dancers who could do amazing moves. I wanted to stretch myself." There certainly is a self-pride that comes from conquering obstacles. Then there is the thrill of performance and the reinforcement given by significant others who come to be the audience.

4. Dance is integral to real life.

Consider how many times . . . you handled a basketball compared to the number of times you skipped to music.

Ruth Murray

John Dewey's idea that school should not be preparation for life, but a part of life, fits here. Dance is an important part of the rituals and ceremonies of our lives—weddings, inaugurations, proms, and holidays. It has been fascinating to watch the response of audiences to entertainment phenomena such as "Lord of the Dance" and "Riverdance." Just as athletic games draw huge crowds, dance attracts entertainment dollars. Certainly, part of the attraction of sports is the movement aspect. We enjoy watching the light airy moves of Michael Jordan or the elegant golf swing of Tiger Woods. While sports is not the same as dance, there is the connection. In sports, as in dance, the body is used as a tool. There are those who would argue that certain individuals make their sport into an art form when they take their moves to a level of beauty that awes and inspires.

5. Dance develops self-confidence.

Graceful movement is just the right amount of energy for what you're doing.

Michael Ballard

One of the first things strangers notice about a good friend of mine is her posture. She sits and stands very erect. When she walks it is with fluidity and grace. The way she holds and moves her body communicates that she is a leader—and she is. A former department chair at a college, she now heads up several community groups, including the Jackson, Michigan, Storyfest. As students learn to control their bodies, endurance and strength develop, enabling them to feel more poised. Satisfaction with one's body and self-confidence increase as students attain mastery of body parts and movements that extend their range of expression. We all want to feel good about our bodies. Dance can develop self-assurance as students have successful experiences in solving problems creatively through dance. *What are all the ways you can walk*

across the room? How would George Washington have stood as he was installed as the first president? Look at this painting of President Washington. When I say "3" hold that pose. Relax. Now, let's do it again and when I say "4" begin to walk around as Mr. Washington would, right after this scene in the picture.

6. Dance is integrated brain–body work.

I see the dance being used as a means of communication between soul and soul—to express what is too deep, too fine for words.

Ruth St. Denis

Gardner (1996) includes dance under body-kinesthetic intelligence, and neurologist Mark Hallett (1999) claims that using the body maximizes brain use. He says athletes at peak performance use close to 100% of their brains—dispelling the myth that humans almost never use more than 10% of brain capability. Dance is intellectual and physical—there is a mind–body connection that "activate[s] far more brain areas than traditional seatwork" (Jensen, 2001, p. 72). Dance involves the whole person in its construction. Through dance we communicate what we think, feel, and value. When students dance ideas from science, social studies, or math, they gain a different view on the subject, because the physical body is engaged, which activates more areas of the brain. During dance, students use kinesthetic intelligence, different from the kind of movement associated with the physical education program. Dance has the added dimension of the esthetic, a potential for creative and inner self-expression, which are crucial for children to be happy and satisfied. "[D]ance provides a primary medium for expression involving the total self (not just a part, like the voice) or totally separated from the physical self (like painting or sculpture)" (Fleming, 1990, p. 5). Savvy teachers help children become "whole" people through the integration of the arts. Dance integration, in particular, involves more holistic learning than any other art because of the brain–body connection.

7. Dance is healthy.
A 1992 ad from the American Heart Association displays a silhouetted child in front of a TV. The boldface caption reads, "Caution: Children Not At Play." Obesity levels of children have risen dramatically as our youth have developed passive television viewing habits. On the average, children now spend about 4 hours a day viewing versus doing. What about during the school day? How much learning time is spent using the body in active physical

ways? How much of the ballooning statistics about "hyperactive" kids has to do with children's bodies rejecting the passive lifestyles and learning environments we've created for them? Dance is exercise, and exercise makes us healthy. It increases blood circulation and muscle tone. Dance also burns up calories. Like any exercise, dance triggers the brain to produce endorphins that are natural pain killers and catecholamine, an alertness hormone. No wonder children enjoy dance; they are out of pain and full of energy. Dancing can even give a person a feeling of being "high" or uplifted, just as any creative activity can. So, dance is another kind of therapy or emotional release to alleviate stress. Dance used before, during, or after a lesson in reading, math, science, or social studies increase physical readiness for cognitive learning by activating more brain areas.

8. Dance calls for creative problem solving and imagination.

[Dance is] the cheapest and most available material to use for creative experiences. It does need space but not as much as we have traditionally thought.

(Fleming, 1990, p. 5)

How many ways can you move across the room? What are all the body parts you can use to make circles? What are all the ways cats move? Leaves? Water? How can you show the idea of "addition" using dance? What are all the words that describe movements? When teachers ask fat questions, such as these, they set up opportunities for creative problem solving. Teachers who encourage risk taking and experimentation, and who give children time to explore ways to use movement to communicate thoughts and feelings, are freeing the unlimited powers of the imagination. That power can be put to use to solve problems in the subject matter under study.

Remember the creative problem-solving process from Chapter 1? It begins with finding problems and then gathering information to solve the problems. Every dance activity should be centered around this idea of exploring movement to unleash creative and artistic thinking. In the regular classroom, this means having students come to understand key concepts about dance and acquire basic communication skills used in this kinesthetic way of knowing.

9. Dance is primary form of communication.

If I could tell you what I mean, there would be no point in dancing.

Isadora Duncan

The importance of movement in communication should not be minimized. Body language was the first language humans undoubtedly used, and nonverbal language retains primacy over the verbal when the two conflict. For example, image someone saying, "I'm delighted to be here" with a sneer on his face. It is fun and effective to ask students to demonstrate examples of "when words and actions conflict" to make this point clear for them. Students involved in dance integration learn effective ways to use the body as a language. Through the use of body, energy, space, and time, they can show understanding of emotion words like boredom, ferocity, defeat, and pride. Students can learn to show comprehension of most vocabulary words—especially verbs and adverbs, through dance. In science and social studies dance can be used to demonstrate understanding of processes such as rotation, cycles, and decay or key concepts such as dependence, interrelationships, and cause–effect. All of these examples show how dance can extend self-expression capabilities.

Dance is a means of *showing* what we know. It enables children to express thoughts and feelings that otherwise may be inexpressible. The kinesthetic mode is the one through which our earliest learning happens. Communication through movement is the most universal form of language. Think about the meanings of an upraised shaking fist or arms stretched high toward the sky or palms open and arms extended. Did you recognize *anger, triumph,* and *invitation* in these gestures? The study of dance is not devoid of words, however. Dance is a way to promote learning throughout the curriculum by developing dance vocabulary and forging conceptual anchors related to movement that can be used across disciplines. As students learn the dance elements of body, energy, space, and time, they also learn how to analyze and categorize their thinking. Many concepts, such as rhythm, space, and shape, are used in music, drama, and the visual arts as well. Other dance concepts such as balance can be extended to areas such as physics.

10. Dance satisfies the need for beauty. There is hardly a sight more beautiful than a graceful human being. When students have opportunities to view dances and participate in dance creation, they increase their esthetic sensitivity. In creative dance the expressive and imaginative potential of children is what is emphasized, so dance can also add beauty to the lives of our students. Maslow (1970) believes the need for beauty is high level and must be met for a person to feel fulfilled or "self actualized". Beauty uplifts us and can give hope in the way a potted flower on a rotted window sill can. It creates a sense that life is worth living. Captivating ethnic dances, such as the hora from Jewish culture, stretch children's concepts of beauty and offer information about how diverse groups celebrate. What's more, hate becomes harder to hold on to for people who give gifts of beauty in the forms of dance, art, and music. The spectacle of a cultural dance performance is a powerful bridge. Even more powerful is sharing in the dance making!

11.   Dance is a path to cultural understanding and expression

Sometimes dancing and music can describe a true image of the customs of a country better than words in a newspaper.
                                                               Gene Kelly

All art forms are vehicles for conveying the ideas and values of their creators. This makes dance an important means of coming to understand values and customs of other cultures. Social studies units are particularly appropriate contexts for using dance. Students feel sensations created by dance forms in particular periods of history (e.g., hip-hop, tap, jazz, ballroom, country line, jitterbug, mazurka). Dances reflect changing values, tastes, economic conditions, and social trends. From the limbo to the lambada there is rich material in these dances to reveal what groups think and feel. Through dance investigations, historical events can be understood from an entirely different point of view. For example, Native American ghost dancers in the 19th century created dances to celebrate the return of the lands taken by the U.S. government. The dancers tried to conjure up the powers of their ancestors and created such a fervor among tribes that the government eventually forbade the dance. When ghost dancing continued, U.S. soldiers attacked and killed a camp of dancers, including many

---

WHY DANCE?

TAKE ACTION 2

There are many other reasons for integrating dance in the regular classroom than the 11 discussed in this book. Think of another reason or choose one of the 11 and develop it with an original example. Be prepared to give clear examples to parents, principals, other teachers, and community members who question the use of dance as a curricular learning tool.

---

children. Students can also view dances and then analyze them for the messages they give about what is important to the dancers and the culture represented.

WHAT DO TEACHERS NEED TO KNOW TO USE DANCE AS A TEACHING TOOL?

The activity is the art.

                                                               Mary Joyce

I believe it can only be done if teachers themselves have had experiences in their professional training (and hopefully before that) which parallel and supplement the expressive, imaginative uses of movement that dance can offer. . . . There is danger that teachers who have had no creative dance in their training and who have been taught only to look and work for efficient, functional movement, will not encourage or even be receptive to a different kind of movement response. [We need teachers who know] children's literature, poetry, music, songs and how to use props for creative movement. More importantly, [we need teachers who have a] sensitivity to children's spontaneous expressiveness, the recognition of imaginative rather than imitative uses of movement. (Fleming, 1990, p. 77)

What's Included in the Study of Dance?

In elementary and middle school, these aspects of dance are studied: (1) the historical, social, and cultural role in our lives, (2) communication through dance by expressing, performing, and responding, and (3) valuing dance for its esthetic contributions. Dance integration includes teaching about dance elements, dancers, choreographers, folk and fad dances, genre or forms, styles, history of dance, tastes and preferences, dance making, music and dance in daily life, and the dance of other cultures. This content and these dance processes can be integrated into other disciplines or can be the body or center of a unit or lesson. (See the four unit bodies and nine-legged model on Post It Page 2–4.) For example, the minuet, a particular dance form or genre, could be integrated into a history unit on early America.

Teachers need to build a repertoire of information about dance. This includes CDs, videos, pictures, books, and other material to use as references for lessons about forms such as ballet and jazz, dances of different time periods and cultures, and important dancers and choreographers. This can begin as simply as creating computer files or traditional file folders on dancers into which tidbits of information are saved from magazine articles. There are numerous biographies of dancers (e.g., *I Feel Like Dancing: A Year with Jacques D'Amboise and the National Dance Institute* by Barboza, 1992) and informational books about various dance forms. Involving students in research on dancers and dance genre enables them to connect literature, social studies, and other art forms as they search for the whys and hows that motivated the creation of dance throughout human history.

Here is a checklist of titles for folders to aid in organizing and collecting information for dance integration:

- Basic elements and concepts used to communicate through dance
- Dance artists: dancers, choreographers
- Styles, forms, and genres of dance
- Actual dances (e.g., the electric slide is a dance in the genre of country line dances)
- Other possibilities: history of dance, science of dance, the math of dance, writing dance (notation systems), sociology of dance, economics and dance, and psychology of dance (e.g., dance therapy)

Definitions: Creative Dance versus Movement

As I type this sentence, I am moving. This is not dance. And yet I can take my hands from the keys and begin to play with the "typing movement." Now I experience the feel of my fingers moving and the shape of my hands on an abstract level. I can use other body parts to create the lightness of touch and the irregular rhythms of typing. I can do this with my toes, torso, and hips. The movement is no longer done to get a job done but to explore how kinesthetics is a way of knowing and feeling.

This chapter has little to do with teachers directing students to mimic, step by step, until a dance is learned. Dance involves creative movement explorations, but it can become a holistic entity, that is, a "sequence of movements which begin, proceed, and finish, can be repeated in similar fashion, and follow a planned and interesting arrangement" (Murray, 1975, pp. 17–18). But for movement to become dance, there must be "expressive interest beyond that of its mere physicality." Dance is a category of art and art is

not created nor understood primarily for function. Murray cautions that "a sequence of learned gymnastic movements, even though they are performed to music, do not make a dance. There must be something present that pertains to the spirit of the performer, and the movement must communicate that spirit" (1975, p. 18). The classroom teacher's purposes are best served by a focus on problem solving. This begins with guided, free exploration and discovery about the nature of movement. In this open-ended approach there is a variety of acceptable solutions. Creating dances and learning about dance aspects should be planned times for students to feel the joy that results from trying out their own ideas to solve dance puzzles.

Don't be surprised to find yourself smiling as you change common movements into dance. So do students. Humor is the natural response to novelty and the discovery that something unexpected makes perfect sense. For many teachers it is this surprising potential of dance to motivate students and free their thinking that convinces them of its curricular importance. Students begin to realize that it not only feels great to find new ways a body can be used, but dance enables us to express thoughts and feelings we can communicate no other way. Dance goes beyond words to reveal truths about people and the world; and dance is a primary vehicle to help us in the universal human search for beauty (Maslow's hierarchy, Post It Page 1–5).

While integrating dance can include teaching students structured folk dances or trendy fad dances, such as the macarena, the mainstay of a classroom teacher's repertoire of dance strategies will not be demonstrating and asking students to learn combinations of memorized steps. If dance is to be a useful and joyful meaning maker, the focus needs to be on the use of the *symbol system* of dance in creative ways to express thoughts and feelings about important life

---

TAKE ACTION 3
ABSTRACT A MOVEMENT

Think about an everyday movement such as washing the dishes or combing your hair. Go beyond "pretending" to do dishes or whatever movement you choose. Explore movement possibilities by moving using different body parts in ways that are unusual. Try doing the movement fast, then very slow. Feel the essence of the movement.

issues. This symbol system, like those of all communication forms such as language, math, art, and music, consists of teachable elements—tools for meaning making.

Creative Movement and Dance

Dance involves becoming conscious of movement. Dance consciousness starts with awareness of body parts: close your eyes and focus on body parts starting with your head, moving slowly down to your toes. During the middle part of the 20th century, creative movement was in its heyday. Based on natural movement, rather than a specific dance genre such as ballet, creative movement was popular in physical education classes. This is logical because dance is movement and, like dance, physical education dwells on using movement to solve problems. The difference is that dance uses kinesthetics in intentional ways to solve problems creatively, and the expression of feelings is integral to the process. In the political fervor over low test scores begun in the 1980s, many dance programs were shelved. The baby was thrown out with the bath water as schools were frightened into getting students to test well. This continues to happen as educators act impulsively without carefully considering research on what causes learning to proceed most successfully. Gardner's (1983) *Frames of the Mind* brought many educators back to the future as he and others showed how *bodily kinesthetic* intelligence is essential to learning. In particular, the revelations from neuroscience suggest the arts are the most productive ways to stimulate high achievement over the long haul of schooling (Jensen, 2001).

Pantomime versus Creative Dance

Pantomime is often confused with creative dance. Pantomime uses movement without words, but it is a drama strategy in which people pretend to be something or someone. Pantomime can lead to imitation, rather than actual creative movement. If teachers are not clear about the different purposes and processes of dance versus pantomime, students end up doing pantomime when the goal is dance.

Movement is more abstract in dance. The focus is on the movement itself, not on pretending to move like an animal, plant, or character problem. If teachers say "move like a cat" students will mime stereotyped paw and claw movements. To cause students to use a dance frame of thinking, the same direction can be given with a changed focus: Show me the shape of a cat's body, how it walks, how its muscles move. How it would walk backwards or on a low level? These directions cause students to explore the kinesthetic options of the concept. Think about involving students in the *movement possibilities* of an idea, rather than in the idea itself. This is particularly important when teaching new concepts in fields such as science or social studies—the goal is an extended perspective that results from creative problem solving by kids.

Detailing the difference between pantomime and creative dance may seem like a minor point, but the teacher who makes this clear can extend students thinking tremendously. Frequently teachers use dance or movement with songs, poems, or other children's literature. Miming Max during the wild rumpus in *Where the Wild Things Are* is not dance. It is a worthy way for students to become part of the story and think about characterization. Creative dance offers another dimension of meaning. For example, children can work on ways to express anger (the emotion that got Max sent to his room) with the body. Movement possibilities can be explored, and a concept, important to the book's theme, is extended. So, the teacher needs to decide if the goal is to "become" or "be" the character (drama/pantomime) or probe the movement extensions of important ideas and feelings in a lesson (dance).

Imagery and Dance

An important way people think and learn is through use of images—visual connections, sound, smell, and tactile associations. But imagery is limited to what is stored in the brain, so it, like pantomime, can restrict thinking through dance. One way to avoid the downside of imagery in dance is to explore dance elements, such as all the ways to move body parts first, and then invite students to "become" through drama. This helps stretch and expand the initial imagery associated with the idea. In other words, when imagery is evoked *after* direct exploration and investigation of movement, there is the chance creative thinking will be extended. Similes and metaphors can be powerful helpers to stretch imaginations for movement: "Show me you are as solid as igneous rock" or "Let me see you shrink as small as you imagine an electron to be." You can also ask for images that lead to movement: "Make your body stretch as if it is being pulled by magnets on either side of you. Use as many body parts as you can" or comment on images that spring from movement: "You're in a round shape, what else do you know that is round in our environment?" This use of imagery enriches conceptual development through movement, rather than activate stereotyped behavior. Finally, images can be used as a basis for movement:

"What kind of movements might a starfish do?" instead of "Pretend you are a starfish and move around." It is a subtle but significant difference in thinking.

Teachers Need Words: Dance Elements Vocabulary

Technique—bodily control—must be mastered only because the body must not stand in the way of a soul's expression.
La Meri

There are a number of systems for categorizing dance tools for meaning making. These concepts develop a conscious awareness of how we move, where, when,

and to what effects. The following is a simple system of remembering dance elements that is useful for classroom teachers and students. (Thanks to Randy Barron, dance educator affiliated with the John F. Kennedy Center for the Performing Arts, for this idea.) It is easy to remember because it is organized around the acronym, BEST: body, energy, space, and time. Post It Page 9–2 is a summary of BEST.

Body Parts, Shapes, Actions. We use all body parts to communicate, both those outside and inside. Think of the ways to move just your little finger or the effect on the body when you tighten inner muscles. Body shape includes ways to form body parts to create everything from pleasant round and curved shapes to

---

POST IT PAGE 9–2

BEST: Basic Dance Elements with Examples

Body
Parts: head, neck, torso (hips, abdomen, shoulders, back), arms and elbows, hands and wrists, fingers, legs, knees and feet (ankles and toes)

Shapes: curved, twisted, angular, small–large, flat–rounded

Actions or moves:

 ◆ Nonlocomotor: stretch, bend, twist, rise, fall, circle, shake, suspend, sway, swing, collapse

 ◆ Locomotor: walk, run, leap, hop, jump, gallop, skip, slide

Energy
Attack: smooth or sharp

Weight: heavy or light

Strength or tension: tight or loose and relaxed

Flow: sudden or sustained, bound or free

Space
Level: low, middle, and high

Direction: forward, backward, sideways, up, down

Size: large and small

Place or destination: where we move to

Pathways: patterns made on the floor or in the air (e.g., circular)

Focus: where the dancer looks

Time
Rhythm: pulse, beat

Speed: time or tempo

Accent: light or strong emphasis

Duration: length

Phrases: dance sentences, patterns, and combinations (e.g., twist, twist, twirl, and freeze)

sharp angry angles and pointed shapes. Then there are all the ways to move in place or through a space. Stationary actions are called *nonlocomotor* and include stretch, bend, twist, rise, fall, circle, shake, suspend, sway, swing, and collapse. Movement through space is called *locomotor* movement and includes actions such as walk, run, leap, hop, jump, gallop, skip, and slide.

Energy is the force a person uses and signals the mood the dancer intends. It includes the person's attack (smooth or sharp), weight (heavy or light), strength or tension (tight or loose), and flow (sudden or sustained).

Space is the personal or shared area in which the body is used. Space is filled up by changing levels (low, middle, and high), directions, size, place or destination, and the pathways (how to get to a destination—directly or in an indirect way). Focus or concentration, or where a person is looking, is also included here.

Time is another element used during movement. It includes rhythm (pulse, beat), speed or tempo, accent or emphasis (light or strong), duration (length), and phrases (dance "sentences," or patterns and combinations of all different kinds of movements) (e.g., "three different middle-level slow, wringing

shapes" is a phrase that may create a message about discomfort or struggle).

Seven *National Standards* for Dance

Dance is not about something. Dance is something.
Mary Joyce, 1994, p. 19

The *National Standards for the Arts* includes dance standards being used across the country as schools frame state and local standards. The *Standards* were used in the construction of the arts section of the National Assessment for Educational Progress (NAEP) and grew out of the *Goals 2000* legislation, so they are a way to focus integration efforts on a national basis. But standards, goals, objectives, and outcomes in curriculum frameworks only help teachers know *what* to teach. They do not explain *how* to teach.

A teaching contract in a school district is a legal promise to teach the curriculum adopted by the board of education—which currently includes teaching to standards and benchmarks in most districts. Each teacher is expected to bring his or her own professional know-how to the job: teaching strategies, ideas

---

TAKE ACTION 4

QUALITIES OF MOVEMENT

Rudolf von Laban (1879–1958) was a dancer and a movement scientist. He studied the elements that create "qualities of movement" and discovered how mood is created by combining eight actions, using different degrees of effort and amounts of space. The eight are: thrust, slash, float, glide, wring, press, flick, and dab. Each is made in a sustained or sudden, strong or light, direct or indirect manner. For example, wringing is a twisting and turning movement that must be sustained. It is strong and involves several body parts going in different directions (versus direct action toward a definite goal). Think like Laban and complete this movement analysis chart:

Action	Sudden/Sustained	Strong/Light	Direct/Indirect
Wring	*Sustained*	*Strong*	*Indirect*
Thrust			
Slash			
Float			
Glide			
Press			
Flick			
Dab			

about materials, and disciplinary and classroom management tools. This means teachers need to structure lessons and units around the school district's performance goals so that students have a better chance of reaching the goals. Therefore, teachers need to know the goals and standards and specify connections between lesson activities and specific goals/ standards. Good teaching includes informing students of lessons goals, as well, and it is the politically astute educator who communicates goals to parents. Parents often feel the rug has been pulled out from under them when assessments show their children aren't making expected progress toward goals they knew nothing about.

The seven dance standards students are expected to meet are summarized in Post It Page 9–3. A full copy of the standards is available from Music Educator's National Conference (see the address in the appendix). All the strategies and activities in this section of the book, and the next chapter, relate to one or more of these standards.

For examples of arts standards developed at the state level, contact the Ohio Department of Education (Columbus, OH). Kentucky also has state standards for the arts that have been widely implemented. Wisconsin's Model Academic Standards for the Arts can be ordered online at http://www.dpl. state.wi.us/ dpl/dltcl/els/pubsales/arts.html.

POST IT PAGE 9–3

Seven National Standards for Dance

Overall focus: Develop self-image, self-expression, and discipline, body awareness, movement exploration, and creative problem solving, appreciation of self and others, cooperation and collaboration, use of musical rhythms, performing for an audience, respect for diversity, and celebration of humanity and cultures.

1. **Identifying and demonstrating movement elements and skills in performing dance.** Example activities: Perform locomotor movements, create shapes, personal space, pathways, move to beat and tempo, show concentration, describe actions and dance elements.
2. **Understanding choreographic principles, processes, and structures.** Example activities: Create dances with a beginning, middle, end structure. Improvise and create new movements. Use partner skills such as leading and copying. Create dance phrases.
3. **Understanding dance as a way to create and communicate meaning.** Example activities: Explain how dance is different from sports and everyday gestures. Discuss what a dance is communicating. Present original dances and explain their meanings.
4. **Applying and demonstrating critical and creative thinking skills in dance.** Example activities: Find multiple solutions to movement problems. Observe two different dances and discuss differences and similarities. Apply esthetic criteria to observed dances. Demonstrate appropriate audience etiquette.
5. **Demonstrating and understanding dance in various cultures and historical periods.** Example activities: Perform folk dances. Share dances from own heritage. Put dance into historical periods based on style and elements. Analyze for values conveyed.
6. **Making connections between dance and healthful living.** Example activities: Set personal goals for a dancer. Discuss healthy practices. Create and use dance warm-ups.
7. **Making connections between dance and other disciplines.** Example activities: Create a dance to explain a concept from another discipline. Respond to dance by making a painting, song, or writing about messages it conveys.

Source: Content *Standards* (material printed in bold type) excerpted from *National Standards for Arts Education*, published by Music Educators National Conference (MENC). Copyright (c) 1994 by MENC. Reprinted with permission. The complete *National Standards* and materials are available from MENC: The National Association for Music Education, 1806 Robert Fulton Drive, Reston, VA 20191 (800-336-3768).

TAKE ACTION 5
CONNECT TO THE STANDARDS

Think about Mr. Moore's lesson using dance to teach states of water. Select the *Standards* you think were the goals of this lesson and give your reasons.

HOW CAN TEACHERS USE DANCE AND MOVEMENT AS TEACHING TOOLS?

A program of little dances once a year for an audience taught under pressure and presented in the school auditorium is not what is meant by [relating to the curriculum].

Murray, 1975, p. 19

General Integration Principles

The general principles for effective arts integration described in Chapter 2 apply to all arts areas. Teachers can choose to teach *with, about, in,* and *through* the arts and that INTEGRATES is one set of 10 general principles to help begin the process. Post It Page 2–5 summarizes all 10 principles synthesized from many integrated arts programs. Here are ones of particular importance for integrating creative dance and movement.

Principle 1: IMMERSION in Dance and Movement

Every classroom needs space for students to move. This can be accomplished by arranging the room in a U shape, putting desks in groups so an open area is left, or simply moving back the desks. It is common knowledge that physical exercise is a way to increase energy and health. Each lesson plan should be examined for ways to use the power of kinesthetic learning. Dance immersion focuses on making movement a part of the start of the day or period, as well as the introduction, development, and conclusion of lessons and units. Most of all dance immersion means realizing that movement is a fundamental means of communication. Dance offers ways to understand and express ideas that will remain locked inside our students if movement is not taught as a meaning-making option.

I remember one student who was in trouble for frequently getting up to sharpen his pencil. When asked why his pencil tip broke so often he honestly replied, "It doesn't. I just need an excuse to move." Hopefully, the curtain has closed on rigid classroom procedures that require children to sit unnaturally on hard chairs for much too long.

Principle 2: NITTY-GRITTY Elements and Concepts

Child's definition of dance: "It's talking. Telling something with your body. Not using words, just using your body to talk.

Fleming, 1990, p. 33

Teach the What and Why of Dance.   Dance is an art form plagued with more than its share of misconceptions that need to change if successful movement integration is to happen. Unfortunately, many students think dance is memorizing steps and using bump and grind motions their parents would find objectionable. In the absence of a clear idea of what creative dance includes, kids tend to focus on learning steps to pop dances; when given "free dance time" they launch into sexualized moves they've seen teen idols use on videos or MTV. Another problem to be confronted is the sexist notion many boys have developed that dance is a girl thing and it might endanger their masculinity. Laying the groundwork for dance integration means dealing with these issues, up front. It is definitely worth the time to sort out these issues with students, and benefits of dance integration make this work most certainly worth the effort.

Discussion-based lessons to explore the definition of dance expose students' prior knowledge. Such discussions provide assessment information that can be used to plan additional lessons. For example, assignments can be made to find dance definition examples and to write personal definitions based on many examples of dance gained from discussions. The goal is for students to form a clear and comfortable idea of how *kinesthetic* intelligence can be used to make meaning. It is not as effective to *give* students a definition of dance. Here are some strategies to help them construct their own:

- Web (map or cluster) what students already know about dance, dancers, choreographers, and the ways people move.

- Do a Venn diagram comparing movement, in general, and in dance. Compare and contrast sports moves with dance to consider what makes something "art" and what is "esthetic" or "beautiful." Use the children's book *Max* by Rachael Isadora, about a boy who discovers the dance–sports connection.

◆ Ask students to find a variety of definitions of dance by doing interviews with people, using reference books or the Internet. They can then synthesize a working definition that makes sense.

Time spent teaching reasons how dance is important in careers, sports, and cultural rituals is time well spent—motivation is grounded in the perception of relevance. Discussions that explore how dance and movement have been a part of each child's life help them discover additional reasons to include dance as a learning tool. Better yet, get the kids moving. Ask them to think about the movement of walking. Then brainstorm different ways to walk: angrily, happily, proudly, triumphantly. Invite students to try different walks and report how each feels. Discuss the difference between *daily* walking and the walking exploration they just did to develop the concept of dance as an intentional way to communicate thoughts and feelings.

Of course, students need to be taught the basic dance elements so that they have tools to construct meaning through movement. As mentioned previously, these lessons are more successful when visual aids, such as word walls and posters of dance elements (BEST), are used to reinforce the concepts. These lessons can be organized in an inductive format so that students are guided to discover ideas after doing movement or after reflecting on movement from a real-life context. The fairly neutral sports context works well because most students can quickly brainstorm sports moves and boys become engaged right off the bat—no pun intended. Kids can then be guided to do the moves with different body parts, in slow motion and using different amounts of energy and space. Within a short time moves from different sports can be combined to create three-part sports dances that begin with a frozen shape, then several moves, and then an ending frozen shape. Inductive or discovery teaching takes a bit more time, but the students will remember and enjoy the lessons more because they were involved emotionally and physically.

It is also useful to address the gender stereotype issue early on when introducing dance as a learning medium. In schools where dance has been successfully integrated, there has been no doubt that boys learn to love to dance. The key to success seems not to be the actual dance activities, but how dance is approached. It does help to have male role models, but all teachers can discuss the history of dance to show how it has persisted as a male activity in many cultures; in fact, there are times when only the males dance, such as the Russian troika, an extremely strenuous dance. Fleming (1990) advises that "boys like percussive rhythms, architectural structures built with bodies, vigorous locomotor patterns (leaps, jumps), and ethnic dance experiences" (p. 49). If this is a special concern, see Mann's article, "Dance education: the ultimate sport" in the August 1999 *Education Update* and read Chapter 5 in Fleming's (1990) book *Children's Dance*. The chapter ends with this observation: "When boys are no longer given dance activities . . . , not only is their cultural, physical, emotional, and aesthetic growth stunted, but also a great disservice is done to dance as an art form. There is something very incomplete about a whole room full of girls dancing. Yet isn't that what a great deal of the dancing is in our culture?" (p. 49).

Principle 3: *TEACHING HABITS for Integrating Dance*

Process versus Product. The purpose of creative dance and movement is the doing of it—the process not the product. This cannot be overemphasized. To convey to students how important kinesthetic learning is, do a bit of action research. Give half the class a set of numbers to learn (8–3–9–6–11–23–87–92). Send them out of the room to study for 10 minutes. With the remaining group, tell them to study kinesthetically by creating dance movements to remember the number sequence—a movement to go with each number. Have them practice the number movements in order, saying the numbers with the movements for 10 minutes. Bring the whole class back together and give them a test to write the number sequence. Ask students to grade their own papers and then compare the scores of the two groups. Regardless of the scores, ask students to tell *how* they learned and how it *felt*. (Usually the dance group does better and enjoys the studying more.)

While there is a place for structured dances in the regular classroom (e.g., when studying Ireland a guest might teach the Irish jig), this is not desired nor feasible daily or even weekly. If dance is to be used as an important learning tool, the emphasis needs to be on process strategies to help students make meaning kinesthetically, creatively, and artistically. This does not mean that dance products won't result from movement explorations. In fact, when students become adept at using dance to understand and express themselves there will be many times when they will create dances for science and social studies. The pride in these creations compels many students to want to share their dances for peer audiences.

Descriptive Feedback, Assessment, and Evaluation. Here are a few pointers to follow up on the suggestions presented in Chapters 1 and 2 about the important habit of giving feedback to facilitate learning:

1. Give clear and focused descriptive feedback (not just vacuous praise) throughout lessons. Describe what students do. Coach them to stretch their imaginations by using lots of "what if" type of questions. Use each child's name in a positive way as feedback is given.

2. Watch and listen. Use powers of observation to see if students are learning the focus of the lesson. Jot down notes about specific student behaviors on cards or sticky notes that can be added to student progress folders. Get a clipboard to make quick observation notes easier to write. This kind of assessment is effective because it captures authentic evidence during the lesson process, as opposed to fabricated "virtual reality" assessments such as traditional tests.

3. Have students self-evaluate after lessons. Ask how fully the concept was explored through movement. How were students challenged? What choices did they have? What did students try that they hadn't tried before?

4. Ask students what they learned that was most important. Write their responses on the board or a chart to give them value. Link these back to lesson objectives and classroom displays, for example, a Arts Word Wall.

5. Give concrete progress indicators: charts, personal checklists of dance elements, positive Post-its (on which you write feedback to give directly to students after a lesson).

Name _____   Date _____

Comments about. . .

Body parts and actions:

Energy:

Space:

Time:

6. Explicitly tell students about their progress. Use charts and checklists to show them what they have learned. Add new dance information to large class webs about dance or use KWL (Know–Want to Know–Learn) charts.

Free versus Guided Lessons. Undirected versus teacher-guided lessons are an issue throughout education today. In dance integration there are particular concerns about preparing students for success by using guided teaching. Here's the problem. If dance integration is initiated by playing music and telling students to do any dance they wish, many students will be embarrassed about moving at all, and others will engage in rigid, and sometimes vulgar, movements they've seen Britney Spears or Michael Jackson use. For this reason, it is recommended that free dance be made available *after teaching dance elements*. Information about movement options makes all the difference, as does warm-up time to explore ways to communicate through the language of the body. This sequence assures student success and builds self-confidence. Students focus more on what their bodies can do and how it can be done—cognitive processes as well as physical are thus engaged.

Meaning making using arts tools grows from experimentation with element concepts. Skill is gained as control grows. "Move any way you want to the music" assumes that students know many ways *to* move. But they may, in fact, have limited experiences, especially on a conscious level. The goal of integrating creative dance and movement is to help students expand communication choices. Once students know many possibilities for using their bodies to respond to music, or any other stimulus, teachers can give time for free creative movement without students feeling awkward. Embarrassment stems from not knowing what to do or doing the "wrong thing." We can teach children many ways to move and that there really aren't "wrong" moves—although there are moves that are not school appropriate! Sequence and balance are the secrets here.

Show versus Tell. Teaching habits, such as asking students to "show" an idea instead of tell it, can be woven throughout lessons. This habit effectively uses the power of learning through dance. Many students would not be able to verbally define "obnoxious" but could use their hands, head, and body posture to do so—the rest of the class will never forget this definition! When students are asked to show, then describe, and relate (e.g., connect dance to their lives)—they begin to form meaningful links between the arts, learning, and life.

Freedom with Structure. Paradoxically, creativity is often enhanced by limitations and structure. Creative dance is no exception. Freedom alone does not ensure creative thinking. Freedom, with structure and focus, does. Students need to be taught the necessary restrictions on space, time, touching others, following directions, obeying signals, and the use of props that make creative dance and movement work. When rules are clear and consistently applied, students learn self-discipline and are helped to think divergently about the specific context in which they are working. None of us can move "any way we want, any time we want" in our homes or at work. Purposeful movement done with concentration on a specific problem is the goal; even in free time dance, guidelines about space and other issues are needed.

Teacher Questioning. Open or fat questions are a mainstay teaching habit in integrating creative dance and movement: *How many ways? What's another way? What if . . . ? What is the shape of . . . ? How might . . . move?* all direct students to think divergently. Alert students to these kinds of questions so that they can also begin to ask these questions of one another, as well as respond to teacher questions. (See the Special Features section in the front of the book for a list of all the Post It Pages on questioning throughout the chapters.)

We Get What We Expect. The hundreds of studies that have examined the influence of teacher expectation make clear how important it is to get in the habit of demanding variety from students. A demonstrated belief in students' creative potential makes it much more likely they will rise to the occasion. For example, teachers need not limit meaningful dance integration to the common three-part sequence of (1) beginning frozen shape, (2) movements, and (3) a frozen ending shape. This is a solid structure to begin with as students learn to use movement to express thoughts about concepts in science or math, but students soon reach the stage where they can construct their own dances. Teachers need to coach students to keep trying out the infinite number of organizational structures that can be used to create dance. Students should be reminded that new dances are created constantly by people who take risks—witness the electric slide or the revival in circle dancing (with new twists). Ask for movements to be done at different speeds and at different levels to stretch students' thinking. Descriptive feedback can be invited from peers to show delight in original ideas produced with minimal prompting.

Teachable Moments and Student Ideas. Once students get comfortable with the general principles of integrating creative dance and movement in science, social studies, math, language arts, and other arts disciplines, teachers can be alert to teachable moments with movement possibilities. There are obvious occasions. When it starts to snow, BEST elements can be explored to develop the concepts of blizzard, snowflake, and sleet. Movements can be abstracted and explored from current events students bring up (e.g., space events such as the recent storms on the sun that resulted in magnetic "belches" or the passing of the Halle–Bopp comet). Invite students to be on the lookout for ideas that can be danced in the units under study.

Choosing Music for Dance. Although there is a close association between music and dance, some dance educators feel recorded music is incidental to dance lessons and should mostly be used for warm-ups, movement exploration, or free dance (Joyce, 1994). Children's songs that just give movement directions to follow are much like coloring books—they do not encourage creative thinking (Stinson, 1988, p. 132). When music is used, it needs to be carefully selected. Choose music for dance that promotes creative, not stereotyped, movement and is rhythmic but not too complicated. Shorter selections of simple classical music (Brahm's Fourth Symphony, Debussy's "Clouds," Wagner's "Forest Murmurs," and Copeland's "Billy the Kid") work well, as do children's songs that suggest, but don't dictate, movement such as those by Ella Jenkins. Electronic and loud music provokes the bump and grind movements inappropriate to school. Begin with listening to the music and then invite students to respond by clapping or tapping feet and then using the whole body. From there, children can be given more space. Go through your personal collections of tapes and CDs and look for music that:

◆ Makes you feel like moving or dancing.

◆ Has a predictable structure; it feels like it goes somewhere.

◆ Has a clear quality (could invite marching or delicate movements).

◆ Has no lyrics, is instrumental (no words), or words that aren't important to the quality (e.g., Enya).

◆ Has different tempos and moods.

◆ Uses a variety of instruments (saxophone, piano, violins, drum, etc.).

◆ Folk music from different countries or ethnic groups or time periods.

◆ Is classical, especially soloists and chamber ensembles (symphonies can overwhelm).

Some musical artists possibilities include Chopin, Yanni, Wynton Marsalis, Kenny G, Enya, George Winston, Paul Winter, Windham Hill, Tomita, and Chuck Mangione. See categories of music especially helpful for classroom teachers in Chapter 11. Here are some useful addresses for resources:

Dancers' Shop
Children's Book & Music Center
2400 Santa Monica Blvd.
Santa Monica, CA 90404
213-829-0215

Festival Folk Shop
160 Turk St.
San Francisco, CA 94102
415-775-3444

Wordtone Music, Inc.
230 Seventh Ave.
New York, NY 10011
212-691-1934

Discipline and Classroom Management. Class control during creative movement comes from teaching students the discipline of dance—how to control their bodies as they move. There is no magic trick or perfect set of techniques to make a class behave. A lot of management has to do with a kind of presence the teacher exudes—a demeanor that says "I'm in charge but we can work together and enjoy learning." Appendix E gives some time-tested techniques and habits used by teachers to establish discipline and interventions for common problems. Here are a few basics particularly important during dance integration:

Show enthusiasm about teaching. The mood of the day is often set by how the teacher greets the class in the morning. Try a bit of sign language or other kinesthetic ways to say "Hello, glad to see you." The book *The Joy of Signing* (Riekehof, 1987) is excellent. Compliment students with descriptive feedback, and ask students to give each other descriptive feedback to create a positive community feeling. Many students initially feel uncomfortable about dance so it is important to create many positive associations with early dance integration efforts.

Dance involves movement and noise! Start with this expectation and make it clear to the principal and other teachers, who may not understand what you are doing. As students gain knowledge about the purpose and nature of dance, they will take it more seriously. As confidence and self-regulation increases, students will be less noisy because they will be more involved. Some lessons can take place outside, in the gym or cafeteria to allow for more space, but let students know dance used to make meaning is not free play or recess. Also, larger spaces can actually increase anxiety and cause some students to become overstimulated.

Structure lessons so that behavior expectations are crystal clear. Chaos derives from loss of clarity about goals and uncertainty about how to achieve them. This doesn't imply a rigid structure, but a general organizational scheme is needed. An enormous variety of strategies and activities can then be selected within any structure. For example, think of all the ways to *introduce* a lesson using pictures, questions, objects, songs, or a movement challenge.

Teach basic rituals for getting attention, start and stop signals, warm-ups, transitions, and dividing into groups. Rituals can be taught creatively with a personal flair: For random small groups, ask students to find others whose names begin with the same letter or who are wearing a particular pattern (stripes, circles). Readjust initial groups to even out numbers, if necessary. This causes students to think in categories and take time to examine details. A drum or tambourine is a good investment because it can be used get attention and for start and stop signals. One favorite attention getter is to start the class with students echoing a rhythm. This causes them to feel different rhythms usable in dance exploration, as well. Patterns can be clapped or drummed: 1–2–3, 1–2–3–4, or 1–2–3–4–5–6–7–8. By changing the stress, students can feel and think about the effect of energy/emphasis in dance or any form of communication. Don't forget to set signals for silence (raised hand palm out) and for "noise" (two hand "taking"), and practice each several times until they are automatic. (See *Joy of Signing* [Riekehof, 1987] for ideas.)

Ground rules can be taught by explaining, posting them, role playing, and games. One idea is to

TAKE ACTION 6

SIGN LANGUAGE

Check out a book of sign language such as *Joy of Signing* (Riekehof, 1987). Make a list of 10 signs to use in your classroom. Students love to learn signs for very good, sit down, line up, listen, dance, funny, yes, no, partner, and other common "words" through this kinesthetic communication system.

draw a huge hand on a poster and call it your Rules of Thumb or High Five rules. Write rules on the fingers and use a raised hand as a signal to think about the rules. Here are common rules teachers use: (1) follow directions: obey cues and signals, (2) respect others (e.g., personal space), (3) be responsible, (4) participate actively (enthusiasm), and (5) concentrate (no talking during movement). Take time to have students role play each rule. Role play nonexamples, or the opposite, so that there is no misunderstanding. It's easy to practice rules in a game format. For example, play "home base" by telling students the goal is to not be the last one to get in their personal spot when they hear "home base." Directions can be given in the form of a challenge to create interest: "Before I count to eight, see if you can get into a perfect circle." Another helpful habit is to invite students to participate, rather than order them to do so: "I'd like to invite all of you to try to make a shape on a low level that you think no one else will think of."

Teach how and why to concentrate and focus. The current teacher outrage about the perceived decline in ability to attend may stem from expecting children to do things they have never been taught. Concentration and focus can be directly taught using games: "Frozen shape" challenges students to make a shape on their personal space and hold it for so many counts. Students enjoy trying to increase the hold time each day and can graph their efforts. This is also a chance to compliment original shapes students create, especially stable ones that have a base and are balanced. Concentration is also helped by removing distractions and limiting the space for dancing. Masking tape or imaginary lines can be used for this purpose.

Rule-breaking consequences. A hierarchy of consequences, appropriate to the transgressions, should be made clear to students. Students are confused by inconsistent teachers. They perceive them as unfair. A consequence hierarchy can be as simple as (1) a warning (verbal or nonverbal), (2) a 1-minute time out, (3) a 5-minute time out and conference with the teacher after the lesson, and (4) loss of a chance to participate in the lesson that day and a phone call to parents. A teacher must be as good as her word: follow through, immediately, when a problem occurs. Students will not believe or respect the teacher who continually threatens and warns without taking the promised action. Of course, hitting another child or disrespect for the teacher calls for a high-level consequence right away (number 4!) and probably would involve the principal. Post general consequences, with the understanding that a teacher must do what is necessary to ensure the class is learning. Discuss consequences explicitly during the same time the ground rules are introduced—usually the first week of school. Finally, there is no substitute for good teacher judgment and common sense.

Teaching habits that help with integration of dance are summarized in Post It Page 9–4.

Principle 4: ENERGIZERS and Routines

Props: Signals and Accompaniment. Simple props, such as a tambourine, drum, or bell, are important tools for teachers to use routinely as start and stop signals and to help children work with rhythms and tempos. Students enjoy learning to use rhythm instruments to beat out rhythms for dance. Wooden spoons and oatmeal boxes work well for this. Whistles are not the best musical instrument for signaling in the arts because they tend to demand and alarm, like a scream, rather than create an esthetic mood. Don't forget that the human voice is a perfect vehicle to accompany or signal. If it is comfortable, sing or hum a rhythm for students (left and right and left and right and stop) or use a special word or phrase to signal for attention or as a start–stop. For example, try famous dancers names as signals: "Isadora Duncan" rolls off the tongue and kids enjoy echoing it.

Energizers and Warm-ups. Creative dance is a great way to start each day. Students can be put in a better frame of mind and body for learning. Begin with easy movement warm-ups such as the ones in Chapter 10. There are also recommended books of dance strategies and activities in the bibliography. For example, Gilbert's (1992) *Creative Dance for All Ages* is full of activities useful to energize and warm-up.

TEACHING HABITS FOR USING DANCE AS A TEACHING TOOL

1. Emphasize process over product.
2. Use descriptive feedback to focus attention on dance elements and concepts.
3. Assessment includes student self-evaluation.
4. Guided lessons are needed before free dancing.
5. Ask students to show rather than tell.
6. Give freedom with structure.
7. Teacher questions should be open or fat.
8. You get what you ask for, so demand variety.
9. Use student ideas.
10. Choose music that promotes creative, not stereotyped, movement.
11. Teach the discipline of dance: how to control the body in motion.
    - Show that you are enthusiastic.
    - Expect movement and noise!
    - Structure lessons.
    - Teach rituals for getting attention, stop signals, transitions, and dividing into groups.
    - Teach ground rules by explaining, posting, role playing, and games.
    - Teach how and why to concentrate and focus.
    - Rules need consequences.

Principle 5: GREAT CHILDREN'S LITERATURE Related to Dance

See the appendix for dance-based children's literature that includes informational books, as well as fiction and poetry. For example, *Sometimes I Dance Mountains* (Baylor, Sears & Longtemps, 1973) is a lovely book with a poetic text that can stimulate many movement explorations before, during, or after the book is read. (Rhythm instruments can be added for background effects.) Isadora's (1976) *Max* can be used to relate dance and sports. Carl Sandburg's "Lines Written for Gene Kelly to Dance To" is a poem that asks the famous dancer to dance such ideas as the alphabet and the wind. The entire poem offers wonderful possibilities. Try it with a musical background, such as Leroy Anderson's "Sandpaper Ballet." (Say a line, turn up the volume, fade down, say the next line, and so on.) There is an annotated sampling of dance-based children's literature in Post It Page 9–5.

Any piece of literature can be examined for potential movement ideas. Invite students to find books about dance or ones with movement. Set up a permanent display spot that highlights dance and movement literature (e.g., use a clear plastic book pocket to display a book and change weekly).

TAKE ACTION 7
CHILDREN'S LITERATURE FOR DANCE

Select a children's book to analyze for dance exploration. Pick a book from the award-winning bibliography in Appendix B or from the Bibliography of Arts-Based Children's Literature. Read the book, look at the pictures, and brainstorm BEST. Go beyond the obvious. For example, in Rylant's *All I See,* the man paints, walks, and floats in his boat. But the book is really about being yourself and using your imagination. Themes related to this idea can be explored, rather than just pantomiming the actions in the book. Think of ways to show an original body shape at different levels. How might you stretch yourself to be as large as you can imagine? What would be the most unusual ways to walk from the easel to the lake? How might the man have walked if he were very happy, in deep thought, or anxious to get in the boat?

DANCE-BASED CHILDREN'S LITERATURE

Ackerman, K. (1988). *Song and dance man.* Random House. (a grandpa relives his vaudeville days)

Archambault, J., Martin, B., & Ted Rand (1986). *Barn dance.* Henry Holt. (the animals of the farm gather together with a skinny little boy for a hoedown in the barn)

Barboza, S. (1992). *I feel like dancing: A year with Jacques d'Amboise and the National Dance Institute.* Crown. (three students spend a year at the Institute)

Bierhorts, J. (1979). *A cry from the earth: Music of the North American Indians.* (information about Indian music, musical instruments, and uses of music)

Gauch, P., & Ichikawa, S. (1992). *Bravo, Tanya.* Philomel. (Tanya loves to dance ballet in the meadow with the music only she hears, but in ballet class she finds it difficult to dance with real music)

Glassman, B. (2001). *Mikhail Baryshnikov: Dance genius.* Gale Group.

Glover, S., & Weber, B. (2000). *Savion!: My life in tap.* Morrow.

Gray, L. (1999). *My mama had a dancing heart.* Scholastic.

Jonas, A. (1989). *Color dance.* Greenwillow. (three dancers show how colors combine through an overlapping scarf dance)

Lobel, A. (1980). "The camel dances." *Fables.* Scott Foresman. (a camel loves to dance ballet and performs for her friends; through this she learns a valuable lesson)

Malcolm, J. (2000). *Drat! We're rats!* Starcatcher.

McKissack, P. (1988). *Mirandy and Brother Wind.* Knopf. (Mirandy tries to capture the wind as her partner for a dance contest)

Patrick, D., & Ransome, J. (1993). *Red dancing shoes.* Tambourine Books. (a girl is given bright, shiny, red dancing shoes that allow her to dance many dances, until something happens and she gets them dirty)

Pavlova, A. (2001). *I dreamed I was a ballerina* (Edgar Degas, Illus.). Simon & Schuster.

Staples, S. (2001). *Shiva's fire.* HarperCollins Children's Books.

Van Laan, N. (1993). *Buffalo dance: A Blackfoot legend.* Little Brown. (story of traditional ritual before buffalo hunts)

Wallace, I. (1984). *Chi Chiang and the dragon's dance.* Atheneum. (a boy gains his grandfather's respect when he performs the dragon's dance)

Walton, R. (2001). *How can you dance?* Penguin Putnam Books for Young Readers. (rhyming text explores many ways to dance, like the leader of a band, like a crab on a sunny day, like a tree as it waves in the breeze)

Waters, K., & Cooper, M. (1990). *Lion dancer: Ernie Wan's Chinese New Year.* Scholastic. (Ernie, a young boy, describes the Chinese New Year and his first Lion Dance performance)

Wells, R. (1999). *Tallchief: America's prima ballerina.* Viking Penguin.

Wood, A., & Rosekrans, H. (1986). *Three sisters.* Dial. (Dot, one of the three pig sisters, wants to be a dancer until she takes her first class)

Principle 6: ADAPT Curriculum and Instruction Models

(Richmond, Virginia) Fourth graders wrote stories during an Indian unit and gradually a dance emerged. Stressing "authenticity rather than the stereotype," the class learned about spatial and floor patterns and were able to notate their original dances. During a study of weather, later in the year, a dance showing children's feelings about cold, by such movements as shivering, freezing, and sliding was created. The class went on to study pulleys and levers, resulting in experimentation with body balance and the concepts of gravity, strength, energy and force. A study of pollution yielded

a pollution dance. Boys created a "Gazinta" math dance based on the operation of division. Teacher DeNette Garber concluded, "Virtually all of our movement activities evolve around some phase of the fourth grade curriculum whether it be language arts, aesthetics, human relations, science, history, math, or current events. These experiences have made me realize that creative movement is not a frill or an extra added attraction." (Fleming, 1990, p. 30)

Unit Structures.   In Chapter 2, four different unit structures were explained for integration. Each of the units is based on one of four centers or bodies with nine legs. See Post It Page 2–4. For example, a teacher or team might plan integrated lessons and units using one or more of the traditional subject areas as a unit body or center, or a unit may be a study of an author–illustrator such as Patricia Polacco (literature-based unit) during which all the arts, as well as math, science, social studies, and reading and language arts, are legs that support the center. Dance and movement would be used as learning tools in such a unit, just as any other leg.

Topics to be explored through dance can also be solicited from students (feelings, weather, fire, water, celebrations, cooking, hiking, weddings, birthday parties, funerals, shopping, work, recess). Students should be asked to list movements that correspond to the topic. Once they explore these movements in unison and then in small groups, they can plan a three-part "frozen shape–moves–frozen shape" dance using choice BEST elements. *Note:* Stinson (1988, p. 51) recommends staying away from the topic of "superheroes" because of the aggressive nature of their actions. Also, stereotyped movements such as sitting "Indian style" or limiting dances to "war dances" during Native American studies should be avoided.

An adaptation of the more common perspective on units is to envision a unit with dance as the body or center. A unit might focus on (1) a dancer or choreographer, (2) a genre or form (jazz, ballet, tap), (3) a problem, theme, topic, or question (e.g., Why do people dance? How do dances emerge?), or (4) a particular book, poem, song, or dance (e.g., *Sometimes I Dance Mountains* by Baylor, Sears, and Longtemps). Major concepts and skills in math, science, social studies, reading and language arts, and the other art forms would be used as support legs. Of course, in any integrated lesson or unit, all bodies and legs should be correlated with courses of study and standards to ensure substantive and focused study.

Post It Page 5–3 is an example unit web for an author–artist study. Examine the ways dance is used in it.

Start Small and Grow.   Rather than plan a whole unit on dance or even one with significant use of dance, teachers and students often feel much more comfortable about trying just one lesson. For example, start with a lesson on body parts related to health or a lesson on the shapes bodies can make on different levels. Relate levels to body language and communication. The key is to make sure first attempts are successful, for you and for students. Another way to begin is to integrate energizing warm-ups to introduce the day or particular lessons—math lessons after lunch could start with counted movements done in patterns: 1-2-3; 1-2-3. Plan short lessons of about 15 minutes at first. If classroom management is an issue, begin with students staying at their desks or help them learn about movement in a personal space or spot marked with a sticky colored dot or piece of masking tape on the floor. Personal dots or spots can serve as "home-base," which can be signaled at any time to control or stop movement. Who knows, interest may expand to dance interests outside of school, such as the "dance discovery club" at Columbus School in Berkeley, California (Fleming, 1990, p. 45).

Structuring Lessons.   By giving children clear language and a predictable lesson structure, they will have the skills to succeed and feel safer about taking risks. Direct instruction can be used to teach basic elements of BEST (body, energy, space, and time) using visual aids such as charts, and lessons can be focused on just one or two dance elements so that students are able to go into some depth, becoming comfortable with the possibilities of each element. Dancing about images such as happiness or sadness or inviting free dance before the elements are grasped can be stumbling blocks to student success. Students may simply get silly (humor may be used to cope) or even withdraw if they don't have the necessary tools. Adapting instructional models such as direct or explicit instruction calls for a three-part lesson framework using the *introduction, development,* and *conclusion* introduced in Chapter 2. (See integrated arts lesson framework in Post It Page 2–2 and the example dance plans in Post It Pages 9–8 and 9–9.) Here are a few pointers related to dance:

Introduction.   Teach elements directly and creatively by telling the name of the element, using visuals, and repeatedly reminding or asking students about the focus element throughout the lesson. Tell or ask students how the lesson goals and objectives (elements of focus) relate to real-life uses and contexts. Get in the habit of asking for examples, rather than telling, so that students do as much or more thinking than the teacher does.

Development (Demonstration and Practice Guided by Teacher Feedback and Coaching). This is a time for students to experiment and explore: Ask *how, what,* and *where* questions about the dance elements. Ask students to move in *place* and then in *space.* Try the movement with different body parts and then with different locomotor movements. Change levels, directions, the time and speed, and energy. Ask students to combine elements. For example, walk at a low level slowly or with energy. *Note:* Teachers need only *model* a movement to help clarify thinking. The goal is not to get students to simply imitate, except in the case of teaching specific folk or ethnic dance step sequences.

Conclusion/Assessment (Opportunities for Students to "Show They Know" They Have Met the Lesson Goals). At this point students should be able to put what they've learned to artistic use in a simple form. If students are to create a dance for classmates to observe, structure is essential. A frozen shape–movements–frozen shape sequence is a *basic* structure students can use to create dances and involves creating a beginning, middle, and end. Encourage students to build in level changes that will make dances more interesting. Ask students to freeze the starting shape so that you and their peers can give descriptive positive feedback on what the shape says and how it feels. Students can be asked to give each other feedback on the element focus and what the dance communicated after a dance sharing. Finally, closure is achieved and important assessment information can be gained from asking students to explain what was learned about dance in general and the lesson focal points, including other subject matter content in the lesson.

Integrated Dance Lesson: Connections and Meaning Making. Dance "suggests vitality of fresh, interdisciplinary and expressive experiences for children . . . active participation, meaningful activity, total involvement, and allegiance to high standards" (Fleming, 1990, p. vii). Loretta Woolard (Richmond, Virginia) is a teacher experienced in integrating dance into science. In a unit on the sea, her second graders increased

their vocabulary and writing when they danced the concepts of waves, shells, fish, gulls, and other aspects of sea life.

> [Children] became better aware of their own potential, discovered spatial relationships, and were able to handle themselves. . . . I now know that a reading experience involves more than just books and words. It involves the child's life and interest as a source, his mind for thinking, his voice for verbalization (stories, poems, songs), his hands for writing, and his whole body for a deeper understanding through creative movement and dance. A child must sense and respond for true learning and understanding. (Fleming, 1990, pp. 24–25)

The point of teaching is to help students create meaning for themselves—to become independent. A lesson that integrates dance begins with the assumption that important concepts and skills will be taught about a subject *and* about dance. The planning begins with meaning: selecting topics, themes, questions, and problems to investigate (see possible unit structures in Chapter 2). To use dance successfully, the lesson focus should be full of movement possibilities—actions and shapes should readily come to mind. Stinson (1988) cautions that "everyday movement often does not go beyond pantomime to become *dance*" (p. 55).

> A theme of "fruits and vegetables," for example, would probably have more possibilities for a sensory awareness session than for a movement session. Some themes involve movement that is mostly pantomime, and they are, therefore, harder to extend to dance. For example, *getting dressed* involves zipping, buttoning, tying, etc. However, all of these movements are so specific that it is harder, though not impossible, to open them up to movement with more possibilities . . . you will have to stretch your imagination . . . and think of such things as tying yourself into a knot or buttoning your hand to your knee. (p. 51)

When dance is used to explore concepts in math, science, social studies, language arts, and reading, the teacher needs to feel comfortable that all the disciplines involved, including dance, are used in respectful ways and not trivialized. It is important to continually reflect on the key concepts and skills that are to be learned for the dance prong of the lesson and for the other curricular area. Both are to be treated as areas of substance. For example, a circle-cycle dance created to a steady beat in a unit on the circulatory system can help students understand the feeling of the heart pumping and beating, the blood moving, and how the whole system operates on a cyclical basis. They can get a better understanding of the word *circulatory* from relating it to the feeling of a circle shape.

Preplanning lessons can be helpful. First, explore the content concepts and skills through movement elements. Do so by thinking of the BEST elements to create questions and directions for students: "Make circles with your head, tongue, wrists, knee." Start with a specific direction and move on to "Think of a way to show a circle that we haven't done yet." Actually write out some questions and directions to use. Imagine yourself teaching the lesson to predict how students may respond.

Once movement possibilities have been squeezed from the topic or theme, it is time for the introduction, development, and conclusion of the lesson. See Post It Pages 9–8 and 9–9 for example plans for third-grade math and dance and fifth-grade health/science and dance. Teachers need to decide on whether they will expect a dance structure as a culmination or if they will just be using warm-ups or isolated dance strategies throughout a lesson. In either case, assess-

ment should be planned to gauge learning in dance and the target curricular area.

The conclusion of the lesson involves students showing what they have learned. They may be asked to demonstrate movements, write or TOT (tell one thing) learned. A "memory minute" can be a time for everyone to close their ideas and review the lesson or a relaxation exercise to *preserve the esthetics* of the lesson. Don't forget that plans need to include strategies for transition, use of space, materials, and even ways to dismiss by groups (e.g., "Your ticket out today is . . ." or "All those that . . . may 'slither' out for a reptiles lesson").

Post It Page 9–6 summarizes preplanning steps for an integrated dance lesson. Post It Page 9–7 shows an actual example. Post It Pages 9–8 and 9–9 are finished lesson plans for integrating math and dance and health and dance.

Build Dances Around Ideas. Any idea can be related to dance by asking questions involving the BEST elements and then connecting elements (locomotor moves in different shapes or levels). Ideas are also given depth by use of contrast: Ask students to do the opposite or show a nonexample. Sustained or continuous movements of the circulatory system can be contrasted with the bound movements of the digestive system such as food being swallowed (moving in clumps).

POST IT PAGE 9–6

PREPLANNING: INTEGRATED LESSON WITH DANCE

Start with one of four "bodies" for lessons:
(1) problem/topic/theme/problem, (2) person, (3) core book, or (4) genre/form, and decide the content focus for the dance exploration.

Brainstorm movements related to:
Body: parts, shapes, actions (nonlocomotor/on the spot and locomotor/traveling)
Energy: attack, weight, strength, flow
Space: direction, pathways, levels, size, destinations, focus
Time: speed, duration, rhythm, patterns/phrases, accent

Plan questions and directions: to cause "exploration" of BEST and concepts from target discipline (e.g., science). Think about lesson introduction, development, and conclusion.

Plan dance composition criteria: for example, frozen shape (5 counts), moves (10 counts), shape (5 counts).

Make plan using *Integrated Plan Form* in Chapter 2: Post It Page 2–2 includes teaching strategies organized into introduction, development, conclusion.

PREPLAN FOR INTEGRATED LESSON WITH DANCE

Start with one of four "bodies" for lessons: *Themes*: *No one likes to feel powerless. We all like to be in control* (core book: *Where the Wild Things Are*).

Brainstorm movements related to:

Body

Energy

Space

Time

Focus on flow (bound versus sustained) and using concentration on speed (fast and slow) to develop feel of control (inside self).

Body: all parts, shapes doing nonlocomotor and locomotor with "powerless qualities" (e.g., floppy, jerky, uncertain).

Questions and directions to cause "exploration" of BEST and concepts from target discipline:

Ask how Max felt when he had to stay in his room—besides angry. Use your hand to show how you can control your foot without touching it, like there is an invisible string attached. Try using a finger to control your knee . . . your elbow. Bend over and hang loose, dangling your fingers and arms. Explore loose and controlled with body parts. Take steps forward and backward as if pulled by an invisible force. Walk across the room using an uneven rhythm that shows you are not in control. Collapse to floor level in a loose way. Move all body parts with lots of control and flow. How does this feel differently? Start at head and move to feet doing controlled, sustained, and slow moves and then faster. Do same with controlled and bound, slow and then fast.

Dance composition criteria: In small groups, make a dance that compares powerlessness with self-control. Start with a frozen shape. Put 5 to 10 moves in your dance. Have a frozen ending shape. Be sure to include different levels and shapes in your dance.

Go now to *Integrated Lesson Plan* framework form (Post It Page 2–2).

LESSON PLAN: INTEGRATED DANCE AND HEALTH (FIFTH GRADE)

Two-Pronged Focus: (1) Circulatory system concepts and (2) dance elements

Standards: 1–4, 6–7 (See Post It Page 9–3.)

Student Objectives: Students should be able to:

1. Show dance phrases that express differing heartbeats (rhythms).
2. Show movement qualities that express changes in the circulatory system (e.g., flow).
3. Use body shapes and personal space to show heart's shapes and movement.
4. Maintain focus.
5. Work cooperatively in groups.

(continued)

Teaching Procedure

Introduction: The teacher will:

1. Signal for attention and tell students to sit in personal space.
2. Remind students about posted rules.
3. Use riddle routine (riddle on board).
4. Ask what they remember about heart and circulatory system. Use visual of circulatory system.
5. Show how to take pulse and move to beat. Use slit drum.
6. Ask "What if. . .?" and "Show me. . .?" beats and rhythms during rest, anger, etc.

Development

1. Read aloud fantasy journey and ask students to show with body shape and focus what is described (about heart changing rhythms).
2. Choral read and move to "Dr. Heart" chant to show heartbeat and blood flow. Repeat and increase rate.
3. Pause to ask about flow (sustained movement) and rhythm or beat (percussive).
4. Play "Tranquility" tape and ask students to create a sustained or percussive movement to go with it.
5. Group students to create a dance with a beginning–middle–end to show flow and beat. Challenge them to include creative use of the "circle."
6. Circulate and give descriptive feedback as students work.

Conclusion

1. Divide class so one-half observes while others dance.
2. Audience gives feedback about concentration, percussive versus sustained beats, and shapes (e.g., circles to represent cycle).
3. Repeat chant.
4. Ask what they learned.

Assessment and Evaluation: Observe students and use checklist with range of evaluation criteria from "clear" to "not present" based on objectives 1 to 5.

POST IT PAGE 9–9

LESSON PLAN: INTEGRATED DANCE AND MATH (THIRD GRADE)

Two-Pronged Focus: (1) fractions and problem solving (2) dance elements: body shapes, levels and choreography

Standards: See Post It Page 9–3.

Student Objectives: Students will:

1. Use high, middle, and low levels and body shapes that are curved, straight, angular, and twisted to show the concepts of: (1) equivalent fractions and (2) fractional parts of wholes and sets that have been divided into as many as 16 parts.
4. Maintain focus.
5. Work cooperatively in groups.

Materials: Two charts, fraction problem cards

Teaching Procedure

Introduction: The teacher will:

1. Signal for students to group into regularly assigned squads. Remind students about posted rules.
2. Tell objectives of today's lesson: fractions and dance.
3. Play inspirational music and do warm up routine.

Development

1. Show charts of four body shapes and three levels. With each student in personal space, call a shape and level in which to freeze, e.g., curved low or straight high.
2. Show fraction chart to review: whole, ½, ⅓, ¼, ⅕, ⅛, 1⁄16. Ask students to show each, e.g., show ½ by dividing into two groups. Do for each, letting students figure out how to arrange themselves.
3. Ask students about equivalent fractions (review from previous lesson). Give examples: ½ = 2⁄4. Tell students they will work in squads to show a fraction problem through dance. Ask how they could create a three part dance for ½–2⁄4 starting with frozen shapes/levels, adding movements, and then ending with a frozen shape. Brainstorm and try their ideas.
4. Break into squads and give each a fraction problem card.
5. Circulate and give descriptive feedback as students work.

Conclusion

1. Performances: Divide class so one-half observes while others dance.
2. Audience observes to figure out fraction problem.
3. Audience gives feedback on what worked.
4. Reverse groups and repeat.
5. Ask what they learned about dance and fractions.

Assessment and Evaluation: Observe students and use checklist with range of evaluation criteria from "clear" to "not present" based on objectives. Photographs of students.

Source: Adapted from: Mr. Crabb and Mrs. Peterson, Lady's Island Elementary School, Beaufort, SC.

TAKE ACTION 8

FINISH THE PLAN

Use the ideas from this chapter to complete the introduction, development, and conclusion for preplanning for the lesson in Post It Page 9–7 on *Where the Wild Things Are.*

PARTICULAR Adaptations for Special Needs. A final consideration under adapting models for curriculum and instruction for dance integration involves a return to thinking about the different adjustments teachers can make for diverse student needs. The 10 adaptations introduced in Chapter 2 (Post It Page 2–7) were to change the *place, amount, rate, target objectives, instruction, curriculum materials, utensils, levels of difficulty, assistance,* and *response.* Using these changes, lessons can be matched to students' ages or stages (e.g., older students may laugh a lot at first because they are unsure of themselves and conscious of changing bodies; laughing is a way people deal with problems). Amount and rate can be adjusted by starting with basic dance warm-ups and doing a thorough job of teaching the BEST elements, one at a time, so that students are comfortable. Target objectives, materials, and response may need to be adjusted for students with physical disabilities; for example, wheelchair-bound students, with limited use of the body, might be given the role of beat keeper or be in charge of start and stop signaling.

Principle 7: TRIPS to Experience Dance

Concert Attendance.   It shouldn't be surprising that figure skating is the most popular Olympic event in terms of audience viewing. Unlike other sports, figure skating combines athleticism with artistry that engages emotions like no other competitive event. This artistry happens to be a kind of dance.

There is no substitute for the emotional impact of the live performance. Dance concert attendance is an invaluable opportunity for children to see skilled amateurs and professionals perform dances from traditional ballet to hip hop. Dance concerts by local companies, including those at colleges, as well as national touring events such as *Riverdance*, expand students' personal visions of career possibilities. They also have the educational opportunity to *dis*band negative cultural and gender stereotypes associated with dance. Nothing is more powerful than a live performance to show children the athletic connections to dance and to help them see strong men and women with the skills, artistry, and confidence to use movement expressively.

Without school-sponsored trips to see live performances, many children experience only in-house assemblies, few of which will be devoted to dance. Just as with other field trips, however, dance expeditions should be carefully selected to align with curricular goals and be an integral part of a unit. Critical to maintaining the integrity of dance excursions is the three-part structure first presented in the Trips sections of Chapter 2: (1) prepare students for the trip; (2) cause them to be mentally focused during the trip; and (3) follow up with debriefing about what was learned.

Pretrip Strategies.   Live performances are different from video or television dramas because the audience shares in the event. There is a feeling of spontaneity that causes the actors to respond to the energy of the audience. Here is a short checklist to help prepare for trips to see live performances:

◆   Students need to be clear about expectations for audience etiquette so that everyone enjoys the performance and the dancers are respected. A discussion of behavior consequences is important to the trip's success. This means the teacher must know the expected behaviors for the site being visited. It is also useful to ask students to role play how to act before, during, and after the concert.

◆   To set the purpose, it is effective to ask students to generate questions they want answered during the trip. Cue sheets (i.e., worksheets listing

things to notice during the performance) help students anticipate what is coming. They can then experience a sense of discovery about the moves dancers make—for example, "That was a triple lutz!" Concept minilessons that focus on key ideas and terms such as *choreographer* or the use of music, sets, and costumes help prepare students to be mindful viewers. Students need guidelines about what they are expected to learn from the field trip, and they should be held accountable. If students know there is to be an assessment after the trip, they are more focused on the trip's purpose and less on socializing with peers. This can be accomplished by reviewing specific study sheets or general questions before the trip that are to be used when they return:

What was the most important thing you learned? What is one thing you could follow up on and find out more about? How did the experience make you feel? Why? What did the trip have to do with what we've been studying? Write about the trip and what you learned about. Show what you learned with art materials, drama, music, or dance and movement. Write a poem about the trip. Write a letter to the teacher convincing her that trips like these are important in school. Write a thank you note to. . . .

◆   Obtain information from the arts organization about the nature of the visit. Some arts organizations provide activity packets to use in advance of the dance concert.

◆   Make a visit to the site prior to the field trip. Check about coat racks, restrooms, seating, and so forth. At this time, try to generate questions or points to focus on in pretrip lessons (e.g., concepts or questions related to displays or other aspects of the upcoming performance). Pick up printed information at the site to share with students.

During the Trip/Concert.   If pretrip steps have been taken carefully, the "during" portion of the trip will be more likely to flow well. Students should know what is expected and be focused. Of course, children need reminders, and behavior signals that can be seen across a theatre are helpful. Agree on signals ahead of time. It is particularly helpful to use sign language for "sit down," "line up," and "listen." It is also important for teachers to participate as learners and viewers, as well as managers of their classes. Teachers should be models of active learning.

Follow-up for the Trip.   Teachers may wish to debrief students before leaving the site and let hosts know some of what the students gained. Students need to be made aware that the teacher will do this so that they can prepare during the visit and not embarrass themselves and their teachers with poor responses. After the dance, it is helpful to have a discussion, and, just as in good literature discussions, it is important to encourage a variety of points of view. Some useful questions include "What did you see? How did it make you feel? What in the dance made you feel that way? What was important in the dance? What was it really about? What was missing? What was the choreographer trying to say?" Of course, responses to field trips can be in many forms, such as journal entries, skits, or artwork. Whatever form responses take, they should be selected to reveal the quantity and quality of the meaning making that students did related to the visit.

Field trips to museums or concerts are not unusual in elementary and middle school. What is unusual is the meaningful integration of these trips. Without pre-trip lessons to prepare students and follow-up assessment, trips can become little more than social time.

Observation Walks and Discovery Trips. Field trips don't have to mean a bus trip. Students often get so excited about trips that they can't get serious about learning. We can take only a few field trips, but short, close-to-school trips can be practice for larger trips and educationally valuable. For example, a walk around the block to discover how people move as they do their work or play can give insight into the Body, Energy, Space, and Time dance elements used in everyday life. Observation walks to see how plants and animals move can be a rich foundation to refine students' use of specific verbs to describe movements.

Principle 8: EVIDENCE of Student Progress/Assessment

Audiences and Performances. Using dance as a teaching tool involves planning for students to both "do and view." When students become audience members, as well as perform for audiences, they learn the "ancient and honorable tradition of dance as art and ritual" (Fleming, 1990, p. 7). The viewing gives ideas for the doing of dance, and doing dance makes students astute viewers. For example, through concert viewing, students can develop a *discriminating* awareness of movement as an artistic medium.

When there is a need for students to exhibit progress through performance, teachers can invite parents and grandparents or use the children themselves. By dividing the class in half and taking turns performing, students are put in both the "do and view" roles. Audience members can be asked to give descriptive feedback after performances so that they see their role as meaningful. This develops social skills and the ability to do analysis and evaluation. Of course, as with all art exhibitions, it is important to stress that there is no right or wrong movements, although some movements are more pleasing or surprising and some do not work as well as others to get across the intentions of the dancers. In any case, students need to learn that applause is a part of good audience etiquette. *Note:* start and stop signals will need to be used to structure performances (e.g., say "curtain," "show time," "close your eyes," "positions," and "lights," as cues).

Videotapes of student dance compositions can be added to portfolio collections related to any unit under study to show how students are using movement to demonstrate learning. These tapes can serve as progress indicators of how students are applyng ideas such as BEST or variations on the three-part dance to "show they know" about key concepts and skills in science, social studies, math, and language arts. In addition, students can re-view past tapes and do self-evaluations of how they have grown in the use of movement as a meaning maker.

Appendix D includes examples of informal assessment tools to use with integrated dance lessons. Also see the general discussion of assessment at the start of Chapter 14.

Principle 9: SPECIALISTS in Dance Are Important

Collaboration. Dancers, dance educators, and physical educators are all potential persons to help integrate dance and movement in a regular classroom. Teachers can begin a collaboration by expressing an interest in using movement throughout the curriculum in conversations with the physical education teacher or, if the school is fortunate to have one, the dance teachers. Classroom teachers need to ask specialists for advice about what they are doing that could be used in the regular classroom. It is a good idea to make an appointment to talk in more depth. A positive way to begin collaboration of this kind is to ask to observe movement lessons. If there is a dance specialist, he can be given a list of units, concepts, and skills to be taught during the month. Specialists can be asked to provide the same information to the classroom teacher so that both can look for possible links. Once a working relationship begins to develop, specialists can be asked to do special lessons with students that connect to classroom lessons. Classroom teachers need to expect to reciprocate.

Reassurance for Classroom Teachers: Common Problems

In the dance, even the weakest can do wonders.

Karl Gross

Any teacher who values creativity and movement can learn to integrate dance. Teachers who feel uncomfortable about dancing in front of students need to understand that it is not necessary to integrate dance throughout the curriculum. Students can be asked or directed to move in certain ways without any demonstration. Lack of a "model" to imitate can actually cause more creative problem solving than if students are shown specific steps. The goal of integrating dance and movement is not to just mimic the teacher.

Another problem that sometimes arises is with the word *dance* itself. If dance is a touchy term, use *creative movement*. Most people will accept that students must know how to move appropriately and parents are supportive of efforts to increase children's self-regulatory skills. Both community members and parents are also impressed by the connections between needed workplace skills and the arts. Dance is an important means of developing the creative thinking so valued by businesses who wish to compete with innovative products and services.

A third concern is a lesson that flops. Many lesson failures occur because the teacher isn't clear about the lesson objectives: what exactly should students know and be able to do by the end of the lesson that they couldn't do or didn't know at the start? Inadequate preparation or lack of structure can also doom a lesson. By using a lesson plan framework, much of this problem can be alleviated. Such a framework includes (1) the arts elements to teach and the content area concepts and skills to be developed and (2) a clear introduction, development, and conclusion that organize the teaching and learning. Keep in mind that too many directions confuse students and that dance is kinesthetic—get students moving as soon as possible. Learning to integrate dance involves trial and error. When something is not working, teachers should feel free to alter *strategies* in the lesson plan while maintaining the dance and other curricular focus. It is important to be flexible, within the parameters of research-based concepts of (1) effective teaching, (2) learning theory, and (3) the principles of arts integration. Chapters 1 and 2 provide an overview of these areas.

Finally, dance construction by the children should not be considered an absolute essential to every integrated lesson. Teachers who do not feel well prepared in dance may initially confine teaching to movement exploration, such as more teacher-directed dance element experimentation. Eventually, students spontaneously begin to construct dance sequences, if they are given experiences that focus on problem solving through movement exploration, invention, and improvisation. Teachers should not rush into having students compose dances. They should feel proud to see that students are enlarging their repertoire of movements and are gaining poise in use and confidence about their bodies.

◆ CONCLUSION

In this chapter, an introduction to integrating dance throughout the curriculum has been discussed with a focus on the role of the general classroom teacher. Rationale was presented for integrating dance *(why)*, information teachers need to know was reviewed *(what)*, and general principles for integrating dance were explained *(how)*. In Chapter 10, specific starter ideas for teaching dance basics and integrating dance throughout the curriculum are organized into three categories.

◆ TEACHER RESOURCES

See Appendix F: *Bibliography of Recommended Reading and Viewing* for additional resources.

Alison, L. (1991). *A handbook of creative dance and drama.* Portsmouth, NH: Heinemann.

Bennett, J. P. (1995). *Rhythmic activities and dance.* Champaign, IL: Human Kinetics.

Berthoz, A. (2000). *The brain's sense of movement.* Cambridge, MA: Harvard University Press.

Choksy, Lois (1987). *120 singing games and dances for elementary schools.* Upper Saddle River, NJ: Prentice Hall.

Creative movement: A step towards intelligence (1993). West Long Branch, NJ: Kultur (80-minute video).

Dana, A. (1991). *All-time favorite dances* (cassette). Long Branch, NJ: Kimbo Educational.

Dance and grow (1994). 60-minute video. Scotch Plains, NJ: Dance Horizons.

Fleming, G. A. (1990). *Children's dance.* Reston, VA: American Alliance for Health, Physical Education, Recreation and Dance.

Hanna, J. (1999). *Partnering dance and education: Intelligent moves for changing times.* Champaign, IL: Human Kinetics.

Landalf, H. (1997). *Moving the earth: Teaching earth science through movement for grades 3–6 (Young Actor Series).* Lyme, NH: Smith & Kraus.

Malam, J. (2000). *Song and dance.* New York: Franklin Watts.

McGreevy-Nichols, S. (1995). *Building dances: A guide to putting movements together.* Champaign, IL: Human Kinetics.

Pica, R. (1995). *Experiences in movement with music, activities, and theory.* Albany, NY: Delmar.

Rowen, B. (1994). *Dance and grow: Developmental dance activities for three- through eight-year-olds.* Pennington, NJ: Princeton Book.

Stinson, S. (1988). *Dance for young children: Finding the magic in movement.* Reston, VA: American Alliance for Health, Physical Education, Recreation and Dance.

◆ BIBLIOGRAPHY AND REFERENCES

Books and Articles

Boston, B. (1996). Educating for the workplace through the arts. Reprinted from *Business Week,* October 28, 1996 issue. Columbus OH: McGraw-Hill.

Donohue, K. (1997). *Imagine! Introducing your child to the arts.* Washington, DC: National Endowment for the Arts.

Fleming, G. A. (Ed.). (1990). *Children's dance.* Reston, VA: American Alliance for Health, Physical Education, Recreation and Dance.

Gardner, H. (1983). *Frames of mind.* New York: Basic Books.

Gardner, H (1996). Learning improved by arts training. *Nature, 381*(580), 284.

Gilbert, A. (1992). *Creative dance for all ages.* Reston, VA: National Dance Association.

Gilbert, A. G. (1977). *Teaching the 3 Rs through movement experiences.* New York: Macmillan.

Griss, S. (1998). *Minds in motion.* Portsmouth, NH: Heinemann.

Hallet, M. (1999, May). *Gray matters: Sports, fitness and the brain.* [Transcript of interview from National Public Radio, available at 800-652-7256.]

Jay, D. (1991). Effect of a dance program on the creativity of preschool handicapped children. *Adapted Physical Activity Quarterly, 8,* 305–316.

Jensen, E. (2001). *Arts with the brain in mind.* Alexandria, VA: Association for Supervision and Curriculum Development.

Joyce, M. (1994). *First steps in teaching creative dance to children* (3rd ed.). Mountain View, CA: Mayfield.

Maslow, A. (1970). *Motivation and personality.* New York: Harper & Row.

Murray, R. L. (1975). *Dance in elementary education: A program for boys and girls* (3rd ed.). New York: Harper & Row.

Pica, R. (1991). *Moving and learning.* Champaign, IL: Human Kinetics.

Riekehof, L. (1987). *The joy of signing* (2nd ed.). Springfield, MO: Gospel Publishing.

Stinson, S. (1988). *Dance for young children: Finding the magic in movement.* Reston, VA: American Alliance for Health, Physical Education, Recreation and Dance.

Children's Literature

Barboza, S. (1992). *I feel like dancing: A year with Jacques D'Amboise and the National Dance Institute.* New York: Crown.

Baylor, B., Sears, B., & Longtemps, K. (1973). *Sometimes I dance mountains.* New York: Atheneum.

Isadora, R. (1976). *Max.* New York: Simon & Schuster.

Other

Baron, R. (1997, February) Scientific thought in motion. Presentation at The Kennedy Center, Washington, DC.

10

Dance Seed Strategies

Introduction

Who can turn a child's mouth into a smile? A child's thoughts into a dream? Who can turn a child's walk into a dance?

                                                              A teacher.

In this chapter there are specific ideas to (1) get students ready for dance, (2) teach basic elements and concepts so that students can use dance as a learning tool, and (3) integrate dance and movement throughout the curriculum. These seed strategies must be grown by developing them to fit student and curricular needs. Seeds can be selected to solve particular teaching and learning problems and adapted using the 10 PARTICULAR variations (Post It 2-6). The strategies are organized into three sections, but many could be placed in several sections. Energizers and elements and concepts do *not* represent integration, as they stand, but are provided to ready students for creative work and teach dance concepts needed if dance is to be used as a way to make meaning.

I. Energizers and Warm-ups

The purposes of energizers and warm-ups are to get the attention of students, actually warm up the body so that it is ready for movement, set mood, and stimulate creative problem solving. Many build concentration and following-directions skills.

Name Moves. Form a circle and ask each student to create a movement to match the syllables in his or her name. The leader begins and demonstrates using a unique level, body part and move, for example, Susan: start at low level and slither up to high level saying "Suuuu-san!" After each student demos her name move, everyone mimics it. Challenge: Repeat everyone's move from the beginning each time to learn names.

Watch My Hand Concentration. Partner students. One is the "hand" and the other must follow the partner's hand with his eyes. Leader should change levels and directions. At teacher's signal, partners reverse roles.

Hang Loose. Use an object to represent the concepts of "relaxed and tense" or "loose and tight" (e.g., scarf versus rock, piece of yarn versus pencil, rag doll versus Barbie doll). Call out a body part and ask students to make it tight and hard, then loose and soft.

No Words. Teacher uses only motions to tell students what to do: "Come forward, turn, sit." Students then get a partner and communicate what to do without words. Don't *show* your partner. Tell with your movements. Repeat without using hands. Afterward, discuss the role of gestures and movements in communication.

Stretches to Music. Direct students to slowly: Inhale, reach up and overhead and to floor with knees bent. Exhale. Repeat to each side. Roll head and shoulders forward and backward, bend arms, do socket rolls, touch head to shoulders, touch knees, touch toes, sit and twist and bend, do slow windmills, toe presses, heel to toe slowly, clasp hands behind and stretch shoulders, spine stretches, squat and press forward (exhale), bend one leg and repeat (exhale). Slow nonrhythmic mood music can be used, and many CDs and tapes are available with nature sounds that work well.

Step In. This is a simple movement activity. Children form a circle and the teacher gives a series of movement directions. For example, "Take two steps in if you know the capital of Ohio. Step back one if you know the state bird."

Weight Shift. Ask students to "Move foot to foot (most basic locomotor step). Go smaller, larger, faster, slower. Expand to leap with body curved forward."

Who Started the Motion. Players stand or sit in a circle. One player is sent from the room while another player is selected to be leader, who leads others through different motions, such as moving hands or tapping feet. Player who left the room comes back in and watches carefully to figure out who is starting the movements as the leader begins a new one.

Cumulative Name Game. Form a circle. The first individual says his or her name and makes a motion. The next person says the name and makes a motion and then everyone repeats the first person's name and motion. The process continues in a cumulative manner until it goes all around.

Hand Warm-up. Teacher directs everyone to make a fist and then show one, then two, then three, then four, and then five fingers. Repeat. Do other hand and then both. Change tempo.

Hug Yourself. Leader calls out body part to hug (e.g., hand hug, finger hug). Encourage creative thinking.

Head, Shoulders, Knees, and Toes. First practice singing the song by this title. Then repeat and ask students to stand in a circle and touch body parts as they are mentioned in the song.

Follow the Leader.   Students imitate actions or words of the leader. For example, move different body parts at different levels. Use the BEST elements for ideas.

"Simon Says" with Dance Elements.   Play "Simon Says" using BEST elements (Post It Page 9–2) and Laban actions (see Take Action 4 in Chapter 9) (e.g., bend, twist). For example, "Simon Says" use your body to show a circle. Relate to units (e.g., time lesson: move clockwise in a circle).

Body Touches.   Do a rhythm or chant (e.g., "Touch your head, head, head . . . touch your toes, toes, toes), and ask students to do the appropriate moves.

Walk Different Ways.   Ask children to walk in the following ways: in place slow and fast, forward, backward, and sideways. Work on posture and alignment: students walk freely as you call out tiny steps, giant steps, on heels, on tiptoe, in place, backward, forward, as lightly as possible (an element of force), or as slowly as possible (an element of time). Use scarves and students throw up scarves and must catch with different parts of the body. Can be done to music. Other materials: balls, hoops, ropes.

Freeze (Self-Control).   Play music or use a tambourine and tell students to move in a specific way using space until the sound stops and they must freeze. When the music begins again, they are to move in their frozen shape. For example, "When drum begins, you are to walk in place to the beat."

Magic Shoes.   Students should imagine they have on magic shoes that allow them to walk in special ways (e.g., on water, on air).

Body Directions.   For example: Show me "up" with your body, "down." How can you make your body go all the way up? All the way down? How high can you get? Show me halfway down. Make yourself so small I can hardly see you. Now as big as you can. Pretend your feet are glued to the floor. Move your body up and down now.

Dancin'

Fantasy Journey (for Concentration). Teacher tells or reads a story or series of movements. For example:

Put your feet into warm water and wiggle your toes. Now put your legs in and swish them around. Make circles in the water. You slip farther into the water and sway your hips back and forth. You are up to your waist. Slowly walk in place in the water. Feel the weight of the water. Now you raise your hands up out of the water and stretch them over your head. You jump up and down. Feel the water. You sink down up to your neck. Let your arms float on top of the water. Press your hands down in the water to your sides and then raise them up. Put your hands on your hips and twist, twist, twist. Now rotate your head forward, to left and back, then right and around again. Oops, the water splashes up your nose, so you wiggle your nose and blow the water from your lips. With your toes you pull the plug and the water begins to drain out. You shiver as it moves below your arm pits. As it reaches your thighs, you raise your knees up and down, up and down. Finally the water drains out. You twirl around and sit down.

Spaghetti Freeze (for Following Directions). Students move as many loose and relaxed ways as they can. Do these in one spot, varying the speed and levels. When the teacher gives a signal, students must freeze in a shape. Students can then be asked to give a one liner about their shape (e.g., how they feel).

Five-Shape Concentration. Goal is to create, number, and remember shapes. Teacher says "one" and each person makes the first shape. On "two," a second different shape is made. This continues through "five." Then the teacher calls numbers at random and students must do the shape they first made for that number.

Slow-Motion Concentration. Each student picks an everyday movement and does it as slowly as possible. Groups can perform by dividing class in half, with audience half giving feedback on focus and concentration.

Circle Back Rub (Relaxation). Form circle and each person puts hands on shoulders of person in front. Leader says "go" and each person rubs the back of the person in front. Leader says "switch" and all turn and do same for person behind them.

Lightning Concentration. Form circle and join hands. Teacher squeezes a rhythm to both the right- and left-hand partners, and the rhythm is passed around the circle until it collides in one person. That person shouts "lightning" and becomes the leader.

Paranoia (Concentration). Group spreads out to fill up space. On signal (e.g., drum beat), they all begin to walk around the room trying to fill up the space and leave no holes. The leader then calls "one" and everyone finds someone to follow around, not letting the person know he's being followed and still trying to fill up the whole space. Then the leader calls "two" and a second person is followed. Finally "three" is called. The leader then alternates numbers and everyone continually switches, but fill up the space.

Popcorn. On signal, the group begins to walk around, filling up space. When leader signals "one," each person identifies a person to track with his eyes. Whenever they actually come near that person, they jump. Next the leader signals "two" and a second person must be tracked, while still tracking the first. When the second person is passed by, you must now freeze for a split second. Everyone is now walking around jumping and freezing. Finally, leader says "three," and a third person is now visually identified by each individual. When that person is passed, say "popcorn." Continue until the leader signals "freeze."

Breathing Warm-up. Slowly breathe in through your right nostril and out through your left. Breathe in slowly, becoming as high and large as you can and then slowly exhale and shrink as small as possible. Breathe in very slowly and exhale slowly, making a single sound. Group can choose to make same sound (e.g., one of short vowel sounds). Breathe in slowly with clenched teeth and out through your nose. Breathe to the rhythm of a piece of music. Put your hands on your abdomen and breathe in slowly and exhale slowly.

Wiggle and Giggle. Ask students to show how they can giggle with a foot, a knee, and on up the body to the head. Shaking and wiggling with controls (signals, numbers) helps students learn self-discipline and focus.

Energizers and Warm-ups for Cooperation

Add On. Groups of four to six form and stand in a line, side to side. At one end a person starts a movement and the next person picks it up and adds to it. The movement travels down the line until the end. The starter then moves to the end and a new starter begins.

Movement Chain. Stand in a line or U shape. On signal, people on the two ends start a movement or a rhythm and send it around until it reaches the end. End people then go to the center of the line, and new end people start new movements or rhythms.

Don't Cross the Line. Pairs face each other and hold on to shoulders. They imagine a line between them.

Each starts pushing but cannot cross the line. The goal is to push hard, but not push each other over. Repeat back to back or side to side.

Buddy Walk. Pairs are back to back, leaning against each other. First, they silently walk around the room. Then they try to sit on the floor and rise up again. Can be done side by side.

Back-to-Back Dancing. Pairs slightly lean against each other and begin dancing with music. Use something slow at first. Each must try to sense what moves to make to keep them together.

Shrink and Stretch. Group forms a circle stretching out so only fingertips touch and moving the body out as much as possible without losing touch. Leader signals "shrink," and the circle moves in and tries to take up as small a space as possible. Then leader says "stretch" again, and so forth.

Balloon Balance or Bust. Group joins hands and forms circle. Several balloons are thrown out and the object is to keep them in the air without dropping each other's hands.

Stuck Together. Pairs must hold a note card between their two body parts (e.g., head to head with card in between). Another card is then added, and so on, until one card falls. Can be done in small groups with one person in the center and others joined to the one person with a card in between. When leader signals, center person must move and group must try to follow without dropping cards.

No Holes. Group spreads out to fill up all available space. On signal (e.g., drum beat), everyone walks around trying to keep the space completely filled. When leader signals "stop," all must freeze. If there is a hole, someone must fill it up.

Body Count. Everyone walks around and fills up the space. Leader then calls out a combination (e.g., three heads and two hands). Students must work together to find others to create this combination of touching body parts.

Spider Web. Everyone in the group must be touching someone else in an appropriate spot. When leader signals to start, everyone moves slowly around the room, always touching someone (e.g., with a foot, hand,

shoulder). When leader signals "stop," everyone must be touching (i.e., connected by the human web).

II. DANCE CONCEPTS AND BEST ELEMENTS

These strategies and activities can be used after you have introduced the BEST dance or movement elements.

Personal Space. Teacher directs students to find a personal spot. Students then explore their personal space, not moving from the spot, by making shapes at low, middle, and high levels.

Movement Words Charts. Challenge students to find all the words they can that go in either the locomotor or nonlocomotor categories. Here are examples:

> *Locomotor:* walk, run, leap, step, jump, hop, lump, jeep, drag, slide, scoot, gallop, skip, crawl, creep, dart, dash, float, fly, glide, patter, pounce, prance, roll, sail, spin, stamp, swoop, tramp, slip.
>
> *Nonlocomotor:* bend, stretch, twist, swing, rock, sway, collapse, curl, dodge, expand, explode, flop, grab, jerk, lean, lift, point, poke, pull, press, push, quiver, rise, shake, shiver, sink, sit, slap, squirm, strike, sway, tap, thrust, tough, turn, wriggle, writhe.

Movement Words Card Sort. Ask students to call out ways to move. Write them on cards. Ask groups to sort the cards into locomotor and nonlocomotor. Next, ask students to list adverbs that qualify each (e.g., walk slowly, fast, with force, directly, in a "shape," using a lot of space, in a rhythm).

Locomotor and Nonlocomotor Action Bingo. Give the definition of these dance concepts. Students cover the word on a bingo card. See Chapter 2 for "big-bingo" idea.

> *Walk:* shift weight from one foot to other with one foot always on the ground.
>
> *Run:* same as walk, but there are moments when neither foot touches the ground.
>
> *Gallop:* this is a step leap with the same foot always leading in an uneven rhythm.
>
> *Leap:* like a run but you are in the air longer with both feet off the ground.

Skip: combines step and hop in an uneven rhythm, and the lead foot alternates.

Jump: weight changes from both feet to both feet.

Hop: requires weight change from one foot to the same foot.

Shake: a wiggle done in place.

Bend: close up your joints.

Stretch: open up your joints.

Push: use your body to move against a resistance.

Pull: use your body away from a resistance.

Twist: rotate in a direction up to the body's limit.

Turn: spin around, whirl, and twirl.

Rise: come up to a higher level.

Sink: move down to a lower level.

Other action words to add include: zoom, slither, scatter, explode, crumple, melt, and tiptoe.

I'm Stuck. Students stand in personal space. Teacher narrates a series of sticky situations and students mime:

> *You are clapping your hands when they suddenly won't come apart. You work them to try to get them to separate. Finally, they pop apart and you reach up to scratch your face. Now your hand is stuck to your face. You are frustrated because you try different ways to pull your hand off, but it is hard. Blop! It comes off and you start to walk around when your left foot sticks solidly to the floor. This time you decide to make the best of it, and you move around all the ways you can with your left foot glued down.*

Variation: Follow up with writing about feelings.

Body Moves and Steps. Use these activities as ways to practice types of moves and steps:

Leap: Pretend to leap over objects or use actual objects (e.g., a log or a rubber swimming pool).

Hop: Use a hoop. Students hop in and out. Hop all the way around the hoop. Change tempo.

Jump: Jump in the following ways: knee straight, landing and taking off only on balls of feet, with feet together, then apart, alternating these, landing on one foot, clicking heels together in air.

Run: Explore running with imagery. Ask the students to run on hot sand, to the finish line, playing basketball, to catch a bus, and so on.

Slide: Slide as if the floor was slick, the floor was warm, you are tired, you are in a hurry.

Step hop: Clap a one–two beat with your hands and instruct students to step on beat 1 and hop on beat 2. Then try it to music.

Stretch: Ask students to stretch as if they are waking up, yawning; ask them how long they can stretch out, how wide.

Bend: Do bends from real life (e.g., to tie shoes, pet a dog, pick up a dime on the floor).

Sit: Have students practice sitting, kneeling, and lying without the use of their hands.

Shake: Ask for images of shaking in real life and do (e.g., a bowl of jelly, a baby's rattle, piece of bacon sizzling on a pan, leaf in the wind, riding on a bumpy road).

Turn, twist, lift: Have students practice turning on feet. Do at different levels and speeds.

Rock and sway: Sway like the wind and then gradually increase the force of the sway so that it is more like rocking. Ask students to sway while walking, slowly, faster, larger, smaller, and so forth (Pica, 1991).

Eight Laban Effort Actions. Practice these actions in different ways by asking students to use different body parts or amounts of energy or by changing the timing (sustained versus quick): *Punch, slash, wring, press, dab, flick, float, glide.* Ask students to try to lead with different parts of body (e.g., glide with your shoulder, flick with a hand, punch with a shoulder). Finally, give three Laban actions and ask students to create a dance with five moves. Dance can be in the three-part frozen shape–movements–shape sequence. Partner and have students teach each other their dances.

Shake It Up. On a signal, everyone shakes and wiggles a body part. When leader says "freeze," all must stop. Begin again. Ask students to give descriptive comments about body shapes when they freeze.

Movement Problems. Start a movement such as arm swinging. Ask problem-solving questions such as "How can you make it smaller? Show me. Now larger. Move the swinging to whole body and then back to just arms. What are the effects of these movements?" Have half the class do and others observe and then reverse. Ask fat questions such as "What did you see? How did it feel?"

Across the Floor. Divide into teams and do as relay. Teacher calls a move (e.g., walk, run, leap, jump, lump, jeep, skip) or a combination, and when he touches the "target," the next person goes.

Walks. Ask students to walk to a variety of drum beats (e.g., half-time, double-time, walk time, march time). Next, direct students to explore other aspects of walking by talking them through a sequence: "Walk in place and then walk around the room without bumping into people. Cover the whole room. Walk with toes first. Walk as if you . . . just got a compliment, were just embarrassed, have a stomach ache, are worried, are expectant, have a heavy load, are in love!" Encourage walks in low, medium, and high levels to music (e.g., Enya).

Imagination Walk. Line up the class and each takes a turn and walks to a destination as others observe and describe. Each go and must walk a *different way* to the other side of the room. Repeat and add energy, change time, use space and body differently, repeat phrases.

Jump–Turn–Freeze. Students walk around and keep an eye on one person. They should not follow the person. Next, add a second person and then, after a while, a third person to the list of others that each student is trying to watch. Students are to keep walking. Then say, "When you pass the first person JUMP!" Continue for a while and then add TURN for the second person and finally FREEZE for the third.

Levels (Space). Students create a shape and then freeze in low, middle, and high levels on a count or signal.

Pathways. Everyone spies a destination and then moves there in a straight pathway and back home, then a curvy pathway and back home, using as little space as possible, with stops and starts inserted, and so forth.

Adopt a Dance. Each person chooses a move or step and gives it a "unique touch." Sustain until you make eye contact with someone and then adopt their dance.

Dance Machine. Each student chooses a move that can be repeated over and over. One student goes to the center and begins her move. One by one all "add on" by touching on some plane and repeating his or her move until all are "one" machine with a variety of moving parts. Machine can be around an idea (e.g., a book or chapter in a book, a concept or feeling).

Pass-It-On Moves. One person in the circle starts a move and others imitate until the moves get all the way around to the starter. The next person to the right then starts a move, and so on. Do to music.

Four Corners Stations. Each group begins at a station with a movement problem (e.g., a warm-up station could have a tape of music or directions, stretch station, wiggle station, walk in place station). At signal, students rotate to next station.

String Shapes. Each person stands in elastic loop (one yard of tied together elastic). They then make movements while holding on to the elastic. Ask the children to then move to music while creating a variety of shapes with the elastic.

Responding to Accent. Clap a phrase accenting the first beat (e.g., think of "I love you" with accent on three different words). Clap the same phrase accenting the last beat. Children move to the phrase, showing the accent by a change of movement (after time element is taught).

Video Response. Watch a video (e.g., a musical with dance in it such as *Oklahoma*) that ties into a lesson's topic and has a dance connection. Have children watch for specific dance elements (BEST) and how they are used to communicate an idea or feeling. This can be a jigsaw cooperative learning activity.

Ribbon or Scarf Dancing. Tape about 2 feet of ribbon to the end of a pencil, creating a wand for each student. In a large space, allow students to experiment with dancing to music with the scarves or ribbons.

Shape Rope. In own space, hold rope up high and drop it. *Look at how rope landed. Make the same shape with your body.* Continue dropping the rope in different ways.

General Space. Use imaginary bubbles or hula hoops. Have students imagine that the hoops are big bubbles around them. Ask them to explore the limits of their hoops or bubbles. Now have them walk around and do moves and steps without touching others' bubbles. Use drum or count to change time, space, energy.

Personal Space. Provide a carpet square or a hula hoop to represent personal space. Ask students to do movements that are low, medium, high. Combine with force, time, and leading with different body parts (e.g., bend slowly leading with your shoulder).

Balancing Moves. Ask students to stand in their spots and do particular moves (e.g., stand on one foot,

TAKE ACTION 1

ADAPT STRATEGIES

Choose a strategy seed idea from *energizers or elements and concepts* and adapt it for science, math, reading and language arts, or social studies. See examples under each curricular area that follows.

on tip toes, twist), but while balancing a book on their heads.

Energy.   Ask for images that move slowly, strong, quick, weak, light. For example, "What moves slowly and lightly?" Compare and contrast movements.

Statues.   Assume a shape. Change on signal to another shape. Say "memorize your body." Do at different speeds. Do three shapes and put together as a shape or statue dance. *Variation:* Move freely around the room until the teacher says "freeze." Students then stand still in a shape and do not move until the teacher says "go." Teacher should give descriptive comments on shapes (e.g., levels, space).

Movement Sentence Add On.   Each person creates a sentence (e.g., three moves or steps) and next person adds on. Do in small groups.

What Did You See or Feel?   Divide notebook paper into four sections. As each of four groups present their dances, audience records impressions in a square for them. After the dances, written comments are shared.

III. CONNECTING DANCE TO OTHER CURRICULAR AREAS

In this section there are examples of seed strategies that use dance to explore concepts and skills in science, social studies, math, and language arts. Courses of study and curriculum guides are useful in identifying dance material suitable in curricular areas, and topics for dance exploration can be solicited from students. To do the latter, ask students for movement ideas related to categories such as feelings, weather, fire, water, celebrations, cooking, hiking, weddings, birthday parties, funerals, shopping, work, and recess. Movements can be explored in unison and then in small groups. A culminating activity is for students to plan a

dance with a beginning, middle, and end around an idea. The three-part freeze–move–freeze dance structure can be used as a starter.

Science Focus

◈ Natural world, systems of the body, seasons, weather, plants, animals, the environment, machines, electricity, magnets, space, gravity, and states of matter

◈ Finding out how and why things happen in the world through careful observation, hypothesis making, and prediction

Webbing.   Choose any topic (see examples in Post It Page 10–1) and web all the kinds of movement associated with it. Use BEST dance elements to expand movements. Break into groups, and each group chooses one or several to explore by doing movement possibilities. Share with class.

Environmental Dance.   Choose a category from Post It Page 10–1 to explore through movement using the principles in Chapter 6.

Environmental Walk.   Explore how to walk in different places: beach on hot sand, deep sand, on an icy hilly walk, crowded city street, in a parade, up a steep hill. Discuss why walks must be changed.

Places to Sit.   Experiment with the effect on the body on places to sit: on a bicycle, on a horse, on a swing, on an airplane, on a step, on a pillow. Make frozen sculptures and ask half the class to view and comment as they would for a museum display. Reverse roles. Combine with photos and art, for example, Rodin's *Thinker*.

Tool Dance.   Explore movements associated with tools: shovel, vacuum, typewriter, saw. Next, label the different movements and discuss common movements.

Mechanical Movements.   Brainstorm things that move in nonorganic ways (e.g., jerky moves of robot or computer). In pairs or small groups, show how to move different body parts at different levels using mechanical movements.

Dance Machines.   Create a group dance based on BEST elements of machines, for example, the elevator, escalator, or computer. (See description of "machine" in Chapter 9.)

Science Insect Dances. Each student or group chooses an insect to explore through movement. Dance should include movements related to eating, life cycle, environmental changes, and their effects.

Real-Life Sounds. Sounds of the body, city, nature, animals, machines, chants, rhymes ("Pease Porridge Hot"), familiar songs ("Row Row Row Your Boat"), and nonsense phrases ("Ziggety Zaggety Zap") can inspire movement. Children's names, names of states, cities, work chants ("heave heave ho, yo yo, heave heave ho") are also sources. Explore the rhythm, size, shape, and energy of sounds. Stress original moves that no one else does.

Ordinary Objects Dance. Use common things such as facial tissue, boxes, paper clips, ropes, and elastic bands to create a dance of inventions in which movement *with the object* is explored, not pantomimed.

States of Water. Students show through dance the molecular movement in a solid, liquid, or gas. Lead students through small-group explorations to move as if melting, condensing, and evaporating. Explore changing from a solid to a liquid and then to a gas. Use different parts of the body, energy, space, and time. Finally, ask each group to create a freeze–move–freeze dance that shows they've learned about molecular movement and structure in the different states of water.

North Pole, South Pole Magnetic Force. Students try to walk as if the floor is a giant magnet. Then suggest that the ceiling is the magnet. Call out the pull on different body parts. Suggest they walk as if the body is an opposite pole of a magnet. How would it move?

Science Movement Questions. Ask students to show different animal movements (use of whole back to move through space, different animal stretches). Ask ways to show movement of breath, bones, and muscles. Show movements to a count of 10 to help with concentration and focus.

Heartbeat. Listen first to heartbeat and then take pulse. Students then move to their own heartbeats using a variety of shapes and moves. Ask "what if . . ." questions: "You got really scared? tired?"

Bird Flight. Students work in groups to create a dance based on different types of bird flight. Include the different formations (space and pathway) birds use, changes in speed and level, and changes in leaders. Think about different body parts. Dance should have a beginning, middle, and end.

Animal Dances. Pick an animal, such as an endangered species, and explore all the ways it moves and under different circumstances (tired, hungry, scared). Use "what if . . ." questions to explore all possibilities. Use children's literature for resource ideas, for example, *The Girl Who Loved Wild Horses* for horse actions.

Weather Dance. All students are frozen in a shape. Weather changes are announced by narrator and they respond by changing levels and shapes for snow, light rain, and raging hailstorm. Begin by restricting movement to one spot and then move to locomotor. *Variation:* Convert to a relay dance in which all start frozen and then begin to move, one at a time, until all are moving. Then reverse the action. This works well if the weather event starts small and slow, escalates, slows, and stops.

Arts Alive. Make action come to life from a painting by creating a freeze, move, freeze dance. For example, use "fighting" art like *Dempsey and Firpo* or *Stag at Sharkey's* by artist George Bellows. Discuss balance, center of gravity, momentum, muscles, and use of light and shade with students.

Life Cycle. Students dance each phase of the life cycle of an animal or plant separately by using BEST elements. After each phase, have them put it together in a dance. Stress that movements can convey feelings. Sounds can be added.

Constellations. Start in frozen shapes of constellations in small groups and then move across night sky to night sounds. *Variation:* Small groups rotate in and out of the "stage" space or come in low, move to high formation, and back to low across the space.

Social Studies Focus

◆　Relationships among human beings, occupations, transportation, communities, governments, customs, cultures, holidays, and use of natural resources.

◆　History, geography (use of maps), civics (citizenship and government) or political science, economics, anthropology, and sociology.

◆　Investigations into cultural diversity and global understanding.

◆　Special questions: How did it used to be and why? Why is it like it is today? What can I do about it? Thinking processes: cause and effect, sequence, gather data, discover relationships, make judgments, draw conclusions and problem

ENVIRONMENTAL SOURCES OF DANCE MAKING

Directions: Think and do movements that show:

Body systems: respiratory, circulatory, digestive, nervous

Body actions: eat, walk, run, hug, hop, skip, sit

Seasons and cycles: life cycles (e.g., butterfly)

Growing things: small to large movements, slow, sustained

Weather: contrasts in nature (e.g., force of tornado versus gentleness of a breeze)

Plants: sizes, shapes, ways they grow

Animals and insects: cats creep, stretch, sneak, roll, slink, ball up, leap

Places or environments: movements at beach, mountains, desert

Machines and mechanical actions: pulleys and levers, tools

Electricity and magnetic forces: north and south poles, pull, repel

Space and solar system: rotate, use of space, size, shape, pathways

Gravity: force, pull, weight

States of matter: solid, liquid, gas

Causes and effects: temperature, wind

Energy: fire, steam, solar, nuclear

Technology: computer, elevator

Inventions and objects: crepe paper, cotton balls, rope scarves, elastic

---

solve about community issues (e.g., economic issues such as school funding or value conflicts related to free speech).

◆ Use of primary source material such as newspapers, art, music, diaries, letters, journals, books, and artifacts, rather than the use of textbooks and gathering data through interviews, surveys, and other investigatory strategies that historians and other social scientists use.

Post It Page 10–2 uses BEST to explore action in social studies.

Real-Life Rituals. Brainstorm patterns of movement in life (greetings, farewells). Divide into pairs and portray each other in a variety of ways using body parts, moves, steps, space, energy, and time.

Work Movements. Brainstorm all the ways people work: picking, washing, sweeping, raking, fixing. Each person creates a work dance based on a real or imaginary prop associated with work (e.g., broom) and

moves in creative ways. Music could be added. Dance should have a beginning, middle, and end.

Trio Dances (to Develop Community). Trios form and each develops a shape and moves around a concept (e.g., loneliness). All group members teach their part to their group. The final dance consists of members doing the dances of all members in a sequence.

Ceremonies. Invent a ceremony related to daily life within the classroom. Create a dance to accompany it and use high, medium, and low levels in the dance, for example, a start-the-day ceremony.

Military Moves. Use military moves to prompt thinking. Research moves used in different countries (e.g., pivot). Learn terms and moves such as left flank, right, center, offense, and defense (Joyce, 1994).

Explore a Country or State. Show terrain by changes in levels as narrator describes a tour of a place. Show the size of the state or country in relation to other countries or states as teacher calls them, for example, Texas–Rhode Island. Use movement to show what you know about a place (products, industries,

SOCIAL STUDIES: TOPICS WITH MOVEMENT POSSIBILITIES

Directions: Choose any topic and then experiment with all movement associated with it. Brainstorm and then explore BEST dance elements related to:

Holidays   Economic development
Customs   Transportation
Legends   Communities
Rituals   Governments
Population density   Cultures and diversity
Directions   Citizenship
Land and water formations   Global understanding
Occupations   Housing
Everyday actions (cook, wash)   Map skills and geography
Social interactions (sharing, cooperation, respect, trust)
Physical environment (e.g., use of natural resources)

Thinking skills: cause and effect, sequencing, gathering data, discovering relationships, making judgments, drawing conclusions.

Big Questions: "How did it used to be and why? Why is it like it is today and what can I do about it?"

---

climate, or plant life by interacting with them through movements and imagination).

Dance a Historical Event.   Brainstorm movements that would have been part of a special event such as the signing of the Declaration of Independence. Do in slow motion, changing rhythm and space. Create the mood of the moment with your body.

Holiday and Season Dances.   Brainstorm movement qualities of Halloween characters (stiff movements of a skeleton) or create a "giving" dance for Thanksgiving (focus on rituals and feasts), or "loving shapes" to rhythms for Valentine's Day. Spring dances can focus on rising and stretching and other growing movements.

Current Events Dances.   Use teachable moments: brainstorm movement possibilities. For example, the Olympic Games can inspire sports dances or dances related to the opening or closing event.

Multicultural Folktale Dance.   Focus on an event in a folktale, for example, Gag's *Millions of Cats:* all the shapes and sizes cats might have been when the old man found them.

Sports Dance.   Create dances using sports moves. Have students plan warm-ups and then move into motions of the actual game. They can play music to go

with the movements and organize final explorations into a freeze–move–freeze dance.

Folk and Ethnic Dances.   Discuss different ways dances have been used through the centuries (ceremonies, prayers, celebrations) and how the forms of dance have evolved, based on common movements used for expressive purposes. Teach a dance or some steps from another culture or time period. Discuss what is represented (rituals for marriage, weather, seasons). When teaching traditional dance steps, it helps to use a "I do, we do, you do" sequence: All face the same direction. Show the whole dance, then practice in unison until all have the basics. Involve children in the process of identifying step components and then join steps to create a whole work or even a new step. Steps do need to be mastered before doing the dance figures in which they are to be used. Mix up partners frequently so no one feels "stuck." (This process deviates from total teacher direction requiring only student imitation.) Folk dances are usually appropriate for students 8 years and up and can begin with short dances based on a dance step such as *walk* in time to music, walk in a circle, forward and backward. Horas and kolas of the Middle East are basically a series of steps and variations on the steps performed without partners in a circle or open circle. Some demand challenging footwork. Common dances include the polka, waltz, schottische, and mazurka. *Variation:* Create original dances around the same topics. An example is the *Irish jig.* Begin by playing Irish folk tunes and or showing a video of Irish folk dancing (e.g., "River-dance"). Ask open questions about the BEST elements and the feel of the dance. Then have students make their own jig using their feet and legs. Hands are held behind the back. Encourage them to kick to the beat, but create new steps, turns, and so forth.

Reading and Language Arts Focus

◈ Reading, listening, speaking, written composition (including handwriting and spelling, grammar, usage, capitalization, and punctuation). Since reading and language arts are processes, they must be connected to a subject to have meaning, that is, something to read and write about.

◈ Goal: *Create* meaning and enjoyment using print through thinking, at every level from memory to critical thinking or evaluation.

◈ The printed word and its components (letters, syllables, spelling patterns), how words combine to make phrases and sentences, and sentences combine to make paragraphs and other forms of discourse, from tongue twisters to novels.

◈ Types of words: antonyms and synonyms, parts of speech and figurative language (metaphor, idiomatic expressions).

Phonics Shapes. Ask students to make soft shapes for soft *c* and *g* words and hard shapes for hard *c* and *g*, for example, *city, ceiling, giraffe; cat, can, go, gone.* For short and long vowels, make sustained movements (vowels are continuous; when given a vowel make your body long or short when you hear the sound of a long or short vowel). Consonants can make "stop" sounds that can be danced using bound moves for *b, p, t,* hard *c, k, d,* hard *g, j, v,* and sustained for consonants such as *s, l, r, m,* and *n.* For consonant blends, students can partner to show "blending." Vowel digraphs can be shown in pairs with one person becoming "silent."

Letters of the Alphabet. Students work in pairs to make letters; use high, medium, and low levels. Stress original ideas and ask students to explain their interpretations. *Variation:* Students make a shape of an object that starts with the letter. Do at different levels and speeds.

Rhyming Words. Give a spelling pattern (*-ack, -ick, -ot, -eek, -id, -op*). Read a poem that contains many words with the pattern or read a list, some of which should have the rhyming pattern. When students hear a word that rhymes with the pattern, they do a creative movement (e.g., make different shapes).

Syllables. Ask students to change BEST dance elements according to number of syllables. Say words aloud. For example, "Hippopotamus has five syllables so make five shapes as I say each syllable." Vary the elements (e.g., time, energy) during word repetitions.

Spelling. Teacher gives a word and students spell it by moving in a floor pattern to "write it" using a chosen pathway to shape the letters. *Variation:* Pairs call words to each other.

Antonyms. Brainstorm movement words and opposites, for example, smooth–jerky, tight–loose. Then (1) call a word and students do it at different levels and speeds, (2) call a word and students do its opposite, and (3) partner students with one person doing the word and the other its opposite. Use with different levels, qualities, and tempo.

Compare and Contrast. Contrast movements such as heavy–light, tight–loose, explosive–smooth, up–down, and wide–narrow by asking students to jump all these ways. Compare ways to do the same move: walk = stride, pace, shuffle, tramp.

Word a Day. Pick a movement word. Students try to squeeze the word for all its possible meanings by exploring it through movement and finding synonyms and related words (e.g., jump = bound, vault).

Word Walls and Webs. Develop and extend vocabulary through movement by asking students to be on the lookout for action and movement words in all their reading. Put up large sheet of paper on a wall. Ask students to add unusual words to the word wall web. At any point, these words can then be used for movement (e.g., slither, sneak, ambulate, dodge, dragged, plod, saunter, amble, trot).

Cause–Effect. Pair students facing each other. One is the *cause* and the other is the *effect*. Cause moves and the effect must respond appropriately (e.g., if cause steps forward, effect must move to keep from being stepped on). Encourage creative effect responses.

Classification. Call out a category or way to classify a movement. Students explore all they can do in that category (e.g., low level, bending, twisting, reaching).

Variation: Students take turns demonstrating three different moves or actions and group must guess the category.

Parts of Speech. *Adverbs example:* Do locomotor/nonlocomotor moves/steps different ways (e.g., merrily, sadly). *Literature verbs:* web ones from a story, put on cards, explore different ways (e.g., run slowly, crawl sneakily). Combine into dances about a chapter or event in a story.

Gestures. Brainstorm everyday gestures used to greet each other or respond (e.g., wave, beckon, stop). Explore ways to do movement (e.g., fast, slow, different body parts, levels).

Tableaux. Get into small groups and use body shape and space to show a concept (e.g., grief, celebration, loneliness). Freeze in the shape.

Math Focus

◆ Daily living situations involving counting, measuring, probability, statistics, geometry, logic, patterns, functions, and numbers.

◆ Problem solving through use of skills (raising questions and answering them, finding relationships and patterns).

◆ Concepts about numbers, operations, and concepts such as bigger, longer, greater than, less, three, four, even, and odd.

◆ The National Council of the Teachers of Mathematics encourages teachers to have children solve problems in many ways, focus on explaining and thinking, rather than just correctness, and using a hands-on approach.

Math is basically the study of quantitative relationships. Dance is also concerned with relationships among shape, time, and size. Through dance, students can come to understand basic math concepts such as add, subtract, divide, and duration (second or minute). Higher-level math skills require sequential thinking, examining situations for important details and patterns. Dance also involves these types of thinking, so dance and math can reinforce one another.

Math Moves Possibilities. Brainstorm all the moves in math; include estimating, adding, multiplying, dividing, patterns, geometric shapes, fractions, lines, curves, and subtracting. Give each group one concept. They are to decide at least three different ways to show their math concept through movement.

Geometric Shapes (Following Directions). Everyone walks around filling up the space. When a leader calls out a shape, all freeze in that shape (circle, triangle, square). Leader should give feedback for unusual ideas (use of energy or space). *Variation:* Students partner to make the shape. Do also with letters of the alphabet.

Telling Time. Use masking tape to make a large clock on the floor. Children move around in the 12 hour spaces by stretching arms to a person in the middle of the clock as a time is called by the teacher. Explore different times: recess time and lunch time and ways to move around (fast, slow, hop, slide).

Shape Dance. Many folk dances are done in a circle, square, or line. Invite a guest to teach one and relate it to the math concept. Challenge students to find other math ideas in the dance (e.g., counting, parallel lines, sequencing—first, second, third).

Get the Facts! Call out math problems for students to solve by jumping, hopping, or walking along a number line. Give a different way to move each time (fast, slow, low, halting, flowing). Sounds, chants, and instruments can be added.

Math Glue. Everyone moves around the room in slow motion. Teacher says "glue 2" and students find others to stick to in that number (everyone must keep moving in slow motion). Teacher then calls "unstick" and continues with a new number.

Twos and Threes. Teach number groups by calling out a way to move and giving the pattern. For example, "Hop in twos with a pause after the two hops." Make into dances of moves grouped into twos and threes.

Angle Dance. Students create a dance that illustrates angles (right, oblique). Each dance should have a beginning, middle, and end and can be locomotor or nonlocomotor. Use freeze, move, freeze form.

Math Dance. Students choreograph a dance to teach to others by creating instructions in math terms. For example, math hop = take two steps forward, slide right, hold for four counts, and hop three times.

Number Shapes. Teacher calls out a signal and students make their bodies into shapes of numbers. They may need to work together. Challenge them to make these shapes combine with time, space, and force.

◈ BIBLIOGRAPHY AND REFERENCES

Books

Joyce, M. (1994). *First steps in teaching creative dance to children* (3rd ed.). Mountain View, CA: Mayfield.

Pica, R. (1991). *Moving and learning*. Champaign, IL: Human Kinetics.

Children's Literature

Gag, W. (1928). *Millions of cats*. New York: Coward-McCann.

Goble, P. (1978). *The girl who loved wild horses*. Scarsdale, NY: Bradbury.

11

Integrating Music Throughout the Curriculum

"This song will live forever."

    Kate Smith, prior to singing Irving Berlin's "God Bless America" in 1938—the first time it was ever publicly sung.

♦ ## CLASSROOM SNAPSHOT

Mr. Bender's Middle School Unit on War Through Music

Just after the Gulf War of 1991 broke out, Lee Greenwood's song "Proud to Be an American" became a hit. My students listened to it all the time. I teach in a small town in Kentucky that proved to be very patriotic throughout this period, and people would stand up whenever and wherever the song was played—bars, restaurants, basketball games. My middle schoolers were very emotionally affected by the song and observed the effect on our community. A class discussion about this became the impetus for an eight-week unit on wars and music.

    Using student interests, we decided to focus on wars in which our country had been involved. They did initial library research, and we listed wars on the board. Students then formed small groups of three to five to research a war to find music and songs produced during the war or about war time. The goals were to find out *why* the songs were written, under what circumstances, and what was expressed through lyrics and music. Students used parents, grandparents, and uncles, aunts, neighbors—even the mayor—as sources, along with the library. Some songs they found right away were

Civil War: "Dixie," "John Brown's Body," "Battle Hymn of the Republic"

Revolutionary War: "Yankee Doodle"

War of 1812: "Star Spangled Banner"

World War I: "Over There"

World War II: "I'll Be Home for Christmas"

Korean War: Theme from M*A*S*H

Vietnam War: "Ballad of the Green Berets"

Many wars: "Marine Hymn"

    We are lucky to have a wonderful music teacher who became enthusiastic about the unit when she saw how hungry the students were for information, sheet music, and old records. She began working on the songs with them. We didn't start intending to create a performance, but the unit culminated in one. Students managed to get old uniforms, and a local history museum volunteered to do a display. Students made transparencies of pictures from history books to project on a large screen to introduce each segment. So many people in the community had been contacted that they were really interested. We ended up needing to schedule two nights for this community event.

    During the performance, students came forward to present their research before each song. Drama and dance were natural parts of the presentations. For example, an Iwo Jima tableau, formed by five boys, was enacted during the World War II songs. Several couples demonstrated the jitterbug during this segment, too. The hour-and-a-half program culminated in the Lee Greenwood piece in which the audience joined in. This was the most integrated unit I've ever taught. The kids learned so much about history from a personal point of view—so much about the emotions expressed in the music. I felt like I was the head of a team of social scientists, rather than a teacher, at some points. Reading and writing just happened naturally. I believe this is the way all learning should be.

INTRODUCTION

Where words leave off, music begins.

Heinrich Heine

"There is clear evidence of an in utero reponse to music" (Jensen, 2001, p. 17). Every child begins life immersed in rhythm—the most basic element of music. The steady beat of mothers' hearts attunes babies to patterned sound. Into the safe, suspended world of the womb also come outside voices with other rhythms and unique timbres. The unborn child physically responds to these external sounds, showing an innate desire to listen and learn. Early on each tiny fetus reacts to phonemes (the smallest sound units in language) such as the percussive consonant sounds of /t/, /p/, and /f/. Phonemic awareness later will form spoken language. As the growing child eavesdrops, the brain grows, absorbs, and makes connections that establish lifetime patterns. If the child's environment is rich in music, the brain's structure will reflect it. Eventually, these silent inner sounds become the foundation for learning to read as children connect them to print and learn to conjure the music of words during silent reading.

Music is so pleasant humans insatiably seek out its beauty. Concerts sell out, CDs are played in our homes and cars, and joggers run with headsets. Teenagers asked to go on a family trip scream "child abuse" if not allowed to listen to favorite music. We never seem to get enough. Once it was common to hear people sing, whistle, and make music on their way to work, at work, and at school. Workers sang in farm fields, musicians played on street corners, and families gathered around the piano after dinner. Then came television, tapes, CDs, and headsets. Somehow a notion developed that a talented few should do the music making. The rest of us became mostly music consumers rather than producers.

Musical Development: Preferences and Tastes

Most children enter school with some musical experiences, and many have well-established preferences. Musical taste seems to be defined in early childhood and not easily altered. The introduction to music often occurs in powerful social contexts such as singing with friends, at church, or listening to the radio as the family travels. This results in positive, even passionate, feelings attached to particular musical artists, styles, or genres.

Music is of central importance in all cultures, but the roles music plays vary greatly. Personal musical tastes develop through the process of acculturation: Children with parents who sing to them and who hear many kinds of music are more likely to sing well and develop diverse tastes. Some cultures expect every member to participate by singing or playing an instrument: In Polynesian culture singing in harmony is valued, and so many Polynesian children sing well. In the Vendan culture (Africa), each child's first rattles and bangs are celebrated and amplified by adults; parents convert baby's rhythms into music, in the same way American parents expand babblings of "ma-ma" into "Mother, yes I am your mother." Most cultures go further to use music in a range of important societal rituals such as weddings and holidays (Page, 1995).

In light of recent brain development research (Jensen, 2001), it is not surprising to learn that Mozart and Haydn grew up in musically fertile environments. Babies, the world over, babble the phonemes of the language around them, and children respond to lullabies and other "comfort music." Foreign language is best learned when the young child's brain is still growing rapidly; this is also true for the language of music. The educational implication is that elementary and middle school years need to be musically rich when children are more open to types of music—from classical to country. Children grow to like and value the music they hear the most, so we need to take advantage of this acceptance of musical diversity by providing experiences in an eclectic range of styles, types, periods, and cultural origins. Such variety sustains interest, engenders a broader attitude, and builds respect for diverse expressions of people. From American jazz to African drums, the world is full of music for students to enjoy and use as a source

---

TAKE ACTION 1

MUSICAL IDENTITY

Take a few minutes to reflect on the music you enjoy. What is special about it? How is your musical identity different from your friends'? your students'?

to understand the different values and customs of other cultures.

Music Is Not My Job?

The authors of the 1997 National Endowment for the Arts report, *American Canvas,* reached the conclusion that many Americans don't see the arts as relevant to life. This low or no value for the arts is attributed partly to "an educational system that at best enshrined the arts as the province of elite cultures" (Larson, 1997, p. 13). Some classroom teachers have lost confidence in their abilities to give their students musical experiences and often claim they lack the resources. It is true that it is no longer common to see a piano in every classroom. Furthermore, it is possible, in some states, for preservice teachers to become licensed without taking a single music course. Generalists and specialists have grown to believe the music teacher should assume sole proprietorship of children's musical education. This attitude further contributes to the perception that music is a domain restricted to the talented and well trained. This narrow view of who is responsible for music education is rather unique, at least in degree, to the United States. In many countries the separation between the talented and untalented is much less stark: Everyone is thought to have ability to express feelings and to think through music. It is unfortunate that music *inside* many American schools has become isolated in a manner so unlike music *outside* school. Compelling evidence supports the full integration of music into the curriculum. Jensen (2001) states, "If this were a court case, the ruling would be that music is valuable beyond a reasonable doubt" (p. 14).

Novice teachers and those with minimal music background may feel uncomfortable doing explicit teaching to develop musical literacy. For those teachers it is recommended that they view music integration as an experience to be offered, rather than a subject to be taught. Most elementary schools have some services of specialists to do the latter. If music integration is conceived as a way to explore, test, and investigate ideas by connecting music to units, the general classroom teacher usually feels more comfortable about giving it a try, and specialists feel less threatened. In this proposal, the focus is on student participation in the process, not perfect singing nor competence in playing an instrument. Another way of putting it is that general classroom teachers are not teaching just for the esthetic experience that music provides, but *through* it. The bottom line is that every child deserves to grow up with music woven into the full fabric of learning, not as an isolated event that happens every other Tuesday.

WHY SHOULD TEACHERS INTEGRATE MUSIC?

Most people will go to their graves with their song still in them.

Benjamin Disraeli

"Flutes have been found in France dating as far back as 30,000 years" (Jensen, 2001, p. 15). This and other evidence implies that music has been used throughout human history. Music has been used by every culture to inspire, tell stories, pass on history, glorify achievements, amuse, relax, and educate. Music is used to express love, anger, despair, and hope. Young adults use music to bond with peers and carve out individual identities. Parents use music to comfort and communicate with infants and toddlers, instinctively singing to fussy babies. We buy music boxes to soothe and intuitively rock in a steady rhythm to calm ourselves and our children. Perhaps, as Jensen suggests, we are "hard wired for music"(p. 14).

Recent investigations of how music affects brain development has piqued the interest of both teachers and parents. For example, one finding is that listening to music only one hour a day may reorganize the brain (Malyarenko et al., 1996). A new industry of private music schools, such as Kindermusik, International (Greensboro, NC), has sprung up as a response to these and other brain studies. Children's communication and perceptual skills have been found to be enhanced by early music experiences. Unconscious listening gives a foundation for conscious listening, and listening *is* a basis for learning. When young children use music to explore their environment, they engage in critical phonemic (sound unit) awareness experiences necessary to speak and read. (Current research in reading disabilities targets lack of phonemic awareness as a determining cause of problems; children who cannot hear distinct sound nuances have trouble decoding words.) Natural music making begins with the babbling songs of babies, and babies can grow into children who can use music to gather information and sort out feelings, ideas, and experiences.

We now know a great deal about the effects of music, and yet the way music affects us is still a bit of a mystery. It is clear that "play" and music arise from instincts to create, express, and experiment, so it isn't surprising that music raises students' interest in subject matter. It is also clear that musical listening experiences and chances to respond to and perform all stimulate imaginative thinking and sharpen problem-solving skills. Music is, in fact, one of the eight alternative ways of knowing counted as a distinct human intelligence (Gardner, 1999). Post It Page 11–1 gives examples of current efforts to use music as a learning tool.

POST IT PAGE 11–1

NEWS BULLETIN: MUSIC RESEARCH YOU CAN USE

The College Board reports for the 1999–2000 school year students with four years of music coursework scored an average of 49 points higher on the combined verbal and math portions of the SAT. The more years students spend in music, the higher the scores. Music Educators National Conference, (*http://www.menc.org/information/advocate/sat.html*).

New York. Over 90 percent of the boys in the Boys Choir of Harlem go to college and 98 percent of graduates from the Choir Academy of Harlem (grades 4–12 arts academy) went to college (Barnet, 2000; Gregorian, 1997).

Pawtucket, Rhode Island. First graders involved in a special music program performed significantly better in math and reading than a comparison group without the music (*Nature,* 1997).

Raleigh, North Carolina. Interest in school subjects is up and so are attendance rates at Bugg Elementary, a school where test scores were below the county average in 1995 and there was little parental involvement. Now, just 2 years into a 4-year pilot program, students listen to Gustav Holst's symphonic suite *The Planets* in science and learn about fractions as they study whole, half- and quarter-notes. The goal: boost reading and math scores.

California. Seventy-eight preschoolers did a better job of improving abstract reasoning skills when given piano lessons rather than computer instruction.

Brooklyn, New York. PS 314 used to be on the state's list of worst schools. Not any more. Since 1989, students have been involved in a cooperative project with the Metropolitan Opera; they attend dress rehearsals and use the plots and settings to help learn history (e.g., *Aida*) and literature (e.g., *Faust*). They are also writing their own operas.

A review of 57 studies showed all the following were increased through arts experiences: self-concept, language, cognitive development, critical thinking, and social skills. Of special note was the positive effect of music participation on self-concept (Trusty & Oliva, 1994).

Cleveland, Ohio. Deforia Lane, director of music therapy and a cancer survivor at Case Western School of Medicine, studied 40 people (half were controls and half got a half-hour of music therapy). The experimental group had a significant increase in healing antibodies in their systems. Remarkably, Dr. Lane had three comatose patients awaken to say they heard the music they'd been immersed in during their unconscious period. Patients' blood pressure, heart, and respiration rates went up and down with the tempo of music selected by finding out their musical tastes from relatives. One man, whose life support was recommended to be ended, awoke and said it was the dulcimer music that drew him back. (Dr. Lane thinks heavy metal or gansta rap could be harmful, because the words and music could stimulate the seizure center, the violence center of the brain.) (*Springfield News Sun,* Saturday, June 7, 1997, p. 1.)

Music therapy has been found successful in illnesses ranging from anorexia or drug addiction to profound mental retardation (e.g., to help autistic children tolerate being touched). It triggers the release of endorphins, our body's natural opiates. It changes the brain waves (e.g., people with Parkinson's have had their walking become more rhythmic over a 3-week period and gain more assured quality and cadence) (National Association for Music Therapy, 8455 Colesville, R. Suite 1000, Silver Spring, MD 20910, 301-589-3300).

Reasons to Integrate Music

A man should hear a little music, read a little poetry, and see a fine picture everyday of his life.

Goethe

1. ***Music is a significant part of life.*** Imagine a day without music. Out would go the radio, our CDs, and much of television. Life without music would be dull. Music adds both spice and comfort to daily existence. Music elements are so embedded in our lives we don't even think about how hard it would be to talk, read, or walk effectively without them. Think of the roles of rhythm, accent, and tempo in saying a simple sentence such as "Turn out the lights." Is it "<u>Turn</u> out the lights," "Turn <u>out</u> the lights," "Turn out the <u>lights</u>," or a gentle whisper of "Turn out the li-i-i-ghts"? It's *all* in the music.

Music is also an important career field. In the last census, more than 130,000 persons listed their livelihoods as musicians or composers; that figure does not include music-related careers such as teachers and music store owners. We spend hundreds of millions of dollars each year on concerts, CDs, tapes, and music videos, making music more than incidental to our economy. There are more than 1,500 orchestras in the United States that generate employment for thousands of people. Music is big business—the 1994–1995 Rolling Stones concerts grossed over $27 million.

Much of school motivation comes from the perception that what is learned is important to life outside the school walls. Music is out there. We need to bring it in and make explicit how it is relevant to life and learning.

2. ***Music is a learning vehicle.***

An educated Iatmul in New Guinea . . . knows between 10,000 and 20,000 clan names. . . . Part of the secret . . . is that he chants the names in a rhythmic way.

Armstrong, 1993

In the thousands of years of human history much teaching has happened through storytelling and song. Songs and chants with attractive rhythms, satisfying repetition, and unforgettable melodies have instilled in people lessons from the past and tenets of their religions. Information and values are still passed along in hymns, military chants, folk, and pop songs. In our lifetimes, the power of song has been deftly used by advertisers to create jingles that compel us to buy products: "You deserve a break today, so get out and get away." We can't get these ditties, with their "get it—rent it—eat it—buy it" messages, out of our heads. This is the *mnemonic* force of music (Chan, Ho, & Cheung, 1998) and most Americans first experience it when learning the alphabet. Children sing the letters to the same melody used for "Twinkle Twinkle Little Star" and "Ba Ba Black Sheep" and the letters are memorized. The number of days in each month is remembered through the sing-song rhythms and rhymes in the poem "Thirty days hath September." At a more advanced level, math performance improved in a study in which one group studied math with a Mozart sonata (thought to activate particular brain regions) and scored an eight-point increase over the nonmusic control group (Campbell, 1997). (Contact the Music and Science Information Computer Archive at the University of California, Irvine, for details on this and other research studies: http://www.musica.uci.edu.)

There is a special term for using music as a learning vehicle—musicogeniceupadia. Through song and music, students can increase general vocabulary, sight word knowledge, use of idiomatic expressions, oral fluency, visual tracking along a line, concentration, understanding of rhyme, rhythm, repetition, alliteration, and syllables, phonemic awareness, concepts of beginning–middle–end, sequence, diction, knowledge of states and capitals, and parts of speech (Douglas & Willatts, 1994). Music is a communication symbol system that develops listening skills and, as previously discussed, listening is an important part of the motivation to learn. In addition, listening to music is a pleasant reinforcing experience, and *critical* listening (close listening to musical elements) develops attending skills. Music also develops important *learning rhythms,* such as the word rhythms in reading necessary to achieve *fluency*—a pulse and phrasing that must be sustained or the message is not constructed.

Why is it easier to learn a song than a series of facts? The brain is attuned to patterns and responds to rhythmic patterns in music, perhaps hearkening back to soothing rhythms in the womb. Learning through music can seem effortless, because the brain almost automatically picks up musical patterns, even when we are not conscious of it happening. Brain imaging technology now enables us to see how music stimulates areas of the brain that were inactive before a music experience. We are attracted to music. It draws our attention. Time spent attending to a task is a major contributor to learning, so if music can increase time on task, might it not be an alternative to drug treatment for attention deficits? This area of research has yet to show conclusive results, but educators are justified in experimenting with coupling music with learning to extend concentration and focus. (See examples of how to learn the bones of the body, the continents, and more with music in Chapter 12.)

3. *Music unites affective, cognitive, and psychomotor domains.*

Music is the shorthand of emotion.

Leo Tolstoy

Music therapy—the systematic use of music to aid in the treatment of disease or illness—has been an accepted medical treatment since the 1950s; the healing, soothing properties of music have been known since drum beats were first heard in Africa. What do we do when we get in the car after a hard day's work? Turn on the radio or put in a favorite CD. Why? Early on we learn how music relaxes, gives energy, and positively alters perceptions of time and mood. Music can even change the state of consciousness; it is not uncommon for people to report *chromesthesia*—seeing colors or images as a result of musical sounds—and experience emotional cathartic effects such as sobbing in response to music. Faster musical rhythms induce smiling, even laughing; endorphins, the body's natural painkillers, are produced as a result. Listening to music causes changes in breath rate, pulse, blood pressure, pupillary muscle tone, and blood flow. Musical sounds charge the brain, activating areas in both hemispheres and stimulating whole-brain involvement. Business and industry use this power of music not only in advertising but to increase attention and energy in the workplace. For example, music is intentionally used to create positive moods and a positive attitude to energize employees. Cognitive (thinking), affective (emotional), and psychomotor (body) responses are needed to function as whole persons and music activates all three. Finally, music is a kind of intelligence, a way of knowing and expressing ideas and feelings. By integrating music, teachers help students become more well rounded and successful because they are drawing on additional avenues of learning.

4. *Music solves problems.*

God made music so we could pray without words.

Anonymous

Music can assist in both solving and enduring problems. Slaves sang to endure, and in a manner,

control suffering. Music can relieve stress, reduce pain awareness, and increase blood flow to stimulated areas of the body. Human existence is defined by the ways we cope with obstacles and problems—music often gives solace during wrenching moments such as funerals, lost loves, and fear ("Whenever I feel afraid I whistle a happy tune"). We hum and rhythmically rock to give physical and mental peace; we sing lullabies to calm cranky children. Singing and humming ease the passing of time or make work more pleasant. Recently, I noticed the use of both music and art to these effects in the Chicago O'Hare airport. In one of the underground tunnels, abstract neon art rhythmically pulses, moving the eye to the tunnel ends, as synthesized music plays. Lyrics softly urge you to "keep walking, keep walking." At first I thought I imagined the messages, but several tunnel trips have convinced me that the power of music to solve problems is being used there. It works; there's never a soul standing around down there.

Teachers learn quickly to play soft, calm music to make transitions in the day or use faster rhythms to rouse students for a lesson requiring mental and physical energy. It is exciting to consider other creative ways to use music to solve classroom problems. From academic to discipline issues, music holds promise. For example, teachers can use warm-ups such as clapping rhythms for students to echo. This entrains students to become one with the teacher's rhythm—and this gets attention. (*Entrainment* is the tendency for two rhythms or pulses to synchronize with each other, like the speed of speaking affects the listener's speed.) Using the concept of entrainment, teachers can use music to transition from high-energy activities to slower, more reflective ones or to energize students with fast-tempo music. The rhythms of the brain imitate external rhythms, and in this way music serves as a mood signal. Slower speech calms, just as slower music does, and a fast tempo causes children to entrain to more active body responses. Physically, we entrain with others as we walk together, pausing or adjusting our gaits. Everything from heart rate to brain waves entrains to the rhythms around us (Armstrong, 1994; Page, 1995).

5. *Music bonds people together.*

Music cures a lot of loneliness.

Anonymous

When we sing together, we are brought closer because collective musical experiences create bonds formed from shared feelings. In singing classrooms the learning community is made strong through ancient powers of rhythm and sound. Group singing can become an inspiring ritual, as evident in the faces of children who show joy during singing that is not otherwise seen at school. Singing together weaves an invisible sound web of group spirit (Page, 1995). Community feeling grows through shared experience, and community building is often the focus of patriotic songs, folk songs, marches, and humorous camp songs. Think of how it feels to sing the "Star Spangled Banner" with hundreds of others right before a basketball game—a uniquely American tradition that foreigners find strange. Songs sung around campfires on chilly nights bring everyone into an envelope of communal sound. Then there are the young lovers who bind themselves together with a trademark "our song" symbolic of mutual feelings. Shared music is nonverbal communication that can bridge gaps between generations and mend fences among disparate groups. For example, during the Civil War, Union and Confederate soldiers, weary from fighting each other by day, joined in songs across the night.

6. Music increases creativity, sensitivity, and self-discipline.

There was once a teacher who taught her fourth graders to sing "I've been working in this classroom all the live long day. I've been learning lots of new things just to pass the time away. Soon we'll hear the bell start ringing and out the door we'll go. Now it's time to get ready, clean up and go on home" (tune: "I've Been Working on the Railroad"). At the end of each day they were energized to prepare to depart—always on a good note. That was a creative teacher, so different from the teacher who struggles to get chores done before dismissal. The pairing of music with other tasks creates an opportunity to respond to common work in uncommon ways. Music is used in the military to accomplish tasks that would otherwise be tedious drills (e.g., marching to a cadence).

Used creatively, music develops the kinds of thinking associated with creative problem solving, such as viewing ideas from a new perspective, and can develop group and independent work skills, such as cooperation and responsibility. Music stimulates creativity because making music involves playing and experimenting with sounds and rhythms. For example, children readily create and adapt hand clap and jump rope rhymes. When teachers engage students in sound experiments, they stimulate the use of brain centers needed for elaborative, original, fluent, and flexible thinking. Why wouldn't teachers make use of the power of this natural creative-thinking motivator in the classroom?

Educators involved in the singing schools of Hungary feel music increases sensitivity, harmony, and cooperation because of its emotional appeal and the need for group work in choirs. In addition, while music can involve language play with lyrics, to produce music requires skill and discipline. To sing or play an instrument *well* demands attention, knowhow, practice, and the desire to improve.

7. Music can develop pride and identity.

Alas for those who never sing, but die with their music in them.
Oliver Wendell Holmes

From early childhood we sing to discover ourselves. Music brings power to children because it gives a mode to express feelings and emotions, as well as release energies in novel ways. Universal questions are asked in favorite songs, questions children would not otherwise be able to articulate (Page, 1995). Childhood ditties can express the ineffable ("Twinkle, twinkle little star, How I wonder what you are"). The "me" egocentrism of childhood eventually morphs into a world of "we" as children discover the importance of peers; song preferences change to a focus on relationships with others. Teenagers become passionate about "their music" as bodies and brains go through sweeping changes triggering foreign feelings. During adolescence, music commonly becomes a means to express identity, a way to associate emerging views of self with things deemed unique symbols of what is important. This use of music to define views and values continues throughout life. As self-identity develops, so do life patterns related to the motivation to learn. Pride is a powerful fuel for the learning engine. By learning a song or to play an instrument, children develop confidence, posture, and poise. Through musical achievements they gain insight into important connections between sustained effort and satisfaction. When children feel proud and know that significant adults share pride in their hard work, it is more likely that self-discipline will grow and be transferred to other areas of life.

8. Music expresses culture and history.

Without music life would be an error.
Nietzsche

Music has been called the "universal language of mankind." Music is so important in some cultures that the act of music making is considered a gift—a gift of beauty through sound. West African cultures view music this way, and in American culture it is a high tribute to have a song written especially for you. Music reveals cultural values, is used to celebrate triumphs, ameliorates the grieving process, expresses fears, gives hope, sustains traditions, and is integral to religion. Recorded history is replete with songs and music that tell stories of heroes, passions, and wars. For example, in our country it is impossible to think of the civil rights movement without recalling the songs of marchers or not to associate World War II with Glenn Miller's big-band sound. At a time in history, each tribe or cultural group had a unique musical identity. Today, diverse kinds of music represent the human family. In the United States we have become culturally diverse in our musical tastes and embrace every genre and style from folk to classical, rock and roll to rap. Blues? Jazz?—all readily available at the local mall. Teachers who share the wondrous varieties of music and celebrate the unique music of cultures and ethnic groups are showing children that diversity is something to be respected and treasured.

9. *Music gives esthetic enjoyment.*

People don't sing because they are happy, they're happy because they sing.

Goethe

Music is a form of celebration, and children need more time to celebrate learning. Music is a form of beauty, and classrooms need all the beautifying they

Painting Chihuly Bellagio

can get. When we help children tap into musical intelligence, we liberate them to make music and add beauty to their personal and shared worlds. Encouraging each child to find a special musical identity gives many options for using a special way of knowing and expressing, plus the possibility of feeling a joyous sense of freedom. This doesn't mean teachers should not let students know a particular *use* of music can be harmful. Music has power that can be used and abused; for example, excessive volume creates permanent auditory loss. Music can also provoke aggressive responses through rhythms and lyrics that are not school appropriate; teachers need to be direct in teaching how any art form that demeans a person or group is questionable. But back to the main point: music is fun and *fun* is fundamental to motivation to learn. Happy children learn better. One way to increase happiness is to sing.

10. *Music can support learning throughout the curriculum.*

Music ability has been found to enhance reading skills (Douglas & Willatts, 1994; Kantrowitz & Leslie, 1997; Lamb & Gregory, 1993) and singing naturally integrates the *language arts* of listening, speaking, and reading. To sing, we must hear in our heads, in the same way we must hear the music of words when reading silently: Which words are to be stressed? what rate? volume? Singing also emphasizes clear enunciation of words, and because we usually sing *words*, vocabulary is built through singing. By pointing out lyrics on a large chart or the overhead, students make the speech-to-print match essential for reading success.

When children learn to compose original songs, collect favorite songs with lyrics, and keep responses to songs and music in journals, they are *writing*—another language arts area. Because of the patterned nature of music, it can be an assist in learning *spelling*

TAKE ACTION 2
MUSICOGENICEUPADIA

Think of a simple song. Brainstorm or web what you could teach about science, social studies, math, and language arts using just that song. The categories mentioned in item 6 will also help you stretch out the *musicogeniceupadic* (learning) possibilities of the song.

as well. When students are taught how to tap out rhythms in words—"en-cy-clo-ped-i-a" (there is a Disney tune for "encyclopedia," too) or to sing the spelling of words, they add an important study mnemonic to their learning repertoires. We can encourage students to create their own word melodies using the universal notes of G, E, and A or any tune. An easy strategy is to break into small groups and give each a word to spell using a melody. Remind them to use the music elements (rhythm, tempo, dynamics, etc.) to create their word melodies (see Post It Page 11–3). Afterward, ask if this helped and why, as a means of using action research to gauge the effects. Keep track of spelling performance to add statistical evidence to the experiment.

Several studies have documented the influence of music on *math*. Graziano, Peterson, and Shaw (1999) documented how proportional math was enhanced through music training. In another study college students who listened to Mozart increased their short-term spatial reasoning (Shaw, 2000). Hearing complex rhythms, even a rhythm rain forest background proved to be three times better than Mozart (Jensen, 2001, citing research by Parsons et al.). In another study preschoolers given 8 months of keyboarding and singing outperformed children with no music on object assembly tasks requiring them to form mental images and move objects to reproduce the images (they showed enhanced long-term spatial reasoning) (Rauscher & Ky, 1995; Rauscher, et al., 1997). Counting songs have long been a part of the early childhood curriculum and for good reason: Through the strategic use of music, teachers help improve skills in measuring, counting, graphing (the five-line staff is a graph), fractions, problem solving, time, and spatial reasoning. See the music-based bibliography in the appendix for collections of math songs such as Baker's (1991) *Raps and Rhymes in Maths* (songs about probability and time).

Music can support *science* learning in a number of ways. As one example, a unit on sound can include a study of how vibration enables us to sing or a musical instrument to be played. Students can explore the nature of sound and learn about musical elements, such as the variety of timbres possible when an object is struck or is used to strike other objects—forks and knives or hands.

A key aspect of *social studies* is learning about cultures. Music fits easily into this area because to understand a culture we must know what the members believe is important; music reveals values. Every culture produces music for similar purposes: to celebrate, mourn, relax, or unite the group. But each culture approaches music differently. While it is rare to hear singing in most work environments in the United States today, in many cultures and countries work songs are still an integral part of life. Music is considered critical to growing crops in areas of the world such as West Africa, where songs and dances are believed to coax plants to grow (Page, 1995). Another cultural difference relates to our Western notion of an audience in one place and musicians in another (on a stage). This concept is foreign to cultures where everyone participates in music creation and everyone is both audience and performer. Fortunately, hundreds of high-quality multicultural materials are now available, including CDs and videos. (See the appendix.) Post It Page 11–2 lists some. For ideas on how to integrate songs for multicultural purposes, as well as stimulate our multiple intelligences, see Page's (1995) *Sing and shine on! A teacher's guide to multicultural song leading.*

Another part of social studies is *history*. Studying the music of a time period can be an exciting introduction to an era: Students can be taught the origins of familiar songs such as "America" that was first a poem Katherine Bates wrote after an inspirational trip out west in 1892. The poem that celebrated the beauty of the country became very popular. People began to sing it to as many as 75 different melodies, including polkas and marches. Eventually a church hymn melody written by Sam Ward called "Our Mother Dear Jerusalem" was coupled with Bates poem and it is this melody we sing today.

TAKE ACTION 3
USE A SPECIAL MUSIC DICTIONARY

Do you know who wrote "Mary Had a Little Lamb" or "Happy Birthday"? One resource for information about these songs and other music is *The New Grove Dictionary of Music and Musicians*, edited by Stanley Sadie (London: Macmillan, 1988). Use it to find the history of songs or about instruments in cultures. For background on folk songs, try Sing Out Corporation, Box 5253, Bethlehem, PA 18025. They publish *Sing Out! The Folk Song Magazine* started by Pete Seeger.

MUSICAL RESOURCES: CULTURES, COUNTRIES, AND ETHNIC GROUPS

George, L. (1987). *Teaching the music of six different cultures.* World Music Press.

Jessup, L. (1988). *World music: A source book for teaching.* World Music Press.

Papp, C. (1988). *Follow the sunset: A beginning geography record with nine songs from around the world* (with tape or CD). Entomography Publications.

Present, G., & Present, S. (1986). *We all live together: Song & activity book and leader's guide.* Hal Leonard.

Walter, C. (1995). *Multicultural music: Lyrics to familiar melodies and authentic songs.* T. S. Denison.

Africa

Atumpan, the talking drums of Ghana. UCLA (1964) 45 min. VHS. (Shows carving of a set of drums for the Ashanti king. Available from UCLA or Original Music.)

Bryan, A. (1991). *All night: All day: A child's first book of African-American spirituals.* Atheneum.

Connelly, B. (1997). *Follow the drinking gourd* (African American). Simon & Schuster.

Floyd, M. (arr.) (1991). *Folksongs from Africa.* Faber Music.

Mattox, C. (1990). *Shake it to the one that you love best: Play songs and lullabies from black musical tradition.* Warren Mattox.

Toop, David (1991). *Rap attack 2: African rap to global hip hop.* Serpent's Tail.

Asia: China, Japan, and Korea

Arthur Barr (producer). (1982). *Discovering the music of Japan* (21 min. video). Instruments introduced, background is provided. Performances of shakuhatchi, koto, and samisen.

Asian Cultural Centre for UNESCO (Books, recordings on Asian music and culture), 6, Fukuromachi, Shinjuku-ku, Tokyo 162 Japan.

Chinese Information Service (information on Chinese music, art, and history), 159 Lexington Ave., New York, NY 10016.

Chinese Music Society of North America, 2339 Charmingfare, Woodridge, IL 60517-2910.

Gritton, P. (arranger). (1991). *Folksongs from the Far East.* Faber Music.

Kinokuniya Bookstores (books and records on Japan and Japanese music and culture), 1581 Webster St., San Francisco, CA 94115.

Kodo: Heartbeat drummers of Japan (28 min. VHS) Kinetic Film and Video. Shows the training of the musicians who form Kodo, a Japanese taiko drum ensemble.

Australia

Australian Institute of Aboriginal Studies, Box 553 City P.O., Canberra, A.C.T., 2600 Australia.

Caribbean and Central and South America

Arthur Barr (producer). (1982). *Discovering the music of Latin America* (Video). Indian and Spanish elements in Latin American music.

Hawaii

Bishop Museum, Education Dept. (materials on music of the Pacific), P.O. Box 6037, Honolulu, HI 96818.

Hawaiian musical instruments (slides and tape). Bishop Museum. Hawaiian instruments such as the dog tooth rattle and the nose flute. Other materials are available from the Bishop Museum.

Hula Supply Center (musical instruments and hula supplies), 2346 King St., Honolulu, HI 96822.

India

Arthur Barr (producer) (1982). *Discovering the music of India* (21 min. video). Music of the South (Carnatic) and North (Hindustani) is introduced, with explanations of melody and rhythm.

Folk musicians of Rajasthan (45 min. VHS). UCLA. Folk traditions of northeast India; includes songs, rituals, and dances.

Folk performers of India (45 min. VHS). UCLA. Nine views of Indian folk traditions; includes magic acts, puppetry, acrobatics, impersonation, and other acts accompanied by music.

God with a green face (16 mm). American Society for Eastern Art. Training and performances of the Kathakali dance drama of southern India. Available from the Center for World Music, San Diego State University.

Gritton, P. (arr.) (1993). *Folksongs from India.* Faber Music.

Indonesia

Indonesian dance drama (30-min. VHS). UCLA Original Music. Balinese shadow play, the puppets of Java, a dance drama, and Sundanese masked dances.

Serama's mask (25 min. video). Coronet Films and Video. A Balinese teenager practices traditional masked dances and carves a mask for a performance.

Israel and the Jewish Culture

Cindy Marshall Productions. *A life of song* (38 min. video). Yiddish folk songs by Ruth Rubin.

Tara Publications, 29 Derby Ave., Cedarhurst, NY 11516. Specializes in Jewish music.

North American

Arthur Barr (producer). (1971). *Discovering American Indian music.* (24 min. video). A survey of many types of Indian music and dance, mostly from the plains and Southwest areas.

Arthur Barr (producer) (1982). *Discovering American folk music.* (video). British and African influences on the music of America are explored. Songs are traced to show changes.

Arthur Barr (producer) (1982). *Discovering country western music.* (video). Traces how the folk music of the mountain people of the South has evolved into popular music.

Barkman, A. (1987). *Rise and shine.* American folk with tape/CD. Moody Press.

Beall, P. (1996). *Wee sing sing-alongs.* American folk with tape/CD. Price Stern Sloan.

Chulas Fronteras (59 min. VHS). Original music. Chicano musicians play conjunto music. Background on the hardships of the farm worker's life.

Cohn, Amy L. (1993) (compiled). *From sea to shining sea: A treasury of American folklore and songs.* Scholastic.

Durell, A. (1989). *The Diane Goode book of American folk tales and songs.* Dutton.

Fichter, G. (1978). *American Indian music and musical instruments.* Random House.

Krull, K. (collected and arranged) (1992). *Gonna sing my head off!: American folk songs for children.* Knopf.

Lewis, R. (1991). *All of you was singing* (African American). Atheneum.

Medearis, A. (1994). *Singing man.* Holiday House.

National Gallery of Art (1991). *An illustrated treasury of songs: Traditional American songs, ballads, folk songs, nursery rhymes.* Rizzoli International.

Pearson, T. (1984). *Old MacDonald had a farm* (American). Dial.

Raffi (1979). *Corner grocery store and other singable songs* (American/French) (tape or CD). Shoreline.

Westcott, N. (1989). *Skip to my Lou* (American). Joy Street Books.

Zemach, H. (1984). *Sing children sing: Songs of Mexico* (with tape or CD). Caedmon.

Organizations

American Folklore Society (publishes *Journal of American Folklore*), 1703 New Hampshire Ave., NW, Washington DC 20009.

Canadian Folk Music Society, 15 Julien St., Pointe Claire, Quebec, Canada.

Center for Intercultural Studies in Folklore and Oral History. American Folklife Society, University of Texas, Austin TX 78712.

Center for Southern Folklore (films, records, photographs, and books on folk culture of the South), 3756 Mimosa Ave., Memphis, TN 38111.

Country Music Association, Inc. (information on country music and the country music industry), 7 Music Circle, Nashville TN 37203.

Country Music Foundation (publishes the *Journal of Country Music*), 700 16th Ave. S., Nashville, TN 37203.

Learning Corporation of America (film: *Black Music in America—From Then Till Now*), 711 Fifth Ave. New York, NY 10022.

University of Oklahoma Productions, Indian Education, 106 E. Constitution, Norman, OK 73069.

Middle East

Arthur Barr (producer). *Discovering the music of the Middle East* (20 min. video). Covers several instruments and styles of music and discusses the spread of Islam.

Other Organizations

American Orf-Schulwerk Association, Executive Hdqtrs., P.O. Box 391089, Cleveland, OH 44139-1098.

International Folk Music Council, Music Dept., Queens University, Kingston, Ont., Canada K7M 6R2 (associated with UNESCO). Information on preservation of folk music and dance.

Music Educator's National Conference (MENC) (publishes *Music Educators Journal*), 1806 Robert Fulton Drive, Reston, VA 22091.

National Geographic Society, Box 2118, Washington, DC 20013-2118 (music of ethnic groups).

Office of International Arts Affairs, Department of State, Washington, DC 20560.

Organization of American Kodaly Educators available: http://oake.org/directory/oake_info.html

Smithsonian Institution, Office of Folklife Programs, 955 L'Enfant Plaza SW, Suite 2600, Washington, DC 20560.

UNESCO: United Nations Educational, Scientific and Cultural Organization, 7 Place de Fontenoy 75700, Paris, France.

UNICEF, The United States Committee, 331 East 38th St., New York, NY 10016 (catalog with books and records on world music, e.g., *Sing, Children Sing* series).

The World Music Institute (ethnic festivals, concert series, mail order for booklets and recordings), 155 West 72 St., Suite 706, New York, NY 10023.

Book Sellers, Publishers, Sources for Recordings and Media

Alcazar's Kiddie Cat 1-902-244-8657 (large catalog of children's music recordings and videos), Box 429,Waterbury, VT 05676.

Anthology Record and Tape Company, 135 West 41st St., New York, NY 10036 (African and Asian).

Canyon Records, 4143 North 16th St., Phoenix, AZ 85016 (Native American music).

Cellar Book Shop, 18090 Wyoming, Detroit, MI 48221 (Philippines, Asia, the Pacific, Australia, and New Zealand).

Children's Book and Music Center, 1-800-443-1856 (offers a preview service; folk and world music), 2500 Santa Monica Blvd., Santa Monica, CA 90404.

Children's Small Press Collection, 1-313-668-8056 (small publisher; many classroom resources), 719 N. Fourth Ave., Ann Arbor, MI 48104.

Dove Music, Box 08286, Milwaukee, WI 53208 (Spanish American music).

Floyd's Record Shop, Post Drawer 10, Ville Platte, LA 70586 (Cajun and Creole music).

G.P.N. Media, 764 Pleasant Ave., Tulare, CA 93274 (videos: African and South American; *Musical Instruments; The Music Machine* series includes Japan and Africa).

Homespun Tapes, Box 694, Woodstock, New York 12498 (tapes, videos on folk and jazz, yodeling).

House of Musical Traditions (books, recordings, and ethnic musical instruments), 7040 Carrol Ave., Takoma Park, MD 20912.

Institute for Music, Health, and Education, Box 1244, Boulder, CO 80306.

Interculture Associates, Box 277, Thompson, CT 06277 (specializes in India).

Ladyslipper, 1-919-683-1570, Box 3130, Durham, NC 27705 (music by women artists).

Music for Little People, 800-836-4445 (audio and video recordings and musical instruments), Box 1460, Redway, CA 95560.

Music of the World, Box 3620, Chapel Hill, NC 27505 (recordings from diverse cultures).

Original Music, RD 1, Box 190, Lasher Rd., Tivoli, NY 12583 (world music; hard to find titles).

Shorey Book Store, 110 Union St., Seattle WA 98104 (Northwest Indian music and culture).

Sing Out, Box 5253, Bethlehem, PA 18015 (publishes *Sing out! The Folksong Magazine* on North American music and *Rise Up Singing!,* an excellent collection; reprints of songs available also).

Tower Records, 1-800-522-5445, 692 Broadway, New York, NY 10012 (all recordings in print).

World Around Songs, Route 5, Burnsville, NC 28714 (series of song books on nearly every culture).

World Music Press, P.O. Box 2565, Danbury, CT 06813 (multicultural books, recordings, videos).

Zephyr Press, 3316 North Chapel Ave., Box 6606-P, Tucson, AZ 85716 (multisensory learning).

Instrument Sources

Carroll Sound, Inc., 351 West 41st St., New York, NY 10036 (drums, percussion, ethnic instruments).

House of Musical Traditions, 7040 Carrol Ave., Takoma Park, MD 20912 (instruments, recordings).

Jag Drums, 88 Hibbert St., Arlington, MA 02174 (ewe barrel, donno, and brekete drums; marimbas).

John's Music Center, 5521-A University Way N.E., Seattle, WA 98105 (ethnic and Orff instruments).

Knock on Wood Xylophones, RD 2 Box 790, Thorndike, MA 04986 (hand-made xylophones).

Lark in the Morning, P.O. Box 1176, Mendocino, CA 95460 (American and European folk).

Latin Percussion, 160 Belmont Ave., Garfield, NJ 07026 (Latin instruments and recordings).

Peripole, Inc., Browns Mills, NJ 08015-0146 (ethnic and Orff instruments).

Rhythm Band, Inc., Box 126, Fort Worth, TX 76101-0126 (ethnic instruments and materials).

Studies of lyrics can show purposes for which the songs were written and help reveal how composers felt—how historic events inspire music (e.g., Berlin wrote "God Bless America" at the brink of World War II). Music can be related to a unit focus, such as transportation systems (canal and railroad songs), and students can discuss what causes certain songs and pieces of music to endure for decades or centuries.

WHAT DO TEACHERS NEED TO KNOW TO USE MUSIC AS A TEACHING TOOL?

The woods would be very silent if no birds sang except those that sang best.

Henry David Thoreau

Classroom teachers who embark on music integration to enhance curricular areas need to be familiar with current patterns of music study in schools. In elementary and middle school, special music classes focus on music's historical, social, and cultural role in life; communication through music by expressing, performing, and responding; valuing music and developing an esthetic sense of it. Topics include music elements, genre and styles, musical tastes, musicians, instruments (including the human voice), composers, and music of diverse cultures (songs and particular musical pieces). Also of importance is the role of beauty and emotion in music as a form of communication. Drawing from this foundation, here is a checklist of titles for computer folders or folder tabs to organize information for music integration:

◆ Basic music elements and concepts used to create and think about music.

◆ Biographical and style information about musicians, composers, songwriters, and singers (e.g., the children's book *Beethoven Lives Upstairs*, available with videotape).

◆ Styles, forms, and genres music (e.g., opera, jazz, country, classical, folk).

◆ Particular examples (e.g., actual songs on CD, tape, and collections of sheet music).

◆ Specific approaches or teaching strategies (e.g., ways to teach a song, Kodaly, Dalcroze).

◆ Poems, quotes, current news articles about music (e.g., collection of poems about music such as

Myra Cohn Livingston's [1995] *Call Down the Moon, Poems of Music)*.

◆ Musical instrument information (e.g., types, history, pictures).

◆ Bibliographies of children's literature that is music related (e.g., *The Philharmonic Gets Dressed* by Karla Kuskin).

◆ Research articles about music integration and mnemonic power of music.

◆ Music ethnography or world music of diverse cultures.

◆ Other possibilities: information about careers in music, music history, science or math of music, economics and music, psychology of music (e.g., music therapy).

Defining Music: When Does Sound Become Music?

It gives a soul to the universe, wings to the mind, flight to the imagination, a charm to sadness, gaiety and life to everything. It is the essence of order and leads to all that is good, just, and beautiful, of which it is the invisible, but nevertheless dazzling, passionate, and eternal form.

Plato on music

Simply put, music is sound organized in time and space. It is aural, kinesthetic, and cognitive, and is dependent on ears for perception, although we also perceive rhythm and beat with our entire body. But what is the difference between sound and music? Consider an African drum beat and the pattern of a baby's feet. Both sound patterns have the musical element of rhythm. Both evoke emotional response. But the drum beat is an *intentional* organization of sounds for the sake of making sound. The sounds evoke feelings and emotions through the use of rhythm, tempo, melody, harmony, pitch, and repetition. These basic components or elements are used to create images and ideas in a musical form. So, music can be thought of as "sound patterns over time *intended* to express moods, ideas, or feelings."

Music Elements That Help Define Music

I am music. I make the world weep, laugh, wonder and worship.
Goethe

While musical elements alone do not create music, classroom teachers need to understand and teach basic elements so that there is a common language to discuss music and students will have concepts to use when creating music. In other words, to integrate music, teachers and students need some tools of music. The caution is for teachers not to kill the joy and spirit of music through overanalysis of a song's elements. Later, in the *How* section and in Chapter 12, there are specific suggestions to teach musical concepts and terms to lay the foundation for successful music integration.

Rhythm is movement of sounds through time. In songs the words usually *match* the rhythm. Try saying and clapping the words "happy birthday to you." Now do the same with "She'll be comin' round the mountain when she comes." Feel the difference in the rhythm? Everything we sing or say has a rhythm that can be varied by changing the tempo, beat, and accent.

Rhythm shows the strong connections between math and music because it is a numerical pattern of beats over time. Rhythm is represented by a series of notes ranging from whole notes (usually 1 beat per measure) to quarter notes (4 beats per measure) to eighth, sixteenth, and even 32nd and 64th notes. So, in order to understand music, one must also understand the math concepts of time and fractions and be able to count beats.

Beat and accent have to do with the rhythmic pulse, such as the steady beat of a clock ticking. The accent is where the strongest emphasis is placed as in *one* two three, *one* two three.

Tempo is the speed, how fast or slow the music is.

Meter is the groupings of rhythms (e.g., triple meter = ¾ [waltz] such as "Happy Birthday").

Syncopation. Syncopated rhythms are uneven, as in jazz. The beat remains steady, however. Try to say "Charlie Parker Played Be Bop" by syncopating it to "Charrrr-lie Parrr-ker Played Be Bop." (He was a great jazz saxophone player.)

Melody is the tune. It is a series (more than one) of musical tones or pitches falling into a recognizable pattern (e.g., in "I'm a Little Teapot" the motions show melodic direction). Melodies may be based on major or minor scales, but you do not need to know what a scale is to make a melody. When we sing words, they become melodies.

An octave is the distance between the first and last notes of our Western scales of eight notes (think of Do Re Mi Fa Sol La Ti Do) or between any pitched note and the next note with the same name (eight notes higher or lower). Most of our folk songs use the eight main notes of the Western scale. There are five other notes that come between the scale notes called sharps and flats, usually the black keys on a piano.

Pitch is the high or low tones in the sound pattern.

Timbre (pronounced "tambur") is the same as tone color and has to do with the unique qualities of a sound (e.g., voices or sounds made by plucking, beating, rattling, or blowing various instruments). In essence, any sound has a timbre that enables you to hear whether you've dropped your keys or a pencil. Children enjoy experimenting with timbres they can create with one body part (e.g., hands or objects such as sticks or even a ruler).

Dynamics is the volume or relative loudness or softness of the sound. Dynamics give emotional intensity. The Italian words *forte, crescendo, piano,* and *pianissimo,* appear in music to indicate dynamics or how loud the music should be played.

Texture is the layering of instruments and/or voices to create a thin or full feeling. Melodies, rhythms, and timbres can be combined to create different textures. Music made by an orchestra is an example of a full texture. We can create texture by combining voices, as in singing a round such as "Frère Jacques."

Harmony is the blending of tones or sounds (e.g., chords). When two or more pitches are blended simultaneously, harmony is made. Children often know about barbershop quartet harmony.

Form is the structure, shape, or pattern of a piece of music or a song, for example, AB (binary form) such as "Fish and Chips," ABA (ternary) such as "Happy Birthday," and ABACA (rondo form). The A's and B's are separate *themes*. It is the order of *repetition* that is the key and largely determines the form of a piece of music. **Musical styles** and **genre** are closely related to form (e.g., jazz versus opera).

Ostinato is simple rhythmic or melodic content repeated over and over to accompany a song. Post It Page 11–3 summarizes music elements.

Musical Instruments

Students want and need to create, explore, and imitate sounds. They enjoy activities involving sound discrimination, classification, sequencing, improvisation, and organization of sounds into songs and music. While classroom teachers may not be able to stock many kinds of instruments, there are ways to explore sounds through a variety of "found," homemade, or inexpensive instruments. See, for example, Hopkins' (1995) *Making Simple Musical Instruments*. Instruments from different cultures can be demonstrated, shown in pictures, and heard

MUSIC ELEMENTS THAT HELP DEFINE MUSIC

Rhythm: movement of sounds through time (matches words not beat). Includes *beat or accent, tempo, meter, and syncopation.*

Melody (tune): a series (more than one) of musical tones falling into a pattern. Includes *pitch.*

Timbre (tambur): tone color or unique qualities of sound.

Dynamics: volume or relative loudness or softness of the sound; gives emotion.

Texture: layering of instruments and/or voices to create a thin or full feeling.

Harmony: the blending of sounds, for example, chords; two or more pitches simultaneously.

Form: structure, shape, or distinct patterns. Related to *style* and *genre.*

Ostinato: simple rhythmic or melodic content repeated over and over to accompany a song.

---

on recordings, as students study uniqueness among peoples. Musical instruments include:

◆ Sound makers (sticks, stones, shakers)

◆ Percussion or rhythm instruments; anything that can be hit or struck, scraped, rubbed (tambourines, triangles, wood blocks, bells, maracas, finger cymbals)

◆ Melody instruments to make tunes (bells, xylophone, tone bars, glasses of water, bamboo flutes, rubber bands, African kalimba)

◆ Harmony instruments (autoharp, guitar, dulcimer)

◆ Orchestral and band (violins, trumpets, organs, accordions, harmonicas, Indian sitar)

◆ Orff xylophone (wooden) and the metallophone (metal); have removable bars so that teachers can choose specific pitches for musical effects (e.g., remove F and B to create a pentatonic scale, five notes with no clashing or dissonant notes that all sound "good"). Recorded versions of Orff instruments can be obtained from Carl Orff and Gunhild Keetman. English version is by Margaret Murray (1959), *Music for Children*, Angel Records.

Composers, Genre, and Styles of Music for Classroom Use

Jazz tickles your muscles, symphonies stretch your soul.
                                          Paul Whiteman

Musical Genre and Styles. It would take more than one course in music history to become familiar with all the music people have created. Teachers who have a music history background start the process of integration with a definite advantage. Most teachers actually know more than they think they do. For example, most of us are familiar with a great deal of classical music from cartoons, such as Bugs Bunny, and advertisers frequently sneak in a bit of Bach or Beethoven to sell a product. Films such as *Platoon* and *Ordinary People* introduced millions to works of composers such as Vivaldi and Pachelbel.

Some styles and genre overwhelm young children. One guideline is to use variety and consider appropriateness. The music specialist will usually be responsible for a sequential music curriculum, leaving the classroom teacher free to explore genres including gospel, jazz, bluegrass, madrigal, marches, lullabies, opera, or barbershop according to preferences, student interests, and connections to curricular goals. Teachers new to music integration are encouraged to begin with genre and styles they know and enjoy so that they can transfer their enthusiasm to their students. Once integration begins, teachers can branch out and explore new types and styles, along with students. Post It Page 11–4 clarifies some of the eras or periods of music commonly used to classify Western *classical* music (music considered to have lasting significance). "Classical" is also a label of one of the periods. Teachers should remember that exposure to non-Western music enlarges children's concept of what is "good" and that 20th-century American music has much to offer, too (the Latin music of the 1930s, big-band music of the 1940s, rock and roll from the 1950s, punk rock and New Age in the 1980s, and the fervor over country music in the 1990s). By the way, to get up on rap, get Stanley's (1992) *Rap, the Lyrics:*

The Words to Rap's Greatest Hits and Toop's, (1991) *Rap Attack 2: African Rap to Global Hip Hop.*

The example works that follow are just that, examples, and are limited to Western culture. They are offered as a place to *begin* as teachers attempt to increase music background. Dates are included for those interested in plotting birthdays on a time line to go along with social studies. Celebrating specific birthdays of composers and other artists is also a routine teachers can use to integrate the arts throughout the school year.

Note: The terms *genre* and *style* are sometimes used interchangeably, but style generally refers to the distinctive way in which musical elements are used; for example, periods of musical development such as the Baroque had a unique style. Style can also refer to media used to make music, for example, keyboard style.

Composers. By introducing students to composers and their music, a "real-person" element is added to music. Children who view videos such as *Beethoven Lives Upstairs,* (and read the picture book by the same title) have an opportunity to learn something of the idiosyncratic man behind the famous music. Just as children become excited about book authors, they can come to identify with the troubles and triumphs of composers and other people who have made music an integral part of their lives. It is inspirational and comforting for children to realize they share many life experiences with famous composers and can create music, just as these individuals did. Of course, introducing students to a diversity of genre, styles, and composers of different racial, ethnic, and cultural backgrounds gives the opportunity to see and hear from added perspectives. This wider view, in turn, permits students to create in a wider array of forms and styles.

For ideas about genre, styles, composers, songs, and other potential questions about *what* to teach, you may want to consult *The Music Teacher's Book of Lists* (Ross & Stangl, 1994).

TAKE ACTION 4
MUSICAL GENRES, STYLES, AND COMPOSERS

Divide a sheet of paper into two columns. List all the genres or styles you can think of on one side and composers on the other. Talk with another person to expand the list and discuss how you know these genres, styles, and composers.

POST IT PAGE 11–4

WESTERN MUSIC: SELECTED PERIODS, COMPOSERS, AND WORKS TO KNOW

Baroque Era: 1600–1750 Ornate, elaborate, flamboyant, marked by strict forms

Bach (1685–1750), German: Brandenburg Concerti and 22 preludes and fugues

Pachelbel (1653–1706), German: Canon in D Major

Vivaldi (1678–1741), Italian: Four Seasons

Handel (1685–1759), German: Messiah, Water Music, and Royal Fireworks Music

Classical Era: 1750–1820 Music without pretense

Haydn (1732–1809), Austrian: Clock Symphony, Surprise Symphony, The Creation, The Seasons

Mozart (1756–1791), Austrian: Operas (*Don Giovanni, Marriage of Figaro, The Magic Flute*), Jupiter Symphony, Coronation concerto for piano, A Little Night Music

Beethoven (1770–1827), German: All nine of his symphonies

Romantic Era: 1820–1900 Often suggests a story or concept, dreamlike

Schubert (1792–1828), Austrian: Unfinished Symphony, The Great Symphony

Schumann (1810–1856), German: Spring Symphony, Papillons (butterflies)

Mendelssohn (1809–1847), German: Scottish Symphony (No. 3) and Italian Symphony (No. 4), Songs without Words

Chopin (1810–1849), Polish: All his piano works

Prokofiev (1891–1953), Russian: Peter and the Wolf

Strauss (1804–1849), Austrian: Waltzes

Liszt (1811–1886), Hungarian: Hungarian Rhapsodies

Donizetti (1797–1848), Italian: Opera *Don Pasquale*

Rossini (1792–1868), Italian: Operas (*The Barber of Seville, William Tell, Cinderella*)

Verdi (1813–1901), Italian: Operas (*La Traviata, Rigoletto, Falstaff, Aida, Otello*)

Puccini (1858–1924), Italian: Operas (*La Boheme, Tosca, Madame Butterfly*)

Berlioz (1803–1869), French: Symphony Fantastique, Romeo et Juliette

Tchaikovsky (1840–1893), Russian: Symphonies 4–6, Swan Lake, The Sleeping Beauty, The Nutcracker, Piano Concerto No. 1 in D minor, Violin Concerto in D major, 1812 Overture

Brahms (1833–1897), German: Symphonies 1–4

Wagner (1813–1883), German: Operas (*Tristan and Isolde, The Flying Dutchman, The Valkyries*)

Post-Romantic Era: 1890–1930 Focuses more on mood or expression of inner experience than telling a story, experimentation with music "without melody"

Mahler (1860–1911), Bohemian: Songs of the Wayfarer, The Song of the Earth, Symphony of a Thousand (No. 8)

Debussy (1862–1918), French: The Sea (La Mer), Prelude to the Afternoon of a Faun

Strauss (1864–1949), German: Don Quixote, Macbeth, operas (*Salome, Elektra*)

Stravinsky (1882–1971), Russian: The Rite of Spring, The Firebird, Petrushka, The Soldier's Tale

Shostakovitch (1906–1975), Russian: Symphony No. 5 in D minor, Piano Quintet

---

Artist-Composer Timeline

American Culture: Songs to Know

It's always touchy to start listing books or topics everyone should know about. That didn't stop the Music Educators National Conference (MENC) from recommending songs they felt all Americans should know and treasure as part of our national common culture. The list is given in Post It Page 11–5. It includes folk songs, Negro spirituals, patriotic songs, a Jewish celebration song, a Japanese folk melody, and many old favorites of the 20th century. MENC is on a campaign to "Get America Singing . . . Again" and this list is intended to get us started. In addition, you may want to survey your own community and school and involve students in compiling a "favorites list." Post It Page 11–6 includes favorite songs recommended by teachers and children from informal surveys.

"I Can't Carry a Tune in a Bucket!" While it is advantageous, it is not necessary for classroom teachers to sing well or be able to read music to integrate music. As in each of the other chapters, reassurance is

POST IT PAGE 11–5

Songs MENC* Thinks We All Should Know

Amazing Grace
America (My Country Tis of Thee)
America the Beautiful
Battle Hymn of the Republic
Blue Skies
Danny Boy
De Colores
Dona Nobis Pacem
Do-Re-Mi
Down by the Riverside
Frère Jacques
Give My Regards to Broadway
God Bless America
Green, Green Grass of Home
Hava Nagila

He's Got the Whole World in His
   Hands
Home on the Range
If I Had a Hammer
I've Been Working on the Railroad
Let There Be Peace on Earth
Lift Ev'ry Voice and Sing
Michael (Row Your Boat Ashore)
Music Alone Shall Live
Oh! Susanna
Oh, What a Beautiful Mornin'
Over My Head
Puff the Magic Dragon
Rock-a My Soul

Sakura
Shalom Chaverim
She'll Be Comin' Round the
   Mountain
Shenandoah
Simple Gifts
Sometimes I Feel Like a
   Motherless Child
Star Spangled Banner
Swing Low, Sweet Chariot
This Land Is Your Land
This Little Light of Mine
Yesterday
Zip-A-Dee-Doo-Dah

*Music Educators National Conference

POST IT PAGE 11–6

Favorite Songs

The following is a list compiled by surveying music teachers, classroom teachers, and children.

Alouette
Alphabet Song
The Ants Go Marching
Baby Bumble Bee
Be Kind to Your Web-footed
   Friends
Bear Song
A Bear Went over the Mountain
Bingo
Boom Boom Ain't It Great to Be
   Crazy
Camptown Races
Chicka Boom
Clementine
Do Your Ears Hang Low?
Down by the Bay
Down in the Valley
Found a Peanut
Go In and Out the Window
Good Night, Ladies

Greasy Grimy Gopher Guts
Green Grass All Around
Hambone
Have You Ever Seen a Lassie?
Head, Shoulders, Knees, and Toes
Hokey Pokey
Home on the Range
I Know an Old Lady
I Wish I Were
If You're Happy
I'm a Nut
In the Good Old Summer Time
It Ain't Gonna Rain
It's a Small World
I've Been Working on the Railroad
John Brown's Body
Kum-Ba-Ya
Little Skunk's Hole
Loop de Loo
Make New Friends

Michael Row Your Boat Ashore
Miss Mary Mack
Mud
My Bonnie Lies over the Ocean
Ninety-nine Miles from Home
Noble Duke of York
Oh, Chester
Old Hogan's Goat
Old MacDonald
On Top of Old
   Smoky/Spaghetti/Pizza
One Bottle of Pop
Over the River
Peanut Butter Song
Polly Wolly Doodle
Pop! Goes the Weasel
Popeye, the Sailor Man
Puff the Magic Dragon
Rise and Shine

She'll Be Comin Round the Mountain	Take Me Out to the Ball Game	This Old Man
Simple Gifts	Ten Little Indians	Turkey in the Straw
Singing Bee	There's a Hole in the Bottom of the Sea	Twinkle, Twinkle
Six Little Ducks	There's a Hole in the Bucket	Up in the Air, Junior Bird Man
		Waltzing Matilda

offered to teachers who are enthusiastic, willing to learn, and able to do creative problem solving. These are the critical teacher attributes for music integration—more important than having a fine voice or music literacy. It is effective for teachers to take the risk to sing *with* and *to* students—being able to read music or play an instrument do give an added dimension to integration efforts. These are desirable, *not necessary,* teacher attributes. A non-Western cultural perspective, where *everyone* is seen as an important music participant, rather than a passive listener, does much to help us consider how music can become an integral part of learning throughout the curriculum. If we consider music as a natural extension of the human spirit it becomes clear that it has a place in every discipline that examines people's courage, creativity, inventiveness, and resiliency. With all that said, consider Post It Page 11–7 on *reading music* intended for those with absolutely no experience, but with a desire to know some basics.

The Nine *National Standards* for Music K–8

Post It Page 11–8 summarizes the music standards for elementary and middle school students. These are a part of the *National Standards for the Arts* presented in each chapter. Classroom teachers need standards in-hand to plan meaningful integrated lessons that teach *about* and *in* art forms, as well as *through*. These standards and other curriculum frameworks help teachers to know *what* to teach but do not explain teaching methodology, integration strategies, nor do they give ideas about materials. These are discussed in the *How* section of this chapter and Chapter 12 is a compendium of strategy starter ideas. All the strategies and activities in this chapter relate to one or more of the *Standards*. Consult your local and state courses of study for ideas tailored to the specific needs of your community. *Note:* For examples of arts standards developed at the state level, contact the Ohio Department of Education (Columbus, OH). Kentucky also

has state standards for the arts that have been widely implemented. Wisconsin's Model Academic Standards for the Arts can be ordered online (http://www.dpl.state.wi.us/dpl/dltcl/els/pubsales/arts.html).

HOW CAN TEACHERS USE MUSIC AS A TEACHING TOOL?

If you can talk, you can sing. If you can walk, you can dance.
Zimbabwe aphorism

Teachers don't need to be able to sing well nor play an instrument to integrate music. They don't need to know how to *read* music, either. A teacher need not even know who Mozart was or what a fugue is. Classroom teachers can integrate music by using ideas such as those discussed next. In so doing they will help students learn how music is another way to make meaning—this time through sound.

To begin with, think of music as another dimension of artistic and creative thinking and consider that all sound has music potential. Knowledge of basic musical elements, introduced previously, enables students to understand music better and can assist them in music making. There are special skills, such as reading and notating music (musical notation is the symbol system that represents elements of rhythm and pitch—the fundamental building blocks of music) that teachers can pursue with students or help those who are interested to find resources or mentors. Most critical to music integration is a positive attitude about being able to use music in meaningful ways throughout the curriculum.

Music Integration Checklist

Two areas make up the bulk of what a classroom teacher does when integrating music: (1) teaching and composing songs and (2) listening to curriculum-related music. Before examining the *How* principles in the

READING MUSIC: QUICK REFERENCE

1. Each note is represented by these letters of the alphabet: ABCDEFG (no note letters above G).
2. Notes are written on a *staff*, which has five lines and four spaces. Each line represents a note, as does each space. The staff looks like this:

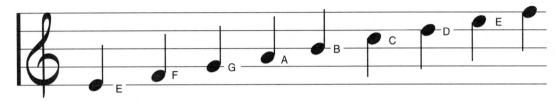

3. To remember the notes on the lines, the phrase "Every Good Boy Does Fine" can be used. For the notes in the spaces, use the acronym FACE. (Treble clef only)
4. Notes can go above or below the five-line staff by adding *ledger* lines. To figure a note on a ledger line, just keep using the A–G sequence; for example, the ledger line (one above) the top staff line would be A because the top staff line is F; the next space is G and, again, the next ledger line would be A.
5. If music has two staffs, one is for the higher notes and the other the lower notes. (It gets confusing to keep adding more and more ledger lines so this is easier.) The top staff is the treble or G clef and has this special sign: 𝄞 The bottom staff is the bass or F clef and has this sign: 𝄢:
6. On a piano, middle C is in the center of the keyboard. To figure out the white notes on either side of it use the A–G sequence. The black keys are the sharps (#) and flats (*b*). A sharp raises a note a half-tone (makes it higher) and a flat lowers it a half-tone.
7. The staff is divided into measures or bars (vertical lines) and can have any combination of notes and rhythms. There are symbols for notes worth different counts or number of beats. For example,

Whole = O   Half =   Quarter =

8. The time signature is two numbers (looks like a fraction) at the start of the staff that tells you the number of beats in a measure (bar) and what kind of note gets one beat, (e.g., 3/4 = 3 beats to a measure and the quarter note gets one beat.).

INTEGRATES model, take a moment to do a self-assessment of strategies you now are comfortable using. Would you . . .

- Teach songs from diverse cultures, for holidays, traditional songs, and others that go with units? (See the appendices Arts-Based Children's Literature [music section] and Recommended Reading and Viewing for resources. Students and their families are also sources of songs and music; consider *co-constructing* the curriculum with your students.)

- Help students learn songs that make up a *cultural repertoire*, including the songs that make up their own cultural repertoire? (See Post It Page 11–5.)

- Present songs and rhythmic activities on CDs or cassettes for pure enjoyment and release of emotion and energy?

- Use activities that make students more aware of musical elements and concepts to help them use musical intelligences and develop vocabulary? (See ideas for teaching in Chapter 12.)

- Invite in guests to play instruments, sing, or share about unique aspects of music?

- Involve students in making and playing simple instruments as a means of *creative expression*?

NINE *NATIONAL STANDARDS* FOR MUSIC (K–8)

Overall focus: creating, performing, responding to music (sing, play instrument, move to music, create own music, read and notate, listen to, analyze, evaluate, understand historical and cultural heritage, that is basic human expression).

1. **Singing, alone and with others, a varied repertoire of music.** Example activities: Learn songs from different cultures, traditional American songs, songs from different genres (lullabies, gospel, rounds, work songs). Observe conductor's cues during singing (change dynamics, sing expressively, use appropriate posture and rhythm).
2. **Performing on instruments, alone and with others, a varied repertoire of music.** Example activities: Echo short rhythms (clap, stamp, etc.). Play rhythm instruments while others sing.
3. **Improvising melodies, variations, and accompaniments.** Example activities: Use "sounds" to create songs with a beginning, middle, and end. Improvise rhythm and ostinato accompaniments.
4. **Composing and arranging music within specific guidelines.** Example activities: Make and use instruments with songs. Find background music to go with poetry or literature readings.
5. **Reading and notating music.** Example activities: Recognize 2/4, 3/4, and 4/4 meter signatures. Read pitch (do re mi . . .) with hand signals.
6. **Listening to, analyzing, and describing music.** Example activities: Do close critical listening to identify music elements and characteristics of styles and genre.
7. **Evaluating music and music performances.** Example activities: Explain personal preferences and why using musical terms.
8. **Understanding relationships between music, the other arts, and disciplines outside the arts.** Example activities: Compare and contrast concepts across art forms (texture, line, rhythm). Connect ways music intersects with reading and language arts, science, social studies, and math.
9. **Understanding music in relation to history and culture.** Example activities: Explain how music expresses cultural and history. Investigate musical careers. Use appropriate audience behavior.

Source: Content Standards (material printed in bold type) excerpted from the *National Standards for Arts Education*, published by Music Educators National Conference (MENC). Copyright © 1994 by MENC. Reprinted with permission. The complete *National Standards* and additional materials are available from MENC; The National Association for Music Education, 1806 Robert Fulton Drive, Reston, VA 20191 (800-336-3768).

- Play a variety of types of music to "stretch students' concepts of the familiar"?
- Sing with students to show you value all voices and are willing to risk sharing your own?
- Cooperate with the music specialist to integrate music throughout the school curriculum?
- Share your own musical tastes and preference—not as what is best, but as a way of celebrating everyone's unique proclivities? Encourage students to share, too?
- Use music to introduce units, such as the "Star Spangled Banner" for study of the War of 1812?
- Offer music as a lesson starter or as a response to a lesson? For example, write a song about a topic or use music as a journal-writing, art, dance, or drama stimulus.
- Connect chants and poetry with music? Help students understand that all reading of words involves adding musical elements to the print?
- Use music to set mood: to slow things down or speed up, to relax, to make transitions?
- Teach basic concepts and skills such as the states and capitals, alphabet, or counting through music?

◆ Learn a few new songs (with limited voice range and notes, e.g., sol, mi, la) for pitch matching, some action songs, and word rhyme songs such as nursery rhymes?

Music Approaches That Influence Integration

The human voice is the most readily available and most important musical instrument for children to explore . . . accompaniment can distract the children's attention from the musical elements of pitch, volume, and timbre, produced by the voice alone.

Zoltan Kodaly

In real life, music is everywhere, all day, every day—on the radio, in department stores, in the hums and whistles of people with whom we work. In regular classrooms music is often viewed as a pleasant, but expendable, aspect of the curriculum—significant music experiences are reserved for music class. But should music be confined to one special class in school, any more than music, outside school, is limited to concerts? If the answer is no, then one next step is to know some approaches *from* music class that can shed light on current integration efforts by helping generalists understand how specialists construct music curricula. The following brief summaries offer background on what specialists do and what is appropriate when using music as a teaching and learning tool. A common thread in most is the *active* involvement of students in making and responding to music through movement. All these approaches connect music to a wide array of curricular areas, from language development to social studies. General classroom teachers can investigate each further by talking with specialists in their schools.

In the 1890s, Swiss educator, Émile Jacques **Dalcroze,** pursued a theory about how control of balance and body movements, along with the use of the senses, prepared children to attend and concentrate—skills necessary for school success. He believed sensory-based learning caused muscles to relax, while maintaining alertness, and helped learning channels to be open for concentration. Dalcroze called his method of teaching music *eurythmics.* In eurythmics, music and movement are inseparable, and the body is used as a natural instrument for the study of rhythm. Dalcroze believed any musical idea could be transformed into movement and any movement could be translated into a musical idea. To start off, Dalcroze students

"become" the music as they listen and move to it. Later they study musical symbols and instruments. It seems incredible that Dalcroze was dismissed from the Geneva Conservatory for encouraging students to remove shoes and experience the musical rhythms through movement. We have him to thank for helping to advance the idea of body-kinesthetic learning widely accepted today.

Dalcroze was joined by Carl **Orff,** in Germany, in emphasizing links between music and movement. (Music and dance were not connected until the turn of the century, because music was considered high art, while dance was deemed common.) In the early part of the 20th century, Orff developed the Orff music education program. He worked off the idea that feeling comes *before* understanding and stressed the thrill of music making through chants, rhythms, and language. The Orff method uses rhymes and proverbs as a basis for teaching rhythm, phrasing, and musical expression. Orff's special instruments, created for children with no technical facility, are still used to enable children to experiment with musical sounds.

Zoltan **Kodaly,** Hungarian composer and early-childhood expert, believed singing should be the basis of a music program, and his work provided impetus for the *singing schools* in Budapest (Hungary is regarded as having one of the best music education programs in the world). He thought children should learn many simple songs, sing in tune, and do conscious listening activities to develop aural skills. Kodaly contended that children can learn complex musical ideas in game situations and all children can become musically literate (reading and writing music) by developing concepts in experiential ways, rather than through rote teaching. Kodaly believed quality musical listening experiences enhance the ability to concentrate and focus and develop thinking skills. He reasoned that language development, reading ability, and coordination were developed when children learn to discriminate sound patterns in music. Kodaly's methods are based primarily on singing nursery songs and doing traditional circle games that include movement. Eventually, children learn musical terms and reading through folk songs. Musical skills are developed through a sequential curriculum so that children learn to sight read and sight sing. Kodaly used a system of hand signs to help children sing and *do* the notes of the scale: do = fist in knocking position; re = palm outstretched down and tilted up; mi = palm down; fa = thumb down; so = handshake; la = first two fingers and thumb make a U (downward); ti = point index finger up (see Choksy, 1974).

Ten Principles for Integration

In this chapter the concept of teaching *with, about, in,* and *through* the arts is applied to music integration using the 10 principles of INTEGRATES. Each principle contains general guidelines to help teachers think of how music integration can proceed. More specific starter ideas are available in Chapters 12 and 13. The latter includes ideas to integrate the arts with the arts.

Principle 1: IMMERSION in Music

Immerse means to totally cover or involve. Teachers can immerse students in music by using it in different ways throughout the day. **Background music** has even been found to enhance test performance by focusing thinking (Cockerton, Moore, & Norman, 1997). Music that is predictable seems to work best. Jazz artists such as Kenny G and environmental music is recommended. Baroque music is used in a school I visited in South Carolina as background during sustained silent reading and writing. They especially liked Bach's Brandenburg Concertos, Handel's Water Music and Vivaldi's Four Seasons. In a California school I've experienced the relaxing sounds of New Age music waft through the halls and cafeteria. One teacher boasted how even the bus drivers were using music to make the ride to and from school more pleasant; the driver and students negotiate radio stations contingent on specific bus behavior. In Illinois an elementary principal and John Phillip Sousa fan plays marches over the intercom every Monday as students and teachers arrive. Here are other immersion ideas gleaned from schools throughout the United States.

◆ *Music in the News:* Hold regular discussions about music-related topics, student interests, and music related to units under study. The newspaper, television, and radio are sources.

◆ *Music to Start the Day:* Invite students to bring in tapes and CDs to share at the start of the day, during recess, or for silent reading and writing times.

◆ *Guests:* Invite singers and musicians to perform for the class; ask students to help in finding potential candidates connected to units under study in science, social studies, and the like.

◆ *Lending Library:* Create a class set of CDs and tapes, similar to a class library of books; ask parents to share tapes and check for PTA help in

this project. Make tape/CD bags to take home with a book and activity. With young children, repeated reading of the lyrics, while listening to the song, is an excellent reinforcement for literacy skills.

◆ *Music Journals:* Write about how music is a part of life.

◆ *Mood and Signal Music:* Play music to calm or to energize, to signal when to change classes or move to other areas.

◆ *Teachable Moment:* Look for opportunities to point out rhythms of words; repeat poetry readings and discuss the musical qualities of poems.

◆ *Compose Songs:* Co-write lyrics with students and improvise on familiar melodies. Focus on writing about concepts and skills learned throughout the curriculum. Simple rhythm instruments can be made or found to perform songs. (See Warren's (1991) *Piggyback Songs for School.*)

Principle 2: NITTY-GRITTY Music Elements and Concepts

Start a Materials Collection.   Basic materials to begin to integrate music include musical instrument-making books, biographies of musicians, finger play books, chants and rhymes books, song collections, music-related children's literature, CDs and tapes, and videos such as *Vivaldi's Four Seasons* and *Beethoven Lives Upstairs.* Start a discography of music to use in units. See Post It Pages 11–10 and 11–11 for music ideas organized by unit topics.

Teach the Elements.   Classroom teachers do not generally have primary responsibility for teaching musical skills and elements. What's more, too much analysis can dispel the magic of music. Teachers can, however, teach and reinforce the basic concepts necessary for students to be successful with lessons involving music integration. For example, basic elements are needed to talk about the music of cultures under study. Elements are labels for words, and words contribute to general vocabulary development; so by teaching elements, students develop language and conceptual anchors to explore ways music can be thought about and created. Here is a sampling of strategies to develop concepts about elements. There are many more ideas in Chapter 12 under Basic Elements and Musical Concepts.

Visual Displays. Offer students a permanent reference. See Chapter 2 for ideas. Word Walls, charts, and banners are possibilities.

Rhythm Power. Use the motivational power of names to explore rhythm. *Name rhythms:* Call a child's name and beat out the rhythm using syllable patterns and accent. Ask students to echo. The teacher can also beat out the rhythm of a name and the *owner* echoes and becomes the leader. For example, "Virginia" would be four claps with the second accented. Relate this to poetry meter patterns. See the "word rhythms" in Post It Page 3–5.

Harmony. Names can also be used to explore harmony. *Name harmonies:* Pair children with long and short names. Pairs take turns beating out their names in rotation and together. Rhythm instruments or body parts can be used. *Variation:* Student pairs sing their names in harmony. *Name duet:* Encourage students to explore combinations they can create with just their names (e.g., Dan–Amber, Dan–Dan–Dan, Amber–Dan–Amber–Dan–Amber–Dan). Vary by changing the tempo of one name, the other, or both. Change the combination of tempo and volume in different ways. What harmonies are created by beating out both names or varying volume and tempo?

Name Melody. Names can be sung, hummed, or played on a keyboard.

Scavenger Hunts. Help students find and notice the music potential of ordinary objects such as keys, pencils, boxes, and bottles filled with beans. Objects can be used to create a tone for each name, as well.

Say It Different Ways. Change volume, rate, pitch, accent, and rhythm patterns: "The rain in Spain falls mainly on the plain."

Principle 3: TEACHING HABITS for Music Integration

Before teaching anyone else, I must teach myself. . . .
                                        Sylvia Ashton Warner

Teachers are people with personality variables and value structures. These have a profound influence on how a person teaches. Probably the most powerful teaching habit for music integration is to continue to grow *personal* musical intelligence by attending concerts, being involved in a choir, taking music lessons, or just being more active in the pursuit of increasing music in your life—at least through the use of tapes and CDs.

Music as a Part of Life. Music is an important way all humans relieve stress and change their moods. Integration of music can be as valuable for the teacher as for the students. A teacher friend, Mrs. Engle, started playing music in her classroom in the mornings as she was getting ready for the day when she first began her teaching career in the 1950s. She played big-band music that she first loved as a teenager. She told me that one morning she was in a rush and left a record on when her fifth graders came in. They were shocked at what the staid Mrs. Engle was listening to. They begged to hear more. Mrs. Engle was surprised the kids liked the "old stuff," but it became a routine to start the day with music. When I started teaching at the school where Mrs. Engle taught, I learned of her reputation for loving music. A tiny, white-haired lady, she retired after 42 years of teaching and credited much of her career longevity to using music to start, and often end, each day in her classroom.

Assess Interests, Abilities, and Preferences. Much can be learned about students' music background through conversations with them, observation, and talks with parents. An interest inventory can be the basis for action research on music integration in a classroom. For example, use an inventory as a pretest at the start of the year and a posttest at the end of the year to see changes in students' skills, knowledge, and attitudes toward learning and music. (See an example inventory in Appendix D.)

Select Quality Music. Children are inundated with music—in the car, on television and radio, in the supermarket. We need to ensure that music chosen for school gives exposure to music they would not otherwise listen to. It needs to be worth using precious school time. Of course, *worthy music* is a subjective concept, but it is important for teachers to develop criteria for quality. For example, if music lyrics are to be examined, then the words should be audible and clear. Some orchestral music can overwhelm students and elicit exaggerated responses. Use a music specialist as a resource, and consult the bibliographies in this chapter and in the appendix for help in finding quality music.

Mood Music. Concertos by Bach or pieces such as Pachelbel's *Canon* can be used to set mood and relax students as information about a topic is presented verbally. There is a great deal of current interest in using music in this manner to set the stage for learning. (See the work of Lozanov, 1978). Consider the use of music therapy, not in the clinical application, but using the concept of music as a motivator, to boost energy and to promote good feelings about school. A listening station or center with calming music can be used by individual students as needed or desired. Try the use of music to deal with anxiety; have a sing-in or play music before tests to relax. Music can be used to create mood and give background for study and writing, too.

Music for Lesson Introductions. To use a piece of music to introduce units, begin by asking students to listen to a piece of music or examine lyrics. Ask them to speculate about what it means, how it feels, the values conveyed, and who wrote it and why. Do a *repeated* listening several times so students develop skills for close listening. The class can be divided into groups to examine designated sections of the lyric.

Real-Life Connections. Focus on the goals of music integration—not to please an audience but to attain personal enjoyment and emotional response; to understand how music is an expression of our humanity and culture, a way of understanding and expressing ourselves. Ask students to brainstorm reasons we use music (e.g., rituals). Discuss the harmful effects of some music. See Scheel and Westefeld's (1999) article on heavy metal music and adolescent suicide! Students need to know that the typical teenager has 40 percent hearing loss caused by more than 90 decibels over a sustained time. Ask students to log or web music in their lives in one day or imagine a single day without music. Do class scavenger hunts for places music happens and the types of music students can find. Regularly ask students to think of connections between songs, music, and topics in math, science, and social studies. Cue them to use their musical intelligences. Finally, discuss how it affects a group when music is integrated. What effects does it have on motivation, attitude, and concentration?

Play with the "Music" of Reading or Talking. A teaching habit that connects music with learning to read and speak is to regularly practice reading and saying words and phrases in different ways. Take a moment to read aloud this sentence: *George Washington was the very first president of the United States of America*. Now, try again and change the dynamics (volume). Try again and change tempo (speed). Once more and change pitch and tone. Finally, try changing the rhythm (group phrases differently and add a regu-

lar beat, e.g., 1–2–3–4). Students can have fun adding musical elements to words and will discover how words really convey very little without the added music. Take time to ask how different versions of the same sentence mean different things based on how the person interprets them through the added music elements. Discuss how different words, phrases, and sentences *feel* different based on how they are said and read. The habit of playing with the musical elements of language will increase reading comprehension and help students speak in more interesting ways and more effectively communicate what they want to say.

Descriptive, Nonjudgmental Feedback. Another important habit is to focus on specific information in response to student efforts. When students create, perform, or respond to music, give them feedback by commenting on musical elements. For example, "You have great volume because you opened your mouth and have upright posture. You are breathing from your diaphragm!" As mentioned in other chapters, praise *controls* others, while descriptive feedback liberates because it is clearer and less value laden.

Sing with Students. Students do not mind if the teacher does not have a fine singing voice if genuine enthusiasm is expressed. Teachers can make the effort to sing with students and show enjoyment of the community built through group singing. Since classroom teachers are not perceived as music specialists, students accept their amateur efforts as natural and normal—especially if teacher singing is a common activity starting in kindergarten. With experience and commitment to music integration, teachers can learn to model how to sing without embarrassment—without being overly concerned about the Western notion that only the talented should sing out. Teachers should take heart in Thoreau's words about how the forest would be a very quiet place if only the talented birds did the singing.

Teach Songs. To learn a song, the singer must be motivated to learn and do close listening to hear specific pitches, grasp the tempo and underlying beat, and identify the rhythmic patterns. In addition, the singer must combine all this into a whole. Here are important song teaching guidelines:

- ◆ *Consider the developmental levels of students* and keep songs for younger students simple—easy lyrics, limited melody (not too high or too low), and a catchy beat. See Jarnow's (1991) *All Ears:*

How to Use and Choose Recorded Music for Children for guidance.

◆ *Combine singing with movement.* Students need to see the teacher move to the song, as well, and show appropriate facial expressions. Sign language can be used to add movement; see Riekehof's (1978) *Joy of Signing* or improvise hand signs or motions. Practice keeping a steady beat together by clapping or use rhythm instruments, and use this as a basis for moving to singing together, doing rounds, and creating harmony later.

◆ *It may be hard to stay in a specific key.* The ideal range for children is usually from about middle C up to G. If songs are pitched too high or low, they have trouble matching the pitch. Usually, students who sing out of tune are not hearing the notes clearly and may need to have a note or phrase isolated for practice. Use the amount of repetitions necessary for students to be successful in matching pitch. Ask students to hear the notes in their heads before they sing them. By taking time to teach careful, close listening, almost all children can learn to sing well. Even intermediate and middle school students, who have not done much singing, can learn to sing well if the teacher takes the time to work on listening carefully to the tune so that intonation is accurate. Don't despair if students aren't perfect singers immediately. Remind yourself and your students that singing in tune, like all important life skills, comes with practice.

◆ *Start with songs student know and like.* See recommended song lists, such as MENC's Top 40 in Post It Page 11–5 or the *Music Teachers Book of Lists* (Ross & Stang, 1994), and consult the music basal in the school district. See anthologies in the bibliography and at the end of this chapter. There is a *Favorite Songs* list that teachers and children in my community selected in Post It Page 11–6. In general, it is recommended that students learn to sing songs without accompaniment so that they learn to listen to themselves and rely on their voices. One easy way to begin is use "Call and response" songs because they are easy; students simply echo what the teacher sings. Begin with keeping a steady beat and clapping or snapping rhythms for students to echo. Students can also become leaders. Here is a favorite chant to use as a call and response: Teacher: *Acka lacka ching/*

(Students echo)/T: *Acka lacka chow/*(Students echo)/ T: *Acka lacka ching ching chow chow/* (Students echo)/ T: *Booma lacka booma alack sis boom bah/* (Students echo)/ T: *Reading Reading/ Rah Rah Rah* (substitute any phrase you want)/(Students echo).

◆ *Sing daily and post lyrics after students hear songs.* (See Bill Harp's article in the bibliography.) Use a chart or pocket chart to write the words large enough for all to see. Pocket charts enable one line to be put up at a time for focus. Sing songs to start the day and cleanup ("I've been working on the railroad"). Instead of giving directions, sing or chant directions; use the universal melody of "na na na NA na"—think of the childhood taunt—and sing "Line up and go home."

◆ *Teach new songs slowly, with many repetitions.* Use nonsense syllables such as "la," "ti," and "tah" to explore singing voice. Encourage students frequently and be supportive about their efforts. Remember, singing requires taking a risk. Tell them that everyone can sing well in their own range if they listen carefully and try their best. To teach a round, make sure students have mastered the whole song first or the song will fall apart during the round. Music is a skill learned through the three Ps: practice, practice, and practice. Neural pathways and muscle tone develop with multiple repetitions.

◆ *Model, imitate, and repeat* are the most typical techniques for teaching songs. Students should hear the whole song first, before seeing the lyrics. This sequence allows students to experience the esthetics of the music first. The whole–part–whole sequence is recommended for introducing all arts: (1) experience the art form as a whole, (2) then work on the skills or individual parts, and then (3) put it all back together again. Give direct instruction line by line or phrase by phrase. Finally, sing the whole song several times to increase fluency and enjoyment. *Note:* Some music educators do recommend starting with the parts and building up to the whole song, rather than having students hear the whole to begin with. Both whole-to-part and part-to-whole methods involve students in listening to a part of a song and then echoing the teacher as the bulk of the lesson. As parts are mastered, the song builds up until students can sing the entire song well. Post It Page 11–9 summarizes steps.

Balance Music Listening and Music Making. There are many reasons to give critical and creative music listening experiences. Listening to music stimulates the right and the left hemispheres of the brain, emphasizes cognitive and affective processes, and enlarges us as whole persons. Because music is primarily an art form created for enjoyment, children need to experience music for the pleasure it brings; we need to give time to *just* listen and *just* sing. Even when students are to do critical thinking (analysis and evaluation) about a piece of music, it is helpful to let them experience the music as a whole, as an enjoyable art form, before breaking it down for study. There are strong connections between forms of listening and forms of oral expression, including singing. When students learn to listen closely, they sing better. When students have many opportunities to listen to a variety of music during morning routines and at other times, they gradually acquire more refined listening skills for identifying how pieces are alike and different and why we respond in so many different ways to music. Giving children a "listen for" or purpose (element, instrument, style, or genre) and doing repeated listening to selections helps develop abilities to do close listening for critical thinking purposes. Try this: Distribute cards with pictures of instruments, and ask children to hold up the card that corresponds with the instrument when they hear its timbre.

Stretch the "Concept of the Familiar." We have a tendency to disdain the strange. If we are serious about teaching tolerance, flexibility, and respect for diversity, music can be a powerful tool in this endeavor. Here are some suggestions. First, don't give students the chance to say they don't like unfamiliar music. Start right in and have them listen with a purpose—to identify instruments they hear, voices, the beat, and so on. Next, ask them to describe what they heard as best they can—not *evaluate* it for preferences, yet. Then, give students many opportunities to hear a piece over and over (at least three times, with different purposes each time) so that they become familiar with it. This simple strategy is effective in expanding musical taste. Make the strange familiar.

Principle 4: ENERGIZERS and Warm-ups

Prepare students for experiences that require risk taking and creative thinking by doing energizers and warm-ups that activate the brain, relax them, and tap into interests. Since performing music is also a physi-

TEACHING SONGS

POST IT PAGE 11–9

Rote Method

1. **Motivate and stimulate interest.** For example, give background on the song. (See *New Grove Dictionary of Music* for ideas.)
2. **Sing the song or play a recording.** The singing should be in your normal voice, not too high pitched or operatic. The range should be appropriate for the students. Teacher enthusiasm is critical at this step, so show it.
3. **Ask students to describe what they heard using music terms (e.g., repetitions, rhythm).**
4. **Echo sing.** Teacher sings a line or phrase and students echo. Go through the whole song this way. Continue to build up the song by repeating previous phrases and adding new ones. If the song is difficult, slow down, but keep a steady beat. If there are unusual words, try doing the whole song echoically in a speaking voice the first time through. Repeat this step as much as necessary.
5. **Display the songs lyrics on a chart, overhead, or pocket chart.**
6. **Sing through many times.** Ask students for ideas on how they can improve and target an element (e.g., dynamics, enunciation).

Rounds

1. Use the rote method to teach the whole song. When it is mastered, go to the previous step 5.
2. Instruct the students to sing softly so that they can hear each other. Establish start and stop hand signals so that you can direct each group. Keep a steady beat.
3. Start with just two parts to keep it simple, with each group singing through twice.

cal activity, the body often needs to be prepared as well. Energizers and warm-ups cause students to use both body and mind. In Chapter 12 there are many ideas to choose from—ones for teaching musical concepts and elements can also be used as energizers. There are also energizers and warm-ups in the other arts chapters that would be appropriate before music-related experiences, for example, drama verbal strategies and dance rhythm strategies. In general, think about doing song sharing, poems, chants, and rhythms that take only a few minutes and cause both mental and physical engagement.

Principle 5: GREAT CHILDREN'S LITERATURE Related to Music

Never has there been more high-quality children's literature available to integrate the arts. There is a plethora of children's literature devoted to music specifically and a variety of genre of music-related children's books (e.g., biographies of musicians). Children's literature can become the basis for a variety of lessons that integrate music. For example, Ambrus's *Seven Skinny Goats* can be used to dance with music signals and to explore different tempos. (Students enjoy trying to dance with one foot stuck to the floor.) *Charlie Parker Played Be Bop* is a striking picture book appropriate for any age. If it is read while playing a tape or CD of "Night in Tunisia," it becomes a magical lesson and can lead to discoveries about genre, styles, and form. (Thanks to teachers at Duxberry Elementary for this idea.) Biographies are particularly important ways for students to get in-depth and personal accounts of individuals with whom they might identify. Biographies are valuable in both science and social studies to add the human element. For example, Krull's *The Lives of Musicians* gives short biographical pieces with interesting facts and a perspective on the historical period in which the musician lived. Post It Pages 11–10 and 11–11 offer a sampling of titles focused on aspects of music and curricular topics. Recording artists can help in locating tapes and CDs. There are many more titles in the Arts-Based Children's Literature bibliography in the appendix.

POST IT PAGE 11–10

MUSIC-BASED LITERATURE BY CATEGORIES

Picture Books Based on Songs

Fox, D. (1987). *Go in and out the window* (various styles). Metropolitan Museum of Art.

Hurd, T. (1987). *Mama don't allow: Starring Miles and the Swamp Band.* Harpercrest.

Karas, B. (1994). *I know an old lady who swallowed a fly.* Scholastic.

Keats, E. (1987). *The little drummer boy.* Aladdin Books.

Mattox, C. (1990). *Shake it to the one that you love the best.* JTG. of Nashville.

Pearson, T. (1984). *Old MacDonald had a farm.* Dial.

Quackenbush, R. (1975). *Skip to my Lou.* Lippincott.

Winter, J. (1988). *Follow the drinking gourd.* Knopf.

Zemach, H. (1966). *Mommy, buy me a China doll.* Follett.

About Orchestras and Bands

Hurd, T. (1987). *Mama don't allow: Starring Miles and the Swamp Band.* Harpercrest.

Johnston, T. (1988). *Pages of music.* Putnam's.

Koscielniak, B. (2000). *The story of the incredible orchestra: An introduction to musical instruments and the symphony orchestra,* Houghton Mifflin.

Kuskin, K. (1982). *The Philharmonic gets dressed.* Harper & Row.

Moss, L. (1995). *Zin! zin! zin!: A violin.* School & Library Binding.

Moss, L. (2001). *Our marching band.* School & Library Binding.

Moss, L. (2002). *Music Is.* School & Library Binding.

Sargent, R. (1968). *Peter and the wolf.* Lancelot.

Williams, V. (1984). *Music, music for everyone.* Greenwillow.

Musical Genre and Styles

Bryan, A. (1991). *All night: All day: A child's first book of African-American spirituals.* Atheneum.

Fleischman, P. (1988). *Rondo in C* (classical). Harper & Row.

Gray, M. (1972). *Song and dance man* (vaudeville). Dutton.

Hart, J. (1982). *Singing bee! A collection of favorite children's songs.* Lothrop Lee & Shepard.

Martin, B. (1986). *Barn dance!* (country). Henry Holt.

Papp, C. (1988). *Follow the sunset: A beginning geography record with nine songs from around the world* (lullabies) (tape or CD). Entomography Publications.

Raschka, C. (1992). *Charlie Parker played bee bop* (bee bop). Orchard Books.

Musical Instruments

Fichter, G. (1978). *American Indian music and musical instruments.* McKay.

Jenkins, E. (1989). *Rhythms of childhood* (with tape or CD). Smithsonian/Folkways.

Wiseman, A. (1979). *Making musical things: Improvised instruments.* Scribner.

Collections of Songs and Singing Games

Barkman, A. (1987). *Rise and shine* (with tape or CD). Moody.

Cote, P. (1995). *Do your ears hang low? Fifty more musical fingerplays.* Scholastic.

Fox, D. (1987). *Go in and out the window.* Metropolitan Museum of Art.

Glazer, T. (1992). *Eye winker, Tom Tinker, chin chopper: Fifty musical fingerplays.* Doubleday.

Hart, J. (1982). *Singing bee! A collection of favorite children's songs.* Lothrop Lee & Shepard.

Jenkins, E. (1989). *You'll sing a song and I'll sing a song* (tape or CD). Smithsonian.

Raffi (1990). *Baby Beluga* (with tape or CD). Crown.

Seeger, M. (1987). *American folk songs for children* (with tape or CD). Cambridge Rounder.

Careers in Music/Composers and Musicians

Fleischman, P. (1988). *Rondo in C.* Harper & Row.

Gmoser, L. (1997). *Great composers.* Smithmark.

Isadora, R. (1979). *Ben's trumpet* (jazz). Greenwillow.

Johnston, T. (1988). *Pages of music.* Putnam's.

Krull, K. (1993). *Lives of musicians.* Harcourt Brace Jovanovich.

Lionni, L. (1979). *Geraldine, the music mouse.* Pantheon.

Mitchell, B., & Smith, J. (1988). *America, I hear you: A story about George Gershwin.* Carolrhoda.

Williams, V. B. (1984). *Music, music for everyone.* Greenwillow.

MUSIC-BASED LITERATURE BY CURRICULAR TOPIC

Abilities and Disabilities

Corcoran, B. (1974). *A dance to still music.* Atheneum.

Keats, E. J. (1964). *Whistle for Willie.* Viking.

McCloskey, R. (1940). *Lentil.* Viking.

White, E. B. (1970). *The trumpet of the swan.* Harper & Row.

Animals

Collection of Brothers Grimm (1988). *The Bremen-town musicians.* McGraw-Hill.

Conover, C. (1976). *Six little ducks.* Crowell.

Hurd, T. (1987). *Mama don't allow: Starring Miles and the Swamp Band.* Harpercrest.

Karas, G. (1994). *I know an old lady who swallowed a fly.* Scholastic.

Knight, H. (1981). *Hilary Knight's the twelve days of Christmas.* Macmillan.

Maxner, J. (1989). *Nicholas Cricket.* Harper & Row.

Pearson, T. (1984). *Old MacDonald had a farm.* Dial.

Prokofiev, S. (1961). *Peter and the wolf.* Franklin Watts.

Steig, W. (1994). *Zeke Pippin.* HarperCollins.

White, E. B. (1970). *The trumpet of the swan.* Harper & Row.

Creativity and Imagination

Isadora, R. (1979). *Ben's trumpet* (jazz). Greenwillow.

Musical Artists and Recordings: Peter Alsop, Linda Arnold, Kim and Jerry Brodey, Frank Cappelli, Tom Chapin, Rick Charette, Charlotte Diamond, Chris Holder, Eric Nagler, Tim Noah, Hap Palmer, Barry Louis Polisar, Rosenshontz, Paul Tracey.

Rylant, C. (1988). *All I see.* Orchard Books.

Cumulative and Repetitive Stories

Dodd, M. (1988). *This old man.* Houghton Mifflin.

Emberley, B. (1967). *Drummer Hoff.* Simon & Schuster.

Karas, G. (1994). *I know an old lady who swallowed a fly.* Scholastic.

Knight, H. (1981). *Hilary Knight's the twelve days of Christmas.* Macmillan.

Martin, B. (1989). *Chicka chicka boom boom.* Simon & Schuster.

Raffi (1987). *Down by the bay.* Crown.

Dance and Movement

Gray, M. (1972). *Song and dance man.* Dutton.

Isadora, R. (1976). *Max.* Macmillan.

Martin, B. (1986). *Barn dance!* Henry Holt.

Seeger, M. (1987). *American folk songs for children* (with tape or CD). Cambridge Rounder.

Fairy and Folk Tales

Collection of Brothers Grimm (1988). *The Bremen-Town musicians.* McGraw-Hill.

Lewis, R. (1991). *All of you was singing.* Atheneum.

Whitehead, P. (1989). *The Nutcracker.* Stoneway Books.

Families and Friends

Griffin, H. (1986). *Georgia music.* Greenwillow.

Pinkwater, D. (1991). *Doodle flute.* Macmillan.

Williams, V. B. (1984). *Music, music for everyone.* Greenwillow.

Holidays

Johnston, T. (1988). *Pages of music* (Christmas). Putnam.

Keats, E. J. (1987). *The little drummer boy* (Christmas). Aladdin Books.

Whitehead, P. (1989). *The Nutcracker* (Christmas). Stoneway Books.

Yolan, J. (1991). *Hark! A Christmas sampler.* Putnam.

Humor

Scieszka, J. (1993). *Your mother was a neanderthal.* Viking.

Language Arts

McMillan, B. (1977). *The alphabet symphony: An ABC book.* Greenwillow.

Math

Karas, G. (1994). *I know an old lady who swallowed a fly.* Scholastic.

Nursery Rhymes and Lullabies

dePaola, T. (1984). *Mary had a little lamb.* Holiday House.

Rounds

Beall, P. (1996). *Wee sing sing-alongs* (with tape or CD). Price Stern Sloan.

School

Giff, P. (1992). *Meet the Lincoln Lions band.* Dell.

Science, Nature, Health

Jenkins, E. (1989). *Rhythms of childhood* (with tape or CD). Smithsonian/Folkways.

Papp, C. (1988). *Follow the sunset: A beginning geography record with nine songs from around the world* (with tape or CD). Entomography Publications.

Social Studies

Kelly, T. (1973). *Yankee Doodle* (Revolution, 1775–83). Performance.

Papp, C. (1988). *Follow the sunset: A beginning geography record with nine songs from around the world* (with tape or CD). Entomography Publications.

Sonneck, O. (1969). *The Star-Spangled Banner* (War of 1812). Da Capo.

Spier, P. (1973). *The Star Spangled Banner.* Doubleday.

Winter, J. (1988). *Follow the drinking gourd* (slavery). Knopf.

Sound Effects

McGovern, A. (1992). *Too much noise.* Demco Media.

Spier, P. (1990). *Crash! Boom! Bang!* Doubleday.

Various Artists (1997). *Sound effects* (with tape or CD). Triangle Books.

Sports

Isadora, R. (1976). *Max.* Macmillian.

Toys

Whitehead, P. (1989). *The Nutcracker.* Stoneway Books.

Zemach, H. (1966). *Mommy, buy me a China doll.* Follett.

Musical Artists Who Record for Children

Peter Alsop	Gemini	Sarah Pirtle
Linda Arnold	Red Grammer	David Polansky
Fran Avni	Greg and Steve	Barry Louis Polisar
Pamela Ballingham	Bill Harley	Raffi
Joanie Bartels	Chris Holder	Rosenshontz
Steve Bergman	Janet and Judy	Phil Rosenthal
Marcia Berman	Ella Jenkins	Kevin Roth
Heather Bishop	Kathi and Milenko	Nancy Rumel and Friends
Kim and Jerry Brodey	Kids on the Block	Pete Seeger
Rachel Buchman	The Kids of Widney High	Sharon, Lois and Bram
Janice Buckner	Lois LaFond	Paul Strausman
Frank Cappelli	Francine Lancaster	Marlo Thomas and Friends
Tom Chapin	John Mccutcheon	Tickle Toon Typhoon
Rick Charette	Marcia Merman	Uncle Ruthie
The Children of Selma	Mary Miche	Bill Usher
Jon Crosse	Eric Nagler	Jim Valley
Charlotte Diamond	Hap Palmer	The Weavers
Jonathan Edwards	Tom Paxton	Weird Al Yankovic
Terrence Farrell	Peter, Paul, and Mary	Patty Zeitli

Principle 6: ROUTINES

Putting predictable routines and rituals in place early in the school year makes a substantial contribution to music integration and enables students to assume increasing responsibility. Once students understand the structure, they should be able to conduct, adapt, and suggest new routines, much like Mrs. Lucas's class did in the Classroom Snapshot in Chapter 2. See Chapter 2 under Routines for additional ideas. Here are some common ones to start music integration:

Use music to signal classroom events, such as recess, lunch, or the end of day.

Have a composer of the day. A few facts about the composer and a musical piece or song can be shared in a morning routine. Students can select favorites from among several songs or pieces of music and display titles with "speech bubbles" around them telling facts or feelings about composers or the music.

Celebrate musicians' birthdays. Often these are printed in the daily newspaper. Play the music the person is famous for to celebrate.

Use background music daily to set mood. Morning music and music played during art making and silent reading and writing times are easy routines to establish. Gentle folk music from diverse traditions or classical music works well. Remember, the rhythms of the brain tend to echo the rhythms of music, and the rhythms can enhance attention and learning (entrainment).

Collect and post music quotes and poems. Livington's *Call Down the Moon,* is a lovely collection of poetry about music. Try a poem a day or a quote a day with this collection. Post quotes from this chapter on music integration.

Do book ads for music-related children's literature. Books ads are advertisements to make others want to read. For "how to," see Book Ads in Chapter 3.

Set up an ongoing display of music-based children's books. Students can even be in charge of supplying a special section of the chalk tray with books they find about music. This can be assigned as a classroom job. Once a spot is established, students can display personal books or library books. A question can be posted above each book to entice readers.

Start the day with singing favorite songs. Familiar songs can be sung with or without posting lyrics. If visuals are used, make song charts using large paper so lyrics are easy to read. Begin with a sing-in of songs students choose. If song charts are used, a few minutes can be used to examine (I Spy game) the lyrics for language patterns being studied (adjectives, homophones, etc.).

Principle 7: ADAPT Curriculum and Instruction Models for Music Integration

To read Schiller's poem Ode to Joy is to know one kind of beauty, yet to hear it sung by a great chorus as the majestic conclusion to Beethoven's Ninth Symphony is to experience beauty of an entirely different kind. . .
                                                                    Bruce Boston, 1996, p. 11

Music integration, based on the models and theories for thinking about curriculum and integration in Chapters 1 and 2, should include considerations about:

- Differentiating or individualizing lessons for students of different ages and stages (see 10 PARTICULAR strategies for special needs)
- Students interests and concerns
- Connections with life-centered issues
- Teaching for depth, not breadth
- Focusing on essential or universal human questions
- Themes versus topics
- Sources for unit and integrated lessons: state and local standards or curriculum guides for science, social studies, reading, language arts, music (see, as an example, Burz & Marshall, 1999)
- The *National Standards for the Arts*
- The variety of integrated unit structures: basic unit types, six interdisciplinary design options, schoolwide topics, centers or stations related to themes
- Multiple intelligences lesson plan formats
- Integrating music with other arts
- Three-part teaching structure in lesson plans: introduction, development, and conclusion

A general discussion of each of the above issues appears in Chapter 2. Here are applications of these ideas that apply specifically to music:

Make Lessons Appropriate to Age and Stage. Children progress through stages of musical development.

Preschool. Even toddlers respond to music by bouncing and rocking. Preschoolers can learn simple songs and love to play with sounds. By age 3 the left hemisphere is more developed so rhythm improves and kids can't get enough of marching, clapping, tapping, and swaying. They are ready for simple keyboard practice, kazoos, and recorders. By age 4, children understand the concepts of rhythm, tempo, volume, and pitch and can create their own songs with improvised lyrics. Of course, children love songs that have suggested actions, such as "Head, Shoulders, Knees, and Toes," and enjoy active engagement through fingerplays, using rhythm instruments, and creative movement or dance. They especially like folk songs, marches, and easy pop songs.

Primary Grades. Usually, children start school able to sing melodies and echo rhythms and melodies during call and response songs. They also probably have established musical preferences. This is the time to introduce many musical genres from classical to hip-hop. Ideally, music lessons would start between the ages of 3 and 8, but the sooner the better, according to brain research that shows distinct differences among those who start lessons early (Jensen, 2001). There is evidence that students have the capability to compose music, as well, so opportunities to both sing and compose (e.g., on a keyboard) should be available. See Sharlene Habemeyer's (1999) *Good Music, Brighter Children* for more information on this topic. Here is a sampling of musical artists for this age group:

The Kids of Widney High

Hap Palmer

Rosenshontz

Pete Seeger

Steve and Greg

Marlo Thomas and Friends

Tickle Tune Typhon

Peter Alsop

Heather Bishop

Tom Chapin

Ella Jenkins

Kids on the Block

Intermediate Grades. By this age the brain is 80 percent developed so if music lessons have not been begun it is unlikely one will become a "world-class"

musician. Musical competence on an instrument is still possible, however (Jensen, 2001, p. 19). Singing in groups, such as school musicals and choirs, is appropriate. Here is a sampling of musical artists for this age group:

Bill Harley

Janet and Judy

Mary Miche

The Weavers

Weird Al Yankovic

Classroom teachers have a lot to build on as they integrate music. As teachers consider what's appropriate for the age and stage of students, it is important to begin with what children already know—start with strengths and interests. One example of this idea is integrating music with reading by asking children to dictate lyrics to a familiar song. Once the chart is created, it can then be read and reread. Sight words, phonic patterns, and special spellings can then be discussed as students play "I Spy" examples of language concepts they see or the teacher suggests a category, for example, all the words that begin with "B." This strategy can be adapted for more mature students by using songs of interest to them as the basis for teaching sentence structure (grammar), usage, alliteration, assonance, consonance, parts of speech, and so forth.

Unit Structures. In Chapter 2, four different integrated unit structures were explained. Each unit is based on one of four centers or bodies with nine legs. See Post It Page 2–4. When integrating music, a teacher or team may plan integrated lessons and units using one or more of the traditional subject areas as the orientation for a unit. Another option is to choose a body or center from the four other unit types: (1) author-artist, (2) genre or form, (3) problem, theme, topic, or question, or (4) single work (poem, book, song). For example, unit 1 could be a study of a musician, such as Charlie Parker, using the book *Charlie Parker Played Be Bop* as a key resource material, with all the arts, as well as math, science, social studies, and reading and language arts as *legs* that would support the body—learning about a person, in this case. Music would be used as a learning tool in such a unit, just as any other leg. A unit might focus on a composer or singer, as well. The second unit type could be planned around a particular genre or form of music (gospel, folk, swing), and the third, which has a problem, theme, topic, or question (e.g., Why and how do people create music? What causes music styles to emerge?), is another option. Finally, a particular book, poem, or song could serve as the unit center (e.g., Hesse's *Out of the Dust*, the 1998 Newbery Award winner, has significant themes about the importance of music in the life of a teenager enduring the Dust Bowl of the 1930s). Other songs the family might have sung would fit into such a unit, including occasions for music in the book (a funeral, wedding, work songs). Major concepts and skills in math, science, social studies, reading and language arts, and the other art forms would be used as support legs. Of course, in any integrated lesson or unit, all bodies and legs should be correlated with courses of study and standards to ensure substantive and focused study. Post It Page 5–13 is an example integrated unit. Take a moment to examine the music ideas in it. See the arts-based bibliography and other bibliographies in this chapter for ideas about children's books.

Start Small and Grow.   Rather than plan a whole unit on music or even one with significant use of music, try just one lesson (e.g., a lesson on the history of a familiar song, such as "Row, Row, Row Your Boat"). The key is to make sure your first attempts are successful, for you and for your students. Begin by integrating energizing warm-ups to introduce the day or particular days for lessons. For example, teach a new song every Monday. Explore the language arts connections by using a song chart and the "I Spy" strategy in which students tell all the types of words and language structures they see in the song. Plan short minilessons of about 10 to 15 minutes at first.

Integrated Music Lessons.   Lessons that meaningfully integrate music begin with careful planning. Brainstorm about music connections (and other web legs) for one of the unit types. For example, a core book unit around Raschka's *Charlie Parker Played Be Bop* could develop the concept of jazz, as well as language arts concepts such as onomatopoeia, rhyme, and language repetition. The power of the book and listening to jazz are bound to make this a memorable learning experience because Charlie Parker was so full of energy and creativity. It's very helpful to use local, state, and national standards and courses of study to get specific concept and skills ideas for teaching and to ensure that lessons are developing the competencies the school district expects. Another critical idea is to

decide how lessons will be ordered in a unit—which will be taught first, second, third, and so on. The flow of lessons is established by thinking about how one will lead into another. For this reason, it is important to think about which lesson will be the introductory one and to plan a culminating lesson to wrap up each unit. The culminating lesson generally involves students in presenting projects worked on throughout a unit. For example, students might write their own jazz "scat" songs and present them to show that they understand syncopation and the use of nonsense words in jazz.

See the lesson format using a two-pronged focus and student objectives in Chapter 2, and refer to the detailed discussion about dividing the teaching strategies into introduction, development, and conclusion. Keep in mind that if students are expected to create a song, structure is very important; for example, adapt lyrics to a familiar tune or, in the case of the Charlie Parker book, write new words to use in place of *be bop, fisk fisk,* and other "scat" words. Plans need to include strategies for transition, use of space, materials, and even ways to dismiss groups: "Your ticket out today is . . ." or "All those that can/know . . . may. . . ." See Post It Page 2–2 for more information on lesson planning.

Guided Music and Language Lesson.   Music and listening, speaking, reading, and writing are integrated in these special guided lessons led by the teacher. This is a special variation on the two-pronged plan format, but it still includes an introduction, development, and conclusion. The instructional steps are *listen closely and think; predict; read; share; write; music response; publish.* These can be posted so that students can eventually guide small- or whole-group lessons. The *guided music and language arts lesson* teaching steps are outlined in Post It Page 11–12.

Integrate Music with Other Arts.   Integrating the arts is about helping students discover the interrelationships that exist in our world and using their creative-thinking gifts to make meaning through all art forms. To achieve this goal, students need to be shown how the arts share common aspects. Basic elements cut across art forms (rhythm, line, shape) and all art forms are created through the creative problem-solving process. We can ease students into the risk taking necessary to do higher-order thinking to create, perform, and respond in the arts by setting the stage with expectations. For example, begin to collect and

POST IT PAGE 11–12

LESSON PLAN: GUIDED MUSIC AND LANGUAGE ARTS

Two-Pronged Focus: (1) Choose from music elements and key concepts and (2) specify reading and language arts skills and concepts; see courses of study for help.

Standards: 6, 8, 9 (See Post It Page 11–8)

Objectives: By the end of the lesson, students should be able to . . . (list specific music and language arts outcomes here).

Teaching Procedure: The teacher will ask students to . . .

◆ **Introduction**

L—*Listen closely and think: Say, "Listen to . . . (a piece of music for a set period of time) to hear and feel everything it is about. No talking at this stage."*

P—*Predict: Next, ask students to write predictions about what the composer is trying to communicate. With younger children the teacher can scribe on a chart or the overhead.*

◆ **Development**

R—*Read: Read about the musician and/or the work. Teachers may read to the students.*

S—*Share: Ask students to share their predictions about the work, whether they were confirmed or rejected in the reading material. This can be done in pairs, small groups, or whole group.*

◆ **Conclusion**

W—*Write: Students do a writing response. Provide students with examples of different writing forms to choose from; see Post It Page 4–2. Focus writing on important ideas learned about the music or composer.*

M—*Music: Give students options of ways to respond to the lesson, using the musical intelligence (see Post It Page 12–1).*

P—*Publish: Student responses are "made public" through displays, oral sharing and singing, and book making (e.g., class big book).*

---

share anecdotes about the struggles and failures most famous artists endure before achieving any measure of success. Share stories about the reactions to highly innovative ideas; Igor Stravinsky's *Rites of Spring* caused a riot when it was first played because it didn't conform to what people thought was good music. If students are shown how people are often uncomfortable with change or the unfamiliar, they can learn to be more open to difference and thus grow in flexibility and tolerance.

Music as a Mnemonic and as a Motivator for Learning. Throughout this chapter there are examples of how music can support learning throughout the curricular areas of science, social studies, math, and reading and language arts. It will be exciting to see future developments in particular research areas. For

TAKE ACTION 5
INTEGRATED MUSIC LESSON

Select a music-based children's book from a Post It Page in this chapter. Use it and the standards from a school district to web *what* could be taught with it about music (concepts, skills, attitudes), and *what* could be taught about language arts and reading. From the *whats* branch off to *hows* (strategies).

---

example, Baroque and Classical music (Mozart, Beethoven, Bach, Vivaldi, Pachelbel, Handel, or Haydn) in 4/4 time has been found to stimulate memory when it is played as background during teaching. (Researchers such as Bulgarian psychiatrist Georgi Lozanov call this "superlearning." Background music for learning is available from Learning in New Dimension, Box 1447, San Francisco, CA 94114.) Teachers can use the mnemonic power of music by putting information into raps or chants to sing math facts or spell words to a rhythm. Rhythm instruments can be used to express ideas through music (e.g., use simple rhythm instruments with a poem or convey ideas learned in a unit on space or even as a means of learning parts of speech), and anytime students write original songs about content areas they are transforming information that entails elaborate thinking.

We are a multicultural country and we need to seek out every means to teach respect for the diversity of people. Songs, musical pieces, and instruments fit well into social studies because of the historical and cultural basis of music. Traditional songs and folk music, passed from generation to generation, help students understand the rules and values of a culture and see how there is a human inclination to create patterns. For example, German songs are often grouped into threes, while Australian songs frequently have beats grouped into twos and fours and are organized using eighth notes. Japanese music is often based on a scale of five notes, rather than the eight-note scale used in Western cultures. Use the bibliographies in the appendix and at the end of the chapter to find collections such as *Rise Up Singing!*, a collection of folk songs including multicultural favorites such as "Hava Nagila" (Hebrew round), "If I Had a Hammer," and "De Colores" (United Farm Workers folk song). Recordings can be purchased to go with the book (tapes and CDs). Campbell's (1994) *Roots and Branches* is another resource that includes background information and songs from more than 25 countries. It comes with a CD. See Post It Page 11–2, organized by cultures and countries. When music is used to explore concepts in content and skill areas (math, science, language arts, and reading), the teacher needs to feel comfortable that all the disciplines involved, including music, are used in respectful ways and not trivialized.

Listening Centers.   Centers or stations with headphones are particularly useful in integrating music. Centers allow students to independently make music a part of their classroom lives. Tapes of environmental sounds can be available at a center for classification

and identification, or music can be selected for free listening. Various musical selections can be at a center for children to listen to, along with information about the composers or as elaborations of ideas introduced in a lesson. Children can match musical selections with the correct composers as a follow up to "close listening" done as a group to discern genre and style characteristics. Students can also be invited to go to listening centers during free time and use them as a source for selecting music to be played for the whole class to enjoy at the start of the day or other group times. This kind of exposure to music has the potential to spur a lifelong interest and further expand a child's musical tastes.

Principle 8: TRIPS for Music Outside of School

When teachers think of music-related field trips, they often think first of visits to hear the local symphony or a special concert, and certainly these opportunities are pivotal in children's musical development. Many communities now have arts coordinators that contact schools to schedule trips and provide pre- and posttrip lesson ideas. The checklist for planning field trips in Chapter 2 will help prepare for such a trip. In addition, in Chapter 7 there are two ideas that apply to music-based field trips: the section on preparing students for live performances and the strategy of using *simulated mind trips* to take students mentally to places they cannot go physically. Both ideas are under the Take Field Trips section in that chapter.

If your community is not so fortunate, use the phone book and check the resources in the community. Very meaningful field trips can be made to music stores or local colleges, if preplanning is done with the speakers and a focus is set for the trip. For example, combine a lesson on running a business with music for the trip to a music store. Then there are the easy field trips that are right there for all of us. Take time to tune in on the sounds of the world. Take listening walks with the class to collect sounds around the school, in the cafeteria, on the playground. Stop and listen closely to the sounds of the classroom or sounds outside the window. Stop and listen for a minute each day to body sounds and rhythms. Ask students to label sounds they hear as fast or slow or high or low. Describe and model sounds made with instruments, and ask students to describe them. Develop the concept of how sounds express emotions. Ask students to make sounds that are tired, happy, or fearful. In general, develop sensitivities to the role that sound plays in how they feel about a place.

Principle 9: EVIDENCE to Document Progress/Assessment

Both students and teachers need evidence that all the work put into music integration is paying off. Ideas mentioned for demonstrating how students have grown in both cognitive and affective areas include keeping portfolios of songs created and collected in anthologies, actual tapes students make, checklists of progress made in using musical elements effectively, journal entries, and other writing about music. Even tests can be used—especially tests to show parents and administrators how music is connected to reading and language arts, math, science, and social studies learning. By sharing student progress made through music integration, in all the forms mentioned, teachers are most likely to win over skeptics. There is additional assessment information in Chapter 14. See examples of assessment tools in Appendix D.

Principle 10: SPECIALISTS in Music Are Important and Necessary

Collaboration with specialists has been discussed in all previous chapters. Music integration should include the music teacher, local musicians, and others with the musical expertise classroom teachers do not possess. Consult the Specialists sections of earlier chapters, including the guidelines in Chapter 2 on artist residencies.

A developing speciality area in music that needs particular attention is the use of technology, especially the computer. Ten years ago teachers would not have considered looking to the technology world for help in music integration. What a difference a decade has made. While most music software is for music reading and history, music-computer specialists can show teachers how to involve students in creating original musical compositions with software. A sequencer is needed to program a background drum beat or harmony—toy stores sometimes have cheap ones that let you do things such as get the three-note C major chord by just pressing the C note, one key. By pressing another button, the chord plays in different rhythms, from waltz to rock. Another button causes the sequencer to play bells, a piano, or a trumpet. Some allow taping of your own voice and play using its unique sounds. Musical software often requires an MIDI (musical instrument digital inter-

face). This is an electric musical keyboard that plugs into a computer. When the notes are played, they appear on the computer, and the computer will then play back what you have played into it. Inexpensive MIDIs can be purchased, but amplifiers or speakers are needed, also reasonably priced. There is software that does not require a MIDI nor any amplification. A book that reviews music software is *The Musical PC* (see Teacher Resources). CD-ROMs can now be purchased that allow students to see and hear orchestras playing, and you can press a button to get background information on composers or instruments. Social studies, math, reading, and language arts experiences are automatically integrated in this type of software experience. Consult sources in your own locale. Here are example sources in the United States.

Computers and music (software and hardware for IBM and Macintosh)
647 Mission Street
San Francisco, CA 94105

Maestro Music, Inc. (software related to reading and understanding music)
2403 San Mateo NE P-12
Albuquerque, NM 87110

Micro Music, Inc. (music hardware and software)
5353 Buford Highway
Atlanta, GA 30340

OPCODE (software related to MIDI)
New Tools for Education
3950 Fabain Way
Palo Alto, CA 94303

◆ CONCLUSION

This chapter is an overview of *why* music should be integrated, *what* classroom teachers need to know and integrate about music, and the basic principles for integration (*how*). In the next chapter more specific ideas are given to teach the tools of music so that students can use it as a way of learning. There are starter strategies for integrating music throughout curricular areas.

◆ TEACHER RESOURCES

See Appendix A: Arts-Based Children's Literature and Appendix F: Recommended Reading and Viewing for more teacher resources such as the following:

Birkenshaw-Fleming, L. (1989). *Come on everybody let's sing*. Toronto, ON: Gordon Thompson Music. Includes many music activities appropriate for the regular classroom.

Campbell, P. (1994). *Roots and branches*. World Music Press. Other cultures; includes CD.

Eddleman, D. (Ed.) (1999). *Great childrens songbook: A treasure chest of music & activities*. New York: Carl Fischer Music Publisher.

Goodkin, D. (1985). *Sally go 'round the sun*. San Francisco: Doug Goodkin. Lessons for Orff instruments. Booklet and tape set available from San Francisco School, 300 Gavin St., San Francisco, CA 94134 (*Mango Walk* [1986] is also available).

Keller, C. (compiled) (1985). *Swine lake: Music and dance riddles*. Upper Saddle River, NJ: Prentice Hall.

Livingston, M. (1986). *Earth songs*. New York: Holiday House. Poetry.

Making music in the classroom (video) (1995). Berkeley, CA: Langstaff Video Project. Cultural songs.

Metropolitan Museum of Art Staff (1987). *Go in and out the window: An illustrated songbook for young people*. New York: Henry Holt.

Mitchell, L. (1991). *One, two, three-echo me!; Ready-to-use songs, games, and activities to help children sing in tune*. West Nyack, NY: Parker.

Mitchell, L. (1992). *The music teacher's almanac: Ready-to-use music activities for every month of the year*. West Nyack, NY: Parker.

Patchen, J. (1996, September). Overview of discipline-based music education. *Music Educator's Journal*, 19–25.

Schiller, P., & Moore, T. (1993). *Where is Thumbkin?* Mt. Rainier, MD: Gryphon House. Hundreds of activities based on familiar songs.

Stanley, L. (Ed.) (1992). *Rap, the lyrics: The words to rap's greatest hits*. New York: Penguin.

Warren, J. (1991). *Piggyback songs for school*. Everett, WA: Warren.

Winters, L. (2000). *Show time!: Music, dance, and drama activities for kids*. Chicago: Chicago Review Press.

Yelton, G. (Ed.) (1991). *The musical PC*. Decatur, GA: MIDI America.

World Wide Web

Independent recorded music guru Paul Stark reports that we can log onto his website, pop a blank CD disc in, and download a complete album. Want to make your own mix? How about a video to go with the music? Stark believes music on the Internet is the delivery system of the future, making CDs and music stores obsolete. Just like old-time jukeboxes, the web makes music instantly available. Stark's site is www.twintone.com if you wish to monitor his progress in bringing high-quality music to consumers via the personal computer. About 800 artists have joined the Internet Underground Music Archive, and anyone on-line can join the thousands who already visit the site each day at www.iuma.com (Silverman, Fran, The Internet Is Becoming a Music Delivery System, *LA Times-Washington Post News Service*, August 11, 1997). Meanwhile, the University of Wisconsin has a huge library of song lyrics, tablature, music pictures, and more: ftp://ftp.uwp.edu.

◆ BIBLIOGRAPHY AND REFERENCES

Books and Articles

Armstrong, T. (1993). *7 Kinds of smart*. New York: Penguin.

Armstrong, T. (1994). *Multiple intelligences in the classroom*. Alexandria, VA: Association for Supervision and Curriculum Development.

Barnet, A. (2000, June). There's joy in harlem. *Reader's Digest*, pp. 130–136.

Boston, B. (1996). Educating for the workplace through the arts. Reprinted from *Business Week*, October 28, 1996. Columbus, OH: McGraw-Hill.

Burz, H., & Marshall, K. (1999). *Performance-based curriculum for music and the visual arts*. Thousand Oaks, CA: Corwin.

Campbell, D. (1997). *The Mozart effect*. New York: Avon.

Campbell, P., Brabson, E., & Tucker, J. (1994). *Roots and branches: A legacy of multicultural music for children.* Danbury, CT: WorldMusic.

Chan, A. S., Ho, Y. C., & Cheung, M. C. (1998). Music training improves verbal memory. *Nature, 396*(607), 128.

Choksy, L. (1974). *The Kodaly method.* Upper Saddle River, NJ: Prentice Hall.

Chroninger, R. (1994). *Teach your kids about music: An activity handbook for parents and teachers using children's literature.* New York: Walker.

Cockerton, T., Moore, S., & Norman, D. (1997). Cognitive test performance and background music. *Perceptual and Motor Skills, I 85,* 1435–1438.

Douglas, S., & Willatts, P. (1994). Musical ability enhances reading skills. *Journal of Research in Reading, 17,* 99–107.

Gardner, H. (1993). *Multiple intelligences: The theory in practice.* New York: Basic Books.

Gardner, H. (1999). *The disciplined mind.* New York: Simon & Schuster.

Graziano, A., Peterson, M., & Shaw, G. (March, 1999). Enhanced learning of proportional math through music training and spatial-temporal training. *Neurologial Research, 21*(2), 139–152.

Gregorian, V. (1997, March 23) Ten things we can do to make our schools better. *Parade Magazine,* pp. 6–7.

Habemeyer, S. (1999). *Good music, brighter children.* Rocklin, CA: Prince.

Hart, A., & Mantell, P. (1993). *Kids make music!* Charlotte, VT: Williamson.

Jarnow, J. (1991). *All ears: How to use and choose recorded music for children.* New York: Viking.

Jensen, E. (2001). *Arts with the brain in mind.* Alexandria, VA: Association for Supervision and Curriculum Development.

Kantrowitz, B., & Leslie, C. (1997, April 14). Readin', writin', rhythm. *Newsweek.* p. 71.

Lamb, S. J., & Gregory, A. H. (1993). The relationship between music and reading in beginning readers. *Educational Psychology, 13,* 19–26.

Larson, G. (1997). *American canvas.* Washington, DC: National Endowment for the Arts.

Lozanov, G. (1978). *Suggestology and outlines of suggestopedy.* New York: Gordon & Breach.

Malyarenko, T. N., Kuraev, G. S., Malyarenko, Y. E., Khvatova, M. V., Romanova, N. G., & Gurina., V. I. (1996). The development of brain's electric activity in 4 yr. old children by long-term sensory stimulation with music. *Human Physiology, 23,* 76–81.

Page, N. (1995). *Sing and shine on! A teacher's guide to multicultural song leading.* Portsmouth, NH: Heinemann.

Rauscher, F., Shaw, G., Levine, L., Wright, E., Dennis, W., & Newcomb, R. (1997). Music training causes long-term enhancement of preschool children's spatial–temporal reasoning. *Neurological Research, 19,* 208.

Rauscher, F., Shaw, G., & Ky, K. (1995). Listening to Mozart enhances spatial-temporal reasoning: Towards a neurophysiological basis. *Neuroscience Letters, 185,* 44–47.

Riekehof, L. (1978). *Joy of signing.* Springfield, MO: Gospel Publishing.

Ross, C., & Stangl, K. (1994). *The music teacher's book of lists.* West Nyack, NY: Parker.

Scheel, K. R., & Westefeld, J. S. (1999, Summer). Heavy metal music and adolescent suicidality: An empirical investigation. *Adolescent, 34*(134), 253–273.

Shaw, G. (2000). *Keeping Mozart in mind.* San Diego: Academic.

Trusty, J., & Oliva, G. (1994). The effects of arts and music education on students' self-concept. *Update: Applications of Research in Music Education, 13*(1), 23–28.

Wallin, N., Merker, B., & Mrown, S. (1999). *The origins of music.* A Bradford book. Cambridge, MA: MIT Press.

Warren, J. (1991). *Piggyback songs for school.* Torrance, CA: Frank Shaffer.

Children's Literature

Ambrus, V. (1970). *Seven skinny goats.* New York: Harcourt, Brace & World.

Baker, A., & Baker, J. (1991). *Raps & rhymes in math.* Portsmouth, NH: Heinemann.

Hesse, K. (1997). *Out of the dust.* New York: Scholastic.

Hill, S. (1990). *Raps and rhymes.* New York: Penguin.

Hopkins, B. (1995). *Making simple musical instruments.* Asheville, NC: Lark.

Krull, K. (1993). *The lives of the musicians: Good times, bad times (and what the neighbors thought).* San Diego: Harcourt Brace Jovanovich.

Kuskin, K. (1982). *The philharmonic gets dressed.* New York: Harper & Row.

Livington, M. (1995). *Call down the moon: Poems of music.* New York: M. K. McElderry.

Nichol, B. (1994). *Beethoven lives upstairs.* New York: Orchard.

Raschka, C. (1992). *Charlie Parker plays be bop.* New York: Orchard.

Stanley, L. (Ed.) (1992). *Rap, the lyrics: The words to rap's greatest hits.* New York: Penguin.

Toop, D. (1991). *Rap attack 2: African rap to global hip hop.* London: Serpent's Tail.

Wallace, R. (1993). *Smart-rope jingles: Jump rope rhymes, raps, and chants for active learning.* Tucson, AZ: Zephyr.

Music Seed Strategies

Introduction

This chapter contains specific ideas to integrate music throughout the curriculum. The ideas are seeds or kernels to stimulate thinking about creative ways to meet student needs and reach curricular goals. It is important to select and adapt these starter ideas to the ages, stages, and interests of students and change them to suit lessons and units. The strategy seeds are organized into sections, but many fit in more than one section. The sections on *energizers and elements and concepts* do *not* represent an integrated focus but are provided to help teach the tools students need to do integrated thinking with music throughout curricular areas. For ideas about integrating music with other arts areas, consult Chapter 13.

I. Energizers and Warm-ups

Note: Also see other energizers and warm-ups in chapters on dance, drama, art, and literature.

Tongue Twisters.   Warm up for singing songs by doing tongue twisters. See more examples in Chapter 8. Here is one for singing: *Tip of the tongue, the teeth, and the lips.* Say it three to five times.

Bingo Scavenger Hunt.   Set up a bingo-type page with musical categories in each box. (Put the categories on the board and have students write them at random in the boxes.) Possible categories are musical genre and styles, composers, singers, musical instruments, musical elements, and particular songs. At a signal, students get up and begin to talk with others to find the names of people who know about the items in the boxes (e.g., a student who likes reggae). The goal is to write down the names of other students until the search results in bingo—across, down, diagonally.

Clap Phrases.   *Record* student suggestions of favorite poems or songs on the board. Then, instead of singing the songs, simply clap the rhythm. On a simpler level, clap sentences: "Hello, how are you?"

Echoing Rhythms.   This is an attention getter to increase focus and concentration. A leader claps, slaps, snaps, or clicks a series of rhythms that are echoed by the rest of the class. Use children's names by dividing them into syllables and giving an accent: Clau' di a. This is adaptable to special phrases or topics such as days of the week, months of the year, animal names, or plants. Make increasingly difficult by turning rhythm patterns into a round: Divide the class in half with a leader for each half to start the pattern at varying times. Repeat twice or thrice.

Question and Answer Songs.   Many songs involve people asking and answering questions, for example, "BaaBaa Black Sheep." Divide the class in half and direct one-half to sing questions and other half the answers.

Join In.   Assemble students in four or five groups to listen to a musical selection. Challenge each group to create a movement pattern involving clapping hands and tapping their feet as the music is played again. Then stop the music. Have students in group 1 do their movements when the music starts. Keep adding more groups until all groups are doing their movements.

Musical Memories (Concentration).   Tell students to close their eyes and imagine different sounds as sounds are described (crickets chirping, wind chimes, jingle bells, a robin singing, someone singing "Twinkle Twinkle Little Star" played on a piano, a baby babble singing). Give students time to create the images.

Time and Tempo.   Explore time and tempo with music by asking children to move at different speeds in response to music. Use slow, fast, staccato (choppy), or legato (smooth) or music that has accelerando (gets faster, e.g., "Beep Beep," the little Nash Rambler song). *Variation:* Beep Beep (accelerando). Class gets into groups according to vehicles (six in a van, four in a car, two on a motorcycle, etc.). Vehicles "drive" around together as the fifties song about the little Nash Rambler plays. They go faster as the music gets faster and slower when the music slows down.

Group Rhythm Mirror (Concentration and Focus). Group forms a circle with an IT in the middle who begins a rhythm or movement. Others must mirror. IT passes the rhythm on by staring at one person, who slowly takes over and changes places with IT. The class observes and begins to mirror the new rhythms and actions when they feel the exchange is complete.

Rhythm Wave.   Group sits or stands in a circle. When leader says "begin," everyone makes his or her own rhythm using hands, feet, or voice. Slowly, by listening to each other, the group becomes one rhythm. Then individuals slowly begin their own new rhythms and a new group rhythm emerges.

Exchange. Two lines are formed on opposite sides of the room. The first pair at one end starts. Each person in the pair begins a unique rhythm and walks toward her partner. As they pass, the two exchange rhythms. Then the next pair goes and on down the line. Focus on unusual rhythms.

Rhythm Pass. Do in groups of four to six. Slap knees on downbeat and back of own hand for other counts. Pass this rhythm around a circle: one person slaps hand of neighbor on "2" and neighbor passes to "3," and so on until the pass is complete and the group is back to each slapping own knees on "1." The last person to receive the pass becomes the new leader.

"Head, Shoulders, Knees, and Toes." First, sing the song through. Then sing and add motions. Practice singing the song together at a slow tempo. Finally, ask students to stand in a circle and do movements as they sing, gradually substituting body part with hums, but continuing the actions: Touch head, touch shoulders, touch knees, touch toes, and so forth.

Shoe Beat. Everyone sits in a circle and removes one shoe. They agree on a song or rhythm pattern to do together during which shoes are passed, left to right, and held. For example, "Mary had a little lamb" could be "pass-pass-hold." If you don't keep the rhythm, the shoes pile up on you!

Balloon Movement. Put on classical musical (e.g., Haydn pastoral) and give small groups each a balloon to waft to the beat of the music. Be sure to discuss behavior expectations and explain how the activity is about concentrating to stay with the beat.

Knock and Respond Rhythms (Attention Getters). When someone knocks on a door to the rhythm "da-da da-da-da," we know to reply "da-da." Create original rhythms by having partners make up ones to demonstrate for the class. Challenge the whole group to learn several knock and respond patterns.

Rhythms Circle. Stand in a circle and with one person as IT. IT creates any rhythmic phrase desired, and it is passed around the circle to the right until it returns to IT. The person to IT's right then becomes IT.

Copycat Songs. Collect songs that invite additional verses such as "If you're happy and you know it" and "The more we are together." Make copycat songs by adding new verses. An example is "On Legs You'll Find Two Legs Behind" to the Scottish tune "Auld Lang Syne."

Word Choirs. Ask for volunteers to form a choir line. Give them a topic such as happiness. When a leader points to each student, he must say or sing a word or make a sound related to the topic. For example, students say "play, laugh, love" for happiness. Create directing signals for students to say or sing their words or sounds and hold or sing at different pitches. Students can learn to conduct the word choirs, and they can be about current units—growing things, other cultures, and the like.

Rainstorm Simulation. This is a rhythm activity. Sit in a circle with eyes closed. A leader begins by rubbing hand palms together. Person to right picks it up until the whole class is participating. Then the leader switches to finger snaps and that moves around the circle. Next is thigh slaps, then foot stomps, with periodical "claps" of lightning. Reverse the order to show the storm dying out.

II. BASIC MUSICAL CONCEPTS AND ELEMENTS

Note: The ideas described here are means to *achieve* integration and do *not* constitute integration, if used in isolation or never connected to other areas of the curriculum.

Hum Melodies. Choose a song that the children know. Hum the first line. If they don't guess it, keep humming the song until someone guesses. Everyone sings the words as soon as they know the song chosen. Then have one of the children take a turn humming a song. Example songs are "I've Been Working on the Railroad" and "Row, Row, Row Your Boat."

Sing the Scales. Warm up voices by singing major and minor scales, with or without words or instruments. Major and minor scale music sheets can be purchased at music supply stores.

Cumulative Melodies. Make a list of songs everyone knows, for example, "Happy Birthday," "Row Row Row Your Boat," and "She'll Be Comin' Round the Mountain." Have each person choose a song to hum. Each child should pick a syllable, for example, "la la" or "ti ti," for humming. The first person starts humming. Then the second person starts humming on top of the other person's song during the second time around, the third person, and so on. Humming all the music at the same time, without words, teaches the concept of *counterpoint* (melodies overlap each other).

Kazoo Melodies. A leader plays a melody on a kazoo and the others must imitate it on kazoos. Make kazoos from combs by folding paper over them or use empty candy boxes—small Milk Dud boxes.

Environment Sounds (Pitch). Listen to sounds in the environment; it's a good idea to tape record common ones. Ask children if the sounds are high or low or in between high and low. Examples are a door bell, mixer, and computer hum.

Guess Who (Timbre). In a group, tell children to close their eyes and someone will be tapped on the shoulder. Whoever is tapped says a word such as "hello." The others guess who spoke. Each time a correct response is given, ask "How did you know who spoke?" The answer will be related to the uniqueness of the person's voice. Repeat the activity. In a following session, play the game again, but have the children *sing* "hello." Stress how each person's speaking voice is unique, and so is the singing voice.

Name That Instrument (Timbre). Have children experiment with various rhythm instruments to become familiar with their sounds. Then ask them to close their eyes as each instrument is played. Stress that each instrument has a unique sound, even though some may sound similar to each other. *Variation:* Use a tape or CD of orchestral instruments or other music instruments (guitar, banjo).

Dynamics Dial. Dynamics has to do with volume. Make a volume dial out of cardboard or use an old clock. Label "soft" to "loud" on the dial with the musical symbols *pp* (very soft), *p* (soft), *mp* (medium soft), *mf* (medium loud), *f* (loud), *ff* (very loud), and *mfz* (loudest). Have children sing a familiar song or talk as someone turns the dial or volume button. The children should sing or speak according to what the dial reads. For example, if the dial said "pp," children sing or talk very, very softly. *Variation:* Teach hand signals to slow dynamics. Make them up or use ones from books such as *Joy of Signing* (Riekehof, 1987).

Conducting Dynamics. Use with musical instruments children have made or purchased ones (Orff or other rhythm instruments). Ask them to play very soft, soft, loud, and very loud. Challenge students to start softly and gradually play louder (*crescendo*) and vice versa (*decrescendo*). One child can then be conductor. The other children play louder as the conductor raises her hands and softer as she lowers her hands. Have the conductor try fast raising of hands to practice sudden dynamic changes.

Sound Effects Textured Story. Read a story (cumulative stories work well and sound stories in Chapter 8) and then assign repetitive words or sound effects for children to perform on cue. For example, every time the word "hen" is heard, children say "cluck cluck cluck" or strike triangles. Involve everyone; sounds can be made by the whole group or individuals. Record results to show textured *layers* throughout the story as sounds enter and reenter.

"Thick and Thin" Voices (Texture). Use poems or stories and assign different numbers of children to participate in solo and choral readings or parts. Ask the children how it sounds when more people are reading compared to less. This should produce "thicker" and "thinner" sounding stories. Repeat the activity using singing voices. Relate to using individual versus multiple instruments by playing recordings of the same song or music done by an orchestra and an individual instrument.

Barbershop Quartet (Harmony). One person sings the main melody while others harmonize or echo the tune to make a barbershop quartet. Some good songs for quartets are "By the Light of the Silvery Moon," "Sweet Adeline," "Down by the Old Mill Stream," and "Down by the Bay." (This is a good time to introduce the terms *soprano, alto, tenor,* and *bass* and the acronym STAB to remember them.)

Cannons and Rounds (Harmony). First, practice *speaking* rounds. Students can also sing along with a tape that features rounds. Once they can sing with a recording, they are ready to sing on their own. Movements can be created for each line and performed while singing, which helps children keep track of where they are. After each group practices and knows its lines, have all groups sing simultaneously.

Picture Form. Play a variety of musical pieces. Discuss repetitive patterns and similar and contrasting sections. Select a piece for discussion. Ask each student to raise his or her right hand when the first line or phrase is heard. Label this A and draw a picture of an object that begins with the letter A. Have children raise the same hand if the next line is similar and draw another A object on the board. If the line is different, have them raise their left hands and draw an item that begins with the letter B. Continue until there is a complete picture to represent all the phrases. Sing the song again and have children raise appropriate hands as symbols are designated. For example, "Mary Had a Little Lamb" would be "ABAC."

Form Books.   Read a book based on a song (e.g., Raffi's "Shake My Sillies Out"). Sing the song by itself. Ask children how form (patterns) is illustrated in the story or song. Then have children illustrate phrases of a favorite song by creating their own books. Children draw a picture for each line of the song. If there is a line that repeats, they should draw the same picture. The final book will be an illustrated example of a song's form.

Repeat a Beat (Ostinato).   Make a sound and repeat it a number of times: tap the window, click your tongue, slap your leg, or repeat a syllable (dum dum dum). Tell children to listen carefully and to count how many times they hear the sound. Then they repeat the sound exactly. Let the children take turns making a sound while others count and repeat the pattern.

Spoken Rounds with Ostinati. Children first memorize a poem. Explain the concept of ostinato (something repeated over and over). Then ask one group to recite the poem, while another group recites an ostinato (a line or word that repeats over and over). The ostinato may be a line they have created, the title of the poem, or a selected line from the poem. When children have practiced the last two activities, break the class into three groups. Two groups perform the poem as a spoken round, while the third group performs the ostinato. An example poem is Silverstein's "Listen to the Mustn'ts" (repeat "mustn'ts"). *Variation:* Use rhythm instruments to create osinati.

Space and Line Walk (Notation).   Make a large musical staff on the floor (with masking tape). Children compete to walk horizontally across a certain space of the staff *without touching* a line, or do this with the lines on the staff. Everyone says or sings notes touched as they walk. *Variation:* Throw bean bags on lines or spaces of the staff and name the notes.

Critical Listening.   This helps students hear notes, phrasing, and rhythm. Choose a jingle from a commercial or use a familiar melody. Sit in a circle and ask each student to sing only one syllable. Go around the circle until it is blended. *Variation:* Use whole words or phrases to help students hear ostinati (repetition).

Instruments Center.   Create a learning center for students to explore the use of instruments. Collect or ask parents to donate old guitars and drums. This is a popular center during inside recess.

Instruments Notation.   Find everyday items— "found sounds" that make music. Even use body parts. The goal is for students to write music for each sound.

First, pairs choose two found sound instruments and decide ways to notate (make symbols for) timbre, pitch, and volume. For example, jingle bells might be small dots to show the high, light sound. Next, pairs write the numbers 1 to 8 across the top of the paper and the names of two instruments at the top of the left margin. Next, put symbols for each instrument under the numbers to show when each should be played. When both are to be played, place them under the same number. Loudness can be shown by drawing a symbol larger or smaller. Pairs then perform.

Music Concentration (Notation). Draw music symbols and different kinds of notes on the chalkboard, for example, quarter, half, and whole notes. Players take turns naming each symbol and remembering it. Students then close their eyes while a symbol is erased. They open their eyes and try to guess what symbol was erased. As more are erased, the students are to name the most recent deletions, as well as the previous ones. Correct answers are reinforced by writing the answer back on the board.

Musical Notation.   Use a favorite children's song to introduce musical notation. First, speak the lyrics while clapping the rhythm. Decide where long, short, and silent sounds occur in the song. Ask children to invent symbols to record musical sounds. Write or draw melodies using circles, squares, or lines for notes. The symbols should show if the melody goes up or down and if the notes are long or short in time; for example, use small circles for short notes and large circles for long notes. Chant the lyrics again while pointing to the symbols. Ask the children again how to represent high and low sounds in the melody, as well as symbols for rhythm. Repeat and then ask children to create symbols to address tempo and dynamics. Sing the complete song while pointing to the symbols.

Body Parts Sound Compositions (Notation and Composition).   Ask children to demonstrate sounds that can be made with their hands, fingers, feet, tongue, lips, cheeks, slapping, and other body parts. Students work in pairs to create a composition using various combinations. *Variation:* Put sounds to any favorite musical recording.

Jives (Rhythm).   Hand and body jives allow children to explore rhythm with their body parts. Examples include "Shimmy, Shimmy Cocoa Puff" and "Hambone." Basically, you slap and brush your hands to a rhythm. See Mattox's (1990) *Shake It to the One That You Love Best.*

Two-Part Rhythm. One group chants and claps a steady beat to the nursery rhyme "Hot Cross Buns," while another groups chants "One a Penny Two a Penny" over and over.

Rhythm Box Beats. Each child needs an empty milk carton or shoe box and a wooden spoon or big pencil. The inside of the box or carton is struck, one side at a time, in the same order to create a 1–2–3–4 beat (common in music). Try at different tempos and put to music by playing along with four-beat songs (see the time signature on sheet music). Next, strike the box using other music beats: 1–2 or 1–2–3 (waltz time).

Follow the Leader Rhythms. Use rhythm instruments, homemade or purchased (sticks, tambourines, drums, cymbals). One child is the leader and plays different rhythms. Everyone echoes the rhythm on his or her instrument (e.g., "ta-tum ta-tum ta-tum tum tum").

Italian Experiments (Tempo, Dynamics). Students can quickly learn the effect of speed on singing or on any task and can expand their vocabularies to incorporate a bit of Italian using this activity. A metronome is needed. Put the following tempos on a chart, set the metronome, and sing a familiar song at each tempo, for example, "Happy Birthday." Ask students to discuss changes in pitch, enunciation, and the like.

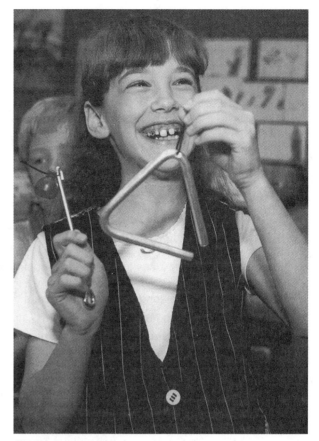

Rhythm Instruments

> Largo = broad (40–60 beats per minute)
>
> Lento = slow (60–66 bpm)
>
> Adagio = at ease (66–76 bpm)
>
> Andante = walking (76–108 bpm)
>
> Moderato = moderate (108–120 bpm)
>
> Allegro = quick/happy (120–168 bpm)
>
> Presto = very fast (168–200 bpm)
>
> Prestissimo = fast as possible (200–208 bpm)

Variation: Extend creative thinking by playing examples of accelerando (e.g., Strauss's "Acceleration Waltz," the 1950s pop song "Beep Beep," and Brahms's "Hungarian Dances" are examples of music that gets faster and faster). Try singing any song using accelerando. Add dynamics changes like *crescendo* and *decrescendo* (get louder and get softer) or use *staccato* (choppy) and *legato* (very smooth). *Variation:* Ask students to create three different shapes and remember them. Repeat the shapes to the different tempos marked by the metronome. Discuss how tempo changes movements (e.g., sustained versus bound).

Musical Instrument Categories. Collect orchestral instrument pictures from magazines and put on cards. Ask children if they know family members whose voices are alike and discuss how people have similar voices, but unique voice sounds, too; this is also true for instruments. Show pictures of instruments grouped in families (percussion, strings, woodwind, and brass). Shuffle cards and have children group them by similar sound. Reinforce efforts based on sound groupings (some may group by size, material, etc.). Explain how instruments are grouped by (1) sound similarity, (2) the way they are played, and (3) the material from which they are made.

Instrument Rummy. Make a deck of 52 cards, with pictures of instruments from the four groups (above) replacing the four groups of face cards. Each player gets 5 cards. Place remaining cards on the table. The object is to acquire sets of four common instruments (string, brass, woodwind, and percussion). The first player draws from the pile and chooses to keep the card or discard it face up. The player with the most instrument sets at the end is the winner.

Homemade Jam. Have a jam session with instruments students have made. Put on music and play along. *Variation:* Create a parade using all the instruments made. (Titles of instrument-making books can be found in the appendix under Arts-Based Children's Literature.)

Musical-Style Party. Have a party where everyone comes dressed as a country, jazz, rock, opera, or other type of musician. Students may choose a specific musician, such as Elvis Presley or Louis Armstrong. *Variation:* Invite students to imitate a favorite musical artist by lip syncing Elvis Presley, Whitney Houston, Alvin and the Chipmunks, Garth Brooks, The Beatles, disco groups, and the like. (Combine with the "style party" above.)

Music Response Options. Students can use their musical intelligences to respond to a book or unit of study using a variety of activities. Nineteen ideas are given in Post It Page 12–1.

POST IT PAGE 12–1

MUSIC RESPONSE OPTIONS

Directions: Use these ideas to respond to a book or area of study.

Songwriting. Write a song about the characters or people, plot, theme, or setting (place or time period).

Sing it, rap it. Choose an important part of the story or event to put to music (sing it, rap it).

Background music read aloud. Choose a part and add rhythm instruments or music.

Scavenger hunt. Find music and songs that relate (same feelings, topics, themes, time period, or culture).

Song list. Make a list of songs the main character would like to listen to or sing.

Match instruments. List musical instruments associated with characters, parts of the plot, the setting, or a topic (e.g., a plant or animal).

Diagram the story plot. Choose musical elements to re-create the action. For example, show rising action with faster rhythm and climax with loud music.

Rhythm plus. Make a list of special words and phrases. Put them to a rhythm or even create a melody. Think about which words or phrases could be repeated over and over (ostinato).

Word choir. List words or feelings for characters, plot, and theme. Groups line up and a category is given (e.g., a character). The "director" then points to each student and she must make a sound or say a word about the character and continue as long as the director indicates. The director keeps pointing at different choir members and indicates dynamics, tempo, and so forth. All can be cued to respond simultaneously.

Opera. Make the story into an opera. Rewrite words so they can be sung (libretto).

Musical instruments. Make musical instruments that characters would have played.

Make a mix. Create a tape or collection of songs and music for your favorite character.

Musical mobile. Use items that relate to the book or topic that will make sounds as they move.

Music fans. List musicians the main character would prefer.

Rock band. If the characters in the book formed a band, what would it be called? What kind of music would they play?

Jingle writing. Write an advertising jingle to sell the book.

Sound collage. List all the sounds in the book. Make a sound collage by re-creating the sounds and organizing them on a tape.

Singing words. Practice reading the story or a section aloud, adding music elements to make the print sing (e.g., change dynamics, tempo, or pitch).

Lip sync. Find a song that a character would sing; for example, what might Jacob sing to Sarah in *Sarah Plain and Tall?*

III. Connecting Music to Curricular Areas

Webbing

Choose any topic and web all the kinds of music associated with it. Break into groups and each group chooses one or several to explore in depth. Share with class.

Science Focus

◆ Natural world, systems of the body, seasons, weather, plants, animals, the environment, machines, electricity, magnets, space, gravity, and states of matter.

◆ Finding out how and why things happen in the world through careful observation, hypothesis making, and prediction.

Science Songs.   Use familiar tunes and have students write words to summarize science learning. See song-writing steps under Reading and Language Arts in this chapter. Here are some examples:

Four Oceans (Tune: BINGO)

There is a planet with four oceans and this is what we call them
Atlantic, Pacific, Indian, Arctic
Atlantic, Pacific, Indian, and Arctic, too.

North South East and West (Tune: I wish I was an Oscar Meyer weiner)

North, south, east, west are directions
Go north to find lots of ice and snow. BRRRR
Go south and the temperature changes
This is where the warm breezes blow. WHEW
Go east to find the Atlantic Ocean
And there you see great big towns
Go west and cross the Rocky Mountains
Keep going 'cause you're Pacific bound.

Invite students to work in groups to create additional verses.

Vibration Study.   Vibrations pass through the eardrum, hammer and stirrups, and the water of the cochlea and are sent as an electrical nerve signal to the brain. We also hear sounds because sound is conducted through our bones. Ask students to cover their ears and hum to hear the sound coming through the bones. Students can try to make as many different timbres as possible with a pencil, hands, and the like.

Bird Song Survey.   In the spring, go on a listening-closely walk to find bird songs. Tape each song and match with bird pictures on return to class. Discuss the differences in melodies, pitches, and rhythms and the different timbres of each bird. *Variation:* Use musical notation to write down bird songs or ask a music teacher to help do so. Students can also write lyrics to bird songs, similar to the "bob white" we use to make the quail song.

Metamorphosis Song.   Use the tune to "The Farmer in the Dell" to describe the metamorphosis process, for example, from a caterpillar to a butterfly. For example, use the refrain *Changes o' changes metamorphosis.*

The butterfly lays eggs. The butterfly lays eggs. REFRAIN
Caterpillars hatch from eggs, caterpillars hatch from eggs. REFRAIN
Caterpillars eat leaves. Caterpillars eat leaves. REFRAIN
Caterpillars spin cocoons. Caterpillars spin cocoons. REFRAIN
Cocoons hold the pupae. Cocoons hold the pupae. REFRAIN
Butterflies hatch out. Butterflies hatch out. REFRAIN

Body Parts Rap.   Use different body parts to create a chant or rap, for example, "Two Hundred Bones" (tap each bone to the rhythm as it is mentioned):

The skull is the head bone, head bone, head bone. The skull is the head bone, head bone, YEAH!
Ribs, vertebrae, pelvis, pelvis. Ribs, vertebrae, pelvis, BONES!
Clavical-collar bone, scapula-shoulder bone.
Two hundred bones, bones, bones, bones (do in decrescendo—get softer).
Humerus, radius-ulna are arm bones, arm bones.
Humerus, radius-ulna are arm bones, Yeah! Femur, tibia-fibula are leg bones, leg bones. Femur, tibia-fibula are leg bones, Yeah!
Two hundred bones in the body, body. Two hundred bones in the body, Yeah!

Variation: Students find additional bones to add to the rap. (Thanks to teachers at Duxberry Elementary for this idea!)

Science Symphonies.   Many pieces of music celebrate or are intended to describe aspects of our world or universe. Start collecting examples to listen to and discuss what they depict through tempo and timbre of instruments. Examples are Grand Canyon Suite, "Flight of the Bumble Bee," Water Music, theme to *2001. Variation:* Discuss how science is shown in songs such as John Denver's "Rocky Mountain High."

ADAPT STRATEGIES

Choose a strategy seed idea from *energizers and warm-ups* or *music elements and concepts* and adapt it for science, math, reading and language arts, or social studies. See examples given under the following curricular areas.

Science and Sound. Explore acoustics by inviting a speaker from a sound system company, or invite a conductor to speak and show a score (which is a graph of frequencies, intensities, and volume changes).

Nature Sounds Orchestra. Students imitate or tape record sounds in nature, such as a bird whistling, dog barking, water splashing, and the wind. Combine sounds to create a nature orchestra. *Variation:* Compose environmental rhythms song: rap or chant by tapping toilet flushes, door shutting, stirring with a metal spoon, clock ticking, and typing.

Musical Season Stories. Play seasonal music without words, and pantomime events from the season. For a spring story, students may mime a flower blossoming. Students may also practice writing about the process of a flower growing from a tiny seed sprout afterward. Vivaldi's The Four Seasons is a piece of classical music that can be used.

Musical Weather Reports and Songs. What would a rainy day sound like? towering cumulus clouds? thunder and lightning? hurricane? Instruct students to create and present weather reports in which the meteorologist makes the sounds as the type of weather is mentioned. *Variation:* Write or find songs about the weather that could be used to introduce or conclude weather reports. Poetry can also be used.

Social Studies Focus

◆ Relationships among human beings, occupations, transportation, communities, governments, customs, cultures, holidays, and use of natural resources.

◆ History, geography (use of maps), civics (citizenship and government) or political science, economics, anthropology, and sociology.

◆ Investigations into cultural diversity and global understanding.

◆ Special questions: How did it used to be and why? Why is it like it is today? What can I do about it? Thinking processes: cause and effect, sequence, gather data, discover relationships, make judgments, draw conclusions and problem solve about community issues (e.g., economic issues such as school funding or values conflicts related to free speech).

◆ Use of primary source material such as newspapers, art, music, diaries, letters, journals, books, and artifacts, rather than the use of textbooks and gathering data through interviews, surveys, and other investigatory strategies that historians and other social scientists use.

States and Capitals Chant. Use drums or sticks to develop a basic beat and compose a mnemonic for chanting cities and states (e.g., Columbus, Ohio; Philadelphia, Pennsylvania; Atlanta, Georgia; Sacramento, California).

Continents Song. Use familiar tunes to summarize factual information (e.g., the names of the seven continents). For example (tune = "She'll Be Comin' Round the Mountain"),

We have seven continents on our globe. We have seven continents on our globe. We have seven great big land forms, seven great big land forms. There are seven continents on the globe.

There are North and South America. Europe, Australia, and Africa. Then there are Asia and Antarctica. Asia and Antarctica. Asia and Antarctica make it seven.

Music and Culture. Explore a culture by listening to its music. Ask students to generate a list of questions. Prompt with examples such as

◆ Why is music created in the culture?

◆ Who makes the music?

◆ How is music made? What instruments are used?

◆ When is music made?

◆ What kind of music is made? How is it different from other music?

◆ How has music in the culture changed over time?

Variation: Challenge students to create an imaginary culture and answer questions about its music.

Multicultural Song Book. Students can collect songs from different cultures and countries by making notebooks of lyrics and music and tapes. *Variation:* Each student selects one country or culture for which to find songs and music. Each student's contribution is put into a class collection that may be copied.

How Instruments Began. Use this idea with a unit on early human history. Explain how our ancestors did not have instruments such as we have today and had to create music from their feelings, experiences, and materials available. Music was made by plucking, blowing, and striking these first instruments. Instruments have been found that were made from bones, rocks, wood, and shells. Invite students to design an instrument that requires plucking, blowing, or striking using a familiar item in their environment. *Variation:* Each student researches an instrument played in the manner of the one he made and presents findings.

Musical Classifieds (Use with Newspaper Unit). Students write or create ads about instruments, musicians, or musical needs. For example: *Lost—Musical instrument, very large percussion type. Black and white in color on main part. Last seen standing on three legs.* Students can read these aloud and attempt to guess each others'. *Suggestion:* Make at least three clues for Lost and Found classifieds, with the first clue very general and the last one the most specific.

Music Current Events. Ask students to find clippings of stories related to music. Set aside time to share "Music in the News." Challenge them to write songs based on news events using familiar tunes with new lyrics—explain that many folk songs are old tunes with new lyrics (e.g., civil rights songs were often based on spirituals).

Multicultural Music and Dances. Integrate the music and dance of each culture and time period studied by analyzing how songs are historical records of how people felt, thought, and acted. Find out the significance of songs, how music even influenced history by studying France's "La Marseillaise" or the Mexican American workers' "De Colores." Possibilities abound: Native American music, Irish jigs, music of the civil rights movement, tribal mountain music, western cowboy tunes, patriotic songs, and African tribal music. Students can come to understand how music helps create identity and explore a people's values and passions expressed in a song; the Apache song, "I Walk with Beauty" (based on a Navajo poem) expresses a concept of beauty related to all things living in harmony. (See Burton's [1993] *Moving within the Circle: Contemporary Native American Music and Dance.*)

Song Sources. Review purposes of songs and various song types (lullabies, work songs, sea chanties, spiritu-

als, patriotic songs, etc.). Ask for examples of social and historical events that use certain types of songs, such as birthdays. Read a book about a historical event and allow children to suggest various types of songs that the characters in the book might sing, play, or compose. Ask them to tell why. This is also a good time to share picture books that are based on songs (e.g., "The Star Spangled Banner" or "Follow the Drinking Gourd"). Discuss how some historical songs were work songs ("I've Been Working on the Railroad") that are now sung for enjoyment or other purposes.

History Time Line. Play a musical selection from different musical periods (Middle Ages, Renaissance, Baroque, Classical, Romantic, and 20th century). After studying each period, create a poster featuring magazine cutouts of corresponding artwork, clothing, architecture, dances, or theatrical productions from each period. When completed, display the posters. Discuss how art reflects societal changes, as well as the materials and technology available in a given time or area. *Variation:* Read about composers of different time periods and place contributions on the time line. Add other significant events (composers' birthdays, song or music events).

Class Community Songs. Write or sing class songs to build community. For example, create a class anthem or write songs to celebrate people, seasons, or special events, such as secretary's day.

History Through Music. Find songs and music that reflect the environment and times, for example, music or songs about specific historical events and values ("Battle Hymn of the Republic"), or examine a song of a period to discover the attitudes and values of the time.

Introduce a Time Period. Play music to introduce a social studies unit. Play music of the period and ask, *What do you hear?* and *What does it tell you about this time?*

Cultural Contrasts. Use a Venn diagram (two overlapping circles) to compare music from countries, cultures, and ethnic groups with familiar music. Use music elements to categorize likenesses and differences.

Song Adaptations. Here are songs teachers have created to help students learn information:

Months of Year (tune = "Ten Little Indians")

January, February, March, and April.
May and June, July and August.
September, October, November, December.
These are the months of the year.

Days of the Week (tune = "My Darling Clementine")

There are seven days (repeat two times)
There are seven days in a week.
(repeat from beginning)
Sunday–Monday, Tuesday–Wednesday,
Thursday–Friday, Saturday! (Repeat)

Reading and Language Arts Focus

- Reading, listening, speaking, written composition (including handwriting and spelling, grammar, usage, capitalization, and punctuation). Reading and language arts are processes that must be connected to a subject to have meaning, that is, something to read and write about.

- Goal: *Create* meaning and enjoyment using print through thinking, at every level from memory to critical thinking or evaluation.

- The printed word and its components (letters, syllables, spelling patterns), how words combine to make phrases and sentences, and sentences combine to make paragraphs and other forms of discourse, from tongue twisters to novels.

- Types of words: antonyms and synonyms, parts of speech, and figurative language (metaphor, idiomatic expressions).

Guided Music and Language Arts Lessons. See the special steps in this type of integrated lesson in Post It Page 11–12.

Teaching Language Arts Skills with Songs. Post It Page 12–2 gives ways to use songs to teach reading, writing, speaking, and listening skills.

Musician Expert. Students pick a musician and do any number of the following activities to become an expert on the person and his or her work. Any of these can culminate in class oral presentations.

- **Collection:** Start finding and saving other works by the person (e.g., tapes, CDs, sheet music).

- **Ape the greats:** Use the mood, style, and techniques of music and songs as a frame for students to create adaptations (e.g., add verses, write new lyrics, own adapted work).

- **Update:** Make or find a modern-day version of the work (e.g., *Hooked on Classics* versions of the classics).

- **Guests and experts:** Invite a local musician, singer, college professor, or conductor to speak about a musician or his or her music or interview a person.

- **Concert:** Go to one!

- **Musician's studio:** Visit the place where a musician works (e.g., a concert hall). Ask to shadow the person for a day.

- **Video:** Watch a video of the musician's life (e.g., *Beethoven Lives Upstairs*).

- **Music show:** Have an event to display the musician's work and students' work together. Set up classroom stations to listen to tapes or CDs.

- **Minidisplay:** Set up a display in the hall, classroom, or special place in the school. Include works by famous musicians and students' works (e.g., compositions, pictures, information about the musician).

- **Vary it:** Do another version of a piece of music (e.g., use just a part of a song or piece of music to play or sing; write different lyrics to a song).

Compose an Opera.   Introduce children to opera using books such as Englander's (1983) *Opera! What's All the Screaming About?*, Price's (1990) *Aida: A Picture Book for All Ages,* or Rosenberg's (1989) *Sing Me a Song: Metropolitan Opera's Book of Opera Stories for Children*, and listen to opera examples. Then choose a familiar story or a folktale. Compose and find songs for each main scene. When words from the story are changed into a form to be sung, they are called a *libretto.* Children can use familiar tunes or compose new ones. Songs can be sung without accompaniment or instruments or taped music can be added. Lead characters can sing their dialog or some parts may be spoken.

Songwriting.   Use these basic steps to show students how to write their own songs. This is an adaptation of a strategy for teaching students to read and write, called the *language experience approach,* in which students work under the guidance of a teacher and then work independently.

1. Choose a topic (e.g., long division in math).
2. Brainstorm words and feelings related to the topic. The teacher can serve as a recorder using a chart, board, or the overhead projector. Ideas can be webbed. *Example:* In long division the steps are divide, multiply, subtract, and bring down. It is done mechanically.

Reading and Language Arts Skills to Teach with Songs

Directions: Make song charts by printing lyrics on poster board or chart paper. Overhead transparencies can also be used so that students can clearly see the lyrics.

- **Echoic reading** of lyrics to work on echoing oral expression elements (volume, rate, tone, pitch, pause, stress, and emphasis).
- **Repeated reading** of lyrics to build reading fluency.
- **Speech-to-print match** made by pointing at lyrics and lines as they are sung.
- **Put each song line on a sentence strip.** Students must put them in the song's order.
- **Students can write out songs** they already know by heart to practice composing, spelling, and handwriting.
- **Singing a word** is another way of stretching its sounds to help with phonemic awareness.
- **Words in songs can be cut apart** and students can sort them into categories (parts of speech, alphabetically, number of syllables).
- **Turn songs into big books** by giving each child or a group a line to illustrate and making a page for each line.
- **Cloze exercises for comprehension.** Use sticky notes on a song chart or white out words on individual song copies. Students "sing" and figure out what's missing.
- **Ballads** (songs that tell stories) can be mapped according to literary elements (characters, plot, theme, style).
- **Word finds.** Students find sight words or word patterns (silent *e, r*-controlled, phonograms, etc.) in lyrics and highlight or circle the target words.
- **Write new verses or song adaptations.** Example: "Down by the Bay." Add any name and rhyming words to make new verses.
- **Song books.** Students make a favorite song into an individual book by illustrating each line of the song. See bookmaking options in Chapter 6.
- **Song anthologies.** Students collect favorite songs in a notebook or file. These can be bound and given as gifts.

3. Students organize ideas. Phrases can be dictated to the teacher as she scribes or students can work in small groups.

4. Lyrics are put in an order and students decide the form, rhythm, melody, tempo, and so forth. For example, will there be a background beat? rhythm instruments? Which lines or words are to be repeated? How fast, slow? What melody? (If students just use the universal melody—the three notes G, E, A—they can make many songs. They all know this because it is the taunt used worldwide: Na na na na na.) Let students know that composers often repeat melodies (listen to pieces to discover this).

5. Make final revisions.

6. Perform: Make a tape, do live sharing, make visuals (e.g., transparencies of lyrics) to accompany. Here is the final version of a long-division rap created by sixth graders in Hays, Kansas:

> *I'm Dr. D. and I'm on the scene*
> *With my division rap that oh so mean*
> *It goes divide, multiply, subtract and bring down (repeat)*
> *Now you can do it wrong or you can do it right*
> *But if you do it wrong you'll be here all night*
> *I say, Divide, multiply, subtract and bring down (repeat)*

If you are interested in additional resource material on songwriting, I recommend Wiggins's (1991)

Composition in the Classroom: A Tool for Teaching. See the bibliography for more resources, including books about rap music.

Sing Letter Sounds. To develop particular letter and sound skills in reading, have students hum melodies using only the target sound. For example, hum "Happy Birthday" just using the /s/ or /b/. This also can be done to teach short vowels. For example, sing "Happy Birthday" with just the short *a* sound. *Variation:* Songs such as "Apples and Bananas" invite students to play with substituting long and short vowel sounds.

Echo Me. Use this activity to explore oral interpretation using the musical concepts of dynamics, pitch, tempo, beat, accent, and rhythm. Recite the alphabet or a nursery rhyme in your normal manner. Repeat and talk very fast or very slow, use a high-pitched voice or deep, bass voice. Break everything into distinct separate syllables or put the accent on every third word. Challenge students to echo you exactly. For example, "Mary Had a Little Lamb" could become mystery or a proclamation simply by varying the delivery. Also try different dialects and foreign accents.

Have a Hootananny. Have weekly sing-alongs from a song collection made by students. Add new songs to the list as they find new favorites. Put some of the lyrics on posters or transparencies and invite students to make their own song books by copying choice songs. Posters and song books are great resources for teaching or reinforcing reading skills. For example, ask students to find words (play I Spy) that fit a specific phonic pattern (silent *e*, vowel digraphs, consonant digraphs, rhyming words, high-frequency phonograms, or rimes). In addition, fluency is increased by doing repeated readings or singing of lyrics.

Finger Plays and Songs. There are many finger plays and songs that can be used to develop vocabulary, reading skills, sequencing, rhyming, and of course musical form (e.g., "Five Little Squirrels" and "Five Green and Speckled Frogs").

Musical Response Journals. Students can keep journals and write in them while listening to a certain selection of music. They may choose to write a story that suits the type of music or a description or write about feelings or images stimulated by the music.

Sing the Vowels. Professional singers practice by singing vowels because vowels are sounds made with the throat loose and open, allowing more sounds to come out. Consonants stop sounds. For example, in a speaking voice: "Happy birthday to you." In a singing voice: "Haa py Birrrthday to youououo." Children can learn about the sounds of vowels and consonants by singing. This is particularly helpful with students who have trouble hearing individual sounds since this stretches sounds and increases phonemic awareness.

Cloze Telegrams. Students can complete telegrams or secret messages that teachers give by writing in the correct musical note on the staff using special staff paper (get at any music supply store). This helps with spelling as well as musical notation. For example, Moz__rt pl__ys __ concert __t Town H__ll (*a* missing). Sousa promot__d to Marin__ band dir__ctor (*e* missing). *Variation:* If an instrument is available, students can play the missing notes.

Read All About It

◈ The life of the musician or singer (biographical information: birth, death, marriage, children, friends)

◈ Who and what most influenced the artist

◈ Time period in which the artist lived

◈ Country or countries where the artist lived

◈ Style in which the artist worked or school of art to which the artist belonged

◈ Influence the artist had on the world of music (what the artist is known for)

◈ Other artists of that period

◈ Particular work the artist did (e.g., the most famous or controversial)

◈ Criticism about the artist and his or her work

Write All About It

◈ Letter to the musician

◈ Letter to the music publishing company to request information about a song, piece, or the musician

◈ Biographical sketch of the musician

◈ Story in a modern setting that includes the music

◈ Description of the music or song

◈ Possible menu that might have been served during the time the piece was created

◈ Report on the customs of the time of the artist

◈ Report on the clothing styles of the time of the artist

◈ Story about how the work came to be

- Report about the period of time
- Paragraph hypothesizing what the musician would do if he or she were alive today
- Play or poem about the musician's life
- Comparison of the work of two musicians
- Time line of the musician's work
- Book for children about a musician, style, or genre of music

Music Dictionary. Students make their own dictionary of musical elements, concepts, song titles, and composers. Use wallpaper to make covers and encourage students to illustrate entries.

Song Charts. Teach reading with song charts made by putting lyrics on poster board or large newsprint. Use sticky notes on the charts to cover certain words for practice at figuring out concealed parts. Cut apart charts and use song line strips in a pocket chart or make big song books from the charts. *Variation:* Give each student or group a line from a song to illustrate for a class big book on the song.

Class Song Books. Create class anthologies of favorite songs, composer fact sheets, song fact sheets, and even riddles about music. For example, brainstorm ideas and make a chart of kids' favorite songs. Have each child sign up to write up the lyrics and research the song. Sing or read from the book each week. Have students make individual song books, song collections, or tape collections to go with their interests and needs (e.g., moods, study music).

Musical Poetry. Use chants, street rhymes, and jump rope rhymes for language arts. Encourage students to make up their own movements and add rhythm instruments (see collections such as Cole and Calmenson's [1990] *"Miss Mary Mack"*).

Song Scavenger Hunts. Use songs as content to find language patterns, or conduct a week-long hunt to find songs in certain categories (e.g., ones with lots of B words, with rhyme, alliteration, about books).

Musical Chair Story. Everyone starts writing a story and goes until the music stops. Each person then passes his story to another person and music begins again. The goal is to write a complete story in a designated number of passes.

Experts. Students choose to do research on a musical instrument or music in a particular culture. They then make a presentation to the class on their findings.

Put It to Music. Find appropriate music to play as favorite poems or stories are read.

Compare and Contrast. Compare versions of same song, for example, "Peter and the Wolf." Use a Venn diagram to note differences in musical elements and instruments.

Foreign Language. Music is a language with a special symbol system. Encourage students who wish to learn to "speak" (sing or play) and read this language by pairing with a mentor. Invite students to share their prowess with the class.

Culture and Language Through Song. Teach students to sing a familiar song in the language of the country under study (e.g., "Frère Jacques" or "Allouette" for France).

Math Focus

- Daily living situations involving counting, measuring, probability, statistics, geometry, logic, patterns, functions, and numbers.
- Problem solving through the use of skills (raising questions and answering them, finding relationships and patterns).
- Concepts about numbers and operations and concepts such as bigger, longer, greater than, less, three, four, even, and odd.
- The National Council of the Teachers of Mathematics encourages teachers to have children solve problems in many ways, focus on explaining and thinking, rather than just correctness, and using a hands-on approach.

Number Lyrics. Students sing familiar songs replacing lyrics with numbers. This can be as simple as singing "Twinkle Twinkle Little Star" and starting with "One, two, three, four . . ." or as challenging as singing odd numbers, even numbers, or by tens or fives.

Musical Math. Give math problems for students to apply music knowledge (adapted from Athey & Hotchkiss, 1995). For example,

Take the number of keys on a piano:	88
Add the number in a quartet:	+4
	92
Add the number in a trio:	+3
	95

Here are some musical facts to construct problems:

1. Solo, quarter-note, quarter-rest
2. Duet, half-note, half-rest
3. Trio, dotted half-note, number of valves on a trumpet, legs on a grand piano
4. Quartet, whole note, whole rest, number of strings on a violin
5. Quintet
6. Number of strings on a guitar; sextet
7. Septet
8. Octave, octet

Rhythm and Sound Math.   Students use rhythm instruments or body sounds to present addition and subtraction problems. For example, pairs present with student A = 2 beats and student B = 4 bells. Class responds with six claps or snaps.

Fraction Pies.   Since music is rhythmically based on subdivisions of time into fractions, students can cut pies into fractions using musical notation. For example, pies could be divided into half with a picture of a half-note in each slice.

Number Water Music.   Use 10 clear glasses. Students measure the side of each glass and subtract one inch from the top. Divide this measurement by 10.

Use a crayon to mark 10 sections on each glass. Fill glasses with water to the lines. Label the first glass 1, the second glass 2, and so on, until the tenth glass is labeled 10. With a teaspoon, gently tap the first glass near the rim. Listen for the sound. As the numbers get higher and water increases, the tones get lower. Have students tap out phone numbers to listen for pitches, and create other addition and subtraction problems to play.

Counting Songs and Chants.   Teach counting songs and chants to help students learn this skill (e.g., "One potato, two potato") and songs such as "The Ants Go Marching" (also good for marching to a one–two beat). See the arts-based bibliography under "Music" for book titles.

Shape Composition.   Students need 15 to 20 pieces of geometric pieces of paper (multiple numbers of 3 to 5 different shapes cut ahead, or they can cut triangles, squares, circles, and diamonds). Review shape names. In groups, students lay out a pattern they like and then decide on a sound for each shape. Rhythm instruments may be used. Groups rehearse and then perform their composition (e.g., square = drum, circle = shaker). Think of how this pattern would sound:

◆ BIBLIOGRAPHY AND REFERENCES

Books

Athey, M., & Hotchkiss, G. (1995). *A galaxy of games for the music class.* West Nyack, NY: Parker.

Riekehof, L. (1987). *The joy of signing.* Springfield, MO: Gospel Publishing.

Wiggins, J. (1991). *Composition in the classroom: A tool for teaching.* Reston, VA: Music Educators National Conference.

Children's Literature

Burton, B. (1993). *Moving within the circle: Contemporary Native American music and dance.* Danbury, CT: World Music.

Cole, J., & Calmenson, S. (1990). *"Miss Mary Mack" and other children's street rhymes.* Long Beach, CA: BeechTree.

Englander, R. (1983). *Opera! What's all the screaming about?* New York: Walker.

Mattox, C. (1990). *Shake it to the one you love best: Play songs and lullabies from the black musical tradition.* El Sobrante, CA: Warren Mattox.

Price, L. (1990). *Aida: A picture book for all ages.* San Diego: Harcourt Brace Jovanovich.

Rosenberg, J. (1989). *Sing me a song: Metropolitan Opera's book of opera stories for children.* New York: Thames & Hudson.

Integrating the Arts with the Arts: Strategy Seed Ideas

CLASSROOM SNAPSHOT

Mrs. Samuel's Kindergarten

Mozart softly plays as the kindergartners arrive. They are each carrying items that focus on the letter *L*, which they place on the *L* table. The bell rings and Mrs. Samuel starts the "Good Morning" song. Children join in and add dance movements. After this song, they sing a daily patriotic song.

Mrs. Samuel invites the children to make a circle. They hold hands and spread out.

"You know how we have clapped the syllables or beats in our names? Well, today, we are going to use our bodies to show the syllables. Let me show you what I mean." Mrs. Samuel says her last name and claps for each syllable. Then she moves a body part for each of the three syllables. The children giggle. "Now, do it with me." She repeats and they join in. "Who wants to try it with her name?"

"I do!" Michelle shouts. Michelle says her own name and claps twice.

"Great! Now, Michelle, show us two ways to move your body—one for each syllable." Michelle grins and kicks her right leg and then her left.

"Let's everyone do it!" Mrs. Samuel announces. And they do. The process continues around the circle until everyone has led the group in clapping and doing creative movements to show his or her name.

After the "greeting circle" ends, the class sings more songs about the days of the week, the months of the year, and a special song about "October." The October song is on a chart stand so children can see the lyrics. They sing the October song several times and Mrs. Samuel invites them to add dance movements. The children do high "tree branch" shapes, sway and turn, and some fall to a low level.

The morning routine continues with a choral reading of the morning message, small group work, and center time. When Mrs. Samuel shakes her tambourine, the children clean up and come to the carpet area to sit on their special spots.

"For group today we are going to think about the letter *L* using our bodies. Let's practice with a small group." Volunteer hands go up and Mrs. Samuel calls on Nicky, Eric, and Jacob to sit in the middle of the circle.

"Think about the shape of uppercase *L*. How can the three of you work together to make that shape? Don't talk. Work together using just movement."

The three children smile and point and move about until they are sitting in the shape of an *L*. The class then works on other ways to show the *L* shape using their bodies and high, medium, and low levels. Finally, they make a giant *L* with the whole class, using lots of floor space.

Mrs. Samuel shakes the tambourine. "Let's go on an *L* hunt!" she enthusiastically announces. The class recognizes this adaptation of "Going on a Bear Hunt" and begins the beat by tapping their legs and chanting, "We're going on an *L* hunt. We're going on an *L* hunt. And what do we see?"

Mrs. Samuel pulls a piece of lace from a can. "Lace!" the children call out. Kaila has brought the lace for "homework." Mrs. Samuel invites him to tell about the lace, and he says it is white, has holes, and is long and soft. It came off his mother's dress.

The class continues chanting and more and more *L* items are shared. Each time an item is seen the children say the name and stretch out the sound of *L* at the beginning. At the end of the *L* hunt Mrs. Samuel shows the children the blank big book she has made and reminds them they will each get a page to write about *L* and do *L* art. The book will belong to the whole class.

Finally, Mrs. Samuel teaches the class a song about Luckless Lucy who looses her locket. She sings it through, and then the children echo her as she sings again, line by line.

"That song has lots of *L*'s," says one child who smiles proudly at his discovery.

"Let's think of all the movements we could add to this song," Mrs. Samuel tells the class. Some children suggest they add props for the locket, leaf, and log in the song. They discuss how to use their bodies to show different kinds of logs and sing the song again adding movement.

Mrs. Samuel shakes the tambourine and asks, "Would you all think of a time when you have been lucky?" Many hands go up. "My goodness, I'm glad there are lots of lucky children here. But, instead of telling your stories, you can write about lucky and unlucky times in your journals this afternoon."

And the day continues. . . .

INTRODUCTION

An ulcer is an unkissed imagination taking its revenge for having been jilted. It is an unwritten poem, it's an undanced dance, it's an unpainted watercolor. It is a declaration that a clear spring of joy has not been tapped and that it must break through muddling on its own.

John Ciardi, poet

This book has focused on integrating the arts with core curricular areas. And yet this is not the only important integration plan. The arts have much in common with one another and are often used in concert, so it is important to consider ideas for integrating the arts *with each other.* This chapter offers starter ideas to do so. There are 10 possible combinations when using any 2 of the 5 arts. Of course, more than 2 can be integrated at a time, and several could be integrated with other curricular areas, making the number of combinations large and the results rich in creative possibilities. The following seed ideas are presented to trigger creative thinking and are best used after becoming familiar with individual arts areas and principles of integration. See the previous chapters on the 5 separate art forms for *why, what,* and *how* to integrate the arts.

Overall Focus of the Arts

These strategy seeds dovetail with the main aims of the arts, which include studying the *historical, social,* and *cultural* roles of the arts in our lives; communicating through art forms by *expressing, performing, responding,* and *valuing* the arts; and developing an *esthetic sense.* Topics include the *basic elements* of each art form, *media, genre, artists,* and *products* (e.g., paintings, plays). The unique focus of each art is summarized in the following list to give clarity about purposes for activities and to encourage development of other integrating-arts-with-arts ideas.

◆ *Literature focus:* Respond to and produce creative writing of all forms and genre, from the tongue twister to the novel. Artistic use of elements such as character, plot, and theme and style elements such as alliteration and onomatopoeia. Learn about authors and artists. Share and perform literature (e.g., oral interpretation of poetry). *Also see Chapter 4.*

◆ *Art focus:* Art elements, artists, pieces of art, art forms, subject matters, styles, history of art, artistic tastes, art making (media and techniques), art in our lives, the art of other cultures, and museums. *Also see Chapter 6.*

◆ *Drama focus:* Drama elements and skills, actors and acting, plays, playwriting, forms, styles, history, drama making with verbal and pantomime, drama and theater in our lives, and the theater and drama of other cultures. *Also see Chapter 8.*

◆ *Dance focus:* Dance elements, dancers, choreographers, folk and fad dances, genre or forms, styles, history of dance, preferences, dance making, music in our lives, and the dance of other cultures. *Also see Chapter 10.*

◆ *Music focus:* Elements, musicians, songs, musical pieces, genre or music forms, styles, history of music, musical tastes, music making with voice and instruments, music in our lives, and the music of other cultures. *Also see Chapter 12.*

1. LITERATURE AND ART (LA)

Art-Based Books. The appendix has a list of children's literature about doing and viewing art, as well as learning about artists and art history. There are books in every genre, from biography to folktales.

Reading Picture Book Art. These general guidelines about using picture books supplement ideas in Chapters 3 through 6.

1. *Teach art elements so that students have words with which to think and talk.* In Chapter 5 each of the elements, types of media, techniques, and styles are explained. See the Post It Pages (Post It Pages 5–4 through 5–7) in Chapter 5 for a summary.

2. *Take time to "decode" the art in picture books.* Use magnifying glasses and paper tubes to isolate and examine the artist's use of line, color, and other art elements, as well as the media, style, and mood. How would the book be different if the art wasn't included or was in a different style (e.g., cartoon versus impressionistic).

3. *Compare the art in different versions of the same story.* Many folktales, such as "Cinderella," "Jack in the Beanstalk," and "Little Red Riding Hood," are available in picture book form. Gather many versions and do big Venn diagrams on bulletin board paper.

4. *Ape the greats.* Using creative problem solving (Chapter 1), students can experiment with various media and styles used by artists of children's books. In addition, students can try out formats of books (e.g., pop-ups, shape books).

5. *Plan author–artist centered units.* By examining an entire body of artwork produced by artists such as Maurice Sendak, Tomie de Paola, or Patricia Polacco, students can become versed in the concept of style, grow to love various styles, and understand the creative process through an up-close, personal look. Esthetic development occurs as preferences form, beginning with exposure. Students can't like what they don't know.

Picture Book Detectives. Children are more attuned to details than adults and will enjoy doing "look closely" activities with magnifying glasses to discover the small, surprising aspects of the visual art in picture books. For example, artists may insert repeated "side notes" (Chris Van Allsburg puts his dog in most books). Have children explore a book to find what the art tells about the following elements:

◆ *Setting* (where and when)

◆ *Characters* (especially body shapes and parts such as hands and faces; also look for how the characters change in the art from the beginning to the end of the book)

◆ *Plot* (the pictures may show events not in the text, even subplots or asides, as in Gilman's *Something from Nothing*, or foreshadow events and create tension with hints and clues)

◆ *Style* (use of exaggeration, humor, how mood is created with color, shapes, line)

◆ *Point of view* (where does the viewer enter the picture?)

In addition, books can be examined to find (1) where the story is extended through art or just illustrates the text and (2) picture book parts (endpapers, gutters, borders, double-page spreads, where the story begins in the art) can be studied. Questions such as "What does the artist do that surprises you?" and "How does the book feel and why?" help children discover esthetic differences by comparing two books in terms of details that artists use and the amount of action or movement in the art. The subtle is significant, and a well-placed bit of line can say volumes.

Mini Museum. Students need a sturdy box to create a display of collected items that relate to a book, story, or poem. Items may be made or found that connect to characters, setting, and theme. Museum tags are added to items with a title, approximate date, and material for each. Set up museums as stations to be visited by groups, with "creators" serving as "docent" guides to talk about the items.

Wanted Posters. After showing examples of wanted posters and portraits, each student selects a book character and creates a poster. A portrait is drawn by examining the general shape of the face and measuring distances between eyes, nose, mouth, and so forth. At the bottom of the poster, students write a description of the character, the place and time last seen, and a contact person. Rewards or other notifications may be added. (Parts of the text may be reread for accurate details.)

Literature Quilts. Each student is given a square of paper (large origami works well) on which he or she uses choice art materials and style to respond to a book everyone has read, a favorite book, an author–artist study, or a genre. Squares are glued on to large, black bulletin board paper. (Use chalk to mark placement until they are glued and then wipe the chalk off.) Make a border by rolling long paper and cutting into slices with a paper cutter. Cut sliced minirolls to make a pattern when it unrolls (just like cutting paper doll strips). Glue onto the quilt, display, and discuss what the quilt shows.

Stretch-to-Sketch. Students interpret what happened to characters and the roles each played by making sketch drawings (quick rough drawings) (Harste, Short, & Burke, 1988). Each character might be sketched in several different story actions to summarize the events. Students present their drawings to explain interpretations and discuss how others saw things differently and why. Drawings can be compared and contrasted.

Art Prediction Cards. You need two copies of a book or a photocopy to cut apart. Pictures are cut out, pasted on tagboard, and put on the chalk tray in "bookological" order. Students observe pictures, without talking, to get clues about the upcoming story. Then students use literary elements to discuss the pictures. Ask "What can you tell about the setting? the characters? the plot? What is the mood? How do you know?" The story is then read and the pictures used for retelling. *Variations:* (1) Students write captions for pictures; (2) before reading, present cards *out of* *order* and ask students to agree about a predicted order. Read the story and rearrange the cards.

Quickdraws. Before reading, students draw for a few minutes about a topic that relates to the upcoming book (Tompkins, 1997). The drawing activates visual imagery. They then use these images while reading to confirm, reject, and modify their ideas—this is active meaning construction.

Sketch Books. Each child has a sketch book to sketch in before, during, or after reading or listening to literature. Sketch book responses can be brought to literature discussions to organize sharing. Prompts for sketches include characters, setting, most exciting points, special objects or symbols, plot, theme, and even style sketches related to special words. For example, Mrs. Tuck is described as a "great potato of a woman" (in *Tuck Everlasting*). Sketches can also be used as a stimulus for writing (e.g., choose a sketch to write a poem or paragraph about).

Poem Match. Students find or write a poem that connects to a work of art. See *Things to Write* and *Say A to Z* in Post It Page 4–2. In addition, see the *poem patterns* in Post It Page 3–5 and a special section on poetry in Chapter 4. Art and poetry can be shared in docent talks and displayed together in a class museum.

Art Story Map. Provide students with portraits, landscapes, and nonrepresentational art (e.g., abstract) to choose from. Students create (write or tell) a story using portraits for characters, a landscape for the setting, and an abstract work for a story problem. Remind them to establish the problem quickly and be descriptive about the setting and characters. Share stories with art displayed.

Story Board. When picture book artists write books, they often begin with a story board—brief sketches or mock-ups of how the finished book might look. Students can make a series of drawings (in order) that tell a story and glue them on a poster board to create a story board about any book.

Art Prewrite. Students create any type of art or collect art (postcards, magazine pictures, sculptures, pottery) to use as topics for writing and then "squeeze" art for writing ideas by brainstorming and webbing ideas. For example, web the five W's and H questions related to a piece of art. Any of the *things to write and say from A to Z* in Post It Page 4–2 can be used as writing forms (caption, letter, list).

Art Media Literature Responses. Making art is an important way for students to respond to any book or poem they've read. Art can also accompany any writing that students produce. For example, after reading a story students can create the following (see Post It Page 5–5 for additional media options):

- Book (pop-up, accordion, big books, minibooks, sewn book)
- Collage—objects (wallpaper, tissue, torn or cut construction paper) glued on
- Craft—handcrafted items such as pottery, weaving, quilt square, or whole quilt
- Drawing—with pencil, charcoal, marker, pen and ink, or crayon
- Enlargement—use overhead projector to blow up a favorite book picture and outline on large paper. Complete art by using tempera, watercolor, collage, and so forth.
- Fiber art—use fabrics and yarn
- Fresco—paint on wet plaster so that paint becomes a part of the material
- Mixed media—paper, wire, paint, fabric, all used in one artwork
- Mobile—3D art that moves
- Painting—tempera, acrylic, watercolor, oil
- Pastel—oil-based chalk art
- Print—pull a print or stamp with found objects, woodcuts, linoleum
- Rubbing—paper is placed on objects and crayon, marker, and the like are used to bring up images
- Sculpture—3D art made from wood clay, metal, found objects, plaster, or paper mâché

Art Subject Matter Literature Responses. Students can respond to important ideas in any piece of literature by creating art with one of these subject matters that connects to the book: landscape (outdoor scene in the story), portrait (a character in the story), cityscape (view of a city in the story), interior (inside a room or building in the story), seascape (a view of a body of water in the story), still life (nonliving objects in the story arranged on a surface), or abstract (color, shape, line, and texture are the focus and are used to express images and feelings).

Visual Poetry. Create shape or concrete poetry written in the shape of the subject of the poem. For a

Author–Artist Timeline and Mapping

whole book of this type of poetry, see Froman's (1974) *Seeing Things: A Book of Poems.*

Masks: Six Dramatic Roles.   According to Temple (1991), story characters fill one or more of six roles, and characters may also change roles. These roles can be used to create masks and puppets throughout the year:

1. The Lion Force: main character
2. The Sun or Object: what the Lion Force wants
3. Mars, the Rival: tries to keep the Lion Force from getting what she or he wants
4. Moon, the Helper: helps Lion Force achieve desired goals
5. Earth, the Receiver: benefits from Lion Force's actions
6. Libra, the Judge: decides if Lion Force may have the Sun or Object

2. ART AND DRAMA (ADR)

Sculpting.   In pairs or groups of four, one person becomes the clay to be sculpted. The others then sculpt the person into specific emotions, concentrating on body shape and levels.

One-Liner Tableau.   Students recreate, in tableau, scenes from photographs, portraits, cartoon strips, and the like. A *series* or cartoon strip can also be performed. Tableaux can be created for scenes before or after a scene in a painting or photo to stimulate creative thinking. After students are "set," teacher taps them one by one and each says a one liner of what they are thinking or feeling. *Variation:* When they are tapped, students come to life, do one action, and then freeze. *Note:* Large, old picture frames can be used to "pose" for drama tableaux and to take pictures of children posing inside the frames.

Storytelling.   Ask students to create stories about a piece of art or several pieces (e.g., two portraits, a landscape, and an abstract work can set up characters, setting, and problem for a good story).

Experts.   Cover half of painting or ask groups to choose a section on which to focus (e.g., foreground, background). Small groups serve as "experts" on their section and report to the whole group after small-group time.

One Minute After.   Ask students to imagine what happened one minute after a piece of art was finished. Divide into groups and allow students to plan a scene. Groups then present to the whole class.

Art Auction. Students prepare information about pieces of art to "sell" the works. Each student then takes a turn at selling and auctioning his art. Give each a sum to spend at the art auction.

Partner Sculptures. Partners take turns sculpting each other by imitating famous character poses or sculptures (e.g., Rodin's *The Thinker*). *Variation:* Half of the class assumes the pose of a famous sculpture while the other half pretends to be museum visitors who tour in pairs and use dialog to show what they see, how they feel, and who they are.

Pretend to Paint. Students imagine they have very tiny paintbrushes and not much space to paint. Narrate a pantomime in which you tell them to keep painting, but the size of the brush and the space keeps getting bigger and bigger. Music can be used to accompany this (e.g., "The Blue Danube" waltz).

Listen and Draw. Partner students and give one person a secret object. They sit back to back and one describes the object while the other tries to draw it as described. Encourage students to tell size, shape, and color and focus on use of visual details. *Variations:* Do by arranging sets of objects or with one partner describing a drawing while the other draws (e.g., a geometric or organic shape).

Photographs. Class pretends to pose in a group photograph that might happen or have happened in a piece of literature (e.g., the family at the fair in *Charlotte's Web*). Students decide about the composition, background, and so forth. Pose and freeze. Ask students to each give a one liner of their thoughts as they pose at this moment in the story.

Statues. Look at famous statues and discuss their emotions and why statues exist. Look closely to see how different parts of the body are arranged. Students assume the pose of a statue and, when tapped, each says a one liner about what he or she is thinking or feeling.

3. DRAMA AND DANCE (DrD)

Dance Freeze. After learning dance elements, put on music without lyrics (new age or classical) and allow students to free dance. When the music stops, they freeze and each gives a one liner about a dance element he or she is using.

Dance in Character. Students think about a famous person or character and how each might dance. When a signal is given, students dance in character. Divide the class in half so that one-half can observe and comment. Reverse.

Famous Dances. Students research a famous dance (e.g., minuet, ballet, waltz). Expert panels present their findings and take questions from the audience. *Variation:* Research dancers.

Musicals and Dance. Watch a musical (e.g., *Oklahoma*) and discuss how dance is used. What does dance communicate about the story and characters that would be missing without the dance?

Verbal Dance. Students create a freeze–move–freeze dance, but actually "talk" as they dance. For example, "low level, low level, flick fingers, flick toes, jump jump, twirl, high level, punch, shrink, collapse."

Dance a Story. Stories abound with characters and situations with movement potential. If the art medium is to be dance, and not drama, only the essence of the character or situation is used. A literal movement translation results in pantomime (drama) not dance. Stories can be danced or pantomimed; both call for targeting a particular event or image, rather than a whole story. An example that combines dance and drama is McCulley's *Mirette on a High Wire*. (Put a strip of masking tape on the floor. Groups take turns balancing in many different ways: one foot, tiptoes along the line—dance movements exploration. Those waiting pantomime the crowd watching and reacting.)

Balance Pantomime. Brainstorm when balance is important (e.g., walking on a wall, crossing a creek on steppingstones). Pantomime situations. Ask half of class to be observers and give feedback. Reverse.

Ball Bounce. Narrate a pantomime in which students start bouncing a small ball (e.g., a tennis ball). Change to a beach ball, basketball, and so on. Tell them to show the size and hardness of the ball with their bodies. Change speeds.

4. DANCE AND MUSIC (DM)

Dance and Movement Songs. There are many action or movement songs, singing games, and song dances available. Hap Palmer, Little Richard, Ella Fitzgerald, and Steve and Greg all have produced movement-oriented song collections on tape and CD for children. Special songs with dances include twist music, hokey pokey, chicken dance, and the pony. Richard Simmons's workout tapes have examples as well. It is important, to keep in mind that following special dance directions will limit creative thinking.

Mood Setting for Dance. Use music to relax students before engaging them in movement. Allow them to move or not move. Example artists are Enya and George Winston.

Repeated Listening to Choreograph a Dance. Play a piece of music and ask students to listen closely to the tempo, mood, and rhythm. Discuss and repeat listening. Brainstorm ways to show the important parts of the music with dance. As a whole or in small groups, create a dance to go with the music. Devise a symbol system to note how to perform the dance (e.g., circles, lines, and squares to show movements).

Sound to Motion. Make different sounds (sound effects tapes, rhythm instruments, bells, etc.) to stimulate creative thinking. Ask students to show the motion that each suggests (e.g., strong? high? low? direction?).

Dynamics! Use a drum, finger cymbals, and other percussion instruments. Ask students to change the size of their body actions according to the sound (e.g., loud makes large movements). Using different instruments helps students understand how timbre can change and still have a loud or soft sound.

Dancing Songs. Many songs are naturally connected to movement (e.g., "The grand ole Duke of York, He had ten thousand men, He marched them up to the top of the hill and marched them down again"). Collect such songs and invite students to add the movements suggested. See the bibliographies for both dance and music in the appendix for ideas. *Variation:* For contrast, ask students to create movements that do not go with the song at all (e.g., what would *not* fit with a lullaby?).

Dancing Animals. Play various types of music to which children can dance. Encourage them to warm up by moving to the music as different animals, concentrating on using animal moves at all the different levels and using a variety of body parts.

Body Melody Match. Select a familiar song. As children sing or listen to the song, lead them in moving up or down in a personal space to illustrate the shape of the melody. Point out that their bodies may move to show the melodic pattern.

Create a Folk Dance. Select a favorite folk song and ask groups to create movements for one line. (Use BEST elements from Chapter 9 to involve arms and feet.) Sing the song and each performs his line.

Cooperative Musical Chairs. Remove chairs, as in the traditional version, but all must find a place to sit when the music stops and help each other do so! No one is eliminated.

Singing with Your Hands. Learn the Kodaly hand signs to add kinesthetics to hearing the scale. See Chapter 11 for the hand movements called Curwen signs that show the scale from "do" up.

Sign Language. Teach songs in sign language or add signs to any song. See Riekehof's (1978) *The Joy of Signing.*

Someone Else's Dance. Contrast how creative problem solving feels with mimicking dance steps modeled by the teacher. Play a familiar piece (e.g., "Dance of the Flowers"). Teach specific movements by modeling and asking them to imitate (use BEST from Chapter 9 to invent five to six dance movements). Ask the students to repeat the dance three to four times until they can do it in unison. Next, play another piece of music and ask students to invent their own movements. To keep this simple, do another piece that might suggest flowers or plants (e.g., Enya's "Trees"). Ask students to practice, and then split the class in half to do performances. The audience half then gives descriptive feedback. After both halves have performed, ask about the differences between the two ways to learn to "dance" to music.

Sheet Music. Use an old sheet and tell children to all hold on around the edge. Put several balloons in the center and put on a tape to move to. The goal is to keep balloons afloat, while keeping the beat of the music.

5. MUSIC AND LITERATURE (ML)

Music-Based Books. The appendix has a list of music-based children's literature such as the picture book *The Star Spangled Banner* (Key, 1973). There are books in every genre, from biography to folktales, including books about making and listening to music.

Musical Literature. Read books to children that are based on music or a song and have them "sing" the story. A variation would be to read stories that are from ballets, such as "The Nutcracker," while playing the music from the ballet in the background.

Story Ballads. Ballads tell tales through lyrics and music. First, share examples, and then students take a familiar story and convert it to a ballad by using rhythm instruments and singing parts of the story. Tell them to use action words as the stimulus for miming or verbal skits during the ballad. Rehearse. The end product can be video or audio taped. *Note:* This is best done in small groups.

Operettas. An opera is a story told with music or song. Students can create an opera for a story they know, such as a fairy tale. For example, use the "Three Little Pigs" and have students choose characters, props and costumes, and melodies to sing the story. Teach students how to write cues in dramatic opera form (e.g., *Enter Big Bad Wolf, shifting eyes from side to side,* or *Trees [chorus] sing*).

Onomatopoeia Poems. Create sound poems by using objects and rhythm instruments. Begin by exploring sounds to make with different objects. Work in small groups to plan a five-line poem that builds from one sound up to five sounds. Decide which sound will be line 1, which two sounds will be line 2, and so on. Encourage thinking about rhythm patterns, accent, tempo, and dynamics. Students rehearse their sound poems, present them, and then write them down using onomatopoeic words. For example,

> Ding
>
> Bang Bang
>
> Shush Shush Shush
>
> Rattle Rattle, Clap Clap
>
> Ding Bang Shush Rattle Donk

Poetry Collections. Collect poems about music (e.g., Shel Silverstein's "Ourchestra"). Display on posters or create individual or class anthologies. Perform poems with rhythm instruments.

Artist Studies. Do units based on biographies of composers, singers, and musicians—even instrument inventors.

Song Story. Students select a song and brainstorm who might have written it and why. Work in groups to write a story that explains how the song came to be. *Variation:* Students can research song origins using references such as the *New Grove Dictionary of Music and Musicians.*

Old Macmajor. Use the tune to "Old MacDonald" to learn the key signatures (from Aurelia Cornett, music teacher):

> Old Macmajor had some keys e-i-e-i-o. And in these keys there were some sharps e-i-e-i-o. With a one sharp G and two sharps D and the key of A has one, two, three. Old Macmajor had some keys e-i-e-i-o. Old Macmajor had some keys e-i-e-i-o. See how easy it can

be e-i-e-i-o. Four sharps gives up the key of E and A has three and two in D and there's just one in the key of G. Old Macmajor had some keys e-i-e-i-o.

Word Rhythms. Find examples of these five phrase patterns in names of classmates, song lyrics, place names, and so forth. Each of the patterns can also be played with rhythm instruments.

1. Iamb = dah DAH: *Do what?* (Iambic pentameter = 5 iambs *"I like to eat my peas without a fork."*)
2. Trochaic = DAH dah: *Rudy, Eileen*
3. Anapestic = dah dah DAH: *Virginia*
4. Dactylic = DAH dah dah: *Claudia* (double dactyl = *Gloria Zittercoff)*
5. Spondaic = DAH DAH: *Go there.*

6. LITERATURE AND DRAMA (LDR)

Showtime. After reading a book, form groups to respond by creating a commercial, a jingle, or a news update or newsbreak to convey something important about the book through the drama. Each group is given a number that will be the order of performance. Give about 10 minutes to plan. The whole group comes back together and the show begins. Group by group they present their drama.

Drama-Based Books. The appendix has a list of drama and theater-based children's literature. There are books in every genre, from biography to fiction, including books about doing and viewing drama and theater.

Puppet Shows. Students can plan the story adaptation, stage, and props to make a story come to life. For example, write a Reader's Theater script (see Chapter 8). Help students map out the story using events in the beginning, middle, and end. Then decide who will make each character, scenery, and so forth. In Chapter 4 there are 10 types of puppets to adapt to story characters. Stages can be made by using a push rod in a doorway to hang a curtain. Presentations can also be made using the overhead projector (shadow puppets). Rather than memorize a script, encourage improvisation. As with all performances, a rehearsal is important to practice with puppets and oral expression.

Choral Reading. Choral reading invites experimentation with words and the use of vocal elements (volume, rate, tone, pitch, pause, and stress and emphasis) to build fluency. Options include (1) leader reads a line and class echoes, (2) leader reads a section and class reads a refrain in the story or inserted for dramatic effect, (3) solo readers read sections and whole group reads the rest, or (4) two groups take turns reading a section. (See the *poetry alive* strategies in Post It Page 4–4.) Do repeated readings for fluency.

Tableau (Freeze Frame).   Students choose a *key moment* (not a complete scene) from a piece of literature. In small groups, they plan facial expressions, body shapes, use of space, and the like to create a frozen scene. Each group takes a turn to perform. The rest shut their eyes and when the tableau group says "curtain," they open their eyes and begin to "look closely" to describe all they see. The focus is on describing details and not just guessing the scene. *Variation:* All groups do the same key moment. Compare and contrast.

Pretend and Write.   Either assign students or let them choose a role from a piece of literature, song, or painting. They write, in role, using one of the many forms of writing (see Post It Page 4–2: letters, wills, chants, lists, etc.). For example, choose to be one of the family members (Anna, Caleb, or Jacob) in *Sarah, Plain and Tall* (after Chapter 2). Write a letter to Sarah introducing yourself and asking her questions. Students can switch letters and become Sarah to write a reply. *Variation:* Do as a guessing game. Don't sign the letters. Be sure to discuss the clues to give to who you are, without coming right out and saying a name or family role.

Twenty Questions.   This old favorite game can be adapted for literature. A student or panel assumes the role of a character. The audience can only ask "yes or no" questions and the question cannot be "Is your name. . . ?" The goal is to guess the identity in 20 or less questions. *Variation:* Form teams to guess and alternate. Periodically ask students to put thumbs up if they know the identity. Coach for better questions by asking, "What would be a question you could ask to really find out an important detail?"

Story Drama.   A play can be created from any story with no scripts to memorize. Start with quality stories with lots of action and believable characters. Dialog can be improvised during the story playing using these steps: (1) Read or tell a story and tell students to listen for dialog, special words, and refrains and to get the gist of the story. (2) Afterward, review the plot and proceed to cast, adding characters, and even crowds so that all can participate. Plan sound effects, music, and

the space to be used. At desks? Create open space? (3) Decide who is to narrate and how to start and end the drama (e.g., will the teacher take a role?). (4) Play the story drama with the teacher coaching. If there are problems in the replaying (e.g., if students don't know when or how to end), assume a character role and facilitate, or be the narrator and tell a conclusion with students following your lead. Circle or cumulative stories work well to begin (e.g., *Henny Penny*), as do episodic plots, such as Marshall's *George and Martha* books (adapted from Heinig, 1993).

Round Robin Retellings.   This is a creative retelling variation in which a known story is retold from another character's point of view. Sit in a circle to retell. Begin with one person telling a line, and move around the circle until the full story has been retold. For example, retell *Cinderella* from a stepsister's viewpoint.

Read Arounds.   After reading a story, each student chooses just one sentence from the story and rehearses to read it aloud (adapted from Tompkins & McGee, 1993). Each student then reads the line using the oral expression elements of volume, rate, tone, pitch, pause, stress, and emphasis to convey the interpretation of meaning. Afterward students discuss why they chose their lines (e.g., the special sound or sense in the passage). *Variation:* Use each line to make a class big book with each page having one line and art.

Poetry Sharing.   See Post It Page 4–4 for a dozen ways to share poetry.

Reader–Responder.   Do in partners, usually with a poem. Reader reads one line and responder orally improvises by saying whatever comes to mind. Continue throughout the poem. For example, reader: "Jack and Jill went up the hill." Responder: "I wonder how high the hill was."

Poem Pantomimes.   Pantomime possibilities exist in many poems. For example, de Regniers's, "Keep a Poem in Your Pocket" is about what a poem can do for you. Students pantomime as the poem is read (narrative pantomime). For example, Beyer's "Jump or Jiggle" poem describes the ways different animals walk, Crane's "Snow toward Evening" describes a calm, peaceful snowy night, and Hillyer's "Lullaby" is a poem about a rowboat drifting along. In Miller's "Cat," movements are described in detail. *Note:* Poetry may not be organized with logical forward action and complete sentences and is hard to edit because of rhyme and rhythm. Select poems for narrative pantomime carefully.

Character Meetings.   Each child chooses a character from a book or story everyone knows. They then partner and have conversations, in character, about their lives, problems, and so forth. Invite pairs to share highlights of conversations with the whole class. *Variations:* (1) Use in social studies with historical characters; (2) at a signal, characters freeze and audience suggests an emotion. When conversation begins again, characters must use the suggested emotion.

Planning Character Improvisation.   Read a story or book and stop after the conflict is introduced. Break into groups to discuss these questions: *What does the character want or need (goals or motives)? What is the problem or conflict? What stands in the way of the character getting what he or she wants? What actions can the character take to deal with the problem (plot)? Where might the character be (place)? What might the character say (e.g., a one liner about the problem)?* These are the same categories contained in a literature storymap. *Note:* It helps to give students a planning sheet with the questions and permit work in groups to plan a scene with a beginning, middle, and end to deal with the questions. A good way to structure is to plan a one liner about the problem to end the scene.

Reader's Theater.   See guidelines and examples in Chapter 8. Scripts can be purchased. See the arts-based bibliography under Doing Drama.

Rhyme Change.   Nursery rhymes and other chants and poems are adaptable to word play activities. Use these as verbal warm-ups and to stimulate creative thinking, for example, "Hickory Dickory Dock, A mouse ran up my . . ." (students supply rhyme). Do all the vowel sounds for phonemic awareness development: Hickory Dickory Dack, Hickory Dickory Deck, etc.

Nursery Rhyme Mime.   Sing or recite nursery rhymes. Divide into groups and have each group plan which rhyme to say and mime, or just mime, for others to guess.

7. DRAMA AND MUSIC (DRM)

Pantomime and Action Songs.   There are numerous songs with actions to mime as the group sings, for example, "If You're Happy and You Know It." *Variation:* Write your own with actions (e.g., if you're happy and you know it laugh out loud, smile a while, show your teeth, grin a lot). Other examples: "Little Bunny Foo Foo," "Grand Old Duke of York," "My Hat It

Has Three Corners," and "This Old Man, He Played One." Coleman (1997) has a collection in his book *Serendipity Encyclopedia*. See the music chapter and arts-based bibliography for more.

Singing Commercials.   Divide students into teams and give each a magazine with picture advertisements. Teams create a song to promote the product in their picture. They may select from familiar tunes or write lyrics to an original tune. Teams then present their commercial jingles.

Pretend to Conduct.   Let students pretend to conduct by learning conducting patterns. Start with learning start and stop signals, and then practice actual patterns, learning "downbeat" and "upbeat." Orchestra members can use different sounds as their instruments (e.g., click, hum, pop, hiss, whistle, etc.). Basic conducting patterns are:

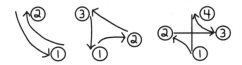

Expert Panels.   Students work in groups and choose a song, composer, musician, or musical style and do research to become well informed. Panels present and then audience members (other students) can ask questions. *Variation:* (1) Groups can all work on the same composer and all be the same person on their panel (i.e., simultaneous casting); (2) panel members can *become* the person or may be people who may have lived during the time of the person.

Interviews.   Students work in groups to list questions to ask musicians, songwriters, conductors, and so forth. Guests are invited to class, and students act as interviewers to find out answers to their questions.

Song Creation Skits.   Students use creative thinking to develop a scene with a beginning, middle, and end to depict how a composer thought of a piece of music or song. Remind students to include conflict in the beginning, and the end of the scene should resolve the problem. Coach them to use start and stop signals and try to make their events believable.

I Heard It First.   Brainstorm a list of songs that are famous: Hallelujah chorus, "Star Spangled Banner," and so on. Students then break into small groups and plan a scene about the first time the music or song was ever heard by an audience and their reactions. Scenes should have a beginning, middle, and end.

Hum Groups.   Put the names of four song titles on slips of paper. Repeat the titles until you have enough for everyone. Students draw a slip and on a signal must sing or hum the melody and try to find others in their group with the same melody. Use songs they know, for example, "Row, Row, Row Your Boat."

One-Minute Instrument Pantomime.   After reading a book such as Isadora's *Ben's Trumpet* or Raschka's *Charlie Parker Played Be Bop* (saxophone), ask students to brainstorm types of instruments. In small groups, one person begins to pantomime playing different instruments, when the leader gives the signal. Group members write down their correct guesses. Change players in the groups at the end of one minute and start again.

Song Pantomimes.   Many songs have characters and actions that can be mimed, such as boat rowing, stars twinkling, or ants marching. Give groups of students song lyrics and ask them to find as many actions as they can and think of creative unusual ways to show the actions.

Narrative Pantomime with Ballads.   As students sing or listen to a story sung through a ballad, they interpret the actions of the song with pantomime. See ideas about developing narrative pantomimes in Chapter 8.

Song Interviews.   Students listen to a song in which several characters occur. Ask students to choose one character and listen again to really find out about the character from the music and lyrics. The teacher can then be in role as an interviewer and use a prop mike to ask the characters questions (e.g., Who are you? What do you want? What are your problems? What will you do about your problems? etc.). This can also be done in pairs, with students taking turns interviewing one another. For example, "Three Blind Mice" has mice, the farmer's wife, and other characters that could be inferred (e.g., farmer, neighbors, representative of the humane society).

8. MUSIC AND ART (MA)

Memphis, Tennessee (1997). High school student Ernest Williams found out how exciting it is to connect art and music. Richard Marx, singer and songwriter, is promoting arts in education by publishing children's art in his CD booklets and Ernest was one of the students selected.

CBSNews

Make Rhythm Instruments.   Many resource books show ways to make rhythm instruments that can be painted and decorated. For example, place papier mâché over a light bulb, let it dry, and then tap it to break it. Paint and you have a shaker. Rainsticks can be made by inserting toothpicks up and down a wrapping paper tube (it helps to make the holes ahead for the students with a drill). Fill tubes with rice or small beans and plug the ends. Sticks can then be painted or covered with collage materials.

Foot Painting.   Put on music and ask students to listen to its rhythm and mood. Spread out a large paper, such as long bulletin board paper. Use shallow trays of tempera; be sure to have students roll up pant legs. Start with a choice of a few colors. Students create art by painting with their feet to the music.

Draw to Music.   Listen to music about a topic (e.g., Grand Canyon Suite). Write or draw to the music and then share how the music communicated messages about the topic.

Musical Mobiles.   Make mobiles from old silverware or other objects that will create music as they move. Use string or wire to tie objects to a stick, pipe, or hanger.

Sound Collage.   Students use magazines to choose pictures of items that produce sounds (animals, machines, people, etc.). Arrange on a large piece of paper, overlapping to form a collage. Students can then share collages by pointing at a picture while the class makes the appropriate sound.

Musical Quilt.   Read a story about how quilts are made. Discuss how quilts portray feelings or events. Tell students they will be composing a song quilt. Decide on an experience, event, or emotion. Divide into small groups. Each group contributes a line to a song. Select a traditional folk tune to accompany the lyrics that children create. Next, children write lyrics on a fabric square or colored paper (e.g., origami paper) using permanent markers. Assemble quilt and sing the squares as a leader points to each.

Musical Rainbow.   Add food coloring to each of eight glasses filled with different amounts of water. (Each should have about one inch more than previous glass.) The eight notes will make a beautiful rainbow when put in order. 1 = clear; 2 = red; 3 = orange; 4 = yellow; 5 = green; 6 = blue; 7 = purple; 8 = clear. Remember, red plus yellow makes orange. Blue plus yellow makes green. Red plus blue makes purple. Under each glass, put a paper with the number of the tone that the glass plays.

Illustrate a Song. Each child chooses a favorite song to illustrate, or the whole class can do the same song to find all the ways one song could be interpreted. Students could create a group mural of a song, or songs can be cut apart, line by line, with children working on illustrating their part. By assembling all the art, the entire song is then depicted (e.g., "Home on the Range" will work).

Sing a Picture. Display a landscape, seascape, or cityscape and ask students to brainstorm all the sounds associated with different parts of the picture. Encourage them to think creatively about what "might be." Come to agreement on a sound for five or six parts of the picture and then discuss the pitch, dynamics, and how many times the sound should be repeated. The teacher then points to each area, and students make the sounds, sustaining them or repeating them, as decided. Next, try harmonizing sounds or doing the sounds of the picture in round form. *Variation:* Use prints with several people and break students into groups to find songs or create songs their character would sing. Come back together and have each group present the songs of their characters.

Finding Musical Elements in Art. After teaching the elements of music, use a piece of art to ask students to find these same elements. For example, folk art and folk music can be compared. Find rhythm in art, texture, tempo, style aspects, and dynamics (areas that are louder or softer).

Media Show and Sound Compositions. Students prepare a sound and art presentation around a choice topic, for example, friends, animals, feelings, weather, culture, or country. They may work in groups or pairs to find a piece of music to play as they present art on transparencies or on an easel as the song is played. Art could be student made or "found art." This could also be done as a computer slide show.

9. ART AND DANCE (AD)

When one looks at the image of a rising arch or tower in architecture or at the yielding of a tree bent by the storm, one receives more than the information conveyed by the image. . . . The body of the viewer reproduces the tensions of swinging and rising and bending so that he himself matches internally the actions he sees being performed outside. And these actions . . . are ways of being alive, ways of being human.

R. Arnheim, 1989, p. 26

Art Dance Connection. Much of art is movement (e.g., draw, paint, and art and dance elements parallel). Dance can awaken the kinesthetic sense and put feelings into motion. Students can dance a painting or paint the dances they create. The kinesthetic center of dance can motivate children to want to move, and the need to express through movement can extend to scribbles, drawing, and painting. Relate the dance elements to other art forms so that students see connections and develop structures for thinking. For example, explore shape in art and dance by painting to music on big paper. Find line, pattern, rhythms, images expressed in art, music, and so forth. Movement possibilities include explorations of lines, shapes, and directions and the use of shape.

Art in Motion. Show artwork with physical motion in it. Discuss how motion is shown and why a particular step is sometimes "frozen" by the artist (e.g., which part of a sneeze would you depict?). Do as a dance with movements before and after: Freeze–move–freeze–move–freeze sequence.

Sound Movement Collages. Sounds of the body, city, nature, animals, machines, children's names, and names of states and cities can all suggest movement. Brainstorm a category with students and then stretch it for movement possibilities. Encourage them to think of the shape, size, rhythm, and energy of the words. Break into groups and ask each group to make a collage (an assemblage of items pasted or glued together) of sounds and movement. Groups can then create a freeze–move–freeze dance and perform. This activity could be followed by a visual art collage around the same topics danced.

Sculpture or Architecture Dances. Display pieces of sculpture or pictures of buildings or furniture. Ask about space, curves, and movements and how each might move if it came to life. Ask students to show the size, energy, and flow with their bodies.

Artists That Move. Set up a station with art books or assign students to locate art that includes movement (e.g., Matisse and Degas). Discuss how artists show movement through line, shape of body, and use of space.

Dance a Painting. Display a print and ask students to brainstorm all the shapes, movements, and emotions (note the word *motion* in this word). Direct attention to the foreground, middle ground, and background in subjects such as landscape, seascape, and still life. Divide into small groups. Each group decides a way to dance the painting, using a beginning–middle–end structure. The goal is not to merely pantomime but to stretch for ideas: What movements came *before* this moment in the art, *during, after,* what is just outside the subject matter (e.g., other people, movements)? After students prepare, take turns presenting. Background or mood music can be added.

Paint a Dance.   Use large paper to capture a dance after doing it. This can begin on a small scale with just painting or drawing certain movements (e.g., curved lines, circles, shaking, turning).

Magic Wand.   Display a full-length portrait such as a narrative scene from history with several figures in it. Students assume figures' positions. When touched by a magic wand, they move in ways the figure might move. Coach them to become conscious of how to bend and walk, the use of curved and straight lines, and positive and negative space. Leader can add emotions: "Move as if you are in a hurry."

Body Painting.   Pretend each body part is a paintbrush and explore a variety of brushstrokes (e.g., broad and sweeping, quick and short, slow and thick).

Negative and Positive Space.   On signal, students make body shapes. Start with "fixed spot" shapes before locomotor. Stress the use of different levels. At freeze signal, all stop and look for "holes" in people's body shapes, made with arms, legs, or fingers. Ask students to squint to see hole shapes—the negative space. *Variation:* Do as partners. Person A makes a shape with holes (negative space) in it, and person B then makes a shape that interacts with the negative space.

Emotion or Color Dance.   Small groups decide on three moves to show an emotion or color and the order and times that each will be repeated. Dances can be accompanied with readings of color poems such as those in O'Neill's (1989) *Hailstones and Halibut Bones.*

10. DANCE AND LITERATURE (DL)

Dance-Based Children's Books.   See the appendix for a bibliography of dance-based literature. There are books in every genre, from biography to folktales, and books about *doing* dance and dancers. Any literature, however, that includes movement or movement imagery has potential use with dance and creative movement.

Character Dance.   Any character in a story or book can be explored through movement by considering all the ways a character might move. For example, how

would Wilbur in *Charlotte's Web* move if he was happy? hungry? afraid? tired? How is his movement different from Charlotte's or Templeton's? How does body shape show something about a character?

Character Walk.   Each person walks around the room as a famous person or character, varying normal level, posture, rhythm, gate, and so forth. When leader says "change," each person tries another walk variation.

Theme Dance.   Any theme from a poem or book can be danced by first brainstorming all the ways to express the theme with body parts, movements, energy, and use of space and time. For example, the theme that courage comes out of fear can be danced in a frozen shape, movements, and frozen shape three-part dance planned and performed by small groups, who will each present a very different interpretation.

Key Topic Dance.   Make a list of important words or topics in a poem or book. Brainstorm all the movements, shapes, levels, energy, and so forth that could be used to convey the topic. Give small groups the choice of a topic or word to plan a dance or a series of creative movements to show it.

Dance Poetry.   A poem about dance can be read as students move creatively, not pantomime, to express its meaning. For example, encourage showing different ways to use the body and space to express the joy of dance in these poems: "Dancing Pants," "Dancin' in the Rain," "Danny O'Dare," by Shel Silverstein. Put poems about dance on poster board to make charts.

Poetry in Motion.   Read aloud a poem for enjoyment, first, and then ask students to interpret movement as a poem is shared. Narrate movement or excerpt words and sentences for students to speak and dance. Music or percussion instruments can be used to highlight poem action. Example poems are "Push Button" by Shel Silverstein, "Jump or Jiggle" by Evelyn Beyer, "The Swing" by Robert Louis Stevenson, and "Jump-Jump-Jump" by Kate Greenaway. Jump rope rhymes are also wonderful ways to energize with rhythmic words. See collections such as the one by Cole, *Miss Mary Mack and Other Children's Street Rhymes* and Booth's *Doctor Knickerbocker and Other Rhymes.*

Line by Line.   Read a poem to students, first. Give each student or group a line from a poem. They then explore all the movement possibilities of the line (e.g., the rhythm of the words, the emotions expressed, the images). Encourage more than pantomiming. The poetry can then be danced line by line as a narrator reads, or groups can each plan to perform just one line.

Write about a Dance.   After any dance or creative movement, students can write about what they did and felt. The BEST elements can give focus to the writing. The writing could be in the form of a story, informational piece, or even a poem (e.g., a couplet or diamante about the dance). For example,

> Shapes
> Round Angled
> Changing Size and Levels
> Dance Shapes Show Feelings
> Frozen Moving Forms

Pointed Curvy

Shapes

Story Tension.   Discuss tension in a story and how characters go about relieving it. Ask, "What point is the climax or most intense part?" Students show with the body this tension in the story.

Characters Alive!   Use a painting or picture from a book with several characters in it. Groups of students become the characters by posing as a frozen picture. They then "come alive" and do three dance moves consistent with the characters. Coach students to do locomotor moves and use low, medium, and high levels. Finally, they return to their original frozen positions.

◆ BIBLIOGRAPHY AND REFERENCES

Books

Arnheim, R. (1989). *Thoughts on art education.* Los Angeles: Getty Center for Education in the Arts.

Harste, J., Short, K., & Burke, C. (1988). *Creating classrooms for authors.* Portsmouth, NH: Heinemann.

Heinig, R. B. (1993). *Creative drama for the classroom teacher.* Upper Saddle River, NJ: Prentice Hall.

Riekehof, L. (1978). *The joy of signing.* Springfield, MO: Gospel Publishing.

Sadie, S. (Ed.). (2001). *New Grove dictionary of music and musicians.* New York: Grove.

Temple, C. (1991). Seven readings of a folktale: Literary theory in the classroom. *New Advocate, 4,* 29.

Tompkins, G. (1997). *Literacy for the 21st century.* Upper Saddle River, NJ: Prentice Hall.

Tompkins, G., & McGee, L. (1993). *Teaching reading with literature: Case studies to action plans.* New York: Merrill.

Children's Literature

Babbitt, N. (1986). *Tuck everlasting.* New York: Farrar, Straus & Giroux.

Beyer, E. (1968). Jump or jiggle. In M. Arbuthnot and S. Root (Eds.), *Time for poetry* (3rd ed.). Glenview, IL: Scott, Foresman.

Booth, D. (1993). *Dr. Knickerbocker and other rhymes.* Toronto: Ticknor and Fields.

Cole, J. (1990). *Miss Mary Mack and other children's street rhymes.* New York: Morrow Junior Books.

Coleman, L. (1997). *Serendipity encyclopedia.* Littleton, CO: Serendipity House.

Froman, R. (1974). *Seeing things: A book of poems.* New York: Crowell.

Gilman, P. (1992). *Something from nothing.* New York: Scholastic.

Greenaway, K. (1968). Jump-jump-jump. In M. Arbuthnot and S. Root (Eds.), *Time for poetry* (3rd ed.). Glenview, IL: Scott, Foresman.

Isadora, R. (1979). *Ben's trumpet* (jazz). New York: Greenwillow.

Key, F. (1973). *The star spangled banner.* Garden City, NY: Doubleday.

Maclachlan, P. (1985). *Sarah, plain and tall.* New York: Harper & Row.

Marshall, J. (1973). *George and Martha.* Boston: Houghton Mifflin.

McCully, E. A. (1992). *Mirette on the high wire.* New York: Putnam.

O'Neill, M. (1989). *Hailstones and halibut bones.* New York: Doubleday.

Raffi (1987). *Shake my sillies out.* New York: Crown.

Raschka, C. (1992). *Charlie Parker played Be Bop* (Be Bop). New York: Orchard.

Silverstein, S. (2000). *Where the sidewalk ends.* New York: HarperCollins.

Silverstein, S. (1981). *A light in the attic.* New York: Harper & Row.

Stevenson, R. L. (1968). The swing. In M. Arbuthnot and S. Root (Eds.), *Time for poetry* (3rd ed.). Glenview, IL: Scott, Foresman.

White, E. B. (1952). *Charlotte's web.* New York: Harper.

Winter, J. (1988). *Follow the drinking gourd.* New York: Knopf.

14

Assessment and Other Frequently Asked Questions

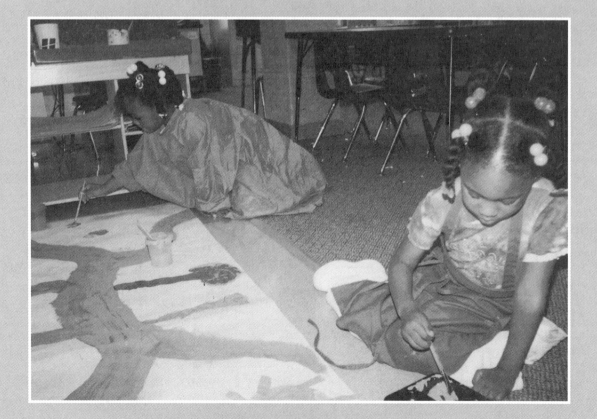

The arts should become a basic part of the K–12 curriculum, not simply for their intrinsic value as a course of study—to help all children and young adults to interpret their world, better understand history—but also for their contribution to students' mastery of other basic areas of the curriculum.

Larson, 1997, p. 167

INTRODUCTION

This final chapter deals with frequently asked questions (FAQs) about assessment and other concerns that often arise during efforts to integrate the arts throughout the curriculum.

FAQs AND ASSESSMENT

1. What about assessment in the arts? Assessment is the process of gathering information to plan or adapt instruction. It is as necessary in the arts as it is in any other curricular area. Indeed, in Western society we demand a degree of excellence in the arts that has precipitated increasingly higher and higher expectations for music, theater, art, dance, and literature. The degree with which we expect artists to grow from assessment and evaluation is comparable only to our expectations that commercial products, such as airbags and car seats, keep us completely safe from harm.

Dilemmas. The dilemma in assessment related to arts integration is how to gather pertinent documentation of student growth without killing the innate artistic spirit. A critical factor in this process is involving students, as completely as possible, in developing and understanding assessment criteria before engaging them in lessons. Students are thus clear about what is expected in advance. This sounds controlling, and yet, in the arts these explicit expectations usually focus most on having students experiment, take risks, and produce original innovations with tool, materials, and techniques.

Another dimension of the assessment dilemma has to do with the use of tools that truly assess what they claim to assess. Valid assessments must also be humane and doable; through their implementation they must uplift, not defeat, learning *with, about, in,* and *through* the arts. Assessment tools and processes must be as creative and diverse as the arts themselves.

Ends driven. Twenty-first century assessment is, for the most part, ends driven. That doesn't mean the emphasis needs to be on arts products, if so the process focus of this book would be in complete contradiction to current trends. Teachers need measurable goals and standards about what students are to *know and be able to do.* Instruction is then designed to move students toward the achievement of goals. Standards exist for assessing both products and the process that engages students in viewing, doing, and listening to the arts.

Performance-based asessment. Some argue that understanding can only truly be assessed, and for that matter, even achieved, through performance; students must do something that puts understanding to work (Perkins, 1998; Wiske, 1997). Walling (2001), on the other hand, warns that performance-based assessment is "a highly useful way of thinking about instruction, but in a postmodernist, constructivist environment . . . —true 'creativity' — [is a] valid ends as well, necessary ends if pluralism and complexity are to be addressed in meaningful ways" (p. 626). One popular example of performance-focused learning and assessment is projects. Project-based units focus on struggling with authentic problems in groups. The process to create the end product that will be assessed includes active exploration and applied learning. Clear evaluation criteria for the projects is either given to students or developed with students in advance. They include expectations for discipline, ability to suspend judgment, use of new perspectives and viewpoints, ability to make creative products, project rigor, and relevance. This approach has its roots in the philosophy of John Dewey and experiments by William Kirkpatrick (Seidel, 1999, p. 85).

Assessing assessment: Four criteria. There are four characteristics that stand out in determining effective assessments. First, assessment should focus on strengths and needs of students, not just on their problems or what they don't know or can't do. This implies that teachers need to use tools such as the Interest Inventory in Appendix D during the first few weeks of school. Second, assessment must also be authentic—it must give documentation in a context that is likely to show what students really know and can do. Paper-and-pencil tests are often criticized for their lack of authenticity, and this is particularly apparent when assessing the arts. Third, assessment needs to be multifactored—not one checklist nor a single anecdotal note is enough to create a portrait of a child's growth. Increasingly, importance is being placed on student self-assessment. Educators have come to acknowledge that self-evaluation often yields greater results as students set goals for their own improvement. Finally, assessment needs to be continuous. We need to collect data from a variety of sources, especially through observing students all year long and noting needs and

Clothesline Art Display

strengths. To make this feasible, some teachers use a clipboard to lay out sticky notes so observations can be easily jotted down and transferred to student folders.

Why assess? It is also important to be clear about the purpose of gathering assessment data. For what is the information to be used? Ideally, assessment information changes how the teacher plans future lessons. Decisions need to be made about the kinds of information to be collected and how it will be collected.

Assessment tools. Common informal assessment tools currently used include the following:

◆ *Interest inventories* and *interviews* are used to find out about students at the start of the year. There is an example in Appendix D.

◆ *Checklists* are used by teachers and students, related to concepts and skills to be learned through specific activities. See samples in Appendix D.

◆ *Rubrics* make a gradient of performance clear, usually on a scale of 1–3 or 1–5. Some districts have written rubrics to make the criteria for letter grades more understandable. See the sample rubric in Appendix D.

◆ *Anecdotal records* are informal notes teachers make about students as they engage in the learning process and as they observe products. See criteria and ideas for anecdotal records in Appendix D.

◆ *Portfolios* are collections of work samples that show progress toward specific goals (usually attached to the front of the portfolio itself). For example, lists of books read and responses to books show progress toward acquiring basic good reader behaviors and learning to transform information to make meaning. Dated entries on audio tapes of children reading can show oral expression growth, especially fluency progress. Journal entries can be evidence of critical and creative thinking as students write about arts experiences used in other curricular areas. It is useful to stick notes on each portfolio item so that it is clear with which goals each item goes. Drama responses and dances can be photographed and videotaped so students can view and reflect on their performances and then set goals to use skills and elements more effectively and creatively.

◆ *Individual conferences* with students are chances to discuss goals and progress and do additional assessment. For example, students may be asked to read a favorite part of a book and give reasons why the section was important or bring a piece of artwork and explain the parts of the creative process intentionally used to make it. A checklist of skills and concepts demonstrated can be included in a child's folder, along with anecdotal notes taken. These short conferences give valuable insight into children's thinking and set the expectation of working toward common goals.

◆ *Student self-evaluation*. Student reflection on learning to use project criteria develops a sense of how the real world operates. From the mechanic to the doctor, there are expectations that each worker will continually reflect on her performance and make necessary adjustments. There are samples of questions for stimulating self-evaluation in Appendix D.

Suggested readings and other resources on assessment are located at the end of this chapter.

2. How do you grade and evaluate in the arts? It is important to distinguish among the concepts of *grades, evaluation,* and *assessment.* Assessment is the process of gathering information or evidence to *plan* meaningful instruction for students. Evaluation is a value judgment placed on work using criteria that answer the question, "How good is it?" Grading is attaching a symbol to the results of evaluation.

Most of us would prefer not to give grades at all, and Jensen (2001) suggests work in the arts be marked as "pass or fail" using criteria such as attendance, participation, and maintaining a portfolio. But the choice to not grade is not always available to teachers. Teachers do have the choice to *not* grade everything but give clear descriptive feedback on progress made during practices. For example, a checklist of what the work represents can be used by both the student and the teacher. See a sample of a checklist in Appendix D. When work in the arts is to be graded, students need to know evaluation criteria before they begin. A grading rubric can be useful and simply describes what each grade means, specifically. A checklist of tasks, based on concept and skill goals, can be given so that students can independently track activities they're doing to reach goals. It is important to discuss with students what makes *quality* work. Consult the *National Standards* and school district standards for help. There is a sample grading rubric in Appendix D. After much exploration and practice, evaluation and grading can happen without destroying students' interest, but this is a delicate area. See Chapter 1 for *creativity squelchers* in Post It Page 1–7.

3. Aren't the arts diluted in an integrated program? Arts-based classrooms cannot substitute for specialized arts classes for students. Integrating the arts into classrooms is intended to *expand* arts experiences. The arts speak for themselves when allowed to become an *integral* part of school—not just extras. When children clamor for more arts experiences that require the knowledge and skills of specialists, parents listen. Communities are sometimes even more ready to support taxes for arts specialists *after the arts have been integrated* into general classrooms.

4. What about art for art's sake? Shouldn't the arts be valued because they are—not because they fix social or academic problems?

Perhaps one day we will hear the news that researchers have shown how the study of reading and mathematics can make us all better artists.
      Playwright Alan Brody, in Larson, 1997, p. 111

There are those that look askance at the practical use of the arts and bewail any view of the arts as fix-its for the economy or to solve drug problems. Some think integrating the arts means lowering of standards and decry efforts of those outside the arts community who view the arts as repositories of practical knowledge and skills. Others actually seem to want an "inner circle" of specialists who control access to the arts and, therefore, culture. Unfortunately, an elitist attitude contributes to isolation of the arts from everyday people, who often believe creativity is the province of a few, talented recipients of years of special training. It is no wonder, when schools experience financial exigency, the solution is frequently to cut areas felt to be unrelated to the majority of students. The arts seem alien, apart, out there, on "museum walls or in concert halls."

5. How do you deal with censorship of the arts (e.g., children's literature)? What is offensive to one person is beautiful to the next. Censorship attempts seem to be on the rise, and any art form is vulnerable. Why? Art is dangerous. It intentionally provokes thought and emotional response—that's why Hitler banned books. It cannot be assumed that all parents want their children to do critical creative thinking and use all learning faculties, including the affective domain. Across the country, complaints related to the arts have been voiced, including challenges to teachers who use children's literature, visual art, and dance. For example, these books have all been accused of the following: Willhoite's *Daddy's Roommate* for condoning homosexuality, Lionni's *Swimmy* (1973) for promoting communism, Sendak's *In the Night Kitchen* (1970) because of nudity in the art, Silverstein's *The Giving Tree* (1973) for being antifeminist, a poem in Silverstein's *A Light in the Attic* about a girl making a milkshake by shaking a cow for suggesting humans engage in sex with animals, and Steig's *Sylvester and the Magic Pebble*, the subject of attack by a police association because police are depicted as pigs in the book. Traditional folktales, especially original versions, are replete with violence causing objections from those who believe children should only be given sugar-coated reading. In my own community, parents objected to Speare's *Witch of Blackbird Pond*, thinking it promotes witchcraft. Any work that deals with religion, sex, nudity, violence, or the occult or uses profanity is particularly prone to complaint. For more information, see Foerstel's (1994) *Banned Books in the USA* and the American Library Association's *Banned Books Week* publications (1984–1993; 1994). There is also a Banned Books page on the Web.

Every school should have a policy for evaluating and selecting books and other art materials (prints, videos, etc.) and a procedure for handling grievances. It is helpful to include a requirement for complaints to be made in writing, with reasons and a signature. Then, if parents object, teachers can follow the policy. Districts need to also allow parents to opt for "substitute" experiences (e.g., books on the same unit topic), but parents do not have the right to prohibit all children from using materials obtained under the school's selection policy. Usually, districts stand behind teachers who use good children's literature or any art considered high quality. It behooves teachers to make sure materials and activities fit the course of study, are appropriate to students' developmental levels, and are defensible. Use recommended book lists, such as the Caldecott, Newbery, and Coretta Scott King awards lists, and be sensitive to a community's values. Call each parent at the beginning of the year, introduce yourself, and explain how you'll be using rich arts experiences throughout the year (for most teachers that's about five calls a night for one week). Have reasons ready. Build an open relationship and encourage parents to visit the class. Parents want their children to be happy and successful, so if you have the research and good results to show that your approach is working, most will be satisfied. People generally call for censorship because they feel threatened and because they don't have all the facts. Share facts, listen to complaints, and see what facts parents have and what other information is needed. Here are resources to help:

◆ American Library Association's Office for Intellectual Freedom has several publications, including *Censorship and Selection: Issues and*

Answers for Schools (Reichman, 2001). The Freedom to Read Foundation can be reached at 800-545-2433.

◆ People for the American Way provides advice and assistance in dealing with censorship in schools: 2000 M St. NW, Suite 400, Washington, DC 20036 (800-326-7329).

◆ The National Coalition Against Censorship can be reached at 212-807-6222.

6. What about parents who object to dancing for religious reasons or ones who think religious books or art about religion have no place in public schools? The concern over dance arises because the word *dance* has come to convey sexual images of bump and grind movements. It is important to provide information to parents *before* beginning to integrate dance. If the word *dance* is inflammatory, call it *movement* or *kinesthetic learning*, which is being honest and politically astute.

As far as religion in public schools is concerned, there is no law against teaching *about* religions or religious groups, but public school teachers *cannot* proselytize students regarding a religious point of view. Units on Native Americans, Jews and the Holocaust, Japan, and so forth, including study of the religions of these groups, are common; it is difficult to understand any culture without studying its religious views. It is interesting how some communities seem to accept the study of many religions but are sensitive to the mention of the Christian religion. In one school a fourth grader drew a picture of Jesus as a response to a book he'd chosen to read. Some teachers demanded his drawing be taken off the Hall Gallery because they thought this violated the principle of separation of church and state! Teachers must know the law and inform those who are not informed.

7. Isn't integrating the arts a lot more work? I liked the ideas of whole language, literature-based instruction, and portfolio assessment, but now I'm exhausted. Humans are known to be willing to work hard if they believe a cause is great. Teachers who enjoy using the arts and see the results in student achievement and motivation do not perceive integrating the arts as forced labor done to get a paycheck. They are energized by accomplishing important goals in different ways, often made easier because students *want* to be involved.

8. How do I find the time to "integrate the arts" with all the other expectations (e.g., inclusion, standardized tests)? The arts are not to be integrated *in addition to* the present curriculum. Integration involves using time differently. Research supports use of the arts to get students to academic proficiency *more efficiently* than traditional approaches, and students enjoy themselves more! Those involved in inclusion are learning about alternative approaches to teaching reading, writing, science, social studies, and math. Teaching *with, about, in,* and *through* the arts is a powerful alternative approach.

9.   It seems we spend too much money on the arts already, for example, the new billion-dollar Getty Museum in Los Angeles. Do we really need to pour more into the arts? These countries spend more per capita on the arts than the United States: United Kingdom 5 times more; Canada, 8 times; France and the Netherlands, 10 times; Germany, 13 times; and Sweden, 15 times more. Less than 0.1% of the Department of Education's $30 billion budget is for arts education.

10.   What if my school is not using the integrated arts philosophy?

The problems of the world cannot possibly be solved by skeptics or cynics whose horizons are limited by the obvious realities. We need men who can dream of things that never were.

John F. Kennedy

Start to share ideas with one or two teachers and your principal. Journal articles and research tidbits (see the **News Bulletins**) can be circulated. Copy the Post It Pages and share. Suggest to staff development committees that workshops be provided on arts integration. Contact local arts agencies to see what they presently offer. Keep in mind that we retain

◆   10 percent of what we read
◆   20 percent of what we hear
◆   30 percent of what we see
◆   50 percent of what we hear and see together
◆   70 percent of what we see, hear, and say
◆   90 percent of what we see, hear, say, and do (drama, dance, make art, sing, write) (Fauth, 1990, pp. 159–87)

11.   How can I feel more creative and help my students to get away from wanting to "copy"? Is it really possible to teach creativity?

A mind once stretched by imagination never regains its original dimensions.

Anonymous

Working in Monet's Garden

Do this activity to see how to activate creative thinking: Line a group up and explain that each will be asked to walk across the room in a way different from everyone else. Start with one person and go down the line. Afterward, discuss how everyone was able to accomplish this "creative" task so easily. Next, here are two children's books that show the values of creative thinking. Use them with adults and children: *The Big Orange Splot* by Daniel Pinkwater and *Imogene's Antlers* by David Small. Discuss the importance of not copying but rather "data gathering" from sources and then "doing your own thing." Try the creativity strategies described in Chapter 1 (and the rest of the book). Repeat them one at a time until they become second nature. For example, try using brainstorming in social studies and science to discuss problems. Keep adding a few strategies at a time. Tell students what you are doing and put up posters about what they can try (e.g., SCAMPER). Consider setting aside 10 minutes of class time each week to discuss how everyone is creative; ask students to discover specific examples by talking with friends, parents, and other relatives. Finally, invite artists and others to class to speak about how they create.

12.   What if I have a very limited budget? How can I get the materials I would need? You don't need a lot of expensive materials. Push back the desks and use the strategies in this book, along with children's literature and other current teaching materials. Check out *more* library books that are arts based, and spruce up the room with art prints (some public libraries lend prints). Playing background music at the start of the day means bringing in a CD player. Eventually, you'll want to have a wider range of art materials such as those recommended in Chapter 5, but to start off, use what's on hand and investigate free community resources such as museums that provide docent-led tours. The public library may have staff to do storytelling. Survey teachers in your school to find what they know and can do in music, art, drama, dance, literature, poetry, and storytelling. Ask about spouses' talents and others they know who would be willing to share (e.g., seniors in the community). There are many talented people out there just waiting to be asked.

13.   Why are the arts specialists the first teachers to be cut when there is a budget crunch? Don't school administrators and board members know the arts research?

A dramatic revolution in cognitive understanding began in the 1970's. Research now substantiates what some teachers and parents already knew intuitively—that the arts are critical to learning.

Murfee, 1995

It is interesting to trace how the arts became dispensable extras. But surveys show most parents now think the arts are as important as reading, writing, math, science, and social studies and favor cuts in administration or sports to pay for arts classes (Harris, 1992). There is a growing consensus among educational policymakers and parents that the arts should be an integral part of education, but support is built on information. Not everyone has had access to the kind of research in the *News Bulletins* of this book. The 1995 pamphlet *Eloquent Evidence: Arts at the Core of Learn-*

ing gives a quick research overview and is available from the President's Committee on the Arts & the Humanities and the National Assembly of State Arts Agencies with the National Endowment for the Arts (see the appendix for addresses and websites). It cites the Improving America's Schools Act, approved by Congress in 1994, as reinforcement of the "importance of the arts in relation to other subjects and as vital subjects in themselves" and provides example studies that show "students with background in the arts are likely to have a richer source of information and insight to draw upon, compared to those who do not study the arts."

14.   Doesn't direct or explicit instruction in the arts interfere with natural creative development? Guided or direct instruction helps children to attain skills, learn to use particular tools, and discover important patterns they will not be likely to find independently. Explicit instruction gives children the confidence to take risks and try new things because they have some know-how. Guided instruction does need to be short and followed by time to experiment to explore creative variations.

15.   Doesn't emphasizing "beauty" focus on looks and appearance when we should focus on more substantial aspects of people and the world?

You may find yourself driving along a highway when you suddenly pass a vista that catches your breath. You stop the car, get out for just a few minutes, and behold the grandeur of nature. This is the arresting power of beauty, and giving in to that sudden longing of the soul is a way of giving it what it needs. Discussions of beauty can sometimes sound ethereal and philosophical, but from the soul viewpoint beauty is a necessary part of ordinary life. Every day we will find moments when the soul glimpses an occasion for beauty, if only passing a store window and stopping for a second to notice a beautiful ring or an arresting pattern in a dress. Moore, 1992, pp. 277–278.

16.   Where can I go to observe teachers already doing this? Contact the schools mentioned in the *News Bulletins* throughout the book. Use the Internet to find out about Arts Propel schools (based on Gardner's multiple intelligences) and the more than 40 A1 schools. (See Ralph Burgard's [1997] *Schools as Communities: Public Education and Social Cohesion*.) In North Carolina there are now 27 A1 schools. Examples: Sunset Park Elementary in Wilmington, North Carolina (reports dramatic increase in parent involvement); Lusher Alternative Elementary in New Orleans, Louisiana. Other resource people to contact are Ron Hughes, principal in Chattanooga, Tennessee, schools; Scott Shuler in the Connecticut Department of Education; Jennifer Davidson at Oakland Intermediate School in Waterford, Michigan; Jayne Ellicott at Ashley River Creative Arts Elementary in Charleston, South Carolina; Cheri Sterman at Binney and Smith School in Easton, Pennsylvania; and Terry Bennett, principal in Beaufort County Schools, South Carolina.

17. How do you begin to collaborate with special teachers of the arts? Begin by asking to sit in on their classes to learn about the arts. Ask about sharing a list of unit topics and skills each of you will address during a semester, and see where there are natural connections. Start slowly and build a respectful relationship that acknowledges that each of you has a different expertise to bring to the common goal of teaching children.

18. How can a teacher who is not artsy integrate the arts? What if I have little or no background in the arts? Almost everyone has more background than they think they do. Think about what you do know and can do in music, art, drama, dance and movement, literature, and poetry. Start small, maybe with a one-minute arts routine such as those described in Chapter 2. Read journal articles such as those in the bibliography in the appendix and watch recommended videos. Find out about teacher workshops such as those sponsored by the Kennedy Center. See addresses, phone numbers, and websites in the appendix. I especially recommend the websites ArtsEdge and ArtsEdNet.

Integrating the arts is about good teaching using brain-based learning. You need not be a dancer, singer, visual artist, or actor to use this research. You do need a basic knowledge of key concepts, principles, techniques, and tools in each of the arts disciplines and a solid foundation in research on child development and learning theory (see discussion on Vygotsky, Piaget, Gardner, Maslow, etc., in Chapter 1). Finally, it is necessary for a teacher to be committed to integrating the arts. Enthusiasm and passion are hard to fake and are major determiners in the success of children in any classroom. Ginott (1985) said it best when he reminded teachers to say to themselves

> I am the decisive element in the classroom. It is my personal approach that creates the climate. It is my daily mood that makes the weather. As a teacher, I possess tremendous power to make a child's life miserable or joyous. I can be a tool of torture or an instrument of inspiration. I can humiliate, humor, hurt or heal. In all situations, it is my response that decides whether a crisis will be escalated or de-escalated and a child humanized or dehumanized.

◆ CONCLUSION

The arts are unique ways humans understand and respond—ways we communicate by receiving and expressing information. They are outgrowths of culture, emotions, values, experiences, and history, created because everyday words are inadequate. As disciplines, the arts are work—brain and body work—that offer unusual perspectives, tools, and techniques to liberate feelings and ideas locked up inside a person. This book has been about tapping a vast potential of the arts to impact learning by giving classroom teachers background to teach *with, about, in,* and *through* the arts.

But great teaching involves more than savoir faire. The goal is not to do what was done *to* you, but to transcend our teachers by using research, theory, curriculum models, and strategies to create an individual teaching style based on a personal philosophy. For meaningful arts integration, this philosophy needs to address beliefs about an esthetic learning environment, the power of belief and expectation, giving students freedom to fail, meaning making about important life-centered issues, the use of teacher demonstration, active learning, opportunities to apply and practice, developing student independence and responsibility, ensuring progress through success, focusing on intrinsic motivation, and the essential role of creative problem solving in learning. We need teachers who will invent, discover, adapt, and twist ideas to solve learning problems, not simply repeat the methods of past generations. We need teachers who believe for every problem there are multiple solutions—the best of which may seem bizarre because they are so creative. But as Dr. Seuss put it, "If you can see things out of whack, you can see things in whack." Of course, this requires risk taking—moving out of a zone of comfort and being willing to experience a degree of dissonance, imperatives for creative thinking. It is the teacher's own knowledge, strategy repertoire, enthusiasm, humor, creativity, and passion that are forces powerful enough to change a child's universe by creating the "what if? classroom." Change the child and we change the future.

◆ TEACHER RESOURCES

Internet

k12artsed@artsedge.kennedy-centr.org

http://www.est.gov.bc.ca/curriculum/irps/music810/mu
toc.htm

ftp://ftp.est.gov.bc.ca/publilc/curric/fak7.pdf

http://www./jwpepper.com

Books and Articles

Armstrong, C. L. (1994). *Designing assessment in art*. Reston, VA: National Art Education Association.

Beattie, D. (1994, March). The mini-portfolio: Locus of a successful performance examination. *Art Education*, pp. 14–18.

Bellanca, J. (1994). *Multiple assessments for multiple intelligences*. Palatine, IL: IRI/ Skylight.

Brandt, R. (1987/88, December/January). On assessment in the arts: A conversation with Howard Gardner. *Educational Leadership*, pp. 30–34.

Khattri, N., Kane, M., & Reeve, A. (1995, November). How performance assessments affect teaching and learning. *Educational Leadership*, pp. 80–83.

MacGregor, R. (1992, November). A short guide to alternative assessment practices. *Art Education*, pp. 34–38.

Manebur, D. (1994, March) Assessment as a classroom activity. *Music Educators Journal*, pp. 23–47.

Wolf, D. (1987/88, December/January). Opening up assessment. *Educational Leadership*, pp. 24–29.

Wolf, D., Bixby, J., Glenn, J., & Gardner, H. (1991). To use their minds well: New forms of student assessment. In G. Grand (Ed.), *Review of research in education* (pp. 31–74). Washington, DC: American Educational Research Association.

Wolf, D. P., & Pistone, N. (1991). *Taking full measure: Rethinking assessment through the arts*. (Locators # NX 282W6). New York: College Entrance Examination Board.

Zimmerman, E. (1992, November). Assessing students' progress and achievements in art. *Art Education*, pp. 14–24.

◆ BIBLIOGRAPHY AND REFERENCES

Books and Articles

Arnheim, R. (1989). *Thoughts on art education*. Los Angeles: Getty Center for Education in the Arts.

Banned Books Week. (1984–1993). Chicago: American Library Association.

Banned Books Week. (1994). Chicago: American Library Association.

Burgard, R. (1997). *Schools as communities: Public education and social cohesion*. Washington, DC: National Endowment for the Arts.

Fauth, B. (1990). Linking the visual arts with drama, movement, and dance for the young child. In J. Stinson (Ed.), *Moving and learning for the young child*. Reston, VA: American Alliance for Health, Physical Education, Recreation, and Dance.

Foerstel, H. (1994). *Banned books in the USA: A reference guide to book censorship in schools and public libraries*. Westport, CT: Greenwood.

Ginott, H. (1985). *Between teacher and child*. New York: Avon.

Harris, L. (1992). *Americans and the Arts VI/Nationwide Survey of Public Opinion*. Washington, DC: Americans for the Arts.

Jensen, E. (2001). *Arts with the brain in mind*. Alexandria, VA: Association for Supervision and Curriculum Development.

Larson, G. (1997). *American canvas*. Washington, DC: National Endowment for the Arts.

Moore, T. (1992). *Care of the soul*. New York: HarperCollins.

Murfee, E. (1995). *Eloquent evidence: Arts at the core of learning*. Washington, DC: President's Committee on the Arts and Humanities and the National Assembly of State Arts Agencies with the National Endowment of the Arts.

Perkins, D. (1998). *The intelligent eye: Learning to think by looking at art*. Santa Monica, CA: Getty Center for Education and the Arts.

Reichman, H. (2001). *Censorship and selection: Issues and answers for schools*. Chicago: American Library Association.

Seidel, S. (1999). Stand and unfold yourself; A monograph on the Shakespeare and Company research study. In E. Fiske (Ed.), *Champions of change*. Washington, DC: Arts Education Partnership and the President's Committee on the Arts and Humanities.

Walling, D. (2001, April). Rethinking visual arts education. *Phi Delta Kappan*, pp. 626–631.

Wiske, M. (1997). *Teaching for understanding: Linking research with practice*. San Francisco: Jossey-Bass.

Children's Literature

Lionni, L. (1963). *Swimmy*. New York: Random House.

Pinkwater, D. (1993). *The big orange splot*. New York: Scholastic.

Sendak, M. (1970). *In the night kitchen*. New York: Harper & Row.

Silverstein, S. (1973). *The giving tree*. New York: Harper & Row.

Silverstein, S. (1981). *A light in the attic*. New York: Harper & Row.

Small, D. (1985). *Imogene's antlers*. New York: Crown.

Speare, E. (1958). *Witch of Blackbird Pond*. Boston: Houghton Mifflin.

Steig, W. (1969). *Sylvester and the magic pebble*. New York: Little Simon.

Appendix A: Arts-Based Children's Literature

Note: The Children's Literature Web Guide (*www.vcalgary.ca/,dkbrown/*) has a bibliography of books with artistic protagonists.

Art

Making Art

Adkins, J. (1975). *Inside: Seeing beneath the surface.* New York: Walker.

Albenda, P. (1970). *Creating painting with tempera.* New York: Van Nostrand.

Arnosky, J. (1982). *Drawing from nature.* New York: Lothrop.

Bang, M. (2000). *Picture this: How pictures work.* New York: SeaStar.

Baumgardner, J. (1993). *60 Art projects for children: Painting, clay, puppets, paints, masks, and more.* New York: Clarkson-Potter.

Belloli, A., & Godard, K. (1994). *Make your own museum.* Boston: Houghton Mifflin.

Blegvad, E. (1979). *Self-portrait: Eric Blegvad.* Reading, MA: Addison Wesley.

Bolognese, D., & Thornton, R. (1983). *Drawing and painting with the computer.* New York: Franklin Watts.

Carle, E. (1974). *My very first book of colors.* New York: Crowell.

Emberly, E. (1991). *Ed Emberly's drawing book: Make a world.* Boston: Little, Brown.

Fine, J., & Anderson, D. (1979). *I carve stone.* New York: Crowell.

Fischer, L. E. (1986). *The papermakers.* Boston: Godine.

Galate, L. (1980). *A beginner's guide to calligraphy.* New York: Dell.

Gibbons, G. (1987). *The pottery place.* San Diego: Harcourt Brace Jovanovich.

Graham, A., & Stoke, D. (1983). *Fossils, ferns, and fish scales: A handbook of art and nature projects.* New York: Four Winds.

Haldane, S. (1988). *Painting faces.* New York: Dutton.

Hauser, J. (1995). *Kids' crazy concoctions: 50 mysterious mixtures for art & craft fun.* Charlotte, VT: Williamson.

Hoban, T. (1974). *Circles, triangles, and squares.* New York: Macmillan.

Hoban, T. (1983). *Round & round & round.* New York: Greenwillow.

Hoban, T. (1986). *Shapes, shapes, shapes.* New York: Greenwillow.

Hyman, T. S. (1981). *Self-portrait: Trina Schart Hyman.* Reading, MA: Addison Wesley.

Irvine, J., & Reid, B. (1987). *How to make pop-ups.* New York: Morrow.

Joe, E. (1978). *Navajo sandpainting art.* Tucson, AZ: Treasure Chest.

Johnson, N. (2001). *National Geographic photography guide for kids.* Washington, DC: National Geographic Society.

Kinney, J., & Kinney, C. (1976). *23 Varieties of ethnic art and how to make each one.* New York: Atheneum.

Kohl, M. (1989). *Mudworks.* Bellingham, WA: Bright Ring.

Kohl, M., & Gainer, C. (1991). *Good earth art: Environmental art for kids.* Bellingham, WA: Bright Ring.

Marks, M. (1972). *OP-tricks: Creating kinetic art.* Philadelphia: Lippincott.

Muller, B. (1987). *Painting with children.* Edinburgh, Scotland: Floris.

Pluckrose, H. (1989). *Crayons.* New York: Watts.

Reid, B. (1989). *Playing with plasticine.* Longbeach, CA: Beechtree.

Sakata, H. (1990). *Origami.* New York: Japan Publishers, U.S.A.

Schulz, C. (2001). *Peanuts: The art of Charles M. Schulz.* New York: Pantheon Books.

Smith, R. (1987). *The artist's handbook: Complete guide to tools, techniques, and materials of painting, drawing and printing.* New York: Knopf.

Solga, K. (1992). *Make sculptures.* Cincinnati: North Light.

Stangl, J. (1986). *Magic mixtures.* Carthage, IL: Teaching Aids.

Striker, S. (1984). *The anti-coloring book.* New York: Holt, Rinehart & Winston. One of a series including *The circus anti-coloring book* and *The newspaper anti-coloring book.*

Takahama, T. (1988). *Quick and easy origami.* New York: Japan Publications.

Terzian, A. (1993). *The kids' multicultural art book: Art & craft experiences from around the world.* Charlotte, VT: Williamson.

Webb, P. H., & Corby, J. (1991). *Shadowgraphs anyone can make.* New York: Running Press.

Weiss, P., & Giralla, S. (1976). *Simple printmaking.* New York: Lothrop.

Zemach, M. (1978). *Self-portrait: Margot Zemach.* Reading, MA: Addison Wesley.

Art as Part of the Book's Theme

Aardema, V. (1967). *Who's in rabbit's house?* New York: Dial Books.

Aardema, V. (1985). *Bimwilli and the Zimwi.* New York: Dial Books.

Abby Aldrich Rockefeller Folk Art Center (1991). *The folk art counting book.* New York: Abrams.

Ackerman, K. (1990). *Araminta's paint box.* New York: Atheneum.

Alcott, L. M. (1994). *Little women.* Boston: Little, Brown.

Alexander, L. (1982). *Kestrel.* New York: Dutton.

Alexander, M. (1995). *You're a genius BLACKBOARD BEAR.* Cambridge, MA: Candlewick.

Allen, C. (1991). *The rug makers.* Austin, TX: Steck-Vaughn.

Allington, R. (1979). *Colors.* Milwaukee, WI: Raintree.

Allison, B. (1991). *Effie.* New York: Scholastic.

Angelou, M. (1994). *My painted house, my friendly chicken.* New York: Clarkson-Potter.

Anholt, L. (1994). *Camille and the sunflowers.* Hauppauge, NY: Barron's Educational Series.

Anno, M. (1989). *Anno's faces.* New York: Philomel.

Asch, F. (1978). *Sand cake.* New York: Parents Magazine Press.

Asch, F. (1981). *Bread and honey.* New York: Parents Magazine Press.

Asch, F. (1985). *Bear shadow.* New York: Simon & Schuster.

Asch, F. (1995). *Water.* New York: Harcourt Brace Jovanovich.

Ata, T., & Moroney, L. (1989). *Baby rattlesnake.* San Francisco: Children's Book Press.

Baker, A. (1994a). *Brown rabbit's shape book.* New York: Larouse Kingfisher.

Baker, A. (1994b). *White rabbit's color book.* New York: Larouse Kingfisher.

Baker, J. (1991). *Window.* New York: Puffin.

Baker, J. (1987). *Where the forest meets the sea.* New York: Greenwillow.

Bang, M. (1985). *The paper crane.* New York: Greenwillow.

Barrett, P., & Barrett, S. (1972). *The line Sophie drew.* New York: Scroll.

Bartalos, M. (1995). *Shadow Willie.* New York: Viking.

Bedard, M. (1992). *Emily.* New York: Doubleday.

Blood, C., & Link, M. (1990). *The goat in the rug.* New York: Aladdin-Macmillan.

Bouchard, D. (1993). *The elders are watching.* Golden, CO: Fulcrum.

Brenner, B. (1989). *The color wizard.* New York: Bantam.

Brown, M. (1984). *There's no place like home.* New York: Parents Magazine Press.

Bulla, C. (1987). *The chalk box kid.* New York: Random House.

Burke-Weiner, K. (1992). *The maybe garden.* New York: Beyond Worlds.

Burns, M. (1994). *The greedy triangle.* New York: Scholastic.

Bush, T. (1995). *Grunt, the primitive cave boy.* New York: Crown.

Byars, B. (1978). *The cartoonist.* New York: Viking.

Canning, K. (1979). *A painted tale.* New York: Barron's.

Carle, E. (1972). *The secret birthday message.* New York: Harper Trophy.

Carle, E. (1974). *My very first book of shapes.* New York: Harper & Row.

Carle, E. (1984). *The mixed-up chameleon.* New York: Crowell.

Carle, E. (1992). *Draw me a star.* New York: Philomel.

Carlstrom, N. W. (1992). *Northern lullaby.* New York: Philomel.

Carrick, D. (1985). *Morgan and the artist.* New York: Clarion.

Castaneda, O. S. (1993). *Abuela's weave.* New York: Lee & Low.

Cazet, D. (1986). *Frosted glass.* New York: Bradbury.

Cazet, D. (1993). *Born in the gravy.* New York: Orchard.

Christiana, D. (1990). *Drawer in a drawer.* New York: Farrar, Straus & Giroux.

Church, V. (1971). *All the colors around me.* Chicago: Afro-American Press.

Clark, A. N. (1955). *The little Indian pottery maker.* Chicago: Melmont.

Clark, A. N. (1957). *The little Indian basket maker.* Chicago: Melmont.

Clement, C. (1986). *The painter and the wild swans.* New York: Pied Piper-Dial.

Coerr, E. (1986). *The Josefina story quilt.* New York: Harper Trophy.

Cohen, J. (1995). *Why did it happen?* New York: Morrow.

Cohen, M., & Hoban, L. (1980). *No good in art.* New York: Greenwillow.

Cole, B. (1989). *Celine*. New York: Farrar, Straus, & Giroux.

Cooney, B. (1982). *Miss Rumphius*. New York: Viking Penguin.

Coville, B. (1991). *Jeremy Thatcher, dragon hatcher*. Harcourt Brace Jovanovich.

Craven, C., & dePaola, T. (1989). *What the mailman brought*. New York: Putnam.

Demarest, C. L. (1995). *My blue boat*. New York: Harcourt Brace.

de Paola, T. (1973). *Charlie needs a cloak*. Upper Saddle River, NJ: Prentice Hall.

de Paola, T. (1991). *Bonjour, Mr. Satie*. New York: Putnam.

de Trevino, E. B. (1965). *I, Juan de Pareja*. New York: Farrar, Straus & Giroux.

Dewey, A. (1995). *The sky*. New York: Green Tiger.

Dillon, L., & Dillon, D. (1994). *What am I?* New York: Blue Sky.

Dixon, A. (1994). *Clay*. New York: Garrett Educational.

Dobrin, A. (1973). *Josephine's imagination*. New York: Scholastic.

Druscher, A. (1992). *Simon's book*. New York: Lothrop, Lee & Shepard.

Dubelaar, T., (1992). *Looking for Vincent*. New York: Checkerboard.

Dunrea, O. (1995). *The painter who loved chickens*. New York: Farrar, Straus & Giroux.

Ernst, L. C. (1986). *Hamilton's art show*. New York: Lothrop.

Feiffer, J. (1993). *The man in the ceiling*. New York: HarperCollins.

Fitzhugh, L. (1964). *Harriet the spy*. New York: Harper & Row.

Fox, P. (1988). *The village by the sea*. Orchard.

Freeman, D. (1987). *Norman the doorman*. New York: Viking Penguin.

French, F. (1977). *Matteo*. New York: Oxford University Press.

Gibbons, G. (1987). *The pottery place*. New York: Harcourt Brace Jovanovich.

Goffstein, M. B. (1980). *An artist*. New York: Harper & Row.

Goffstein, M. (1985). *An artist's album*. New York: Harpercrest.

Goffstein, M. (1986). *Your lone journey: Paintings*. HarperCollins.

Grifalconi, A. (1990). *Osa's pride*. Boston: Little, Brown.

Harwood, P. A. (1965). *Mr. Bumba draws a kitten*. Minneapolis: Learner.

Heyer, M. (1986). *The weaving of a dream*. New York: Puffin.

Hort, L. (1987). *The boy who held back the sea*. New York: Dial.

Isadora, R. (1977). *Willaby*. New York: Macmillan.

Isadora, R. (1988). *The pirates of Bedford Street*. New York: Greenwillow.

Isadora, R. (1991). *Swan lake*. New York: Putnam.

Jarrell, R. (1964). *Bat poet*. New York: Macmillan.

Jenkins, J. (1992). *Thinking about colors*. New York: Dutton.

Johnson, C. (1955). *Harold and the purple crayon*. HarperCollins.

Keats, E. J. (1962). *The snowy day*. New York: Viking.

Kesselman, W., & Cooney, B. (1980). *Emma*. New York: Doubleday.

Knox, B. (1993). *The great art adventure*. New York: Rizzoli.

Koch, K., & Farell, K. (1985). *Talking to the sun*. New York: Metropolitan Museum of Art.

Konigsburg, E. L. (1975). *Second Mrs. Giaconda*. New York: Atheneum.

Leaf, M. (1987). *Eyes of the dragon*. New York: Lothrop, Lee & Shepard.

Lobel, A. (1968). *The great blueness and other predicaments*. New York: Harper & Row.

Lobel, A. (1980). *Fables*. New York: Harper & Row.

MacAgy, D., & MacAgy, E. (1978). *Going for a walk with a line*. New York: Doubleday.

Markun, P. M. (1993). *The little painter of Sabana Grande*. New York: Bradbury.

Martin, B. (1992). *Brown bear, brown bear, what do you see?* New York: Henry Holt.

Mayers, F. (1991a). *The ABC: Museum of Fine Arts, Boston*. New York: Abrams.

Mayers, F. (1991b). *The ABC: Museum of Modern Art, New York*. New York: Abrams.

Mayhew, J. (1989). *Katie's picture show*. New York: Bantam.

McPhail, D. (1978). *The magical drawings of Mooney B. Finch*. New York: Doubleday.

Minarik, E. (1968). *A kiss for Little Bear*. New York: Harper & Row.

Mori, K. (1993). *Shizuko's daughter*. New York: Henry Holt.

Munsch, R. (1992). *Purple, green and yellow*. Toronto: Annick.

O'Kelley, M. L. (1983). *From the hills of Georgia: An autobiography in paintings*. Boston: Atlantic Monthly.

O'Neal, Z. (1980). *Language of goldfish*. New York: Viking.

O'Neal, Z. (1985). *In summer light*. New York: Viking Kestrel.

Parr, L. (1991). *A man and his hat*. New York: Philomel.

Paterson, K. (1990). *The tale of Mandarin ducks*. New York: Lodestar.

Paulsen, G. (1988). *Island*. New York: Franklin Watts.

Paulsen, G. (1991). *Monument*. New York: Delacorte.

Peet, B. (1989). *Bill Peet: An autobiography*. Boston: Houghton Mifflin.

Picard, B. L. (1966). *One is one*. New York: Henry Holt.

Pilkey, D. (1990). *'Twas the night before Thanksgiving*. Orchard.

Pinkwater, D. (1993). *The big orange splot*. New York: Scholastic.

Polacco, P. (1988). *The keeping quilt*. New York: Simon & Schuster.

Polacco, P. (1997). *In Enzo's splendid gardens*. New York: Philomel.

Reiner, A. (1990). *A visit to the art galaxy*. New York: Green Tiger.

Rockwell, A. (1993). *Mr. Panda's painting*. New York: Macmillan.

Rodari, F. (1991). *A weekend with Picasso*. New York: Rizzoli.

Rylant, C. (1982). *When I was young in the mountains*. New York: Dutton.

Sanford, J. (1991). *Slappy Hooper: The world's greatest sign painter*. New York: Warner.

Schick, E. (1987). *Art lessons*. New York: Greenwillow.

Small, D. (1987). *Paper John*. New York: Farrar, Straus & Giroux.

Spier, P. (1978). *Oh, were they ever happy!* New York: Doubleday.

Spilka, A. (1964). *Paint all kinds of pictures*. New York: Hill & Wang.

Sutcliff, R. (1978). *Sun Horse, Moon Horse*. New York: Dutton.

Tallarico, T. (1984). *I can draw animals*. New York: Simon & Schuster.

Testa, F. (1982). *If you take a paintbrush: A book of colors*. New York: Dial.

Trevino, E. (1965). *I, Juan de Pareja*. New York: Farrar, Straus & Giroux.

Tuyet, T. (1987). *The little weaver of Thai-Yen village*. Emeryville, CA: Children's Book Press.

Wadell, M., & Langley, J. (1988). *Alice the artist*. New York: Dutton.

Watson, W. (1994). *The fox went out on a chilly night*. New York: Lothrop, Lee & Shepard.

Wilhelm, J. (1988). *Oh, what a mess*. New York: Random House.

Williams, V. B. (1986). *Cherries and cherry pits*. New York: Greenwillow.

Xiong, B. (1989). *Nine-in-one, Grr, Grr*. Emeryville, CA: Children's Book Press.

Art History and Appreciation

Alcron, J. (1991). *Rembrandt's beret*. New York: Tambourine.

Bearden, R., & Henderson, H. (1972). *Six black masters of American art*. Osceda, WI: Zenith.

Behrens, J. (1977). *Looking at the beasties*. Chicago: Children's Press.

Behrens, J. (1982). *Looking at children*. Chicago: Children's Press.

Blanquet, C. (1994). *Miro: Earth and sky. Art for children*. New York: Chelsea House.

Blizzard, G. (1992). *Come look with me: Exploring landscape art with children*. Charlottesville, VA: Thomasson-Grant.

Bohn-Ducher, M., & Cook, J. (1991). *Understanding modern art*. London: Osborn House.

Bolton, L. (1970). *The history and techniques of the great Masters: Gaugin*. Edison, NJ: Booksales.

Bonafoux, P. (1987). *Van Gogh: The passionate eye*. New York: Abrams.

Bonafoux, P. (1991). *A weekend with Rembrandt*. New York: Rizzoli International.

Boutan, M. (1995). *Van Gogh: Art activity pack* and *Monet*. San Francisco: Chronicle.

Brown, L. K., & Brown, M. (1986). *Visiting the art museum*. New York: Dutton.

Burdett, L. (1995). *A child's portrait of Shakespeare*. Buffalo, NY: Blackmoss.

Cachin, F. (1991). *Gaughin: The quest for paradise*. New York: Abrams.

Ceserani, G. P., & Ventura, P. (1983). *Grand constructions*. New York: Putnam.

Chapman, L. *Discover Art, Vol. 1–6*. Worchester, MA: Davis.

Chase, A. E. (1966). *Looking at art*. New York: Crowell.

Collins, D. R. (1989). *The country artist: A story about Beatrix Potter*. Minneapolis: Carolrhoda.

Collins, P. L. (1972). *I am an artist*. Brookefield, CT: Millbrook.

Conner, P. (1982a). *Looking at art: People at home*. New York: Atheneum.

Conner, P. (1982b). *Looking at art: People at work*. New York: Atheneum.

Contempre, Y. (1978). *A Sunday afternoon on the Island of Jatte*. Paris: Dululot.

Craft, R. (1975). *Brueghel's the fair*. New York: Lippincott.

Crespi, F. (1995). *A walk in Monet's garden*. Boston: Little, Brown.

Cummings, P. (1992). *Talking with artists*. New York: Bradbury.

Cummings, R. (1982). *Just imagine: Ideas in painting*. New York: Scribner.

Cummings, R. (1979). *Just look: A book about paintings*. New York: Scribner.

Davidson, M. B. (1984). *A history of art*. New York: Random House.

Deem. G. *Art school: An homage to the masters.* San Francisco: Chronicle.

Dobrin, A. (1975). *I am a stranger on earth: The story of Vincent Van Gogh.* New York: Warne.

Drucker, M. (1991). *Frida Kahlo: Torment and triumph in her life and art.* New York: Bantam.

Elderfield, J. (1978). *The cut-outs of Henry Matisse.* New York: Brogiller.

Epstein, V. S. (1978). *History of women artists for children.* Denver, CO: VSE.

Galli, L. (1996). *Mona Lisa: The secret of the smile.* New York: Bantam Doubleday Dell.

Gardner, J. M. (1993). *Henry Moore: From bones and stones to sketches and sculptures.* New York: Four Winds.

Gates, F. (1982). *North American Indian masks: Craft and legend.* New York: Walker.

Gherman, B. (1986). *Georgia O'Keefe.* New York: Atheneum.

Glubok, S., & Nook, G. (1972). *The art of the New American.* New York: Macmillan.

Greenberg, J., & Jordan, R. (1991). *The painter's eye: Learning to look at contemporary American Art;* (1993) *The sculptor's eye: Looking at contemporary American art.* New York: Delacorte.

Greenfield, H. (1991). *Marc Chagall.* New York: Abrams.

Harrison, P. (1995). *Claude Monet.* New York: Sterling.

Hart, T. (1993). *Michelangelo.* Hauppuage, NY: Barron's Educational Series.

Highwater, J. (1978). *Many smokes, many moons: A chronology of American Indian history through Indian art.* New York: Lippincott.

Holmes, B. (1979). *Enchanted worlds: Pictures to grow up with.* New York: Universal.

Isaacson, P. M. (1993). *A short walk around the pyramids and through the world of art.* New York: Knopf.

Janson, H. W., & Janson, A. F. (1992). *History of art for young people.* New York: Abrams.

Kennet, F., & Measham, T. (1979). *Looking at paintings.* New York: Van Nostrand Reinhold.

Kinghorn, H., Badman, J., & Lewis-Spicer, L. (1998). *Let's meet famous artists.* Minneapolis, MN: Denison.

Klein, M., & Klein, N. (1972). *Kalbe Kollwitz: Life in art.* New York: Holt, Rinehart & Winston.

Krull, K. (1995). *Lives of the artists: Masterpieces, messes, and what the neighbors thought.* San Diego: Harcourt Brace.

Lepscky, A. (1984). *Pablo Picasso.* Woodbury, NY: Barron's.

LeTord, B. (1995). *A blue butterfly: A story about Claude Monet.* New York: Bantam Doubleday Dell.

Luchner, L., & Kaye, G. (1971). *A child's story of Vincent van Gogh.* Morristown, NJ: Silver Burdett.

McLanathan, R. (1991). *Leonardo da Vinci.* New York: Abrams.

Messinger, L. M. (1988). *Georgia O'Keefe.* New York: Thomas & Hudson.

Messinger, L. M. (1991). *For our children.* Burbank, CA: Disney Press (to benefit Pediatric AIDS Foundation).

Meyer, S. (1990). *Mary Cassatt.* New York: Abrams.

Milande, V. (1995). *Michelangelo and his times.* New York: Henry Holt.

Mondays, G. (1975). *Norman Rockwell's Americana ABC.* New York: Dell.

Muhlberger, R. (1993). *What makes a Monet a Monet?* New York: Viking.

Munthe, N., & Kee, R. (1983). *Meet Matisse.* Boston: Little, Brown.

Nelson, M. (1972). *Maria Martinez.* New York: Dodd Mead.

Newlands, A., & National Gallery of Canada Staff (1989). *Meet Edgar Degas.* New York: Harper.

O'Neal, Z. (1986). *Grandma Moses: Painter of rural America.* New York: Viking Kestrel.

Peppin, A. (1980). *The Usborne story of painting.* Tulsa, OK: EDC.

Peter, A. (1974). *Paul Gaugin.* (Art for Children). New York: Doubleday.

Pluckrose, H. (1987). *Crayons.* New York: Franklin Watts.

Price, C. (1977). *Arts of clay.* New York: Scribner.

Priess, B. (1981). *The art of Leo and Diane Dillion.* New York: Ballantine.

Proddow, P. (1979). *Art tells a story: Greek and Roman myths.* New York: Doubleday.

Provenson, A., & Provenson, M. (1984). *Leonardo da Vinci: The artist, inventor, scientist in three-dimensional, movable pictures.* New York: Viking.

Raboff, E. (1982a). *Marc Chagall.* Garden City, NY: Doubleday.

Raboff, E. (1982b). *Pablo Picasso.* Garden City, NY: Doubleday.

Raboff, E. (1982c). *Paul Klee.* Garden City, NY: Doubleday.

Raboff, E. (1987 and 1988). Art for Children Series: *da Vinci; Rembrandt; Renoir; Matisse; Michelangelo; Raphael; Velasquez; van Gogh.* New York: Lippincott.

Richardson, J. (1993). *Inside the museum: A children's guide to the Metropolitan Museum of Art.* New York: Metropolitan Museum of Art, Abrams.

Richmond, R. (1992). *Children in art.* Nashville, TN: Ideals Children's Books.

Rockwell, A. (1971). *Paintbrush and peace pipe: The story of George Catlin.* New York: Atheneum.

Rodari, F. (1991). *A weekend with Picasso.* New York: Rizzoli International.

Schwartz, L. (1992). *Rembrandt.* New York: Abrams.

Sills, L. (1989). *Inspirations: Stories about women artists*. Nills, IL: Whitman.

Skira-Venturi, R. (1990). *A weekend with Renoir; A weekend with Degas*. New York: Rizzoli.

Strand, M. (1986). *Rembrandt takes a walk*. New York: Clarkson.

Sturgis, A. (1994). *Introducing Rembrandt*. Boston: Little, Brown.

Sullivan, C. (Ed.) (1989). *Imaginary gardens: American poetry and art for young people*. New York: Abrams.

Swain, S. (1988). *Great housewives of art*. New York: Penguin.

Tobias, T. (1974). *Isamu Noguchi: The life of a sculptor*. New York: Crowell.

Turner, R. (1991). *Georgia O'Keefe*. Boston: Little, Brown.

Venezia, M. (1988–1991). Getting to Know the World's Great Artists Series: *Picasso; Rembrandt; van Gogh; da Vinci; Mary Cassatt; Edward Hopper; Monet; Botticelli; Goya; Paul Klee; Michelangelo*. Chicago: Children's Press.

Ventura, P. (1984). *Great painters*. New York: Putnam.

Ventura, P. (1989). *Michelangelo's world*. New York: Putnam.

Waldron, A. (1991). *Claude Monet*. New York: Abrams.

Walker, L. (1994). *Roy Lichenstein: The artist at work*. New York: Dutton Lodestar.

Walters, A. (1989). *The spirit of Native America: Beauty and mysticism in American Indian art*. San Francisco: Chronicle.

Waterfield, G. (1982). *Looking at art: Faces*. New York: Atheneum.

Winter, J. (1991). *Diego*. New York: Knopf.

Woolf, F. (1993). *Picture this century: An introduction to twentieth-century art*. New York: Doubleday.

Woolf, H. (1989). *Picture this: A first introduction to paintings*. New York: Doubleday.

Yenawine, P., & Museum of Modern Art (1991). Series on Modern Art: *Colors; Lines; Shapes; Stories*. New York: Delacorte.

Zhensun, A., & Low, A. (1991). *A young painter: The life and paintings of Wang Yani, China's extraordinary artist*. New York: Scholastic.

Photography

Allen, M., & Rotner, S. (1991). *Changes*. New York: Macmillan.

Arnold, C. (1991). *Snake*. New York: Morrow.

Barrett, N. (1988). *Pandas*. New York: Watts.

Bauer, J. (1995). *Thwonk!* New York: Dutton.

Behrens, J. (1986). *Fiesta*. San Francisco: Children's Book Press.

Brenner, B. (1973). *Bodies*. New York: Dutton.

Brown, T. (1986). *Hello, Amigos*. New York: Henry Holt.

Brown, T. (1987). *Chinese New Year*. New York: Henry Holt.

Burton, J. (1991). *See how they grow series: Kitten; Puppy*. New York: Lodestar.

Cobb, V. (1990). *Natural wonders*. New York: Lothrop.

Cornish, S. (1974). *Grandmother's pictures*. Freeport, ME: Bookstore Press.

Cousteau Society Series. (1992). *Dolphins; Penguins; Seals; Turtles*. New York: Simon & Schuster.

Doubilet, A. (1991). *Under the sea from A to Z*. New York: Crown.

Eye Openers Series. (1991). *Baby animals; Jungle animals; Pets; Zoo Animals*. New York: Aladdin.

Feeney, S. (1980). *A is for aloha*. Honolulu: University Press of Hawaii.

Feeney, S. (1985). *Hawaii is a rainbow*. Honolulu: University Press of Hawaii.

Goldsmith, D. (1992). *Hoang Auk: A Vietnamese-American boy*. New York: Holiday House.

Hewett, J. (1990). *Hector lives in the United States now: The story of a Mexican-American child*. New York: Lippincott.

Hirschi, R. (1990a). *Spring*. New York: Dutton.

Hirschi, R. (1990b). *Winter*. New York: Dutton.

Hirschi, R. (1991). *Fall*. New York: Dutton.

Hoban, T. (1985a). *A children's zoo*. New York: Greenwillow.

Hoban, T. (1985b). *Is it larger? Is it smaller?* New York: Greenwillow.

Hoban, T. (1990). *Exactly the opposite*. New York: Greenwillow.

Johnson, N. (2001). *National Geographic photography guide for kids*. Washington, DC: National Geographic Society.

Kuklin, S. (1991). *How my family lives in America*. New York: Bradbury.

Lehrman, F. (1990). *Loving the earth: A sacred landscape book for children*. Berkeley, CA: Celestial.

Le Tord, B. (1999). *A bird or two: A story about Henri Matisse*. Grand Rapids, MI: Eerdmans.

Marshall, J. P. (1989). *My camera at the zoo*. Boston: Little, Brown.

Meltzer, M. (1986). *Dorothea Lange: Life through the camera*. New York: Puffin.

Miller, M. (1991). *Whose shoe?* New York: Greenwillow.

Morris, A. (1989a). *Bread, bread, bread*. New York: Lothrop, Lee & Shepard.

Morris, A. (1989b). *Hats, hats, hats*. New York; Lothrop, Lee & Shepard.

Morris, A. (1990). *Loving*. New York: Lothrop, Lee & Shepard.

Oliver, S. (1990). *My first look at seasons*. New York: Random House.

Rauzon, M. (1992). *Jungles*. New York: Doubleday.

Ricklin, N. (1988). *Grandpa and me*. New York: Simon & Schuster.

Robbins, K. (1991). *Bridges*. New York: Dial.

Schlein, M. (1990a). *Elephants*. New York: Aladdin.

Schlein, M. (1990b). *Gorillas*. New York: Aladdin.

Stanley, D. (2000). *Michelangelo*. New York: HarperCollins.

Steichen, E. (1985). *The family of man*. New York: Museum of Modern Art.

Waters, K., & Slorenz-Low, M. (1990). *Lion dancer: Earnie Wan's Chinese New Year*. New York: Scholastic.

Wilkes, A. (1991). *My first green book*. New York: Knopf.

Winter, J. (1998). *My name is Georgia: A portrait*. New York: Harcourt.

DRAMA

Doing Drama (includes pantomime and verbal activities)

Aardema, V. (1975). *Why mosquitoes buzz in people's ears*. New York: Dial.

Adoff, A. (1981). *Outside/inside poems*. New York: Lothrop, Lee & Shepard.

Ahlberg, J., & Ahlberg, A. (1986). *The jolly postman's or other people's letters*. Boston: Little, Brown.

Alexander, L. (1992). *The fortune tellers*. New York: Dutton.

Alexander, S. (1980). *Whatever happened to Uncle Albert?: And other puzzling plays*. New York: Houghton Mifflin/Clarion.

Bailey Babb, K. (1990). *Beginning readers theatre: Presentation masks and scripts for young readers*. Denver, CO: Skipping Stone.

Barchers, S. (1993). *Reader's theatre for beginning readers*. Englewood, CO: Teacher Ideas.

Bayer, J. (1984). *My name is Alice*. New York: Dial.

Bemelmens, L. (1939). *Madeline*. New York: Viking Penguin.

Bennett, J. (collected) (1987). *Noisy poems*. New York: Oxford University Press.

Berger, B. (1984). *Grandfather Twilight*. New York: Philomel.

Blos, J. (1984). *Martin's hats*. New York: Morrow.

Bodecker, N. M. (1974). *"Let's marry," said the cherry*. New York: Atheneum.

Boiko, C. (1981). *Children's plays for creative actors: A collection of royalty-free plays for boys and girls*. Boston: Plays.

Boiko, C. (1985). *Children's plays for creative actors: A collection of royalty free plays for boys and girls*. Boston: Plays.

Bradley, A. (1977). *Paddington on stage*. Boston: Houghton Mifflin.

Cameron, P. (1961). *"I can't," said the ant*. New York: Coward-McCann.

Caras, R. (1977). *Coyote for a day*. New York: Windmill.

Carle, E. (1969). *The very hungry caterpillar*. New York: Philomel/Putnam.

Carlson, B. W. (1973). *Let's pretend it happened to you*. Nashville: Abingdon.

Carlson, B. W. (1982). *Let's find the big idea*. Nashville: Abingdon.

Carroll, L. (1989). *Jabberwocky*. New York: Abrams.

Caruso, S., & Kosoff, S. (1998). *The young actor's book of improvisation: Dramatic situations from Shakespeare to Spielberg, Vol. 1,* Portsmouth, NH: Heinemann.

Cauley, L. B. (retold) (1979). *The ugly duckling*. New York: Harcourt Brace Jovanovich.

Chaconas, D. (1970). *The way the tiger walked*. New York: Simon & Schuster.

Charlip, R. (1980). *Fortunately*. New York: Four Winds.

Chess, V. (1979). *Alfred's alphabet walk*. New York: Greenwillow.

Cole, J. (1987). *The magic schoolbus inside the earth*. New York: Scholastic.

Collins, M. (1976). *Flying to the moon and other strange places*. New York: Farrar, Straus & Giroux.

Corbett, S. (1984). *Jokes to tell your worst enemy*. New York: Dutton.

Cunningham, J. (1970). *Burnish me bright*. New York: Pantheon.

Day, A. (1985). *Good gog, Carl*. New York: Green Tiger.

de Paola, T. (1979). *Charlie needs a cloak*. Upper Saddle River, NJ: Prentice Hall.

Dunn, S. (1990). *Crackers and crumbs. Chants for whole language*. Portsmouth, NH: Heinemann.

Eastman, P. D. (1960). *Are you my mother?* New York: Random House.

Emberley, B. (1967). *Drummer Hoff*. Upper Saddle River, NJ: Prentice Hall.

England, A. W. (1990). *Theatre for the young (Modern Dramatists)*. New York: St. Martin's.

Fraser, P. (1982). *Puppets and puppetry: A complete guide to puppetmaking for all ages*. New York: Stein & Day.

Friedman, L. (2001). *Break a leg!: The kid's guide to acting and stagecraft*. New York: Workman.

Gag, W. (1928). *Millions of cats*. New York: Coward-McCann.

Galdone, P. (1968). *The Bremen town musicians*. New York: McGraw-Hill.

Georges, C., & Cornett, C. (1986). *Reader's theatre*. Aurora, NY: Developers of Knowledge.

Gerke, P. (1996a). *Multicultural plays for children: Grades K–3 (Young Actors Series), Vol. 1*. Lyme, NH: Smith & Kraus.

Gerke, P. (1996b). *Multicultural plays for children: Grades 4–6 (Young Actors Series), Vol. 2*. Lyme, NH: Smith & Kraus.

Gerstein, M. (1984). *Roll over!* New York: Crown.

Gibbons, G. (1985). *Lights! Camera! Action! How a movie is made*. New York: Crowell.

Goffstein, M. (1987). *An actor*. New York: Harper & Row.

Grimm, J., & Grimm, W. *Rumpelstiltskin*. (Several editions)

Guarino, D. (1991). *Is your mama a llama?* New York: Scholastic.

Hackbarth, J. (1994). *Plays, players, and playing: How to start your own children's theater company*. Colorado Springs, CO: Piccadilly.

Haley, G. (1970). *A story—A story*. New York: Atheneum.

Haskins, J. (1982). *Black theater in America*. New York: Crowell.

Heide, F. P. (1971). *The shrinking of treehorn*. New York: Holiday House.

Hutchins, P. (1976). *Don't forget the bacon*. New York: Greenwillow.

Jennings, C. (1988). *Plays children love: A treasury of contemporary & classic plays for children, Vol. 2*. New York: St. Martin's.

Jennings, C. A., & Harris, A. (1981). *Plays children love: A treasury of contemporary and classic plays for children*. Garden City, NY: Doubleday.

Jennings, C. A., & Harris, A. (Eds.) (1988). *Plays children love, Vol. 2*. New York: St. Martin's.

Johnson, C. (1955). *Harold and the purple crayon*. New York: Harper & Row.

Juster, N. (1989). *A surfeit of smiles*. New York: Morrow.

Kahl, V. (1955). *The duchess bakes a cake*. New York: Scribners.

Kamerman, S. (1988). *The big book of Christmas plays: 21 modern and traditional one-act plays for the celebration of Christmas*. Boston: Plays.

Kamerman, S. (1989). *The big book of comedies: 25 one-act plays, skits, curtain raisers, and adaptations for young people*. Boston: Plays.

Kamerman, S. (1991). *The big book of folktale plays: One-act adaptations of folktales from around the world, for stage and puppet performance*. Boston: Plays.

Kamerman, S. (1994). *The big book of large-cast plays: 27 one-act plays for young actors*. Boston: Plays.

Kamerman, S. (1996). *Big book of skits: 36 short plays for young actors*. Boston: Plays.

Kase-Polisini, J. (1989). *Drama as a meaning maker*. Lanham, MD: University Press of America.

Keats, E. J. (1964). *Whistle for Willie*. New York: Viking.

Keller, C. (1985). *Astronauts: Space jokes and riddles*. New York: Simon & Schuster.

Kellogg, S. (1971). *Can I keep him?* New York: Dial.

Kline, S. (1993). *Who's Orp's girlfriend?* New York: Putnam.

Knight L. M. (1990). *Readers theatre for children: Scripts and script development*. Englewood, CO: Teachers Idea.

Kohl, M. (1999). *Making make-believe: Fun props, costumes and creative play ideas*. Beltsville, MD: Gryphon House.

Kuskin, K. (1982). *The philharmonic gets dressed*. New York: Harper & Row.

Laughlin, M. K., & Latrobe, K. H. (1990). *Reader's theatre for children*. Englewood, CO: Teacher Ideas.

Malkin, M. (1979). *Training the young actor: An idea book (for students from seven to fourteen)*. South Brunswick, Australia: Barnes.

Martin, J. (1997). *Out of the bag: The paper bag players book of plays*. New York: Hyperion.

McDermott, B. (1976). *The Golem: A Jewish legend*. Philadelphia: Lippincott.

McGovern, A. (1967). *Too much noise*. Boston: Houghton Mifflin.

McGowan, D. (1997). *Math play!* Charlotte, VT: Williamson.

McNulty, F. (1979). *How to dig a hole to the other side of the world*. New York: Harper & Row.

Miller, H. (1971). *1st plays for children*. Boston: Plays.

Munsch, R. (1980). *The paper bag princess*. Toronto: Annick.

Murray, B. (1995). *Puppet and theater activities: Theatrical things to do and make*. Honesdale, PA: Boyds Mills Press; distributed by St. Martin's.

Numeroff, L. J. (1985). *If you give a mouse a cookie*. New York: Harper & Row.

Parish, P. (1963). *Amelia Bedelia*. New York: Harper & Row.

Pollock, J. (1997). *Side by side: Twelve multicultural puppet plays (School Library Media, No. 13)*. Lanham, MD: Scarecrow.

Rey, H. A. (1941). *Curious George*. Boston: Houghton Mifflin.

Rosenfeld, S. (1970). *A drop of water*. Irvington-on-Hudson, NY: Harvey House.

Ross, L. (1975). *Mask-making with pantomime and stories from American history*. New York: Lothrop, Lee & Shepard.

San Souci, R. (1989). *The talking eggs*. New York: Dial.

Scieszka, J. (1989). *The true story of the 3 little pigs by A. Wolf.* New York: Viking.

Scull, M. (1990). *The skit book: 101 skits for kids.* Hamden, CN: Linnet.

Sendak, M. (1963). *Where the wild things are.* New York: Harper & Row.

Seuss, Dr. (1940). *Horton hatches the egg.* New York: Random House.

Seuss, Dr. (1961). *The Sneetches.* New York: Random House.

Sharmat, A. (1989). *Smedge.* New York: Macmillan.

Shaw, E. (1971). *Octopus.* New York: Harper & Row.

Small, D. (1985). *Imogene's antlers.* New York: Crown.

Smith, M. (1996). *The Seattle Children's Theatre: Seven plays for young actors (Young Actors Series).* Lyme, NH: Smith & Kraus.

Stanley, D., & Venneman, P. (1992). *Bard of Avalon: The story of Shakespeare.* New York: Morrow.

Steptoe, J. (1987). *Mufaro's beautiful daughters.* New York: Lothrop, Lee & Shepard.

Stevens, C. (1999). *Magnificent monologues for kids.* South Pasadena, CA: Sandcastle.

Stevenson, J. (1977). *"Could be worse!"* New York: Morrow.

Stone, R. (1975). *Because a little bug went ka-CHOO!* New York: Random House.

Straub, C. (1984). *Mime for basic beginners.* Boston: Plays.

Swortzell, L. (1997). *Theatre for young audiences: Around the world in 21 plays.* New York: Applause.

Thaler, M. (1974). *Magic letter riddles.* New York: Scholastic.

Thayer, E. L. (1988). *Casey at the bat.* Boston: Godine.

Tolstoy, A. (1968). *The great big enormous turnip.* New York: Franklin Watts.

Tresslet, A. (1964). *The mitten.* New York: Lothrop, Lee & Shepard.

Tripp, V. (1994a). *Addy's theater kit: A play about Addy for you and your friends to perform.* Middletown, WI: Pleasant.

Tripp, V. (1994b). *Felicity's theater kit: A play about Felicity for you and your friends to perform.* Middletown, WI: Pleasant.

Tripp, V. (1994c). *Kirsten's theater kit: A play about Kirsten for you and your friends to perform.* Middletown, WI: Pleasant.

Tripp, V. (1994d). *Molly's theater kit: A play about Molly for you and your friends to perform.* Middleton, WI: Pleasant.

Tripp, V. (1994e). *Samantha's theater kit: A play about Samantha for you and your friends to perform.* Middleton, WI: Pleasant.

Turkle, B. (1976). *Deep in the forest.* New York: Dutton.

Ungerer, T. (1986). *Crictor.* New York: Harper & Row.

Van Allsburg, C. (1984). *The mysteries of Harris Burdick.* Boston: Houghton Mifflin.

Van Allsburg, C. (1986). *The stranger.* Boston: Houghton Mifflin.

Viorst, J. (1972). *Alexander and the terrible, horrible, no good, very bad day.* New York: Atheneum.

Walsh-Bellville, C. (1986). *Theater magic: Behind the scenes at a children's theater.* Minneapolis: Carolrhoda.

Westcott, N. B. (1988). *The lady with the alligator purse.* Boston: Little, Brown.

White, M. (1993). *Mel White's Readers Theatre anthology: Twenty-eight all-occasion readings for storytellers.* Colorado Springs, CO: Meriwether.

White, W. (1986). *Stories for telling: A treasury for Christian storytellers.* Minneapolis: Augsburg.

White, W. (1997). *Speaking in stories: Resources for Christian storytellers.* Minneapolis: Augsburg.

Wiesner, D. (1991). *Tuesday.* New York: Clarion.

Winter, P. (1976). *The bear and the fly.* New York: Crown.

Winther, B. (1992). *Plays from African tales.* Boston: Plays.

Wolf, A. (1993). *It's show time!: Poetry from the page to the stage.* Asheville, NC: Poetry Alive!

Wood, A. (1985). *King Bidgood's in the bathtub.* New York: Harcourt Brace Jovanovich.

Young, E. (1989). *Lon Po Po: A Red-Riding Hood story from China.* New York: Philomel.

Zemach, M. (1976). *It could always be worse.* New York: Farrar, Straus & Giroux.

Drama as Part of the Book's Theme

Berenstain, S., & Berenstain, J. (1986). *The Berenstain bears get stage fright.* New York: Random House.

Booth, C. (1992). *Going live.* New York: Scribner.

Boyd, C. (1994). *Fall secrets.* New York: Puffin Books.

Brandenberg, F. (1977). *Nice new neighbors.* New York: Scholastic.

Brown, M. (1983). *Arthur's April fool.* New York: Little, Brown.

Byars, B. (1992). *Hooray for the Golly sisters!* New York: Harper Children's Books.

Cohen, M. (1985). *Starring first grade.* New York: Greenwillow.

Coville, B. (1987). *Ghost in the third row.* New York: Bantam.

dePaola, T. (1978). *The Christmas pageant.* Houston, TX: Winston.

dePaola, T. (1979). *Flicks.* New York: Harcourt Brace Jovanovich.

dePaola, T. (1983). *Sing, Pierrot, sing: A picture book in mime*. New York: Harcourt Brace Jovanovich.

de Regniers, B. (1982). *Picture book theatre: The mysterious stranger and the magic spell*. San Francisco: (Seabury Press) Harper & Row.

Freeman, D. (1970). *Hattie: The backstage bat*. New York: Viking.

Fujikawa, G. (1981). *The magic show*. New York: Grosset & Dunlap.

Gerrard, R. (1992). *Jocasta Carr: Movie star*. New York: Farrar, Straus & Giroux.

Giff, P. (1984). *The almost awful play*. New York: Viking.

Giff, P. (1992). *Show time at the Polk St. school*. New York: Delacorte.

Greydanus, R. (1981). *Hocus pocus, magic show!* Mahwah, NJ: Troll.

Grimm, J., & LeCain, E. (illus). (1978). *The twelve dancing princesses*. New York: Viking.

Holabird, K. (1984). *Angelina and the princess*. New York: C. N. Potter.

Howard, E. (1991). *Aunt Flossie's hats (and crab cakes later)*. Boston: Houghton Mifflin.

Kroll, S. (1986). *The big bunny and the magic show*. New York: Holiday House.

Kroll, S. (1988). *Looking for Daniela: A romantic adventure*. New York: Holiday House.

Leedy, L. (1988). *The bunny play*. New York: Holiday House.

Lepscky, I. (1989). *William Shakespeare*. New York: Barron's Educational Series.

Marshall, E. (1981). *Three by the sea*. New York: Dial.

Marshall, J. (1993). *Fox on stage*. New York: Dial.

Martin, A. M. (1984). *Stage fright*. New York: Holiday House.

McCully, E. A. (1992). *Mirette on the high wire*. New York: Putnam.

Morley, J. (1994). *Entertainment: Screen, stage, and stars*. New York: Franklin Watts.

Robinson, B. (1972). *The best Christmas pageant ever*. New York: Harper & Row.

Sendak, M. (1960). *The sign on Rosie's door*. New York: Harper & Row.

Thee, C. (1994). *Behind the curtain*. New York: Workman.

Tryon, L. (1992). *Albert's play*. New York: Atheneum.

DANCE

Doing Dance

Barlin, A. (1993). *Goodnight toes!: Bedtime stories, lullabies, and movement games*. Pennington, NJ: Princeton Book.

Bennett, J. (1995). *Rhythmic activities and dance*. Champaign, IL: Human Kinetics.

Brady, M. (1997). *Dancing hearts: Creative arts with books kids love*. Golden, CO: Falcrum.

Esbensen, B. (1995). *Dance with me*. New York: HarperCollins.

Krementz, J. (1976). *A very young dancer*. New York: Dell.

LaPrise, L. (1996). *The hokey pokey*. New York: Simon & Schuster.

Southgate, M. (1996). *Another way to dance*. New York: Delacorte.

Walton, R. (2001). *How can you dance?* Penguin Putnam Books for Young Readers.

Weiwsan, J. (1993). *Kids in motion: A creative movement and song book*. Milwaukee, WI: Hal Leonard.

Dance in a Book's Theme

Ackerman, K., & Gammell, S. (1988). *Song and dance man*. New York: Knopf.

Asch, F. (1993). *Moondance*. New York: Scholastic.

Auch, M. (1993). *Peeping beauty*. New York: Holiday House.

Baylor, B. (1973). *Sometimes I dance mountains*. New York: Scribner.

Berenstain, S., & Berenstain, J. (1993). *The Berenstain bears gotta dance!* New York: Random House.

Binford, D. (1989). *Rabbits can't dance!* Milwaukee, WI: Gareth Stevens.

Bornstein, R. (1978). *The dancing man*. New York: Seabury.

Carter, A. (1989). *The twelve dancing princesses*. New York: Lippincott.

Daly, N. (1992). *Papa Lucky's shadow*. New York: Margaret K. McElderry Books.

Edwards, R. (1994). *Moles can dance*. Cambridge, MA: Candlewick.

Elliot, D. (1979). *Frogs and the ballet*. Ipswich, MA: Gambit.

Esbensen, B. J. (1995). *Dance with me* (poems). New York: HarperCollins.

Freeman, D. (1996). *A rainbow of my own*. New York: Viking.

French, V. (1991). *One ballerina two*. New York: Lothrop.

Gauch, P. (1989a). *Bravo, Tanya*. New York: Putnam.

Gauch, P. (1989b). *Dance, Tanya*. New York: Philomel.

Getz, A. (1980). *Humphrey the dancing pig*. New York: Dial.

Giannini, E. (1993). *Zorina ballerina*. New York: Simon & Schuster.

Gray, L. M. (1995). *My Mama had a dancing heart*. New York: Orchard.

Greene, C. (1983). *Hi, clouds.* Chicago: Children's Press.

Hoff, S. (1994). *Duncan the dancing duck.* New York: Dial.

Holabird, K. (1992). *Angelina dances.* New York: Random House.

Hollinshead, M. (1994). *Nine days wonder.* New York: Philomel.

Hurd, E. (1965). *The day the sun danced.* New York: Harper & Row.

Hurd, E. (1982). *I dance in my red pajamas.* New York: Harper & Row.

Isadora, R. (1980). *My ballet class.* New York: Greenwillow.

Keats, E. J. (1962). *The snowy day.* New York: Viking.

Komaiko, L. (1992). *Aunt Elaine does the dance from Spain.* New York: Doubleday.

Kuklin, S. (1989). *Going to my ballet class.* New York: Macmillan.

Landry, A. (1964). *Come dance with me.* New York: Heineman.

Lasky, K. (1994). *The solo.* New York: Macmillan.

Lionni, L. (1963). *Swimmy.* New York: Pantheon.

Lowery, L. (1995). *Jitter with bug.* Boston: Houghton Mifflin.

Marshall, J. (1990). *The cut-ups carry on.* New York: Viking.

Martin, B. (1970). *The wizard.* New York: Holt, Rinehart & Winston.

Mathers, P. (1991). *Sophie and Lou.* New York: Harper-Collins.

Mayer, M. (1971). *The queen always wanted to dance.* New York: Simon & Schuster.

McCully, E. A. (1990). *The evil spell.* New York: Harper & Row.

McPhail, D. (1985). *The dream child.* New York: Dutton.

Medearis, A. S. (1991). *Dancing with the Indians.* New York: Holiday House.

Mott, E. C. (1996). *Dancing rainbows: A pueblo boy's story.* New York: Cobblehill Books/Dutton.

Myers, W. (1972). *The dancers.* New York: Parents Magazine Press.

Noll, S. (1993). *Jiggle, wiggle, prance.* New York: Puffin.

Oxenbury, H. (1983). *The dancing class.* New York: Dial.

Patrick, D. L. (1993). *Red dancing shoes.* New York: Tambourine.

Richardson, J. (1987). *Clara's dancing feet.* New York: Putnam.

Rockwell, A. (1971). *The dancing stars: An Iroquois legend.* New York: Crowell.

Scheffrin-Falk, G. (1991). *Another celebrated dancing bear.* Scribners.

Schroeder, A. (1989). *Ragtime turnpie.* Boston: Little, Brown.

Schumaker, W. (1996). *Dance!* Niles, IL: Harcourt Brace Jovanovich.

Sendak, M. (1962). *Alligators all around.* New York: Harper & Row.

Sendak, M. (1963). *Where the wild things are.* New York: Harper & Row.

Shannon, G. (1982a). *Dance sway.* New York: Greenwillow.

Shannon, G. (1982b). *Dancing the breeze.* New York: Greenwillow.

Simon, C. (1989). *Amy, the dancing bear.* New York: Doubleday.

Skofield, J. (1984). *Nightdances.* New York: Harper & Row.

Spinelli, E. (1993). *Boy, can he dance!* New York: Four Winds.

Wallace, I. (1984). *Chin Chang and the Dragon's Dance.* New York: Atheneum.

Waters, K., & Slovenz-Low, M. (1990). *Lion dancer: Earnie Wan's Chinese New Year.* New York: Scholastic.

Wood, A. (1986). *Three sisters.* New York: Dial.

Zion, G., & Graham, M. (1951). *All falling down.* New York: Harper & Row.

Dance History and Appreciation

Alice in wonderland in dance (videorecording) (1993). New York: V.I.E.W. Video.

Anderson, H. C. (1991). *The red shoes.* New York: Simon & Schuster.

Bailey, D. (1991). *Dancing.* Milwaukee: Raintree.

Barboza, S. (1992). *I feel like dancing: A year with Jacques D'Amboise and the National Dance Institute.* New York: Crown.

Bottner, B. (1979). *Myra.* New York: Macmillan.

Cinderella: A dance fantasy. (1993). New York: V.I.E.W. Video.

Dood, C., & Soar, S. (1988). *Ballet in motion: A three-dimensional guide to ballet for young people.* New York: Lippincott.

Edom, H., & Katrak, N. (1998). *Starting ballet.* Willington, DE: Usborne.

Fonteyn, M. (1989). *Swan Lake.* San Diego: Gulliver.

Glassman, B. (2001). *Mikhail Baryshnikov: Dance genius.* Farmongton Hills, MI: Gale Group

Glover, S., & Weber, B. (2000). *Savion!: My life in tap.* New York: Morrow.

Gray, L. (1999). *My mama had a dancing heart.* New York: Scholastic.

Gross, R. B. (1980). *If you were a ballet dancer.* New York: Dial.

Haskins, J. (1990). *Black dance in America: A history through its people*. New York: Crowell.

Hoffman, E. T. (1984). *The Nutcracker*. New York: Crown.

Isadora, R. (1991). *Swan Lake*. New York: Putnam.

Klein, N. (1983). *Baryshnikov's Nutcracker*. New York: Putnam.

Malcolm, J. (2000). *Drat! we're rats!* Sydney, Australia: Starcatcher.

Pavlova, A., Edgar Degas (Illustrator) (2001). *I dreamed I was a ballerina*. New York: Atheneum.

Schick, E. (1992). *I have another language, the language is dance*. New York: Macmillan.

Sorine, S. R. (1981). *Our ballet class*. New York: Knopf.

Staples, S. (2001). *Shiva's fire*. Glenview, IL: HarperCollins.

Verdy, V. (1991). *Of swans, sugarplums, and satin slippers: Ballet stories for children*. New York: Scholastic.

Wells, R. (1999). *Tallchief: America's prima ballerina/Maria Tallchief*. New York: Viking Penguin.

Werner, V. (1992). *Petrouchka*. New York: Viking.

MUSIC

Making Music

Adams, P. (1975). *This old man*. New York: Grossett & Dunlap.

Aliki (1974). *Go tell Aunt Rhody*. New York: Macmillan.

Aliki (1968). *Hush, little baby*. Upper Saddle River, NJ: Prentice-Hall.

Axelrod, A. (1991). *Songs of the Wild West*. Metropolitan Museum of Art. New York: Simon & Schuster.

Bangs, E. (1976). *Yankee Doodle*. New York: Parents Magazine Press.

Bantok, N. (1990). *There was an old lady*. New York: Viking Penguin.

Barbareski, N. (1985). *Frog went a-courting*. New York: Scholastic.

Bierhorst, J. (1979). *A cry from the earth: Music of the North American Indians*. New York: Atheneum.

Bolam, K., & Bolam, J. (arr.). (1992). *Folksongs from Eastern Europe*. London: Faber Music.

Bolam, K., & Gritton, P. (arr.). (1993). *Folksongs from the Caribbean*. London: Faber Music.

Brett, J. (1990). *The twelve days of Christmas*. New York: Putnam.

Bryan, A. (1991). *All night, all day: A child's first book of African-American spirituals*. New York: Atheneum.

Bunting, J. (1980). *My first recorder and book*. New York: Barron's.

Campbell, P., Brabson, E., & Tucker, C. (1994). *Roots and branches* (with CD). Danbury, CT: World Music.

Child, L. (1987). *Over the river and through the woods*. New York: Scholastic.

Cole, J., & Calmenson, S. (1991). *The eentsy, weentsy spider: Fingerplays and action rhymes*. New York: Mulberry.

Cooney, B., & Griego, M. C. (1981). *Tortillitas para Mama and other nursery rhymes*. New York: Henry Holt.

Coonover, C. (1976). *Six little ducks*. New York: Crowell.

Corp, R. (arr.). (1991). *Folksongs from the British Isles*. London: Faber Music.

Corp, R. (arr.). (1992). *Folksongs from North America*. London: Faber Music.

Corp, R. (arr.). (1993). *Folksongs from Ireland*. London: Faber Music.

Cracre, L. (1989). *Arroz con leche: Popular songs and rhymes from Latin America*. New York: Scholastic.

Currie, S. (1992). *Music in the Civil War*. Cincinnati: Betterway.

de Regniers, B. (1970). *Catch a little fox*. New York: Seabury.

Disney Press. (1991). *For our children*. Burbank, CA: Author.

Emberly, B. (1969). *London Bridge is falling down*. Upper Saddle River, NJ: Prentice Hall.

Emberly, B. (1969). *One wide river to cross*. Upper Saddle River, NJ: Prentice Hall.

Emberly, B. (1969). *Simon's song*. Upper Saddle River, NJ: Prentice Hall.

Fiarotta, N. (1993). *Music crafts for kids: The how-to book of music discovery*. New York: Sterling.

Floyd, M. (arr.). (1991). *Folksongs from Africa*. London: Faber Music.

Garson, E. (compiler). (1968). *The Laura Ingalls Wilder songbook*. New York: Harper & Row.

Gauch, P. (1978). *On to Widecombe Fair*. New York: Putnam.

Gill, M., & Pliska, G. (1993). *Praise for the singing: Songs for children*. Boston: Little, Brown.

Girl Scouts of U.S.A. (1980). *Canciones de nuestra cabana: Songs of our cabana*. New York: Author.

Glass, P. (1969). *Singing soldiers: A history of the Civil War in song*. New York: Grosset & Dunlap.

Glazer, T. (1980). *Do your ears hang low? Fifty more musical fingerplays*. New York: Doubleday.

Glazer, T. (1982). *On top of spaghetti*. New York: Doubleday.

Glazer, T. (1988). *Tom Glazer's treasury of songs for children*. New York: Doubleday.

Glazer, T. (1990). *The Mother Goose songbook*. New York: Doubleday.

Griego, F. M. (1980). *Tortillas para Mama*. New York: Holt, Rinehart & Winston.

Gritton, P. (arr.) (1991). *Folksongs from the Far East.* London: Faber Music.

Gritton, P. (arr.) (1993). *Folksongs from India.* London: Faber Music.

Hart, A. (1993). *Kids make music! Clapping & tapping from Bach to rock.* Charlotte, VT: Williamson.

Hazen, B. (1973). *Frere Jacques.* Philadelphia: Lippincott.

Hoban, T. (1973). *Over, under, through and other spatial concepts.* New York: Macmillan.

Houston, J. (1972). *Song of the dream people: Chants and images of the Indians and Eskimos of North America.* New York: Atheneum.

Jeffers, S. (1974). *All the pretty horses.* New York: Scholastic.

Keats, E. J. (1972). *Over in the meadow.* New York: Scholastic.

Kellogg, S. (1976). *Yankee Doodle.* New York: Parents' Magazine Press.

Kennedy, J. (1983). *Teddy Bear's picnic.* San Marcos, CA: Green Tiger.

Kent, J. (1973). *Jack Kent's twelve days of Christmas.* New York: Parents' Magazine Press.

Kidd, R., & Anderson, L. (1992). *On top of Old Smokey: Collection of songs and stories from Appalachia.* Nashville, TN: Ideals Children's Books.

Knight, H. (1981). *The twelve days of Christmas.* New York: Macmillan.

Koontz, R. (1988). *This old man: The counting song.* New York: Putnam.

Kovalski, M. (1987). *The wheels on the bus.* Boston: Little, Brown.

Krull, K. (1989). *Songs of praise.* San Diego: Harcourt Brace Jovanovich.

Langstaff, J. (1974). *Oh, a hunting we will go.* New York: Atheneum.

Leedy, L. (1988). *The bunny play.* New York: Holiday House.

Livingston, M. (1986a). *Earth songs.* New York: Holiday House.

Livingston, M. (1986b). *Sea songs.* New York: Holiday House.

Magers, P. (1987). *Sing with me animal songs.* New York: Random House.

McNally, D. (1991). *In a cabin in a wood.* New York: Cobblehill Dutton.

National Gallery of Art (1991). *An illustrated treasury of songs: Traditional American songs, ballads, folk songs, nursery rhymes.* New York: Rizzoli International.

Oram, H., Davis, C., & Kitamura, S. (1993). *A creepy-crawly song book.* New York: Farrar, Straus & Giroux.

Parker, R. (1978). *Sweet Betsy from Pike: A song from the Gold Rush.* New York: Viking.

Paterson, A. B. (1972). *Waltzing Matilda.* New York: Holt, Rinehart & Winston.

Peek, M. (1981). *Roll over! A counting song.* Boston: Houghton Mifflin.

Peek, M. (1987). *The balancing act: A counting song.* New York: Clarion.

Peek, M. (1988). *Mary wore her red dress and Henry wore his green sneakers.* Boston: Houghton Mifflin.

Poddany, E. (1967). *The cat in the hat songbook: 19 Seuss-songs for beginners.* New York: Random House.

Quackenbush, T. C. (1973). *She'll be coming 'round the mountain.* New York: Dial.

Quakenbush, T. C. (1975). *The man on the flying trapeze.* Philadelphia: Lippincott.

Rae, M. M. (1989). *The farmer in the dell.* New York: Scholastic.

Raffi (1987). *Down by the bay.* New York: Crown.

Raffi (1989). *The Raffi everything grows songbook.* New York: Crown.

Rounds, G. (1989). *Old MacDonald had a farm.* New York: Holiday House.

Seeger, P. (1989). *Abiyoyo.* New York: Scholastic.

Silberg, J. (1989). *My toes are starting to wiggle! and other easy songs for circle time.* Overland Park, KS: Miss Jackie Music.

Spier, P. (1961). *The fox went out on a chilly night.* New York: Doubleday.

Spier, P. (1967). *London Bridge is falling down.* New York: Doubleday.

Stanley, L. (Ed.) (1992). *Rap, the lyrics: The words to rap's greatest hits.* New York: Penguin.

Toop, D. (1991). *Rap attack 2: African rap to global hip hop.* London: Serpent's Tail.

Walter, C. (1995). *Multicultural music: Lyrics to familiar melodies and authentic songs.* Minneapolis: Denison.

Walther, T. (1981). *Make mine music.* Boston: Little, Brown.

Warren, J. (1991). *Piggyback songs for school.* Everett, WA: Warren.

Wessells, K. (1982). *The golden songbook.* New York: Golden.

Westcott, N. (1980). *I know an old lady who swallowed a fly.* Boston: Little, Brown.

Westcott, N. (1989). *Skip to my Lou.* Boston: Little, Brown.

Williams, V. (1988). *Music, music for everyone.* New York: Morrow.

Winter, J. (1988). *Follow the drinking gourd.* New York: Knopf.

Wirth, M. (comp.) (1983). *Musical games, finger plays, and rhythmic activities for early childhood.* West Nyack, NY: Parker.

Wiserman, A. (1979). *Making musical things*. New York: Scribner.

Yokum, J. (1986). *The lullaby songbook*. San Diego: Harcourt Brace Jovanovich.

Yolen, J. (1989). *The lap-time song and play book*. San Diego: Harcourt Brace Jovanovich.

Yolen, J. (1992). *Jane Yolen's Mother Goose songbook*. Honesdale, PA: Caroline House/Boyds Mills.

Making Instruments

Doney, M. (1995). *Musical instruments*. New York: Franklin Watts.

Elliott, D. (1984). *Alligators and music*. Boston: Harvard Common.

Fiarotta, N. (1995). *Music crafts for kids: The how-to book of music discovery*. New York: Sterling.

Hawkinson, J. (1969). *Music and instruments for children to make, Vol. 1*. Chicago: Whitman.

Hopkin, B. (1995). *Making simple musical instruments*. Asheville, NC: Lark.

Palmer, H. (1990). *Homemade band: Songs to sing: Instruments to make*. New York: Crown.

Wilt, J. (1978). *Listen!: 76 listening experiences for children, including 60 rhythm and musical instruments to make and use*. Waco, TX: Creative Resources.

Music as Part of Book's Theme

Alexander, L. (1970). *The marvelous misadventures of Sebastian*. New York: Dutton.

Ambrus, V. (1969). *Seven skinny goats*. San Diego: Harcourt Brace Jovanovich.

Angell, J. (1982). *Buffalo nickel blues band*. New York: Bradbury.

Baer, G. (1989). *Thump, thump, rat-a-tat-tat*. New York: Harper & Row.

Bang, M. (1985). *The paper crane*. New York: Greenwillow.

Baylor, B., & Himler, R. (1982). *Moon song*. New York: Scribner.

Birdseye, T., & Bammell, S. (1988). *Airmail to the moon*. New York: Holiday House.

Blake, Q. (1991). *All join in*. Boston: Little, Brown.

Bodecker, N. M. (1981). *The lost string quartet*. New York: Atheneum.

Bottner, B. (1987). *Zoo song*. New York: Scholastic.

Boynton, S. (1979). *Hester in the wild*. New York: Harper & Row.

Brandt, K. (1993). *Pearl Bailey with a song in her heart*. Mahwah, NJ: Troll.

Brett, J. (1991). *Berlioz the bear*. New York: Putnam.

Brooks, B. (1986). *Midnight hour encores*. New York: Harper & Row.

Buffett, J., & Buffett, S. J. (1988). *The jolly man*. New York: Harcourt Brace Jovanovich.

Bunting, B., & Zemach, K. (1983). *The travelling men of Ballycoo*. New York: Harcourt Brace Jovanovich.

Burningham, J. (1984). *Granpa*. New York: Crown.

Byars, B. (1985). *The glory girl*. New York: Puffin.

Card, O. S. (1980). *Songmaster*. New York: Dial.

Carle, E. (1996). *I see a song*. New York: Scholastic.

Carlson, N. (1983). *Loudmouth George and the cornet*. Minneapolis: Carolrhoda.

Clement, C. (1988). *The voices of the wood*. New York: Penguin.

Crews, D. (1983). *Parade;* (1982). *Carousel*. New York: Greenwillow.

de Paola, T. (1983). *Sing, Pierrot, sing*. San Diego: Harcourt Brace Jovanovich.

Duder, T. (1986). *Jellybean*. New York: Viking.

Dupasquier, P. (1985). *Dear Daddy*. New York: Bradbury.

Edwards, P. K., & Alisson, D. (1987). *Chester and Uncle Willoughby*. Boston: Little, Brown.

Fleischman, P., & Wentworth, J. (1988). *Rondo in C*. New York: Harper & Row.

Freeman, L. (1953). *Pet of the Met*. New York: Viking.

Gilson, J. (1979). *Dial Leroi Rupert, DJ*. New York: Lothrop.

Gioffre, M. (1985). *Starstruck*. New York: Scholastic/Apple.

Goffstein, M. B. (1972). *A little Schubert*. New York: Harper & Row.

Goffstein, M. (1977). *Two piano tuners*. New York: Farrar, Straus & Giroux.

Greenfield, E. (1988). *Nathaniel talking*. New York: Writers & Readers.

Grimm, J., & Grimm, W. (E. Shub & J. Domanska, trans.). (1980). *The Brementown musicians*. New York: Greenwillow.

Haas, I. (1981). *The little moon theatre*. New York: Atheneum.

Haley, G. E. (1984). *Birdsong*. New York: Crown.

Hantzig, D. (1989). *Pied Piper of Hamlin*. New York: Random House.

Hasley, D., & Gammel, S. (1983). *The old banjo*. New York: Macmillan.

Hedderwick, M. (1985). *Katie Morag and the two grandmothers*. London: Bodley Head.

Hentoff, N. (1965). *Jazz country*. New York: Harper & Row.

Hilgartner, B. (1986). *A murder for Her Majesty*. New York: Harper & Row.

Hill, D. (1978). *Ms. Glee was waiting*. New York: Atheneum.

Hoban, R. (1976). *A bargain for Frances*. New York: Harper & Row.

Hoffman, E. T., & Sendair, M. (1984). *The Nutcracker*. New York: Crown.

Hogrogian, N. (1973). *The cat who loved to sing*. Palmer, AK: Aladdin.

Hughes, S. (1983). *Alfie gives a hand*. New York: Mulberry Books.

Jeffers, S. (1974). *All the pretty horses*. New York: Macmillan.

Johnson, J. W. (1976). *God's trombones*. New York: Viking Penguin.

Johnston, T. (1988). *Pages of music*. New York: Putnam.

Keats, E. J. (1971). *Apt. 3*. New York: Macmillan.

Keller, C. (compiled) (1985). *Swine lake: Music and dance riddles*. Upper Saddle River, NJ: Prentice Hall.

Kherdian, D., & Hogrogian, N. (1990). *The cat's midsummer jamboree*. New York: Putnam.

Kidd, R. (1988). *Second fiddle: A sizzle & splat mystery*. New York: Lodestar.

Komaiko, L., & Westman, B. (1987). *I like music*. New York: Harper & Row.

Koscielniak, B. (2000). *The story of the incredible orchestra: An introduction to musical instruments and the symphony orchestra*. St. Charles, IL: Houghton Mifflin.

Krementz, J. (1991). *Very young musician*. New York: Simon & Schuster.

Kroll, S., & Lobel, A. (1988). *Looking for Daniela*. New York: Holiday House.

Lasker, D. (1979). *The boy who loved music*. New York: Viking.

Leodhas, S. N., & Hogrogian, N. (1965). *Always room for one more*. New York: Henry Holt.

Lionni, L. (1979). *Geraldine, the music mouse*. New York: Random House.

Lisle, J. T. (1986). *Sirens and spies*. New York: Bradbury.

Lobel, A. (1966). *The troll music*. New York: Harper & Row.

MacLachlan, P. (1988). *The facts and fictions of Minna Pratt*. New York: Harper & Row.

Marshall, J. (1973). *George and Martha: Encore*. Boston: Houghton Mifflin.

Martin, B., Archambaut, J., & Endicott, J. (1988). *Listen to the rain*. New York: Henry Holt.

Martin, B., Archambault, J., & Rand, T. (1986). *Barn dance*. New York: Henry Holt.

Martin, B., & Rand, T. (1988). *Up and down on the merry-go-round*. New York: Henry Holt.

Maxner, J., & Joyce, W. (1989). *Nicholas Cricket*. New York: Harper & Row.

Mayer, M. (1974). *Frog goes to dinner*. New York: Scholastic.

McCaffrey, A. (1976). *Dragonsong*. New York: Macmillan.

McCloskey, R. (1940). *Lentil*. New York: Viking Penguin.

Menotti, G., & Lemieux, M. (1986). *Amahl and the night visitors*. New York: Morrow.

Moss, L. (1995). *Zin! zin! zin! : A violin*. New York: Simon & Schuster.

Moss, L. (2001). *Our marching band*. New York: Putnam.

Moss, L. (2002). *Music is*. New York: Putnam.

Newton, S. (1983). *I will call it Georgie's blues*. New York: Viking.

Old, W. (1996). *Duke Ellington: Giant of jazz*. Hillside, NJ: Enlsow.

Paterson, K. (1985). *Come sing, Jimmy Jo*. New York: Dutton.

Paulsen, G. (1985). *Dogsong*. New York: Bradbury.

Peyton, K. M. (1971). *The Pennington Series*. New York: Crowell.

Plume, I. (1980). *The Bremen-Town musicians*. New York: Harper & Row.

Purdy, C. (1994). *Mrs. Merriwether's musical cat*. New York: Putnam.

Raschka, C. (1992). *Charlie Parker played be bop*. New York: Orchard.

Ray, M. L. (1994). *Pianna*. San Diego: Harcourt Brace Jovanovich.

Rayner, M. (1993). *Garth pig steals the show*. New York: Dutton.

Rylant, C., & Gammell, S. (1985). *The relatives came*. New York: Morrow.

Schick, E. (1977). *One summer night*. New York: Greenwillow.

Schick, E. (1984). *A piano for Julie*. New York: Greenwillow.

Schroeder, A., & Fuchs, B. (1989). *Ragtime tumpie*. Boston: Little, Brown.

Sendak, M. (1981). *Outside over there*. New York: Harper & Row.

Shannon, G. (1981). *The piney woods peddler*. New York: Morrow.

Shannon, G., Aruego, J., & Dewy, A. (1981). *Lizard's song*. New York: Greenwillow.

Sharmat, M. (1991). *Nate the great and musical note*. New York: Dell.

Showell, E. (1983). *Cecilia and the blue mountain boy*. New York: Lothrop.

Skofield, J., & Gundersheimer, D. (1981). *Night dances*. New York: Harper & Row.

Stecher, M. (1980). *Max the music maker*. New York: Lothrop.

Steig, W. (1994). *Zeke Pippin*. New York: HarperCollins.

Stevens, B. (1990). *Handel and the famous sword swallower of Halle*. New York: Philomel.

Stevermer, C. (1992). *River rats*. New York: Harcourt Brace Jovanovich.

Stock, C. (1988). *Sophie's knapsack*. New York: Lothrop.

Taylor, S. (1985). *All-of-a-kind family*. New York: Dell.

Thomas, I. (1981). *Willie blows a mean horn*. New York: Harper & Row.

Treschel, G. (1992). *The lute's tune*. New York: Doubleday.

Turkle, B. (1968). *The fiddler of High Lonesome*. New York: Viking.

van Kampen, V., & Eugen, I. C. (1989). *Orchestranimals*. New York: Scholastic.

Voight, C. (1983). *Dicey's song*. New York: Atheneum.

Walter, M. (1989). *Mariah loves rock*. New York: Macmillan.

Walter, M. P., & Tomes, M. (1980). *Ty's one-man band*. New York: Scholastic.

Wharton, T. (1991). *Hildegard sings*. New York: Farrar, Straus & Giroux.

Wildsmith, B. (1988). *Carousel*. New York: Knopf.

Williams, V. B. (1983). *Something special for me*. New York: Greenwillow.

Wood, A., Woo, A., & Wood, D. (1988). *Elbert's bad word*. New York: Harcourt Brace Jovanovich.

Yolen, J. (1983). *Commander Toad and the big black hole*. New York: Putnam.

Yorinks, A., & Egielski, S. (1988). *Brave, Minsky!* New York: Farrar, Straus & Giroux.

Zolotow, C., & Tafuri, N. (1982). *The song*. New York: Greenwillow.

Music History and Appreciation

The adventures of Peer Gynt: A puppet production (video-recording) (1995). Los Angeles: Laser Light Video.

Ammons, M. (1995). *Music A.D. 450–1995*. Greensboro, NC: Mark Twain Media, Carson-Dellosa.

Anderson, D. (1982). *The piano makers*. New York: Pantheon.

Arnold, C. (1985). *Music lessons for Alex*. New York: Clarion.

Autexier, P. (1992). *Beethoven, the composer as hero*. New York: Abrams.

Bain, G., & Leather, M. (1986). *The picture life of Bruce Springsteen*. New York: Franklin Watts.

Bayless, K., & Ramsey, M. (1990). *Music: A way of life for the young child*. New York: Merrill.

Beck, I. (1995). *Peter and the wolf*. New York: Atheneum.

Berliner, D. C. (1961). *All about the orchestra and what it plays*. New York: Random House.

Bierhorst, J. (1979). *A cry from the earth: Music of the North American Indians*. New York: Four Winds.

Brighton, C. (1990). *Mozart: Scenes from the childhood of the composer*. New York: Doubleday.

Busnar, G. (1979). *It's rock and roll*. New York: Messner.

Bye, L. D. (1985). *Students' musical dictionary*. Pacific, MO: Bayside.

Bye, L. D. (1986). *Mel Bay's student's guide to music theory: A book of music fundamentals*. Pacific, MO: Parker.

Bye, L. D. (1988). *Students' guide to the great composers: A guide to music history for students*. Pacific, MO: Bayside.

Carnival of the animals: A puppet production (videorecording) (1996). Los Angeles: Laser Light Video.

Commins, D. B. (1961). *All about the symphony orchestra and what it plays*. New York: Random House.

Deitch, K. M. (1991). *Leonard Bernstein: America's maestro*. Lowell, MA: Discovery Enterprises.

Downing, J. (1990). *Mozart tonight*. New York: Messner.

Emberely, R. (1980). *Jungle sounds*. Boston: Little, Brown.

Emberely, R. (1989). *City sounds*. Boston: Little, Brown.

Englander, R. (1983). *Opera! What's all the screaming about?* New York: Walker.

English, B. L. (1980). *You can't be timid with a trumpet*. New York: Lothrop.

Fonteyn, M. (1987). *Swan Lake*. New York: Harcourt Brace.

Fornatale, P. (1987). *The story of rock n' roll*. New York: Morrow.

Gass, I. (1970). *Mozart: Child wonder, child composer*. New York: Lothrop.

Glass, P. (1969). *Singing soldiers: A history of the Civil War in song*. New York: Grosset & Dunlap.

Greene, C. (1992). *John Philip Sousa, the marching king*. Chicago: Children's Press.

Greens, C. (1992). *Johann Sebastian Bach: Great man of music; Ludwig Van Beethoven, musical pioneer*. Chicago: Children's Press.

Haas, I. (1977). *The Maggie B*. New York: Atheneum.

Hargrove, J. *Pablo Casals*. Chicago: Children's Press.

Hart, M. (1990). *Drumming at the edge of magic: A journey into the spirit of percussion*. New York: Harper & Row.

Haskins, J. (1986). *Diana Ross: Star supreme*. New York: Puffin.

Haskins, J. (1987). *Black music in America*. New York: Crowell.

Hayes, A. (1991). *Meet the orchestra*. San Diego: Harcourt Brace Jovanovich.

Hayes, A. (1995). *Meet the marching Smithereens*. San Diego: Harcourt Brace Jovanovich.

Helprin, M., & Van Allsburg, C. (1990). *Swan lake*. Boston: Houghton Mifflin.

Hughes, L. (1982). *Jazz*. New York: Franklin Watts.

Jones, K. M. (1994). *The story of rap music*. Brookfield, CT: Millbrook.

Kendall, C. W. (1985). *More stories of composers for young musicians*. Edwardsville, IL: Toadwood.

Kendall, C. W. (1993). *Stories of women composers for young musicians*. Edwardsville, IL: Toadwood.

Lasker, D., & Lasker, J. (1979). *The boy who loved music*. New York: Viking.

Lepsky, I. (1982). *Amadeus Mozart*. New York: Baron's Educational Series.

Lillegard, D. (1987). *Woodwinds*. Chicago: Children's Press.

Mann, W. (1982). *James Galway's music in time*. Upper Saddle River, NJ: Prentice Hall.

McKissack, P. (1991). *Louis Armstrong: Jazz musician*. Hillside, NJ: Enslow.

Meyerowitz, J. (narrator) (1993). *George Balanchine's The Nutcracker*. Boston: Little, Brown.

Mitchell, B. (1987). *Raggin': A story about Scott Joplin; America, I hear you: A story about George Gershwin*. Minneapolis: Carolrhoda.

Monceaux, M. (1994). *Jazz: My music, my people*. New York: Knopf.

Monjo, F. N., & Brenner, F. (1975). *Letters to Horseface: Being the story of Wolfgang Amadeus Mozart's journey to Italy*. New York: Viking.

Mundy, S. (1980). *The Usborne story of music*. Tulsa, OK: EDC.

The Nutcracker: A puppet production (videorecording). (1995). Los Angeles: Laser Light Video.

Parker, J. (1995). *I wonder why flutes have holes and other questions about music*. New York: Kingfisher.

Peter and the wolf: A puppet production (videorecording) (1995). Los Angeles: Laser Light Video.

Pillar, M. (1992). *Join the band!* New York: HarperCollins.

Previn, A. (Ed.) (1983). *Andre Previn's guide to the orchestra*. New York: Putnam.

Price, L. (1990). *Aida: A picture book for all ages*. San Diego: Harcourt Brace Jovanovich.

Rosenberg, J. (1989). *Sing me a song: Metropolitan Opera's book of opera stories for children*. New York: Thames & Hudson.

Sabin, F. (1990). *Mozart, young music genius*. Mahwah, NJ: Troll.

Sabin, L. (1992). *Ludwig van Beethoven: Young composer*. Mahwah, NJ: Troll.

San Souci, R. (1992). *The firebird* (retold). New York: Dial.

Schaff, P. (1980). *The violin close up*. New York: Four Winds.

Schonberg, H. (1981). *The lives of the great composers*. New York: Norton.

Schulman, J. (adap.) (1991). *Story of the Nutcracker* (cassette). New York: HarperCollins.

Simon, C. (1992). *Seizi Owaza: Symphony conductor*. Chicago: Children's Press.

Simon, H. W. (1989). *100 Great operas and their stories*. New York: Doubleday.

Spier, P. (1973). *The star-spangled banner*. New York: Doubleday.

Stevens, B. (1983). *Ben Franklin's glass harmonica*. Minneapolis: Carolrhoda.

Stevens, B. (1991). *Handel and the famous sword swallower of Halle*. New York: Philomel.

Suggs, W. W., & Arno, E. (1971). *Meet the orchestra*. New York: Macmillan.

The Swan Lake story (videorecording). (1993). New York: V.I.E.W. Video.

Tames, R. (1991). *Frederick Chopin*. New York: Franklin Watts.

Terkel, S. (1975). *Giants of jazz*. New York: Crowell.

Thompson, W. (1991, 1993). *Pyotr Ilyich Tchaikovsky; Claude Debussy; Franz Schubert; Wolfgang Amadeus Mozart; Ludwig van Beethoven; Joseph Haydn*. New York: Viking.

Venezia, M. (1995). *Aaron Copland;* (1994) *George Gershwin;* (1995) *George Handel*. Chicago: Children's Press.

Ventura, P. (1989). *Great composers*. New York: Putnam.

Weil, L. (1982). *Wolferl: The first six years in the life of Wolfgang Mozart*. New York: Holiday House.

Weil, L. (1989). *The magic of music*. New York: Holiday House.

Wildlife symphony (video). (1993). Pleasantville, NY: Reader's Digest.

Wilson, R. (1991). *Mozart's story*. London: A. & C. Black.

Wolff, V. E. (1991). *The Mozart season*. New York: Henry Holt.

Zin! Zin! Zin!: A violin (video). (1996). Lincoln, NE: The Library.

Appendix B: Award-Winning Children's Literature *

THE RANDOLPH CALDECOTT MEDAL for the most distinguished picture book for children published in the United States during the preceding year. Sponsored by American Library Association.

1938 *Animals of the Bible, A Picture Book* by H. D. Fish. Illus. by D. Lathrop (P). HONORS: *Seven Simeons: A Russian Tale* (Trad., P), *Four and Twenty Blackbirds* (Trad., P).

1939 *Mei Li* by T. Handforth (Realism, P). HONORS: *The Forest Pool* (Realism, P), *Wee Gillis* (Realism, P), *Snow White and the Seven Dwarfs* (Trad., P), *Barkis* (Realism, P), *Andy and the Lion* (Fant., P).

1940 *Abraham Lincoln* by I. Aulaire & E. P. d'Aulaire (Biog., P). HONORS: *Cock-a-Doodle-Doo* (Animal Realism, P), *Madeline* (Realism, P), *The Ageless Story* (Bible, P).

1941 *They Were Strong and Good* by R. Lawson (Biog., P). HONORS: *April's Kittens* (Realism, P).

1942 *Make Way for Ducklings* by R. McCloskey (Animal Fant., P). HONORS: *An American ABC* (Alphabet, P), *In My Mother's House* (Info., P), *Paddle-to-the-Sea* (Info., P), *Nothing at All* (Animal Fant., P).

1943 *The Little House* by V. Burton (Fant., P). HONORS: *Dash and Dart* (Realism, P), *Marshmallow* (Realism, P).

1944 *Many Moons* by J. Thurber. Illus. by L. Slobodkin (Modern folktale, P). HONORS: *Small Rain: Verses from the Bible* (Bible, P), *Pierre Pigeon* (Realism, P), *The Mighty Hunter* (Fant., P), *A Child's Good Night Book* (Realism, P), *Good Luck Horse* (Trad., P).

1945 *Prayer for a Child* by R. Field. Illus. by E. Jones (Realism, P). HONORS: *Mother Goose: Seventy-Seven Verses with Pictures* (Trad., P), *In the Forest,* (Fant., P), *Yonie Wondernose* (Realism, P), *The Christmas Anna Angel* (Mod. folktale, P).

1946 *The Rooster Crows* selected and Illus. by M. and M. Petersham (Mother Goose rhymes, P). HONORS: *Little Lost Lamb* (Realism, P), *Sing Mothers Goose* (Nursery songs, P), *My Mother Is the Most Beautiful Woman in the World* (Trad., P), *You Can Write Chinese* (Info., P).

1947 *The Little Island* by G. MacDonald. Illus. by L. Weisgard (Fant., P). HONORS: *Rain Drop Splash* (Info., P), *Boats on the River* (Info., P), *Timothy Turtle* (Animal Fant., P), *Pedro, the Angel of Olvera Street* (Realism, P), *Sing in Praise: A Collection of the Best Loved Hymns* (Info., P).

1948 *White Snow, Brite Snow* by A. Tresselt. Illus. by R. Duvoisin (Realism, P). HONORS: *Stone Soup: An Old Tale* (Trad., P), *McElligot's Pool* (Fant., P), *Bambino the Clown* (Realism, P), *Roger and the Fox* (Realism, P), *Song of Robin Hood* (Trad., I–U).

1949 *The Big Snow* by B. and E. Hader (Animal realism, P). HONORS: *Blueberries for Sal* (Realism, P), *All Around the Town* (Alphabet, P), *Juanita* (Realism, P), *Fish in the Air* (Fant., P).

1950 *Song of the Swallows* by L. Politi (Realism, P). HONORS: *America's Ethan Allen* (Biog., P), *The Wild Birthday Cake* (Realism, P), *The Happy Day* (Animal Fantasy, P), *Henry—Fisherman* (Realism, P), *Bartholomew and the Oobleck* (Mod. folktale, P).

1951 *The Egg Tree* by K. Milhous (Realism, P). HONORS: *Dick Wittington and His Cat* (Trad., P), *The Two Reds* (Fant. P), *If I Ran the Zoo* (Fant., P), *T-Bone, the Baby-Sitter* (Realism, P), *The Most Wonderful Doll in the World* (Realism, P).

1952 *Finders Keepers* by Will (pseud. for W. Lipkind). Illus. by Nicolas (N. Mordvinoff) (Mod. Folktale, P). HONORS: *Mr. T. W. Anthony Woo* (Mod. Folktale, P), *Skipper's John's Cook* (Realism, P), *All Falling Down* (Info., P), *Bear Party* (Animal Fant., P), *Feather Mountain* (Mod. folktale, P).

1953 *The Biggest Bear* by L. Ward (Realism, P). HONORS: *Puss in Boots* (Trad., P), *One Morning in Maine* (Realism, P), *Ape in a Cape: An Alphabet of Odd Animals* (Alphabet, P), *The Storm Book* (Info., P), *Five Little Monkeys* (Animal Fant., P).

1954 *Madeline's Rescue* by L. Bemelmans (Realism, P). HONORS: *Journey Cake, Ho!* (Trad., P), *When Will the World Be Mine?* (Animal Fant., P), *The Steadfast Tin Soldier* (Mod. folktale, P), *A Very Special House* (Fant., P), *Green Eyes* (Animal Fant., P).

1955 *Cinderella, or the Little Glass Slipper* by C. Perrault. Trans. and Illus. by M. Brown (Trad., P). HONORS: *Book of Nursery and Mother Goose Rhymes* (Nursery rhymes, P), *Wheel on the Chimney* (Realism, P), *The Thanksgiving Story* (Hist. Fic., USA, P).

*P = primary ages 4–8; I = intermediate; I–U and U = young adult ages 13+.

1956 *Frog Went A-Courtin'*, retold by J. Langstaff. Illus. by F. Rojankovsky (Trad., P). HONORS: *Play with Me* (Realism, P), *Crow Boy* (Realism, P).

1957 *A Tree Is Nice* by J. Udry. Illus. by M. Simont (Info., P). HONORS: *Mr. Penny's Race Horse* (Animal Fant., P), *1 is One* (Counting, P), *Anatole* (Animal Fant., P), *Gillespie and the Guards* (Realism, P), *Lion* (Animal Fant., P).

1958 *Time of Wonder* by R. McCloskey (Realism, P). HONORS: *Fly High, Fly Low* (Animal Fant., P), *Anatole and the Cat* (Animal Fant., P).

1959 *Chanticleer and the Fox* by Chaucer. Adapted and Illus. by B. Cooney (Trad., P). HONORS: *The House That Jack Built* ("La Maison Que Jacques a Batie"): A Picture Book in Two Languages (Info., P), *What Do You Say, Dear? A Book of Manners for All Occasions* (Fant., P), *Umbrella* (Realism, P).

1960 *Nine Days to Christmas* by M. Ets and A. Labastida. Illus. by M. Ets (Realism, P). HONORS: *Houses from the Sea* (Info., P), *The Moon Jumpers* (Realism, P).

1961 *Baboushka and the Three Kings* by R. Robbins. Illus. by N. Sidjakov (Trad., P). HONORS: *Inch by Inch* (Animal Fant., P).

1962 *Once a Mouse*, retold by M. Brown (Trad., P). HONORS: *The Fox Went out on a Chilly Night* (Trad., P), *Little Bear's Visit* (Animal Fant., P), *The Day We Saw the Sun Come Up* (Info., P).

1963 *The Snowy Day* by E. J. Keats (Realism, P). HONORS: *The Sun Is a Golden Earring* (Mod. folktales, P–I), *Mr. Rabbit and the Lovely Present* (Animal Fant., P).

1964 *Where the Wild Things Are* by M. Sendak (Fant., P). HONORS: *Swimmy* (Animal Fant., P), *All in the Morning Early* (Trad., P), *Mother Goose and Nursery Rhymes* (Trad., P).

1965 *May I Bring a Friend?* by B. de Regiers. Illus. by B. Montresor (Fant., P). HONORS: *Rain Makes Applesauce* (Fant., P), *The Wave* (Trad., P–I), *A Pocketful of Crickets* (Realism, P).

1966 *Always Room for One More* by S. Nic Leodhas (pseud. for L. Alger). Illus. by N. Hogrogian (Trad., P). HONORS: *Hide and Seek* (Realism, P.), *Just Me* (Realism, P), *Tom Tit Tot* (Trad., P).

1967 *Sam, Bangs and Moonshine* by E. Ness (Realism, P). HONORS: *One Wide River to Cross* (Bible, P).

1968 *Drummer Hoff*, adapted by B. Emberley. Illus. by Ed Emberley (Trad., P). HONORS: *Frederick* (Animal Fant., P), *Seashore Story* (Realism, P), *The Emperor and the Kite* (Mod. folktales, P).

1969 *The Fool of the World and the Flying Ship: A Russian Tale* by A. Ransome. Illus. by U. Shulevitz (Trad., P). HONORS: *Why the Sun and the Moon Live in the Sky: An African Folktale* (Trad., P).

1970 *Sylvester and the Magic Pebble* by W. Steig (Animal Fant., P). HONORS: *Goggles* (Realism, P), *Alexander and the Wind-up Mouse* (Animal Fant., P), *Pop Corn and Ma Goodness* (Mod. folktale, P), *Thy Friend, Obadiah* (Hist. Fic., New England, 1700s, P), *The Judge: An Untrue Tale* (Mod. Folktales, P).

1971 *A Story, A Story: An African Tale* by G. Haley (Trad., P). HONORS: *The Angry Moon* (Trad., P), *Frog and Toad Are Friends* (Animal Fant., P), *In the Night Kitchen* (Fant., P).

1972 *One Fine Day* by N. Hogrogian (Traditional, P). HONORS: *If All the Seas Were One Sea* (Trad., P), *Moja Means One: Swahili Counting Book* (Counting, P), *Hildilid's Night* (Mod. Folktale, P).

1973 *The Funny Little Woman*, retold by A. Mosel. Illus. by Dutton (Trad., P). HONORS: *Hosie's Alphabet* (Alphabet, P–I), *When Clay Sings* (Info., P), *Snow-White and the Seven Dwarfs* (Trad., P), *Anansi the Spider: A Tale from the Ashanti* (Trad., P).

1974 *Duffy and the Devil*, retold by H. Zemach. Illus. by M. Zemach (Trad., P). HONORS: *Three Jovial Huntsmen* (Trad., P), *Cathedral: The Story of Its Construction* (Info., I–YA).

1975 *Arrow to the Sun*, adapted and Illus. by G. McDermott (Trad., P). HONORS: *Jambo Means Hello: Swahili Alphabet Book* (Alphabet, P).

1976 *Why Mosquitoes Buzz in People's Ears*, retold by V. Aadema. Illus. by L. and D. Dillon (Trad., P). HONORS: *The Desert Is Theirs* (Info., P), *Strega Nona* (Trad., P–I).

1977 *Ashanti to Zulu: African Traditions* by M. Musgrove. Illus. by L. and D. Dillon (Info., P–I). HONORS: *The Amazing Bone* (Fant., P), *The Contest* (Trad., P), *Fish for Supper* (Realism, P), *The Golem: A Jewish Legend* (Trad., P–I), *Hawk, I'm Your Brother* (Realism, P–I).

1978 *Noah's Ark* by P. Spier (Bible/Wordless, P). HONORS: *Castle* (Info., ages 8–YA), *It Could Always Be Worse* (Trad., P).

1979 *The Girl Who Loved Wild Horses* by P. Goble (Trad., P). HONORS: *Freight Train* (Info. Concept, P), *The Way to Start a Day* (Info., P–I).

1980 *Ox-Cart Man* by D. Hall. Illus. by B. Cooney (Hist. Fic., New England, 1800s, P–I). HONORS: *Ben's Trumpet* (Realism, P), *The Treasure* (Trad., P), *The Garden of Abdul Gasazi* (Fant., P).

1981 *Fables* by A. Lobel (Animal Fant., P). HONORS: *The Bremen-Town Musicians* (Trad., P), *The Grey Lady and the Strawberry Snatcher* (Fant./Wordless, P), *Mice Twice* (Animal Fant., P), *Truck* (Concept, P).

1982 *Jumanji* by C. VanAllsburg (Fant., P). HONORS: *A Visit to William Blake's Inn: Poems for Innocent and Experienced Travelers* (Biog./Poetry, I), *Where* *the Buffaloes Begin* (Trad., ages P), *On Market Street* (Alphabet, P), *Outside Over There* (Fant., I).

1983 *Shadow* by B. Cendrars. Trans. and Illus. by M. Brown (Trad., I). HONORS: *When I Was Young in the Mountains* (Realism, P–I), *A Chair for My Mother* (Realism, P).

1984 *The Glorious Flight: Across the Channel with Louis Bleriot* by A. and M. Provensen (Hist. Fic., France, 1909, P–I). HONORS: *Ten, Nine Eight* (Counting, P), *Little Red Riding Hood* (Trad., ages P–I).

1985 *Saint George and the Dragon,* adapted by M. Hodges. Illus. by T. S. Hyman (Trad., P–I). HONORS: *Hansel and Gretel* (Trad., P), *The Story of Jumping Mouse* (Trad., P–I), *Have You Seen My Duckling?* (Animal Fant., P).

1986 *The Polar Express* by C. Van Allsburg (Fant., P–I). HONORS: *The Relatives Came* (Realism, P–I), *King Bidgood's in the Bathtub* (Fant., P–I).

1987 *Hey, Al* by A. Yorinks. Illus. by R. Egielski (Fant., P–I). HONORS: *The Village of Round and Square Houses* (Trad., P–I), *Alphabatics* (Alphabet, P), *Rumpelstiltskin* (Trad., P–I).

1988 *Owl Moon* by J. Yolen. Illus. by J. Schoenherr (Realism, P). HONORS: *Mufaro's Beautiful Daughters* (Trad., P–I).

1989 *Song and Dance Man* by K. Ackerman. Illus. by S. Gammell (Realism, P–I). HONORS: *Free Fall* (Fant./Wordless, P–I), *Goldilocks and the Three Bears* (Mod. Folktale, P), *Mirandy and Brother Wind* (Trad., P–I), *The Boy of the Three-Year Nap* (Trad., P–I).

1990 *Lon Po Po: A Red Riding Hood Story from China.* Trans. and Illus. by E. Young (Trad., P). HONORS: *Hershel and the Hannukkah Goblins* (Mod. Folktale, P–I), *The Talking Eggs* (Trad., P–I), *Bill Peet: An AutoBiog* (Biog., P–I), *Color Zoo* (Concept, P).

1991 *Black and White* by D. Macaulay (Mystery, P–I). HONORS: *Puss 'n Boots* (Trad., P), *"More, More, More" Said the Baby: 3 Love Stories* (Realism, P).

1992 *Tuesday* by D. Wiesner (Fant./Wordless, P–I). HONORS: *Tar Beach* (Multicultural, African American, P–I).

1993 *Mirette on the High Wire* by E. McCully (Realism, P–I). HONORS: *Seven Blind Mice* (Mod. Folktale, P–I), *The Stinky Cheese Man and Other Fairly Stupid Tales* (Mod. Folktale, P–I), *Working Cotton* (Realism, African American, P–I).

1994 *Grandfather's Journey* by A. Say (Biog., P–I). HONORS: *Peppe the Lamplighter* (Realism, P–I), *In the Small, Small Pond* (Pattern, P), *Owen* (Animal Fant., P), *Raven: A Trickster Tale from the Pacific Northwest* (Trad. Native American, P), *Yo! Yes?* (Realism/Multicultural, P–I).

1995 *Smoky Night* by E. Bunting. Illus. by D. Diaz (Realism/ Multicultural, P). HONORS: *Swamp Angel* (Mod. Folktale, P–I), *John Henry* (Trad., P–I), *Time Flies* (Wordless, P–I).

1996 *Officer Buckle and Gloria* by P. Rathmann (Contemp. Fic., P). HONORS: *Alphabet City* (Concept [alphabet], P), *Zin! Zin! Zin!: A Violin* (Info. [Music instruments], P–I), *The Faithful Friend* (Fant., P–I), *Tops & Bottoms* (Fant., P).

1997 *Golem* by D. Wisniewski (Legend, P–I). HONORS: *Hush!: A Thai Lullaby* (Contemp. Fic., P), *The Graphic Alphabet.* (Concept [alphabet], P), *The Paperboy,* (High Fant., P), *Starry Messenger* (Biog. [Galileo], P–I).

1998 *Rapunzel* by P. O. Zelinsky (Folktale, P). HONORS: *Harlem: A Poem* (Poetry, I–U), *The Gardener* (Hist. Fic. [Depression], P), *There Was an Old Lady Who Swallowed a Fly* (High Fant., P).

1999 *Snowflake Bentley* by J. Martin (Biog., P–I), HONORS: *Duke Ellington* (Biog., P–I), *No, David!* (Fic., P), *Tibet: Through the Red Box* (Fic., P–I), *Snow* (Fic., P).

2000 *Joseph Had a Little Overcoat* by S. Taback (Folktale, P), HONORS: *A Child's Calendar* (Poetry, P), *Sector 7* (Wordless Fant., P.), *When Sophie Gets Angry— Really, Really Angry* (Fic., P).

2001 *So, You Want to Be President* by J. St. George (Nonfic., P–I). HONORS: *Casey at the Bat* (Ballad, P–I), *Cliic-Clack-Moo* (Fant., P), *Olivia* (Fant., P.).

2002 *The Three Pigs* by D. Weisner (Folktale-Fant., P), HONORS: *The Dinosaurs of Waterhouse Hawkins* (Biog., P–I), *Martin's Big Words: The Life of Martin Luther King, Jr.* (Biog., P), *The Stray Dog* (Fic., P).

THE JOHN NEWBERY MEDAL for the most distinguished contribution to children's literature published during the preceding year. Presented by the American Library Association.

1922 *The Story of Mankind* by H. W. Van Lonn (Info., U). HONORS: *The Great Quest* (Hist. Fic., New England, 1826, U), *Cedric the Forester* (Hist. Fic., England, 1200s, U), *The Old Tobacco Shop* (Fant., U), *The Golden Fleece and the Heroes Who Lived before Achilles* (Trad. Fant., U), *Windy Hill* (Realism, I–U).

1923 *The Voyages of Doctor Doolittle* by H. Lofting (Fant., I).

1924 *The Dark Frigate* by C. Hawes (Hist. Fic., England, 1600s, I–U).

1925 *Tales from Silver Lands* by C. Finger. Illus. by Paul Honore (Trad. Fant., I–U). HONORS: *Nicholas* (Fant., Little People, I–U), *Dream Coach* (Fant., I-U).

1926 *Shen of the Sea* by A. Chrisman. Illus. by E. Hasselriis (Fant., Literary Tale, I–U). HONORS: *The Voyagers* (Trad./Info., I–U).

1927 *Smoky, the Cowhorse* by W. James (Animal Realism, I–U).

1928 *Gay-Neck, The Story of a Pigeon* by D. Mukerji. Illus. by B. Artzybasheff (Animal Realism, I–U). HONORS: *The Wonder Smith and His Son* (Trad. Fant., Ireland, I–U), *Downright Dencey* (Hist. Fic., New England, 1812, I–U).

1929 *The Trumpeter of Krakow* by E. Kelly. Illus. by A. Pruszynska (Hist. fic., Poland, 1400s, U). HONORS: *The Pigtail of Ah Lee Ben Loo* (Fant./Poetry, I–U), *Millions of Cats* (Pict. Book; Fant., P), *The Boy Who Was* (Hist. Fic., Italy through 3000 years, I–U), *Clearing Weather* (Hist. Fic., USA, 1787, U), *The Runaway Papoose* (Realism/Multicultural, I–U), *Tod of the Fens* (Hist. Fic., England, 1400s, U).

1930 *Hitty: Her First Hundred Years* by R. Field. Illus. by D. Lathrop (Hist. Fant., I–U). HONORS: *The Tangle-Coated Horse and Other Tales: Episodes from the Fionn Saga* (Trad., I–U), *Vaino: A Boy of New Finland* (Hist. Fic., Finland, 1920s, U), *Pran of Albania* (Realism, U), *The Jumping-off Place* (Realism, I–U), *A Daughter of the Seine* (Biog., U), *Little Blacknose* (Fant., I–U).

1931 *The Cat Who Went To Heaven* by E. Coatsworth. Illus. by L. Ward (Fant., I–U). HONORS: *Floating Island* (Fant., I), *The Dark Star of Itza* (Hist. Fic., Mayan Empire, U), *Queer Person* (Hist. Fic./Multicultural, Native American, I–U), *Mountains Are Free* (Hist. Fic., Switzerland, U), *Spice and the Devil's Cave* (Hist. Fic., Portugal, 1400s, U), *Meggy McIntosh* (Hist. Fic., Scotland, USA, 1775, I–U), *Garram the Hunter: A Boy of the Hill Tribes* (Realism, Africa, I–U), *Ood-Le-Uk, the Wanderer* (Realism, Alaska, U).

1932 *Waterless Mountain* by L. Armer. Illus. by S. Armer (Realism/Multicultural, Native American, I–U). HONORS: *The Fairy Circus* (Fant., P–I), *Calico Bush* (Hist. Fic., USA, 1743, I–U), *Boy of the South Seas* (Realism, I–U), *Out of the Flame* (Hist. Fic., France, 1500s, I–U), *Jane's Island* (Realism, I–U), *The Truce of the Wolf and Other Tales of Old Italy* (Trad. Fant., I–U).

1933 *Young Fu of the Upper Yangtze* by E. Lewis. Illus. by K. Wiese (Realism, U). HONORS: *Swift Rivers* (Hist. Fic., USA, 1835, U), *The Railroad to Freedom* (Biog., U), *Children of the Soil* (Realism, I–U).

1934 *Invincible Louisa: The Story of the Author of "Little Women"* by C. Meigs (Biog., I–U). HONORS: *The Forgotten Daughter* (Hist. Fic., Italy, 2nd century B.C., U), *Swords of Steel* (Hist. Fic., USA, 1859, U), *ABC Bunny* (Picture book, Fant./Alphabet, P), *Winged Girl of Knossos* (Hist. Fic., Ancient Greece, U), *New Land* (Realism, I–U), *The Apprentice of Florence* (Hist. Fic., Italy, 1400s, U), *The Big Tree of Bunlahy: Stories of My Own Countryside* (Fant., I–U), *Glory of the Seas* (Hist. Fic., USA, 1850s, U).

1935 *Dobry* by M. Shannon. Illus. by A. Katchamakoff (Realism, I–U). HONORS: *The Pageant of Chinese History* (Info., U), *Davy Crockett* (Biog., U), *A Day on Skates: The Story of a Dutch Picnic* (Realism, P).

1936 *Caddie Woodlawn* by C. Brink. Illus. by K. Seredy (Hist. Fic., USA, 1860s, I–U). HONORS: *Honk: The Moose* (Realism, I–U), *The Good Master* (Realism, I–U), *Young Walter Scott* (Biog., U), *All Sails Set* (Hist. Fic., USA, 1851, U).

1937 *Roller Skates* by R. Sawyer. Illus. by V. Angelo (Realism, I–U). HONORS: *Phoebe Fairchild: Her Book* (Hist. Fic., New England, 1830s, I–U), *Whistler's Van* (Realism, I–U), *The Golden Basket* (Realism, P–I), *Winterbound* (Realism, U), *Audubon* (Biog., U), *The Codfish Musket* (Hist. Fic., USA, 1780s, U).

1938 *The White Stag* by K. Seredy (Trad., ages 10–YA). HONORS: *Bright Island* (Realism, U), *Pecos Bill* (Trad., I–U), *On the Banks of Plum Creek* (Hist. Fic., USA, 1870s, I–U).

1939 *Thimble Summer* by E. Enright (Realism, I–U). HONORS: *Leader by Destiny: George Washington, Man and Patriot* (Biog., U), *Penn* (Biog., U), *Nino* (Realism, I–U), *"Hello, the Boat!"* (Hist. Fic., USA, 1817, I–U), *Mr. Popper's Penguins* (Animal Fant., I–U).

1940 *Daniel Boone* by J. Daughtery (Biog., I–U). HONORS: *The Singing Tree* (Hist. Fic., Eastern Europe, 1910s, I–U), *Runner of the Mountain Tops* (Biog., U), *By the Shores of Siver Lake* (Hist. Fic., USA, 1880s, I–U), *Boy with a Pack* (Hist. Fic., USA, 1837, I–U).

1941 *Call It Courage* by A. Sperry (Realism, I–U). HONORS: *Blue Willow* (Hist. Fic., USA, 1930s, I–U), *Young Mac of Fort Vancouver* (Hist. Fic., Canada, early 1800s, U), *The Long Winter* (Hist. Fic., USA, 1800s, I–U), *Nansen* (Biog., U).

1942 *The Matchlock Gun* by W. Edmonds. Illus. by P. Lantz. (Hist. Fic., Colonial America, 1757, I–U). HONORS: *Little Town on the Prairie* (Hist. Fic., USA, 1881, I–U), *George Washington's World* (Info./Biog., I–U), *Indian Captive: The Story of Mary Jemison* (Hist. Fic., USA, 1750s, I–U), *Down Ryton Water* (Hist. Fic., England, Netherlands, 1600s, U).

1943 *Adam of the Road* by E. Gray. Illus. by R. Lawson (Hist. Fic., England, 1290s, I–U). HONORS: *The Middle Moffat* (Realism, I–U), *"Have You Seen Tom Thumb?"* (Biog., U).

1944 *Johnny Tremain* by E. Forbes. Illus. by L. Ward (Hist. Fic., Boston, 1770s, U). HONORS: *These Happy Golden Years* (Hist. Fic., USA, 1880s, I–U), *Fog Magic* (Mod. Fant., I–U), *Rufus M.* (Realism, I–U), *Mountain Born* (Animal Realism, I–U).

1945 *Rabbit Hill* by R. Lawson (Animal Fant., P–I). HONORS: *The Hundred Dresses* (Realism, P–I), *The Silver Pencil* (Realism, ages 10–YA), *Abraham Lincoln's World* (Info./Biog., U), *Lone Journey: The Life of Roger Williams* (Biog., U).

1946 *Strawberry Girl* by L. Lenski (Hist. Fic., Florida, early 1900s, I–U). HONORS: *Justin Morgan Had a Horse* (Animal Realism, I–U), *The Moved-Outers* (Multicultural, I–U), *Bhisma, the Dancing Bear* (Realism, I–U), *New Found World* (Info., ages 10–YA).

1947 *Miss Hickory* by C. Bailey. Illus. by R. Gannett (Fant./Toys, P–I). HONORS: *The Wonderful Year* (Realism, I–U), *The Big Tree* (Info., I–U), *The Heavenly Tenants* (Fant., I–U), *The Avion My Uncle Flew* (Realism, U), *The Hidden Treasure of Glaston* (Hist. Fic., England, 1172, U).

1948 *The Twenty-one Balloons* by W. Pene duBois (Fant., I–U). HONORS: *Pancakes—Paris* (Realism, ages 8–11), *Li Lun, Lad of Courage* (Realism, I–U), *The Quaint and Curious Quest of Johnny Longfoot, The Shoe-King's Son* (Trad., I–U), *The Cow-Tail Switch, and Other West African Stories* (Trad., I–U), *Misty of Chincoteague* (Animal Realism, Horse, I–U).

1949 *King of the Wind* by M. Henry. Illus. by W. Dennis (Hist. Fic., Morocco, Europe, 1700s, I–U). HONORS: *Seabird* (Info., I–U), *Daughter of the Mountains* (Realism, I–U), *My Father's Dragon* (Fant., P–I), *Story of the Negro* (Info., U).

1950 *The Door in the Wall* by M. de Angeli (Hist. Fic., England, 1300s, I–U). HONORS: *Tree of Freedom* (Hist. Fic., USA, 1780s, I–U), *The Blue Cat of Castle Town* (Trad., U), *Kildee House* (Realism, I–U), *George Washington* (Biog., I–U), *Song of the Pines* (Hist. Fic., USA, 1850s, U).

1951 *Amos Fortune, Free Man* by E. Yates. Illus. by N. Unwin (Biog., I–U). HONORS: *Better Known as Johnny Appleseed* (Biog., U), *Gandhi, Fighter without a Sword* (Biog., U), *Abraham Lincoln, Friend of the People* (Biog., I–U), *The Story of Appleby Capple* (Fant., P).

1952 *Ginger Pye* by E. Estes (Realism, I–U). HONORS: *Americans before Columbus* (Info., U), *Minn of the Mississippi* (Info., P–I), *The Defender* (Realism, I–U), *The Light at Tern Rock* (Realism, P–I), *The Apple and the Arrow* (Biog., I–U).

1953 *Secret of the Andes* by A. Clark. Illus. by J. Charlot (Realism/Multicultural, Native American, I–U). HONORS: *Charlotte's Web* (Animal Fant., P–I), *Moccasin Trail* (Hist. Fic., USA, 1830s, U), *Red Sails to Capri* (Hist. Fic., Italy, 1826, I–U), *The Bears on Hemlock Mountain* (Hist. Fic., USA, 1800s P–I), *Birthdays of Freedom* (Info./Biog., U).

1954 *And Now Miguel* by J. Krumgold. Illus. by J. Charlot (Hist. Fic., New Mexico, 1940s, I–U). HON-

ORS: *All Alone* (Realism, I–U), *Shadrach* (Animal Realism, I–U), *Hurry Home, Candy* (Animal Realism, I–U), *Theodore Roosevelt, Fighting Patriot* (Biog., I–U), *Magic Maize* (Realism, I–U).

1955 *The Wheel on the School* by M. DeJong. Illus. by M. Sendak (Realism, I–U). HONORS: *The Courage of Sarah Noble* (Hist. Fic., USA, 1707, I–U), *Banner in the Sky* (Hist. Fic., Europe, 1860s, I–U).

1956 *Carry on, Mr. Bowditch* by J. Latham (Biog., U). HONORS: *The Golden Name Day* (Realism, I–U), *The Secret River* (Fant., P–I), *Men, Microscopes, and Living Things* (Info., U).

1957 *Miracles on Maple Hill* by V. Sorensen. Illus. by B. and J. Krush (Realism, I–U). HONORS: *Old Yeller* (Animal Realism, I–U), *The House of Sixty Fathers* (Hist. Fic., China, 1940s, I–U), *Mr. Justice Holmes* (Biog., I–U), *The Corn Grows Ripe* (Realism, I–U), *The Black Fox of Lorne* (Hist. Fic., Scotland, 10th Cent., I–U).

1958 *Rifles for Watie* by H. Keith. Illus. by P. Burchard (Hist. Fic., USA, 1860s, I–U). HONORS: *The Horescatcher* (Realism, U), *Gone-Away Lake* (Realism, I–U), *The Great Wheel* (Hist. Fic., USA, 1890s, I–U), *Tom Paine, Freedom's Apostle* (Biog., U).

1959 *The Witch of Blackbird Pond* by E. Speare (Hist. Fic., USA, 1860s, I–U). HONORS: *The Family under the Bridge* (Realism, I–U), *Along Came a Dog* (Animal Realism, I–U), *Chucaro: Wild Pony of the Pampa* (Animal Realism, I–U), *The Perilous Road* (Hist. Fic., USA, 1860s, I–U).

1960 *Onion John* by J. Krumgold. Illus. by S. Shimin (Realism, I–U). HONORS: *My Side of the Mountain* (Realism, U), *America Is Born* (Info., I–U), *The Gammage Cup* (Fant., Little People, I).

1961 *Island of the Blue Dolphins* by S. O'Dell (Hist. Fic., USA, 1800s, Multicultural/Native American, I–U). HONORS: *America Moves Forward* (Info., I–U), *Old Ramon* (Realism, I–U), *The Cricket in Times Square* (Animal Fant., P–I).

1962 *The Bronze Bow* by E. Speare (Hist. Fic., Jerusalem, 1st Cent. A.D., U). HONORS: *Frontier Living* (Info., I–U), *The Golden Goblet* (Hist. Fic., Ancient Egypt, I–U), *Belling the Tiger* (Fant., P–I).

1963 *A Wrinkle in Time* by M. L'Engle. (pseud. for Leclaire Alger) (Fant., I–U). HONORS: *Thistle and Thyme* (Trad. Fant., I–U), *Men of Athens* (Biog., U).

1964 *It's Like This, Cat* by E. Neville (Realism, I–U). HONORS: *Rascal* (Animal Realism, I–U), *The Loner* (Realism, I–U).

1965 *Shadow of a Bull* by M. Wojciechowska (Realism, I–U). HONORS: *Across Five Aprils* (Hist. Fic., USA, 1860s, U).

1966 *I, Juan de Pareja* by E. de Trevino (Biog., I–U). HONORS: *The Black Cauldron* (Fant., Quest, I–U), *The Animal Family* (Fant., U), *The Noonday Friends* (Realism, I–U).

1967 *Up a Road Slowly* by I. Hunt (Realism, I–U). HONORS: *The King's Fifth* (Hist. Fic., Spain, 1500s, I–U), *Zlateh the Goat and Other Stories* (Fant., I–U), *The Jazz Man* (Realism, I–U).

1968 *From the Mixed-up Files of Mrs. Basil E. Frankweiler* by E. L. Konigsburg (Realism, I–U). HONORS: *Jennifer, Hecate, Macbeth, William McKinley, and Me, Elizabeth* (Realism, I–U), *The Black Pearl* (Realism, I–U), *The Fearsome Inn* (Fant., I–U), *The Egypt Game* (Realism, I–U).

1969 *The High King* by L. Alexander (Fant., Hero-Quest, I–U). HONORS: *To Be a Slave* (Info., U), *When Shlemiel Went to Warsaw and Other Stories* (Fant., I–U).

1970 *Sounder* by W. Armstrong. (Hist. Fic., Southern USA, early 20th Cent., U). HONORS: *Our Eddie* (Realism, U), *The Many Ways of Seeing: An Introduction to the Pleasure of Art* (Info., I–U), *Journey Outside* (Fant., U).

1971 *Summer of the Swans* by B. Byars (Realism, U). HONORS: *Kneeknock Rise* (Fant., I–U), *Enchantress from the Stars* (Fant., Sci. Fic., U), *Sing Down the Moon* (Hist. Fic., USA, 1860s, U).

1972 *Mrs. Frisby and the Rats of NIHM* by R. O'Brien (Animal Fant., I–U). HONORS: *Incident at Hawk's Hill* (Hist. Fic., Canada, 1870/Animal Realism, I–U), *The Planet of Junior Brown* (Realism, U), *The Tombs of Atuan* (Fant., Quest, I–U), *Annie and the Old One* (Pict. Book; Realism/Multicultural, Native American, I–U), *The Headless Cupid* (Realism, Mystery, I–U).

1973 *Julie of the Wolves* by J. George (Realism/Multicultural, Native American, U). HONORS: *Frog and Toad Together* (Pict. Book; Animal Fant., P), *The Upstairs Room* (Hist. Fic., Holland, 1940s, I–U), *The Witches of Worm* (Realism, I–U).

1974 *The Slave Dancer* by P. Fox (Hist. Fic., USA, Africa, 1840s, U). HONORS: *The Dark Is Rising* (Fant., Quest, I–U).

1975 *M. C. Higgins, the Great* by V. Hamilton (Realism/Multicultural, African American, U). HONORS: *Figgs & Phantoms* (Realism, U), *My Brother Sam Is Dead* (Hist. Fic., Colonial America, 1700s, I–U), *The Perilous Guard* (Hist. Fic., England, 1558, U), *Philip Hall Likes Me. I Reckon Maybe* (Realism/Multicultural, African American, I–U).

1976 *The Grey King* by S. Cooper (Fant., Hero-Quest, U). HONORS: *The Hundred Penny* (Realism/Multicultural/African American, I–U), *Dragonwings*

(Hist. Fic., San Francisco, 1903–1909/Multicultural, Chinese American, U).

1977 *Roll of Thunder, Hear My Cry* by M. Taylor (Hist. Fic., Mississippi, 1934/Multicultural/African American, I–U). HONORS: *Abel's Island* (Animal Fant., I–U), *A String in the Harp* (Fant., I–U).

1978 *The Bridge to Terabithia* by K. Paterson (Realism, I–U). HONORS: *Anpao: An American Indian Odyssey* (Trad. Fan./Muticultural, Native American, I–U), *Ramona and Her Father* (Realism, P–I).

1979 *The Westing Game* by E. Raskin (Realism, Mystery, I–U). HONORS: *The Great Gilly Hopkins* (Realism, I–U).

1980 *A Gathering of Days: A New England Girl's Journal, 1830–32* by J. Blos (Hist. Fic., New England, 1830s, U). HONORS: *The Road from Home: The Story of an Armenian Girl* (Hist. Fic., Turkey, Greece, 1907–1924, U).

1981 *Jacob I Have Loved* by K. Paterson (Hist. Fic., USA, 1940s, U). HONORS: *The Fledging* (Fant., I–U), *A Ring of Endless Light* (Fant./Sci. Fic., I–U).

1982 *A Visit to William Blake's Inn: Poems for Innocent and Experienced Travelers* by N. Willard. Illus. by A. and M. Provensen (Pict. Book/Poetry, I–U). HONORS: *Ramona Quimby, Age 8* (Realism, P–I), *Hungary, 1939–1944* (Hist. Fic., U).

1983 *Dicey's Song* by C. Voigt (Realism, I–U). HONORS: *The Blue Sword* (Fant., Quest, U), *Dr. DeSoto* (Pict. Book/Animal Fant., P), *Graven Images* (Fant., I–U), *Homesick: My Own Story* (Biog., I–U), *Sweet Whispers, Brother Rush* (Fant./Multicultural, African American, U).

1984 *Dear Mr. Henshaw* by B. Cleary (Realism, I–U). HONORS: *The Sign of the Beaver* (Hist. Fic., Colonial America, I–U), *A Solitary Blue* (Realism, I–U), *Sugaring Time* (Info., I–U), *The Wish Giver* (Fant., I–U).

1985 *The Hero and the Crown* by R. McKinley (Fant., Quest, U). HONORS: *Like Jake and Me* (Pic. Book; Realism, P–I), *The Moves Make the Man* (Realism, Multicultural/African American, U), *One-Eyed Cat* (Realism, I–U).

1986 *Sarah, Plain and Tall* by P. MacLachlan (Hist. Fic., USA Western Frontier, 1800s, I–U). HONORS: *Commodore Perry in the Land of the Shogun* (Info., I–U), *Dogsong* (Realism, Multicultural/Native American, U).

1987 *The Whipping Boy* by S. Fleischman. (Hist. Fic., Medieval England, I–U). HONORS: *On My Honor* (Realism, I–U), *Volcano: The Eruption and Healing of Mount St. Helens* (Info., I–U), *A Fine White Dust* (Realism, I–U).

1988 *Lincoln: A PhotoBiog* by R. Freedman (Biog., I–U). HONORS: *After the Rain* (Realism, U), *Hatchet* (Realism, I–U).

1989 *Joyful Noise: Poems for Two Voices* by P. Fleischman (Poetry, I–U). HONORS: *In the Beginning: Creation Stories from Around the World* (Trad. Fant., I–U), *Scorpions* (Realism/Multicultural/African American, Hispanic American, U).

1990 *Number the Stars* by L. Lowry (Hist. Fic., Denmark, 1940s, I–U). HONORS: *Afternoon of the Elves* (Realism, I–U), *Shabanu, Daughter of the Wind* (Realism, U), *The Winter Room* (Realism, U).

1991 *Maniac Magee* by J. Spinelli (Realism, I–U). HONORS: *The True Confessions of Charlotte Doyle* (Hist. Fic., England, USA, 1830, I–U).

1992 *Shiloh* by P. Naylor (Animal Realism, I–U). HONORS: *Nothing but the Truth* (Realism, I–U), *The Wright Brothers: How They Invented the Airplane* (Info./Biog, I–U).

1993 *Missing May* by C. Rylant (Realism, U). HONORS: *The Dark-Thirty: Southern Tales of the Supernatural* (Mod. Fant./Ghost Stories/African American, I–U), *Somewhere in Darkness* (Realism, African American, I–U), *What Hearts* (Realism, U).

1994 *The Giver* by L. Lowry (Mod. Fant., I–U). HONORS: *Crazy Lady* (Realism, I–U), *Dragon's Gate* (Hist. Fic., China, USA West, 1860s, U), *Eleanor Roosevelt: A Life of Discovery* (Biog., I–U).

1995 *Walk Two Moons* by S. Creech (Realism, Native American, ages 11–14). HONORS: *Catherine, Called Birdy* (Hist. Fic., England, 1200s, I–U), *The Ear, the Eye, the Arm* (Mod. Fant., U).

1996 *The Midwife's Apprentice* by K. Cushman (Hist. Fic., Medieval Eng., I–U). HONORS: *What Jamie Saw* (Fic., Child Abuse, I–U), *The Watsons Go to Birmingham—1963* (Hist. Fic., African American, I–U), *Yolonda's Genius* (Contemp. Fic., I), *The Great Fire* (Info., Chicago's Fire, I–U).

1997 *The View from Saturday* by E. L. Konigsburg (Contemp. Fic, I). HONORS: *A Girl Named Disaster* (Contemp. Fic., I–U), *The Moorchild* (Fant., I), *The Thief* (Fant., P–I), *Belle Prater's Boy* (Contemp. Fic., I–U).

1998 *Out of the Dust* by K. Hesse (Contemp. Fic., I–U). HONORS: *Lily's Crossing* (Hist. Fic., I–U), *Ella Enchanted* (Fant., I–U), *Wringer* (Contemp. Fic., I–U).

1999 *Holes* by L. Sachar (Fic., I). HONORS: *A Long Way from Chicago* (Hist. Fic., I).

2000 *Bud, Not Buddy* by C. Curtis (Contemp. Fic., I–U). HONORS: *Getting Near to Baby* (Contemp. Fic., I–U), *Our Only May Amelia* (Contemp. Fic., I), *26 Fairmount Avenue* (Biog,. I).

2001 *A Year Down Yonder* by R. Peck (Hist. Fic., I). HONORS: *Because of Winn-Dixie* (Fic., I), *Hope Was Here* (Fic., I–U), *Joey Pigza Loses Control* (Contemp. Fic., U), *The Wanderer* (Fic., I–U).

2002 *A Single Shard* by L. Park (Hist. Fic., I–U). HONORS: *Everything on a Waffle* (Contemp. Fic., I–U), *Carver: A Life in Poems* (Poetry, I–U).

Appendix C: Arts Organizations, Addresses, and Internet Sites

American Alliance for Theater and Education (AATE)
c/o Arizona State University Theater Department, Box 873411, Tempe, AZ
85287

American Arts Alliance
805 15th St., N.W.
Suite 500
Washington, DC 20005
(202)289-1776; Fax: (202)371-6601
Website: www.artswire.org/~aaa/

Principal advocate for America's professional nonprofit arts organizations.

Americans for the Arts
1285 Avenue of the Americas, Floor 3, Area M, New York, NY 10022
http://www.artsusa.org/index.html

Resource and leadership development, information services, public awareness and education.

Dance USA
633 E Street NW, Washington, DC 20004
(202)628-0144

Getty Center for Education in the Arts
1875 Century Park East, No. 2300
Los Angeles, CA 90067
(213)277-9188
Website: www.artsednet.getty.edu

Dedicated to improving arts education in the nation's K–12 public schools. The Center is one of the J. Paul Getty Trust's seven divisions. The Center coordinates partnerships among arts agencies and schools and disseminates information about art education programs.

Project Zero, Harvard Graduate School of Education
321 Longfellow Hall, Appian Way
Cambridge, MA 02138
(617)495-4342
http://pzweb.harvard.edu

International Society for the Performing Arts
17 Purdy Avenue
P.O. Box 909
Rye, NY 10580 USA
(914)921-1550; Fax: (914)921-1593
Website: www.ispa-online.org/

An international network dedicated to advancing the field of the performing arts.

The Kennedy Center's Partnerships in Education
Kennedy Center for the Performing Arts
Washington, DC 20566
(202)416–8000

Coalition of statewide, nonprofit organizations working in partnership to support policies, practices, and partnerships that ensure that the arts are woven into the fiber of American education.

Website: www.artsedge.kennedy-center.org

Lincoln Center Institute
Lincoln Center for the Performing Arts, Inc.
70 Lincoln Center Plaza
New York, NY 10023-6594
(212)875-5535; Fax: (212)875-5539

Created to fulfill a commitment to esthetic education through educational partnerships with schools. *Cities:* Albany, Binghamton, Buffalo, New York City, Rochester, Syracuse, and Utica; Philadelphia; Wilmington, DE; Nashville and Memphis, TN; Bowling Green, OH; Lincoln, NE; Houston, TX; Tulsa, OK; San Diego, CA; and Melbourne, Australia.

Music Educators National Conference (MENC)
1902 Association Drive
Reston, VA 22091
(703)860-4000

National Art Education Association (NAEA)
1916 Association Drive
Reston, VA 22091
(703)860-8000

Comprised of nearly 15,000 art educators and anyone concerned about quality art education.

National Arts Education Research Center

University of Illinois at Urbana–Champaign
1114 West Nevada Street
Urbana, IL 61801
(217)333-1027

National Assembly of State Arts Agencies (NASAA)

http://www.nasaa-arts.org

Each of the 50 states has an arts agency to support excellence in and access to the arts by supporting established and emerging artists and arts organizations.

National Dance Association

1900 Association Drive
Reston, VA 22091
(703)476-3421

National Endowment for the Arts

1100 Pennsylvania Avenue NW
Washington, DC 20506
(202)682-5426

NEA's website is divided into
(1) "arts.community—a hyperlinked periodical with features and news about the arts; (2) "Guide to the National Endowment for the Arts," an overview of the grant-making programs; a hyperlinked list of state and regional arts organizations is also available; (3) "Arts Resource Center," includes a catalog of publications (some free), contact information for a broad range of national arts service organizations, and a library of on-line publications.

National Foundation for Advancement in the Arts (NFAA)

100 North Biscayne Blvd., No. 1801
Miami, FL 33132
(305)371-9470

Mission is to identify emerging artists and raise consciousness and appreciation for the arts.

New England Foundation for the Arts,

330 Congress Street, 6th Floor
Boston, MA
(617)951-0010
http://www.nefa.org/

Links the public and private sectors in a regional partnership to support the arts.

OPERA America

1156 15th Street NW, Suite 810
Washington, DC 20005
(202)293-4466
http://www.operaam.org/

Its fundamental mission is to promote opera. Provides resources on arts education leadership, professional development, plus resources of interest to administrators, performers, and educators.

Very Special Arts

Kennedy Center for the Performing Arts
Washington, DC 20566
(202)662-8899

Promotes arts education and creative expression involving children and adults with disabilities.

INTERNET WEBSITES ON THE ARTS

A. Pintura Art Detective
www.eduweb.com/pintura/index.html

The Art Geek
www.dhc.net/~artgeek

The Art Room
www.arts.ufl.edu/art/rt_room/

The Art Teachers Connection
www.inficad.com/~arted

Arts Edge: The Kennedy Center's website for lesson plans and other resources
http://artsedge.kennedy-center.org

Arts Education Means Business
http://www.winternet.com/~maae/business.html

Arts Education in Public Elementary and Secondary Schools: surveys and support
http://artsedge.kennedy-center.org/db/nea/survey.html

Arts in Education: Congressional support for the arts
http://www.ed.gov/legislation.ESEA?sec10401.html

Arts Resource Connection: Minnesota's Center for Arts Education Arts Resource Connection
http://www.mcae.k12.mn.us/art_connection/art_connection.html

Arts Wire: The New York Foundation for the Arts: Arts Wire is a national computer-based communications network for the arts community. http://www.artswire.org

ArtsEdNet: The Getty Center's extensive curriculum, lesson plans, and resources http://www.artsednet.getty.edu/

ArtsNet: arts management and cultural diversity resources http://artsnet.heinz.cmu.edu/

Association for the Advancement of Arts Education (information page) http://www.aaae.org/aboutaaae.html

Association for the Advancement of Arts Education: Connections http://www.aaae.org/

Association for the Advancement of Arts Education—Other Web Links http://www.aaae.org/othersites.html

Bell's & Blue Web'n http://www.kn.pacbell.com/wired/bluewebn/

Crayola Arts Education: share ideas, lesson plans, news on arts advocacy http://www.crayola.com

Culturefinder: The Internet Address for the Performing Arts: Provides a cultural event database, which initially contains schedule information for over 200 events, plus information about performing arts products, reviews, and news. http://culturefinder.mediapolis.com/

Daily Report Card (Interviews and Quotes) http://www.utopia.com/mailings/reportcard/

Education Survey http://www.aaae.org/caesumm-p.html

The Educational Theatre Association (ETA) teaching production http://www.etassoc.org

eWorld: Learning Museum: virtual tours of 24 world-famous art, history, and science museums. http://www.eworld.com/learning/museum.html

The Foundation Center: guides to grant and research writing. http://www.fdcenter.org

GeoCities the Tropics: vast information on museums, art styles and periods, art education and advocacy.

http://www.geocities.com/thetropics/1009/index.html

The Incredible Art Department: Student work, cartoons, lesson plans, links, news, jobs, chat rooms, awards. http://www.in.net/~kenroar/

Infusion Program http://aspin.asu.edu?~rescomp/targeted/augusta.html

KODAK Picture http://www.kodak.com/digitalImaging/pictureThis/picThisHome.shtml (Send email postcards.)

Learning in Motion's Top Ten List http://www.learn.motion.com/lim/links/linkmain

Leonard Bernstein Center for Education through the Arts

www.nashville.org/mc/leonard_bernstein.html

Minnesota Center for Arts Education: resources, links, lessons. http://www.mcae.k12.mn.us/

National Art Education Association: Links to art education sites for art educators, artists, and administrators. http://www.arts.arizona.edu/arted/12-1-arted.html

National Endowment for the Arts http://arts.endow.gov.

On Broadway: season summaries, educational resources. http://artsnet.heinz.cmu.edu:80/OnBroadway/

Schools, Communities, and the Arts: A Research Compendium http://aspin.asu.edu/~rescomp/intro.html

Storytelling, etc. http:falcon.jmu.edu/~ramseyil/drama.htm

Theatre Education Literature Review http://www.aaae.org/theatre/thfront.html

Theatre Education Literature Review Cont'd http://www.aaae.org/theatre/theatre5.html

Virtual Museums http://www.icom.org/vlmp

World Wide Arts Resources: more than 500 types of resources and links to 1,000 websites. http://www.wwar.com

World Wide Web Virtual Library http://www.icom.org

CHILDREN'S LITERATURE INTERNET SITES

ALAN: The Assembly on Literature for Adolescents
http://english.byu/Alan/alanfoun.htm

American Library Association (ALA)
http://www.ala.org/

The Canadian Children's Book Centre
Promotes Canadian books.
http://home.echo-on.net/~ccbc/

Carol Hurst's Children's Literature WebSite
http://www.carolhurst.com/

Child Study Children's Book Committee
http://www.bnkst.edu/bookcommittee/booklist.html.

Children's Authors and Illustrators and Their Books
http://www.acs.ucalgary.ca/~dkbrown/authors.htm.

Children's Book Council (CBC): Complete text of pamphlet "Choosing a Children's Book"
http://www.cbcbooks.org/text.html

The Children's Catalog, Bank Street College Library
http://www.bnkst.edu/library/cats.html

Children's Literature: Electronic Resources
http://www.ccn.cs.dal.cal~aa331/childlit.html.

Children's Literature Web Guide
http://www.ucalgary.ca/~dkbrown/

Fairrosa Cyber Library of Children's Literature
http://www.users.interport.net/~fairrosa/lists/adoption.html

Harold D. Underdown (a book editor)
http://www.users.interport.net/~hdu/newhdu.htm

International Reading Association's Reading Online (IRA)
www.readingonline.org

Internet Discussion Groups: Use net news group to discuss children's books
http://www.rec.arts.books.childrens

Kay Vandergriff's Children's Literature Home Page
www.scils.rutgers.edu/special/kay/childlit.html

LibrarySpot: gateway to websites of 2,500 libraries
http://www.libraryspot.com

The National Library of Canada: Annotated Canadian children's books in English and French. Online: *The Art of Illustration: A Celebration of Contemporary Canadian Children's Book Authors.*
http://www.nlc-bnc.ca/

OzKidz Literature: Australian literature for children
http://www.gil.com.au/ozkidz/Ozlit/ozlit.html

Society of Children's Book Writers and Illustrators
http://www.scbwi.org/

A Writer's Best Friend: Inkspot: Resources for writers with sections for young writers
http://www.inkspot.com/

Appendix D: Assessment Tools

SAMPLE 1: ARTS FOR LIFE INTEREST INVENTORY

Name _____ Nickname _____ Birthday _____ Favorite Color _____

INTEREST INVENTORY

What are your favorite
- Foods?
- Sports?
- Toys?
- TV shows?
- Movies?
- Things about school? your least favorite?
- Book?
- Favorite songs? music?

1. Do you have any pets?
2. What do you enjoy doing with your family?
3. What books have you read that you enjoyed?
4. What do you do well?
5. How do you like to spend your free time? What hobbies do you have?
6. Where have you traveled?
7. If you could be anywhere right now, where would you be?
8. Do you belong to any clubs or organizations?
9. Do you play or would you like to play a musical instrument?
10. Do you like to draw?
11. Do you like to dance? What dances do you know?
12. Have you ever been to a library? a museum?
13. Have you ever been in a play? watched a play?
14. Do you read the newspapers or magazines at home?
15. What things have you written? Any poetry?
16. What types of art do you like? photography ____ puppets ____ weaving ____ drawing ____ charcoal ____ pastels/chalk ____ pen and ink ____ painting ____ acrylics ____ watercolor ____ print making ____ woodcuts ____ sculpture ____ paper ____ collage ____ papier mâché ____ mobiles ____ diorama ____ carving ____ felt tip markers ____
17. Who do you admire? Why?
18. Do you like to pretend?
19. Do you like storytelling?
20. What makes you laugh? How do you make other people laugh?

21. Do you own any art?

22. If you could meet an artist (musician, visual artist, dancer, actor, writer), who would it be? Why? What three questions would you ask him or her?

23. If you could visit any country, which one would it be? Why?

24. Would you like to visit an art gallery ____ museum ____; go to a play ____ concert ____?

25. If you had the opportunity to create a work of art, what would you use? What would it be about?

26. What type of literature do you enjoy? picture books ____ poetry ____ fables ____ folktales ____ fairy tales ____ myths ____ legends ____ epics ____ historical fiction ____ science fiction ____ realistic fiction ____ informational ____ autobiographies ____ biographies ____

27. If you could read a biography or autobiography about an artist, which one would it be?

28. If you could write a book, what would it be about?

29. What would you like to know more about or be able to do?

SAMPLE 2: INTEGRATED ARTS LESSONS: TEACHER SELF-EVALUATION

Directions: After lessons, reflect on your teaching using these questions. These can be used in conjunction with a video tape of teaching and peer observation.

1. How satisfied were you with the overall lesson? Why?

2. To what extent did students learn important concepts and skills about BOTH an art area and another curricular area?

3. To what extent did students meet the lesson objectives? What assessment and evaluation evidence do you have for this?

4. How effective was the lesson *introduction* in providing students with focus on lesson objectives?

5. How was mood set in the lesson?

6. How interested were the students in the lesson? What evidence do you have for interest?

7. What adaptations were made for special student needs? (See Post It Page 2–6.)

8. What strategies were used that caused students to be physically and mentally active?

9. How did you show enthusiasm for the focus art form? How did students respond?

10. How did you cause students to be involved in creative and artistic ways? (questions, coaching, etc.)

11. How did the lesson feel? How comfortable were you and the students during the lesson?

12. What discipline prevention/intervention and management strategies were used and to what effect?

Comment on how each of the following 10 INTEGRATES principles guided you:

- IMMERSION in the art form
- NITTY-GRITTY concepts and skills
- TEACHING HABITS
- ENERGIZERS and warm-ups
- GREAT CHILDREN'S LITERATURE
- ROUTINES

- ◆ ADAPTED curriculum frameworks
- ◆ TRIPS
- ◆ EVIDENCE for assessment
- ◆ SPECIALISTS

SAMPLE 3: OBSERVATIONAL CHECKLIST: ARTISTIC AND CREATIVE SKILLS

Directions: Observe students during listening, viewing, and doing experiences in the arts. Rate each child using a 1–5 scale with 5 = very evident and 1 = not evident. Alternative: date when behavior is evident (3 or more)

Student Name _____

Dates   **Response Characteristics**

   1. Uses the arts to communicate ideas and feelings.
   2. Intentionally uses creative problem-solving strategies such as SCAMPER and brainstorming.
   3. Uses arts vocabulary to describe what is seen, heard, and felt.
   4. Uses a variety of arts tools, media, and techniques.
   5. Seeks alternative ways to understand and express through the arts.
   6. Takes risks to offer personal interpretations or feelings and try new things.
   7. Gives supporting evidence for opinions involving personal taste.
   8. Compares and contrasts using prior arts experiences.
   9. Builds on previous arts experiences.
  10. Notices details and patterns.
  11. Is open to and respectful of alternative perspectives.
  12. Shows interest in arts reflections and discussions.
  13. Offers both first impressions and revisions of impressions.
  14. Works collaboratively.
  15. Works independently.
  16. Is aware of special strengths in arts areas.

SAMPLE 4: DRAMA RUBRIC

Directions: Rate the degree to which each student shows evidence of the following drama skills. Level 1 = "low evidence." Level 2 = "some moderate evidence." Level 3 = "the highest level" and is described below. Assessment should be dated, e.g., by grading period. Discuss the rubric with students at the start of the school year.

Level 3

Body: Very able to coordinate and control body. Uses appropriate energy. Displays sensory awareness and expression. Uses gestures and facial expressions skillfully to communicate through pantomime and to accompany verbal work. Responds appropriately to nonverbal communication of others.

Verbal expression: Speaks clearly. Uses appropriate variety in volume, rate, tone and pitch, pause, stress, emphasis, and inflection. Is fluent and can improvise dialog.

Focus: Can concentrate and stay involved. Makes others believe in the realness of the character. Follows directions.

Imagination: Uses flexible creative thinking to solve drama problems. Contributes unique ideas and elaborates on others' ideas. Shows spontaneity.

Evaluation: Gives constructive feedback and uses suggestions of others. Can self-evaluate and adapt own behavior.

Social skills: Works cooperatively with groups: listens and responds to others.

Audience etiquette: Attend, listen, and responds appropriately to others' performances.

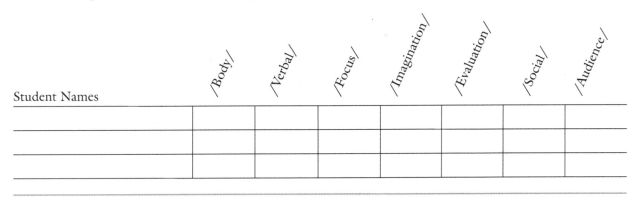

Student Names	Body	Verbal	Focus	Imagination	Evaluation	Social	Audience

SAMPLE 5: ART PROJECT EVALUATION

Directions: Art-making projects will be graded using the following criteria. Your "Reflections" paper will be used, along with your project and any drafts as documentation. Use this rubric to self-evaluate before turning in your work. The scale of 1 to 5 will be used:

1 = no evidence
2 = little evidence
3 = moderate evidence
4 = good evidence
5 = strong evidence

Criteria	Rating
Directions for assignment followed	_____
Information gathered from sources	_____
Risk taking and Experimentation (tools, techniques and media)	_____
Original (new to you) ideas incorporated	_____
Project completeness	_____
Organized reflections with examples	_____
Met deadline	_____

What did you learn most from this project?

How did you feel about your product?

What obstacles did you have to overcome during the process of creating your product?

Would you like to publicly share or display your art?

SAMPLE 6: DANCE REFLECTION

Student Name _____ Date _____

1. How did you feel about the dance making and sharing?
2. What did you contribute to the group work on dance making?
3. What was the most interesting thing about the process of creating the dance or the dance itself?
4. What problems or obstacles came up during the dance creation? How were they solved?
5. How do you take risks and experiment with the dance elements of BEST?
6. How did you encourage other students?
7. How did you show involvement and concentration? To what extent are you becoming more self-disciplined?
8. What did you learn that you can now use in other lessons or in life?
9. What would you like to change to make future dance making better?

SAMPLE 7: ANECDOTAL RECORDS: INTEGRATED DANCE LESSONS

Directions: Place a sticky note for each student on a clipboard. During dance planning in groups and during dance sharing note observations about individuals on each of their sticky notes. Place sticky notes in student folders or portfolios.

Comment on:

◆ Collaboration skills
◆ Risk-taking and experimentation
◆ Positive attitude
◆ Use of various body parts and moves
◆ Use of energy
◆ Use of space
◆ Use of time
◆ Concentration
◆ Dance form: beginning–middle–end
◆ Creativity (ideas used in new ways)

SAMPLE 8: MUSIC SELF-EVALUATION

Student Name _____ Date _____

1. How have you learned to use music to express your ideas and feelings in other subjects?
2. What have you learned about making music that has helped you?
3. What have you learned about listening to music?
4. What music concepts and skills do you now have that you didn't have before?
5. What were your favorite music integrated lessons or projects? Why?
6. What would you like to learn more about in music?
7. How comfortable are you when we sing together in class?
8. What would you like to share with the class that is related to the idea of music as a way to learn in school and in real life?

SAMPLE 9: LITERATURE CHECKLIST

Student Name _____

Concept or Skill   **Date Observed**

1. Chooses to read in free time.
2. Has favorite authors.
3. Has favorite genre.
4. Uses literary elements to discuss and evaluate books.
5. Uses books and authors as "models" for own writing.
6. Uses art elements to comment on illustrations.
7. Connects personal experiences to books.
8. Shares feelings about books.
9. Shares insights from books.
10. Responds to books through a variety of art forms.
11. Prepares for book discussions.
12. Leads book discussion.
    - Has discussion starters.
    - Listens actively.
    - Encourages others.
    - Has discussion ender.

Appendix E: Discipline Prevention and Intervention Strategies

DISCIPLINE PREVENTION

- Create an inviting environment. Think of the classroom as a *living* room. Bring in rugs, art, plants, and music.

- Really be the teacher you would want for yourself. Model expectations for attitude, courtesy, respect, and enthusiasm for learning. Listen to students using "active listening" techniques.

- Enjoy the kids and let them know it. Tell them they are the best! Laugh with students and share their humor. No sarcasm. Start with a riddle, cartoon, or poem related to the lesson. Write down specific positive behaviors on Post-its and give them to students to keep in a "Positive Post-its" folder. Put names on the board for positive contributions to class.

- A *few* rules or consequences are necessary. Post them. Start out firm and allow students to "earn" more and more freedom. *Examples:* **I Care** rules and **Fighting Fair** rules. (Focus on respect and courtesy. Be a model!) Involve students in making rules: role play, "Show me how you'll look when you are really listening" and "In groups of three, show me a scene of showing respect."

- Teach with variety. Change methods. Integrate the arts!

- Explain the real-life connections between school and school work.

- Do give choices within limits (e.g., "When you finish . . . you can either . . . or . . .").

- Interest and attention are essential! Research shows that interest accounts for as much as 25 times the variance in success. Get attention before starting a lesson. Use signals (e.g., a rhythm, secret word, chant, sign language). Stop if you don't have attention and state your expectation in a direct, businesslike way (e.g., "I need . . ." Use Every Pupil Response [EPR]).

- Set up predictable classroom routines: Open and end the day with poem, song, riddle, or cartoon. Assign jobs and responsibilities for running the class. Post a daily agenda. Tell students the lesson focus and goals.

- Cause students to believe you know important things. Let them know you read books, like to dance, sing, and draw. No one wants to be around blah know-nothing teachers who can't do anything and seem to have few interests. Ask open, or fat, questions to get more thought and participation (e.g., "What did you learn
about . . . ?" versus "Who was the main character?").

- Intrinsic motivation is more important than concrete rewards. The research is clear: Extrinsics can harm interest. Use stickers and stamps sparingly and only as "symbols" of hard work. Focus on learning for its own worth and how it relates to the real world. If you use extrinsics, they must: (1) be intermittent and phased out as soon as possible, (2) be focused on privileges students want versus "things," and (3) show students they are making progress toward the reinforcer. Use frequent daily or hourly points to start out with, rather than some vague "certificate" at the end of the week.

- Proximity. Stand or sit close and circulate around the room as you teach. Vary the pattern to give each child a chance to be close to you. *Yardstick*: walk about three steps toward a nonlistener and he will usually be brought back to the lesson *or* stand between one or more students making a disturbance. Use the *two-finger touch* technique or touch a student's paper or desk as you walk around to focus attention.

- Let students sit where they want until they show they cannot learn in that spot. Show them how to establish personal space.

- Expect that students will have bad days, too. Give a coupon to turn in homework late one time a grading period. Allow use of the "pass" option, occasionally, during questioning.
- Send silent signals to student. Use sign language to praise, nod your head, make eye contact.

Discipline Interventions

- Ignore behavior unless it interferes with learning. Follow up with a private conference with students who perpetually are problems. Some teachers keep a camera handy to take pictures (even if there isn't film in it).
- Never threaten, but if you make a promise, carry it out. Be consistent.
- Talk to repeat offenders individually and privately. Focus the conference on what you observed, what you expect and why, and ask, "What can you do to solve *your* problem?" Do not humiliate since you wouldn't want this done to you. Set behavior goals.
- Encourage shy or hesitant speakers. Nod your head "yes" and smile as they speak.
- Remember to start fresh each day. Greet children and make them feel welcome. Be positive at the start and throughout each day. Prevent problems by displaying an enthusiastic "can-do, will-do, want-to-do" attitude.
- Volume (teacher's) should be lowered or use silence and pauses to get attention.
- Elevate students with descriptive feedback versus praise. Say, "John, you have three different colors on your quilt piece so far" (praise just controls and may be empty).
- Never *casually* (in a gossip manner) discuss student problems with other teachers. This is unprofessional and may put unfair labels on kids. Never talk about a student in front of other students—as if they aren't listening.
- Time outs away from the group should include a chance to return to the group when there is agreement to follow the rules: ask what rule was broken and discuss how the child will behave the next time if confronted with a similar situation.
- Institute consequences that are hierarchical and appropriate. *A warning is a courtesy we all appreciate.* Take away one minute of recess at a time, instead of a whole recess. Never assign sentence writing as a consequence because this makes writing seem like a punishment! Do not allow some students to "get away" with not doing their share of cleanup or not take responsibility after an activity in the classroom. Loss of privilege is appropriate here.
- On the spot assistance: Make eye contact, move toward the student, and state your expectation (e.g., "Joe, I want you to sit in your chair and start writing"). Give THE EYE. Attack the problem, not the person. Mention names as you teach (e.g., "This morning Pat was saying she thought . . . and now . . ."). Say a child's name before asking a question to help them "tune in."
- Negative remarks don't solve problems. "Stop talking and get back to work" (negative) versus "Susan, what do you need to do and how can I help you do it?" (positive).
- State what you want children TO DO versus NOT TO DO. Instead of "Don't talk," say "Listen." Address the group as a first step: "There are people who are talking who need to listen."

Appendix F: Bibliography of Recommended Reading and Viewing

This bibliography is in addition to the references that appear at the ends of chapters. Films and videos are given in the last section on this appendix.

THE ARTS (GENERAL)

Altieri, J. L. (1995). Pictorial/oral and written responses of first grade students: Can aesthetic growth be measured? *Reading Horizons, 35*(4), 273–286.

Anderson, T. (1995, March/April). Rediscovering the connection between the arts: Introduction to the symposium on interdisciplinary arts education. *Arts Education Policy Review,* pp. 10–12.

Anderson, W. M., & Lawrence, J. E. (1982, September). Approaches to allied arts. *Music Educator's Journal, 69*(1), 31–35.

Barrie, J. (1986). G. H. Bantock's conceptualization of the relationship between the expressive arts and education. *Journal of Aesthetic Education, 20*(2), 41–50.

Best, D. (1974). *Expression in movement and the arts.* London: Lepus.

Bloom, B. (1956). *Taxonomy of educational objectives.* New York: Longman.

Boyer, E. (1995). *The basic school: A community for learning.* Princeton, NJ: Carnegie Foundation for the Advancement of Teaching.

Brandt, R. (1987/88, December/January). On assessment in the arts: A conversation with Howard Gardner. *Educational Leadership,* pp. 30–34.

Brewer, C. B., & Campbell, D. (1991). *Rhythms of learning.* Tucson, AZ: Zephyr.

Broudy, H. S. (1977). How basic is aesthetic education? or is it the fourth *r*? *Language Arts, 54,* 631–637.

Casey, M. B., & Tucker, E. (1994, October). Problem-centered classrooms. *Kappan,* pp. 139–143.

DeMille, R. (1981). *Put your mother on the ceiling: Children's imagination games.* Santa Barbara, CA: Santa Barbara Press.

Edwards, B. (1979). *Drawing on the right side of the brain.* Los Angeles: Jeremy P. Tarcher.

Eisner, E. (1983). *Beyond creating.* Los Angeles: Getty Center for Education in Art.

Epstein, T. (1994, March). Sometimes a shining moment: High-school students' representations of history through the arts. *Social Education,* pp. 136–141.

Farrell, G. (1991, May). Drawbridges and moats: The arts and the middle school classroom. *Middle School Journal,* pp. 28–29.

Feeney, S., & Moravcik, E. (1987). A thing of beauty: Aesthetic development in young children. *Young Children, 42*(6), 7–15.

Fisher, L. (1994, June). The arts curriculum. *Curriculum Leader,* pp. 1–7.

Fowler, C. (1994, November). Strong arts, strong schools. *Educational Leadership,* pp. 4–9.

Galda, L. (1984). Narrative competence: Play, storytelling and story comprehension, in A. Pellegrini and T. Yawkey (Eds.), *The development of oral and written language in social contexts* (pp. 105–117). Norwood, NJ: Ablex.

Gallas, K. (1991, February). Arts as epistemology: Enabling children to know what they know. *Harvard Educational Review, 61*(1), 40–50.

Gardner, H. (1989a). *To open minds: Chinese clues to the dilemma of contemporary education.* New York: Basic Books.

Gardner, H. (1989b). Zero-based arts education: An introduction to ARTS PROPEL. *Studies in Art Education,* 71–83.

Gibbs, N. (1995, October 25). The EQ factor. *Time,* pp. 60–68.

Gingrich, D. (1974). *Relating the arts.* New York: Center for Applied Research in Education.

Ginsberg, H., & Opper, S. (1969). *Piaget's theory of intellectual development.* Upper Saddle River, NJ: Prentice Hall.

Goleman, D. (1995). *Emotional intelligence: Why it can matter more than IQ.* New York: Bantam.

Gopher://gopher.ed.gov.1001/00/initiatives/goals/overview/file (Internet).

Gowan, J. C. (1967). *Creativity: Its educational implications.* San Diego: Knapp.

Gowan, J. C. (1972). *Development of the creative individual.* San Diego: Knapp.

Greene, A. (1995). Schools, communities, and the arts: A research compendium. Morrison Institute for Public

Policy School of Public Affairs, Arizona State University and National Endowment for the Arts.

Hamblen, K. (1985, September). Developing aesthetic literacy through contested concepts. *Art Education,* 19–24.

Hanna, J. L. (1992, April). Connections: Arts, academics and productive citizens. *Kappan,* pp. 601–607.

Hoyt, L. (1992, April). Many ways of knowing: Using drama, oral interactions, and the visual arts to enhance reading comprehension. *Reading Teacher, 45*(8), 580–584.

Khattri, N., Kane, M., & Reeve, A. (1995, November). How performance assessments affect teaching and learning. *Educational Leadership,* pp. 80–83.

Lazear, D. (1991). *Seven ways of knowing.* Palatine, IL: Skylight.

Lazear, D. (1992). *Seven ways of teaching.* Palatine, IL: Skylight.

Lee, M. A. (1993, June). Learning through the arts. *Journal of Physical Education, Recreation, and Dance,* pp. 42–46.

MacGregor, R. (1992, November). A short guide to alternative assessment practices. *Art Education,* pp. 34–38.

Manebur, D. (1994, March). Assessment as a classroom activity. *Music Educators Journal,* pp. 23–47.

Oddleifson, E. (1994, February). What do we want our schools to do? *Kappan,* pp. 446–451.

Ohio's model competency based program. Comprehensive arts education (1996). Columbus: State Department of Education.

Olshansky, B. (1995, September). Picture this: An arts-based literacy program. *Educational Leadership,* pp. 44–47.

Parnes, S. (1966). *Creative behavior guidebook.* New York: Scribner.

Remer, J. (1990). *Changing schools through the arts.* New York: American Council for the Arts.

Schaefer, C. (1973). *Developing creativity in children: An idea book for teachers.* Buffalo, NY: Developers of Knowledge.

Slywester, R. (1993/1994, December/January). What the biology of the brain tells us about learning. *Educational Leadership,* pp. 46–51.

Sukraw-Ebert, J. (1988, January). Arts not apart, but a part. *Principal,* pp. 11–14.

Tardif, T. Z., with Sternberg, R. J. (1988). What do we know about creativity? In R. J. Sternberg (Ed.), *The nature of creativity* (pp. 429–440). New York: Cambridge University Press.

Torrance, E. P. (1970). *Encouraging creativity in the classroom.* Dubuque, IA: Brown.

Warner, S. (1989). *Encouraging the artist in your child.* New York: St. Martin's.

Integration of the Arts

Aaron, J. (1994, May). Integrating music with core subjects. *Music Educators Journal,* pp. 33–36.

Alejandro, A. (1994, January). Like happy dreams—integrating visual arts, writing, and reading. *Language Arts,* pp. 12–21, 71.

Altieri, J. L. (1991, September). Integrating literature and drama. *Reading Teacher,* pp. 45, 74–75.

Amdur, D. (1993, May). Arts and cultural context: A curriculum integrating discipline-based art education with other humanities subjects at the secondary level. *Art Education,* pp. 12–19.

Anderson, W., & Lawrence, J. (1991). *Integrating music into the classroom* (2nd ed.). Belmont, CA: Wadsworth.

Beane, J. (1995, April). Curriculum integration and the disciplines of knowledge. *Kappan,* pp. 616–622.

Burnaford, G. (1994, July). The challenge of integrated curricula. *Music Educators Journal,* pp. 44–47.

Cardarelli, A. F. (1979). *Twenty-one ways to use music in teaching the language arts.* Evansville: Indiana State University.

Dean, J., & Gross, I. (1992, April). Teaching basic skills through art and music. *Kappan,* pp. 613–618.

Donlan, D. (1974, October). Music and the language arts curriculum. *English Journal, 63*(7), 86–88.

Dunn, P. (1995, March/April). Integrating the arts: Renaissance and Reformation in arts education. *Arts Education Policy Review,* pp. 32–37.

Friedlander, J. L. (1992, November/December). Creating dances and dance instruction—an integrated-arts approach. *Journal of Physical Education, Recreation, and Dance,* pp. 49–52.

Gardner, H., & Boix-Mansilla, V. (1994, February). Teaching for understanding—within and across the disciplines. *Educational Leadership,* pp. 14–18.

Gilbert, A. G. (1977). *Teaching the three Rs through movement experiences.* Minneapolis: Burgess.

Irwin, R., & Reynolds, J. K. (1995, March/April). Integration as a strategy for teaching the arts as disciplines. *Arts Education Policy Review,* pp. 13–19.

Kalb, V. (1990, Summer). Curriculum connections: Literature—helping children experience the arts. *School Library Media Journal,* pp. 249–250.

Katz, S., & Thomas, J. (1992). *Teaching creatively by the working word: Language, music, and movement.* Upper Saddle River, NJ: Prentice Hall.

Ross, E. (1994). *Using children's literature across the curriculum.* Bloomington, IN: Phi Delta Kappa.

Roucher, N., & Lovano-Kerr, J. (1995, March/April). Can the arts maintain integrity in interdisciplinary learning? *Arts Education Policy Review,* pp. 20–25.

Scheinfield, D., & Steele, T. (1995, January). Expressive education: Arts-integrated learning and the role of the artist in transforming the curriculum. *New Art Examiner,* pp. 22–27.

Silva, C., & Delgado-Larocco, E. L. (1993, October). Facilitating learning through interconnections: A concept approach to core literature units. *Language Arts, 70,* 469–474.

Slay, J., & Pendergast, S. (1993, May). Infusing the arts across the curriculum: A South Carolina school lifts students' self-esteem through arts study. *School Administrator,* pp. 32–35.

Thompson, K. (1995, November). Maintaining artistic integrity in an interdisciplinary setting. *Art Education,* pp. 39–44.

Weisskopf, V. (1981). Art and science. *Leonardo, 14*(3), 238–242.

Williams, D. (1995). *Teaching mathematics through children's art.* Portsmouth, NH: Heinemann.

CHILDREN'S LITERATURE

Benton, M. (1995, Spring). From 'A rake's progress' to 'Rosie's walk': Lessons in aesthetic reading. *Journal of Aesthetic Education, 29,* 33–46.

Brozo, W. (1988). Applying the reader response heuristic to expository text. *Journal of Reading, 32,* 140–155.

Cohen, D. (1968). The effect of literature on vocabulary and reading achievement. *Elementary English, 45,* 209–213, 217.

Cullinan, B. (Ed.). (1992). *Invitation to read: More children's literature in the reading program.* Newark, DE: International Reading Association.

Devescovi, A., & Baumgartner, E. (1993). Joint-reading a picture book: Verbal interaction and narrative skills. *Cognitive Instruction, 11*(3/4), 299–323.

Dishner, E., Bean, T., Readance, J., & Moore, D. (Eds.). *Reading in the content areas: Improving classroom instruction,* 2nd ed. Dubuque, IA: Kendall/Hunt.

Fallen, J. R. (1995, March). Children's literature as a springboard to music. *Music Educator's Journal, 81,* 24–27.

Forte, I., & Schurr, S. (1995). *Using favorite picture books to stimulate discussion and encourage critical thinking.* Nashville, TN: Incentive.

Funk, H. D., & Funk, G. D. (1992, Spring). Children's literature: An integral facet of the elementary school curriculum. *Reading Improvement, 29,* 40–44.

Galda, L., & Kiefer, B. (1991, February). Children's books: Accent on art. *Reading Teacher, 44*(6), 406–414.

Glazer, J. (1997). *Introduction to children's literature* (2nd ed). Upper Saddle River, NJ: Prentice Hall.

Hancock, M. R. (1993, December). Exploring the meaning-making process through the content of literature response journals: A case study investigation. *Research in the Teaching of English, 27,* 335–368.

Hara, K. (1995, Spring). Teacher-centered and child-centered pedagogical approaches in teaching children's literature. *Education, 115,* 332–338.

Hennings, D. G. (1992). *Beyond the read aloud: Learning to read through listening to and reflecting on literature.* Bloomington, IN: Phi Delta Kappa.

Hillman, J. (1995). *Discovering children's literature.* Upper Saddle River, NJ: Prentice Hall.

Johnson, P. H., et al. (1995, July). Assessment of teaching and learning in "literature-based" classrooms. *Teaching Education, 11,* 359–371.

Johnson, T., & Louis, D. (1987). *Literacy through literature.* Portsmouth, NH: Heinemann.

Jones, H. J., et al. (1994/1995, Winter). A themed literature unit versus a textbook: A comparison of the effects on content acquisition and attitudes in elementary social studies. *Reading Research and Instruction, 34,* 85–96.

Kiefer, B. (1995). *The potential of picturebooks: From visual literacy to aesthetic understanding.* Upper Saddle River, NJ: Prentice Hall.

Krening, N. (1992). Authors of color: A multicultural perspective. *Journal of Reading, 36*(2), 124–129.

Lamme, L. L. (1979, April). Song picture books—A maturing genre of children's literature. *Language Arts, 56*(4), 400–407.

Lamme, L. L. (1990, December). Exploring the world of music through picture books. *Reading Teacher, 44*(4), 294–300.

Lukens, R. (1990). *A critical handbook of children's literature* (4th ed.) Glenview, IL: Scott, Foresman/Little, Brown Higher Education.

Madura, S. (1995, October). The line and texture of aesthetic response: Primary children study authors and illustrators. *Reading Teacher, 49,* 110–118.

McCabe, A. (1996). *Chameleon readers: Teaching children to appreciate all kinds of good stories.* New York: McGraw-Hill.

McCord, S. (1995). *The storybook journey: Pathways to literacy through story and play.* Upper Saddle River, NJ: Prentice Hall.

Miller-Hughes, K. A. (1994, December). Making the connection: Children's books and the visual arts. *School Arts, 94,* 32–33.

Mitchell, F. (1990, December). Introducing art history through children's literature. *Language Arts, 67,* 839–846.

Norton, D. (1995). *Through the eyes of a child: An introduction to children's literature* (4th ed.). Upper Saddle River, NJ: Prentice Hall.

Ogle, D. (1986). K–W–L: A teaching model that develops active reading of expository text. *Reading Teacher, 39,* 564–570.

Pantaleo, S. (1995). What do response journals reveal about children's understandings of the working of literary texts? *Reading Horizons, 36*(1), 76–93.

Peterson, R., & Eeds, M. (1990). *Grand conversations: Literature groups in action.* New York: Scholastic.

Richards, P. O. (1994, September). Thirteen steps to becoming a children's literature expert. *Reading Teacher, 48,* 90–91.

Rose, L. (1996). *Developing intelligences through literature: Ten theme-based units for growing minds.* Tucson, AZ: Zephyr.

Rostankowski, C. (1994, Fall). A is for aesthetics: Alphabet books and the development of the aesthetic in children. *Journal of Aesthetic Education, 28,* 117–127.

Rothlein, L., & Meinbach, A. M. (1996). *Legacies: Using children's literature in the classroom.* New York: Harper-Collins.

Sipe, L. R. (1993, September). Using transformations of traditional stories: Making the reading–writing connection. *Reading Teacher, 47,* 18–26.

Slaughter, J. P. (1994, Summer). The readers respond—a key component of the literary club: Implementing a literature-based reading program. *Reading Improvement, 31,* 77–86.

Smardo, F. (1984, April). Using children's literature as a prelude or finale to music experiences with young children. *Reading Teacher, 37*(8), 700–705.

Stewig, J. (1988). *Children and literature* (2nd ed.). Boston: Houghton Mifflin.

Van Kraayenoord, C. E., & Paris, S. G. (1996, March). Story construction from a picture book: An assessment activity for young learners. *Early Childhood Research Quarterly, 11,* 41–61.

ART

Anderson, T. (1981, November). Wholes and holes: Art's role in holistic education. *Art Education,* pp. 36–39.

Arnold, A. (1995, Winter). Opening windows to stories through art. *Journal of Youth Services in Libraries, 8,* 204–207.

Baumgardner, J. M. (1993). *60 art projects for children.* New York: Clarkson-Potter.

Beattie, D. K. (1994, March). The mini-portfolio: Locus of a successful performance examination. *Art Education,* pp. 14–18.

Blandy, D., Pancsofar, E., & Mockensturm, T. (1988, January). Guidelines for teaching art to children and youth experiencing significant mental/physical challenges. *Art Education,* pp. 60–66.

Caldwell, H., & Moore, B. (1991). The art of writing: Drawing as preparation for narrative writing in the primary grades. *Studies in Art Education, 32*(4), 207–219.

Chalmers, F. G. (1987, September). Beyond current conceptions of discipline-based art education. *Art Education,* pp. 58–61.

Chertok, B., Hirshfield, G., & Rosh, M. (1992). *Meet the masterpieces.* New York: Scholastic.

Dalke, C. (1984, November). There are no cows here: Art and special education together at last. *Art Education,* pp. 6–9.

Englebaugh, D. (1994). *Art through children's literature: Creative art lessons for Caldecott books.* Englewood, CO: Teacher Ideas.

Evans, J., & Moore, J. E. (1992). *How to teach art to children.* Monterey, CA: Evan Moor.

Gainer, R. S. (1983, November/December). At home in art. *Childhood Education,* pp. 102–109.

Galda, L. (1993, March). Visual literacy: Exploring art and illustration in children's books. *Reading Teacher, 46*(6), 506–516.

Godfrey, R. (1992, April). Civilization, education, and the visual arts: A personal manifesto. *Kappan,* pp. 596–600.

Greco, R. (1996/1997, December/January). Introducing art history through children's literature. *Reading Teacher, 50,* 365.

Greer, W. D. (1984). Discipline-based art education: Approaching art as a subject of study. *Studies in Art Education, 25*(4), 212–218.

Hamblen, K. (1987). What general education can tell us about evaluation in art. *Studies in Art Education, 28*(4), 246–250.

Hart, K. (1988). *I can draw: Ideas for teachers.* Portsmouth, NH: Heinemann.

Herberholz, B., & Hanson, L. (1995). *Early childhood art.* Madison, WI: Brown & Benchmark.

Herberholz, D., & Herberholtz, B. (1994). *Artworks for elementary teachers: Developing artistic and perceptual awareness.* Madison, WI: Brown & Benchmark.

Herman, G. (1992). *Kinetic kaleidoscope: Exploring movement and energy in the visual arts.* Tucson, AZ: Zephyr.

Hurwitz, A., & Day, M. (1995). *Children and their art: Methods for the elementary school.* Orlando, FL: Harcourt Brace.

Jefferson, B. (1964). The color book craze. *Bulletin F.* Washington, DC: Association for Childhood Education International.

Linderman, M. G. (1990). *Art in the elementary school: Drawing, painting, and creating for the classroom.* Ames, IA: Brown.

Massey, S., & Darst, D. (1992). *Learning to look: A complete art history and appreciation program for grades K–8.* Upper Saddle River, NJ: Prentice Hall.

Parrott, J. (1986). Developing excellence through curriculum in art. *Journal of Aesthetic Education, 20*(3), 69–80.

Perkins, D. N. (1987/88, December/January). Art as an occasion of intelligence. *Educational Leadership,* pp. 36–42.

Rowe, G. (1987). *Guiding young artists: Curriculum ideas for teachers.* Melbourne: Oxford University Press.

Seely, C., & Hurwitz, A. (1983, May). Developing language through art. *School Arts,* pp. 20–22.

Simpson, J. (1996, January). Constructivism and connection making in art education. *Art Education,* pp. 53–59.

Smith, N. (1993). *Experience and art: Teaching children to paint.* New York: Teachers College Press.

Smout, B. (1990, February). Reading, writing, and art. *Reading Teacher,* pp. 430–431.

Stover, L. (1988, September). What do you mean, we have to read a book for art class? *Art Education,* pp. 8–13.

Wachowiak, F., & Clements, R. (1993). *Emphasis art: A qualitative art program for elementary and middle schools.* New York: HarperCollins.

DRAMA

Barchers, S. (1993). *Reader's theatre for beginning readers.* Englewood, CO: Teacher Ideas.

Bray, E. (1995). *Playbuilding: A guide for group creation of plays with young people.* Portsmouth, NH: Heinemann.

Collins, R. (1997). Storytelling: Water from another time. *Drama Teacher, 5*(2), 6.

Comeaux, P. (1994, Winter). Performing poetry: Centering the language arts program. *Contemporary Education,* pp. 77–81.

Cottrell, J. (1987). *Creative drama in the classroom, grades 1–3 and 4–6.* Lincolnwood, IL: National Textbook.

Fennessey, S. (1995, September). Living history through drama and literature. *Reading Teacher, 49,* 16–19.

Flynn, R., & Carr, G. (1994, January). Exploring classroom literature through drama: A specialist and a teacher collaborate. *Language Arts,* pp. 38–43.

Fox, M. (1987). *Teaching drama to young children.* Portsmouth, NH: Heinemann.

Hackbarth, J. (1994). *Plays, players, and playing: How to start your own children's theater company.* Colorado Springs, CO: Piccadilly.

Harmon, R. (1994). *Teaching a young actor: How to train children of all ages for success in movies, TV, and commercials.* New York: Walker.

Harp, B. (1988, May). Is all of that drama taking valuable time away from reading? *Reading Teacher,* pp. 938–940.

Heathcote, D., & Bolton, G. (1995). *Drama for learning.* Portsmouth, NH: Heinemann.

Heinig, R. B. (1987). *Creative drama resource book for kindergarten through grade 3* and *Creative drama resource book for grades 4 through 6.* Upper Saddle River, NJ: Prentice Hall.

Heller, P. (1995). *Drama as a way of knowing.* Galef Institute. York, ME: Stenhouse.

Henderson, L. C., & Shanker, L. C. (1978). The use of interpretive dramatics versus basal reader workbooks. *Reading World, 17,* 239–243.

Landy, R. (1986). *Drama therapy: Concepts and practices.* Springfield, IL: Thomas.

Laughlin, M. K., & Latrobe, K. H. (1990). *Reader's theatre for children.* Englewood, CO: Teacher Ideas.

Livo, N., & Rietz, S. (1987). *Storytelling activities.* Littleton, CO: Libraries Unlimited.

McDonald, M. R. (1986). *Twenty tellable tales: Audience participation folktales for the beginning storyteller.* New York: Wilson.

Martinez, M. G. (1993, May). Motivating dramatic story reenactments. *Reading Teacher, 46,* 682–688.

Mazor, R. (1978, March). Drama as experience. *Language Arts, 55*(3), 328–333.

O'Neill, C., Lambert, A., Linell, R., & Warr-Wood, J. (1977). *Drama guidelines.* Portsmouth, NH: Heinemann.

Ross, E., & Roe, B. (1977, January). Creative drama builds proficiency in reading. *Reading Teacher,* pp. 383–387.

Sawyer, R. (1942). *The way of the storyteller.* New York: Viking.

Scher, A., & Verrall, C. (1981). *One hundred plus ideas for drama.* Portsmouth, NH: Heinemann.

Scher, A., & Verrall, C. (1987). *Another one hundred plus ideas for drama.* Portsmouth, NH: Heinemann.

Spolin, V. (1963). *Improvisation for the theatre.* Evanston, IL: Northwestern University Press.

Spolin, V. (1986). *Theatre games for the classroom: A teacher's handbook.* Evanston, IL: Northwestern University Press.

Stewig, J. (1983). *Informal drama in the elementary language arts program.* New York: Teachers College Press.

Verriour, P. (1985). Face to face: Negotiating meaning through drama. *Theory into Practice, 24*(3), 181–186.

Wagner, B. J. (1979, March). Using drama to create an environment for language development. *Language Arts, 56*(3), 268–274.

Wagner, B. J. (1988, January). Research contents: Does classroom drama affect the arts of language? *Language Arts, 65*(1), 46–54.

Ward, W. (1981). *Stories to dramatize*. New Orleans: Anchorage.

Way, B. (1981). *Audience participation: Theatre for young people*. Boston: W. H. Baker.

White, M. (1993). *Mel White's readers theatre anthology: Twenty-eight all-occasion readings for storytellers*. Colorado Springs, CO: Meriwether.

Wolf, A. (1993). *It's show time!: Poetry from the page to the stage*. Asheville, NC: Poetry Alive!

DANCE

Allen, B. (1988, November/December). Teaching training and discipline-based dance education. *Journal of Physical Education, Recreation, and Dance*, pp. 65–69.

Barlin, A. L. (1979). *Teaching your wings to fly: The nonspecialist's guide to movement activities for young children*. Santa Monica, CA: Goodyear.

Barlin, A. L., & Greenberg, T. (1980). *Move and be moved: A practical approach to movement with meaning*. Los Angeles: Learning through Movement.

Benzwie, T. (1988). *A moving experience: Dance for lovers of children and the child within*. Tucson, AZ: Zephyr.

Boorman, J. (1969). *Creative dance in the first three grades*. Toronto: Longman Canada.

Exiner, H., & Lloyd, P. (1973). *Teaching creative movement*. Sydney: Angus & Robertson.

Exiner, H., & Lloyd, P. (1987). *Learning through dance: A guide for teachers*. Melbourne, Australia: Oxford University Press.

Griss, S. (1994, February). Creative movement: A language for learning. *Kappan*, pp. 78–80.

Hanna, J. (2000, June). Learning through dance. *American School Board Journal*, pp. 47–48.

Kane, K. A. (1994, May). Stories to help students understand movement. *Strategies, 7*, 13–17.

Lee, A. (1985). *A handbook of creative dance and drama*. Portsmouth, NH: Heinemann.

Lee, P. (1994, February). To dance one's understanding. *Kappan*, pp. 81–82.

Mettler, B. (1980). *The nature of dance as a creative art activity*. Tucson, AZ: Mettler Studio.

National Dance Association. (1990). *Guide to creative dance for the young child*. Reston, VA: Author.

Pesetsky, S., & Burack, S. (1984). *Teaching dance for the handicapped: A curriculum guide*. Lansing, MI: Michigan Dance Association.

Preston-Dunlop, V. A. (1980). *Handbook for dance in education* (2nd ed.). Estover, Plymouth, England: Macdonald & Evans.

Schwartz, V. (Ed.). (1989, November/December). A dance for all people. *Journal of Physical Education, Recreation, and Dance*, pp. 49–64.

Silk, G. (1989, November/December). Creative movement for people who are developmentally disabled. *Journal of Physical Education, Recreation, and Dance*, pp. 56–58.

Werner, P. (Ed.). (1974, December). Movement, music, and children's literature. *Physical Education, 31*(4), 216–218.

Willis, C. (1995, May/June). Creative dance—how to increase parent and child awareness. *Journal of Physical Education, Recreation, and Dance, 66*(6), 16.

Witkin, K. (1978). *To move, to learn*. New York: Schocken.

Zirulnik, A., & Abeles, J. (Eds.) (1985). *Resource lists for children's dance*. Lansing: Michigan Dance Association.

MUSIC

Ameigh, T. (1993, January). Learn the language of music through journals. *Music Educators Journal*, pp. 30–32.

Bennett, P., & Bartholomew, D. (1997). *Songworks I: Singing in the education of children*. Belmont, CA: Wadsworth.

Best, H. (1992, November). Music curricula in the future. *Arts Education Policy Review*, pp. 2–7.

Bibbins, P. (1993, July). More than music: A collaborative curriculum. *Music Educators Journal*, pp. 23–26.

Boshkoff, R. (1991, October). Lesson planning the Kodaly way. *Music Educators Journal*, pp. 30–34.

Campbell, D. (1997). *The Mozart effect*. New York: Avon.

Collett, M. J. (1991, November). Read between the lines: Music as a basis for learning. *Music Educators Journal*, pp. 42–45.

Davidson, L. (1990, May). Tools and environments for musical creativity. *Music Educators Journal*, pp. 47–51.

Deither, B. (1991, December). Using music as a second language. *English Journal*, pp. 72–76.

Goodkin, D. (1994, July). Diverse approaches to multicultural music. *Music Educators Journal*, pp. 39–43.

Grant, J. M. (1995). *Shake, rattle & learn*. York, ME: Stinhouse.

Judy, S. (1990). *Making music for the joy of it*. Los Angeles: Jeremy P. Tarcher.

Kaplan, D. (1985, January). Music in the classroom: A new approach. *Learning, 13*(5), 28–31.

Lehman, P. (1993, March). Why your school needs music. *Arts Education Policy Review,* pp. 30–34.

Levene, D. (1993). *Music through children's literature: Theme and variations.* Englewood, CO: Teacher Ideas.

Livo, N. J. (1975, April). Multiply music with books and add art. *Elementary English, 52*(4), 541–544.

Lynch, S. (1994). *Classical music for beginners.* New York: Writers and Readers.

Manins, S. (1994, March). Bridge building in early childhood music. *Music Educators Journal,* pp. 37–41.

Mann, R. (1979, March). The effect of music and sound effects on the listening comprehension of fourth grade students. Paper presented at the Annual Convention of the Association for Educational Communications and Technology. New Orleans.

Markel, R. (1983). *Music for your child: A complete guide for parents and teachers.* New York: Facts on File.

McGirr, P. I. (1994/1995, Winter). Verdi invades the kindergarten: Using song picture books. *Childhood Education, 71,* 74–79.

Merritt, S. (1990). *Mind, music, and imagery: 40 exercises using music to stimulate creativity and self-awareness.* New York: NAL/Plume.

Miller, A., & Coen, D. (1994, February). The case for music in the schools. *Kappan,* pp. 459–461.

Nash, G., & Repley, J. (1990). *Music in the making: Optimal learning in speech, song, instrument instruction, and movement for grades K–4.* Van Nuys, CA: Alfred.

Painter, W. (1989). *Musical story hours: Using music with storytelling and puppetry.* Hamden, CT: Library Professional Publications.

Phillips, K. (1993, September). A stronger rationale for music education. *Music Educators Journal,* pp. 17–19.

Present, G. (1986). *We all live together: Song & activity book and leader's guide.* Milwaukee, WI: Hal Leonard.

Reaser, D. (1993, March). Let's speak music! *Education Digest,* pp. 66–68.

Seeger, A. (1992, May). Celebrating the American music mosaic. *Music Educators Journal,* pp. 26–29.

Shaffer, G. (1982, September). Music teaches poetry, poetry teaches music. *Music Educator's Journal, 69*(1), 40–42.

Speake, C. (1993, February). Create an opera with elementary students. *Music Educators Journal,* pp. 22–26.

Stover, L. (1989, October). Read a book for music class? Are you serious? *Music Educators Journal, 76*(2), 48–52.

Warner, L. (1982, January/February). 37 music ideas for the nonmusical teacher. *Childhood Education, 58*(3), 134–137.

Whitaker, N. (1994, July). Whole language and music education. *Music Educators Journal,* pp. 24–28.

VIDEOGRAPHY

American storyteller video series. (1987). New York: H. W. Wilson.

Art education in action. (1994). (Video, 112 min.). Los Angeles: J. Paul Getty Trust.

The art of learning. (1993). (Video, 46 min). Santa Monica, CA: Getty Center for Education in the Arts.

The arts and children: A success story. (Video, 15 min.). Goals 2000 Arts Education Partnership. Motivational video on why the arts should be integrated. Classroom examples and interviews.

Artscape. (1994). Princeton, NY: Films for the Humanities. Series of children's videos on art.

Arts for life. (1990). (Video, 15 min.). J. Paul Gerry Trust. Excellent rationale for arts integration.

Art's place. (1994). Princeton, NY: Films for the Humanities. Series of children's videos on art.

The arts: Tools for teaching. (1994). (Video). Washington, DC: John F. Kennedy Center for the Performing Arts.

Aurand Harris demonstrating playwriting with children. (1983). (24 min. video). Cleveland, OH: Edward Feil Production. Teaching playwriting to fifth and sixth graders.

Brighten your road. (1986). Allen, TX: KLM Teaching Resources.

Creative beginnings. (1991). (Video, 59 min). New York: Ambrose Video.

Creative movement: A step towards intelligence. (1993). (Video, 80 min.). West Long Branch, NJ: Kultur.

Creativity: A way of learning. (Video, 11 min.). NEA Distribution Center, Academic Bldg., Saw Mill Rd., West Haven, CT 06516. Explores how to encourage creativity.

Dance and grow. (1994). (Video, 60 min.). Heightstown, NJ: Princeton Book Company.

Dorothy Heathcote talks to teachers. (1973)(62 min: two parts on drama). Chicago: Northwestern University.

Drama with the kindergarten. (1987). (Video). Tempe, AZ: Arizona State University. Three drama approaches.

Introduction to creative drama & improvisation. (1990). Indianapolis: DVC.

Humor in music: What is a melody? (1993). (113 min.). New York: Sony Classical.

Literary visions. (1992). South Burlington, VT: Annenberg/CPB Collection (5 vol., 30 min./each).

The lively art of picture books. (1957). Weston, CT: Weston Woods (57 min.; older, but a classic piece).

Master class. (1992). New York: Columbia University Media and Society Seminars Collection. PBS Video. West Tisbury, MA: Vineyard Video.

Max made mischief: An approach to literature. (1977). (Video, 30 min.). University Park, PA: Pennsylvania State AV Services.

One of a kind. (Film, 58 min.). Phoenix Films, Inc., 470 Park Ave. South, New York, NY, 10016. Use of puppets. Troubled child gains emotional release. Good for special education.

Picture thoughts. (1994). (Video). Columbia, MD: Hamilton Associates.

Playing: Pretending spontaneous drama with children. (Film, 20 min.). Community Services Dept., Pittsburgh Child Guidance Center, 201 De Soto St., Pittsburgh, PA., 15213.

Poetry is words that I sing! (1988). (Video, 30 min.). Berkeley: University of California Extension Media Center.

The role of art in general education. (1988). (Video). Los Angeles: Getty Center for Education in the Arts.

Statues hardly ever smile. (Film, 25 min.). Brooklyn Museum, Eastern Parkway and Washington Ave., Brooklyn, NY, 11238. Creative drama in a museum.

Teaching in and through the arts. (1995). (Video, 25 min.). Santa Monica, CA: Getty Center for Education in the Arts. Classroom examples, elementary through high school, are shown.

Three looms waiting. (52 min. film). BBC. Distributed by Time-Life Films, 43 W. 16th St., New York, NY, 10016. Dorothy Heathcote working with children.

Traditional expressions. Santa Cruz, CA: Multi-Cultural Communications. Several multicultural art projects are demonstrated, including mask making and aboriginal dot painting.

What do you see? (Video, 25 min). Chicago: Art Institute of Chicago.

What is Kodaly music education? An historical overview. (1992). Wellesley, MA: KCA (48 min.).

What's a good book? (1982). (Video, 27 min.). Weston, CT: The Studios.

Why are the arts essential to education reform? (1993). (Video). Los Angeles: J. Paul Getty Trust.

Why man creates. (Film, 25 min.). Pyramid Films, Box 1048, Santa Monica, CA 90406.

Seed Strategies Index

Subject Index

About the Author

Claudia Cornett is Professor Emerita at Wittenberg University and a recipient of the Distinguished Teaching Award. During her tenure at Wittenberg she directed the Reading Center and taught graduate and undergraduate courses in all aspects of literacy methodology and integration of literature and the arts. Before moving to the college level she received her Ph.D. from Miami University, taught grades 1 through 8, and was a reading specialist.

Claudia is the author of both books and articles about the strategic use of humor, bibliotherapy, children's literature, learning styles, integrated arts, and the teaching of reading. She regularly gives keynote talks and does staff development for educators throughout the United States, Canada, and Europe. Her most popular workshop is "Learning through Laughter," presented on the lecture circuit for Phi Delta Kappa. Claudia also developed and is featured in *Sounds Abound*, an instructional television series on early literacy that is broadcast on PBS stations.

Claudia lives with her husband, a retired school superintendent, on an island in South Carolina. She can be reached at ccornett@wittenberg.edu.